*Major Problems
in the History
of the American South*

MAJOR PROBLEMS IN AMERICAN HISTORY SERIES

GENERAL EDITOR
THOMAS G. PATERSON

Major Problems in the History of the American South
Volume II: The New South

DOCUMENTS AND ESSAYS

SECOND EDITION

EDITED BY

PAUL D. ESCOTT

WAKE FOREST UNIVERSITY

DAVID R. GOLDFIELD

UNIVERSITY OF NORTH CAROLINA, CHARLOTTE

SALLY G. McMILLEN

DAVIDSON COLLEGE

ELIZABETH HAYES TURNER

UNIVERSITY OF HOUSTON—DOWNTOWN

HOUGHTON MIFFLIN COMPANY   BOSTON   NEW YORK

For Lauren and David
Eleanor and Erik
Blair and Carrie
Meg and Laura
and to our students

Editor-in-Chief: Jean L. Woy
Senior Associate Editor: Frances Gay
Senior Project Editor: Janet Young
Editorial Assistant: Nasya Laymon
Associate Production/Design Coordinator: Jodi O'Rourke
Assistant Manufacturing Coordinator: Andrea Wagner
Senior Marketing Manager: Sandra McGuire

Cover image: *Westfield Blast Furnace, 1931,* by Roderick Mackenzie. Collection of the Birmingham Museum of Art, Birmingham, Alabama; Museum Purchase.

Printed in the U.S.A.

Library of Congress Catalog Card Number: 98-72022

ISBN: 0-395-87140-9

6 7 8 9 10 11 12-CS-07 06 05

Contents

C H A P T E R 6
Race, Violence, Disfranchisement, and Segregation
Page 155

C H A P T E R 7
Southern Religion and the Lost Cause
Page 187

CHAPTER 8

The Progressive South in the Age of Jim Crow: Promise and Paradox
Page 215

CHAPTER 9

New Women, New South, New Prospects
Page 255

C H A P T E R   1 0
In Search of the Modern South
Page 287

C H A P T E R   1 1
Turning Points? The New Deal and World War II
Page 317

CHAPTER 14
The South Lives (Moves) On
Page 416

Preface

The historian David M. Potter once wrote that the South has been "a kind of Sphinx on the American land." Nothing in the two volumes of *Major Problems in the History of the American South* will challenge that description of a great American enigma. The documents and essays in these volumes demonstrate that the search to know what the South was and what it is remains at the core of southern history.

William Faulkner made the observation that in the South the past is not dead; it is not even past. Some students of southern history may well recognize this statement to be true; others will decide that the South has moved beyond its past, becoming more like the rest of the nation. Or, perhaps the rest of the nation has become more like the South. In any case, today the South is less a geographical entity than a state of mind, offering a panorama of almost bewildering diversity. Writers and historians have yet to agree on what makes the region's culture and history different. For all who have sought to discover its essence, the challenge has been in the pursuit and in the insights that come from what the scholar Fred Hobson has called "the southern rage to explain." We hope that the selections in this book will encourage readers to pursue that quest to understand the South's past.

Like the first edition of *Major Problems in the History of the American South,* this revised Volume II on the New South follows a basically chronological tour of southern history, from the dislocations of Reconstruction to the conservative turn of politics in the recent South. We have selected documents that evoke the atmosphere, personal experiences, and events of the times. In choosing the essays, we have provided historical perspective on some of the major issues that southerners have confronted. We have included provocative interpretations of those key issues. We present, in both the documents and essays, a variety of viewpoints, inviting readers to reach their own conclusions about major interpretive problems in southern history.

After receiving guidance from instructors who teach southern history, in this second edition we have reduced the length of this volume by one chapter and by shortening chapters throughout the volume. Chapter 11 now covers the New Deal and World War II. Freedom struggles of the 1950s and 1960s are covered in Chapter 12, and race, politics, and religion in the recent South are covered in Chapter 13.

In this edition we have also included new documents in each chapter, most of which were taken from the personal observations of people living at the time. We have created a new chapter on women (Chapter 9) and have added documents and articles in other chapters that reflect the perspective of gender as well as the latest scholarship in that field. We have included more information about the Trans-Mississippi West, focusing on Mexican Americans in Texas (Chapter 6) and drought victims in Oklahoma (Chapter 11). Documents and articles on sharecroppers in

North Carolina (Chapter 3), coal miners in Appalachia and Alabama and textile workers in the Carolinas (Chapter 4), and women workers in New Deal agencies (Chapter 11) represent the new labor scholarship. Race relations continue to be one of the major themes of this volume, as indicated by the new essays on this topic in Chapters 6, 12, and 13. The conservative turn in southern politics since the civil rights movement is reflected in essays that analyze party politics at the local, state, and national level in Chapter 13.

This book follows the same general format as other volumes in the *Major Problems in American History* series. Each chapter begins with a brief introduction to its topic, followed first by documentary readings and then by essays that illuminate the central theme. Head notes that place the readings in historical and interpretive perspective introduce each chapter's primary sources and essays. A "Further Reading" section, suggesting important books and articles for those who wish to explore the subject in more depth, closes each chapter.

Many friends and colleagues have contributed to these volumes. For help with the second edition, we want to thank Carlos Blanton, John B. Boles, Laura Edwards, Elna Green, Randal Hall, John Inscoe, Charles Israel, Paul Levengood, Bruce McMillen, J. Russell Snapp, Randy Sparks, Pamela Tyler, and Marjorie Wheeler.

Detailed and extremely helpful written reviews of draft tables of contents were provided by Bradley G. Bond, University of Southern Mississippi; Jane Turner Censer, George Mason University; Peter A. Coclanis, University of North Carolina, Chapel Hill; Elna C. Green, Sweet Briar College; John C. Inscoe, University of Georgia; Lawrence N. Powell, Tulane University; Ann W. Ellis Pullen, Kennesaw State University; and Charles Reagan Wilson, University of Mississippi. And we are grateful for the very helpful reviews of the first edition that were provided by Clarence L. Mohr, Tulane University; Theodore Ownby, University of Mississippi; Christopher Phillips, Emporia State University; Joseph P. Reidy, Howard University; J. B. Smallwood, Jr., University of North Texas; and Peter Wallenstein, Virginia Polytechnic Institute.

We received documents and sound advice from the Library of Congress Prints and Photographs Division, the Southern Baptist Historical Library and Archives, the *Journal of Southern History,* and Rice University. Thomas G. Paterson, the editor of the *Major Problems in American History* series, provided timely assistance and encouragement. And the editors at Houghton Mifflin, Jean Woy, Frances Gay, and Janet Young, have kept us on track, even when part of the manuscript went astray through the mail.

Without the unlimited support and patience of our families, this project would not have been completed. This volume is dedicated to our children—all eight of them—and to our students. May they always view the South with unclouded vision.

P. E.
D. G.
S. M.
E. H. T.

Major Problems
in the History
of the American South

CHAPTER
1

What Is the South?

Historian Michael O'Brien noted that "no man's South is the same as another's." Although there is general agreement that the South is (or at least was, at some time) distinct from other regions of the United States, there is no consensus on either the nature or the duration of that difference. Definitions of the South have stressed everything from the obvious (for example, climate and white supremacy) to the obscure (the geographical line below which grits replace hash browns).

Part of the problem is that there are many Souths. Those who lived in the South Carolina lowcountry were different in terms of ethnicity, accent, ideology, occupation, religion, music, and language from the people of the southern Appalachians. Distinctions exist within states—lowcountry versus upcountry, Piedmont versus coastal plains, and Delta versus piney woods. These disparities have led some to contend that the South is more a state of mind than a geographical region.

Yet some thing or things draw these disparate areas together, and observers since the earliest settlements have tried to identify what constitutes "the South." The task is more than a mere intellectual exercise. As with the study of any ethnic group, distinction helps to define identity. And the study of the South has helped to define our national identity as well. The South has often served as a counterpoint, both good and bad, to the rest of the country. In learning what is special about the South and how it became that way, we are learning about our national culture as well.

ESSAYS

W. J. Cash's *The Mind of the South* is among the most eloquent and forceful statements of a southern identity, though the Charlotte journalist's emphasis on the continuity of southern history has provoked sharp responses from some historians, among them Yale University's C. Vann Woodward. The first two essays present Cash's and Woodward's differing views. Defining southern distinctiveness is a major academic industry and in fact, as historian David L. Smiley notes in the next essay, has become a distinctive element in itself. Assuming the South's difference, the obvious question is, "Different from what?" John B. Boles, professor of history at Rice University and managing editor of the *Journal of Southern History,* notes the complex task of identifying the South's distinct character and how individuals continue to try to rediscover and embrace its uniqueness.

The Continuity of Southern History

W. J. CASH

There exists among us by ordinary—both North and South—a profound conviction that the South is another land, sharply differentiated from the rest of the American nation, and exhibiting within itself a remarkable homogeneity.

As to what its singularity may consist in, there is, of course, much conflict of opinion, and especially between Northerner and Southerner. But that it is different and that it is solid—on these things nearly everybody is agreed. Now and then, to be sure, there have arisen people, usually journalists or professors, to tell us that it is all a figment of the imagination, that the South really exists only as a geographical division of the United States and is distinguishable from New England or the Middle West only by such matters as the greater heat and the presence of a larger body of Negroes. Nobody, however, has ever taken them seriously. And rightly.

For the popular conviction is indubitably accurate: the South is, in Allen Tate's phrase, "Uncle Sam's other province." And when Carl Carmer said of Alabama that "The Congo is not more different from Massachusetts or Kansas or California," he fashioned a hyperbole which is applicable in one measure or another to the entire section.

This is not to suggest that the land does not display an enormous diversity within its borders. Anyone may see that it does simply by riding along any of the great new motor roads which spread across it—through brisk towns with tall white buildings in Nebraska Gothic; through smart suburbs, with their faces newly washed; through industrial and Negro slums, medieval in dirt and squalor and wretchedness, in all but redeeming beauty; past sleepy old hamlets and wide fields and black men singing their sad songs in the cotton, past log cabin and high grave houses, past hill and swamp and plain. . . . The distance from Charleston to Birmingham is in some respects measurable only in sidereal terms, as is the distance from the Great Smokies to Lake Pontchartrain. And Howard Odum has demonstrated that the economic and social difference between the Southeastern and Southwestern states is so great and growing that they have begun to deserve to be treated, for many purposes, as separate regions.

Nevertheless, if it can be said there are many Souths, the fact remains that there is also one South. That is to say, it is easy to trace throughout the region (roughly delimited by the boundaries of the former Confederate States of America, but shading over into some of the border states, notably Kentucky, also) a fairly definite mental pattern, associated with a fairly definite social pattern—a complex of established relationships and habits of thought, sentiments, prejudices, standards and values, and associations of ideas, which, if it is not common strictly to every group of white people in the South, is still common in one appreciable measure or another, and in some part or another, to all but relatively negligible ones.

It is no product of Cloud-Cuckoo-Town, of course, but proceeds from the common American heritage, and many of its elements are readily recognizable as being simply variations on the primary American theme. To imagine it existing outside this continent would be quite impossible. But for all that, the peculiar history of the South has so greatly modified it from the general American norm that, when viewed as a whole, it decisively justifies the notion that the country is—not quite a nation within a nation, but the next thing to it.

To understand it, it is necessary to know the story of its development. And the best way to begin that story, I think, is by disabusing our minds of two correlated legends—those of the Old and the New Souths.

What the Old South of the legend in its classical form was like is more or less familiar to everyone. It was a sort of stage piece out of the eighteenth century, wherein gesturing gentlemen moved soft-spokenly against a background of rose gardens and dueling grounds, through always gallant deeds, and lovely ladies, in farthingales, never for a moment lost that exquisite remoteness which has been the dream of all men and the possession of none. Its social pattern was manorial, its civilization that of the Cavalier, its ruling class an aristocracy coextensive with the planter group—men often entitled to quarter the royal arms of St. George and St. Andrew on their shields, and in every case descended from the old gentlefolk who for many centuries had made up the ruling classes of Europe.

They dwelt in large and stately mansions, preferably white and with columns and Grecian entablature. Their estates were feudal baronies, their slaves quite too numerous ever to be counted, and their social life a thing of Old World splendor and delicacy. What had really happened here, indeed, was that the gentlemanly idea, driven from England by Cromwell, had taken refuge in the South and fashioned for itself a world to its heart's desire: a world singularly polished and mellow and poised, wholly dominated by ideals of honor and chivalry and *noblesse*—all those sentiments and values and habits of action which used to be, especially in Walter Scott, invariably assigned to the gentleman born and the Cavalier.

Beneath these was a vague race lumped together indiscriminately as the poor whites—very often, in fact, as the "white-trash." These people belonged in the main to a physically inferior type, having sprung for the most part from the convict servants, redemptioners, and debtors of old Virginia and Georgia, with a sprinkling of the most unsuccessful sort of European peasants and farm laborers and the dregs of the European town slums. And so, of course, the gulf between them and the master classes was impassable, and their ideas and feelings did not enter into the makeup of the prevailing Southern civilization.

But in the legend of the New South the Old South is supposed to have been destroyed by the Civil War and the thirty years that followed it, to have been swept both socially and mentally into the limbo of things that were and are not, to give place to a society which has been rapidly and increasingly industrialized and modernized both in body and in mind—which now, indeed, save for a few quaint survivals and gentle sentimentalities and a few shocking and inexplicable brutalities such as lynching, is almost as industrialized and modernized in its outlook as the North. Such an idea is obviously inconsistent with the general assumption of the South's great difference, but paradox is the essence of popular thinking, and millions—even in the South itself—placidly believe in both notions.

These legends, however, bear little relation to reality. There was an Old South, to be sure, but it was another thing than this. And there is a New South. Industrialization and commercialization have greatly modified the land, including its ideology. . . . Nevertheless, the extent of the change and of the break between the Old South that was and the South of our time has been vastly exaggerated. The South, one might say, is a tree with many age rings, with its limbs and trunk bent and twisted by all the winds of the years, but with its tap root in the Old South. Or, better still, it is like one of those churches one sees in England. The facade and towers, the windows and clerestory, all the exterior and superstructure are late Gothic of one sort or another, but look into its nave, its aisles, and its choir and you find the old mighty Norman arches of the twelfth century. And if you look into its crypt, you may even find stones cut by Saxon, brick made by Roman hands.

The mind of the section, that is, is continuous with the past. And its primary form is determined not nearly so much by industry as by the purely agricultural conditions of that past. So far from being modernized, in many ways it has actually always marched away, as to this day it continues to do, from the present toward the past.

The Discontinuity of Southern History

C. VANN WOODWARD

Among the major monuments of broken continuity in the South are slavery and secession, independence and defeat, emancipation and military occupation, reconstruction and redemption. Southerners, unlike other Americans, repeatedly felt the solid ground of continuity give way under their feet. An old order of slave society solidly supported by constitution, state, church and the authority of law and learning and cherished by a majority of the people collapsed, perished and disappeared. So did the short-lived experiment in national independence. So also the short-lived experiment in Radical Reconstruction. The succeeding order of Redeemers, the New South, lasted longer, but it too seems destined for the dump heap of history.

Perhaps it was because Cash wrote toward the end of the longest and most stable of these successive orders, the one that lasted from 1877 to the 1950's, that he acquired his conviction of stability and unchanging continuity. At any rate, he was fully persuaded that "the mind of the section . . . is continuous with the past," and that the South has "always marched away, as to this day it continues to do, from the present toward the past." Just as he guardedly conceded diversity in advancing the thesis of unity, so he admits the existence of change in maintaining the thesis of continuity, change from which even the elusive Southern "mind" did not "come off scot-free." But it was the sort of change the French have in mind in saying. *"Plus ça change, plus c'est la même chose."* Tidewater tobacco, up-country cotton, rampaging frontier, flush times in Alabama and Mississippi, slavery, secession, defeat, abolition, Reconstruction, New South, industrial revolution—*toujours la même chose!* Even the Yankee victory that "had smashed the Southern world" was "almost entirely illusory," since "it had left the essential Southern mind and will . . . entirely unshaken. Rather . . . it had operated enormously to fortify and confirm that mind and will." As for Reconstruction, again, "so far from having reconstructed the Southern mind in the large and in its essential character, it was still this Yankee's fate to have strengthened it almost beyond reckoning, and to have made it one of the most solidly established, one of the least reconstructible ever developed."

The continuity upon which Cash is most insistent is the one he sees between the Old South and the New South. He early announces his intention of "disabusing our minds of two correlated legends—those of the Old and the New South." He promises in Rankean terms to tell us "exactly what the Old South was really like." He concedes that there was a New South as well. "Nevertheless, the extent of the change and of the break between the Old South that was and the New South of our time has been vastly exaggerated." The common denominator, the homogenizing touchstone is his "basic Southerner" or "the man at the center." He is described as "an exceedingly simple fellow," most likely a hillbilly from the backcountry, but fundamentally he is a petit bourgeois always on the make, yet ever bemused by his vision of becoming, imitating, or at least serving the planter aristocrat. Cash's crude Irish parvenu is pictured as the prototype of the planter aristocrat. Cash is confused about these aristocrats, mainly I think because he is confused about the nature and history of aristocracy. He admires their "beautiful courtesy and dignity and gesturing grace," but deplores their "grotesque exaggeration" and their "pomposity" and suspects that the genuine article should have been genteel. He grudgingly acknowledges their existence, but denies the legitimacy of their pretenses—all save those of a few negligible Virginians. He seems to be saying that they were all bourgeois, that therefore the Old South was bourgeois too, and therefore essentially indistinguishable from the New South. New and Old alike were spellbound by the spurious myth of aristocracy. This and the paradoxical fact that those parvenu aristocrats actually took charge, were a real ruling class, and the continuity of their rule spelled the continuity of the New South with the Old.

The masses came out of the ordeal of Civil War with "a deep affection for these captains, a profound trust in them," a belief in the right "of the master class to ordain and command." And according to Cash, the old rulers continued to ordain and command right on through the collapse of the old order and the building of the new. He detects no change of guard at Redemption. So long as the industrialists and financiers who stepped into the shoes of the old rulers gave the Proto-Dorian password and adopted the old uniforms and gestures, he salutes them as the genuine article. In fact they were rather an improvement, for they represent "a striking extension of the so-called paternalism of the Old South: its passage in some fashion toward becoming a genuine paternalism." Cash enthusiastically embraces the thesis of Broadus Mitchell's "celebrated monograph" that the cotton-mill campaign was "a mighty folk movement," a philanthropic crusade of inspired paternalists. The textile-mill captains were "such men as belonged more or less distinctively within the limits of the old ruling class, the progeny of the plantation." Indeed they were responsible for "the bringing over of the plantation into industry," the company town. Even "the worst labor sweaters" were "full of the ancient Southern love for the splendid gesture," fulfilling "an essential part of the Southern paternalistic tradition that it was an essential duty of the upper classes to look after the moral welfare of these people."

To the cotton mills the neopaternalists add the public schools for the common whites and thus "mightily reaffirm the Proto-Dorian bond." The common poverty acted as a leveler (back to the Unity thesis) and brought "a very great increase in the social solidarity of the South," a "marked mitigation of the haughtiness" of the old captains, now "less boldly patronizing," and "a suppression of class feeling that went beyond anything that even the Old South had known." The common white felt "the hand on the shoulder . . . the jests, the rallying, the stories . . . the confiding reminders of the Proto-Dorian bond of white men." That, according to Cash, was what did in the Populist revolt and the strikes of the lint-head mill hands as well. For from the heart of the masses came "a wide, diffuse gratefulness pouring out upon the cotton-mill baron; upon the old captains, upon all the captains and preachers of Progress; upon the ruling class as a whole for having embraced the doctrine and brought these things about."

Of course Cash professes not to be taken in by Progress like the rednecks and the lint-heads. He realizes that Progress and Success had their prices and he sets them down scrupulously in the debit column of his ledger. "Few people can ever have been confronted with a crueler dilemma" than the old planter turned supply merchant to his former huntin' and fishin' companion as sharecropper: "The old monotonous pellagra-and-rickets-breeding diet had at least been abundant? Strip it rigidly to fatback, molasses, and cornbread, dole it out with an ever stingier hand . . . blind your eyes to peaked faces, seal up your ears to hungry whines. . . ." And that sunbonnet, straw-hat proletariat of the paternalistic mill villages? By the turn of the century they had become "a pretty distinct physical type . . . a dead white skin, a sunken chest, and stooping shoulders. . . . Chinless faces, microcephalic foreheads, rabbit teeth, goggling dead-fish eyes, rickety limbs, and stunted bodies. . . . The women were characteristically stringy-haired and limp of breast at twenty, and shrunken hags at thirty or forty." Something admittedly was happening to the captains, too, what with "men of generally coarser kind coming steadily to the front." And in "all the elaborate built-up pattern of leisure and hedonistic drift; all the slow, cool, gracious and graceful gesturing of movement," there was a sad falling off, a decay of the ideal. "And along with it, the vague largeness of outlook which was so essentially a part of the same aristocratic complex; the magnanimity. . . ."

Admitting all that, "But when the whole of this debit score of Progress is taken into account, we still inevitably come back to the fact that its total effect was as I have said." *Plus ça change!* "Here in a word, was triumph for the Southern will . . . an enormous renewal of confidence in the general Southern way." In [Henry W.] Grady's rhetoric, "Progress stood quite accurately for a sort of new charge at Gettysburg." To be sure, Southern Babbitts eventually appeared, but even they were "Tartarin, not Tartuffe . . . simpler, more naïve, less analytical than their compatriots in Babbittry at the North. . . . They go about making money . . . as boys go about stealing apples . . . in the high-hearted sense of being embarked upon capital sport." Yet, like the planter turned supply merchant or captain of industry, "they looked at you with level and proud gaze. The hallmark of their breed was identical with that of the masters of the Old South—a tremendous complacency." And Rotary, "sign-manual of the Yankee spirit"? Granting "an unfortunate decline in the dignity of the Southern manner," it was but "the grafting of Yankee backslapping upon the normal Southern geniality. . . . I am myself," Cash wrote, "indeed perpetually astonished to recall that Rotary was not invented in the South." And does one detect "strange notes—Yankee notes—in all this talk about the biggest factory, about bank clearings and car loadings and millions"? Strange? Not for Jack Cash. "But does anybody," he actually asked, "fail to hear once more the native accent of William L. Yancey and Barnwell Rhett, to glimpse again the waving plume of, say, Wade Hampton?"

How could he? How could any historian? He sometimes reminds one of those who scribble facetious graffiti on Roman ruins. He betrays a want of feeling for the seriousness of human strivings, for the tragic theme in history. Looking back from mid-twentieth century over the absurd skyscrapers and wrecked-car bone piles set in the red-clay hills, how could he seriously say that the South believed it "was succeeding in creating a world which, if it was not made altogether in the image of that old world, half-remembered and half-dreamed, shimmering there forever behind the fateful smoke of Sumter's guns, was yet sufficiently of a piece with it in essentials to be acceptable." A great slave society, by far the largest and richest of those that had existed in the New World since the sixteenth century, had grown up and miraculously flourished in the heart of a thoroughly bourgeois and partly puritanical republic. It had renounced its bourgeois origins and elaborated and painfully rationalized its institutional, legal, metaphysical, and religious defenses. It had produced leaders of skill, ingenuity, and strength who, unlike those of other slave societies, invested their honor and their lives, and not merely part of their capital, in that society. When the crisis came, they, unlike the others, chose to fight. It proved to be the death struggle of a society, which went down in ruins. And yet here is a historian who tells us that nothing essential changed. The ancient "mind," temperament, the aristocratic spirit, parvenu though he called it—call it what you will, *panache* perhaps—was perfectly preserved in a mythic amber. And so the present is continuous with the past, the ancient manifest in the new order, in Grady, Babbitt, Rotary, whatever, *c'est la même chose.*

I am afraid that Cash was taken in by the very myth he sought to explode—by the fancy-dress charade the New South put on in the cast-off finery of the old order, the cult of the Lost Cause, the Plantation Legend and the rest. The new actors threw themselves into the old roles with spirit and conviction and put on what was for some a convincing performance. But Cash himself, even though he sometimes took the Snopeses for the Sartorises, plainly saw how they betrayed to the core and essence every tenet of the old code. "And yet," he can write,

> And yet—as regards the Southern mind, which is our theme, how essentially superficial and unrevolutionary remain the obvious changes; how certainly do these obvious changes take place within the ancient framework, and even sometimes contribute to the positive strengthening of the ancient pattern.
>
> Look close at this scene as it stands in 1914. There is an atmosphere here, an air, shining from every word and deed. And the key to this atmosphere . . . is that familiar word without which it would be impossible to tell the story of the Old South, that familiar word "extravagant."
>
> [Then, after a reference to the new skyscrapers in the clay hills:]
>
> Softly; do you not hear behind that the gallop of Jeb Stuart's cavalrymen?

The answer is "No"! Not one ghostly echo of a gallop. And neither did Jack Cash. He only thought he did when he was bemused.

After some years in the profession, one has seen reputations of historians rise and fall. The books of Ulrich Phillips and later Frank Owsley began to collect dust on the shelves, and one thinks of Beard and Parrington. In America, historians, like politicians, are out as soon as they are down. There is no comfortable back bench, no House of Lords for them. It is a wasteful and rather brutal practice, unworthy of what Cash would agree are our best Southern traditions. I hope this will not happen to Cash. The man really had something to say, which is more than most, and he said it with passion and conviction and with style. Essentially what he had to say is something every historian eventually finds himself trying to say (always risking exaggeration) at some stage about every great historical subject. And that is that in spite of the revolution—any revolution—the English remain English, the French remain French, the Russians remain Russian, the Chinese remain Chinese—call them Elizabethans or Cromwellians, Royalists or Jacobeans, Czarists or Communists, Mandarins or Maoists. That was really what Cash, at his best, was saying about Southerners, and he said it better than anybody ever has—only he rather overdid the thing. But in that he was merely illustrating once more that ancient Southern trait that he summed up in the word "extravagant." And, for that matter, his critic, poured in the same mold, may have unintentionally added another illustration of the same trait. If so, Jack Cash would have been the first to understand and not the last to forgive. Peace to his troubled spirit.

Quest for a Central Theme

DAVID L. SMILEY

In the history of Southern history in America the central theme has been the quest for the central theme. Local and state historians, students of regionalism and sectionalism, along with authors of American history surveys, have agreed in accepting the hypothesis that there is an American South and that it has had, historically, a unifying focus at its center. Furthermore, it has become customary among many historians to emphasize sectionalism as a key factor in American political history and to seek the causes for the apparent division of national patriotism. The man in the street, though his views may be hazy or overemotional, is confident that there are distinctive social and political patterns, perhaps traceable to a unique agricultural base, which combine to make the regions below the Potomac a recognizable entity, and most Americans at one time or another have engaged in the pursuit of a central theme in Southern history.

In its broadest sense the attempt to generalize regional folkways into an American South is part of the search for a national identity. Since the days of Noah Webster's early crusade for American English orthography and usage and Ralph Waldo Emerson's 1837 appeal for an American culture—Oliver Wendell Holmes called it "our intellectual Declaration of Independence"—Americans have earnestly sought to define the elusive qualities of their civilization and have squirmed uncomfortably

David L. Smiley, "The Quest for the Central Theme in Southern History." *South Atlantic Quarterly,* 71:3 (Summer 1972), pp. 307–25. Copyright © 1972, Duke University Press. All rights reserved. Reprinted with permission.

when critics such as Harriet Martineau or Charles Dickens ridiculed their efforts. There are interesting parallels between the national response to Dickens' *American Notes* and the Southern umbrage at the publication of Fanny Kemble's *Georgia Journal.* Still, the search for a national identity went on, and alongside it, as if in overt denial of a homogeneous national character, the search for Southern distinctiveness continued.

The reasons for the dichotomy in the national personality are complex and often obscure. At the same time that it served the purposes of American patriotism to sound a bold trumpet for a native civilization, it was politically advantageous to assent to the proposition that that civilization contained two "nations," opposites in fundamental aspects. The subsequent defeat of one "nation" by the other had the effect, on both sides, of inspiring each to glamorize its superior civilization and to denigrate that of the other as alien, un-American, and lacking in enduring and essential values. Especially was this activity prevalent among Southerners, where it took the form of reverence for the Lost Cause and allegiance to the cult of the Old South. In paying homage to a mythical past they were but acting out a characteristic common to peoples defeated by material or military force, i.e., the tendency to emphasize the superiority of less tangible qualities which their civilization allegedly produced in great quantity. This happened in the post–Civil War South at a thousand veterans' campfires, in political orations on days set aside to the memory of the dead, and in graduation addresses replete with scholarly appurtenances, and soon the emphasis began to appear in presumably objective histories and biographies of the Confederacy and its leaders.

In these expressions, down to the latest Rebel yell or defiant wave of the Confederate battle flag, there was the axiomatic acceptance of the belief that there was in fact an American South and that it possessed clearly defined traits which set it apart from the rest of the nation. In some instances, notably in the rhetoric of ambitious politicians and regional promoters, these assumptions conveyed overtones of immediate advantage to the author. A widely accepted central theme or distinguishing characteristic of the American South, for example, might affect a person's vote for or against a party, a personality, or a platform. On other occasions it might encourage or discourage decisions concerning the migration of industries and the choice of sites for capital investments, or the transfer of individual talents to sunnier climes or a more favorable labor situation.

At the same time, other statements of the central theme emerged from the labors of those committed to the highest obligations of scholarship: to sift the evidence and to generalize its meaning into an idea whose purpose is to enlarge understanding and to stimulate additional study and thought. In each case the motivation, though vastly different in purpose and effect, remains confused and unclear, and a study of the themes and forces which have attracted scholarly attention is significant in illuminating the problems and clarifying the objectives of the broader quest for national identity.

Basically and historically the effort to express the essence of the American South in a central theme has turned upon two related streams of thought. One has been to emphasize the causal effects of environment, while the other has put uppermost the development of certain acquired characteristics of the people called Southern. The work of the scholar Ulrich B. Phillips well illustrates the dual thrust of the endeavor. The South, he declared in a famous article, was a section dominated by racial conflict. It was "a land with a unity despite its diversity, with a people having common joys and common sorrows, and, above all, as to the white folk a people with a common resolve indomitably maintained—that it shall be and remain a white man's country." The "cardinal test of a Southerner and the central theme of Southern history," he said, was the desire to preserve the supremacy of the white race.

A few months after the article appeared, however, Phillips published *Life and Labor in the Old South,* in which he defined the South in terms of environmental causation. "Let us begin by discussing the weather," he wrote, "for that has been the chief agency in making the South distinctive." Behind the central theme of white supremacy Phillips could now discern a determinative meteorological pattern. Climate encouraged the production of staple crops, he declared, and staple crops promoted the plantation as the most efficient institution for their cultivation; the plantation's demand for large quantities of cheap labor led to slave importations; the presence of large numbers of Africans resulted in turn in a continuing race problem and the effort to maintain white supremacy. The acquired characteristic of racism now became a "house that Jack built" upon the foundation of a causative weather pattern.

Although critics have eroded much of Phillips' work, searchers for the central theme continued to follow the twin trails that he blazed. Generally they have undertaken to document either the theme of a dominant pattern of life or they have looked beyond the characteristic itself to seek geographical, meteorological, or psychological determinants of the significant traits. Sometimes a student has combined all of these in a single sentence. "The South," wrote Wendell H. Stephenson, "is a geographical location, a group of factors that differentiated the region and its inhabitants from other sections of the United States, and a state of mind to which these factors gave rise."

Thus, in one way or another, seekers for the central theme in Southern history have illustrated Phillips' observations that the South was either the home of a peculiar behavior pattern—all but universally present among people who considered themselves Southern and all but universally absent elsewhere in the land (the inheritance theory)—or a place where men's lives were molded by impersonal forces of climate or geography (the environmental view).

Perhaps the earliest assumption among those in quest of the central theme has been that the South is the product of a dictatorial environment. Phillips himself spoke of climate, in the form of heavy rainfall and an overheated sun, as causative factors in Southern life. Deluges eroded the topsoil, packed plowed lands, and ran off in floods, he said, and these rains conditioned the soils of the South. The sun was "bakingly hot"; it parched vegetation and enervated Europeans. Clarence Cason agreed that the South was a hot land. It was that part of the United States where the mercury reached 90 degrees in the shade at least one hundred afternoons a year. According to the climate theory, the tyrant sun slowed life to a languid crawl, impelled men to choose the shaded sides of streets, and induced cooks to concoct gastronomical delights to tempt heat-jaded appetites. It also dictated an emphasis upon staple crops, and as a consequence influenced the labor system of the South. Cason related with approval the Mississippi proverb that "only mules and black men can face the sun in July" in support of the comforting philosophy that only dark-skinned menials, presumably equipped by an all-wise Creator to endure the heat, should perform physical labor.

The idea that the central theme of Southern history may be found in the environment, in a causal relationship between a tropical climate and a peculiar way of life, has been a persistent one. in 1778 Judge William Henry Drayton told the South Carolina Assembly that "from the nature of the climate, soil and produce of the several states, a northern and southern interest naturally and unavoidably arise," and this view found ready acceptance. In his *Notes on Virginia* Thomas Jefferson remarked that "in a warm climate, no man will labor for himself who can make another labor for him." For this reason, he said, "of the proprietors of slaves a very small proportion indeed are ever seen to labor." Not only did the sun dictate a Southern interest and an aversion to toil; it also purified the Anglo-Saxon blood lines. In 1852 a newspaper editor pointed out that South Carolina lay in the same latitude as Greece and Rome, which was a "pretty good latitude for a 'breed of noble men.' " Six years later an observer commented that the "gentleman and lady of England and France, born to command, were especially fitted for their God given mission of uplifting and Christianizing the Negroes because they were softened and refined under our Southern sky." These views continued into the present century. Hamilton J. Eckenrode declared that in the warm climate of the American South a superior Nordic race became "tropicized" and thus improved in quality, and Francis B. Simkins also defined the South as the result of an adjustment of Anglo-Saxon peoples to a subtropical climate. He went on to deplore the modern preference for sun-tanned women and architectural styles that broke with the ante-bellum tradition, and—perhaps with tongue in cheek—he regarded all admiration for Southern temperatures as a form of Yankee carpetbaggery. "Because of the tyranny of books and magazines imported from strange climates," he said, Southerners had lost their fear of the sun, and in so doing had denied their birthright. They were "prompted to construct artificial lakes, treeless lawns, and low-roofed houses without porches or blinds."

Such is the environmental view—the causal effects of climate upon Southern folkways—and its inaccuracies are manifest. There is no unity in Southern climate, for the section includes startling variations in pattern and is wholly temperate rather than tropical in nature. William A. Foran pointed out that it was climate of opinion rather than climate in fact that influenced the configurations of life and thought among Europeans inhabiting the Southern regions of North America. "The Great South of 1860," Foran said, "began at Mason's and Dixon's line, just twenty-five miles south of the Liberty Bell on Independence Square, and ranged on through fifteen degrees of latitude." It encompassed almost every type of North American climate, "from pleasantly-tempered Virginia and magnolia-scented Charleston to the arctic blizzards of Texas. . . . Can historians speak glibly of a southern climate, much less of a tropical one," he asked, "of a land whose rainfall varies from zero to seventy inches a year?"

But the important question concerns the causal relationship between high temperatures and a distinctive life style. Even if there were a demonstrable meteorological unity to Southern weather, that would not of itself determine a particular social order, an agricultural pattern, or a way of life. That it did so in fact is the basic assumption of the advocates of the environmental theory. Yet climate neither forecast nor foreordained a staple crop-slave labor-race segregation cycle such as Phillips and others have described. Edgar T. Thompson explicitly rejected the Phillips thesis. "The plantation was not to be accounted for by climate," he said; the climate-plantation-slavery syndrome was instead a defense mechanism. "A theory which makes the plantation depend upon something outside the processes of human interaction, that is, a theory which makes the plantation depend upon a fixed and static something like climate," he declared, "is a theory which operates to justify an existing social order and the vested interests connected with that order."

Whatever forces produced the plantation—perhaps a complex combination of the English manorial tradition and the immediate need for a social unit that could provide a measure of economic independence and military defense—it has existed in low-country regions of the South as an important institution. Many seekers for the central theme have considered it, therefore, as the distinctive characteristic of Southern life. First used to describe a group of "planted" colonists, the word came to mean a system of farming with tenants, indentured servants, peons, or slaves working under the direction of proprietors who owned great estates and who used their wealth and social position to play active roles in their communities' affairs. As a close-knit social and political group, the planters exerted an influence that was indeed often predominant. In some regions they were able to define their interests as those of the entire population, and their way of life as typical of the whole. With the enthusiastic co-operation of nostalgic novelists, poets, song composers, and advertising agents, the plantation and its gentlemen of distinction became the epitome of the Southern ideal. For a generation prior to the Civil War its proponents were able to impose the "plantation platform" of opposition to national banks, internal improvements at federal government expense, and tariffs of protection upon the policies of the general government. At the same time, opponents of the Jeffersonian agricultural Arcadia and the Calhounian logic of dominant particularism came to view the plantation as the symbol of all that was evil or amiss about America. It represented wealth amassed by exploiting an immoral labor system, disunionist and antinationalistic sentiments, support for policies that tied the whole country to a humiliating economic colonialism, and political power resting upon a snobbish and superficial aristocracy. For these reasons, enemies of the plantation regarded it as "un-American." Still, it served as a definition of the South. The plantation system was an ancient one; in varying forms it antedated the rise of chattel slavery, and after emancipation it persisted in fact and fancy as a distinctive entity. It was also fairly well distributed over the coastal plains and river valleys, regions earliest settled and seat of preponderant voting strength, and it extended into a roughly similar topography as settlement advanced into the Southwest. The plantation pattern of production was therefore general enough to serve as an archetype, however superficial, of a recognizable Southern society.

The great estate, with its paternalistic Massa and Missus, and the values it allegedly conserved, has provided much of the romantic Southern tradition. "The plantation," said Sheldon Van Auken, "is central to any understanding of the South." Since before there were white men in New England, he declared, it has been the most significant aspect of a South differentiated by it from the rest of the nation. More than other forms of economic and social organization the plantation provided security to laborers and a satisfying way of life to its operators. It set the standards for the entire South, Van Auken concluded, and it has remained the ideal image of the South. Earlier, Francis P. Gaines studied the plantation as a Southern tradition and declared that "the supremacy of the great estate in the thinking of the South cannot be successfully challenged."

But despite the plantation's exalted place in tradition, at no time was it the typical pattern of life in the Southern regions. It was a hothouse flower that could not hold its own in the low country and could not survive the cooler breezes of the uplands. Many students, including both Gaines and Van Auken, pointed out that the plantation did not penetrate into the hilly regions where yeoman farmers predominated and where a different way of life prevailed; except for isolated regions in the Virginia tidewater and the South Carolina low country, it did not monopolize life anywhere. The Owsleys have demonstrated that the plantation was not typical even of the Alabama black belt and was becoming less important in the decade of the 1850's. And according to Avery Craven, by 1860 Virginia and Maryland had "come largely to the small farm and the small farmer." The governor of Virginia reported that the state was no longer characterized by the "large plantation system," but had developed into an agriculture of "smaller horticultural and arboricultural farming.". . .

The plantation was, presumably, the home of other significant factors in the Southern image—the planter and his code of honor, and the institution of slavery—and students turned to these as central characteristics. As Avery Craven put it, "Only two factors seem to have contributed to the making of anything Southern—an old-world country-gentleman ideal and the presence of negroes in large numbers." The small minority of well-to-do planters lived in conscious imitation of the old English squires, stocking their homes with books and musical instruments, importing furnishings and clothing, and providing tutors for their children. In their personal relationships the more refined among them practiced a gallant chivalry. "When you institute a comparison between the men of the North and the South, does it not result in favor of those of the South?" a speaker in the Kentucky constitutional convention of 1849 asked. "Has not the South acquired for itself a character for frankness, generosity, high-toned honor, and chivalry which is unknown in the North?"

This was the country-gentleman ideal as a characteristic of the South. Though many planters ignored the demands of the code, in theory it set Cavalier Southerner apart from Roundhead Yankee. It provided a theme for the Southern Agrarians, who saw in it a conservative civilization which had, in the words of John Crowe Ransom, come "to terms with nature." Living "materially along the inherited line of least resistance," the planters sought "to put the surplus of energy into the free life of the mind." But to emphasize the country-gentleman as the typical inhabitant of the Southern regions, and to pretend that he alone possessed a code of disinterested obligation to public service or polite manners, ignored a host of other types equally Southern and overlooked commendable contributions to statecraft made by men who lived in other quadrants of the country.

Much more common as a unifying factor was another by-product of the plantation system of production, slavery and the Negro. Thomas P. Govan declared that the South was that part of the United States in which slavery continued for sixty years after it was abandoned elsewhere, but was in all other respects similar to the rest of the country. The only important sectional conflict in America, he said, arose from the fact that Negroes were held as slaves; emancipation eliminated the single

Southern distinctive and removed the cause of its desire to be independent. The subsequent insistence upon white supremacy, Govan contended, merely meant that Southerners acted like other men of European origins when they confronted large numbers of people of differing ethnic types. To define the South as the land of white supremacy, he concluded, overlooked the very real racism among non-Southern Americans and incorrectly suggested that only Southerners were capable of bigotry and intolerance. Yet Charles S. Sydnor cited the presence of the Negro as the most popular of the monocausationist theories explaining the differences between Southerners and other Americans.

The plantation also fostered a rural environment with its strange mixture of the polished and the primitive, and some students have defined the South in terms of its folkways. Andrew N. Lytle stated the central theme as a "backwoods progression" of an agrarian Arcadia, and others of the Agrarian School have emphasized the essential "South-ness" of a slowed pace of life, enjoyment of living, and leisure for contemplation and meditation. John Hope Franklin saw a different product of a rural South. It was a land of violence whose peoples possessed a "penchant for militancy which at times assumed excessive proportions." The Southern reputation for pugnacity, he added, "did not always command respect, nor even serious consideration; but it came to be identified as an important ingredient of Southern civilization."

Another critique of the Agrarian School came from David Potter. Declaring that the agrarian formula fitted the South remarkably badly, he defined the section as a place where older folkways persisted. "The culture of the folk survived in the South long after it succumbed to the onslaught of urban-industrial culture elsewhere," he said. "It was an aspect of this culture that the relations between the land and the people remained more direct and more primal in the South than in other parts of the country." In addition, relationships of people to one another "imparted a distinctive texture as well as a distinctive tempo to their lives." Americans regarded the South with a kind of nostalgia, he noted; its basis was not an ideal utopian society that never existed, but a "yearning of men in a mass culture for the life of a folk culture which really did exist."

Thus the climate and its alleged offspring, the plantation, the planter, the staple crop, and the Negro, all set in a rural scene surrounded by primitive folkways, have provided students with the ingredients for a central theme. Another avenue into the character of the Southern regions has been to pursue the second of Phillips' hypotheses and to describe the South on the basis of social patterns. Charles S. Sydnor suggested both the problem and the possibilities. Southern historians, he pointed out, studied a region which had no definite boundaries and therefore faced the prior necessity of delimiting their subject. In doing so, they pioneered in the study of social history. They considered the distinctive traits of the people called Southern and then sought "to discover the geographical incidence of these characteristics." Thus the student of the South "was driven from the problem of area back to the prior problem of essence," Sydnor declared; "his initial task was to discover what the Old South was. From the nature of the case he was compelled to be a social historian."

Elaborating upon his own analysis, in another article Sydnor listed some distinctively Southern culture patterns. Among them he described an inherited way of life modeled after that of the English gentry, slavery, malaria, hookworm, lynching, farm tenancy, the advocacy of states' rights, mockingbirds, and a unique attitude toward law and order. Following Sydnor's suggestions, other South-seekers offered additional criteria: the South is the place where people celebrate Christmas but not the Fourth of July with fireworks; it is where cooks add salt pork to the extended boiling of green vegetables; it is the domain of hominy grits; it is the land of one-party politics, one-horse plowing, and one-crop agriculture. Charles F. Lane declared that "the preference for the mule as a draft animal is one of the least-considered traits characterizing Southern culture" and proposed a map showing the mule population of the country as a way of marking boundaries around the South.

Other observers defined the South as the center of Protestant evangelical fundamentalism. Edwin McNeill Poteat declared that "the South is religiously solid" in much the same way that it was, to him, politically solid. To most Southerners heresy remained heresy, he said, and "they still in the main submit readily to demagogy in the pulpit, and enjoy the thrill of denominational competition." The religious South exhibited a "more homogeneous quality than any other section," Poteat concluded. There was some agreement with this idea. "The distinctiveness of the Old South," said Francis B. Simkins, "is perhaps best illustrated by its religion. Historic Protestantism was reduced to the consistencies of the Southern environment without sacrificing inherent fundamentals." Charles W. Ramsdell noted that religious fundamentalism was a Southern characteristic, and pointed out its effects in the reaction to the biological discoveries of the evolution of species, the effort to prohibit the manufacture and sale of beverage alcohol by constitutional amendment, and the resurgence of the Ku Klux Klan.

Another proposal in the quest for cultural distinctives held that the South was a collection of "settlement characteristics." The geographer Wilbur Zelinsky catalogued these traits as the pattern in which men house themselves. "In the course of field observations of house types, urban morphology, farmsteads, and other settlement characteristics," he said, "I have discovered a constellation of traits that are apparently co-terminous with the South and function collectively as a regional label." Some of the traits he emphasized were houses placed well back from the street and from each other, low or nonexistent curbings, sidewalk arcades in front of town shops, a central location for courthouses in county seats, a large number of rural nonfarm homes, a lack of "spatial pattern" to farm buildings, and a high rate of building abandonment. "The observer can be reasonably certain that he is within the Southern culture area when the bulk of these traits recur with great frequency," Zelinsky concluded, "and particularly when they are assembled into one or another of the regional house types."

Related to the description of the South as a land of rather slovenly dwelling patterns is David Bertelson's idea that the distinguishing characteristic of Southerners is laziness. By his definition, however, they were afflicted not with a lack of energy but with a dearth of social unity. Southerners sought individual rather than social goals and were motivated by a desire for private gain, he said. They were prototypes of the "robber barons" who sought wealth without social responsibility, and were so thoroughly committed to economic motivation that the relatively un-self-seeking abolitionists baffled them. To Bertelson the South was an individualistic, chaotic economy in an America whose other inhabitants held some idea of community purpose, and this gave Southerners a sense of apartness and led both to the formation and to the failure of the Confederacy. Before and during the war, he said, the idea that labor meant liberty for private gain destroyed all efforts to create community and strengthened the view of outsiders that Southerners were lazy.

A similar view was that of Earl E. Thorpe, who also argued that freedom was a chief characteristic of Southerners. To Thorpe, however, its emphasis was upon sexual license. Easy access to black females who "desperately wanted displays of recognition and affection" meant that there was less repression in the South than elsewhere, and freedom led to romanticism, hedonism, and pugnacity. The Southern white male, confronting the criticism of a more inhibited outside world, became militant in the defense of his society and his frequently deceived womenfolk. Thorpe thus described a Freudian South lying just below the land of Id, a harem of sexual freedom rather than a place of economic individualism.

Another recent proposal, offered by C. Vann Woodward, held that the only distinguishing feature that may survive the social revolution of the post-1945 era is the memory of the Southern past. "The collective experience of the Southern people," he said, has made the South "the most distinctive region of the country." It was an experience that repudiated the most cherished aspects of the American self-image, for it was a record of poverty in a land of plenty, pessimism and frustration among a people wedded to optimism and unending success, and guilt complexes in a naively innocent America. Indeed, Woodward comes close to saying that the central theme of Southern history is Southern history. However helpful the idea may be in interpreting the dreary years after Appomattox, it ignores the peculiarities and events that caused such an aberrant history in the first place.

Another currently popular thesis, also based upon the harsh unpleasantness that surrounds much of Southern existence, contends that the Southerner is more inclined to romanticism than are other Americans. The Southerner is distinguished by his preference for fantasy and myth. "The quality that makes him unique among Americans," said T. Harry Williams, is his ability to conjure up "mind-pictures of his world or of the larger world around him—images that he wants to believe, that are real to him, and that he will insist others accept." George B. Tindall suggested the possibility that "we shall encounter the central theme of Southern history at last on the new frontier of mythology," and he listed some of the myths about the South that have at one time or another gained support: the Pro-Slavery South, the Confederate South, the Demagogic South, the States' Rights South, the Lazy South, and the Booster South. "There are few areas of the modern world," he declared, "that have bred a regional mythology so potent, so profuse and diverse, even so paradoxical, as the American South." Here again the searcher finds the results of an allegedly distinctive South, one of the inheritance family of character traits, but provides little illumination as to its cause.

The effort to locate the South by defining it as a single characteristic produced still another statement of the central theme. Outlined by Avery Craven and Frank L. Owsley and amplified by others, it argued that the South was the product of attacks from without. In this view the South was a state of mind, a conscious minority reacting to criticism by forging a unity as a defense mechanism. Opposition drew people together in defense of their peculiarities when their natural course would have been to fight among themselves. It began, according to Craven, with the tariff controversy in the 1820's and it became full grown in the abolition crusade.

Frank L. Owsley further developed the theme that the South came into being only when it became the victim of outside attack. "There was very little defense or justification of slavery until the commencement of a vigorous abolitionist assault from the North," he said. But "the attack upon slavery and the South resulted in the development of a philosophical defense of slavery. . . . So violent and dangerous did this new crusade appear to Southerners that a revolution in Southern thought immediately took place." Owsley declared that attacks upon the South had continued since the Civil War, but these merely succeeded in making the section more united than before. Charles W. Ramsdell, B. B. Kendrick, and A. B. Moore, along with others, defended the "outside attack" thesis, while Frank E. Vandiver emphasized an "offensive-defensive" pattern of Southern response to external criticism. Implicit in this argument is the assumption that a united South began as a Yankee invention.

The contention that the idea of a South grew out of external attacks produced its corollary—that the South was the result of a conscious effort to create a sense of unity among a diverse population with conflicting interests. In the effort, Southern leaders used all available arguments—climate, race, soil, staple-crop similarities, the agrarian philosophy with its country-gentleman ideal and the plantation as a romantic tradition, and slavery as a positive good. Some of them dramatized, if they did not actually invent, attacks from without as aids to their campaign for sectional unity. "If there is a central theme," said Robert S. Cotterill, "it is the rise of Southern nationalism." The study of the emergence of a divergent nationalism attracted many scholars. The South "was an emotion," Avery Craven wrote, "produced by an assumption on the part of outsiders of a unity there which did not exist, by propaganda within which emphasized likenesses rather than differences and created a unity of fear where none other existed."

In the conscious effort to create a South, every hint of attack from outside the section came as a godsend. William Lloyd Garrison and his abolition newspaper might well have passed unnoticed had not Southern publicists called attention to him by putting a price upon his head. Critics of the Southern system such as Elijah P. Lovejoy in Illinois and Cassius M. Clay in Kentucky found themselves the objects of violent mob resistance. In 1859 Edmund Ruffin, an energetic Southern unifier, expressed gratitude for the John Brown raid upon Harpers Ferry because of its beneficial effects upon "the sluggish blood of the South," and he took it upon himself to send samples of Brown's pikes to the governors of the slave states lest they forgot. After the war, Reconstruction again called forth a movement for white unity in the face of political and economic coercion—new attacks from without—and into the twentieth century there appeared leaders willing to evoke memories of the past as weapons against proposed changes in existing social or educational arrangements.

The flaw in the hypothesis of a movement to unify a people in the face of real or imaginary attacks from without has two aspects. First, as with all devil theories of historical motivation, it assumes almost magical powers of clairvoyance among promoters of the movement; and second, what it describes are but activities common to politicians practicing their profession wherever found, not uniquely Southern behavior at all. It was not surprising that Southern leaders should appeal for unanimity in support of their programs and candidacies; indeed, it would require explanation had any not done so. And that they could have foreseen the consequences of their conduct places a severe strain upon credulity.

From this confusing and sometimes contradictory survey of central themes in Southern history and life the suspicion emerges that the American South defies either location or analysis. It appears to be in fact an enigma challenging comprehension, "a kind of Sphinx on the American land." Its geographical boundaries are imprecise at best, and the characteristics of its population resist valid generalization. To say this is not to say that the South does not exist; it is to suggest that it exists only as a controlling idea or belief upon which men acted, risked, and died. The idea of the South is real; it is one of the most important ideas in American history, and that gives it significance.

The South idea has played a fundamental role in national development. In the early days of the Republic, as part of the debate between Thomas Jefferson and Alexander Hamilton which formed the basis of the first party divisions under the Constitution, the idea of a South contributed to the definition of public policy. As the internal dispute became more heated, it entered into the compromises that Americans made over the admission of Missouri, in the tariff settlement in 1833, and in the agreements of 1850. The idea appeared in party platforms and in the selection of candidates, and in 1860 it was an essential element in the division within the Democratic party.

The idea of a South produced an internal civil war whose outcome established the American nation. That result might have occurred in the absence of civil war, and also without the South idea, temporarily expressed as a Confederacy of states hostile to national union. But as it happened, the emergence of American nationality depended upon the idea of a South that posed a challenge to national citizenship and solidarity. In the postwar settlement—the constitutional amendments comprised in the peace treaty between the sections—the idea of the South profoundly affected the nature of the re-established Union upon national and pluralistic foundations. Later, when war emotions had cooled and industrial production expanded, it was the idea of the South that influenced the form and the content of the reactionary compromises of 1877. In the twentieth century the idea of a South re-emerged as men debated the meaning of national citizenship and the civil liberties the nation owed its citizens.

The American South is therefore not a place or a thing; it is not a collection of folkways or cultural distinctives. It is an idea. Those of whatever persuasion or tradition who believe themselves to be Southern are indeed Southern, and the South exists wherever Southerners form the predominant portion of the population. The study of the idea of Southness is thus a part of intellectual history, or, because it is an exercise in faith, it belongs among the academic offerings in the department of religion.

Perhaps a more fruitful question for students of the American South would be, not *what* the South is or has been, but *why* the idea of the South began, and *how* it came to be accepted as axiomatic among Americans. Whose interests were served when people spoke and thought of the South as an entity? How did the agents of the opinion-forming and opinion-disseminating institutions transmit the idea that allegiance to a section should transcend loyalty to the nation? What have been the effects upon American history of the belief in the idea of a South? Answers to these questions will go far to remove the study of the South from the realm of classifying and cataloguing to the tasks of probing causes and effects and the weighing of motivations. These are the true functions of the historian.

The Difficulty of Consensus on the South

JOHN B. BOLES

Any prospective reader of a book of essays on the modern South might expect a certain consensus of viewpoints, a commonly accepted definition of the region, even a general agreement about the South's past, if not its future. . . . No single conclusion, no mutually accepted point of view emerges. What the South is, whether it is persisting as a distinct region or vanishing into a great homogenous American culture, or whether that "loss" should be applauded, regretted, or prevented by some intellectual cardiopulmonary contraption, remains a riddle that different individuals answer differently. It has always been so with the South. Everyone has a ready image of the region, but the closer one comes to examine the South, the more the differences merge into similarities, and vice versa. Like a giant sphinx on the American land—as one historian called it—Dixie beckons investigators even as it resists explication. Therein of course lies its attraction.

The South is both American and something different, at times a mirror or magnifier of national traits and at other times a counterculture. That difference has been good, bad, and indefinable, but it has long been felt. . . . The South still challenges those who try to separate image from reality, stereotype from myth. Accepting the difficulty of consensus, wary of simple truths, adventurous readers will find here hard thinking, suggestive analysis, but ultimately no single key to understanding the South. And that makes the whole endeavor not futile but exciting. The southern character is too complex for easy answers, and southerners—at least the publishing kind—enjoy the perennial search for southern identity.

For at least two centuries Americans have recognized a distinctive South, and perhaps there is no more enduring regional image in the American mind than that of a Dixie different from the rest of the nation. In a famous letter to the Marquis de Chastellux, dated September 2, 1785, Thomas Jefferson compared the characteristics of northerners and southerners by listing their traits in parallel columns:

In the North they are	In the South they are
cool	fiery
sober	voluptuary
laborious	indolent
persevering	unsteady
independant [*sic*]	independant [*sic*]
jealous of their own liberties, and just to those of others	zealous for their own liberties, but trampling on those of others
interested	generous
chicaning	candid
superstitious and hypocritical in their religion	without attachment or pretensions to any religion but that of the heart

Essay, "The Difficulty of Consensus on the South," by John B. Boles from the introduction to *Dixie Dateline,* © 1983. Reprinted by permission.

Jefferson was so certain that these traits conformed to geographical setting that he wrote: "An observing traveller, without aid of the quadrant, may always know his latitude by the character of the people among whom he finds himself."

Jefferson ascribed the South's peculiarities to "that warmth of their climate," a judgment echoed almost a century and a half later by U. B. Phillips of Yale University. Georgia-born Phillips, the first great southern historian, commenced his classic account of the Old South with the sentence, "Let us begin by discussing the weather, for that has been the chief agency in making the South distinctive." We are less concerned here with the role of climate or the accuracy of Jefferson's classification than with the underlying assumption of southern distinctiveness. That idea grew slowly. Historians still debate when the South emerged as a self-consciously separate section, perceived as such also by the nation as a whole. Taking their cue from Jefferson and pronouncements made by delegates from several southern states during and shortly after the chaos of the American Revolution, some historians argue that the "South"—as distinct from the geographically southern colonies—existed as early as 1776, set apart even then by slavery.

Historians of course are no more likely to agree than are economists or theologians. Few scholars accept this early a date for the existence of full-blown southern identity. Instead, most view the long generation following the Treaty of Paris (1783) as the high-water-mark of southern Americanism, when southerners were at the liberal forefront of national decisionmaking and in fact controlled four of the first five presidential administrations. Washington, Jefferson, Madison, and Monroe were nation-builders, not dismantlers of the Union. For many twentieth-century southern liberals, these founding fathers represented the true South, the Great South, before slavery interests and John C. Calhoun led the region down the seductive path of sectionalism, then secession, Civil War, and Reconstruction, to sharecropping and colonial status within the nation.

There is a pleasing symmetry to this view, for it allows one to think of the history of southernness as a kind of long aberration, ended perhaps in 1976 when southerner Jimmy Carter became president. The great break occurred sometime between the War of 1812—when even John C. Calhoun was a fiercely nationalistic "war hawk"—and the early 1830s, by which time the nullification crisis in the South and the rise of modern antislavery activities in the North called forth a militant southern sectionalism. Perhaps the pivotal year was 1819, when the debate over the admission of Missouri as a state raised the critical question of the expansion of slavery. In that year also the deep economic depression—the Panic of 1819—highlighted profound economic differences between North and South. In retrospect it seems that a southern recognition of divergent values, contrasting social and economic systems, and an emerging distinctive culture began that eventful year, a full century and a half after the slavery-plantation system had developed.

Once the perception arose that the South had a unique destiny, events were interpreted to prove the perception. Old realities were observed in a new light. Many contemporaries saw the divisive issues and dilemmas of the next four decades as springing from the essential dichotomy between North and South. From this perspective the Civil War became necessary, even irrepressible, for a southern nation had arisen with manifold interests so different that continued union was impossible. Thus the Civil War, the apex of southern separateness, appears almost predetermined, with the long and often arduous century afterwards being merely the slow process by which the South was brought back into the Union, first legally in 1876, then politically in 1976, and not quite yet economically.

In this sense of the South's finally rejoining the nation, some commentators heralded Jimmy Carter's election to the presidency as ending the region's long sojourn as a separate province. How appropriate it seemed, on the nation's 200th birthday, for the great sectional rapprochement to occur. Yet those who thought that the nation was finally done with things distinctly southern were ill-prepared for the next few years. Punsters quickly labeled the Carter-Mondale team "Grits and Fritz," and Jimmy's brother Billy added a new dimension to the stereotype of the Good Ole Boy. With toe-tapping country music in the White House and recipes for catfish in the *New York Times,* southern fried chic seemed to suit the national taste. The subtitle of John Egerton's book, *The Southernization of America,* was perhaps more appropriate than its title, *The Americanization of Dixie.* The upshot of the matter was the question, with the South becoming more like the North, or vice versa, was there validity any more to the hoary concept of the distinctive South? Journalists vied with sociologists and historians to describe the death of Dixie. Their efforts proved premature.

Of course even an attempt to eulogize the South implies the assumption of regional distinctiveness, and the origin of that assumption lies intertwined with much of American history. For two centuries Americans North and South have felt a need to define the Dixie difference. In the antebellum days of slavery and plantations the South's economy and its labor system differentiated it from the rest of the nation, but southerners, feeling defensive about their peculiar institution and not a little guilty, sought to apotheosize their society. Real regional differences were exaggerated and elaborated upon. Like whistling in the dark to dispel fears and doubts, southerners tried, largely successfully, to persuade themselves that theirs was a higher form of civilization than the frenzied, industrial North. According to the plantation legend, the South produced gentlemen rather than vulgar businessmen; a leisurely life of manners and lofty thoughts rather than a hurried, pell-mell struggle for ever-higher profits; a working class of contented slaves, not sullen, unruly factory laborers. Thus the myth of the Old South emerged, but not entirely because it soothed southern consciences. Many northern intellectuals, dismayed by the social changes being wrought by the incipient Industrial Revolution, helped create the plantation legend and then used it to criticize the changing North. The Old South of moonlight and magnolias, of carefree hospitality and happy-go-lucky Sambos, served both regions as myths usually do, relieving social tensions and reconciling conflicting values.

During the generation before the Civil War both North and South conspired to create an image of the South, an illusion that never bore close resemblance to reality. For their contrasting needs Americans in the two regions constructed self-serving portraits of the Old South, an exotic, romantic "touched-up" portrait with the diversity, the conflict, the frontier aspects of the South removed. In the aftermath of Appomattox, white southerners, suffering a depression of both morale and money, sought to recoup some of their pride by romanticizing the Old South with a vengeance, constructing a never-never land of mess, magnolias, mansions, and mammies. Many southern clergy found meaning in Confederate defeat by arguing that God was thereby testing the South for a higher purpose, the reformation of the nation along the lines of evangelical Protestantism. Southern traditions were united with biblical themes to produce a religion of the Lost Cause, a faith that practically equated the heritage of Dixie with Holy Scripture.

Following Reconstruction, secular advocates of an urban, industrial "New South" of profits and progress helped sell their program, legitimate themselves as southern, and assuage vague guilt feelings about imitating the Yankees by piously glorifying the Old South. Joel Chandler Harris, for example, wrote booster editorials by day and Uncle Remus stories by night, seemingly without noticing the conflict. Ever since, students have labored under the heavy burden of myth and contradiction. In fact, much historical scholarship in the twentieth century has been an attempt to demythologize the popular notions of southern history. The list of myths debunked is long—the Lazy South, the Romantic South, the Cavalier South, the New South. Historians point out again and again, for example, that the large majority of southern whites in 1860 did not own slaves; that Reconstruction was not a "blackout of honest government"; that slaves were not happy Sambos; that Sunbelt notions to the contrary, the South is still the nation's poorest region. But the myths live on. Now historians are turning their attention to the function of myths, how they have helped shape southern history by forging unity, offering rationales for action, providing a common goal.

After acknowledging the prevalence of several mythical Souths and then trying to analyze the reality behind the facade, one quickly realizes that more riddles abound. Even defining the South quickly transcends geography to become a problem in cultural and intellectual history. Simple geography brings difficulties. The Mason-Dixon Line does not suffice as a boundary between North and South, for such a division would assign Delaware to the South. If we were to consider the former Confederate states as delimiting the South, we would be excluding Maryland and Kentucky, two important slave states, as well as Missouri. Some expansive Sunbelt theoreticians would lump the Southeast along with New Mexico, Arizona, and much of California and call the broad swath of geography "the southern rim," meanwhile searching in vain for parallels between southern California and South Carolina. In this century migrations of southerners northward and northerners southward have blurred the boundaries. Much of southern Illinois and Indiana have a southern cast, as do sections of Detroit; and Bakersfield, California, is a southern enclave in the West. The Virginia suburbs of Washington, D. C., the coastal areas of the Florida peninsula, and the cosmopolitan suburbs of Houston and Atlanta have been so penetrated by persons of northern birth as to lead to a proliferation of delicatessens and the easy availability—even home delivery—of the *New York Times.* Where does the South begin and end?

To make matters worse, any geographical concept of the South conveys the false impression of homogeneity. Expressions such as "the Solid South" have created the image of a monolithic region, a huge, warm, culturally flat region of slow-talking people who prefer grits with breakfast and their pork barbecued. Yet within the South there is variety of every kind: geological, climatic, cultural, ethnic. Even the favored styles of barbecue differ. The piedmont and mountain areas of Virginia, North Carolina, and Tennessee are as different from the coastal plains of Louisiana as Savannah is from Dallas. The Texas Germans and Czechs, the Louisiana Cajuns, and the North Carolina Moravians are people very different from the First Families of Virginia (the FFVs) and the aristocracies of Charleston and New Orleans. The mountain folk of the Appalachian valleys share little with Texas wildcatters or Georgia blacks. Yet all are southerners. One of the important roles of myth has been to create an illusion of unity out of this diversity. Similarly, students of the region, seeking to impose order on a crazy-quilt topic, have labored mightily to find a central theme of southern history with which to comprehend the whole. In many ways the search for a central theme has been the central theme of southern history; that quest now has added urgency because of the perception that the South is slowly, before our very eyes, disappearing as a definable entity.

Despite the historical uses and convenience of myths and stereotypes in characterizing or describing the region, most students of the South accept the truth that there really is something different about Dixie. From Jefferson's day the climate has frequently been interpreted as having played a major role in making the South distinctive. According to this view, a long growing season allowed the South to satisfy world demand for tobacco and cotton. The successful introduction of these crops led in turn to the rise of the broad-acred plantation system with its need for cheap labor, a need ultimately met by Negro slavery. Here then were the essential ingredients of southern history: a rural, agricultural region dominated by large planters, with a suppressed racial minority on the bottom. In tangible, measurable ways, the antebellum South was different from the antebellum North. From this fact emerged images of the romantic Old South, as well as the idea, expressed best in 1928 by U. B. Phillips, that the essence of southernism was "a common resolve indomitably maintained" that the South "shall be and remain a white man's country." Whether "expressed with the frenzy of a demagogue or maintained with a patrician's quietude," this was, according to Phillips, "the cardinal test of a Southerner and the central theme of Southern history." The myth of a planter aristocracy, the theme of an agrarian republic, the identification of the South with gracious living or white domination or rural-dominated Bible-Belt religion or one-party politics—all have evolved from the old assumption that environment shaped events.

The economy and society that were made possible and produced by the climate gave rise to a people who possessed certain characteristics, and many observers have shifted their attention away from the immediate consequences of climate and focused on those acquired human traits that seem to define southerners. Rather than its crops, it is its people and their character that distinguish the region. Because geography fails, we turn to defining the South as a region possessing a unique folk culture, or having experienced a history very unlike the rest of the nation. The South becomes a way of living, a sense of belonging, a state of mind. W. J. Cash's great book, *The Mind of the South,* is the classic of this genre, although in his emphasis on southerners' feeling instead of thinking, on their simple hedonism mixed with a rigid Puritanical streak, Cash came close to arguing that the South did not have a mind. Southerners, it seems, *are* more violent, more religious, more conservative, more fatalistic than nonsoutherners. Thinking does affect behavior. Statistics show that the southern death rate from tornadoes, for example, is significantly higher than elsewhere, and the best explanation is that southerners ignore warnings and neglect to build storm cellars in the belief that if your time has come, you can't escape, and if your time has not come, then why bother with precaution. Southerners also speak differently, whether with a Georgia drawl or an East Texas twang, and have an infatuation with words, a tendency to express themselves not in straightforward analytical prose but with detailed, richly textured stories. . . . The love affair with talk may explain the world-renowned outpouring of southern fiction, as well as the disproportionate number and influence of southern journalists and historians—people who, after all, mainly tell stories. Even that most southern of music, labeled "country," is peculiarly concerned with the stories that unfold in the lyrics.

In recent decades the quest to understand southern distinctiveness has produced more emphasis on the human dimension. David Potter, a Georgia-born historian who taught at Rice, Yale, and Stanford universities, argued that southern identity inhered in what he called a unique folk culture. In this folk society a sense of belonging, a relatedness of people to people and people to land, persisted amidst a national culture that was increasingly urban and technological. This identification with place and family seemed to be particularly true among rural southerners, and the South remained largely rural until after World War II. The urban areas in the South today are still peopled mostly by rural folk who have migrated to the cities in search of jobs. They have brought with them their tastes in food, music, sports, and religion. In subtle ways they have changed the cities, and certainly their urban residence has changed their expectations, even if it has not rendered them completely urbane. During the decade of the 1970s, Dixie was the only region of the nation in which urban growth outpaced rural growth. The rising generation of city-born southerners will determine whether the South can survive urbanization and remain recognizably southern. If southernness is merely an artifact of rurality, then it will soon be gone with the winds of change and growth. Sociological data shows, however, that educated, urban southerners continue to attend church far more regularly than their counterparts nationally and identify themselves with their homeplaces with greater intensity than northerners—an indication that southern values will persist in the cities.

Realizing that the bulldozer revolution of urban sprawl and industrialization would eventually end the South's rural isolation, and that the Supreme Court's desegregation decision in *Brown* v. *Board of Education of Topeka* in 1954 would ultimately end the white South's intransigence on race, C. Vann Woodward sought the essence of southernness in the region's peculiar historical experience. According to Woodward, what had made the South different was not its relative absence of cities, its agrarian traditions, its inordinate concern with race, or its political practices, but rather the way it had been treated by time itself.

Writing a generation ago, Woodward contrasted the nation's history of prosperity—being the people of plenty—with the South's long travail of poverty, stretching from the rise of sharecropping to the trough of the Great Depression, when President Franklin D. Roosevelt called the region the nation's number one economic problem. Moreover, although no nation in all history had succeeded like the United States, winning all its wars and spreading its banner from sea to shining sea, the South had failed, and failed utterly, in its one great attempt to have a separate national destiny. And while the nation—born in liberty, protector of the Union, and emancipator of the slaves—basked in innocence, the South had to live with the guilt of slavery and secession bearing heavily on its soul. Thus, Woodward concluded, in a nation marked by success, prosperity, and innocence, the South was set apart by its failure, poverty, and guilt. That collective experience, shared by all southerners, gave them a sense of identity, a common heritage apart from the national norm. The South's history, a past that was not dead, defined the southern character. A sense of tragedy, a recognition of frailty and limits to endeavor marked the regional psyche. Because the southern experience has been more akin to the world experience than the northern experience has been, southern literature both fictional and historical attracts an enormous audience abroad. Moreover, two quintessential southern musical forms, jazz and country, enjoy a global acceptance. The southern encounter with history has ironically produced an intensely localistic people with universal dilemmas and international appeal.

Of course, in the years since Woodward made his influential analysis, the nation has undergone a series of shocks. In the aftermath of Vietnam, Watergate, and the discovery of poverty in the land of plenty—what Michael Harrington called "The Other America"—the national experience no longer seems so different from that of the South. And with the South solving its racial problems arguably more satisfactorily than the North, with Sunbelt prosperity narrowing the regional income gap, and with a recent southern president, one might even argue that the regions have flip-flopped. Such of course is not the case, but southerners now feel much freer of that scorn once directed their way, and are finding "Snowbelt" envy much more gratifying.

The southern folk culture that has experienced a history unlike the rest of the United States is in many ways biracial. In the South blacks and whites have lived together, cheek by jowl, for more than three hundred years. Nothing and no one in the South has escaped the mutual influences of the two races. Black values and styles have helped shape the white culture, and vice versa, to such an extent that today it is impossible to separate the strands. Southerners are truly both the white and black inhabitants of the region. Hearing Elvis Presley borrow from black vocal traditions or Charlie Pride singing Hank Williams, or eating southern home cooking, or listening to southern preachers or gospel singers, who can deny that we truly are one at the same time that we are two people?

But the question remains: where is and what is the South today? Efforts to reappraise the South seem to proliferate shortly after every period of change. At the end of the 1950s, Arkansas journalist Harry Ashmore wrote a perceptive book entitled *An Epitaph for Dixie,* but historian Francis B. Simkins of Virginia countered with *The Everlasting South.* Parallel titles could be supplied down to the present, with concern ever being raised about *The Americanization of Dixie,* then laid aside with reflections on *The Enduring South.* As change erodes the characteristics that were once thought to define the South—poverty, rurality, educational and "cultural" backwardness, segregation, Democratic hegemony—the South's separate existence seems threatened. With that threat of loss, writers of every sort start examining the region, hunting for surviving fossils of the past or subtle new forms of southern identity, and lo, that very concern with self-identity betrays a very southern habit of wanting to know who you are and from whence you came. That concern with family, with place, with "relatedness" that so epitomizes the southerner produces a spate of regional analysis and nostalgia and, yes, even pious self-congratulation that keeps the South alive. Whether one assumes that there is still a tangible essence that sets the region apart or that one must, in the face of modernization and homogenization, "Dixiefy Dixie" . . . to keep the image alive artificially, the search for southern identity has continued for at least two centuries and shows no signs of faltering or concluding.

With the South, as with much else, a great deal lies in the eye of the beholder. High technology, interstate highways, and industrial growth may threaten one vision of the South, but recorded country music, fast food outlets for fried chicken and biscuits and sausage, C-B radios in eighteen-wheelers crackling with good-ole-boy talk from their drivers, and the working poor who have moved from the fields to the factories keep alive memories of the past. Southern speech patterns and that signal form of ethnic identification, gastronomic preferences, show sure signs of resisting change. While the architecture and form of southern cities appear as standardized as American cities elsewhere, . . . in human terms the texture of life in them reveals surprising continuity with the rural past. Yet popular images often lag behind changing reality, and the myth of southern distinctiveness may ultimately be more tenacious, and more significant, than actuality. Perceptive journalists . . . can document that southern universities are more than holding their own and subscribing to national standards for research, tenure, and curricula. Yet a "manual" like *The Insiders' Guide to the Colleges* (1971) stereotypically includes most southern universities under the category "Hard Playin', Hard Drinkin', Hard Lovin' Southern Schools." How do myth, perception, and reality merge in the popular mind? The acceptance of diversity, real or imagined, can make a real difference. As long as southerners believe in, fear, or desire a regional identity, or worry about whether one exists, there will be a South. What that South is, precisely speaking, no one can say.

And surely few will not admit that the loss of many "southern characteristics" is a great blessing. The South's long heritage of spirit-breaking poverty, of ignorance and religious prejudice, of savage racism and brutal violence, of irrelevant politics and undemocratic control, took a heavy toll on all southerners. To the extent that *that* South has died, humanity has triumphed. Better schools and improved job opportunities have freed thousands from poverty and given them immeasurably better lives. While city dwellers acknowledge a twinge of nostalgia for life back on the farm, the higher pay, greater scope of entertainment, and educational and medical advantages of urban life keep them in town. Even so, many still identify with their rural homeplaces and intend to retire and be buried there. For the huge majority of southerners, black and white, the South today is certainly a much better place to live than it was a generation ago. The beneficial changes in race relations alone represent a fundamental reshaping of the social, cultural, and political landscape, and give promise of improving relations in the future. The tide of black migration has turned back toward the South, and southern blacks are finding new purpose and meaning in their original American homeland. Even today one is surprised, driving into Montgomery from Atlanta, to see overhead the large green interstate sign proclaiming the "Martin Luther King, Jr., Expressway," but what could be a better symbol of the changing South?

In one sense this whole endeavor of defining and making predictions about the continuity of southernness has an abstract, ersatz quality about it. Most southerners take their sense of regional identity for granted even if they cannot articulate its nature. Perhaps one even has to be a southerner to know really what it is. For southerners, after all, grew up with a perception of differentness that had its roots in that long-ago time when slavery gave a concreteness that has since evaporated to the idea of separate cultures. That folk memory of distinction, imbibed with their mothers' milk, predisposes southerners to assume their distinctiveness, even when tangible evidence is wanting. And for generations, except when threatened by or contrasted to outsiders, the search for regional self-identity was what kept novelists and historians and journalists in business; the folk simply were southerners. The magnitude of the change in recent years, however, has brought urgency, a sense of potential loss, not only to aspiring authors but to average persons who can instinctively sense that they are drifting away from their old world. Often loss brings reflection and renewed appreciation, and exactly that seems to be happening with southernness.

People are suddenly eating homestyle cooking and saying "y'all," purposely being southern as a personal statement of identity. People are no longer ashamed to be southerners. A perception that the South might be disappearing in a cultural sense has led to a discovery of its importance in personal and national terms. Ninety years ago the census revealed that the American frontier was closed; three years later a great historian discovered "The Significance of the Frontier." . . . [S]omething similar might be happening in the South's largest and most rapidly changing city. Houston's phenomenal growth in population and prosperity has changed its motto from the "Magnolia City" to the "Urban West." A new culture is emerging, neither completely southern nor western. But as Houston becomes less like the Texas of old, with its heritage of openness and individuality, native Houstonians (and transplanted rural Texans) eagerly try to recapture that old ethic. Cowboy chic began not as a movie gimmick but as a grassroots attempt to recapture and hold on to a way of life and a mythical identity that was rapidly disappearing. Moreover, the thousands of mobile Americans from California, Michigan, and New York who have moved to Houston—rootless searchers for economic opportunity and advancement—seize upon the cowboy image in an attempt to legitimate their residence and show that they "belong." While the western cowboy seems to have conquered the southern cavalier in Texas, partly because of the more favorable popular associations of the cowpoke with freedom and "good" and partly because the cowpuncher is a more national hero, Houston's cowboy renaissance may suggest the future of southernness.

As the South disappears in demographic, economic, and political terms, there seems to be a corresponding effort to rediscover and revivify at least certain components of the southern way of life. Opinion molders sense the popular concern, and thus symposia, books, clothing, musical fads, and even college curricula—witness the proliferation of "southern institutes"—speak to that concern. In a very real sense, southerners did not exist until about 1819, when they began to perceive themselves as an identifiable group. The underlying socioeconomic factors that gave substance to the perception existed for more than a century before the perception arose. Self-identification as "southern" was the essence of southernness, and that perception has acquired a life of its own, in large part independent of material reality. Southernness is now almost an intellectual construct, "the flesh made word,". . . . Having a distinctiveness to lose makes possible a recognition of loss, and that triggers a process of retrospection and nostalgia that bodes well to keep the South alive and thriving. The South will continue to exist, if only by an act of the will. After all, . . . they aren't having symposia in Phoenix to discuss the everlasting West.

⚓ *F U R T H E R   R E A D I N G*

David Bertelson, *The Lazy South* (1967)
John B. Boles, ed., *The Dixie Difference* (1983)
———, *Dixie Dateline* (1983)
———, *The South Through Time* (1995)
James Branch Cabell, *Let Me Lie* (1947)
W. J. Cash, *The Mind of the South* (1941)
James C. Cobb, *The Most Southern Place on Earth: The Mississippi Delta and the Roots of Regional Identity* (1992)
Albert E. Cowdrey, *This Land, This South: An Environmental History* (1983)
F. Garvin Davenport, *Myth and Southern History* (1970)
Carl N. Degler, *Place over Time: The Continuity of Southern Distinctiveness* (1977)
———, "Thesis, Antithesis, Synthesis: The South, the North, and the Nation," *Journal of Southern History* 53 (1987), 3–8
Paul D. Escott, ed., *W. J. Cash and the Minds of the South* (1992)
John Hope Franklin, *The Militant South* (1956)
Patrick Gerster and Nicholas Cords, eds., *Myth and Southern History* (1974)
Larry J. Griffin and Don H. Doyle, eds., *The South as an American Problem* (1995)
Fred C. Hobson, *Tell About the South: The Southern Rage to Explain* (1983)
C. Hugh Holman, *The Immoderate Past: The Southern Writer and History* (1977)
Lewis M. Killian, *White Southerners* (1970)
Florence King, *Southern Ladies and Gentlemen* (1975)
Jack Temple Kirby, *Media-Made Dixie* (1978)
A. Cash Koeniger, "Climate and Southern Distinctiveness," *Journal of Southern History* 54 (1988), 21–44
Bill C. Malone, *Southern Music, American Music* (1979)
Sharon McKern, *Redneck Mothers, Good Ol' Girls, and Other Southern Belles* (1979)
Grady McWhiney, *Southerners and Other Americans* (1973)
U. B. Phillips, "The Central Theme of Southern History," *American Historical Review* 34 (1928), 30–43
David M. Potter, "The Enigma of the South," *Yale Review* 51 (1961), 142–151
John Shelton Reed, *One South: An Ethnic Approach to Regional Culture* (1982)
John Herbert Roper, ed., *C. Vann Woodward: A Southern Historian and His Critics* (1997)
Francis Butler Simkins, *The Everlasting South* (1963)
William R. Taylor, *Cavalier and Yankee* (1961)
Frank E. Vandiver, ed., *The Idea of the South: Pursuit of a Central Theme* (1964)
Charles Reagan Wilson and William Ferris, eds., *Encyclopedia of Southern Culture* (1989)
C. Vann Woodward, *The Burden of Southern History*, 3rd ed. (1993)
———, *The Future of the Past* (1989)
Howard Zinn, *The Southern Mystique* (1964)

Reconstructing the South

⚓

At one time, historians echoed the assessment of Reconstruction prevailing among white southerners: that Reconstruction had been a disastrous episode in which un-scrupulous northern carpetbaggers, aided by traitorous scalawags and unqualified blacks, seized power in southern governments and inaugurated an orgy of corrup-tion, robbery, and misrule. But the civil rights movement and new historical re-search since 1960 have led to a complete revision of this once standard interpretation. While noting the importance of many white southerners' opposition to racial and other changes, revisionist studies have presented a much more bal-anced assessment of the personnel and policies of Reconstruction.

The two most important political and social questions facing the nation after the Civil War were how to bring the former Confederate states back into the Union and how to ensure civil liberties to the newly freed slaves. How did Congress address these two issues? What did Congress require of the former Con-federate states during Reconstruction? What policies did Republican governments follow? What was the response of white southerners? How did ex-slaves gain their rights after emancipation, and how did they create new lives for themselves and their families? What was the role of the Freedmen's Bureau? What impact did the Ku Klux Klan and other terrorist organizations have on Reconstruction? These are just some of the many questions that arise in the study of Reconstruc-tion from 1865 to 1877.

⚓ *D O C U M E N T S*

Congress's involvement in Reconstruction is summarized in Documents 1 and 2: the three Reconstruction Amendments—13 (emancipation), 14 (black citizenship), and 15 (black male voting rights)—and the Military Reconstruction Act of 1867. These were passed in part because southern state governments had returned ex-Confederates to of-fice and state legislatures had enacted Black Codes, restricting the freedom of ex-slaves. In Document 3, we see a report from J. R. Johnson, a Freedmen's Bureau superintendent. He quotes a corporal in the U.S. Colored Troops, who wrote of the hopes and aspirations of millions of freedpeople for civil rights. Legal marriage was a right that had been denied slaves but was granted after emancipation. They saw it as be-ing at the foundation of all their rights because it allowed them to establish households independent of white interference. In the turbulent years just after the war, courts bound out or apprenticed children—particularly black children—to households that could support them. Former masters of slave children were eager to get them back under apprenticeship conditions that resembled slavery. Document 4 provides an example of the difficulties freedpeople faced in retaining rights to their own children. To gain control over their children, they often had to use the courts. White southerners reacted negatively to the "occupation" by federal troops and to the election of northern settlers (carpetbaggers), blacks, and southern whites who had remained loyal to the Union (scalawags) to state and national office. Document 5 contains excerpts from the *Raleigh (N.C.) Sentinel* that reveal how quickly southern opponents of Congress's measures began to construct the legend of Reconstruction misrule. Documents 6 and 7—the transcript of a congressional hearing and Instructions to Red Shirts—reveal a great deal about white hostility and about the creation of the KKK and the paramilitary group known as the Red Shirts, who supported gubernatorial candidate Wade Hampton. These instructions make clear that white Democrats were determined to regain control of the government at any price. Thomas Nast in Document 8 comments graphically in *Harper's Weekly* on the issues of Reconstruction.

1. Constitutional Amendments 13, 14, and 15

Amendment XIII [Adopted 1865]

Section 1.   Neither slavery nor involuntary servitude, except as a punishment for crime whereof the party shall have been duly convicted, shall exist within the United States, or any place subject to their jurisdiction.

Section 2.   Congress shall have power to enforce this article by appropriate legislation.

Amendment XIV [Adopted 1868]

Section 1.   All persons born or naturalized in the United States, and subject to the jurisdiction thereof, are citizens of the United States and of the State wherein they reside. No State shall make or enforce any law which shall abridge the privileges or immunities of citizens of the United States; nor shall any State deprive any person of life, liberty, or property, without due process of law; nor deny to any person within its jurisdiction the equal protection of the laws.

Section 2.   Representatives shall be apportioned among the several States according to their respective numbers, counting the whole number of persons in each State, excluding Indians not taxed. But when the right to vote at any election for the choice of Electors for President and Vice-President of the United States, Representatives in Congress, the executive and judicial officers of a State, or the members of

---

These are Constitutional Amendments 13, 14, and 15.

the legislature thereof, is denied to any of the male inhabitants of such State, being twenty-one years of age and citizens of the United States, or in any way abridged, except for participation in rebellion, or other crime, the basis of representation therein shall be reduced in the proportion which the number of such male citizens shall bear to the whole number of male citizens twenty-one years of age in such State.

Section 3.   No person shall be a Senator or Representative in Congress, or Elector of President and Vice-President, or hold any office, civil or military, under the United States, or under any State, who, having previously taken an oath, as a member of Congress, or as an officer of the United States, or as a member of any State legislature, or as an executive or judicial officer of any State, to support the Constitution of the United States, shall have engaged in insurrection or rebellion against the same, or given aid or comfort to the enemies thereof. Congress may, by a vote of two-thirds of each house, remove such disability.

Section 4.   The validity of the public debt of the United States, authorized by law; including debts incurred for payment of pensions and bounties for services in suppressing insurrection or rebellion, shall not be questioned. But neither the United States nor any State shall assume or pay any debt or obligation incurred in aid of insurrection or rebellion against the United States, or any claim for the loss of emancipation of any slave; but all such debts, obligations, and claims shall be held illegal and void.

Section 5.   The Congress shall have power to enforce, by appropriate legislation, the provisions of this article.

Amendment XV [Adopted 1870]

Section 1.   The right of citizens of the United States to vote shall not be denied or abridged by the United States or by any State on account of race, color, or previous condition of servitude.

Section 2.   The Congress shall have power to enforce this article by appropriate legislation.

2. The Military Reconstruction Act, 1867

Whereas no legal State governments or adequate protection for life or property now exists in the rebel States of Virginia, North Carolina, South Carolina, Georgia, Mississippi, Alabama, Louisiana, Florida, Texas, and Arkansas; and whereas it is necessary that peace and good order should be enforced in said States until loyalty and republican State governments can be legally established: Therefore

---

This document can be found in the United States of America Statutes at Large, Volume 13, pp. 428–29.

Be it enacted, . . . That said rebel States shall be divided into military districts and made subject to the military authority of the United States . . .

Sec. 2. . . . It shall be the duty of the President to assign to the command of each of said districts an officer of the army, not below the rank of brigadier general, and to detail a sufficient military force to enable such officer to perform his duties and enforce his authority within the district to which he is assigned.

Sec. 3. . . . It shall be the duty of each officer assigned as aforesaid to protect all persons in their rights of persons and property, to suppress insurrection, disorder, and violence, and to punish, or cause to be punished, all disturbers of the public peace and criminals, and to this end he may allow local civil tribunals to take juris-diction of and to try offenders, or, when in his judgment it may be necessary for the trial of offenders, he shall have power to organize military commissions or tribunals for that purpose; and all interference under color of State authority with the exercise of military authority under this act shall be null and void. . . .

Sec. 5. . . . When the people of any one of said rebel States shall have formed a constitution of government in conformity with the Constitution of the United States in all respects, framed by a convention of delegates elected by the male citizens of said State twenty-one years old and upward, of whatever race, color, or previous condition, . . . and when such constitution shall provide that the elective franchise shall be enjoyed by all such persons as have the qualifica-tions herein stated for electors of delegates, and when such constitution shall be ratified by a majority of the persons voting on the question of ratification who are qualified as electors of delegates, and when such constitution shall have been submitted to Congress for examination and approval, and Congress shall have approved the same, and when said State, by a vote of its legislature elected under said constitution, shall have adopted the amendment to the Constitution of the United States, proposed by the thirty-ninth Congress, and known as article four-teen, and when said article shall have become a part of the Constitution of the United States, said State shall be declared entitled to representation in Congress, and senators and representatives shall be admitted therefrom on their taking oaths prescribed by law, and then and thereafter the preceding sections of this act shall be inoperative in said State: *Provided,* That no person excluded from the privilege of holding office by said proposed amendment to the Constitution of the United States shall be eligible to election as a member of the convention to frame a constitution for any of said rebel States, nor shall any such person vote for members of such convention.

Sec. 6. . . . Until the people of said rebel States shall be by law admitted to rep-resentation in the Congress of the United States, any civil governments which may exist therein shall be deemed provisional only, and in all respects subject to the paramount authority of the United States at any time to abolish, modify or control, or supersede the same; and in all elections to any office under such provisional gov-ernments all persons shall be entitled to vote, and none others, who are entitled to vote under the provisions of the fifth section of this act; and no person shall be eli-gible to any office under any such provisional governments who would be disquali-fied from holding office under the provisions of the third article of said constitutional amendment.

3. J. R. Johnson Preaches on Marriage Covenants and Legal Rights, 1866

Freedmen's Village, Va. June 1st 1866.

Dear Col: I have the honor to report to you concerning my efforts as Supt. of Marriages in 5th Dist Va. from April 25th, to May 31st, (inclusive) 1866. . . .

On the evening of April 25th, I preached on the subject of Marriage to the soldiers at Fort Corcoran, 107. U.S.C.I. co. A & co E. Capt. Goff of co. A. and commander of the Fort, was present, and assisted me, by reading the Circular on Marriage, explaining it—and adding earnest remarks, which exerted much influence on the minds of the soldiers. I record for him my *thanks* for such timely, and efficient assistance. I addressed the soldiers at that Fort several other times, on the same theme: these occasions included two Sabbath evenings. At the close of service on one of those evenings—Corporal Murray (of co A), said:—

"Fellow Soldiers:—

I praise God for this day! I have long been praying for it. The Marriage Covenant is at the foundation of all our rights. In slavery we could not have *legalised* marriage: *now* we have it. Let us conduct ourselves worthy of such a blessing—and all the people will respect us—God will bless us, and we shall be established as a people." His character is such, that every word had power.

I have preached & lectured, or *talked* publicly five times at Freedmens Village. From Apr 26 to May 30th, gave fifteen certificates: six to soldiers of 107 USCI Fort Corcoran; three to 107. Vienna Fairfax county—one-107 Freedmens Village—one 107 Alx——; and four couples of citizens, all of Alexandria co. Nearly three weeks of sickness prevented me from accomplishing more. Yesterday, 31st of May, we gave seventy nine certificates in Freedmens Village. We have much more to do. Rev R S Laws, Rev D A. Miles & lady teachers, much help me. Spent last Sabbath with Capt Ross, of Vienna & the way is open for work in that region. Yours

J. R. Johnson

4. Edward Coleman Seeks Child Custody, 1866

Clarksville Va. July 31 1866

Edward Coleman

States that he had nephew and niece bound out to a Mr. Young of Henderson and the children finding out where he (Coleman) lived came over to see him with the intention of remaining but Mr. Young finding out where they were came and took them away. Also that he has bought land and has a home to bring the children

---

From Ira Berlin and Leslie Rowland, eds., *Families and Freedom: A Documentary History of African American Kinship in the Civil War Era* (New York: New Press, 1997), pp. 168, 170.

From Edward Coleman to Freedmen's Bureau, 31 July 1866, Letters Received, Assistant Superintendent's Office, Oxford, Bureau of Refugees, Freedmen, and Abandoned Lands, RG 105. National Archives.

up on without any expence to any one and that he feels that he has the best right to them.

Clarksville, Va. July 31 1866

To the Office of Granville Co., N.C.

Sir

I had a nephew and niece bound out by some officer in your county last year to a Mr. Young of Henderson N.C. since which time they have found out where I am living and came over to see me with the intention of remaining but Mr. Young finding out where they were sent and got them and carried them back to Henderson. I have bought land and have a house to bring the children to and will raise them without any expense to any one. I feel perfectly able to take them and support them and I feel that I have the best right to them.

Respectfully yours,

Edward Coleman

Bu. R.F. and A.L. [Bureau of Refugees, Freedmen, and Abandoned Lands] Office Sub. Dist of Oxford N.C.

Aug. 3rd 1866

Edward Coleman:

Your letter of July 30th is received. The children were legally bound to Mr. Young as far as I have any means of knowing. If you wish to recover them you must do so through the civil courts. I am powerless in the case.

Respectfully,

W.W. Jones

Capt. V.R.C. and Asst. Supt.

5. A Southern Newspaper Denounces Reconstruction, 1869

That the State has been cursed and almost ruined by a class of "carpet bag" vultures from the North, aided by degenerate and too often corrupt natives, is patent to anybody who opens his eyes. We have not been slow to tell the people of the villainies that have been perpetrated and are yet being perpetrated, day and night, by the present State government, at the expense and injury of the people, black and white. We intend to continue to do so regardless of cost or consequences.

Our firm conviction is that the people will not tolerate these villainies a great while longer; the day of reckoning cometh, and it will be terrible. The "carpet bagger" race will then hurry off to some other field of spoils and laugh at the calamity

---

This document originally apeared in the *Raleigh Daily Sentinel*, August 6, 1869, page 2 under the title, "The Day of Reckoning Will Come."

of their dupes and co-workers in iniquity; but the *native* culprit must answer at the bar of public opinion, and in many cases at the bar of the Court for high crimes. We tell the native scalawags that the day is not far distant, when the thin vail that now hides their crimes from public gaze will be withdrawn, and they will be exposed to the scorn and indignation of an outraged people. Yes, and that small class of our people who claim to be good and true men, who, for the sake of a little gain, have *secretly* colluded with the bad wretches who have plundered and impoverished the people without mercy, they, too, will be exposed. Yes, we repeat, the day will be mercilessly exposed. And such perpetration or crime will thenceforth be a *stench* in the nostrils of all decent men, white and black. Everybody will bate them, mock and hiss at them as they pass by. The Penitentiary fraud will be exposed, the Railroad frauds will be exposed; it will yet be known how much money was used to corrupt the members of the Legislature, who used it, who paid it, and where it came from; it will yet be known how many warrants have been made on the Treasury not authorized by law. We have the best of reasons for saying that the passage of the Railroad acts cost the State tens and hundreds of thousands of dollars. The people will yet ferret out those who so recklessly and criminally spent the treasure of the people. Yes, gentlemen, the day of reckoning will come. Mark what we say! Let every man watch how he connects himself even innocently with those who have so outraged the State and the people.

6. Congressional Testimony on the Ku Klux Klan, 1871

Ben Hill on the Klan

Question. You have not studied this organization?

Answer. I have only investigated a few cases for the purpose of ascertaining who were the guilty offenders. One reason for investigating the few cases was upon the attempt to reconstruct Georgia some time ago, and these Ku-Klux outrages were made to bear very, very heavily against even Union parties [who opposed returning Georgia to military rule]. I wanted to know if that was the case, and if so, I wanted the people to put down the Ku-Klux. . . .

Question. Can you state any particulars you may have heard in reference to the attack on [Jourdan] Ware?

Answer. Yes, sir; I can state what I heard. A body of about twenty-five or thirty disguised men went one night and met him upon the road. (I think this was the case of Jourdan Ware.) I am not certain that they went to his house. I believe they met him on the road, somewhere or other, and demanded of him his arms and his watch. I believe he gave up his arms, and they shot him upon his refusal to surrender the watch, and he died a day or two afterward.

Question. Did you ever hear that there was any accusation of his having done anything wrong?

This document can be found as part of the United States of America's Congress' testimony taken by the Joint Select Committee to inquire into the Condition of Affairs: Georgia, volume 1, p. 308; volume II, pp. 770–71.

Answer. No, sir; I think not, except I believe I did hear that there was some complaint of his impudence, or something of that sort.

Question. We hear from a great many witnesses about the "impudence" of negroes. What is considered in your section of the country "impudence" on the part of a negro?

Answer. Well, it is considered impudence for a negro not to be polite to a white man—not to pull off his hat and bow and scrape to a white man, as was always done formerly.

Question. Do the white people generally expect or require now that kind of submissive deportment on the part of the negroes that they did while the negroes were slaves?

Answer. I do not think they do as a general thing; a great many do.

Question. Are there many white people who do require it?

Answer. Yes, sir; I think there are a great many who do require it, and are not satisfied unless the negroes do it.

Question. Suppose that a negro man has been working for a white man, and they have some difference or dispute in relation to wages, will your people generally allow a negro man to stand up and assert his rights in the same way and in the same language which they would allow to a white man without objection?

Answer. O, no sir, that is not expected at all.

Question. If the colored man does stand up and assert his rights in language which would be considered pardonable and allowable in a white man, that is considered "impudence" in a negro?

Answer. Yes, sir; gross impudence.

Question. Is that species of "impudence" on the part of the negro considered a sufficient excuse by many of your people for chastising a negro, or "dealing with him?"

Answer. Well, some think so. . . .

Question. In your judgment, from what you have seen and heard, is there something of a political character about this organization?

Answer. I think it is entirely political.

Question. What makes you think so?

Answer. Because the parties who are maltreated by these men are generally republicans. I have never known a democrat to be assaulted. . . .

Question. Give the committee your judgment in relation to the object with which this organization has been gotten up. What do its members intend to attain by it?

Answer. Well, sir, my opinion is that the first object of the institution of the Ku-Klux, or these disguised bands, was to cripple any effect that might be produced by Loyal Leagues. That is my opinion—that this organization was an offset to the Loyal Leagues.

Question. But the Ku-Klux organization kept on increasing after the Loyal Leagues were disbanded?

Answer. Yes, sir.

Question. What, in your opinion, is the object of keeping up the Ku-Klux organization and operating it as they do? What do they intend to produce or effect by it?

Answer. My opinion is, that the purpose was to break down the reconstruction acts; that they were dissatisfied with negro suffrage and the reconstruction measures and everybody that was in favor of them.

Question. Do you think this organization was intended to neutralize the votes of the negroes after suffrage had been extended to them?

Answer. Yes, sir, I think so.

Question. How? By intimidating them?

Answer. Any way. Yes, sir, by intimidation.

Question. Making them afraid to exercise the right of suffrage?

Answer. Yes, sir.

Question. Do you believe that the organization and its operations have, in fact, produced that effect?

Answer. I think they have to some extent.

Question. What is the state of feeling which has been produced among the colored people by this armed, disguised organization, and the acts they have committed?

Answer. Well, in my section of the country, the colored people, generally, are afraid now, and have been for some time, to turn out at an election. They are afraid to say much, or to have anything to do with public affairs. I own a plantation on Coosa River, upon which I have, perhaps, about 40 negroes, and some of them have been pretty badly alarmed, afraid to say much. Some have lain out in the woods, afraid to stay at home.

7. Instructions to Red Shirts in South Carolina, 1876

1. That every Democrat in the Townships must be put upon the Roll of the Democratic Clubs. . . .
2. That a Roster must be made of every white and of every Negro in the Townships and returned immediately to the County Executive Committee.
3. That the Democratic Military Clubs are to be armed with rifles and pistols and such other arms as they may command. They are to be divided into two companies, one of the old men, the other of the young men; an experienced captain or commander to be placed over each of them. . . .
12. Every Democrat must feel honor bound to control the vote of at least one Negro, by intimidation, purchase, keeping him away or as each individual may determine, how he may best accomplish it.
13. We must attend every Radical meeting that we hear of whether they meet at night or in the day time. Democrats must go in as large numbers as they can get together, and well armed, behave at first with great courtesy and assure the ignorant Negroes that you mean them no harm and so soon as their leaders or speakers begin to speak and make false statements of facts, tell them then and there to their faces, that they are liars, thieves and rascals, and are only trying to

This document can be found in William A. Sheppard, *Red Shirts Remembered: Southern Brigadiers of the Reconstruction Period,* pp. 46–50. Copyright © 1940 Ruralist Press, Inc.

mislead the ignorant Negroes and if you get a chance get upon the platform and
address the Negroes.

14. In speeches to Negroes you must remember that argument has no effect upon
them: they can only be influenced by their fears, superstitions and cupidity. Do
not attempt to flatter and persuade them. . . . Treat them so as to show them,
you are the superior race, and that their natural position is that of subordination
to the white man. . . .

16. Never threaten a man individually. If he deserves to be threatened, the necessities of the times require that he should die. . . .

29. Every club must be uniformed in a red shirt and they must be sure and wear it
upon all public meetings and particularly on the day of election.

30. Secrecy should shroud all of our transactions. Let not your left hand know what
your right hand does.

8. Thomas Nast Views Reconstruction, 1865, 1874

"Worse Than Slavery"

This cartoon appeared in *Harper's Weekly*, October 24, 1874 (Volume 18, p.878).

Columbia.—"Shall I Trust These Men, And Not This Man?"

This cartoon was published August 5, 1865, and also appears in Morton Keller, *The Art and Politics of Thomas Nast* (New York: Oxford University Press, 1968), plate 55.

✠ E S S A Y S

In the first essay, Laura F. Edwards focuses on freedpeople, their right to marriage, and their resistance to Black Codes, which apprenticed their children (read legally stole and gave them) to former slave owners. As Edwards argues in this gendered interpretation, the establishment of marriages and families provided the most compelling justification for full civil and political rights. Historian William C. Harris reexamines both the actions and the motives of the much-maligned carpetbaggers. Although some northerners in the Reconstruction South were corrupt or scoundrels, Harris shows in the second essay that most of those called carpetbaggers had quite different, and often laudable, motives. Their chief crime was to challenge traditional racial, political, and social arrangements in the region. In the third selection, Eric Foner delineates with care the role that blacks played in Reconstruction and the importance of the Ku Klux Klan.

"The Marriage Covenant Is at the Foundation of All Our Rights"

LAURA F. EDWARDS

. . . Federal army chaplains and northern missionaries had strongly encouraged slaves who escaped to union lines to marry legally, but many needed no prompting. In July 1865, nearly a year before passage of the legislative act requiring ex-slaves to register their marriages, an Episcopal minister in Warren County [N.C.] married 150 African-American couples in the course of just two days. Over the county line in Granville [N.C.], many of the 878 couples who registered their unions in compliance with the legislative act may have already formalized their vows, just as their Warren neighbors had done. The great majority recorded their unions in July and August of 1866, well before the deadline. The derisive comments of skeptical white observers only underscored freedpeople's enthusiasm. According to a *New York Tribune* correspondent, white North Carolinians viewed "this eagerness among the darkeys to get married" a "good joke." A Lumberton minister concurred, noting that "whites laugh at the very idea of the thing" and "do not believe the negroes will respect those relations more than the brutes."

For freedpeople, however, marriage was no joke. It provided a way to establish the integrity of their relationships, to bring a new security to their family lives, and, above all, to affirm their freedom. Even the most sympathetic whites did not fully grasp the meanings freedpeople attached to legal marriage. Many, southern as well as northern, commended the popularity of marriage among ex-slaves, interpreting it as a sign of their moral and social improvement. Some even mistakenly assumed that freedpeople were accepting the definition of marriage as a relationship primarily of "obligations" and "responsibilities." All these interpretations missed the mark, as the words of one black corporal in the U.S. Colored Troops suggest. Explaining to his troops the implications of Virginia's 1866 act legitimating slave mar-

Adapted from *Gendered Strife & Confusion: The Political Culture of Reconstruction.* Copyright © 1997 by the Board of Trustees of the University of Illinois. Used with the permission of the University of Illinois Press and the author.

riages, he maintained: "The Marriage Covenant is at the foundation of all our rights. In slavery we could not have *legalised* marriage: *now* we have it . . . and we shall be established as a people." The local Freedmen's Bureau superintendent applauded the speech along with the black troops in the audience. But for these troops and for other freedpeople, marriage had become entangled with freedom in a way it had not for the Freedmen's Bureau superintendent. If the prohibition of marriage had underscored their dependent position and the precariousness of their family ties in slavery, the act of marriage now symbolized the rejection of their slave status. As the corporal's words reveal, marriage was as much about rights as obligations.

Freedpeople's resistance to the apprenticeship provisions in the state's Black Code provides a particularly striking example of their position. If the apprenticeship system looked bad on paper, it was even worse in practice. Like Harriet Ambrose and Eliza Moore, children were bound without their parents' consent, often without any notification whatsoever of the proceedings, and even kidnapped from their homes. The experience of Robert Lee Pool, of Granville County, was not unusual. When Pool's mother decided to leave the Cannady plantation where they had been enslaved, their former master was not willing to let them go. Although he seized their personal possessions in an attempt to keep them on the plantation, Pool and his mother did manage to slip away. Cannady immediately began searching for them. When he found them in nearby Franklin County, he kidnapped Pool, who was playing in the yard. Cannady could no longer force Pool's mother to remain on the plantation, but the apprenticeship laws allowed him to keep Pool. Pool's mother apparently enlisted the help of the Freedmen's Bureau, because two Union soldiers were sent to retrieve both her son and her personal belongings. The soldiers reached the Cannady plantation only to discover that Cannady was in court, apprenticing Pool. "Never the lest," as Pool remembered later in life, "those blue jacket Yankee officers went there and had my mother's belongings loaded on the wagon and ordered me to get on the wagon. And they marched with those big pistols in their belts and Mrs. Cannady did not open her mouth only to hollow and cry at the last of me." Pool was lucky. In this instance, might triumphed over the law. The "blue jacket Yankee officers" notwithstanding, the legal claim of Pool's mother to her son was tenuous, at best. Other planters, moreover, were far more persistent than Cannady, who did not bother Pool or his mother again. Not all apprenticeship incidents ended this happily.

The application of the apprenticeship laws infuriated African Americans. How could they be free, if their children could still be taken from them as easily as they had been during slavery? The uproar echoed across the South, as denunciations mounted in frequency and intensity between 1865 and 1867. The delegates to a statewide freedmen's convention in 1866 described apprenticeship as the system in which "our children, the dearest ties of which bind us to domestic life, and which makes the tie of home endearing, are ruthlessly taken from us, and bound out without our consent." Singling out the practice for particular criticism among their other complaints, they resolved to "do all in our power to prevent its further continuance." Ultimately, however, it was freedpeople themselves, not their leaders, who dealt the most successful blows to those laws that granted planters the power to acquire custody of freed children.

Many individual parents went to great lengths to keep their children out of the hands of former masters. Fan, a Granville County slave who had been moved to

Kentucky before the war by her master, David Yarbrough, absolutely refused to apprentice her daughter Barbra to Yarbrough or any other white master. Fan clearly treasured her independence and her ability to protect the interests of her daughter. Her position, however, emerges through the words of Yarbrough, who found her actions not just puzzling, but personally insulting. Responding to relatives in Granville County who had inquired after the welfare of the family's ex-slaves, he wrote in 1867 that Fan was "doing no good on the top side of earth." He went on to explain: "Fan is the meanest negro living almost she cant get a home at all. . . . She had 4 or 5 homes last year going from pillow [pillar] to post + dragging her 4 children after her. She says white people cant whip her children I offered her $50 for Barbra last year + she would not hear to it carrin her off + got only $15 for her last year so Nick says. She lives near Nick's House. Nick told me that she was doing no good for herself nor nobody else + if he was in my place he would have Barbra bound to us." As it turns out, Yarbrough had taken Nick's advice and applied to the county court to apprentice Barbra. He expected "no difficulty as the Legislature has pass[ed] an act giving the refusal to former owners."

David Yarbrough, however, may have encountered more difficulty than he expected. When evasion proved unsuccessful, African Americans began challenging the apprenticeship system directly, through the courts. They were an unlikely forum, since local court officials were the ones who apprenticed children in the first place. Indeed, before congressional Reconstruction and the subsequent redrawing of North Carolina's constitution, local courts remained as undemocratic as they had been before the war. The office of magistrate remained appointive and, with the exception of those appointed by [North Carolina] Governor William W. Holden during his brief term as provisional governor, most magistrates were wealthy and politically conservative. Very much aware of their power, these elite men did not hesitate to use it as a political weapon. In his assessment of Reconstruction's progress in Granville County, for instance, Freedmen's Bureau agent Thomas Hay focused his concerns on the local courts: "I sincerely believe, that nearly every white man in the Counties of Warren, Franklin and Granville who was a Secessionist . . . is one at this day, and if the U.S. Troops should be withdrawn from this State at this time, leaving the great body of Magistrates unchanged and the County Courts not reconstructed, the future of the Freedmen would be *dark* indeed." This was no exaggeration. As Granville County's court records indicate, magistrates defined freedpeople's legal rights very narrowly, even within the context of the already restrictive Black Code. In this context, freedpeople's suits against apprenticeship acquire that much more significance. It was against great odds that they claimed access to the judicial process on the same footing as other free people.

African Americans often enlisted the aid of the Freedmen's Bureau in their efforts to move the wheels of local justice. Indeed, the sheer number of complaints to the bureau testifies to the persistent opposition of African Americans and the role they played in making apprenticeship a political issue. Both the bureau and the local courts apprenticed children at first. The bureau officially objected to racial distinctions in the treatment of white and black children, but its otherwise ambiguous guidelines did not forcefully establish parental claims over those of white planters. Agents' interpretations of these rules varied widely. Some regularly bound out children to white planters, while others saw the potential for abuse and made every effort to place children within the black community. Local courts, however, simply ignored the bureau's sketchy guidelines and apprenticed children at will. As 1865 gave way to 1866, both local agents and officials in the bureau's state office grew increasingly concerned over the local courts' actions. In Granville County and across the state, agents shepherded cases through the local courts and sometimes canceled indentures themselves. At the state level, the bureau issued directives defending parental rights. Yet even the most sympathetic bureau officers would not have been so aware of the blatant inequities of the system if not for the freedpeople themselves, who kept agents' attention riveted on the issue, whether they liked it or not. Thomas Hay, bureau superintendent for the subdistrict of Warren, which included Granville County, canceled seventy-seven indentures in the first eight months of 1867 alone. Representing only successful complaints, this figure gives just a partial accounting of freedpeople's opposition.

The case of Richard Hester reveals the underlying logic to their resistance. Hester, a former slave, tried to obtain custody of his two grandsons in 1867. Unable to block their apprenticeship in court, he turned to the Freedmen's Bureau. Daniel Paschall, a sympathetic white planter and local magistrate, offered to write to the bureau on Hester's behalf. As Paschall explained in the letter: "My course on the bench of our county court has been to bind the colored children to colored friends where it was in proof that they were capable and had the means of feeding and clothing, but in many instances was overruled, if this case was before me on the bench, I should give these boys to Richard Hester." Paschall's position, however, was very different from that of Richard Hester. Paschall promoted the binding of children to family and friends when appropriate, but he did not question the right of the court to apprentice black children. Hester did. He did not want the court's permission to apprentice his grandchildren; he wanted custody of them as their grandfather. He thus challenged the court's guardianship power and its right to apprentice his grandchildren to anyone at all. Ultimately, Hester was able to proceed with the case on his own terms. With the backing of the Freedmen's Bureau, he filed a motion in the local court, asking that the contracts "be cancelled" and that his grandsons "be placed in the custody and care of him, the said Dick Hester."

Coleman Edward would have applauded the decision. The year before he had petitioned the bureau to obtain custody of his niece and nephew, who had been apprenticed to a Granville County planter. "I have bought land and have a house to bring the children to and will raise them without any expense to any one," Edward wrote. But even if he were not so well situated, Edward still would have maintained that the children had no business living with a white master. As he put it, "I have the last right to them."

Such claims become more remarkable in comparison with similar cases during slavery. With no thought of the mother's or the child's desires, the courts regularly apprenticed the children of all unmarried free black women. If a white woman was poor or if her partner was black, even her race would not save her children from a court-ordered indenture. In the antebellum period, as Victoria Bynum has shown, poor white and free black women opposed the system in the best way their limited power would permit: they challenged mistreatment of their children and influenced where they would be placed. After emancipation, African Americans, in particular, questioned the system itself.

In rejecting their ex-masters' claims to their children, freedpeople insisted on the sanctity of their households and their own rights as parents. Apprenticeship, they argued, was a violation of their domestic relations. In the words of a group of petitioners from Maryland: "Our homes are invaded and our little ones seized at the family fireside." Legal marriage, which gave freedpeople the materials necessary to construct a wall of privacy around their households, proved particularly useful in their efforts. Positioned within these households as husbands and wives, they could now mobilize the law to support their claims to their children. . . .

By the time Congress entered the fray, a good many freedpeople had already chipped away enough of the existing system to expose its weaknesses. Congressional Reconstruction then bolstered their position. The Fourteenth and Fifteenth Amendments prohibited racial discrimination in the construction and exercise of the law and granted full political rights to African-American men. In 1868, when a Republican-dominated convention gathered in Raleigh to draft a new constitution, it restructured the state's judicial system. Sweeping away all impediments that kept African Americans from enjoying the same rights under the law as whites, the constitution also further democratized the courts by making the key positions of magistrate and judge elective. The results were quite dramatic in Granville County, where 50 percent of the population was African American and where many whites had reluctantly supported the Confederacy. Republican magistrates and judges presided over cases; African Americans and poor whites sat on juries; and Republican sheriffs, deputies, and jailers kept the peace. Together these changes made the courts more responsive to the concerns of African Americans and marginalized whites. The term "more responsive," however, was strictly relative; the courts did not completely reverse themselves to advocate the interests of these people alone. The elite white Republicans who so often presided over the courts operated from a very different political perspective from that of rank-and-file Republicans. Furthermore, the courts by no means abandoned wealthy white Democrats. . . . [T]hese two groups had a powerful common interest in the protection of property. Nonetheless, the change in the courts was perceptible, and it bolstered confidence in the system. African-American households now occupied the same legal position as white households, and blacks were granted the legal power to protect their households in their own right. Not coincidentally, apprenticeship cases all but disappeared.

Carpetbaggers in Reality

WILLIAM C. HARRIS

The tainted reputation of the carpetbagger during the post–Civil War period is undergoing a remarkable revision. Viewed for decades as the chief of villains in the melodrama known as Radical Reconstruction, the carpetbagger, or northerner who went south after the war and engaged in politics, has attracted during the last few years a number of defenders among historians of the postwar era. The image that

From "The Creed of the Carpetbaggers" by William C. Harris, *Journal of Southern History* XL (May 1974), pp. 199–224. Copyright © 1974 by the Southern Historical Association. Reprinted by permission of the Managing Editor.

now emerges, though far from exculpating them for their failures and abuses of power, represents carpetbaggers as basically decent individuals who in most cases entered the South seeking the main chance through commercial and planting endeavors rather than through political activity. Many became insolvent as a result of the disastrous agricultural failure of 1866, and some of the less enterprising abandoned the region at this time, returning to the North to inveigh against the inhospitable South. Only after the passage of the military Reconstruction Acts of 1867, enfranchising blacks and temporarily disfranchising the former leadership class in the South, did many of the remaining northerners become involved in the politics of their adopted states. Regarded as liberators by the freedmen, the influence of these newcomers among the new citizens virtually ensured their rapid rise to positions of state and local leadership in the young Republican organizations of the region.

In office, the performance of the carpetbaggers was mixed in the opinion of present-day historians. While some were extravagant and corrupt, others, like Governors Adelbert Ames of Mississippi and Daniel Henry Chamberlain of South Carolina, "were economy-minded and strictly honest." Even those who pursued material gain through political power often did so in collaboration with acquisitive southern Democrats. Of course, the carpetbaggers disturbed race relations in the South: to have done otherwise would have been an abject abandonment of the freedmen to the devices of unsympathetic southern whites. But carpetbaggers, revisionist historians find, did not incite blacks to violence against their former masters; in fact, they frequently took the position of their conservative neighbors on inflammatory racial issues, notably the question of social integration. . . .

The politically active carpetbag class in Mississippi was never very numerous, probably at no time exceeding two hundred men and never including the majority of the postwar northern settlers in the state. Most of the newcomers from above the Ohio were of the farmer class and, either because of their fear of ostracism by local whites or their hostility to the advanced doctrines of Negro rights, shunned affiliation with the Republican party. On the other hand, carpetbaggers, or those northerners who joined and labored for the Republican party, generally were the most affluent and best educated of the northern immigrants in the state. And these men frequently accumulated considerable property in Mississippi before entering politics. Such elite qualities were especially true of carpetbaggers whose influence was statewide, but evidence exists that a number of relatively obscure members of this political class, those who organized and led local Republican clubs and Union Leagues, often serving in county and town offices, were also men of means and some erudition.

Carpetbagger ideology in Mississippi was a product of the intense republican idealism that swept the North during the Civil War era, finding its most profound expression in the minds of young, educated officers in the Union Army. Generally men of some mobility even before the war, the northerners who came to the state after the conflict had never felt the constraints of provincial ties usually characteristic of life in a single community. To an impressive extent their allegiance was to the stirring national ideals produced by the sectional conflict and the subsequent northern commitment to freedom; their vision was broad and optimistic, with a belief in progress through the revitalized republican institutions of the Founding Fathers.

The principal goal of the carpetbaggers was the eradication of the vestiges of slavery and rebellion which they believed still existed in the South. They sought to

replace these baneful anachronisms with the progressive spirit of Union and freedom. These were broad and ambiguous concepts, but northerners in Mississippi
thought they knew their precise meaning and the requirements for fulfilling them.
In their view, slavery and secession were coexistent if not synonymous; similarly,
Union and freedom were paired. The slavery-secession syndrome, according to
these agents of a new order for the state, had not only caused the internecine war but
had also been the reason for the destitution, economic inefficiency, ignorance, intolerance, and violence they found to a deplorable extent in the postwar South. "The
effects of the [slave] institution upon the character of its devotees," a leading carpetbagger observed after living in the state for two years, "are a thousandfold more
appalling than the most vivid imagination ever dreamed. What slavery failed to
touch has been wrecked by secession and treason. The social, business, religious,
and political history of the south will show more bad faith, deception, and treachery
in a single State [there] than in all the States of the north together." Not until the
"hydra-headed monster" of secession had been completely expelled could the South
and Mississippi hope to be regenerated and become like the progressive states of
the North.

Secession and rebellion had become institutionalized in the Democratic party,
carpetbaggers believed, and it followed that the national agency for the redemption
of the South should be the Republican party. Triumphant in the war against Democratic copperheads and secessionists, the Republican party must ensure in Reconstruction that Union sacrifices had not been made in vain. Specifically, the South
should be reconstructed along lines that would guarantee loyalty to the Union, bona
fide freedom for blacks, and tolerance of the opinions of all. Despite the intensity of
their views, most carpetbaggers in Mississippi would probably not have agreed
with [Governor] Adelbert Ames that Reconstruction was merely an extension of the
Civil War and that their purpose in the state was "Mission with a large M," but most
of them accepted the necessity of certain changes in the South designed to preserve
the fruits of the national victory. . . .

Once in power, carpetbaggers, who proved to be the predominant element in
the Republican administrations from 1870 to 1876, set about to implement the progressive features of the new constitution. Shunning a conception of themselves as
revolutionary agents or as ultra-Radicals, these northerners were nonetheless convinced that certain reforms were essential before Mississippi could advance into the
mainstream of American life. After five years of peace the state still suffered from
lawlessness, violence, ignorance, and intolerance of the rights of those who dis-
agreed with the white majority. These vestiges of the blighted past, they believed,
must be stamped out before the spirit of progress and equality could take permanent
root in the state.

In the minds of the reformers the most important prescription for the retrogres-
sive ills of Mississippi society was a comprehensive system of public schools for
both races. Even the shadowy Ku Klux Klan owed its existence to the ignorance of
the masses, according to carpetbagger Amos Lovering, a former Indiana judge.
Such lawless activities as those practiced by the Klan, he declared, could only be
permanently suppressed through the power of "universal education in morals and
mind." Charles W. Clarke, the thirty-year-old native of Vermont who drafted the
public-school article in the constitution, asserted that education was "the energizing

agent of modern civilization" and a necessity for the continuance of republican government and institutions. Furthermore, Clarke and others of his class believed that education was the answer to the race problem in southern society. Enlighten the white masses and their prejudices against Negroes would fade away, they argued; at the same time schooling for the blacks would elevate them to a position in society nearly equal to whites, and their irresponsible behavior in freedom would inevitably cease. In the Republican press, on the campaign stump, and in the legislature, carpetbaggers trumpeted the virtues of public education. Much of their rhetoric was simply promotional, but the emphasis and zeal with which they pursued educational reform suggest strongly the faith of these northerners in its remedial and progressive qualities.

On the question of mixed schools most carpetbaggers preferred to remain silent or ambiguous, hoping to avoid a commitment to equality for blacks that would arouse the prejudices of the bulk of white Republicans, incite conservatives to violent opposition, and inevitably destroy the infant school system. Some, like their southern white neighbors, were simply antagonistic to any social mixing of the races, although they generally were able to keep their racism subdued for political, if for no other, reasons. A few northerners such as Clarke, Henry R. Pease, the state superintendent of education, and Albert T. Morgan probably favored the principle of integration, but they shied away from public statements suggesting that they questioned the dual arrangement established by the legislature of 1870. The only white Republican in Mississippi during Reconstruction to advocate publicly the integration of the public schools was a scalawag and a former slaveholder, Robert W. Flournoy.

After only one year's experience with the free school system, Superintendent Pease reported outstanding progress, including a remarkable improvement in white attitudes toward public education, despite the burning of several Negro schools by the Klan. But difficulties developed as the financial costs of the system proved greater than anticipated, and the goodwill of whites toward it declined. As a result Pease and his associates turned to the federal government for aid. Writing in the state educational journal, Hiram T. Fisher asserted: "It is the utmost folly to talk about establishing free schools permanently in the South without national aid. . . . The little that has been done [already] . . . far surpasses anything that the friends of education can or will do in the South for the next twenty years if they are compelled to rely solely upon their own resources." Congress, he declared, must act before it was too late to save free schools in the financially depressed region. Although viewed as radical and unconstitutional in most quarters, the demand for federal aid received the strong support both of Mississippi carpetbaggers of Radical tendencies and those of the moderate persuasion as well.

To effectuate these demands for national aid, carpetbag congressman Legrand Winfield Perce of Natchez on January 15, 1872, introduced in the House of Representatives a bill to apply the annual proceeds from the sale of federal lands to education in the states. Even though the measure did not single out the South for special treatment, the amended version of the bill had this effect, since it provided that the distribution of the funds during the first ten years would be based on the proportion of illiterates in the population of each state, a category in which the southern states clearly led the nation. The first federal-assistance bill for public school to be given serious consideration by Congress, the far-reaching Perce proposal passed the House but failed in the Senate. . . .

Though never achieving the society of virtue and enlightenment that the educational program was supposed to produce, the carpetbag principle of free schools did not die in Mississippi when the Republican political edifice collapsed. The conservative Redeemers of the late 1870s and the 1880s, despite their public resolves to purge the state of carpetbag innovations and to economize in state expenditures, found it desirable to maintain the semblance of the comprehensive system of public education that their bitter enemies had established during Reconstruction.

Even though public education was the cornerstone of the carpetbaggers' reform program, they realized somewhat vaguely that other measures were also required to transform Mississippi into a progressive commonwealth. Perhaps most carpetbaggers, especially those of moderate leanings, believed that the adoption of the Fifteenth Amendment and the establishment of Republican civil rule in the state made further legislation guaranteeing fundamental rights unnecessary. The ferociousness of Ku Klux Klan attacks in 1870 and 1871 and the continuation of general lawlessness, however, convinced many that additional laws, either state or federal, along with a vigorous enforcement, were essential to the security of the new order. In the United States Senate during the zenith of Klan activity in the South, Adelbert Ames, who was always suspicious of the intentions and behavior of southern whites, led the effort to reawaken Republicans in Mississippi, and especially blacks, to the dangers posed by the resurgence of the "Ku Klux Democracy." At the same time, encouraged by his Radical colleagues in Mississippi, the young, idealistic native of New England urged Congress to apply the full power of the army to end the spreading political violence in the South.

Moderate carpetbaggers, on the other hand, sought frantically to prevent this, believing, as so many of their brethren in the North did, that "The ready resort to the military is one of the most dangerous precedents which we can establish as a party." In an effort to prevent federal intervention, Governor Alcorn and his associates, including carpetbaggers, secured the passage of a state Ku Klux Klan law, legislated against the carrying of concealed weapons, and organized the militia. When these measures failed, many moderate carpetbaggers abandoned their reservations and supported the federal Klan law of 1871, designed to put down terror societies in the South.

Northerners in Mississippi were even more reluctant to accept the necessity for further legislation protecting the rights of blacks. During the early, exuberant days of the new order they seemed genuinely to believe that the ballot for blacks and universal education for whites would lead to an end of racial hostility and prejudice in the state. Many carpetbaggers obviously held racial attitudes similar to those of native whites, but it is also clear that an impressive number of them viewed black inferiority as only temporary, and they believed that Negroes would soon come up to or approach closely the standards set by whites. At any rate, most northerners in the state interpreted black capacity in a far more sympathetic light than did their white neighbors. . . .

Representative of carpetbag opinion on the treatment of blacks in public was the position of Governor Ridgely C. Powers, generally a moderate in politics, who signed the civil rights bill in 1873. Addressing the state Senate in 1870, he explained that he could "see some reason for refusing to ride in the same car or steamboat, or for declining to sit in the same assembly with drunkards, gamblers, robbers and murderers, but to refuse to come into such proximity with men because they happened to bear a different complexion from my own, would be to acknowledge a mean prejudice, unworthy of an age of intelligence. . . . The time, I apprehend, has past for estimating a man by the color of his skin rather than by the qualities of his heart, or the strength of his intellect." . . .

. . . As might be expected, carpetbaggers were caught up in the mania for railroad construction, although most of them probably did not view such internal improvements as the *sine qua non* for economic rehabilitation and progress that conservatives did. On one occasion the editor of the Jackson *Mississippi Pilot* had to reassure his readers that, regardless of its concern with other issues, the Republican leadership in the state had no intention of slighting Mississippi railroads. As "the great civilizer of nations," railroads, carpetbaggers asserted, should receive the financial support of all levels of government—federal, state, county, and community. Such aid would be repaid in many ways: lands would appreciate in value, economic activity would be stimulated, new enterprises would arise, tax revenues would increase, and a large number of immigrants would be attracted to Mississippi. The Vicksburg *Times and Republican* confidently claimed that the railroads "will certainly bring prosperity and population" to the state.

Although equally as interested as the old citizens in promoting internal improvements, leading carpetbaggers warned against haphazardly conceived railroad projects. Unlike overanxious conservative leaders during the Johnsonian period, they urged legislative planning for the construction of roads that would serve the general interests of the state. As Stafford of the Jackson *Mississippi Pilot* put it, railroads should be constructed for the benefit of Mississippi and her people "without regard to section, locality, race, color, or previous condition." The provision in the constitution against extending the state's credit to aid private corporations, Stafford and others of his class believed, should be no barrier; they fully expected the legislature to evade the clause by providing direct assistance to the railroads. When the chips were down, transplanted northerners, as much as their conservative associates in railroad development, abandoned their good intentions and succumbed to local influences and interests in supporting the construction of roads that would benefit only their own communities or districts.

Black Activism and the Ku Klux Klan

ERIC FONER

In 1867, politics emerged as the principal focus of black aspirations. In that annus mirabilis, the impending demise of the structure of civil authority opened the door for political mobilization to sweep across the black belt. Itinerant lecturers, black and white, brought the Republican message into the heart of the rural South. A black Baptist minister calling himself Professor J. W. Toer journeyed through parts

Excerpt from *Reconstruction: America's Unfinished Revolution 1863–1877* by Eric Foner. Copyright © 1988 by Eric Foner. Reprinted by permission of HarperCollins Publishers, Inc.

of Georgia and Florida with a "magic lantern" exhibiting "the progress of reconstruction. . . . He has a scene, which he calls 'before the proclamation,' another 'after the proclamation' and then '22nd Regt. U. S. C[olored] T[roops] Duncan's
Brigade'." Voting registrars instructed freedmen in American history and government and "the individual benefits of citizenship." In Monroe County, Alabama,
where no black political meeting had occurred before 1867, freedmen crowded
around the speaker shouting, "God bless you," "Bless God for this." Throughout the
South, planters complained of blacks neglecting their labor. Once a week during the
summer of 1867, "the negroes from the entire county" quit work and flocked to
Waco, Texas, for political rallies. In Alabama, "they stop at any time and go off to
Greensboro" for the same purpose. On August 1, Richmond's tobacco factories
were forced to close because so many black laborers attended the Republican state
convention.

So great was the enthusiasm that, as one ex-slave minister later wrote, "Politics
got in our midst and our revival or religious work for a while began to wane." The
offices of the black-controlled St. Landry (Louisiana) *Progress,* where several hundred freedmen gathered each Sunday to hear the weekly issue read aloud, temporarily displaced the church as a community meeting place. More typically, the church,
and indeed every other black institution, became politicized. Every AME [African
Methodist Episcopal] preacher in Georgia was said to be actively engaged in Republican organizing, and political materials were read aloud at "churches, societies,
leagues, clubs, balls, picnics, and all other gatherings." One plantation manager
summed up the situation: "You never saw a people more excited on the subject of
politics than are the negroes of the south. They are perfectly wild."

The meteoric rise of the Union League reflected and channeled this political
mobilization. Having originated as a middle-class patriotic club in the Civil War
North, the league now emerged as the political voice of impoverished freedmen.
Even before 1867, local Union Leagues had sprung up among blacks in some parts
of the South, and the order had spread rapidly during and after the war among
Unionist whites in the Southern hill country. Now, as freedmen poured into the
league, "the negro question" disrupted some upcountry branches, leading many
white members to withdraw altogether or retreat into segregated branches. Many
local leagues, however, achieved a remarkable degree of interracial harmony. In
North Carolina, one racially mixed league composed of freedmen, white Unionists,
and Confederate Army deserters, met "in old fields, or in some out of the way
house, and elect candidates to be received into their body."

By the end of 1867, it seemed, virtually every black voter in the South had enrolled in the Union League or some equivalent local political organization. Although the league's national leadership urged that meetings be held in "a
commodious and pleasant room," this often proved impossible; branches convened
in black churches, schools, and homes, and also, when necessary, in woods or
fields. Usually, a Bible, a copy of the Declaration of Independence, and an anvil or
some other emblem of labor lay on a table, a minister opened the meeting with a
prayer, new members took an initiation oath, and pledges followed to uphold the
Republican party and the principle of equal rights, and "to stick to one another."
Armed black sentinels—"a thing unheard of in South Carolina history," according
to one alarmed white—guarded many meetings. Indeed, informal self-defense

organizations sprang up around the leagues, and reports of blacks drilling with weapons, sometimes under men with self-appointed "military titles," aroused considerable white apprehension.

The leagues' main function, however, was political education. "We just went there," explained an illiterate North Carolina black member, "and we talked a little; made speeches on one question and another." Republican newspapers were read aloud, issues of the day debated, candidates nominated for office, and banners with slogans like "Colored Troops Fought Nobly" prepared for rallies, parades, and barbecues. One racially mixed North Carolina league on various occasions discussed the organization of a July 4 celebration, cooperation with the Heroes of America (itself experiencing a revival among wartime Unionists in 1867), and questions like disenfranchisement, debtor relief, and public education likely to arise at the state's constitutional convention. A York County, South Carolina, league "frequently read and discussed" the Black Code, a reminder of injustices in the days of Presidential Reconstruction.

The detailed minute book of the Union League of Maryville, Tennessee, a mountain community with a long-standing antislavery tradition, offers a rare glimpse of the league's inner workings. It records frequent discussions of such issues as the national debt and the impeachment of President Johnson, as well as broader questions: "Is the education of the Female as important as that of the male?" "Should students pay corporation tax?" "Should East Tennessee be a separate state?" Although composed largely of white loyalists—mainly small farmers, agricultural laborers, and town businessmen, many of them Union Army veterans—and located in a county only one-tenth black, the Maryville league chose a number of black officers, called upon Tennessee to send at least one black to Congress, and in 1868 nominated a black justice of the peace and four black city commissioners, all of whom won election.

The local leagues' multifaceted activities, however, far transcended electoral politics. Often growing out of the institutions blacks had created in 1865 and 1866, they promoted the building of schools and churches and collected funds "to see to the sick." League members drafted petitions protesting the exclusion of blacks from local juries and demanding the arrest of white criminals. In one instance, in Bullock County, Alabama, they organized their own "negro government" with a code of laws, sheriff, and courts. (The army imprisoned its leader, former slave George Shorter.)

This hothouse atmosphere of political mobilization made possible a vast expansion of the black political leadership (mostly, it will be recalled, freeborn urban mulattoes) that had emerged between 1864 and 1867. Some, like the Charleston free blacks who fanned out into the black belt spreading Republican doctrine and organizing Union Leagues, did have years of political activism behind them. Others were among the more than eighty "colored itinerant lecturers" financed by the Republican Congressional Committee—men like William U. Saunders, a Baltimore barber and Union Army veteran, James Lynch, who left the editorship of the *Christian Recorder* to organize Republican meetings in Mississippi, and even James H. Jones, former "body servant" of Jefferson Davis. Of the black speakers who crisscrossed the South in 1867 and 1868, Lynch was widely regarded as the greatest orator. "Fluent and graceful, he stirred the audience as no other man did or could do," and his eloquence held gatherings of 3,000 freedmen or more spellbound for hours at a time.

Not a few of the blacks who plunged into politics in 1867 had been born or raised in the North. Even in South Carolina, with its well-established native leadership, Northern blacks assumed a conspicuous role. One white participant in the state's first Republican convention, "astonished" by "the amount of intelligence and ability shown by the colored men," singled out Ohio-born William N. Viney, a young veteran (he was twenty-five in 1867) who had purchased land in the low country and, after the passage of the Reconstruction Act, organized political meetings throughout the region at his own expense. Many Northern blacks, like Viney, had come south with the army; others had served with the Freedmen's Bureau, or as teachers and ministers employed by black churches and Northern missionary societies. Still others were black veterans of the Northern antislavery crusade, fugitive slaves returning home, or the children of well-to-do Southern free blacks who had been sent north for the education (often at Oberlin College) and economic opportunities denied them at home. Reconstruction was one of the few times in American history that the South offered black men of talent and ambition not only the prospect of serving their race, but greater possibilities for personal advancement than existed in the North. And as long as it survived, the southward migration continued. As late as 1875, twenty-two year old D. B. Colton came to South Carolina from Ohio and promptly won a position as election manager. As a consequence, Northern black communities were drained of men of political ambition and of lawyers and other professionals. Having known discrimination in the North—Jonathan C. Gibbs had been "refused admittance to eighteen colleges" before finding a place at Dartmouth—black migrants carried with them a determination that Reconstruction must sweep away racial distinctions in every aspect of American life.

Even more remarkable than the prominence of Northern blacks was the rapid emergence of indigenous leadership in the black belt. Here, where few free blacks had lived before the war, and political mobilization had proceeded extremely unevenly before 1867, local leaders tended to be ex-slaves of modest circumstances who had never before "had the privilege" of expressing political opinions "in public." Many were teachers, preachers, or individuals who possessed other skills of use to the community. Former slave Thomas Allen, a Union League organizer who would soon win election to the Georgia legislature, was a propertyless Baptist preacher, shoemaker, and farmer. But what established him as a leader was literacy: "In my county the colored people came to me for instructions, and I gave them the best instructions I could. I took the New York Tribune and other papers, and in that way I found out a great deal, and I told them whatever I thought was right." In occupation, the largest number of local activists appear to have been artisans. Comprising 5 percent or less of the rural black population, artisans were men whose skill and independence set them apart from ordinary laborers, but who remained deeply embedded in the life of the freedmen's community. Many had already established their prominence as slaves, like Emanuel Fortune, whose son, editor T. Thomas Fortune, later recalled: "It was natural for [him] to take the leadership in any independent movement of the Negroes. During and before the Civil War he had commanded his time as a tanner and expert shoe and bootmaker. In such life as the slaves were allowed and in church work, he took the leader's part." The Union League catapulted others into positions of importance. James T. Alston, an Alabama shoemaker and musician and the former slave of Confederate Gen. Cullen A. Battle, had "a stronger influence over the minds of the colored men in Macon county" than any other individual, a standing he attributed to the commission he received in 1867 to organize a local Union League.

And there were other men, respected for personal qualities—good sense, oratorical ability, having served in the army, or, like South Carolina Republican organizer Alfred Wright, being "an active person in my principles." Calvin Rogers, a Florida black constable, was described by another freedman as "a thorough-going man; he was a stump speaker, and tried to excite the colored people to do the right thing. . . . He would work for a man and make him pay him." Such attributes seemed more important in 1867 than education or political experience. "You can teach me the law," wrote one black Texan, "but you cannot [teach] me what justice is." Nor, in a region that erected nearly insuperable barriers against black achievement, did high social status appear necessary for political distinction. "All colored people of this country understand," a black writer later noted, "that what a man does, is no indication of what he is."

In Union Leagues, Republican gatherings, and impromptu local meetings, ordinary blacks in 1867 and 1868 staked their claim to equal citizenship in the American republic. Like Northern blacks schooled in the Great Tradition of protest, and the urban freemen who had dominated the state conventions of 1865 and 1866, former slaves identified themselves with the heritage of the Declaration of Independence, and insisted America live up to its professed ideals. In insistent language far removed from the conciliatory tones of 1865, an Alabama convention affirmed its understanding of equal citizenship:

> We claim exactly *the same rights, privileges and immunities as are enjoyed by white men*—we ask nothing more and will be content with nothing less. . . . The law no longer knows white nor black, but simply men, and consequently we are entitled to ride in public conveyances, hold office, sit on juries and do everything else which we have in the past been prevented from doing solely on the ground of color. . . .

Violence . . . had been endemic in large parts of the South since 1865. But the advent of Radical Reconstruction stimulated its further expansion. By 1870, the Ku Klux Klan and kindred organizations like the Knights of the White Camelia and the White Brotherhood had become deeply entrenched in nearly every Southern state. One should not think of the Klan, even in its heyday, as possessing a well-organized structure or clearly defined regional leadership. Acts of violence were generally committed by local groups on their own initiative. But the unity of purpose and common tactics of these local organizations makes it possible to generalize about their goals and impact, and the challenge they posed to the survival of Reconstruction. In effect, the Klan was a military force serving the interests of the Democratic party, the planter class, and all those who desired the restoration of white supremacy. Its purposes were political, but political in the broadest sense, for it sought to affect power relations, both public and private, throughout Southern society. It aimed to reverse the interlocking changes sweeping over the South during Reconstruction: to destroy the Republican party's infrastructure, undermine the

Reconstruction state, reestablish control of the black labor force, and restore racial subordination in every aspect of Southern life. . . .

By and large, Klan activity was concentrated in Piedmont counties where blacks comprised a minority or small majority of the population and the two parties were evenly divided. But no simple formula can explain the pattern of terror that engulfed parts of the South while leaving others relatively unscathed. Georgia's Klan was most active in a cluster of black belt and Piedmont cotton counties east and southeast of Atlanta, and in a group of white-majority counties in the north-western part of the state. Unknown in the overwhelmingly black South Carolina and Georgia lowcountry, the organization flourished in the western Alabama planta-tion belt. Scattered across the South lay counties particularly notorious for rampant brutality. Carpetbagger Judge Albion W. Tourgée counted twelve murders, nine rapes, fourteen cases of arson, and over 700 beatings (including the whipping of a woman 103 years of age) in his judicial district in North Carolina's central Pied-mont. An even more extensive "reign of terror" engulfed Jackson, a plantation county in Florida's panhandle. "That is where Satan has his seat," remarked a black clergyman; all told over 150 persons were killed, among them black leaders and Jewish merchant Samuel Fleischman, resented for his Republican views and repu-tation for dealing fairly with black customers.

Nowhere did the Klan become more deeply entrenched than in a group of Pied-mont South Carolina counties where medium-sized farms predominated and the races were about equal in number. An outbreak of terror followed the October 1870 elections, in which Republicans retained a tenuous hold on power in the region. Pos-sibly the most massive Klan action anywhere in the South was the January 1871 as-sault on the Union county jail by 500 masked men, which resulted in the lynching of eight black prisoners. Hundreds of Republicans were whipped and saw their farm property destroyed in Spartanburg, a largely white county with a Democratic major-ity. Here, the victims included a considerable number of scalawags and wartime Unionists, among them Dr. John Winsmith, a member of "the old land aristocracy of the place" wounded by Klansmen in March 1871. In York County, nearly the entire white male population joined the Klan, and committed at least eleven murders and hundreds of whippings; by February 1871 thousands of blacks had taken to the woods each night to avoid assault. The victims included a black militia leader, found hanging from a tree in March with a note pinned to his breast, "Jim Williams on his big muster," and Elias Hill, a self-educated black teacher, minister, and "leader amongst his people." Even by the standards of the postwar South, the whipping of Hill was barbaric: A dwarflike cripple with limbs "drawn up and withered away with pain," he had mistakenly believed "my pitiful condition would save me." Hill had al-ready been organizing local blacks to leave the region in search of the "peaceful liv-ing, free schools, and rich land" denied them in York County. Not long after his beating, together with some sixty black families, he set sail for Liberia.

Contemporary Democrats, echoed by subsequent scholars, often attributed the Klan's sadistic campaign of terror to the fears and prejudices of poorer whites. (More elevated Southerners, one historian contends, could never have committed these "horrible crimes.") The evidence, however, will not sustain such an interpretation. It is true that in some upcountry counties, the Klan drove blacks from land desired by impoverished white farmers and occasionally attacked planters who employed freedmen instead of white tenants. Sometimes, violence exacerbated local labor shortages by causing freedmen to flee the area, leading planters to seek an end to Klan activities. Usually, however, the Klan crossed class lines. If ordinary farmers and laborers constituted the bulk of the membership, and energetic "young bloods" were more likely to conduct midnight raids than middle-aged planters and lawyers, "respectable citizens" chose the targets and often participated in the brutality.

Klansmen generally wore disguises—a typical costume consisted of a long, flowing white robe and hood, capped by horns—and sometimes claimed to be ghosts of Confederate soldiers so, as they claimed, to frighten superstitious blacks. Few freedmen took such nonsense seriously. "Old man, we are just from hell and on our way back," a group of Klansmen told one ex-slave. "If I had been there," he replied, "I would not want to go back." Victims, moreover, frequently recognized their assailants. "Dick Hinds had on a disguise," remarked an Alabama freedmen who saw his son brutally "cut to pieces with a knife." "I knew him. Me and him was raised together." And often, unmasked men committed the violence. The group that attacked the home of Mississippi scalawag Robert Flournoy, whose newspaper had denounced the Klan as "a body of midnight prowlers, robbers, and assassins," included both poor men and property holders, "as respectable as anybody we had there." Among his sixty-five Klan assailants, Abram Colby identified men "not worth the bread they eat," but also some of the "first-class men in our town," including a lawyer and a physician.

Personal experience led blacks to blame the South's "aristocratic classes" for violence and with good reason, for the Klan's leadership included planters, merchants, lawyers, and even ministers. "The most respectable citizens are engaged in it," reported a Georgia Freedmen's Bureau agent, "if there can be any respectability about such people." Editors Josiah Turner of the Raleigh *Sentinel,* Ryland Randolph of the Tuscaloosa *Monitor* (who years later recalled administering whippings "in the regular *ante bellum style*"), and Isaac W. Avery of the Atlanta *Constitution* were prominent Klansmen, along with John B. Gordon, Georgia's Democratic candidate for governor in 1868. When the Knights of the White Camelia initiated Samuel Chester in Arkansas, the pastor of his church administered the oath and the participants included Presbyterian deacons and elders "and every important member of the community." In Jackson County, Florida, the "general ring-leader of badness . . . the generalissimo of Ku-Klux" was a wealthy merchant; elsewhere in the black belt, planters seem to have controlled the organization. Even in the upcountry, "the very best citizens" directed the violence. "Young men of the respectable farming class" composed the Klan's rank and file in western North Carolina, but its leaders were more substantial—former legislator Plato Durham, attorney Leroy McAfee (whose nephew, Thomas Dixon, later garbed the violence in romantic mythology in his novel *The Clansman*), and editor Randolph A. Shotwell. As the Rutherford *Star* remarked, the Klan was "not a gang of *poor trash,* as the leading Democrats would have us believe, but men of property . . . respectable citizens." . . .

. . . Violence had a profound effect on Reconstruction politics. For the Klan devastated the Republican organization in many local communities. By 1871, the party in numerous locales was "scattered and beaten and run out." "They have no leaders up there—no leaders," a freedman lamented of Union County, South Carolina. No party, North or South, commented Adelbert Ames, could see hundreds of its "best and most reliable workers" murdered and still "retain its vigor." Indeed, the black community was more vulnerable to the destruction of its political infrastructure by violence than the white. Local leaders played such a variety of roles in schools, churches, and fraternal organizations that the killing or exiling of one man affected many institutions at once. And for a largely illiterate constituency, in which political information circulated orally rather than through newspapers or pamphlets, local leaders were bridges to the larger world of politics, indispensable sources of political intelligence and guidance. Republican officials, black and white, epitomized the revolution that seemed to have put the bottom rail on top. Their murder or exile inevitably had a demoralizing impact upon their communities.

The violence of 1869–71 etched the Klan permanently in the folk memory of the black community. "What cullud person dat can't 'membahs dem, if he lived dat day?" an elderly Texas freedman asked six decades later. The issue of protection transcended all divisions within the black community, uniting rich and poor, free and freed, in calls for drastic governmental action to restore order. To blacks, indeed, the violence seemed an irrefutable denial of the white South's much-trumpeted claims to superior morality and higher civilization. "Pray tell me," asked Robert B. Elliott, "who is the barbarian here?"

More immediately, violence underscored yet again the "abnormal" quality of Reconstruction politics. Before the war, Democrats and Whigs had combated fiercely throughout the South, but neither party, as Virginia Radical James Hunnicutt pointed out, advised its supporters "to drive out, to starve and to perish" its political opponents. Corrupt election procedures, political chicanery, and even extralegal attempts to oust the opposition party from office were hardly unknown in the North, but not pervasive political violence. "I never knew such things in Maine," commented an Alabama carpetbagger. "Republicans and Democrats were tolerated there." Democracy, it has been said, functions best when politics does not directly mirror deep social division, and each side can accept the victory of the other because both share many values and defeat does not imply "a fatal surrender of . . . vital interests." This was the situation in the North, where, an Alabama Republican observed, "it matters not who is elected." But too much was at stake in Reconstruction for "normal politics" to prevail. As one scalawag pointed out, while Northern political contests focused on "finances, individual capacity, and the like, our contest here is for life, for the right to earn our bread . . . for a decent and respectful consideration as human beings and members of society."

Most of all, violence raised in its starkest form the question of legitimacy that haunted the Reconstruction state. Reconstruction, concluded Klan victim Dr. John Winsmith, ought to begin over again: "I consider a government which does not protect its citizens an utter failure." Indeed, as a former Confederate officer shrewdly observed, it was precisely the Klan's objective "to defy the reconstructed State Governments, to treat them with contempt, and show that they have no real existence." The effective exercise of power, of course, can command respect if not spontaneous loyalty. But only in a few instances had Republican governments found the will to exert this kind of force. Only through "decided action," wrote an Alabama scalawag, could "the state . . . protect its citizens and vindicate its own authority and *right to be*." Yet while their opponents acted as if conducting a revolution, Republicans typically sought stability through conciliation.

✢ *F U R T H E R   R E A D I N G*

Eric Anderson and Alfred A. Moss, Jr., *The Facts of Reconstruction: Essays in Honor of John Hope Franklin* (1992)

Peter Bardaglio, *Reconstructing the Household* (1995)

Michael Les Benedict, *A Compromise of Principle* (1974)

Ira Berlin et al., *Slaves No More* (1992)

Carol R. Bleser, *The Promised Land* (1969)

Orville Vernon Burton, *In My Father's House Are Many Mansions* (1985)

Randolph B. Campbell, *Grassroots Reconstruction in Texas, 1865–1880* (1998)

Dan T. Carter, *When the War Was Over* (1985)

Paul Cimbala, *Under the Guardianship of the Nation* (1997)

Richard N. Current, *Those Terrible Carpetbaggers* (1988)

David Donald, *The Politics of Reconstruction* (1965)

Edmund L. Drago, *Black Politicians and Reconstruction in Georgia* (1982)

W. E. B. Du Bois, *Black Reconstruction* (1935)

Paul D. Escott, *Many Excellent People* (1985)

Eric Foner, *Reconstruction* (1988)

———, *Freedom's Lawmakers: A Directory of Black Officeholders During Reconstruction* (1993)

William Gillette, *Retreat from Reconstruction, 1869–1879* (1979)

William C. Harris, *Day of the Carpetbagger* (1979)

Thomas Holt, *Black over White* (1977)

Elizabeth Jacoway, *Yankee Missionaries in the South* (1979)

Jacqueline Jones, *Soldiers of Light and Love* (1985)

Peter Kolchin, *First Freedom* (1972)

J. Morgan Kousser and James M. McPherson, eds., *Region, Race, and Reconstruction* (1982)

Leon F. Litwack, *Been in the Storm So Long* (1979)

Edward Magdol, *A Right to the Land* (1977)

Jay R. Mandle, *Not Slave, Not Free: The African-American Experience Since the Civil War* (1992)

Robert C. Morris, *Reading, 'Riting, and Reconstruction* (1981)

Donald Nieman, ed., *Freedom, Racism, and Reconstruction* (1997)

Otto H. Olsen, ed., *Reconstruction and Redemption in the South* (1980)

Claude F. Oubre, *Forty Acres and a Mule* (1978)

Michael Perman, *Reunion Without Compromise* (1973)

———, *The Road to Redemption* (1984)

Lawrence N. Powell, *New Masters* (1980)

George C. Rable, *But There Was No Peace* (1984)

James Roark, *Masters Without Slaves* (1977)

Willie Lee Rose, *Rehearsal for Reconstruction: The Port Royal Experiment* (1964)

Leslie A. Schwalm, *A Hard Fight for We: Women's Transition from Slavery to Freedom in South Carolina* (1997)

Kenneth M. Stampp, *The Era of Reconstruction, 1865–1877* (1965)

Mark W. Summers, *Railroads, Reconstruction, and the Gospel of Prosperity* (1984)

Albion W. Tourgee, *A Fool's Errand* (1879)

Allen W. Trelease, *White Terror* (1971)

Ted Tunnell, *Crucible of Reconstruction* (1984)

Charles Vincent, *Black Legislators in Louisiana During Reconstruction* (1976)

Xi Wang, *The Trial of Democracy: Black Suffrage and Northern Republicans, 1860–1910* (1997)

Vernon L. Wharton, *The Negro in Mississippi, 1865–1890* (1947)

Sarah Woolfolk Wiggins, *The Scalawag in Alabama Politics, 1865–1881* (1977)

Joel Williamson, *After Slavery* (1966)

CHAPTER
3

Land and Labor in the New South

In the aftermath of the Civil War, southerners turned once again to the land. Fields, pastures, streams, and woods remained much as they had always been, but the relationship of people to land changed with the demise of slavery. A new land and labor system developed between landowners and a landless labor force that was striving to make a living in a cash-poor economy. Former slaveowners, anxious to see a return on their idle lands, and landless laborers developed a system that included sharecropping, tenant farming, and crop liens. The results were tragically disappointing for many workers and for farmers, some of whom succumbed to debt peonage and lost ownership of the land. By 1880, per capita income for southerners was one-third that of the rest of the nation.

All scholars agree that one fundamental, underlying reason for poor returns in agriculture was a worldwide decline in cotton prices. Demand was growing much more slowly than between 1800 and 1860, and the South's booming production led only to depressed prices. Then why did the South maintain its heavy reliance on cotton? The answer lies in the sharecropping and furnishing systems, which locked farmers and farm workers into the production of a crop whose price was falling.

What was sharecropping and how did it develop? What role did merchants, landowners, and laborers—black and white—play in the sharecropping system? Did it benefit sharecroppers and tenant farmers, or did it lead to abuses? What role did race play in the system? Historians still ponder these questions because they relate to larger issues concerning the South's overall economic health. How did the region's economy fare under this system, and to what extent was the system responsible for the South's slower economic recovery after the Civil War?

☦ DOCUMENTS

Document 1 is a contract executed in January 1886 between a sharecropper and a landowner in North Carolina; it is typical of innumerable contracts made in the South in the last decades of the nineteenth century and well into the twentieth. Document 2 is an agricultural lien, or "crop lien," which gave assurance to the landowner that his expenses for "furnishing" the cropper with food and supplies during 1876 would be repaid. The crop lien customarily accompanied any sharecropping agreement. (This document also pledged the cropper's real and personal property, if necessary, to repay the man who furnished him or her.) In Document 3, Nate Shaw, a black sharecropper in Alabama, describes some of his experiences with the sharecropping system. His account both explains the system and reveals its special dangers to a black family, given pervasive racism. Note the important role that Mrs. Shaw played in defending their interests. Document 4 provides a different and more positive view of sharecropping by William Alexander Percy, a white man who in the 1930s became the head of a large landowning family in Mississippi. In Document 5, William Owens, a white boy from East Texas, describes the rhythms of life on a small farm. Fatherless, he credits the family's survival to the energy and resourcefulness of his mother and grandmother. Finally, small farmers and farm laborers increasingly found themselves left out of any New South prosperity, as their comments to the North Carolina Bureau on Various Subjects in Document 6 plainly show.

1. A Sharecropping Contract, 1886

This contract made and entered into between A. T. Mial of one part and Fenner Powell of the other part both of the County of Wake and State of North Carolina—

Witnesseth—That the Said Fenner Powell hath barganed and agreed with the Said Mial to work as a cropper for the year 1886 on Said Mial's land on the land now occupied by Said Powell on the west Side of Poplar Creek and a point on the east Side of Said Creek and both South and North of the Mial road, leading to Raleigh, That the Said Fenner Powell agrees to work faithfully and dilligently without any unnecessary loss of time, to do all manner of work on Said farm as may be directed by Said Mial, And to be respectful in manners and deportment to Said Mial. And the Said Mial agrees on his part to furnish mule and feed for the same and all plantation tools and Seed to plant the crop free of charge, and to give the Said Powell One half of all crops raised and housed by Said Powell on Said land except the cotton seed. The Said Mial agrees to advance as provisions to Said Powell fifty pound of bacon and two sacks of meal pr month and occationally Some flour to be paid out of his the Said Powell's part of the crop or from any other advance that may be made to Said Powell by Said Mial. As witness our hands and seals this the 16th day of January A.D. 1886

Witness   *A. T. Mial* [signed]   [Seal]

                                                           his

W. S. Mial [signed]   *Fenner X Powell*   [Seal]

                                                          mark

---

This document can be found in the Alonzo T. and Millard Mial Papers, North Carolina Division of Archives and History.

2. A Crop Lien, 1876

No. 123.—Lien Bond secured by Real and Personal Property.

STATE OF NORTH CAROLINA,

Wake County.

Articles of Agreement, Between *Alonzo T. Mial* of said County and State, of the first part, and *A. Robert Medlin* of the County and State aforesaid, of the second part, to secure an Agricultural Lien according to an Act of General Assembly of North Carolina, entitled "An Act to secure advances for Agricultural purposes":

Whereas, the said *A. R. Medlin* being engaged in the cultivation of the soil, and being without the necessary means to cultivate his crop, *The Said A. T. Mial* ~~have~~ has agreed to furnish goods and supplies to the said *A. R. Medlin* to an amount not to exceed *One Hundred and fifty* Dollars, to enable him to cultivate and harvest his crops for the year 1876.

And in consideration thereof, the said *A. R. Medlin* doth hereby give and convey to the said *A. T. Mial* a LIEN upon all of his crops grown in said County in said year, on the lands described as follows: *The land of A. R. Medlin adjoining the lands of Nelson D. Pain Samuel Bunch & others.*

And further, in Consideration thereof, the said *A. R. Medlin* for One Dollar in hand paid, the receipt of which is hereby acknowledged, have bargained and sold, and by these presents do bargain, sell and convey unto the said *A. T. Mial his* heirs and assigns forever, the following described Real and Personal Property to-wit: *All of his Stock horses, Cattle Sheep and Hogs—Carts and Wagons House hold and kitchen furnishings.* To Have and to Hold the above described premises, together with the appurtenances thereof, and the above described personal property, to the said *A. T. Mial his* heirs and assigns.

The above to be null and void should the amount found to be due on account of said advancements be discharged on or before the *1st* day of *November* 1876: otherwise the said *A. T. Mial his* executors, administrators or assigns, are hereby authorized and empowered to seize the crops and Personal Property aforesaid, and sell the same, together with the above Real Estate, for cash, after first advertising the same for fifteen days, and the proceeds thereof apply to the discharge of this Lein, together with the cost and expenses of making such sale, and the surplus to be paid to the said *A. R. Medlin,* or his legal representatives.

IN WITNESS WHEREOF, The said parties have hereunto set their hands and seals this *29th* day of *February,* 1876.

his

A. Robert X *Medlin,* [seal]

mark

A. T. Mial [signed], [seal]

Witness: *L. D. Goodloe* [signed]

A lien bond between A. Robert Medlin and Alonzo T. Mial: 1876. All italicized words were handwritten in the original. This document is from the Alonzo T. and Millard Mial Papers, North Carolina Division of Archives and History.

3. Nate Shaw's Story (c. 1910), 1971

I didn't make two good bales of cotton the first year I stayed with Mr. Curtis. Sorry land, scarce fertilizer, Mr. Curtis not puttin out, riskin much on me and I a workin little old fool, too. I knowed how to plow—catch the mule out the lot, white man's mule, bridle him, go out there and set my plow the way I wanted—I knowed how to do it. Bout a bale and a half was what I made.

The second year he went out there and rented some piney wood land from Mr. Lemuel Tucker, sixteen acres bout a half mile from his plantation and he put me on it. Well, it was kind of thin but it was a king over Mr. Curtis's land. I worked it all in cotton; what little corn I had I planted on Mr. Curtis's place. Well, I made six pretty good bales of cotton out there for Mr. Curtis and myself. When I got done gatherin, wound up, by havin to buy a little stuff from Mr. Curtis at the start, in 1907—it sort of pulled the blinds over my eyes. It took all them six bales of cotton to pay Mr. Curtis. In the place of prosperin I was on a standstill. Second year I was married it took all I made on Mr. Tucker's place, by Mr. Curtis havin rented it from Mr. Tucker for me, to pay up 1908's debts and also 1907's debts—as I say, by me buyin a right smart to start me off to housekeepin, cleaned me. I had not a dollar left out of the cotton. And also, Mr. Curtis come in just before I moved off his place—I was determined to pay him and leave him straight; in fact, I reckon I just had to do it because he'd a requested it of me, moving from his place, clean up and leave myself clear of him.

Mr. Curtis had Mr. Buck Thompson to furnish me groceries. Mr. Curtis knowed all of what Mr. Thompson was lettin me have; kept a book on me. See, he was standin for everything Mr. Thompson gived me; he paid Mr. Thompson and I paid him—the deal worked that way—out of my crop. So he made somethin off my grocery bill besides gettin half my crop when the time come.

Took part of my corn to pay him. He come to my crib, him and Mr. Calvin Culpepper come together to my crib and got my corn, so much of it. And what I had he got the best of it, to finish payin him on top of them six bales of cotton.

Then I moved to Mr. Gus Ames', 1908. Mr. Ames' land was a little better than Mr. Curtis's, but it was poor. Worked his pet land hisself and whatever he made off me, why, that was a bounty for him. I didn't make enough there to help me.

Hannah was dissatisfied at it, too. We talked it over and our talk was this: we knew that we weren't accumulatin nothin, but the farmin affairs was my business, I had to stand up to em as a man. And she didn't worry me bout how we was doin—she knowed it weren't my fault. We was just both dissatisfied. So, we taken it under consideration and went on and she was stickin right with me. She didn't work my heart out in the deal. I wanted to work in a way to please her and satisfy her. She had a book learnin, she was checkin with me at every stand. She was valuable to me and I knowed it. And I was eager to get in a position where I could take care of her and our children better than my daddy taken care of his wives and children.

Mr. Curtis and Mr. Ames both, they'd show me my land I had to work and furnish me—far as fertilize to work that crop, they'd furnish me what *they* wanted to;

didn't leave it up to me. That's what hurt—they'd furnish me the amount of fertilize they wanted regardless to what I wanted. I quickly seed, startin off with Mr. Curtis in 1907, it weren't goin to be enough. First year I worked for him and the last year too he didn't allow me to use over twenty-two hundred pounds of guano—it come in two-hundred-pound sacks then—that's all he'd back me up for all the land I worked, cotton and corn. It was enough to start with but not enough to do any more. Really, I oughta been usin twice that amount. Told him, too, but he said, "Well, at the present time and system, Nate, you can't risk too much."

I knowed I oughta used more fertilize to make a better crop—if you puts nothin in you gets nothin, all the way through. It's nonsense what they gived me—Mr. Curtis and Mr. Ames, too—but I was a poor colored man, young man too, and I had to go by their orders. It wasn't that I was ignorant of what I had to do, just, "Can't take too much risk, can't take too much risk." . . . But you had to do what the white man said, livin here in this country. And if you made enough to pay him, that was all he cared for; just make enough to pay him what you owed him and anything he made over that, why, he was collectin on his risk. In my condition, and the way I see it for everybody, if you don't make enough to have some left you aint done nothin, except givin the other fellow your labor. That crop out there goin to prosper enough for him to get his and get what I owe him; he's makin his profit but he aint goin to let me rise. If he'd treat me right and treat my crop right, I'd make more and he'd get more—and a heap of times he'd get it all! That white man gettin all he lookin for, all he put out in the spring, gettin it all back in the fall. But what am I gettin for my labor? I aint gettin nothin. I learnt that right quick: it's easy to understand if a man will look at it. . . .

If you want to sell your cotton at once, you take it to the market, carry it to the Apafalya cotton market and they'll sample it. Cotton buyin man cuts a slug in the side of your bale, reaches in there and pulls the first of it out the way and get him a handful, just clawin in there. He'll look over that sample, grade that cotton—that's his job. What kind of grade do it make? You don't know until he tells you. If it's short staple, the devil, your price is cut on that cotton. Color matters too, and the way it was ginned—some gins cuts up the cotton, ruins the staple.

They had names for the cotton grades—grade this, or grade that or grade the other. Didn't do no good to argue with the man if you didn't agree with the grade. Thing for you to do if he graded your cotton, examined it and gived you a low bid, take it to the next man.

Much of it is a humbug just like everything else, this gradin business. Some of em don't pay you what that cotton's worth a pound. They want long staple, clean cotton: the cleaner and the prettier it is and the nearer it comes to the specification of the staple they lookin for, the more they'll offer you. Generally, it's a top limit to that price and that's what they call the price cotton is bringin that year. If it's forty-cent cotton or six-cent cotton, it don't depend much on *your* cotton. It's a market price and it's set before you ever try to sell your cotton, and it's set probably before you gin your cotton and before you gather it or grow it or even plant your seed.

You take that cotton and carry it around to the cotton buyers. You might walk in that market buildin to a certain cotton buyer and he'll take your sample and look it over, look it over, give it a pull or two and he just might if he's very anxious for cotton, offer you a good price for it. But if he's in no hurry to buy your cotton and he gives you a price you don't like you can go to another buyer.

Heap of em buyin that cotton to speculate; he got plenty of money, wants to make more money, he buyin that cotton for himself and he don't care what company buys it from him. Maybe he might be buyin for a speculatin company, a company what does business in speculation. Or he might be buyin for a company that uses that cotton. Or if he can handle the matter, he buys for two companies.

Niggers' cotton didn't class like a white man's cotton with a heap of em. Used to be, when I was dealin with them folks in Apafalya, some of em you could have called em crooks if you wanted to; they acted in a way to bear that name, definitely. Give a white man more for his cotton than they do you.

I've had white men to meet me on the streets with a cotton sample in my hand, say, "Hello, Nate, you sellin cotton today?" White men, farmers like myself, private men; some of em was poor white men.

I'd tell em, "Yes, sir, I'm tryin. I can't look like get what my cotton's worth."

"What you been offered?"

"Well, Mr. So-and-so—"

"O, I see here such-and-such a one offered you so-and-so-and-so—"

Heap of times the scaper that I offered to sell him my cotton had a knack of puttin his bid on the paper that the cotton was wrapped up in. I didn't want him to do that. The next man would see how much this one bid me and he wouldn't go above it.

And so, I'd have my cotton weighed and I'd go up and down the street with my sample. Meet a white man, farmin man like myself, on the street; he'd see what I been offered for my sample—the buyer's marks would be on the wrapper—or I'd tell him. And he'd take that sample, unwrap it, look at it; he'd say, "Nate, I can beat you with your own cotton, I can get more for it than that."

Aint that enough to put your boots on! The same sample. He'd say, "Let me take your sample and go around in your place. I can beat what they offered you."

Take that cotton and go right to the man that had his bid on it and he'd raise it; right behind where I was, had been, and get a better bid on it. I've gived a white man my sample right there on the streets of Apafalya; he'd go off and come back. Sometime he'd say, "Well, Nate, I helped you a little on it but I couldn't help you much."

And sometime he'd get a good raise on it with another fellow out yonder. He'd bring my sample back to me with a bid on it. "Well, Nate, I knowed I could help you on that cotton."

That was happenin all through my farmin years: from the time I stayed on the Curtis place, and when I moved to the Ames place and when I lived with Mr. Reeve, and when I moved down on Sitimachas Creek with Mr. Tucker, and when I lived up there at Two Forks on the Stark place, and when I moved down on the Pollard place and stayed there nine years. Colored man's cotton weren't worth as much as a white man's cotton less'n it come to the buyer in the white man's hands. But the colored man's labor—that was worth more to the white man than the labor of his own color because it cost him less and he got just as much for his money. . . .

I come up to my house one day—I was out checkin on my fences—and my wife told me there was a card in the mailbox tellin me to come to the bank in

Apafalya and sign papers on my place. I said, "If I go, any way I go, you goin with me." See, she had book learnin and she could read and write. So I told her, "Well, we'll go to Apafalya this evenin, right after dark."

She was right down with me. Sometimes she'd say, "Darlin, you know what's best to do. But you can't decide *what* to do until you knows every side of the proposition. And bein that you can't read and write, it's profitable for us all for you to make me your partner."

I told her, one day, and many a time, "I'm married to you. And I think my best business should be in your hands. If anybody knows the ins and outs of it, you the one to know. But so far as workin in the field, I aint never had a high opinion of that and I intend to always be that way. Your business is at the house, mine's out in the field."

She was a girl that her mother would put all her business in her hands—her mother couldn't read and write. You could drop any sort of paper in front of Hannah and she could pick it up and read it like a top. She was pretty far advanced in education. She wasn't a graduate but she understood anything and could talk it off, too. She was, in a way of speakin, the *eyes* and I was the mouthpiece.

So, when I went there to sign them papers, I told her, "You goin with me."

I wanted her to read them papers to me; I knowed they weren't goin to do it. All I had to do was sign, but I wanted to know what I was signin.

Watson had taken over the place from the federal government and it was him I had to sign with. My wife and I jumped in the car and went right on to Apafalya. Got there and walked in—weren't nobody there in the bank but Mr. Grace and Mr. Watson. O good God, the doors flew right open and I broke out; I couldn't help it, I got red hot. I was signin—called it signin papers on that place. I knowed what I was signin before I signed; that's what brought the devil up.

"Hi, hello, Nate."

"Hello, Nate."

"How do you do, Mr. Watson, Mr. Grace."

Said, "Well, you come here to sign your papers, didn't you?"

I said, "Yes sirs, that's why I'm here."

Pushed it through the window for me to sign. My wife was standin right there and I just handed it to her. That's when I found out the devil was in the concern; that kept crossin my mind all the time and that kept me, to a great extent, from signin any notes at all with Watson.

Hannah turned away, stepped off a step or two, whipped that paper right over in a jiffy. She come back with it and touched me on my arm. I listened to her. She said, "Darlin, that paper covers everything you got: your mules, wagon, all your tools and your cows and hogs and everything you got's on that paper."

Good God, when she told me that I hollered. I just pushed the paper back to em through the bars. I said, "I won't sign that paper, noway under the sun it could be fixed like it is."

I'd expected to come there that night and sign papers on the land—Watson knowed what I had—not reach out and take my mules, my wagon, my hogs, my cows, on that paper. And if I'd a signed it like they was preparin me to do, I could have lost it all. Just be late payin on the land and they would take everything I had. I had sense enough through my wife to see what they was tryin to do to me. Woooooooooo, I meant to buck it.

I said, "Aint that land sufficient to stand for itself and not none of my personal property on it? I can't carry it nowhere."

Tried to saddle everything I had. Right there I burst like a butterbean in the sun. I wouldn't sign that note for Jesus Christ. I just stuck that paper back through them bars—I knowed the type of him. I felt a fire in my heart; told my wife, "Let's go."

If I couldn't do better I was goin to move away from there. Soon as I told my wife, "Let's go," and got nearly to the door, "Come back, come back, Nate, we can change the paper; come back, come back, we can change it."

I just say now I was a fool—I went back. They changed that paper to suit me and I signed it. It just spoke for the land then. So I signed to buy the place from Mr. Watson and if I couldn't make the payments all they could do was take it back. . . .

4. William Alexander Percy Views Sharecropping, 1941

I have no love of the land and few, if any, pioneer virtues, but when Trail Lake became mine after Father's death, I must confess I was proud of it. I could reach it in three quarters of an hour. It was a model place: well drained, crossed by concrete roads, with good screened houses, a modern gin, artesian-well water, a high state of cultivation, a Negro school, a foolish number of churches, abundant crops, gardens and peach trees, quantities of hogs, chickens, and cows, and all the mules and tractors and equipment any place that size needed.

Father had operated it under the same contract that Fafar used on the Percy Place. The Negroes seemed to like it and I certainly did. I happen to believe that profit-sharing is the most moral system under which human beings can work together and I am convinced that if it were accepted in principle by capital and labor, our industrial troubles would largely cease. So on Trail Lake I continue to be partners with the sons of ex-slaves and to share fifty-fifty with them as my grandfather and Father had done.

In 1936 a young man with a passion for facts roved in from the University of North Carolina and asked to be allowed to inspect Trail Lake for the summer. He was Mr. Raymond McClinton, one of Doctor Odum's boys, and the result of his sojourn was a thesis entitled "A Social-Economic Analysis of a Mississippi Delta Plantation." That's coming pretty stout if you spend much of your time trying to forget facts and are stone-deaf to statistics. But some of his findings were of interest even to me, largely I suspect because they illustrated how Fafar's partnership-contract works in the modern world. In 1936, the year Mr. McClinton chose for his study, the crop was fair, the price average (about twelve cents), and the taxes higher than usual. Now for some of his facts:

Trail Lake has a net acreage of 3,343.12 acres of which 1,833.66 are planted in cotton, 50.59 are given to pasture, 52.44 to gardens, and the rest to corn and hay. The place is worked by 149 families of Negroes (589 individuals) and in 1936 yielded 1,542 bales of cotton. One hundred and twenty-four of the families work under Fafar's old contract, and twenty-five, who own their stock and equipment, under a similar contract which differs from the other only in giving three-fourths instead of one-half of the yield to the tenant. The plantation paid in taxes of all kinds $20,459.99, a bit better than $6.00 per acre; in payrolls for plantation work $12,584.66—nearly $4.00 an acre. These payrolls went to the Negroes on the place. The 124 families without stock of their own made a gross average income of $491.90 and a net average income of $437.64. I have lost Mr. McClinton's calculation of how many days of work a plantation worker puts in per year, but my own calculation is a maximum of 150 days. There is nothing to do from ginning time, about October the first, to planting time, about March the fifteenth, and nothing to do on rainy days, of which we have many.

These figures, as I read them, show that during an average year the 124 families working on Trail Lake for 150 days make each $437.64 clear, besides having free water and fuel, free garden plot and pasturage, a monthly credit for six months to cover food and clothing, a credit for doctor's bills and medicine, and a house to live in. The Negroes who receive this cash and these benefits are simple unskilled laborers. I wonder what other unskilled labor for so little receives so much. Plantations do not close down during the year and there's no firing, because partners can't fire one another. Our plantation system seems to me to offer as humane, just, self-respecting, and cheerful a method of earning a living as human beings are likely to devise. I watch the limber-jointed, oily-black, well-fed, decently clothed peasants on Trail Lake and feel sorry for the telephone girls, the clerks in chain stores, the office help, the unskilled laborers everywhere—not only for their poor and fixed wage but for their slave routine, their joyless habits of work, and their insecurity. . . .

Share-cropping is one of the best systems ever devised to give security and a chance for profit to the simple and the unskilled. It has but one drawback—it must be administered by human beings to whom it offers an unusual opportunity to rob without detection or punishment. The failure is not in the system itself, but in not living up to the contractual obligations of the system—the failure is in human nature. The Negro is no more on an equality with the white man in plantation matters than in any other dealings between the two. The white planter may charge an exorbitant rate of interest, he may allow the share-cropper less than the market price received for his cotton, he may cheat him in a thousand different ways, and the Negro's redress is merely theoretical. If the white planter happens to be a crook, the share-cropper system on that plantation is bad for Negroes, as any other system would be. They are prey for the dishonest and temptation for the honest. If the Delta planters were mostly cheats, the results of the share-cropper system would be as grievous as reported. But, strange as it may seem to the sainted East, we have quite a sprinkling of decent folk down our way.

Property is a form of power. Some people regard it as an opportunity for profit, some as a trust; in the former it breeds hubris, in the latter, noblesse oblige. The landed gentry of Fafar's time were of an ancient lineage and in a sober God-fearing tradition. Today many have thought to acquire membership in that older caste by acquiring land, naked land, without those ancestral hereditaments of virtue which change dirt into a way of life. On the plantation where there is stealing from the Negro you will generally find the owner to be a little fellow operating, as the saying goes, "on a shoe-string," or a nouveau riche, or a landlord on the make, tempted to take more than his share because of the mortgage that makes his title and his morals insecure. These, in their pathetic ambition to imitate what they do not understand, acquire power and use it for profit; for them the share-cropper system affords a golden opportunity rarely passed up.

5. William A. Owens Describes Tenant Farm Life in 1906

My mother was then in a family of women who had lost most of their men: her grandmother, born Missouri Ann Cleaver, who lived on the Pin Hook road between the graveyard and the store; her mother, Alice Chennault, who had married off her two daughters and was "living around"; her mother's sister, Ellen Victoria, Aunt Vick; her mother's half-sister, Elizabeth Penelope Haigood, who lived across Little Pine Creek on the Novice road. All her life she had seen these women doing the work of men—plowing, cutting wood, feeding stock. In the beginning of winter she had to take up the work of a man and do what she could for the children. . . .

My grandmother . . . came to live with her, to help with the children and to keep house while my mother went to the field. She had raised a family without a man. So could any woman who wanted badly enough to hold her children together. At the time she was a tall raw-boned woman of fifty and, as the people said of her, "as stout as e'er a man." The strongest daughter of the stronger Missouri Ann, she had survived the hard times of the Civil War, the walk from Camden, Arkansas, to Blossom Prairie, the hardships of making a living at Pin Hook. She had buried a husband and a son. It was time for her to take a rest, but rest had to be farther along the road. . . .

In Pin Hook, November is often wet and gray but rarely wintry. Monroe and Dewey could go to school, barefoot because there was no money for shoes that year. In December and January they would have to miss some days when blue northers swept down and left ice on the ruts in the road, but they were pushed to get as much learning as they could while they could. To give them the chance, my mother cut and hauled wood to keep fires going in the fireplace and cookstove. At night she helped them with their lessons in front of the fire.

Three months of schooling and then they had to stop. By the first warm days of February plowing had to start and Monroe had to be a hand in the field. They hitched Old Maud, the bay mare, to a kelly turning plow and began to flatbreak the land my father had plowed the year before, taking it a square at a time, first for corn and then for cotton. Hour after hour my mother went, holding the plow in the ground, guiding the mare with rope lines looped over her shoulders. When she was too tired to manage both, Monroe held the lines. It was backbreaking, heartbreaking work, going as they did from first light till first dark. Breaking the land was only the beginning. Planting and cultivating still had to come. . . .

By the middle of March the garden had to be started and the hens set. New shoots of poke and dandelion and peppergrass were beginning to show along the rail fences and turnrows. My grandmother took on the jobs of garden and chickens, and picking "sallet" greens. The older children could trail after her. I had to be taken to the field, to lie on a quilt on the ground.

All that spring I spent my days in the field, sleeping, waking, crying when I was hungry or needed changing. When I was big enough to crawl, my mother tied me to a stake to keep me from going off into the woods where there were snakes and scorpions and long blue santafees with yellow stingered legs. Where the rows were long, she tied me in the middle of the field. When she was plowing and Monroe planting, she staked me between them, where one or the other could keep an eye on me.

My toys were the dirt, and a stick to dig the dirt. No one could live closer to the earth than I did. I dug the sand, I rolled in it, I covered myself with it. Before my first year had passed I had eaten the peck of dirt everyone, Pin Hook people said, is entitled to. I had learned the feel, the smell, the taste of earth.

That year and later I learned, hardly knowing I was learning it, how farm life is shaped by the land and the seasons—by what will grow and the days or weeks or months of growing time—of making the best of sun and rain and seed in the earth. In Pin Hook, corn had to be planted in late February or early March, the time of sandstorms out west. There were days when the sky was overcast with a cloud of red dust, and the sun shone through a muddy red. Corn planted then was in the ground on time. Corn planted later might twist and burn and never tassel in the drouth of late July and August. Cotton planting had to wait till the ground was warm. All in the month of May it had to be planted, plowed, chopped, to make it ready for fast growing in the hot moist days of June. Farming was going right for anybody who could say, "I found me a cotton bloom Fourth of July." In the heat of summer, crops had to be "laid by" with a last running of the Georgia stock down the middles. Once they were through laying by, Pin Hookers could rest a little before gathering time.

Gathering time came and my mother began to take heart. The crop was light, but she had made a crop. The land had not been lost; the children were still all together. My mother knew that she could go on. She could gather this year's crop. She could plant the next. She could see that the children got to school when they were not in the field.

Gathering corn came first, each trip down the field with the wagon taking a swath five rows wide. My mother took two rows on one side, Monroe took two on the other. The other children "carried the down row," the row of stalks knocked down by the wagon. I rode in the front of the wagon, with boards between me and the pile of pale yellow shucks.

Cotton picking came next. Grown-ups and older children dragged long canvas sacks down the middles, picking two rows at a time, their fingers working down the stalks, pulling out the white lint, leaving yellow burrs among the green leaves. The smaller children picked in flour sacks, and cried when the points of cotton burrs pricked their fingers. I rode on my mother's sack, or slept on a pile of cotton in the wagon.

Potato digging had to come before frost, while the sand was still warm and dry. The diggers had to work close to the earth. First the rows were turned up with a kelly turning plow. Then the diggers went on their hands and knees, grabbling in the earth with their fingers. It was a job for children. They could crawl and roll in the dirt as much as they liked. In moments of rest they could build sand houses and tunnels over their bare feet.

On the farm, sights and smells go with the seasons, and I learned them the first year, with each following year only a relearning: the green of young corn, the white of cotton blossoms slowly turning pink, the burnt brown of grass under an August sun; the sweetness of corn in silk and tassel, the dryness of dust in a cotton middle, the new-clothes smell of cotton lint when the face is pressed down into it.

The year passed. I was one year old, my father one year in the grave. Work had been hard, but there was enough to live on: milk and cornbread, sweet potatoes and black-eyed peas. Cotton money had to go for doctor bills and medicine. Times were bad, but they could be worse. Next year they would be better. At night they could be truly thankful when, after the Bible reading, they knelt beside hickory-bottomed chairs for the prayers they made themselves.

"If our health holds out," my mother and grandmother said.

6. Tenants and Farmers Assess the New South, 1887–1889

Extracts from Letters to the Bureau on Various Subjects from Tenants and Farm Laborers in the Different Counties of the State

1887

A. R.—There is general depression and hard times and almost broken spirits among the tenant farmers. There are many things that contribute somewhat to this bad state of things but the one great cause is the outrageous per cent. charged for supplies bought on credit; it is sapping the life of North Carolina.

F. M. S.—The poor cannot clothe their children decently enough for a school room because of the exorbitant rate of interest they are charged for supplies; they are obliged to pay whatever the merchants charge. This is a most pressing evil and should be stopped by law or it will soon swallow us body and soul.

T. D. H.—Some think they pay only 25 or 30 per cent. for what they buy on crop liens, but if they will figure it out, they will see it is 100 to 200 per cent. per annum on the amount they buy over cash prices. There would be an over supply of labor if they would work. Negroes with some education will not work on the farm if they can help it. They have a keener desire for education than the whites and attend school much better.

W. J. M.—I think the present depressed condition of the farming interest is largely due to the mortgage system in buying supplies. There is no chance for improvement where this system is in operation.

J. M. B.—There is no man and no county that can long exist on 50 per cent. charged on everything eaten by farmers; unless a remedy is found the county will be ruined very soon.

O. E.—There ought to be a law passed forbidding any man planting more than ten acres in cotton to the horse.

This document is taken from the *First Annual Report of the Bureau of Labor Statistics of the State of North Carolina,* W. N. Jones, Commissioner (Raleigh: Josephus Daniels, State Printer and Binder, Presses of Edwards and Broughton, 1887), and *Third Annual Report of the Bureau of Labor Statistics of the State of North Carolina for the Year 1889,* John C. Scarborough, Commissioner (Raleigh: Josephus Daniels, State Printer and Binder, Presses of Edwards & Broughton, 1890).

J. S. M.—The condition of the farmers is bad and will get no better until we adopt some system and unite in our efforts to better ourselves and stop looking to others to help us; we must depend upon ourselves. When we become united we can get all the legislation we need; not till then.

J. L. H.—Merchants require a mortgage on whatever property tenant has, besides the crop. They are more strict this year than ever before. There were many that could not pay out last year. Tenants pay an advance of at least 25 per cent. on the average.

J. H. R.—The system of buying on time and using guano has broken up many farmers, and has driven so many to the towns to seek employment that wages have been greatly reduced. If this state of things continues it will soon put all the land in the hands of a few men and ruin all classes.

F. W. R.—Attendance at school ought to be enforced by law; the schools are now usually taught in winter when the child of the poor man is poorly clad and hence unable to attend; in summer they must work, and so they do not attend school. This should not be so—we must get out of this condition or we shall go backward as a people and State.

S. A. H.—Many whites do not send their children to school for want of proper clothes. The people are in a bad condition and most of their lands are mortgaged, in most cases too irredeemably. I see no hope for the county to get better unless the government comes to their help and lends them money at 1 per cent. to redeem their land and gives them twenty years to pay out. Wages have decreased on farms owing I believe to the tariff.

S. S.—We farmers work very hard, but get in no better condition. Evidently there is something wrong. The towns flourish, while in the country, where the producing element is, the people get worse off. We do not mind the work—were raised to it—but would like to get something for it.

W. H. B.—The mortgage system is working its deadly way into this county, and making sad havoc where its tempting offers are once entered into. Alas! one never gets out from its magic embrace until he dies out or is sold out. I wish this ruinous law could be repealed, and with it the homestead law, which is the father of the mortgage system.

L. P.—The trouble in this county is the awful time prices that we have to pay the merchants, not less than 50 per cent. The price of labor is low and it should be higher, but the farmer can't afford to pay even present prices, because the high per cent. keeps him down. The homestead law should be repealed and then the lien law and the high time prices would have to go.

P. H. H.—The poor tenant and farm laborers and in many cases landowners, are in a bad condition, mostly on account of the heavy per cent. charged by merchants for supplies.

J. E. D.—Labor is down; so is the farmer. The merchant is the prosperous man now. Half of the farms are mortgaged to the commission merchants, who charge 50 per cent. above cash prices. Half of the farmers of this county are bound to merchants by the mortgage system.

1889

Remarks.—In my opinion, the greatest evil with the farmers here is, that the landowners will rent their lands and hire their teams to tenants, and furnish provisions;

the consequence is, the tenant gets so far in debt to the landlord that, before the crop is laid by, the tenant gets dissatisfied and fails to work the crop as it ought to be, and, therefore, raises bad crops and the land is left in bad condition. If the landlord would hire the labor, his land would be in better condition and labor would be better also.

Remarks.—The year in this section was not favorable to farming. Spring late. The heavy rain-fall in June and July injured the general crop badly, particularly cotton. The sweet-potato crop not good—too much rain. Had a killing frost on the nights of October 5 and 6, which did considerable damage.

Remarks.—I will name a few evils the farmer has to contend with, viz: The price of everything produced by the farmer is fixed by the merchant, or purchaser, as well as everything bought by the farmer, and high rates for transportation on railroads. The first evil mentioned can be overcome by the farmers paying cash for what they purchase, and cooperation. The second should be overcome by proper legislation—a Railroad Commission Bill.

Remarks.—The mortgage system, with the consequent high prices exacted for supplies, and the one-crop (cotton) system hangs like an incubus about this people and have well-nigh ruined them financially. The system of working the public roads now in vogue with us is very unsatisfactory with us, not to say unjust. Capital or property and labor should both be taxed to keep up the public highways. My idea would be to value an able-bodied man, with nothing but his head, say at $500 or $1,000 each, as the exigencies of the case might demand, and then require every $500 or $1,000 worth of capital or property to contribute a like amount, either in labor or its equivalent in money. I have given this matter much thought and this strikes me as the most equitable and feasible plan. Our public school system in this part of the State is very inefficient.

Remarks.—Time was in this vicinity nearly every farmer not only supported himself and family from the products of the farm, but had something to spare as well. That time has passed away, I fear, forever. Then very little cotton was raised, and the farmers looked well to grain crops, horses, cattle, hogs and sheep. There was not much opulence, but much of substantial independence. Now, instead of being a year before, they are a year, at least behind, and, toil as they may, too many of them at the close of the year, when the books are opened, find the balance-sheet against them, "though every nerve was strained." The mortgage system, which hangs like a pall of death over many an honest, hard-working man, will ruin any business interest in this country. No farmer can borrow money, or buy on crop-time, at an advance of from thirty to fifty per cent. No farmer can farm successfully without some money; the present rates offered him amounts to prohibition. I cannot, in the brief space allowed, recount many of the ills now affecting us, or make any suggestion in the palliation of them. To be brief, farmers are very much dispirited at the outlook, while they have worked harder for the last two years than at any time within my knowledge.

✢   *E S S A Y S*

In the first essay, historian Jonathan Wiener explores the relationship between class structure and economic development in the South. He begins by discussing class conflict and the plantation system during the early years of Reconstruction and argues that the South's labor system was essentially different from that of the North. He shows how the system of "bound labor" was detrimental to the South's overall economy and destructive to human incentive, especially to freedpeople. One might well ask, how did African Americans survive? Sharon Ann Holt answers this in her essay by closely observing the multifaceted methods small farmers used to supplement their incomes and alleviate the negative effects of sharecropping. Although pervasive racism and class prejudice continued to create economic inequities, a family's maintenance often depended on the creative use of the household economy, wage earning, and farming skills.

Bound Labor in Southern Agriculture

JONATHAN M. WIENER

. . . The social history of the immediate postwar period . . . indicates that [southern] planters reached different conclusions about what constituted economic rationality. They believed that the most profitable course was to maintain the plantation as a centralized unit of production. By using supervised gang laborers who were paid wages and incorporated into the organizational structure of the antebellum plantation, the planters hoped to preserve economies of scale and centralized management. . . .

. . . Planters organized to limit the free market in labor and to force freedmen to work on plantation gangs, sought to enlist the Freedmen's Bureau in the same effort, and worked in the state legislatures to establish repressive laws. Some turned to terror—to the Ku Klux Klan—to force blacks to labor in plantation gangs. Planters throughout the South in the years immediately following the war organized to limit competition among themselves. At a typical meeting in the fall of 1867, planters in Sumter County, Alabama, unanimously resolved that "concert of action" was "indispensable" in hiring labor. Thus, all would offer the same terms to the freedmen, and none would "employ any laborer discharged for violation of contracts." Other planters held similar meetings in places like Sumter, South Carolina, and Amite County, Mississippi, followed by statewide meetings of planter representatives. The report of the Freedmen's Bureau in 1866 complained of the planters' "community of action," and the Joint Congressional Committee on Reconstruction heard evidence on the same phenomenon. As one planter explained the strategy to John Trowbridge in 1866, "The nigger is going to be made a serf, sure as you live. It won't need any law for that. Planters will have an understanding among themselves: 'You won't hire my niggers, and I won't hire yours,' then what's left for them? They're attached to the soil, and we're as much their masters as ever." Planters went beyond these informal organizations and used state power to enforce the interests of their class and prevent those individualists among them who desired to engage in market economics. "Enticement" acts passed in every Southern state immediately after the war made it a crime to "hire away, or induce to leave the ser-

From Jonathan M. Wiener, "Class Structure and Economic Development in the American South, 1865–1955," from *American Historical Review* (October 1979). Reprinted by permission of the author.

vice of another," any laborer "by offering higher wages or in any other way whatsoever." The criminal defined by this law was not the black who left his plantation,
but the planter who sought a free market in labor.

. . . Louisiana law . . . made it a crime to "feed, harbor, or secrete any person
who leaves his or her employer," and enticement laws in most states provided that
farm laborers hired away by better offers could be forcibly returned to the original
employers. Vagrancy acts were even more extreme efforts to control the mobility of
labor. The definition of vagrancy usually included "stubborn servants . . . , a laborer
or servant who loiters away his time, or refuses to comply with any contract . . .
without just cause." Planters could thus enlist local courts in keeping "their" laborers on their plantations.

The planters' bitter opposition to the presence of the Freedmen's Bureau did
not stop them from seeking to enlist the bureau's agents in an effort to tie blacks to
the land. Planters put intense and calculated social pressure on the Union representatives in their midst. As early as 1864, a War Department report warned that officials in charge of the freedmen were "received into the houses of the planters and
treated with a certain consideration," so that, under the "influences" that the
planters brought to bear, officials often ("without becoming fully conscious of it")
became "the employers' instrument of great injustice and ill-treatment toward . . .
colored laborers." A black-belt newspaper explained in 1866 that Union officials
who were "gentlemen" were "received ito the best families . . . on probation" but
those who kept "company with Negroes . . . could not get into society." When the
Freedmen's Bureau opened an office in the Alabama black belt, "the white people
. . . determined to win their good will," according to Walter L. Fleming. "There
were 'stag' dinners and feasts, and the eternal friendship of the officers, with a few
exceptions, was won." Fleming gave more credit to the persuasive power of stag
dinners with planters than the feasts probably deserved, but he was undoubtedly
correct in describing the planters' intentions as well as the effect of their efforts:
some agents of the Freedmen's Bureau helped planters get freedmen to work on
terms agreed to by planter organizations and often sided with planters in disputes
with freedmen.

Finally, some planters restricted blacks' freedom to move by resorting to terror.
Historians concerned with the politics of Reconstruction have overlooked the extent to which the Klan in the black belt was an instrument of the planter class for the
control of labor. Planters played a major role in organizing and directing Klan activities there; and Klan terror contributed to the repression of black labor, primarily by
threatening those who contemplated emigration. As early as 1866, masked bands
"punished Negroes whose landlords had complained of them." According to the
Congressional testimony of one planter, when blacks "got together once to emigrate
. . . , disguised men went to them and told them that if they undertook it they would
be killed," in order to keep "the country from being deprived of their labor." In the
words of a black belt lawyer, the Klan was "intended principally for the negroes
who failed to work." And Allen W. Trelease has shown that the Klan pursued blacks
who "violat[ed] . . . labor contracts by running away."

Despite the planters' use of informal organization, formal law, the Freedmen's
Bureau, and the Klan, they failed to preserve the plantation as a centralized unit cultivated by gangs of wage laborers. To understand this failure, it is necessary to look

beyond the abstract logic of the market and focus on the relatively concrete process of class conflict between planters and freedmen. Rational as the planters' effort was, preservation of the centralized plantation confronted an insurmountable obstacle: the freedmen's refusal to agree to it. Their widespread resistance to working for wages in gangs, which appears in the sources as a "shortage of labor," played a crucial role in the reorganization of agriculture after the war. Such shortages were reported throughout the plantation South in the immediate postwar years. Robert Somers, who visited the South in 1871 and wrote a book about his experiences, titled his chapter on the Alabama black belt "Despair of the Planters for Labor." Reports by the Freedmen's Bureau and the Boston textile firm of Loring and Atkinson concurred. The freedmen's idea of a rational system of production differed from that of the planters; the blacks hungered for land. Eugene Genovese has quoted a plantation mistress's description of a typical situation at the war's end: "our most trusted servant . . . claims the plantation as his own." The Joint Congressional Committee on Reconstruction noted the freedmen's fierce "passion . . . to own land," and the Montgomery *Advertiser* agreed that blacks were "ravenous for land." The freedmen made their claim on the basis of a kind of labor theory of value; as a "Colored Convention" proclaimed in Montgomery in May 1867, "the property" that the planters held was "nearly all earned by the sweat of our brows, not theirs." And an exslave wrote in 1864, "we wants land—dis bery land dat is rich wid de sweat ob we face and de blood ob we back."

By creating a "shortage of labor," the freedmen defeated the planters' efforts to preserve the plantation as a single, large-scale unit worked by gangs. Increasingly in 1867 and 1868, planters divided their plantations into small plots and assigned each to a single family. In establishing decentralized family sharecropping as the prevailing organization of cotton production after the war, the planters made a major concession to the freedmen and their resistance to the slavelike gang system. The Selma *Southern Argus,* one of the most articulate and insightful voices of the planter class, admitted this explicitly: sharecropping was "an unwilling concession to the freedman's desire to become a proprietor . . . , not a voluntary association from similarity of aims and interests." Thus, class conflict shaped the form of the postwar plantation more than did purely economic forces operating according to the logic of the free market. . . .

. . . The North's economy depended on the market mechanism to allocate "free" labor; capitalists competed for labor and laborers were free, at least in theory, to move in response to better offers. This was the "classic capitalist" route to industrial society. Until the Great Depression of the 1930s, planters in the postwar South used more directly coercive methods of labor allocation and control. These restrictions on the South's labor market distinguished the planter from the Northern bourgeois, turned the sharecropper into a kind of "bound" laborer, and made the development of postwar Southern capitalism qualitatively different from the Northern pattern.

To argue that Northern agricultural laborers enjoyed freedoms denied to their Southern counterparts is not to say that the capitalist development of the North eliminated exploitation, oppression, or poverty. But their characteristic forms were different in kind from those under which Southern sharecroppers labored. The typical laborer in the "bonanza" wheat farms of the Northern plains was a migrant wage worker who was oppressed not by peonage but by seasonal unemployment and the need to travel great distances over the course of the year. The terms of disparagement for these workers—"tramps," "bums," "riffraff"—precisely described their mobility, their absence of ties to the land. In other areas of the North, agricultural laborers worked primarily as "hired hands" on family farms and received wages by the month or, during the harvest season, by the day. Farm labor took other forms in the truck gardens of the East and on the great farms of California's central valley. Studies of tenancy in the Midwest contain no evidence that debt peonage was widespread. Northern farm laborers were "forced to be free," the fate of labor wherever agriculture develops in classic capitalist fashion.

The most important institution in the South's system of bound labor was debt peonage. Pete Daniel's work on this central element in postwar Southern history is indispensable. Tenants began each season unable to finance the year's crop and had to seek credit from their landlords or the local merchants, who required that the tenant remain until the debt was paid, however many seasons that took. Hard-working tenants could be made to stay by exaggerating their indebtedness through dishonest bookkeeping; undesirable ones could be ordered to move on, with their debts transferred to a new landlord. The movement of tenants among landlords preserved the system's repressive nature as long as the debt moved with the tenant, as typically it did. Movement alone does not, therefore, disprove the existence of debt peonage. Its extent is difficult to measure precisely; no doubt it varied along with economic cycles. Most contemporaries and historians describe it as a characteristic feature of cotton agriculture in the postwar South, and one study has found that 80 percent of the sharecroppers in Alabama had an indebtedness of more than one year's standing.

Debt peonage was not limited to sharecroppers; nor were they necessarily more exploited and oppressed by the labor-repressive system than were cash renters, usually regarded as one step up the socioeconomic ladder. During the 1890s, when cotton prices reached their low point for the century, renting replaced sharecropping at an astonishing rate. Higgs, for one, has taken this shift to rental labor as a sign of progress, "a response to the growth in the number of experienced black farmers to whom landlords were willing to grant such contracts." An alternative interpretation is more plausible: the economic collapse during that decade made it more profitable for landlords to collect rent instead of a share of the cotton crop from their tenants. Landlords, therefore, responded to the depression by forcing their tenants to assume the full extent of the risk, a risk in which the planters had previously shared. Landlords could still require tenants to obtain credit from them, thereby earning interest and tying their renters to the land by debt peonage until another season, when cotton might become profitable once again; then renters could be turned back into sharecroppers.

The actions of the planter class during the Mississippi River flood of 1927 are revealing. High water covered fifty miles on each side of the channel, submerging the delta plantation district and driving four hundred thousand black tenants from their homes. The planters believed, according to William Alexander Percy, one of their leaders, that "the dispersal of our labor was a longer evil . . . than a flood." They insisted that laborers not be permitted to leave the region so that the tenants could be returned to the plantations when the waters receded. The Red Cross and the National Guard operated refugee camps and helped the planters by acceding to their demand that the camps be "closed"—fenced and locked—so that the blacks could not get out and labor recruiters from other areas could not get in. The governor of Mississippi himself denounced labor recruiters who offered employment elsewhere to victims of the flood. Planters argued that, since labor contracts had already been signed for the 1927 season and since advances had been made to tenants, blacks had to go back and work after the flood, even though it became clear that the waters would not recede quickly enough to permit any planting. The Red Cross distributed emergency supplies not to the blacks inside the locked camps but to the local planters, some of whom billed their tenants after passing on the supplies, creating further indebtedness. The NAACP [National Association for the Advancement of Colored People] denounced the "peonage" practiced in refugee "concentration camps," but the planters succeeded in preventing blacks from leaving the region and in tightening the bonds that tied the tenants to their landlords.

The regional apparatus of involuntary servitude that prevailed between Reconstruction and World War II extended well beyond debt peonage; it also consisted of five different kinds of laws, all of which worked to restrict the free market in labor: enticement statutes, which made it a crime for one planter to hire laborers employed by another; emigrant agent laws, which severely restricted the activities of out-of-state labor recruiters; contract enforcement statutes, which made it a criminal offense for tenants to break contracts with landlords; vagrancy statutes, drawn broadly enough to permit landlords to enlist the aid of local courts to keep laborers at work; and the criminal surety system, backed up by the system of convict labor, which permitted convicts to serve their sentences laboring for private employers. Enticement acts were revived in eight out of ten Southern states after Reconstruction and survived with amendments into the mid-twentieth century. An Alabama statute from 1920 outlawed even attempted enticement. Like the enticement laws, emigrant agent acts were intended to control competition among white employers rather than to punish workers who moved. They sought to prevent the activities of out-of-state labor recruiters by levying prohibitive license fees. In the Carolinas, the license cost one thousand dollars per county, with a penalty for unlicensed recruiting of up to five thousand dollars or two years in prison. Six states of the Deep South passed such laws between 1877 and 1912, and three more did so between 1916 and 1929.

Other laws limited the freedom of laborers to move. Vagrancy acts forced workers to sign labor contracts. Penalties and apparently enforcement as well increased between 1890 and 1910 in response to the rise of agrarian insurgency. Georgia's law of 1895 provided for a fine of one thousand dollars or six to twelve months on the chain gang for those found without employment. The vagrancy acts permitted sheriffs to function as labor recruiters for planters, rounding up "vagrants" at times of labor shortage. Additional laws upheld labor contracts. Late in the nineteenth century six states passed "contract enforcement" and "false pretenses" statutes, which held that a worker's unjustified failure to work constituted "*prima facie* evidence of the intent to injure or defraud the employer." An Alabama law of 1903 did not permit the defendant to rebut testimony about his intentions. Under "criminal surety" laws, employers were permitted to pay the fines of individuals convicted under contract enforcement or vagrancy proceedings; the convict had to work for that employer until his earnings repaid the fine. Thus a laborer whose work displeased his landlord could not only be convicted of a crime but also be compelled by the court to labor for the same employer. The alternative for convicts was the chain gang, and almost anything was preferable to its brutality. A distinctly Southern institution, it was reserved primarily for convicts who refused to sign criminal surety contracts or who were unable to get any landlord to pay their fine and hire them.

Thus, the Southern states established a net of laws to limit the mobility of labor. Vagrancy acts forced workers to sign labor contracts; contract enforcement and false pretenses laws prevented them from leaving. If they left nevertheless, the criminal surety system could return them to the employer, who was backed by the threat of the chain gang. Enticement and emigrant agent statutes prevented another employer from seeking their labor. In the North a laborer whose work displeased his employer could be fired; in the South he could be convicted of a criminal offense. This web of restrictive legislation distinguished the South's labor system from that of the classically capitalist North.

How successful were these laws? It is difficult to tell. William Cohen has suggested that one measure is the extent of their litigation in higher courts, an expensive and time-consuming practice—undertaken, presumably, only if enforcement were of great importance. The Alabama criminal surety law came before the state supreme court at least sixteen times between 1883 and 1914, and the Georgia contract enforcement law was litigated in appellate courts on eighty different occasions between 1903 and 1921. These cases suggest fairly extensive reliance on the law to repress labor, for those argued in the appellate courts were only the tip of the iceberg. The mere threat of prosecution usually sufficed to bring about the desired result; and, since only a handful of sharecroppers had the resources to appeal a conviction, planters, sheriffs, and local judges had virtually a free hand. Informal practice extended the law; extralegal and illegal acts were often undertaken to accomplish the same ends. In September 1901 local officials in the Mississippi black belt rounded up "idlers and vagrants" and drove them "into the cotton fields," where the farmers were "crying for labor." In February 1904 police in Newton, Georgia, made "wholesale arrests of idle Negroes . . . to scare them back to the farms from which they emanated." In 1908 the steamer *America* docked at a Natchez wharf, seeking to recruit black laborers. White businessmen established a local committee, whose methods according to one Southern reporter were "so emphatic that the negroes concluded to abandon their idea of leaving."

Legal and illegal efforts to restrict the mobility of labor in the South did not, of course, completely succeed; they only made it difficult. But the planter class did not require that every laborer be tied to his landlord, only that most, too frightened to leave, remain in order to preserve the low-wage, labor-intensive system of production. The most resourceful, energetic, and determined were always able to escape from their landlords and from the region, and more did so each year—but not because the planters made no effort to stop them. The typical departure occurred under cover of darkness, with family and neighbors sworn to secrecy. Large-scale black migrations from the South took place only twice between Reconstruction and the Depression: the "Kansas Fever" exodus of 1879–80 [a large migration of blacks to Kansas and other midwestern states] and the migration during World War I. Aside from these two movements, the migration rate from Southern states was significantly lower than that from other areas of the country, another measure of the success of repressive law and regional practice.

Freedpeople Working for Themselves

SHARON ANN HOLT

In early June of 1880, Mr. E. G. Butler stopped at the home of Thomas Sanford in Oxford, North Carolina. A thriving town of almost 1,400 people, Oxford was the seat of Granville County and the marketing center of a bustling trade in bright leaf tobacco. Butler's call was on business, his business as the county's federal census enumerator. In addition to his wife and children, Thomas Sanford included in the record of his household two servants, Ottawa Lee, a black man, and Nancy Lee, a mulatto woman. He guessed their ages to be about fifty and forty years respectively.

Several days later Butler unknowingly entered the home of those very same Lees and counted them a second time in his census tally. Speaking for themselves, Nancy and Ottawa Lee revealed rather different lives than Thomas Sanford had described. They noted that they were husband and wife, a connection not recorded in the first enumeration. Mr. Lee was thirty-six, not fifty, and Mrs. Lee was twenty-six, not forty. The couple shared their home with Mrs. Lee's widowed sister, Ann Norman, who worked as a washerwoman. And, while acknowledging that they were both domestic servants by trade, the Lees informed Butler that they also owned two acres of land, worth about $150.

The bureaucratic accident of double-counting has preserved two versions of the lives of Ottawa and Nancy Lee, and the differences between the two accounts are eloquent. The first enumeration includes only the portion of their lives that fell within Thomas Sanford's domain. . . . The Lees were residents of Sanford's home only part of the time; they also kept a household of their own, which they shared with a wage-earning sister. When the Lees were counted as dependents of Thomas Sanford, the structure of the enumeration highlighted a difference in their skin color and made their marriage invisible. The enumeration taken under their own roof recorded their marriage and failed to distinguish their color. Most important, in Sanford's household the Lees are listed only as servants, while in their own they appear both as servants and as landowners.

While Butler's mistake may have slightly distorted his population count, it actually brings economic reality sharply into focus. Butler's record reveals that the Lees lived two lives within one; while they worked as wage-earning servants in the Sanford household, they led another life as a family of small proprietors. Their economic livelihood encompassed not only wages from Thomas Sanford but also Ann Norman's earnings and the produce of a small family farm.

Sharon Ann Holt, "Making Freedom Pay: Freedpeople Working for Themselves, North Carolina, 1865–1900," *Journal of Southern History,* LX (May 1994), pp. 229–62. Copyright © 1994 by the Southern Historical Association. Reprinted by permission of the Managing Editor. The notes for this piece have been omitted.

Freedpeople like the Lees generated resources for themselves from manifold activities within their households in arrangements that whites like Sanford scarcely knew existed. Major historical studies of the postbellum period have tended to re-produce the priorities of the census, bypassing evidence of small-scale household production and building their analyses of freedpeople's lives around the economic dependency associated with wage labor and various forms of tenancy. . . .

It is not surprising that historians and economists have riveted on tenancy and left household production largely unstudied, because the significance of the house-hold labor of freedpeople is far from obvious. Nothing about the activity in freed-people's homes signals that this is labor that deserves special attention. Slaves, too, had raised chickens, hunted game, tended small food crops, and produced textiles, as had poor southern white farmers and, indeed, rural householders almost every-where. What seems to distinguish freedpeople from both their enslaved parents and their white farming neighbors is their confinement in tenant farming, not their com-petence in household production. The very nature of household work further com-pounds the temptation to disregard it; most of the primary produce of the household economy is immediately consumed, making its tracks almost undetectable. Assum-ing that freedpeople's household work was as ephemeral in value as it was in sub-stance, economic historians have seen the world largely as Thomas Sanford saw it—a place where freedpeople worked for whites, period.

Two aspects of the lives of freedpeople, however, combine to direct attention to the work they did for themselves in the household economy. The first is the post-emancipation reduction in field labor, recorded in the countless complaints made to newspapers and government officials by frustrated southern labor managers unable to get a sufficiency of hands into the fields. The second is the achievement of the emancipated slaves in laying the foundation for black-controlled community life by establishing schools and churches and purchasing farms. That these developments occurred at the same time and that each was a direct result of emancipation raises several questions. Where had the "missing" labor gone? Whence came the re-sources to build these new communities? And could the household economy be the link between the two phenomena?

The household economy was one of two means that freedpeople used to gener-ate resources. The other, most often, was some form of tenant farming, which, by the terms of their contracts with employers, demanded the weekday labor of adult males. The household economy was a miscellany of productive activities that con-sumed the days, nights, and weekends of every other member of the household and the after-hours labor of adult males. This two-sided economy was a complex struc-ture that defies conventional characterizations.

The two parts of freedpeople's economic lives cannot properly be contrasted under such rubrics as *public* versus *private, cash* versus *non-cash,* or *women's work* versus *men's work.* Both household production and contract work were public in the sense that their existence was known and their merchandise was traded openly; trade in both sectors involved cash as well as goods; and women and men of both races participated in both domains. Nor can the two kinds of economic activity properly be designated *primary* and *secondary,* a hierarchy that replicates the landlord's perspective. Though the household economy produced much less in total value each year than contract work, it could hardly have been of secondary concern to freedpeople, since it was virtually their only source of discretionary income.

Moreover, the two types of work were more entangled than a hierarchical distinction suggests: household production coexisted with and was linked vitally to the structure of farm tenancy. Tenants gained access to houses and to land for gardens by contracting with planters. Planters, in turn, boosted their profits by keeping tenant shares low and rations short, leaving tenant families to sustain themselves through gardening and home manufacturing. Without a contract, moreover, freedpeople, and especially freedmen, risked harassment and arrest under vagrancy statutes. Contract-based farming for a landlord cleared the way socially, as well as providing the physical location, for the home-based economy to operate, while household production partially indemnified landlords against the disintegration of a severely exploited labor force.

The most meaningful distinction between home-based and contract-based production turns on differences of power and control. The surplus from the household economy was available to freedpeople to spend as they pleased, while the fruits of contract work were not—at once a modest and a momentous difference. Landlords controlled the way contract work was paid for, providing, in return for labor, fixed items, like the use of a house, regular allotments of food, and occasional clothing. Any wages due over and above the value of these allowances were generally paid by a note from the landlord, often good only for specific provisions and redeemable only at the local store. Tenants had to have houses, food, clothing, and store goods; contract work was valuable because it provided them. But because landlords controlled the timing, the substance, and the method of payment for contract work, freedpeople could only rarely use their contract wages for the independent work of community building. The rewards of household production, meager though they were, came to freedpeople directly. Such cash and produce, controlled by freedpeople themselves, could be applied to the creation of schools and churches and to the purchase of farms. . . .

. . . The term *household economy* does not describe a physical geography of production so much as a social and economic geography that reflects the flow of resources into and out of households. Conceptually, the freedpeople's household economy begins where landlord entitlement ends.

Household production included house-bound activities like manufacturing baskets, shoes, hats, and clothing for use or sale. Hauling, gardening, hunting, and foraging must also be reckoned within the household economy, though they took place outside the home itself. Moreover, to reveal fully the ways that households functioned as centers of resource production, the definition of the household economy must also include waged work by women, children, and the old, as well as after-hours or off-season wage-earning by men. Though wage-earning is conventionally considered the antithesis of household production, among the freedpeople wages functioned in precisely the same way as activities like truck farming or raising chickens. If wives and children earned wages, then they did so at the expense of other productive work for their families, and the proceeds of their outside labor were as a matter of course turned over to the family exchequer. Occasional wage-earning by all family members was one among many productive strategies that farm families exercised on their own behalf. Because wages flowed into the family and remained there for the family to control, wage-earning should be considered with, not apart from, other modes of home production.

Though household production was nested intimately within the structure of plantation economics, few planters or merchants recognized that it generated surpluses for tenants themselves. Their ignorance was no accident. Black tenants purposefully concealed their economic achievements from whites, and in this regard the small sale and perishability of household production served their purposes exactly. Household production was not lucrative enough to attract the attention of the landlords and merchants who directed the contract work of tenants. . . . The absence of white supervision, besides being a good in itself, allowed black households to conceal the extent of their independent activity and the degree of autonomy that it underwrote.

However common and personally gratifying freedpeople's modest independent income may have been, such small capital would remain of trifling historical importance except for its significant effect on the society beyond individual households. The impact of freedpeople's household production on community development depended not only on their small savings but also on their successful use of credit. Judicious use of certain kinds of credit made their small surpluses large enough to provide meaningful support to schools, churches, and family farms. Credit thus became an important bridge, though a rickety and dangerous one, between household production and community uplift.

Credit presented a different face to the freedpeople than it did to poor whites, though in fact property ownership, rather than race itself, was the decisive factor in shaping the meaning of credit. Since credit could boost the power of their meager household surpluses, freedpeople, and especially the landless, could approach credit as an opportunity for accumulation and advancement. Those, white or black, who already owned small farms tried to protect their hold on land and possessions by avoiding indebtedness. They mobilized household production less to accumulate new goods than to prevent staple crop production and market relations (including credit) from overwhelming their relative self-sufficiency. In short, the propertied of both races saw loss and entanglement in credit, while the propertyless saw a potential opportunity. Analysis of how the freedpeople borrowed, therefore, ties the small-scale operations of the household economy to credit and land distribution, the large shaping forces of the postbellum economy.

Household production by freedpeople, then, was neither the miscellany of meaningless chores it seems at first glance nor a romantic routine of friendly barter in quilts and cheese. It was a major enterprise on a minor scale, providing crucial evidence of what freedpeople did for themselves, and of how their goals and efforts shaped the economic life of the South as a whole. The former slaves found in the home economy a productive venture that could help them—at the margins—not only to cope with but also to alter the conditions of their lives. Household production soaked up the labor that former masters longed to see in the fields, and it provided the fuel to develop and fulfill the individual and community aspirations of the emancipated slaves. . . .

Labor power was the freedpeople's greatest resource, and home-based production allowed them to employ everyone in the household to the fullest extent. Household production occupied the very young and the very old as well as employing adults in their prime; disabled members made significant contributions alongside the more able-bodied. Freedpeople drew on productive skills that they had developed as slaves as well as on the new opportunities that freedom made possible. As they had under slavery, families gardened and foraged, they chopped and hauled, they spun and sewed, and they saved by doing without. Freedom offered the chance to earn wages, to send members off to seek distant, seasonal employment, and to raise and sell staple crops on their own behalf.

Each person's particular contribution was conditioned by age, gender, overall ability, and immediate need. Children contributed heavily to work around the house. If they were not watching infant siblings, young children might carry water to workers in the fields, forage for and trade berries and wild eggs, tend the family garden, or collect kindling. Joseph Adams, farming in Goldsborough, North Carolina, in the 1870s, speculated that his garden vegetables—probably raised by his children—might have enabled him to save three or four dollars each month. Adams does not say who took care of the family garden, but he does note that his wife cooked out for a local family and that he himself had only half of every other Saturday off, during which time he tended a patch of cotton and corn. With both adults working away from the home, it seems likely that it was the children who brought the family fresh vegetables. Children might also card cotton, piece quilts, and help their mother or an older sister wind yarn. In the mid-1870s, nine-year-old Elizabeth Johnson stayed up late helping her grandmother make quilts and rose early to hawk produce from her grandfather's garden. Children were available to run errands into town or carry messages to neighbors. Children contributed to millinery, draying, and other income-producing enterprises; through their foraging, which they often combined with play, they also provided food for the family table.

As they grew older, boys might begin to hunt and fish with their fathers, or help with wood cutting or hauling for pay if the family owned a wagon. William Scott recalled that "when we farmed share cr[o]p dey took all we made. In de fall we would have to split cord wood to live through de winter." Girls, too, sometimes hunted or hauled; more often, they did domestic work. They might sew dresses, apply ribbons to hats, weave baskets, or candle eggs until well past dark. Most of these tasks continued as children grew. After about age ten, field labor was added to the list. As an alternative to farm labor, older girls might go out to work in the homes of nearby whites. Older boys, if fortunate, might learn a trade; more often they, too, chose between domestic service and farm labor.

If young household members worked hard, so did the elder ones. Age and infirmity by themselves rarely ended a person's working life. Sarah Louise Augustus reported that her grandmother, a former slave named Sarah McDonald, worked until her death of pneumonia at age 110. The elder Sarah was, by her granddaughter's account, an accomplished and experienced nurse. At 110 years of age, she commuted about sixty miles by train between her home in Fayetteville, North Carolina, and a nursing job for a family in Raleigh. When she missed a connecting train one rainy night, she sat in the station all night in wet clothing, took sick the next day, and died. Sarah McDonald's story was echoed in the reports of other former slaves who worked for wages into their nineties and beyond. . . .

Activities performed inside the home did not exhaust a family's productive capacity. While children and elders worked in or around the house as much as possible, adults in their prime ventured farther afield to earn wages and grow staple crops. James E. O'Hara, a prominent Edgecombe County black man who served in the United States Congress from 1883 to 1887, counted "three or four hundred colored men" heading south each spring to work until fall in the turpentine fields, presumably leaving their families behind to tend the crops. Margaret Thornton, a former slave raised in Harnett County, North Carolina, earned wages year-round as a nurse and laundress, despite her husband's protests. Five years old at emancipation, she explained, "I wus brung up ter nurse an' I'se did my share of dat. . . . I has nursed 'bout two thousand babies I reckins. I has nursed gran'maws an' den dere gran'chiles." Her account suggests that her mother may also have nursed and passed on the skill to Margaret. Mrs. Thornton commented on the relationship of her nursing to the income of her whole family: "Tom [her husband] never did want me ter work hard while he wus able ter work, but I nursed babies off an' on all de time he lived[.] When he wus in his death sickness he uster cry case I had ter take in washin'. Since he's daid I nurses mostly, but sometimes I ain't able ter do nothin'." Despite her husband's wish to support the family by his own work, the Thorntons found it necessary for Margaret to earn as well. This arrangement may have been more satisfactory to Margaret Thornton than to Tom. Her work clearly created a network of connections that spanned several generations in satisfied families. Those families may even have helped her support herself or provided charity to her after her husband's death.

Harvest time brought the highest wage rates of any part of the year, offering a bonanza to families who could send family members into the fields to pick. . . . With laborers' wages around ten dollars per month, these harvest earnings [$6-$11] represented a genuine windfall. Wage-earning, like the rest of household production, could be year-round or occasional, and there were opportunities for men and women alike. Each household evaluated its needs and skills in an effort to formulate at least an adequate, if not an optimal, mix of productive activities.

Besides earning wages picking other people's crops, freedpeople also grew staples on a small scale for themselves. Joseph Adams, whose family had a vegetable garden and whose wife cooked for a local family, tended a "patch" of cotton in addition to his tenant field. Mattie Curtis grew cotton in Franklin County, North Carolina. She supported her family with the proceeds of her cotton crops and eventually bought and cleared fifteen acres. Curtis anticipated hostility toward her success, however, which made her wary; when she carried her first bale to town and failed to locate the cotton market, she gave up and went home rather than ask directions, fearing to reveal that the cotton, and the income it would produce, belonged solely to her. . . .

Awareness of how the freedpeople's household economy worked leads almost ineluctably to a further question: how did freedpeople use the resources they amassed? Household production can be considered critical to the advancement of freedpeople only if the resources developed within it did more than meet a family's basic needs for food and shelter. There is evidence that fulfillment of the desires that animated the freedpeople after emancipation—for religious autonomy, for literacy, and for farms of their own—depended heavily on household production. Freedpeople did indeed use resources drawn from the household economy to staff, house, and endow their churches; to build, equip, and sustain primary schools; and to purchase, pay taxes on, and sustain their farms.

Before emancipation, some communities of slaves had been able to create in-dependent, often clandestine, religious institutions, and one of their first projects as freedpeople was to bring those assemblies out of hiding. Congregations commonly began by building a rudimentary sanctuary for worship along with a Sabbath school for educating both children and adults. Deeds recorded in Granville County indicate that black congregations often paid market price or higher for the plots they bought for their churches. New Corinth Baptist Church purchased its one-acre lot from a member for ten dollars, about the price of an acre of good farmland. The trustees of Flat Creek Baptist Church paid twenty-five dollars for their one-acre building site. Blue Wing Grove Church, an exception to the pattern, acquired one acre for one dollar from two members, C. A. and Louisa B. Tuck, "in consideration of [their] love and respect for religious and educational advantages." In Promised Land, South Carolina, Elizabeth Rauh Bethel records that "in 1875 James Fields [freed-man and local community leader] sold one acre of his land to the Mt. Zion African Methodist Episcopal Trustees for forty dollars. In 1882 Wells Gray [another leading citizen of the town] sold two acres of his land to the Crossroads Baptist Church Board of Deacons for thirty-two dollars.". . .

Freedpeople built and rebuilt their churches several times as the size and means of congregations expanded. The congregation of Huntsville Baptist Church, another Granville County institution, began meeting in a brush arbor in the 1830s and then built a log church after emancipation; the log structure was replaced in turn by a clapboard building. Finally, in the 1920s, the congregation built the sturdy brick sanctuary that stands today. St. Paul's AME church in Rockingham County, North Carolina, kept a record of one of its building-fund drives, and the record illustrates the importance of small contributions from the congregation in the repeated build-ing and rebuilding of a sanctuary. The members of St. Paul's had built their first ed-ifice in 1878, and probably another one after that. In 1909 church members set out once again to raise funds to build a new sanctuary. The ledger kept during that fund drive indicates that the drive lasted nearly a year and a half and raised somewhat less than $100, mostly in pledges from church members of one, two, and five dol-lars. The ledger also records contributions from churchwomen of money and of ap-ples, oranges, and cakes, the food designed presumably for a fund-raising dinner. Some of the revenue came from a species of beauty contest wherein the young woman who collected the most cash in tribute to her beauty was declared the win-ner, and all proceeds went to the building fund. With that money, supplemented by donations of labor, wood, and homemade vestments, the congregation ultimately assembled a small, clapboard church with a bell tower. It stood until 1987, when the abandoned structure finally collapsed in a storm.

Efforts like those made at Huntsville Baptist and St. Paul's AME were repeated across the postbellum South as black congregations built and rebuilt their sanctuar-ies, expanding and upgrading them as the means of the assembly would permit. Fund-raising was a permanent aspect of church life; when the money was not re-quired for building, the collections underwrote salaries, bought supplies, and pro-vided charity. Each contribution was small, and indeed, the total was small—it was enough largely because it had to be. Church members' households could not pro-duce any more.

As much as freedpeople helped their churches, they did even more for their schools. Freedpeople's schools and churches, at first, were often one and the same.

The minister and his family might be the only literate members of a rural black community, and they were expected to teach as well as preach. Moreover, one-half to two-thirds of all pupils reported to be in school between 1866 and 1870 attended Sabbath schools rather than day or night schools.

Much was expected of schooling in the postbellum South, by both freedfolk and philanthropists, and perhaps for that reason school development is the most thoroughly documented private effort of the period. Many instances of critical support provided by the freedpeople are in the records; however, the importance of their work for schools has received scant attention. To support missionary schools, freedpeople paid tuition, purchased lots, and built school buildings, though often of the most rough-and-ready sort. They paid, housed, and fed missionary teachers, and they raised or contributed funds for such essentials as books, slates, maps, and heating stoves. Older students helped in the overcrowded classrooms by serving as assistant teachers, hearing the recitations of pupils just inferior to themselves in skill. Alongside the schooling sponsored on their behalf by missionaries, white churches, and northern philanthropists, freedpeople ran their own schools, independent of assistance.

The Freedmen's Bureau sent John W. Alvord, the bureau's newly appointed school superintendent, on a fact-finding tour of the defeated Confederacy in the summer of 1865. Only months after emancipation and a year or more before northern teachers arrived in force, Alvord estimated that over 500 black-run schools were already in operation. This number grew, and in his second report, dated July 1866, Alvord noted to his superior that "we estimated in January [1866] that the entire educational census of the bureau was 125,000 pupils. We now, with increased means of information and greater assurance of certainty, estimate that, beyond the 90,778 pupils as officially reported, there are, including the above irregular and Sabbath schools, with colored soldiers and individuals who are learning at home, one hundred and fifty thousand (150,000) freedmen and their children [studying their books]." Many independent schools continued to operate long after missionary teachers had arrived, especially in remote areas where it was too dangerous for northerners to venture. As late as 1869, when the missionaries had been active in the field for several years, James W. Hood, North Carolina's State Superintendent of Colored Schools, found that 41 percent of the state's black pupils were being taught in private, independent schools. . . . A number of so-called missionary or Freedmen's Bureau schools were in fact independent schools that the philanthropic societies simply absorbed. . . . Freedpeople in Warrenton wrote to officers of the AMA, offering to pay a teacher $10 a month, provide a home and schoolhouse, and fill the school with eighty to ninety scholars. AMA teacher David Dickson reported from outside Fayetteville, North Carolina, that "the building which we have for schools is now rented and we have collected $26.50 for rent, wood, &c this month." In Fayetteville proper, freedpeople had purchased a lot for $140, built a school with $3,800 from the Freedmen's Bureau and the AMA, furnished the building with another $400 gift, and funded $200 worth of improvements out of their own pockets.

Freedpeople's support did not end once a school had opened; it was used to provide food, firewood, and funds to further the work of the teachers. . . . Freedpeople also worked to reconstruct and refine the drafty, ramshackle school buildings in which AMA teachers met their classes. In Beaufort during the winter of 1866, "the thrifty portion" of the local community pledged $212 and the time of their best carpenters to erect a solid, draft-free building. In Smithville the teacher collected

$22.50 from the pupils, most of which was spent on a stove, with a bit left over to purchase books and slates. David Dickson's pupils outside Fayetteville paid for "fuel, lights, and books" and offered to pay for an assistant if Dickson required one.

As late as 1876, four years after the opening of public schools in North Carolina, freedpeople continued to subsidize the education supposedly provided to them by the state. In Raleigh, parents pledged to pay ten cents a week to keep the local school open after state appropriations ran out. Another AMA school in Raleigh, which met in the sanctuary of Long Church, reported a successful "exhibition and concert on Thursday . . . for the purpose of raising some money to pay for repairs of church." Besides repairing their sanctuary/schoolroom, the pupils at Long Church routinely contributed "about enough for light and fuel." Indeed, the contributions continued for at least a generation. In the early twentieth century, 7 percent of black schoolchildren still met in crude log schoolhouses and 44 percent of them were still sitting on homemade benches.

To speak of the work of missionary, Freedmen's Bureau, or even public schools in the South after the war without explicit acknowledgment of freedpeople's own contributions obscures the commitment and resourcefulness of the many black communities that created and sustained these schools. The very first schools were already joint enterprises, not gifts, and long after schooling officially became the responsibility of state governments, black schools continued to draw deeply at the well of their [pupils'] resources. The support offered to the schools—labor, firewood, food, and bits of cash—[was] precisely the type of goods most readily generated within the household economy.

Building and supporting their churches and schools did not exhaust the freedpeople's means nor fulfill all their dreams. There was still the hope of owning a farm, a dream long cherished and suddenly, thanks to freedom, just barely within reach. When freedmen all over the South met in conventions in 1865 and 1866 to draft memorials to their state constitutional conventions, the liberty to worship, the opportunity to learn, and a legal guarantee of equal rights stood at the top of their lists of desiderata. Right behind, and in their minds necessary to all the rest, was protection of their right to own property. Freedpeople wanted farms of their own, believing that farm ownership was essential to their long-term prosperity. As hope for the redistribution of Confederate properties receded, freedpeople began acquiring land directly. Household production played as crucial a role, though a different one, in this process as it did in the support of churches and schools. The proceeds of household production alone were too small to purchase farm acreage, but borrowing could make the proceeds larger. Freedpeople's savings became seed money in the risky business of southern credit, with home production as a kind of mortgage insurance. The mixture of household production and credit, with an occasional stroke of good luck, could help a family gain and keep a farm. . . .

Freedpeople found their opening not in the widely used and justly reviled annual crop lien but in a less rigid instrument, the short-term chattel mortgage. Chattel mortgages were by no means free of risk, since creditors usually demanded collateral worth much more than the loan amount. Just as store owners built their high interest rates into the prices of their wares, so creditors built their risk calculations into the amount of collateral that they demanded. However, for any individual black farmer making the choice between the high cost of lien-based credit and the high cost of chattel-based credit, the chattels held one important advantage. Chattel mortgages were much more flexible than annual liens in time, terms, and collateral. . . . Under a chattel mortgage, the period of borrowing could be as short as a week or a month, and lenders accepted livestock, farm equipment, and household goods as collateral in addition to crops. Chattel mortgages, in other words, allowed freedpeople to borrow against home production, which they could control, rather than against future crops, which they could not. Though freedpeople commonly used the annual lien to support their planting and harvesting operations, the rest of their economic lives, including buying and selling land, equipment, and livestock, depended upon the credit available through chattel mortgages. The flexible terms of chattel mortgage credit played to the strengths of the household economy, making household production essential to the successful manipulation of chattel loans. At the price of some risk, small infusions of credit greased the slow machinery of accumulation, while the value of goods produced in the household helped indemnify the family against possible loss.

Those who sought to buy land had first to acquire mortgageable goods. The need for and terms of chattel mortgage credit tended to oblige freedpeople to follow a common pattern of accumulation of goods preceding land purchase, and this pattern can be discerned in census and tax records. Families usually began with the acquisition of chickens, which were the cheapest livestock available and the only farm animals not subject to taxation. Chickens provided eggs, meat, and feathers, all goods that could be sold, traded, or consumed in place of store-bought goods. Properly managed, chickens could rather quickly generate the dollar or two needed to purchase a pair of pigs. Like chickens, pigs were directly productive, representing both pork and piglets. With good fortune, pigs and chickens together might soon underwrite the purchase of a cow, which represented the first major threshold of accumulation. John O. Kelly, a freedman from Raleigh, explained the link between owning a cow and escaping tenancy to the Senate investigating committee in 1879. "There are not many who are going to live but if they have got a cow and such things as that." Kelly assured the senators that "they will do business for themselves." Any family able to save enough to buy a cow would be tempted to try to purchase an acre of land and move off the tenant farm. . . .

In the complex economic life of North Carolina's freedpeople, all signs point to the center, to the household as a critical turbine of production. Operating from within their own households, freedpeople tried every kind of productive activity that might generate resources they could use, from humble efforts to raise potatoes to extensive and carefully organized forays into staple crop agriculture. They fought for control over their own labor, limiting the claims of landlords to the time of women and children and fighting off their landlords' attempts to fasten extra work on adult males. The resources they scratched together in this variegated process became the seeds of larger communal endeavors as well as the foundation of private family hopes. Schools were kept open and teachers supported with food, wages, stoves, and supplies by the families of their pupils. Churches were respectably housed and Sunday schools provided with books and slates because the community dug into its pockets to provide. For a family seeking a farm on which to stake its future, the care and management of chickens, pigs, cows, and credit became the milestones on their road. Moreover, because household production was by its very nature modest in scale and unremarkable in content, these projects could proceed right under the collective nose of a society that was openly hostile to black aspirations. Within the restrictions imposed by tenancy, poverty, and persecution, freedpeople found ways to shape their own future. Household production provided what the freedpeople required—a way to accumulate a surplus, a way to push desperation just far enough away from the door to make room for hope, to provide reasons for effort, and to deliver the resources needed for the uplift of the community.

⚓ *F U R T H E R   R E A D I N G*

Charles S. Aiken, *The Cotton Plantation South Since the Civil War* (1998)
Armando C. Alonzo, *Tejano Legacy: Rancheros and Settlers in South Texas, 1734–1900* (1997)
Pete Daniel, *The Shadow of the Plantation* (1972)
Ronald F. Davis, *Good and Faithful Labor* (1982)
Stephen J. DeCanio, *Agriculture in the Postbellum South* (1975)
Charles L. Flynn, Jr., *White Land, Black Labor* (1983)
Eric Foner, *Nothing but Freedom* (1983)
Thavolia Glymph and John J. Kushma, eds., *Essays on the Postbellum Southern Economy* (1985)
Robert Higgs, *Competition and Coercion* (1977)
Samuel C. Hyde, ed., *Plain Folk of the South Revised* (1997)
Gerald D. Jaynes, *Branches Without Roots* (1986)
Jacqueline Jones, *Labor of Love, Labor of Sorrow* (1985)
Jay Mandle, *The Roots of Black Poverty* (1978)
———, *Not Slave, Not Free* (1992)
Daniel A. Novack, *The Wheel of Servitude* (1978)
William Alexander Percy, *Lanterns on the Levee* (1941)
Peter J. Rachleff, *Black Labor in the South* (1984)
Roger L. Ransom and Richard Sutch, *One Kind of Freedom* (1977)
Lawrence D. Rice, *The Negro in Texas* (1971)
Theodore Rosengarten, *All God's Dangers* (1975)
Edward Royce, *The Origins of Southern Sharecropping* (1983)
Thad Sitton and Dan K. Utley, *From Can See to Can't: Texas Cotton Farmers on the Southern Prairies* (1997)
Peter Wallenstein, *From Slave South to New South* (1987)
Michael Wayne, *The Reshaping of Plantation Society* (1983)
Harold Woodman, *King Cotton and His Retainers* (1968)
Gavin Wright, *Old South, New South* (1986)
———, *The Political Economy of the Cotton South* (1978)

Industry, Workers, and the

Myth of the New South

☫

After the Civil War, southern leaders publicly recognized the need for what they had formerly foresworn: industry in the South. Following Reconstruction a vision appeared of a New South invigorated by industrial and economic progress. Advocates of this new South urged southerners to change some of their traditional ways and imitate the victorious Yankees in habits of thrift, labor, and industry.

By 1900 the South had changed. A southern textile industry, replete with factories and mill villages, had reached sizable development in the Piedmont of Virginia, the Carolinas, Georgia, and into Alabama. Nearly 100,000 men, women, and children worked at below national average wages to turn out mostly cotton and some wool cloth, hosiery, thread, and bagging. Other industries also attracted workers, although salaries were low and conditions dangerous: Coal mining in Appalachia and in northern Alabama accompanied the development of iron and steel plants. South-wide railroads, lumber and logcutting operations, and cigarette and chewing tobacco companies expanded. Finally, after 1902 the discovery of huge oil reserves in Texas brought wildcatters, roughnecks, and eventually national oil companies to the South, making Houston the region's largest city.

But had southerners changed along with increasing industrialization? New South advocates promised a better life for industrial workers. Was it better? Who benefited from this New South—factory owners, investors, farmers, workers, labor unions? How did mill workers respond to the "habits of industry" imposed on them by factory owners? How were race relations affected during this period of industrial growth? How were labor grievances settled? And finally, why did some black and white workers form interracial labor unions while others did not? What role did gender play in this process?

☫ D O C U M E N T S

Two of the foremost exponents of the New South were Atlanta newspaper editor Henry Grady and Carolina industrialist Daniel Augustus Tompkins. Both often spoke before northern audiences, boasting that with the war behind it, the South was changing; northerners could trust southern capitalists with loans and purchase orders and could rely on its social policies, especially regarding African Americans. The excerpts from their speeches and writings in Documents 1 and 2 cover some of their major ideas and suggest the tone of the New South myth. The notion that enthusiasm for textile development grew into a public-spirited, community movement was enshrined in the early historical writings of Broadus Mitchell, seen here in Document 3, an excerpt from his book written in 1921. Hopes for industrial prosperity animated Warren C. Coleman, a black entrepreneur. In Document 4, he calls on others of his race to support his plans for a cotton mill run by African Americans. Those who worked in the South's factories had a different view of their benefits. When asked about their conditions by a North Carolina state agency, the Bureau of Labor Statistics, mill workers identified many areas of dissatisfaction, noted in Document 5. In Document 6 Bertha Miller of Thomasville, North Carolina, describes her upbringing "in the country" and her transition to mill factory work at the age of eleven. Note the realities of mill work for young women before 1915. Document 7 is a series of photographs depicting coal mining villages in Appalachia and miners at work.

1. Speeches by Henry W. Grady on the New South, 1886, 1889

From Speech Before Boston's Bay State Club, 1889

I attended a funeral once in Pickens county in my State. . . . This funeral was peculiarly sad. It was a poor "one gallus" fellow, whose breeches struck him under the armpits and hit him at the other end about the knee—he didn't believe in *decollete* clothes. They buried him in the midst of a marble quarry: they cut through solid marble to make his grave; and yet a little tombstone they put above him was from Vermont. They buried him in the heart of a pine forest, and yet the pine coffin was imported from Cincinnati. They buried him within touch of an iron mine, and yet the nails in his coffin and the iron in the shovel that dug his grave were imported from Pittsburg. They buried him by the side of the best sheep-grazing country on the earth, and yet the wool in the coffin bands and the coffin bands themselves were brought from the North. The South didn't furnish a thing on earth for that funeral but the corpse and the hole in the ground. There they put him away and the clods rattled down on his coffin, and they buried him in a New York coat and a Boston pair of shoes and a pair of breeches from Chicago and a shirt from Cincinnati, leaving him nothing to carry into the next world with him to remind him of the country in which he lived, and for which he fought for four years, but the chill of blood in his veins and the marrow in his bones.

Now we have improved on that. We have got the biggest marble-cutting establishment on earth within a hundred yards of that grave. We have got a half-dozen woolen mills right around it, and iron mines, and iron furnaces, and iron factories. We are coming to meet you. We are going to take a noble revenge, as my friend, Mr.

These speeches can be found in Joel Chandler Harris' *Life of Henry W. Grady* (New York: Cassel Publishing Company, 1890).

Carnegie, said last night, by invading every inch of your territory with iron, as you invaded ours twenty-nine years ago.

From Grady's Speech, "The New South," Delivered to the New England Club in New York, 1886

We have established thrift in city and country. We have fallen in love with work. We have restored comfort to homes from which culture and elegance never departed. We have let economy take root and spread among us as rank as the crabgrass which sprung from Sherman's cavalry camps, until we are ready to lay odds on the Georgia Yankee as he manufactures relics of the battlefield in a one-story shanty and squeezes pure olive oil out of his cotton seed, against any down-easter that ever swapped wooden nutmegs for flannel sausage in the valleys of Vermont. Above all, we know that we have achieved in these "piping times of peace" a fuller independence for the South than that which our fathers sought to win in the forum by their eloquence or compel in the field by their swords.

It is a rare privilege, sir, to have had part, however humble, in this work. Never was nobler duty confided to human hands than the uplifting and upbuilding of the prostrate and bleeding South—misguided, perhaps, but beautiful in her suffering, and honest, brave and generous always. In the record of her social, industrial and political illustration we await with confidence the verdict of the world.

But what of the negro? Have we solved the problem he presents or progressed in honor and equity toward solution? Let the record speak to the point. No section shows a more prosperous laboring population than the negroes of the South, none in fuller sympathy with the employing and land-owning class. He shares our school fund, has the fullest protection of our laws and the friendship of our people. Self-interest, as well as honor, demand that he should have this. Our future, our very existence depend upon our working out this problem in full and exact justice. We understand that when Lincoln signed the emancipation proclamation, your victory was assured, for he then committed you to the cause of human liberty, against which the arms of man cannot prevail—while those of our statesmen who trusted to make slavery the corner-stone of the Confederacy doomed us to defeat as far as they could, committing us to a cause that reason could not defend or the sword maintain in sight of advancing civilization.

Had Mr. Toombs said, which he did not say, "that he would call the roll of his slaves at the foot of Bunker Hill," he would have been foolish, for he might have known that whenever slavery became entangled in war it must perish, and that the chattel in human flesh ended forever in New England when your fathers—not to be blamed for parting with what didn't pay—sold their slaves to our fathers—not to be praised for knowing a paying thing when they saw it. The relations of the southern people with the negro are close and cordial. We remember with what fidelity for four years he guarded our defenseless women and children, whose husbands and fathers were fighting against his freedom. To his eternal credit be it said that whenever he struck a blow for his own liberty he fought in open battle, and when at last he raised his black and humble hands that the shackles might be struck off, those hands were innocent of wrong against his helpless charges, and worthy to be taken in loving grasp by every man who honors loyalty and devotion. Ruffians have maltreated him, rascals have misled him, philanthropists established a bank for him, but the South, with the North, protests against injustice to this simple and sincere people. To liberty and enfranchisement is as far as law can carry the negro. The rest must be left to conscience and common sense. It must be left to those among whom his lot is cast, with whom he is indissolubly connected, and whose prosperity depends upon their possessing his intelligent sympathy and confidence. Faith has been kept with him, in spite of calumnious assertions to the contrary by those who assume to speak for us or by frank opponents. Faith will be kept with him in the future, if the South holds her reason and integrity. . . .

The old South rested everything on slavery and agriculture, unconscious that these could neither give nor maintain healthy growth. The new South presents a perfect democracy, the oligarchs leading in the popular movement—a social system compact and closely knitted, less splendid on the surface, but stronger at the core—a hundred farms for every plantation, fifty homes for every palace—and a diversified industry that meets the complex need of this complex age.

The new South is enamored of her new work. Her soul is stirred with the breath of a new life. The light of a grander day is falling fair on her face. She is thrilling with the consciousness of growing power and prosperity. As she stands upright, full-statured and equal among the people of the earth, breathing the keen air and looking out upon the expanded horizon, she understands that her emancipation came because through the inscrutable wisdom of God her honest purpose was crossed, and her brave armies were beaten.

2. D. A. Tompkins on the New South, c. 1900

First Speech Excerpt

The South is in a state of change. A condition of civilization which grew upon the basis of the institution of slavery is dying and fading away. A condition of civilization based upon the new conditions imposed by the results of the late war has commenced to grow, and its growth is healthy and vigorous. . . .

The people who have adapted themselves to the new conditions imposed by the results of the Civil War constitute what we are beginning to hear called the New South. They have divorced from their minds the idea that for a Southern man there is no occupation but raising cotton with negro labor, and that free negro labor constitutes a curse to a country. . . .

All along the Piedmont belt there are men who have attained to such success as entitles them to distinction. . . . Atlanta is full of enterprises and enterprising men, and the growth of that city is a fair example of the results of Southern raw material and Southern labor combined. Here, too, the diversity of enterprise is marked. Here it is possible to contract for the products of cotton or cottonseed. Here are the headquarters of marble companies supplying marble as fine as the Italian stone. Granite is supplied for paving the streets of cities to the north and west. Here are manufactured cotton gins, steam engines, and various machines used in the preparation of cotton for the market. In Macon, J. F. Hanson is the successful manager of two

This document can be found in George Taylor Winston, *A Builder of the New South,* pp. 84–86, 89–90, 125–26, 127–28. Copyright © 1920 Doubleday, Page & Company.

splendidly equipped cotton factories; and at Columbus there are the Eagle and Phoenix Mills, than which none in Massachusetts has been more successful.

In Alabama, O. O. Nelson, of Montgomery, and George O. Baker, of Selma, have been foremost in the development of the new industry of crushing cottonseed for its products. And in connection with the growth of the iron interest the names of Doctor Caldwell of Birmingham, and A. H. Moses of Sheffield, are more than well known in connection with the growth of two cities and the marvellous multiplication of the original dollars invested by the corporations of which they are the heads. Both these gentlemen undertook the management of the affairs of the companies they now represent at a time when prospects did not look bright, and when the stock of the respective companies was not particularly marketable. Under their management the properties they control have increased in value more than any other properties in the United States have ever been known to do before. While these places stand conspicuous for their growth from almost nothing to marvellous wealth, other places have grown also, and other men in lesser degrees have done excellent work in Chattanooga, Anniston, South Pittsburg, etc., etc.

With all this improvement and marvellous progress how is it that we now and then see in a well-written public journal that the South is growing poorer? It is because the editor lives amongst people who have not yet consented to give up antebellum ways and ideas.

Second Speech Excerpt

The factories in North Carolina now manufacture about 300,000 bales of cotton into cloth and yarn a year. For this work there are employed in round numbers 30,000 operatives. This work is done with about one million spindles. It must be understood, of course, that I speak in figures that are even and somewhat approximate, but that are near enough the exact figures to illustrate this argument with reasonable accuracy.

In order to manufacture the entire cotton crop of the South into plain white and coarse colored goods there would be required something like 30,000,000 spindles and 1,000,000 operatives. The population of the Southern States may be reckoned at 20,000,000. Does anybody doubt that out of this 20,000,000 there is idle time enough wasted, even by those who would be willing to work, to furnish 1,000,000 good operatives in cotton factories? Go into any ordinary cotton market town where no cotton factories have as yet been built, and at any time from 7 A.M. to 10 P.M. count the people who are loafing, and the number found would more than make up the quota of people for its share of the workers necessary to manufacture the cotton crop. This loafing habit; this superabundance of people who are capable of working but who are loafing in the country and in towns where there are no factories, is conspicuous by comparison with the town where manufacturing enterprises have been established. By the same comparison the dilapidation of the houses is conspicuous; the poverty of the farmers in the adjacent country and the wretched condition of the roads are more than conspicuous.

Happily these old conditions are passing away. In many sections they have already passed away. The people of the South are naturally enterprising and resourceful. In the early days of the republic the south was the manufacturing end of the union. The first steamship ever to cross the ocean went out of Savannah. The South

Carolina railway, when it was building, was the greatest engineering enterprise of the world. According to the United States census of 1810, the manufactured products of Virginia, the Carolinas, and Georgia, exceeded in value and variety those of the entire New England States. This is mentioned in no disparagement of New England but rather to show that our forefathers were men of enterprise and that they had confidence to venture on their own judgment. They never waited for somebody to come from somewhere and develop their resources for them. If they thought a cotton factory or a railroad would be a good thing they built it. The only mistake they made was in thinking that the colored brother as a slave was a good thing. The growth of slavery dried up a well-developed manufacturing tendency in the South. . . .

For more than a quarter of a century the political and social conditions in the South have been very unfavorable for the development of material interests. The generation that is now passing away has withstood a test of Anglo-Saxon civilization—fighting against the strong prejudices of other people of their own blood living at a distance, and against semi-barbaric influences at home that were supported and urged on by those prejudices. This contest is well nigh over. It is no wonder that during its progress so little advance was made in material prosperity; but it is a wonder that the production of cotton has kept ahead of that of other advancing cotton-growing countries. This result alone, together with the saving of civilization and the preservation of the social status of the South, shows the ability of the people of the South to carry to the maximum limit the white man's burden. In the same time Egypt and India, both under English control, have been pushing forward in the production of cotton, becoming our serious competitors. . . .

It is my firm belief that in the near future no community can afford to be without its cotton factory, its cottonseed oil mill, and its fertilizer works.

3. The Myth of the "Cotton Mill Campaign," 1921

Notices of ceremonies held when a mill commenced operation convey sometimes touchingly the pride of a community in the plant and the public character of the enterprise. Townspeople were like children with a very precious new toy; newspapers described the arrangement of the machinery in the factory with the keenest interest.

The potency of associative effort, so marked in Southern cotton mill building in this period, overcame timidity that might have been prompted by a frank and individual canvass of attending economic facilities. "The mill at Albemarle, North Carolina, had its origin in the desire of the Efirds to have a mill at the town. Whether there existed real advantages or not, the people would make it appear that there were advantages for that particular location. Many mills were located at places where there was the spirit for them, rather than where they would be, economically, most successful." A Marylander knowing the industry thoroughly said there was little community interest in his State, but that "down South the community interest was very strong. Every little town wanted a mill. If it couldn't get a big one, it would take a small one; if not a sheeting, then a spinning mill."

Broadus Mitchell, *The Rise of Cotton Mills in the South.* pp. 129–132; 134–135. Copyright © 1921 Johns Hopkins University Press.

"A good deal of patriotism developed," said a not impressionable mill man, "and every town would vie with others in building mills. Some people took stock and sold it at a discount when it was apparent that the mill would be operated. They were willing to give so much to secure the mill for the town." There is no stronger indication of the different spirit characterizing the building of mills in the eighties as contrasted with earlier periods than the fact that after 1880 many plants were located within the corporate limits of towns and cities. In the earlier enterprises community spirit had not counted, and even the mills of the seventies, such as Piedmont, were taken to the water powers. Eager discussion as to the comparative advantages of water and steam power marked this transition. From being an excuse for the town, the cotton mill came to be erected to invigorate a place that was languishing. It has been said that at least half the South Carolina mills were community enterprises. Later, when the commercial spirit was more pronounced, factories were built just outside the corporation to escape town taxes.

In the case of some investors with whom assistance to the town was an indirect motive, the creation of a payroll, putting more money in circulation, was the causal stimulus. An editorial recommended the Charleston Manufacturing Company "as a means of enlarging the common income. . . . The employment given to hundreds of persons . . . will increase the value of house-property at once. They who earn nothing can't spend much. It was calculated last year that every $228 invested in cotton manufactures in South Carolina supported one person. . . . It is evident that the building of half-a-dozen cotton factories would revolutionize Charleston. Two or three million dollars additional poured annually into the pockets of the shopkeepers . . . would make them think that the commercial millennium had come.

To give employment to the necessitous masses of poor whites, for the sake of the people themselves, was an object animating the minds of many mill builders. One does not have to go outside the ranks of cotton manufacturers to find denials of this, but a study of the facts shows how frequent and normal was the philanthropic incentive. . . .

No undertaking was born more emphatically in the impulse to furnish work than the Salisbury Cotton Mills. All the circumstances of the founding of this factory were singularly in keeping with the philanthropic prompting. The town of Salisbury, North Carolina, in 1887 had done nothing to recover from the war. It was full of saloons, wretched, unkempt. It happened that an evangelistic campaign was conducted; Mr. Pearson, remembered as a lean, intense Tennesseean, preached powerfully. A tabernacle was erected for the meeting, which lasted a month and, being undenominational, drew from the whole town and countryside. The evangelist declared that the great morality in Salisbury was to go to work, and that corruption, idleness and misery could not be dispelled until the poor people were given an opportunity to become productive. The establishment of a cotton mill would be the most Christian act his hearers could perform. "He gave Salisbury a moral dredging which made the people feel their responsibilities as they had not before, and made them do something for these folks. There had been little talk of manufacturing before Pearson came; there had been some tobacco factories in the town, but they had failed. The Salisbury Cotton Mills grew out of a moral movement to help the lower classes, largely inspired by this campaign. Without the moral issue, the financial interest would have come out in the long run, but the moral considerations brought the matter to a focus."

4. A Black Entrepreneur Builds a Cotton Mill, 1896

Please allow me to call the attention of the public to the fact that a movement is on foot to erect a cotton mill at Concord to be operated by colored labor. The colored citizens of the United States have had no opportunity to utilize their talents along this line. Since North Carolina has fairly and justly won for herself in the Centennial at the World Fair at Chicago and at the Atlanta Exposition the honored name of being "the foremost of the States," she will further evidence the fact if she is the first to have a cotton mill to be operated principally by the colored people. We are proud of the spirit and energy of the white people in encouraging and assisting the enterprise and will our colored people not catch the spark of the new industrial life and take advantage of this unprecedented opportunity to engage in the enterprise that will prove to the world our ability as operatives in the mills thereby solving the great problem "can the Negroes be employed in cotton mills to any advantage"? And now that the opportunity is before us, experience alone will determine the question and it behooves us to better ourselves and do something, and as one man . . . [make] the effort that is to win for us a name and place us before the world as industrious and enterprising citizens.

Don't think for a moment that this desireable and enviable position can be obtained by merely a few of our people, but on the other hand, it will require the united effort of the race. Then when the people of the white race who are our friends clearly see that we are surely coming, they will "come over into Macedonia and help us." The enterprise will be just what we make of it. There is nothing to gain but everything to lose by allowing the enterprise to prove a failure.

In case of a failure, it will be due to mere neglect. If it proves a success, it will be to the honor and glory of the race. If racial weakness is set forth, it will only strengthen the sentiment already expressed about us. We can see the finger of Providence directing our cause, for we believe that God helps only those who help themselves. If we show no desire to succeed in this, and in all the enterprises designed for the industrial and financial development of the race, then it can be proven that our Liberty is a failure. We cannot afford to be idle or lukewarm in this matter. There is too much connected with it that would not let our conscience rest if we did not make the effort to carry out the plan. Can there be any among us who do not wish to see the moral, intellectual, religious and industrial character of our people elevated to a higher and broader plan[e] of civilization and true usefulness? There is no middle ground. We are either going forward or backward. The watchword is onward and upward, and if we ever expect to attain the heights of industrial usefulness, we must fall in line and march shoulder to shoulder in one solid phalanx along the road that leads to fortune and fame.

When we grasp the opportunities offered for the betterment of our condition, we are performing the great task which will at last determine our future position in the ranks of the great nations of the world. The markets of Madagascar, Zanzibar and other tropical regions where there are millions of inhabitants are open for all goods that can be produced in the mills.

Let us not be discouraged but move onward with the enterprise, with that spirit and determination that makes all things possible for those who strive in real earnest.

5. Mill Workers' Comments on the New South, 1887

Superintendent Cotton Mill—Ten hours are enough for a day's work, where children are worked from twelve years old and up, and I think the mills of this section are willing to it, if all would adopt it. I think there should be a law making all run 60 hours per week, and compelling parents to send their children to school. I work 11½ hours per day, at $75 per month. Have four in family and one at school. Live in my own house.

Employee—There are about 225 to 250 hands engaged at different classes of work in this mill, about 100 of them children—many of them very small children, under 12 years of age. Wages are about as good here as at any mill in the State and I think better than at many of them, the only trouble about wages is that they are not paid in cash—trade checks are issued with which employees are expected to buy what they need at the company's store, which is not right. The same system is practised I am told, at the most of the cotton mills in the State, but that does not make it right and just. The tobacco factories in this town pay the cash every week. Any man who has ever tried it knows there is a great difference in buying with cash. This, with the long hours required for a day's work, (12 hours) is the only cause for complaint; the officers are kind and close attention to work and sobriety and morality is required of all who work here.

Employee—I work in the cotton mills. They employ men, women and children—many children who are too small to work, they should be at school; the parents are more to blame than are the mill-owners. The hands in the mills in this section are doing very well, and if they only received their pay weekly in cash instead of "trade checks," and store accounts they would not complain if they were paid in cash and were allowed to buy for cash where they pleased, it would be much better. Ten hours are enough for a day's work. I believe the mills here would be willing to it if there was a law making all conform to it. I believe compulsory education would be a benefit too.

Employee—This mill runs day and night. The day hands commence work at 6 o'clock in the morning and run tell 7 o'clock at night. They stop at 12 o'clock for dinner and ring the bell at 12:30 o'clock. I contend that the hands are in actual motion 13 hours per day. The trade check system is used here, and is not as good as cash, at this place nor any other place. If the hands trade their checks to any other firm, and they present them for cash, this firm demands a discount of 10 per cent. The best trade check used in this county is not worth over 75 per cent. Some of the checks used in this county are almost worthless. This long-hour system is destroying

---

This document can be found in the First Annual Report of the Bureau of Labor Statistics of the State of North Carolina, W. N. Jones, Commissioner, 1887, and the Third Annual Report of the Bureau of Labor Statistics of the State of North Carolina, John C. Scarborough, Commissioner, 1889.

the health of all the young women who work in the mills. The employment of children in the mills at low wages keeps a great many men out of employment. Our Legislature should do something in regard the long-hour system and trade checks, and compel employers to pay cash for labor; then, you see, competition in trade would take place, and we could save some of our earnings, which would enable us to have night schools and improve our condition much in the way of education.

6. Bertha Miller Recalls Her Days as a Cotton Mill Girl (1915), 1984

I was born in Randolph County ninety years ago. I wanted to be a farmer. Yeah, but I didn't get to be one. I was raised on a farm and I like a farm. I'd rather plow than do any other kind of work I've ever done in my life. We rented our land, we didn't own it, but we had all we wanted to tend. We raised corn, wheat, barley, tobacco, and enough cotton to make quilts and stuff like that. That was the best living I ever did, was living on a farm. We'd go possum hunting, rabbit hunting, cut wood together, work on the farm, and me and my daddy, we'd plow. I remember old Doc Phillips come walking by one day. Doc Phillips brought me in this world and all my younguns too. We lived side by side down in the country. So that day he come walking by and I was plowing corn. He stopped there at the house and hollered for me to come in the house. He said, "You're going to get killed on that thing." And I said, "No I ain't. I reckon I got enough sense to plow." I wasn't nothing but a youngun then.

My grandpap used to live with us. He made coffins. He lived with us for years, then he went back to his little home in the country and that's where he died. My daddy, he was a hard worker. I remember he got sick after we come to town. He worked down at the cotton mill for several years until he got down, plumb down, and wanted to go back home to the farm. That's where he died. My mother was a little old bitty thing, weighed about ninety pounds. She was a good Christian woman. When we moved here from the country, she went out there at the cotton mill and went to work. We all did.

I was so little for my age that at three years old, old Doc Phillips told my mother, he said, "Lou, give Pug,"—he always called me Pug—"a chew of tobacco." That was going to make me grow. So Ma cut me off a little chew of tobacco and I just chomped on it. First thing I knew my head started going around maybe ninety miles an hour and oh I was sick. I just laid down on the porch and vomited like a dog. I thought I was going to vomit my insides out. But I kept tasting it along and finally one day I said, "Give me a dip of snuff, maybe it won't make me sick." But it did. Still I kept dipping it a little longer 'til I got to where I dipped it regular. Then I started to grow. When I worked in the mill, just about all the girls in there dipped snuff. They dipped to keep the lint out of their throats. You never saw a woman smoking cigarettes back then. The awfullest looking sight I ever saw was a woman smoking a cigarette. I thought, Lord help.

From *Hard Times Cotton Mill Girls: Personal Histories of Womanhood and Poverty in the South* by Victoria Morris (Ithaca, NY: ILR Press, 1986). Used by permission of Cornell University Press.

Bertha Miller, *right,* with a friend, about
1915. (Photo courtesy of Victoria Byerly)

I was eleven years old when I went to work in the mill. They learnt me to knit.
Well, I was so little that they had to build me a box to get up on to put the sock in the
machine. I worked in the hosiery mill for a long time and, well, then we moved back
to the country. But me and my sister Molly finally went back up there in 1910 and I
went to work in the silk mill. Molly went to work in the hosiery mill. I come over here
in 1912 and boarded with Green Davis and Lou. They kept four other mill girls besides me. We all worked in the Amazon Cotton Mill. When we weren't working in the
mill, there wasn't nothing much to do only sit around there and laugh and talk. Us
girls, we'd wash our clothes and stuff like that. That's all there was to do. There
weren't no place to go. We'd go to the show every once in a while, but it was so far to
walk to town. Still, we had a good time. Mrs. Welch lived beside of us and she had
three girls. We'd all get together and sing and go on. Me, Berthie, Nan, and all of us,
we'd get in one room and we'd sing religious songs and laugh and talk. We'd have a
good time and enjoyed ourselves right there in the house. Weren't allowed to go
nowhere. Didn't get out and frolic around at night. We'd just sit right there at home
and talk about what we was going to do when we got old enough to get married and
all such things as that. We worked twelve hours a day for fifty cents. When paydays
come around, I drawed three dollars. That was for six days a week, seventy-two
hours. I remember I lacked fifty cents having enough to pay my board.

7. Appalachian Coal Mines and Laborers

An Early Coal Mine, Miller's Creek, Kentucky. (Special Collections Library, Alice Lloyd College, Pippa Passes, Kentucky)

From Ronald D. Eller, *Miners, Millhands, and Mountaineers: Industrialization of the Appalachian South, 1880–1930* (Knoxville: University of Tennessee Press, 1982).

(*right*) From *Coal Towns* by Crandall A. Shifflett. Reprinted by permission of the Eastern Regional Coal Archives, Craft Memorial Library, Bluefield, West Virginia.

Company Mining Town, Red Ash, Kentucky in Whitley County. (The Filson Club Historical Society, Louisville, KY).

Miner at Goodwill mine, West Virginia, 1937. (Courtesy of Eastern Regional Coal Archives/Craft Memorial Library/Bluefield, West Virginia 24701)

✠ E S S A Y S

Historian C. Vann Woodward began the scholarly reevaluation of the New South with his seminal book *Origins of the New South*. In the first selection, Woodward examines the "cotton mill campaign," and argues that mill ownership was in the hands of a class of southerners who were not connected to the antebellum planters but rather represented a new rising middle class. The second article, by a team of researchers from the University of North Carolina, explores the lives of mill workers using their own testimony and documents. Taking the perspective of the workers rather than the mill owners explodes the myth of southern labor's docility. The workers emerge from these interviews as much less unwitting victims than participants, however circumscribed, in their own destinies. The final essay, by Daniel Letwin, explores the rise of union activism among black and white workers in Alabama's coalfields and asks how it was possible for them to engage in biracial union organizing in a region where separation of the races was the norm.

The Rise of Southern Industry

C. VANN WOODWARD

The dramatic elements in the rise of the Southern cotton mill gave the movement something of the character of a "crusade." The successful competition with New England, the South's old political rival, the popular slogan, "bring the factories to the fields," and the organized publicity that attended every advance, have combined to enshrine the cotton mill in a somewhat exalted place in Southern history. Burdened with emotional significance, the mill has been made a symbol of the New South, its origins, and its promise of salvation. Facts that embarrass this interpretation of cotton-mill history have been somewhat neglected.

Rising in the Old Order, the cotton mills of the South showed a rather remarkable tenacity and even prosperity in the troubled decades that followed secession. Of the three leading cotton-manufacturing states of the South, North Carolina doubled the value of her output between 1860 and 1880, Georgia tripled her antebellum record, and South Carolina quadrupled hers. These gains continued right through the supposedly blighting years of Reconstruction. The case of a large Augusta mill was by no means unique. Running some 30,000 spindles and 1,000 looms, this mill paid cash dividends averaging 14.5 per cent a year during the seventeen years following 1865 and laid aside a surplus of about $350,000. These and other facts call into serious question the tradition of dating the beginning of the cotton-mill development of the South from 1880.

In the eighties the rate of cotton-mill expansion was simply accelerated, but it was accelerated to a speed never attained in earlier years, a pace vastly exceeding the rate of growth outside the South. In his report on the cotton-textile industry in the Census of 1890, Edward Stanwood wrote that "the extraordinary rate of

Reprinted by permission of Louisiana State University Press from *Origins of the New South 1877–1913* by C. Vann Woodward, pp. 131–135, 153–155. Copyright © 1951 by Louisiana State University Press and The Littlefield Fund for Southern History, University of Texas; copyright © renewed 1972 by C. Vann Woodward.

growth in the south" during the eighties was "the most important" aspect of the period. In 1900 he was even more emphatic, saying that "The growth of the industry in the South is the one great fact in its history during the past ten years." The number of mills in the South mounted from 161 in 1880 to 239 in 1890, and to 400 in 1900—an increase of 48.4 per cent in the eighties and 67.4 in the nineties. This, as compared with a national increase of 19.7 and 7.5 per cent in the two decades, and an apparent decrease in New England. A great number of the new mills, moreover, were equipped with more up-to-date machinery than the mills of the old textile regions. The first factory operated entirely by electricity was located in the South, and many improvements first found their way into the country through that region. The increase in the number of mills reveals only a fraction of the expansion. In the four leading states of North and South Carolina, Georgia, and Alabama—in which virtually all the increase took place—the average number of spindles per mill increased from 3,553 in 1880 to 10,651 in 1900. In total number of spindles the same states rose from 422,807 in 1880 to 1,195,256 in 1890, a gain of 182.7 per cent; and in the next decade the total mounted to 3,791,654 or an additional increase of 217 per cent in the nineties. Between 1880 and 1900 the total number of operatives in all Southern mills rose from 16,741 to 97,559; the number of bales consumed, from 182,349 to 1,479,006; the capital invested, from $17,375,897 to $124,596,874. Not untypical of the relative rate of expansion was the increase in capital invested in cotton manufactures, which, between 1890 and 1900 amounted to 131.4 per cent in the South as compared with 12.1 per cent in New England.

Both the historians and the promoters of the cotton-mill campaign have held that the movement was motivated by "moral incitement" and became "a form of civic piety" in the South. While the incentives common to most industrialization were admittedly present, "the moral considerations brought the matter to a focus." The cotton-mill executives were "thinking for the whole people." The extent of this motivation should be carefully explored, but it is well to point out first that in the early years of the movement, according to the census report of 1900, "the return upon investment in Southern cotton mills has greatly exceeded that upon factories in the North." In 1882 an average of 22 per cent profit was received on investments in Southern mills, under good and bad management—and there was much of the latter. There were failures as well as successes among the new mills. But profits of 30 to 75 per cent were not unheard of in those years.

As important as these inducements undoubtedly were, they cannot account for the public zeal that, in the Carolinas, Georgia, and Alabama, converted an economic development into a civic crusade inspired with a vision of social salvation. Not only did this process occur in cities like Charleston, Atlanta, and Charlotte, with their efficient chambers of commerce, big newspapers, and Northern visitors and settlers, but even more typically in isolated Piedmont towns. Old market villages of a few hundred citizens that had drowsed from one Saturday to the next since the eighteenth century, were suddenly aflame with the mill fever and "a passion for rehabilitation." Stock was often subscribed in small holdings. Among the professions from which early mill executives were called, Broadus Mitchell lists lawyers, bankers, farmers, merchants, teachers, preachers, doctors, and public officials. City dailies and country weeklies devoted columns to the crusade and itinerant evangelists added the theme to their repertoire. With a headlong zeal not uncharacteristic of the region in war as in peace, the Southeast embraced the cotton mill. "Even machinery was wrapped with idealism and devotion," according to one account.

Much was made by mill promoters of the philanthropic motive of giving "employment to the necessitous masses of poor whites." Undoubtedly this motive was sincere in some cases. Its force, however, is somewhat diminished by evidence submitted by the promoters themselves. Francis W. Dawson of Charleston, one of the most forceful propagandists for cotton mills, wrote in 1880 that employment in the mills subjects the poor whites "to elevating social influences, encourages them to seek education, and improves them in every conceivable respect." In the same editorial he stated that in South Carolina there were at that time "2,296 operatives, upon whom 7,913 persons are dependent for support. The amount paid out in wages monthly is $38,034." The average worker and dependent thus enjoyed an income of a little over twelve cents a day. In the same article Dawson estimated that the profits of these factories "ranged from 18 to $25\frac{1}{2}$ per cent a year . . . under the most unfavorable circumstances." The profit motive did not necessarily preclude the philanthropic motive, but it does seem to have outweighed it in some instances.

The question of the relative proportion of Southern and Northern capital in the Southern cotton mills is hedged with difficulties. Acknowledging the importance of Northern investment in Georgia and in areas of other states, authorities are in substantial agreement that after the seventies and before the depression years of the nineties, when Northern capital moved southward in quantities, the initiative lay with the South, and the chief source of capital was local. One writer finds "no evidence of any cotton mill established in North Carolina by Northern interests before 1895." This could not be said of any other mill state. A widespread practice was to raise only part of the required capital locally and then issue a large percentage of the stock of a new mill to Northern textile machinery and commission firms. Dependence upon these absentee firms, which often charged exorbitant rates of interest and employed injurious marketing practices, resulted in milking off a sizable proportion of profits. . . .

Within the little islands of industrialism scattered through the region, including the old towns as well as the new, was rising a new middle-class society. It drew some recruits from the old planter class, but in spirit as well as in outer aspect it was essentially new, strikingly resembling the same class in Midwestern and Northeastern cities. Richmond, former capital of the Confederacy, observed the social revolution within its walls with complacency: "We find a new race of rich people have been gradually springing up among us, who owe their wealth to successful trade and especially to manufactures. . . . [They] are taking the leading place not only in our political and financial affairs, but are pressing to the front for social recognition. . . . 'The almighty dollar' is fast becoming a power here, and he who commands the most money holds the strongest hand." . . .

The facts of the record would not seem to warrant the contention that "whereas in England many from the middle class became captains of industry, here [in the

South] the characteristic leadership proceeded from the aristocracy." According to this interpretation, the English industrialists were "small men who struck it lucky," whereas the Southern mill men were "gentlemen." A study of the background of 254 industrialists in the South of this period reveals that "about eighty per cent came of nonslave-owning parentage." Out of a total of 300 studied only 13 per cent were of Northern birth. Professor John Spencer Bassett, the historian, who took a peculiar delight in the rise of the new and the decline of the old ruling class, wrote that "The rise of the middle class has been the most notable thing connected with the white population of the South since the war. . . . Everywhere trade and manufacturing is almost entirely in the hands of men who are sprung from the non-planter class, and . . . the professions seem to be going the same way." As for the old planters, a decadent class, Bassett thought, "They have rarely held their own with others, and most frequently they have been in the upper ranks of those who serve rather than those who direct business. . . . But the captains of industry . . . are men who were never connected with the planter class." A shrewd New England observer corroborated the Southerner's view when he wrote in 1890: "now, like a mighty apparition across the southern horizon, has arisen this hope or portent of the South,—the Third Estate,—to challenge the authority of the old ruling class." He advised his section against "exclusive observation of the old conflict of races" in the South. "For the coming decade, the place to watch the South is in this movement of the rising Third Estate. What it demands and what it can achieve in political, social, and industrial affairs . . . on these things will depend the fate of this important section of our country for years to come."

Mark Twain on a Southern junket in the eighties was brought face to face with these men of the New South: "Brisk men, energetic of movement and speech; the dollar their god, how to get it their religion." Somewhat awkwardly, but with great show of self-assurance, this new man adjusted to his shoulders the mantle of leadership that had descended from the planter. Some considerable alteration was found necessary: less pride and more "push," for example. Punctilio was sacrificed to the exigencies of "bustle," and arrogance was found to be impracticable in the pursuit of the main chance.

The Lives and Labors of the Cotton Mill People

JACQUELYN DOWD HALL, ROBERT KORSTAD, AND JAMES L. LELOUDIS II

Textile mills built the new South. Beginning in the 1880s, business and professional men tied their hopes for prosperity to the whirring of spindles and the beating of looms. Small-town boosterism supplied the rhetoric of the mill-building campaign, but the impoverishment of farmers was industrialization's driving force. The post–Civil War rise of sharecropping, tenantry, and the crop lien ensnared freedmen, then eroded yeoman society. Farmers of both races fought for survival by

Jacquelyn Dowd Hall, Robert Korstad, and James L. Leloudis II, "Cotton Mill People: Work, Community, and Protest in the Textile South, 1880–1940," *American Historical Review* 91 (April 1986), pp. 245–286. Reprinted by permission of the authors.

clinging to subsistence strategies and habits of sharing even as they planted cash crops and succumbed to tenantry. Meanwhile, merchants who had accumulated capital through the crop lien invested in cotton mills. As the industry took off in an era of intensifying segregation, blacks were relegated to the land, and white farmers turned to yet another strategy for coping with economic change. They had sold their cotton to the merchant; now they supplied him with the human commodity needed to run his mills. This homegrown industry was soon attracting outside capital and underselling northern competitors. By the end of the Great Depression, the South-east replaced New England as the world's leading producer of cotton cloth, and the industrializing Piedmont replaced the rural Coastal Plain as pacesetter for the region. . . .

Nothing better symbolized the new industrial order than the mill villages that dot-ted the Piedmont landscape. Individual families and small groups of local in-vestors built and owned most of the early mills. Run by water wheels, factories flanked the streams that fell rapidly from the mountains toward the Coastal Plain. Of necessity, owners provided housing where none had been before. But the set-ting, scale, and structure of the mill village reflected rural expectations as well as practical considerations. Typically, a three-story brick mill, a company store, and a superintendent's house were clustered at one end of the village. Three- and four-room frame houses, owned by the company but built in a vernacular style familiar in the countryside, stood on lots that offered individual garden space, often supple-mented by communal pastures and hog pens. A church, a company store, and a modest schoolhouse completed the scene. By 1910 steam power and electricity had freed the mills from their dependence on water power, and factories sprang up on the outskirts of towns along the route of the Southern Railway. Nevertheless, the urban mill village retained its original rural design. Company-owned villages survived in part because they fostered management control. Unincorporated "mill hills" that surrounded towns such as Charlotte and Burlington, North Carolina, and Greenville, South Carolina, enabled owners to avoid taxes and excluded workers from municipal government. But the mill village also reflected the workers' her-itage and served their needs.

Like the design of the mill village, the family labor system helped smooth the path from field to factory. On farms women and children had always pro-vided essential labor, and mill owners took advantage of these traditional roles. They promoted factory work as a refuge for impoverished women and children from the countryside, hired family units rather than individuals, and required the labor of at least one worker per room as a condition for residence in a mill-owned house. But this labor system also dovetailed with family strategies. The first to arrive in the mills were those least essential to farming and most vulnera-ble to the hazards of commercial agriculture: widows, female heads of house-holds, single women, and itinerant laborers. By the turn of the century, families headed by men also lost their hold on the land. Turning to the mills, they sought not a "family wage" that would enable a man to support his dependents but an arena in which parents and children could work together as they had always done.

The deployment of family labor also helped maintain permeable boundaries between farm and mill. The people we interviewed moved with remarkable ease from farming to mill work and back again or split their family's time between the two. James Pharis's father raised tobacco in the Leaksville-Spray area of North Carolina until most of his six children were old enough to obtain mill jobs. The family moved to a mill village in the 1890s because the elder Pharis "felt that all we had to do when we come to town was to reach up and pull the money off of the trees." From the farm Pharis saved his most valuable possession: his team of horses. While the children worked in the mill, he raised vegetables on a plot of rented ground and used his team to do "hauling around for people." Betty Davidson's landowning parents came up with the novel solution of sharing a pair of looms. "My father would run the looms in the wintertime," Davidson remembered, "and go to and from work by horseback. And in the summertime, when he was farming, my mother run the looms, and she stayed in town because she couldn't ride the horse. Then, on the weekends, she would come home."

This ability to move from farming to factory work—or combine the two—postponed a sharp break with rural life. It also gave mill workers a firm sense of alternative identity and leverage against a boss's demands. Lee Workman recalled his father's steadfast independence. In 1918 the superintendent of a nearby cotton mill came to the Workmans' farm in search of workers to help him meet the demand for cloth during World War I. The elder Workman sold his mules and cow but, contrary to the superintendent's advice, held on to his land. Each spring he returned to shoe his neighbors' horses, repair their wagons and plows, and fashion the cradles they used to harvest grain. "He'd tell the superintendent, 'You can just get somebody else, because I'm going back to make cradles for my friends.' Then he'd come back in the wintertime and work in the mill." This type of freedom did not sit well with the mill superintendent, but the elder Workman had the upper hand. " 'Well,' he told them, 'if you don't want to do that, I'll move back to the country and take the family.' "

Although Lee Workman's father periodically retreated to the farm, his sons and daughters, along with thousands of others, eventually came to the mills to stay. There they confronted an authority more intrusive than anything country folk had experienced before. In Bynum, North Carolina, the mill owner supervised the Sunday School and kept tabs on residents' private lives. "If you stubbed your toe they'd fire you. They'd fire them here for not putting out the light late at night. Old Mr. Bynum used to go around over the hill at nine o'clock and see who was up. And, if you were up, he'd knock on the door and tell you to cut the lights out and get into bed." Along with surveillance came entanglement with the company store. Mill hands all too familiar with the crop lien once again found themselves in endless debt. Don Faucette's father often talked about it. "Said if you worked at the mill they'd just take your wages and put it in the company store and you didn't get nothing. For years and years they didn't get no money, just working for the house they lived in and what they got at the company store. They just kept them in the hole all the time."

The mill village undeniably served management's interests, but it also nurtured a unique workers' culture. When Piedmont farmers left the land and took a cotton mill job, they did not abandon old habits and customs. Instead, they fashioned familiar ways of thinking and acting into a distinctively new way of life. This adaptation occurred at no single moment in time; rather, it evolved, shaped and reshaped by successive waves of migrations off the farm as well as the movement of workers from mill to mill. Village life was based on family ties. Kinship networks facilitated migration to the mill and continued to play a powerful integrative role. Children of the first generation off the land married newcomers of the second and third, linking households into broad networks of obligation, responsibility, and concern. For many couples, marriage evolved out of friendships formed while growing up in the village. One married worker recalled, "We knowed each other from childhood. Just raised up together, you might say. All lived here on the hill, you see, that's how we met." . . .

Cooperation provided a buffer against misery and want at a time when state welfare services were limited and industrialists often refused to assume responsibility for job-related sickness and injury. It bound people together and reduced their dependence on the mill owners' charity. When someone fell ill, neighbors were quick to give the stricken family a "pounding." "They'd all get together and help. They'd cook food and carry it to them—all kinds of food—fruits, vegetables, canned goods." Villagers also aided sick neighbors by taking up a "love offering" in the mill. . . .

Community solidarity did not come without a price. Neighborliness could shade into policing; it could repress as well as sustain. Divorced women and children born out of wedlock might be ostracized, and kinship ties could give mill supervisors an intelligence network that reached into every corner of the village. Alice Evitt of Charlotte remarked that "people then couldn't do like they do now. They was talked about. My daddy would never allow us to be with people that was talked about. This was the nicest mill hill I ever lived on. If anybody done anything wrong and you reported them, they had to move." . . .

Given such tensions, we were struck by how little ambivalence surfaced in descriptions of mill village life. Recollections of factory work were something else again, but the village—red mud and all—was remembered with affection. The reasons are not hard to find. A commitment to family and friends represented a realistic appraisal of working people's prospects in the late nineteenth- and early twentieth-century South. Only after World War II, with the expansion of service industries, did the Piedmont offer alternatives to low-wage factory work to more than a lucky few. Until then, casting one's lot with others offered more promise and certainly more security than the slim hope of individual gain. To be sure, mill people understood the power of money; they struggled against dependency and claimed an economic competence as their due. Nevertheless, they had "their own ideas . . . about what constitute[d] the 'good life.' " Communal values, embodied in everyday behavior, distanced mill folk from the acquisitiveness that characterized middle-class life in New South towns.

This is not to say that mill village culture destroyed individuality. On the contrary, it conferred status and dignity that the workplace could seldom afford. Although mill ways encouraged group welfare at the expense of personal ambition, they did support individual accomplishment of a different sort. The practice of medicine provides one example, music another.

Folk medicine formed an important part of workers' "live-at-home" culture. Until well into the twentieth century, mill hands simply could not afford medical fees; besides, they viewed doctors with distrust and fear. In emergencies, the village turned to its own specialists. Among the earliest of these in Bynum was Louise Jones's mother, Madlena Riggsbee. "She was what you'd say was a midwife. She could just hold up under anything. Unless they were bound and compelled to have the doctor, they'd usually get her to go." In the 1920s and 1930s, the company retained the services of a physician, paid for with funds withheld from workers' checks. But in the eyes of the villagers, he was a partner—indeed a junior partner— to Ida Jane Smith, a healer and midwife who was one of the most respected figures in the community. "Lord, she was a good woman," Carrie Gerringer recalled. "She knowed more about younguns than any doctor."

If the midwife was the most prestigious member of the female community, the musician held that place among men. String bands had been a mainstay of country gatherings, and they multiplied in the mill villages where musicians lived closer together and had more occasions to play. Mastery of an instrument brought a man fame as the local "banjo king" or expert guitar picker. Musicians sometimes played simply for their own enjoyment. Paul Faucette and a small group of friends and kinfolk used "to get together on the porch on Saturday night and just have a big time." On other occasions, they performed for house dances and community celebrations. Harvey Ellington remembered that on Saturday night "you'd have a dance in somebody's house—they'd take the beds and all out, and then we'd just play." The dance might end before midnight, but the musicians' performance often continued into the morning. "We'd be going home and decide we didn't want to go to bed. So we'd take the fiddle and the guitar and the banjo and stop at the corner and harmonize—do what they call serenade. The people would raise their windows and listen. That's the best sounding music, wake up at night and hear somebody playing."

Special talents won Harvey Ellington and Madlena Riggsbee places of honor in their neighbors' memories. But most villagers never achieved such distinction. They lived in quiet anonymity, often guided and strengthened by religious faith. Most textile workers were evangelical Protestants, and many worshipped in churches built and financed by factory owners. On one level, these churches proved helpful, maybe even essential, to the mills. Like their counterparts in other industrializing societies, they inculcated the moral and social discipline demanded by factory life. Still, there was another side to evangelical religion, one that empowered the weak, bound them together, and brought them close to God. At springtime revivals, faith turned to ecstasy. "People got happy and they shouted. They'd sing and hug each other—men and women both." When the Holy Spirit moved individuals to confessions of sin, the entire body of worshippers joined in thanksgiving for God's saving grace.

The physical and social geography of the mill village, then, was less a product of owners' designs than a compromise between capitalist organization and workers' needs. For a more clear-cut embodiment of the manufacturers' will, we must look to the factory. The ornate facades of nineteenth-century textile mills reflected their builders' ambitions and the orderly world they hoped to create. The mill that still stands at Glencoe is an excellent example. Situated only a few hundred yards from the clapboard houses that make up the village, the mill is a three-story structure complete with "stair tower, corbelled cornice, quoined stucco corners, and heavily stuccoed window labels." In contrast to the vernacular form of the village, the architecture of the factory, modeled on that of New England's urban mills, was highly self-conscious, formal, and refined.

At Glencoe, and in mills throughout the Piedmont, manufacturers endeavored to shape the southern yeomanry into a tractable industrial workforce. Workers' attitudes toward factory labor, like those toward village life, owed much to the cycles and traditions of the countryside. Owners, on the other hand, sought to substitute for cooperation and task orientation a labor system controlled from the top down and paced by the regular rhythms of the machine. Barring adverse market conditions, work in the mills varied little from day to day and season to season. Workers rose early in the morning, still tired from the day before, and readied themselves for more of the same. For ten, eleven, and twelve hours they walked, stretched, leaned, and pulled at their machines. Noise, heat, and humidity engulfed them. The lint that settled on their hair and skin marked them as mill workers to the outside world. The cotton dust that silently entered their lungs could also kill them.

Owners enforced this new pattern of labor with the assistance of a small coterie of supervisors. As a rule, manufacturers delegated responsibility for organizing work and disciplining the help to a superintendent and his overseers and second hands. A second hand in a pre–World War I mill recalled, "You had the cotton, the machinery, and the people, and you were supposed to get out the production. How you did it was pretty much up to you; it was production management was interested in and not how you got it." Under these circumstances, supervision was a highly personal affair; there were as many different approaches to its problems as there were second hands and overseers. As one observer explained, "There was nothing that could be identified as a general pattern of supervisory practice."

At times, discipline could be harsh, erratic, and arbitrary. This was particularly true before 1905, when most workers in southern mills were women and children. Even supervisors writing in the *Southern Textile Bulletin* admitted that "some overseers, second hands, and section men have a disposition to abuse the help. Whoop, holler, curse, and jerk the children around." James Pharis remembered that "you used to work for the supervisor because you were scared. I seen a time when I'd walk across the road to keep from meeting my supervisor. They was the hat-stomping kind. If you done anything, they'd throw their hat on the floor and stomp it and raise hell."

In the absence of either state regulation or trade unions, management's power seemed limitless, but there were, in fact, social and structural constraints. Although manufacturers relinquished day-to-day authority to underlings, they were ever-present figures, touring the mill, making decisions on wages and production quotas, and checking up on the help. These visits were, in part, attempts to maintain the appearance of paternalism and inspire hard work and company loyalty. At the same time, they divided power in the mill. Workers had direct access to the owner and sometimes saw him as a buffer between themselves and supervisors, a "force that could bring an arbitrary and unreasonable [overseer] back into line." Mack Duncan recalled that in the early years "most all the mill owners seemed like they had a little milk of human kindness about them, but some of the people they hired didn't. Some of the managers didn't have that. They were bad to exploit people." Under these circumstances, the commands of an overseer were always subject to review. Workers felt free to complain about unjust treatment, and owners, eager to keep up production, sometimes reversed their lieutenants' orders. Federal labor investigators reported in 1910 that "when an employee is dissatisfied about mill conditions he may obtain a hearing from the chief officer of the mill . . . and present his side of the case. Not infrequently when complaints are thus made, the overseer is overruled and the operative upheld."

Authority on the shop floor was further complicated by social relations in the mill village. Before the introduction of industrial engineers and college-trained foremen in the 1920s and 1930s, most supervisors worked their way up through the ranks. . . .

A personal style of labor management posed but one obstacle to the imposition of strict discipline. Mill owners also faced the limitations of existing technology. The small size of most mills before World War I made it difficult to coordinate production in a way that kept all hands constantly at work. . . .

Mill owners and workers alike had to accommodate themselves to a work environment not entirely of their own choosing. Factory labor did not allow the independence and flexibility of labor on the farm, but neither did it meet the standards of rigor and regularity desired by owners. An informal compromise governed the shop floor. "We worked longer then in the mill than they do now," explained Naomi Trammell, "and made less, too. But we didn't work hard. I done all my playing in the mill." . . .

World War I marked a turning point in the development of the southern textile industry. Stimulated by wartime demand, new mills sprang up, old ones operated around the clock, wages rose, and profits soared. But, when peace came, overexpanded businesses went into a tailspin. The situation worsened when tariff policies and the advent of textile manufacturing in other parts of the world cut into the southern industry's lucrative foreign markets. A sudden change in clothing styles added to manufacturers' troubles. Young women in the 1920s hiked their skirts six inches above the ankle, then all the way to the knee, causing consternation among their elders and panic in the textile industry. All in all, the depression that hit the rest of the country in 1929 began for textile manufacturers in the immediate postwar years.

Mill officials greeted the armistice with a rollback of workers' wages. But, to the owners' surprise, mill hands refused to abandon small but cherished advances in their standard of living. When wage cuts were announced in 1919, thousands of workers joined the American Federation of Labor's United Textile Workers (UTW). "They are in deadly earnest," reported the Raleigh *News and Observer,* "and almost religiously serious in their belief in the union." Manufacturers were equally determined not to employ union members, and in many cases they simply shut their factory gates to all workers. As the conflict dragged on, threats of violence mounted. Armed strikers patrolled the mill villages, intent on enforcing community and union solidarity. Manufacturers eventually agreed to a settlement but insisted that "the adjustment . . . shall not be construed as a recognition by the mills of collective bargaining." Similar confrontations occurred throughout the Piedmont until 1921, when a severe business downturn crippled union locals and gave management the upper hand. But workers had made their message clear: mill owners would no longer be able to shore up profits simply by cutting wages.

The impasse created in 1921 by hard times and workers' protests set the stage for a new era of corporate consolidation. As smaller firms went bankrupt, more aggressive competitors gobbled them up. J. Spencer Love, who took over faltering mills in Alamance County and eventually built Burlington Mills into the world's largest textile enterprise, set the pace. Love's generation led the region to ascendancy in the production of synthetics and helped effect a permanent shift of cotton manufacturing from New England to the Piedmont. These "progressive mill men" also set out to find new solutions to problems of profitability and labor control. The methods they adopted aimed at altering the structure of work and breaking the bonds between supervisors and the mill village community. But their freedom of action depended on a ballooning labor supply. . . .

In 1927 resistance to management tactics by individuals and small groups gave way to labor conflict on an unprecedented scale. The battle opened in Henderson, North Carolina, where workers struck for restoration of a bonus withdrawn three years before. Then on March 12, 1929, young women in a German-owned rayon plant in Elizabethton, Tennessee, touched off a strike wave that spread quickly into the Carolinas. The involvement of the communist-led National Textile Workers Union and the shooting deaths, first of the police chief and then of Ella May Wiggins, the strikers' balladeer, brought Gastonia, North Carolina, a special notoriety. But the carnage was even worse in nearby Marion, where deputies opened fire on demonstrators, wounding twenty-five and killing six. In 1930, revolt hit the massive Dan River Mill in Virginia—a model of welfare capitalism.

Responding to these workers' initiatives, the UTW tried to remedy its neglect of southern labor. Most energetic was the American Federation of Hosiery Workers, an autonomous UTW affiliate, represented by Alfred Hoffman, an intrepid organizer who popped up in virtually every trouble spot until his militancy landed him in a Marion jail. But even Hoffman usually arrived after the fact, and a number of the less well known but more successful walkouts ran their course with no official union involvement at all. In 1929, thousands of South Carolina workers formed their own relief committees, held mass meetings, and negotiated modifications in the stretch-out—all without help from the UTW. Similarly, in 1932, in High Point, North Carolina, hosiery workers sparked sympathy strikes at textile mills and furniture plants and used automobile caravans to spread walkouts to nearby towns. Fearing a "revolution on our hands," officials conceded most of the workers' demands.

Whether independently organized or union led, each walkout was shaped by local circumstances. But more important than the differences were the experiences strikers shared. In community after community, mill folk turned habits of mutuality and self-help to novel ends. Union relief funds were paltry at best, and survival depended on neighborly sharing. Many of the Marion strikers "had a good garden, and they'd divide their gardens with people that didn't have any." Those who held back found themselves donating anyway. Sam Finley remembered frying chickens for hungry picketers—supplied by a boy who could "get a chicken off the roost and leave the feathers." Baseball games, picnics, and barbecues buoyed spirits and fostered solidarity. As in the routines of daily life, women workers were essential to this mobilization of community resources. "The women done as much as the men," Lillie Price asserted. "They always do in everything." . . .

In these ways, workers fashioned a language of resistance from established cultural forms. But the young people who led the protests had also come of age in a society different from the one their parents had known. Most had grown up in the mill villages or moved as children from the countryside. They did not see themselves as temporary sojourners, ready to beat a retreat to the land, or as displaced farmers for whom "it was heaven to draw a payday, however small." Their identities had been formed in the mill village; they had cast their fate with the mills.

Interracial Unionism and Gender in the Alabama Coalfields, 1878–1908

DANIEL LETWIN

One summer day in 1878, Willis J. Thomas, an African American coal miner and an organizer for the Greenback-Labor party in the Birmingham mineral district, stopped in the town of Oxmoor to post signs announcing a public meeting where he was scheduled to speak. The notice addressed itself to both black and white voters. As he nailed one to the door of the Eureka Iron Company storehouse, Thomas was accosted by a group of Democrats, who warned him that he was courting trouble and that he had best make himself scarce. Thomas coolly withdrew from his vest pocket a piece of paper, perhaps documenting his association with the Greenback-Labor party or his legal right to post the announcements, and invited the men to read it. Nonplussed, they handed it back and left.

"Our country is going to the dogs!" one of the Democrats muttered afterward to an acquaintance, unaware that he was speaking to a Greenbacker. "To think that a Negro has that much authority in a good Democratic state, is enough to make a white man commit suicide." Such a development, he feared, threatened to undo the work of the Redeemers: "Three years ago if a Negro dared to say anything about politics, or public speaking, or sitting on a jury, or sticking up a notice, he would be driven out of the county, or shot, or hung in the woods." Especially alarming

From Daniel Letwin, "Interracial Unionism, Gender, and 'Social Equality' in the Alabama Coalfields, 1878–1908," *Journal of Southern History*, LXI (August 1995), pp. 519–54. Copyright © 1995 by the Southern Historical Association. Reprinted by permission of the Managing Editor. The notes for this piece have been omitted.

was Thomas's influence among whites. "Some white men that heard nigger Thomas," he fretted, "say he is the best speaker in Jefferson county, white or black. . . ."

The scene that so scandalized this Democrat was not an isolated one in the Alabama coal region. Thomas was merely the most prominent of a number of African Americans active in building the Greenback-Labor party around the newly developed mineral district. Nor did the fading of Greenbackism by the close of the decade spell the end of interracial organization; black and white coal miners joined forces on an even larger scale in the 1880s under the banner of the Knights of Labor. In the early 1890s the United Mine Workers of Alabama displaced the Knights as a bastion of interracial unionism in the New South. To be sure, none of these movements fully confronted the prevailing assumptions of white supremacy. None eliminated racial strains or hierarchies within their ranks or overcame stubborn veins of antipathy to interracial mobilization among the miners. Still, their egalitarian rhetoric, and their very existence as racially mixed enterprises, made these organizations a conspicuous—and, to many, unnerving—exception to the rising tide of Jim Crow.

Recent years have brought growing attention to long-neglected instances of interracial organization across the late-nineteenth- and early-twentieth-century South. Historians have uncovered union collaboration among black and white workers in such disparate settings as the timberlands of Louisiana, the docks of New Orleans, the urban trades of Richmond and Birmingham, and the coalfields of southern and central Appalachia. Just as C. Vann Woodward has exploded the encrusted myth that segregation was somehow encoded in southern history, the recent scholarship on labor has shaken loose the traditional depiction of black and white workers locked in an unrelieved cycle of exclusion, conflict, and mutual alienation. Rather, it has shown their relationship to be historically variegated, ranging from hostility to solidarity. Even if episodes of interracial cooperation were less common and lasting than those of antagonism and defeat, they restore the question mark to the interaction of class and race among American workers. Varied and complex, at times openly defiant of the dominant norms and at times scrupulously bent to the contours of Jim Crow, labor interracialism has been the subject of sharply conflicting historical interpretation. At the core of this literature lies the question of explanation: what prompted black and white workers to collaborate in labor campaigns even though they were segregated by race in nearly all other areas of their lives? There is, of course, no single answer. The recent spate of case studies has shed light on three broad dynamics that encouraged or enabled black and white workers to organize collectively in the face of formidable barriers: a determination to resist the efforts of employers to divide and weaken them along racial lines; a sense of shared identity rooted in common class experience; and the readiness of interracial unions to incorporate elements of white supremacy.

These characteristics go a long way toward explaining the anomaly of interracial unionism in a segregated society. The first section of the discussion to follow will explore how these strands of self-interest, solidarity, and accommodation to the larger racial order converged to shape the nature of interracial unionism in the

Birmingham district. Yet they do not on their own completely explain the presence of labor interracialism in the Jim Crow South. In the Alabama coalfields one further circumstance—the gender-specific composition of the labor force—contributed significantly, if inconspicuously, to this remarkable tradition. The second section will argue that, in workplaces occupied only by men, such as coal mines, the spectacle of blacks and whites engaged in collective activity was less viscerally threatening than it was in settings where interracial association involved both sexes.

Birmingham, Alabama, was founded in the foothills of Appalachia in 1871, at the initiative of investors eager to develop the area's rich deposits of coal and iron. By the end of the century the Birmingham district had emerged, albeit in fits and starts, as the industrial centerpiece of the New South. The labor force of the coalfields was racially mixed from the beginning. In the early years, whites made up a small majority of the miners; over the 1880s and 1890s, the proportion of African Americans in the workforce increased, until by the turn of the century they were in the majority. Significant numbers of both blacks and whites worked as skilled pick miners, generally in the same mines although seldom in the same rooms. Blacks figured predominantly, but not exclusively, among the laborers who worked under the supervision of skilled miners, either black or white. At many mines, convicts leased from the state or the counties, overwhelmingly black, were used as cheap and controllable labor.

As in other mineral regions around the country, the Alabama coalfields were the sites of chronic tensions between the miners and the operators. Living conditions, the company store, rent levels, wages, the weighing and screening of coal, the hours and conditions of work, the subcontracting of unskilled labor, the leasing of convicts, the operators' power to fire, dock, and otherwise penalize the miners, the miners' right to unionize and to receive contractual recognition—all provoked rancorous and at times bloody conflict. Alabama miners particularly detested the overarching power wielded by many coal and iron operators. Writing from Carbon Hill in 1890, one miner complained bitterly that the operators "assume the power to buy and sell alike. They dictate to us when we shall work, how we shall work, how long we shall work, how much work shall be done, and the amount of pay they shall pay for the labor performed. Labor has no rights. . . ." Miners responded to meager pay, harsh conditions, and overbearing employers in a variety of ways. Many acted individually, moving from mine to mine, alternating between mining and farming, shifting among different occupations around the district, or balancing mining with other activities, such as hunting, fishing, gardening, and varied forms of leisure.

But it was through organization that Alabama's miners most visibly asserted their grievances and aspirations. The appearance of the Greenbackers coincided with the first surge of coal and iron production during the late 1870s. Throughout 1878 and 1879 Greenback-Labor clubs proliferated across the coalfields. Through regular meetings, contributions to the *National Labor Tribune,* and participation in political campaigns, the Greenback-Labor party gave Alabama's first generation of miners a collective voice. The concerns that Greenback miners articulated ranged from the swelling power of finance and industrial capital throughout the nation and the corrupt hegemony of Redeemer governments around the South to the immediate issues of low pay, unsafe mine conditions, and, most heatedly, the leasing of convicts. While Greenbackism enjoyed substantial appeal among the miners in statewide elections of the late 1870s and the early 1880s, it faded as an active movement in the mineral district by the end of 1880. A significant portion of Greenback miners, however, was absorbed by another, more broadly structured movement, the Knights of Labor.

Drawing on and elaborating the Greenbackers' moral critique of Gilded Age America and the Redeemed South, the Knights of Labor first set down roots in Alabama in 1879. Birmingham rapidly emerged as one of the hubs of southern Knighthood, claiming dozens of local assemblies and nearly 4,000 members during the peak years of 1886 and 1887. The Knights not only pursued a legislative agenda focused heavily upon the concerns of the mining district but also extended miners' activism into the workplace itself. Throughout the 1880s skirmishes occurred between miners and operators, chiefly strikes or lockouts. . . . By 1890 a more militant Miners' Trade Council (MTC) had supplanted the Knights and affiliated with a new organization, the United Mine Workers of America (UMW).

Founded in early 1890 in Columbus, Ohio, the UMW thereafter provided the structure for labor organization in the Alabama coalfields. Blending the Knights of Labor's promotion of mutualism, independence, and decent conditions with the militancy of the MTC, the Alabama UMW struck a chord from the beginning. Economic depression and stubborn resistance from the operators stymied unionism over the first half of the 1890s, but the economic recovery of 1897 breathed new life into the UMW. By the spring of 1898, the miners' union, District 20 of the UMW, claimed more than 1,000 members; over the next several years, its numbers surged, reaching a peak in 1903 of 14,000 members, organized into ninety-five locals. Although the union continued to encounter pockets of indifference among miners and resistance from employers, these years of economic buoyancy ushered in the first era of contractual recognition by the Alabama operators. Dramatically, if unevenly around the district, the UMW enhanced the miners' material livelihood and feeling of independence. The gains did not last. When the economic boom subsided, the operators rolled back their accommodation to organized labor, provoking a strike in 1904 that ground on for two years before the miners finally conceded defeat. After a general strike was crushed in 1908, the Alabama UMW lay in ruins, not to revive until World War I.

The Greenback-Labor party, the Knights of Labor, and the United Mine Workers each approached a crossroads familiar to unions in multiracial settings through much of American history. One path for white unionists, the one more commonly chosen during the late nineteenth and early twentieth centuries, was to exclude African Americans or to banish them to peripheral branches of the organization. The alternative was to organize all workers in the trade, regardless of race; and the Greenbackers, the Knights, and the UMW each followed the course of racial inclusion, even while Jim Crow grew increasingly prevalent. Interracial unionism was a stark anomaly in the otherwise segregated world of the Birmingham coal towns. In no other area of life did black and white miners stray so far from the spirit of white supremacy. In virtually all aspects of the mining community, blacks and whites oc-cupied separate spheres: each town had black and white residential areas, black and white schools, black and white churches, black and white fraternal lodges, black and white athletic clubs, black and white brass bands. These dual, mutually insular worlds seldom attracted public comment, so naturally did they reproduce the pre-vailing racial arrangements of the New South.

The insularity was by no means absolute. Blacks and whites did interact on the margins of daily life in the mining camps, on terms that ran the gamut from amica-ble to hostile. Occasionally, tensions erupted into gruesome violence, most often by whites against African Americans. Such confrontations are grim reminders that, however powerfully class relations shaped the miners' livelihood and world-view, their loyalties—their very self-identities—remained heavily affected by the South's racial order. Nonetheless, one is struck by the infrequency of visible conflict. The most notable characteristic of the black-white relationship in the mining communi-ties was the clean separation of the two races. . . .

The interracialism of these successive movements emerged in a variety of ways. Each organization established biracial structures—dual networks of black and white "clubs" with the Greenbackers, "local assemblies" with the Knights, and "local unions" with the UMW. Within each association, blacks and whites shared leadership roles—organizing local bodies, recruiting members, represent-ing miners in their dealings with the operators, delivering speeches, and con-tributing reports of current struggles to local or national organs. The interracial character of union leadership became most conspicuous as the UMW reasserted its presence at the turn of the century. Even as segregation calcified into law and disfranchisement constitutions were adopted across the South—Alabama's was ratified in 1901—African American miners continued to figure prominently among the elected officials, convention delegates, and organizers of UMW Dis-trict 20.

The Greenback-Labor party, the Knights, and the UMW each functioned in the mineral district as a biracial collaboration: black clubs, assemblies, and unions were generally mobilized by black organizers; their white counterparts, by white leaders. Still, the color line yielded to extensive interaction between black and white miners. Blacks and whites frequently attended common gatherings, whether to conduct business or partake in festivities. Willis J. Thomas, the charismatic African American Greenbacker whose brush with the Democrats opened this es-say, spoke with widely noted influence at racially mixed events. In the Knights of Labor era, white and black local assemblies cultivated close working relationships. "The fraternal visits [between black and white assemblies] are productive of much good and encouraging to our members," a Knight from Warrior Station reported. At a Birmingham rally in 1887, black and white leaders shared a platform before a racially mixed crowd of 5,000 Knights. There was "no color line in our fight," the Knights' *Alabama Sentinel* proclaimed in 1887. The UMW sustained this tradition of biracial meetings, organizing efforts, and social affairs through the 1890s and 1900s.

Reluctance to be drawn into reflexive promotions of white supremacy sur-faced with particular clarity during strikes. During 1884 and 1885, for example, black and white miners at the coal town of Warrior struck together to oppose the introduction of Italian contract labor by a newly arrived, northern-based company. Like any group, the Warrior miners sharpened their sense of identity against the foil of "outsiders." Of interest here is where they drew the line between their "legitimate" selves and the "outsiders": not between white and black but rather between regional and northern capital, American and Italian workers, and above all, between independent and "pauper" labor—"that terrible curse upon American soil," in the words of local Knight E. R. Harris. On no known occasion during this era did white miners mobilize to exclude African Americans as such from the mines.

During the 1890s and 1900s the prospects for interracial collaboration faced new tests, as the operators began to introduce black strikebreakers en masse during major conflicts, such as district-wide strikes in 1890–1891, 1894, 1904–1906, and 1908. The UMW worked strenuously to deflect the racial wedge, exhorting black and white miners to march "shoulder to shoulder . . . together in our struggle of right against might." Such appeals paid off substantially, as African American miners remained widely committed to the union. "We, the colored miners of Alabama, are with our white brothers," read a typical sign at a mass rally at the outset of the 1894 strike. During large-scale strikes, word came regularly from around the district that miners of both races were "as firm as ever," "still solid," and so forth. . . .

The interracial practices of the Greenback-Labor party, the Knights of Labor, and the United Mine Workers were heavily anchored in the impulse for self-preservation. For white miners particularly, subordinating the color line to the struggle against a shared adversary reflected a recognition of an immutable demographic circumstance. Commonly, in American industry the initial contact between black and white workers involved an "invasion" by blacks of white turf, often as strikebreakers. By contrast, the Alabama coalfields had been racially mixed from the beginning; moreover, the lines dividing skilled from unskilled, striker from strikebreaker, even free miner from leased convict, did not correspond absolutely to that between black and white. Whatever their preferences might otherwise have been, the first generation of Birmingham miners had little say over the racial arrangement of the labor force; the presence of African Americans in skilled as well as unskilled occupations was a fait accompli. The concept of a racially defined workplace thus had little chance to take root. Convicts, strikebreakers, Italian "paupers," distant capital—these were the "intruders" upon the terrain of the "real miners," a group that encompassed both blacks and whites.

Recognizing these realities, labor organizations made the case for interracialism largely in the language of collective self-interest: all miners, they argued, were in the same boat. . . .

More powerfully than rhetoric alone, the experience of interracial collaboration inspired some miners to reassess their premises about race. Following a speech by Willis Thomas to a racially mixed gathering of Greenbackers, one white member rose to praise Thomas's club as the best order, white or black, in the state, adding that he had never thought such work could be carried on by black people.

When Thomas was nominated for a district-wide position in the Greenback-Labor party, the white club in Warrior declined to run a candidate against him, asserting that all members knew Thomas and preferred him to anyone else. Likewise, many white miners in the Knights of Labor came to reconsider their assumption that African Americans could not be trusted as allies. "The Knights of Labor in Alabama have had but little cause for complaint against the colored Assemblies," the *Sentinel* observed in late 1887, "much less than was feared by some of our white brothers."

The UMW, too, was enlivened by a genuine bond among black and white miners, a solidarity fostered by the experience of labor conflict. The union press regularly highlighted such moments. The Birmingham *Labor Advocate* celebrated a victorious strike at Corona in 1893 and 1894 as a model of interracial harmony. Reported one miner: "A great many white men will say, 'what are you going to do with the nigger?' Let me tell you something. The best men we have today are negros *[sic]*." Nor did the role of imported black strikebreakers in the devastating defeat of 1894 extinguish the UMW's vision of interracial camaraderie. "I am proud of the white and colored men," wrote a *Labor Advocate* agent fresh from a tour of the coal areas in 1895. "I . . . find a very fraternal feeling between them, which will prove beneficial to both races, if they will only keep getting to know . . . 'that an injury to one is the concern of all'." Such episodes suggest that the willingness of white miners to organize with African American miners, however rooted in self-interest, had opened at least some to experiences that altered their racial attitudes.

Yet as striking as the interracial policies of the Greenbackers, the Knights, and the UMW may have been, each ventured only so far beyond the racial orthodoxies of the New South. Even as they bristled over the operators' manipulation of the color line, all three trimmed their racial strategies to the tenets of segregation and white superiority—a tack that, as with the boldest of their interracial practices, drew upon a fluid mix of self-preservation and true conviction. The ambiguities of labor interracialism surfaced in the structures and practices of the organizations. Although racially divided clubs, assemblies, and locals simply reflected broader patterns in the miners' lives, the color line remained deliberate and pronounced in each group, most visibly in the UMW. The union declined to hold district meetings at halls that barred African Americans, but, within those halls, blacks and whites sat separately; they adjourned from common conventions to attend separate banquets; they marched in the same Labor Day parade but retired to picnic in separate parks. Nor did the union repudiate hierarchies of race in its own leadership. District 20 offices, filled annually by election, were distributed between the two races according to a carefully constructed formula. The office of president was reserved for whites; vice president, for African Americans; secretary-treasurer, for whites. The various committees usually comprised a modest majority of whites. District convention delegations were similarly apportioned by set ratios of black to white members. If the union's interracialism flowed largely from pragmatic concerns, so too did the determination to contain it within a clear racial hierarchy. For example, in 1904, when a convention delegate called for the direct election of officers by the full membership (rather than indirect election by delegates), the district president promptly quashed the notion. Direct vote, he and others cautioned, might lead to the election of a black president, which could only mean the destruction of the union. A black delegate concurred, assuring the gathering that members of his race would oppose the popular vote, not despite, but because African Americans would probably capture all the offices in District 20—and thus doom the union in a Jim Crow environment. . . .

By the turn of the century, the resurgent Alabama UMW had turned virtually mute on political developments, neither contesting nor endorsing the Jim Crow constitution of 1901. Even some black unionists acknowledged that the issue of the franchise lay beyond the ken of organized labor, going so far as to concede, in the tone of Booker T. Washington, that African Americans had been implicated by irresponsible behavior in their own disfranchisement. During the 1904 strike, for instance, Vice President Greer urged the black members to "prove to the white man and the world that we are fit for a union. We have been given the right [to] suffrage, it has been justly said, too soon. It was taken away from us because some of us sold our votes for $1. Let us not throw away our union birthright." By the early 1900s, then, District 20's support for racial inclusion evaporated in the sphere of politics, where the color line appeared less offensive or less disruptive or more unassailable than in other areas of the miners' struggle.

Throughout the ups and downs of the Greenback-Labor party, the Knights of Labor, and the United Mine Workers, the outer confines and inner contradictions in the cooperation between black and white miners—an indissoluble blend of genuine sentiment and self-protective savvy—had a mixed effect upon the fortunes of organized labor. By limiting the reach and diluting the potency of labor interracialism, these constraints simultaneously blunted the movement's threat to the broader racial order and gained it greater room in which to operate. The clashing imperatives of labor unity and white supremacy yielded an interracialism that was highly qualified, often cramped, and at times severely circumscribed. . . .

The foregoing has illustrated how three overlapping concerns—self-interest, solidarity, and an inclination to accommodate or embrace as well as to challenge white supremacy—converged to shape and explain the interracialism of the Greenbackers, the Knights of Labor, and the United Mine Workers. Precisely because of their explanatory power, these concerns have obscured another factor that could figure in the persistence of interracial unionism in the New South: the gender composition of the labor force.

In contrast to most areas of the mining community, the mines themselves were an exclusively male environment. As in many other contemporary trades, women had no presence at any stage in the production process. To the miner's wife fell the myriad tasks of social reproduction: bearing and rearing children, cooking, cleaning, washing clothes, tending gardens and livestock, and the like. But this division of labor only began to suggest the masculine character of coal mining. Dark, grimy, arduous, and always dangerous, mining encompassed qualities popularly associated with the burdens of manhood. The mine constituted nothing less than a subterranean world unto itself; in few followings were these "masculine" features so powerfully concentrated or was the absence of women so pronounced or jealously guarded. If women had no place in the steel mills, on the docks, or at the construction sites of industrializing America, their presence was literally taboo in the coal mines. Miners' unions reflected this reality: they were essentially male institutions—although, notably, less so during major strikes, when they expanded more fully into community enterprises.

The absence of women from the mines and their marginal place in labor organization served quietly, but significantly, to open up space for an interracial labor movement in the constraining environment of Jim Crow. The drive toward segregation was, after all, steeped in notions of gender. Lurking beneath fevered allusions to "social equality" were the frightful images of miscegenation, amalgamation, the despoiling of cherished white womanhood. "Nowhere were the ethics of living Jim Crow more subtle and treacherous," Jacquelyn Dowd Hall observes, "than when they touched on the proper conduct of black men toward white women. . . . Any transgression of the caste system was a step toward 'social equality'; and social equality, with its connotations of personal intimacy, could end only in interracial sex." The specter of social equality cannot be reduced entirely to sexual imagery, for it was defined in numerous ways and invoked in diverse settings. Yet sexual associations lent the term its deepest emotional power. "Sex was the whip," Nell Irvin Painter writes, "that white supremacists used to reinforce white solidarity. . . ." Indeed, the singular power of the social equality charge flowed from its formidable capacity to link African American empowerment and interracial activity in wide-ranging endeavors—schooling, worship, casual recreation, political campaigns, social movements—to the lurid imagery of interracial sex. The admission of blacks into the white section of a theater, a Charleston newspaper noted crisply in 1886, "points unquestionably to social equality. Social equality means miscegenation." While this fear cannot on its own, of course, explain the spread of Jim Crow, it did serve to reinforce the segregation impulse, to embarrass any tendency towards racial mixing in the social world, to render it intolerable, even unimaginable. In the words of Neil McMillen, "the injunction against 'amalgamation' " was "the first law of white supremacy."

"The more closely linked to sexuality," Edward Ayers has observed, "the more likely was a place to be segregated." The critical link between racial separation and the sanctity of white womanhood lost much of its resonance in the coal mines, where women, black and white, were decidedly absent. Thus, the spectacle of black and white miners collaborating in labor organizations, though disquieting to many, did not so readily agitate the wellsprings of segregationist sentiment as, for example, did blacks and whites attending the same churches or schools. . . .

The miners' associations and their adversaries both sensed the connection between gender and interracial unionism, and so it became a terrain of battle. Increasingly during this period, and most especially during peaks of conflict, opponents of labor organization sought to inject the race issue into public consciousness to the acute discomfort of organized labor, which knew that whenever race overshadowed other issues, the union was at a disadvantage. In turn, gender-based imagery became the device through which the opponents of unionism sought most tenaciously to rivet public attention upon the union's interracial character. Overheated charges that miners' unions were agents of social equality—which the Birmingham *News* opined in 1904 could be tolerated only by "cranks, freaks, enthusiasts, and mis-guided people"—were the most ritualistic expression of this tactic. "It is a lamenta-ble condition," the *Age-Herald* declared in representative fashion during the 1908 strike, "that incites and permits ignorant negro leaders to address assemblies of white women and children as social equals, advising as to moral and social questions. . . ."

In their determination to shake the charge [of social equality], UMW advocates sought to cast their movement in narrowly economic terms. The cause of the UMW, White testily insisted, was merely "an industrial one." However real the tone of irri-tation and however obligatory the disclaimer, such defenses had a bloodless, disin-genuous ring. The UMW was never, after all, a purely bread-and-butter or workplace-centered association. "No less than" their husbands, the women in the coal towns "worked in the all-pervasive atmosphere of the coal company and its su-perintendent," Priscilla Long has noted. The breadth of concerns that the union addressed, from mine safety to company stores, from wages to housing, expanded its scope into the wider community. So too did the UMW's almost evangelical promotion of mutualistic and egalitarian values—a sweeping moral vision that en-dowed the union with a status approaching what Herbert Gutman described as a "secular church." Never did the union emerge more fully as a community institution than during major strikes. The mass evictions of miners' families, the provocative intrusion of troops and company guards, the integral roles of both women and men in confronting strikebreakers and sustaining the morale and material livelihood of the community—these developments turned labor battles into broad-based, social struggles. Even though the union was centered in the all-male arena of work and its activities were primarily conducted by the miners themselves, its significance dur-ing labor conflicts inevitably embraced the broader community. The UMW's ex-pansive presence in the mining towns during strikes certainly empowered the miners, but it also left the union open to the public impression that its interracialism meant the social equality of blacks and whites.

The charge of social equality did not, on its own, defeat the Alabama miners in 1908. It was only one weapon in the daunting arsenal available to the operators and their allies—but it was powerful. By inflaming public fears of race-mixing, the alle-gation played a vital, perhaps a pivotal role in breaking the strike. Amid the virulent Jim Crow atmosphere of 1908, the gender-exclusive character of mining could not exempt interracialism from the sexually charged implications of social equality. But for many years the all-male composition of the labor force had allowed blacks and whites more room for shared activity in the union movement than had existed in other areas of their social world.

✢ *F U R T H E R   R E A D I N G*

Edward L. Ayers, *The Promise of the New South* (1992)
Dwight B. Billings, Jr., *Planters and the Making of a "New South"* (1979)
Orville V. Burton and Robert C. McMath, eds., *Toward a New South?* (1982)
David L. Carlton, *Mill and Town in South Carolina, 1880–1920* (1982)
James C. Cobb, *Industrialization and Southern Society, 1877–1984* (1984)

———, "Beyond Planters and Industrialists: A New Perspective on the New South," *Journal of Southern History* 54 (February 1988), 45–68.

John Milton Cooper, Jr., *Walter Hines Page* (1977)

Don H. Doyle, *New Men, New Cities, New South: Atlanta, Nashville, Charleston, Mobile, 1860–1910* (1990)

Paul D. Escott, *Many Excellent People* (1985)

Walter J. Fraser, Jr., and Winfred B. Moore, Jr., eds., *From Old South to New* (1981)

Paul M. Gaston, *The New South Creed* (1973)

David R. Goldfield, *Cotton Fields and Skyscrapers* (1982)

Steven Hahn, *The Roots of Southern Populism* (1983)

Daniel Letwin, *The Challenge of Interracial Unionism* (1997)

Melton A. McLaurin, *Paternalism and Protest* (1971)

———, *The Knights of Labor in the South* (1978)

Broadus Mitchell, *The Rise of Cotton Mills in the South* (1921)

Sydney Nathans, *The Quest for Progress* (1983)

Stephen H. Norwood, "Bogalusa Burning: The War Against Biracial Unionism in the Deep South, 1919," *Journal of Southern History* 63 (August 1997), 591–628

Gail W. O'Brien, *The Legal Fraternity and the Making of a New South Community, 1848–1882* (1986)

Harold L. Platt, *City Building in the New South* (1982)

Howard Rabinowitz, *Race Relations in the Urban South* (1978)

———, *The First New South* (1992)

Crandall A. Shifflett, *Patronage and Poverty in the Tobacco South* (1982)

Laurence Shore, *Southern Capitalists* (1986)

Bryant Simon, *A Fabric of Defeat: The Politics of South Carolina Millhands, 1910–1948* (1998)

John F. Stover, *The Railroads of the South, 1865–1900* (1955)

Nannie M. Tilley, *The Bright-Tobacco Industry, 1860–1929* (1948)

Allen Tullis, *Habits of Industry: White Culture and the Transformation of the Carolina Piedmont* (1989)

Peter Wallenstein, *From Slave South to New South* (1987)

Michael Wayne, *The Reshaping of Plantation Society* (1983)

David E. Whisnant, *All That Is Native and Fine: The Politics of Culture in an American Region* (1983)

Jonathan M. Wiener, *Social Origins of the New South* (1978)

C. Vann Woodward, *Origins of the New South* (1951)

Annette Wright, "The Aftermath of the General Textile Strike: Managers and the Workplace at Burlington Mills," *Journal of Southern History* 60 (February 1994), 81–112

Robert H. Zieger, ed., *Southern Labor in Transition* (1997)

C H A P T E R
5

From Redeemers to Populists

At the close of Reconstruction in 1877, white southern men, many of them former Confederates, regained the right to vote in state and national elections, ran for office, and resumed control of the state assemblies; every southern state had a Democratic majority by 1886. The result was an era of political domination known as Redemption; its followers were called Redeemers, Bourbons, or Conservatives. They created a solidly Democratic South, or the "Solid South." State after state rewrote its constitution, instituted low taxes, and provided minimal government services. Development of industry at the expense of workers' needs stole the attention of most politicians, who remained comparatively unresponsive to farmers, industrial laborers, and African Americans. There were episodic attempts to overthrow the Redeemers: the Virginia Readjusters, the Greenbackers, and the Knights of Labor had enthusiastic followings. Finally by the late 1880s, harsh economic conditions— worldwide overproduction of cotton, falling prices for farm products, the crop lien and sharecropping systems, scarcity of capital, and abuses of the convict leasing system—accompanied by a sense of political impotence led to a massive political upheaval called the Populist movement. It had begun with the Grange, a farmers' educational and social organization, and had continued with the rise of the National Farmers' Alliance, the Colored National Farmers' Alliance, and, eventually, the Southern Alliance. Finally, the movement culminated in the creation of the People's party, a third party that by 1892 had a political platform and millions of voting followers.

The Populists demanded far-reaching changes in the nation's monetary system and thereby frightened both bankers and leaders of the New South's budding industries. Finding the Democratic party unsupportive, the Populists demanded greater democracy in the political system and began courting the votes of black southerners. This step brought racial issues to center stage, and as a result the battles over Populism involved not only economic questions but also an alleged threat to white supremacy and fears of a return to "black rule."

Historians continue to debate these questions: How did the South become the "Solid South"? Who benefited from Conservatives' gains? Were the Populists radicals or would-be capitalists seeking needed economic reforms? Why did their movement create such deep divisions in southern society? Why did Populism ultimately fail? What were the consequences for farmers, laborers, and African Americans in the South?

Farmers' Alliances provided men, women, and children isolated on farms with opportunities for social contact as well as political strategizing. Document 1, a series of letters from Texas women to the *Southern Mercury,* describes Alliance encampments where recreation followed politics. Talk of political reform led to discussions of women's rights and gender roles as seen from the perspective of farm women. A wellspring of Populist strength was the suffering and frustration of thousands of southern farmers, many of whom were in debt and had lost or feared losing their land. Their pent-up anger is conveyed in Document 2, containing selections from letters of North Carolina farmers to a state agency explaining the reasons for farmers' poor conditions. The political demands and program of the Populist party are summarized in the Ocala platform, Document 3. Note its proposal for a subtreasury system and changes in the nation's money supply. Georgia's Tom Watson, the most prominent Populist leader in the South, described the problems of southern farmers in an article in the *Arena,* a national magazine. By then the nation was experiencing a debilitating depression with 20 percent unemployment. His strategy for relief called for political cooperation across racial lines, which became highly controversial. The selections from his article reprinted as Document 4 provide clues to the extent and limit of racial tolerance among Populists. The Populist economic doctrines came under attack, but Democrats more often focused on white supremacy and the need to dominate blacks in the South. Document 5 reveals a Populist speaker's maneuvering around the racial issue in 1898, when the Populists were in decline and the Democrats' white supremacy campaign in North Carolina was gaining ground.

1. Letters from Alliance Women in Texas, 1888

An Alliance Encampment

July 31, 1888. Americus, Marion County. Mrs. V.A. Taylor.

EDITOR MERCURY: Variety is the spice of life so I concluded this time to send you a short letter describing the events of last Saturday, viewed through the spectacles of an Alliance picnicker (to wit, myself).

First there was the hurry and bustle of the morning's packing provisions, placing baskets and children in the wagon so as to consume as little space as possible for we must take in friends on the way until we are pretty thoroughly jammed. No inconvenience I assure you however for our sub-Alliance which had been invited to join the Lasater Alliance in a day of general boom, fun and frolic must be well represented, hence the cram in all available vehicles. A drive of eight miles over rough roads, under a blazing sun did not in the least damp the ardor and enthusiasm and we arrived there with keen zest for the enjoyments of the day, meeting old friends and forming of new acquaintances under the auspices of being united in fraternal love.

I look upon this Alliance movement as the most potent abettor of Christianity that was ever originated, but hold! I am not going to moralize just now. The

"Women in the Texas Populist Movement: Letters to the Southern Mercury," by M. K. Barthelme. Published by Texas A & M University Press, 1997.

program of the day was first music; second, essay on the principles, aims and possibilities of the Alliance, by your scribe; third, lecture by Bro. Macready who was sent to us by Dr. [C.W] Macune; and I have only to say if the Dr. is as successful in running that Exchange as he is in getting hold of good material for speeches, it is bound to succeed; fourth, dinner, and that in quality and quantity all that could be desired. After dinner, music, then as he expressed it a sort of "fill up the time talk" by Bro. D. R. Hale, but let me whisper in your ear that those are the kind of "fill up talks" it pays one to listen to. His happy hits and telling anecdotes fill us with mirth and enjoyment while his unlimited zeal fires us with enthusiasm for the cause. Next, short speeches from the candidates for county office and there seemed to be less palaver this year than ever before. I believe that class of office-seeker is becoming extinct or do not dare to show themselves among Alliance people.

Toward the end, I allowed certain side issues, viz. music and dancing, to divert my attention from the graver questions of the day, but I had an excuse. I took my little ones where for the first time they might behold displays of the terpsichorean art; not that I cared to witness, oh no (?) but like school teachers and preachers who have to carry the little ones to circuses and menageries, sacrificed my wishes in order to please and interest the children.

The sinking sun reminded us of the weary miles we had to plod upon our homeward way and bidding goodbye to friends departed with the kindest of feelings in our hearts, our loyalty to the Alliance strengthened.

Defending the Woman's Sphere

July 31, 1888. Bexar County. Corn Bread.

EDITOR MERCURY: I have seen so much said about "woman's rights" I thought I would beg admittance to you, dear paper, to say a few words. Although I have not been one of you, yet I feel a deep interest in all you do; for does not a vow which is made before the high heavens bind us? We are the housewives, the makers of the home, and the home makes the nation. It puts me all out of patience to hear some of the ladies talk about their "woman's rights." How can any true wife and mother walk up to the polls on election day amid a crowd of gaping men, perhaps some of them drunk and some of them using slang. I don't mean all when I say some. You have no right to do such a thing, dear ladies, that is your husbands' and brothers' and fathers' business, not yours. Then you must know that if you are to be a man's equal in these things you must help to make the living. My husband is a farmer and I think I would much rather be a housewife than be a "woman's rights" woman: not that I do not believe in us all having our rights; if you only knew it, we have more rights than a man has, "the housewife makes the home and the home makes the nation."

Dear ladies, are you not the counselor of all your household? Do you not know why your husbands object to your going to the polls? It is because as a masculine woman you are no longer the dear little girl whom he promised to love, honor and cherish. Be contented as we are and make the home pure (if the men can't make the laws so) and stand by them. The ladies had better keep out of politics.

First Mention of Frances Willard, Advocate of Temperance and Suffrage; First Letter from Ann Other

May 31, 1888. Ennis, Texas. Ann Other.

WHERE SHALL WE LOOK FOR HELP?

EDITOR MERCURY: As we are searching for facts on this subject, and I sincerely believe that none of us are writing for argument's sake, let us look candidly on the matter and sift each point, and try to give fair and unprejudiced opinion on the arguments. . . . Now, sister Rebeca *[sic],* . . .

You class the decline of patriotism with the rise of the popularity of universal suffrage and "woman neglecting her duty in her proper sphere." Now will someone kindly tell me what is her proper sphere? I have always heard the expression, but have failed to locate it by any series of studies I have taken up. I am obliged to conclude it is whatever the state of society dictates to her.

Men have intruded and wrestled from her what were formerly her legitimate occupations. And her present effort is only to recover a useful sphere in life by those who have become weary for others to do that which God intended she should do for herself.

Women used to be our bakers, brewers, dry-salters, butter-makers, cooks, dressmakers, cheese-makers, confectioners, jam and jelly makers, pickle makers, soap makers, spinners, weavers, sock makers, lace makers, embroiders, and mid-wives. Thus crowded out of her old fields of labor by men's intrusion and invention, she must either accept a life of idleness, and be satisfied with such as her brothers see proper to give her, or she must demand a more useful and energetic life. . . .

Have you not seen Frances E. Willard's address before the senate committee? For fear you have not, I will quote a little from it: "I suppose these honorable gentlemen think that we women want the earth, when we only want one half of it. Our brethren have encroached upon the sphere of women. They have very definitely marked out that sphere and then they have proceeded with their incursions by the power of invention, so that we women, full of vigor and full of desire to be active and useful and to react upon the world around us, finding our industries largely gone, have been obliged to seek out new territory and to preempt from the sphere of our brothers, as it was popularly supposed to be, some of the territory that they have hitherto considered their own. So we think it will be very desirable indeed that you should let us lend a hand in their affairs of government." It is said that if women are given the right to vote, it will prevent their being womanly; how it is a sentiment of chivalry in some good men that hinders them from giving us the ballot. They think we should not be lacking in womanliness of character, which we most certainly wish to preserve but we believe that history proves they have retained that womanliness, and if we can only make men believe that, the ballot will just come along sailing like a ship with the wind beating every sail.

2. Farmers Describe the Crisis, 1890s

Remarks.—The average farmer in our county, under existing circumstances, cannot make much money over his living. Wages are low, but on account of the scarcity of money the farmer can't afford to give better wages. I think that we need—that the times imperatively demand—a greater volume of circulating currency. I am nearly eighty-four years old and have seen such a great scarcity of money but twice; when Andrew Jackson vetoed the National Bank bill and during the great negro speculation; but those depressions did not last so long.

Remarks.—Owing to the low price of products the farmers are behindhand. We think the trouble lies in our financial system. With a better system of finance than we have, and with the push and energy that our farmers have, they would certainly overcome all their troubles in a few years. But there will have to be changes in the policy of our National Government before we get much relief. The Farmers' Alliance is doing a grand work on this line.

Remarks.—The farmers in my vicinity are much rejoiced at the result of their labor for 1890. Cotton crops are especially good, but, as the results of bad legislation, the cotton, in many instances, will have to be sold for less than the cost of production, caused principally by an insufficient circulation of money to purchase the agricultural products. . . .

Remarks.—The cotton crop is above an average; it is the best that has been made in this township since I have been farming (or in ten years). I think the greatest evil that exists in this county is the high rate of interest. It is that that makes the poor poorer and the rich richer. We have to pay eight per cent. per annum and a premium of ten per cent. in advance, making eighteen per cent. per annum. The average farmer is poorer than he was ten years ago, and getting poorer every year. I think the next Legislature ought to fix the rate of interest at about five or six per cent., and make it a misdemeanor to charge any more.

Remarks.—The present debts heavily oppress the people. In fact many are forced to give a mortgage or crop lien at the beginning of the year. We have reached a crisis when many cannot run a farm without first pledging it as security for supplies. Do away with the National Banks and abolish all trusts and combines with the abolition of the tariff, and give us the Sub-Treasury Bill; it would afford much relief. . . .

Remarks.—. . . Our people are not only not prosperous, but are growing poorer as the years go by. Not a man in all my knowledge is making a dollar to lay up for the future or to enlarge his operations. With farmer and mechanic it is a *pull for life*. Farm laborers get poor wages, because the farmer owning the land and hiring labor is not in condition to pay good wages, and laborers are, for the same reason, not regularly employed, but are strolling over the country a large part of the time looking for work. Scarcely any progress is made on farms, and for these reasons the ne-

These documents can be found in the Fourth Annual Report of the Bureau of Labor Statistics of the State of North Carolina, John C. Scarborough, Commissioner, 1890; the Fifth Annual Report of the Bureau of Labor Statistics of the State of North Carolina, John C. Scarborough, Commissioner, 1891; and in the Tenth Annual Report of the Bureau of Labor Statistics of the State of North Carolina, B. R. Lacy, Commissioner, 1896.

groes, who constitute the bulk of our farm laborers, are being driven, from necessity, to leave the State in large numbers. This is to our hurt. If hands could be employed regularly the year round it would be to the great advantage of farmers and laborers. With all this, I think there are not so many mortgages given now as for the past few years.

What is to become of the country under these conditions I cannot imagine. Farming is the great "king-wheel" which moves every other branch of business when it moves easily and prosperously. Without success and prosperity in farming, no prosperity can come to other business in our section of this country. . . .

Remarks.—Farming pays in this country; but, on account of high interest and scarcity of money, it pays the wrong man. We are oppressed with debt, time prices and high interest. These hinder business of every kind. Manufactured articles are kept up to usual prices, while the products of farm labor drop lower every year. The need of more money in circulation is felt by the farmers all over the country. . . .

Remarks.—Times here are very close in money matters. Sometimes they are higher, at others lower. I could not sell anything for cash at present. The money men have closed in on us farmers again. I believe in money being worth its value, but I do not believe in it being shut off entirely. What is this done for? Only to make slaves of the farmers. How is this to be remedied—free silver? I think so. Is it to reduce the homestead exemption? I think so. Has it been any benefit to the farmer? I think not. Do our leaders legislate more for the sake of party than for the good of the country? I think the majority do. Is the farmer as honorable as anybody else? I think he is. God made all men equal.

Remarks.—High interest on money is one of our drawbacks. It oppresses the person who borrows it. Great bodies of land owned by one man or company of men is a drawback to our county. Manufacturing ought to be the moneyed men's object, and not the oppression of agriculture. It is demoralizing to the people to take what belongs to man as a gift from God and force men to be tenants or slaves on the soil of a free country. High taxes, big salaries to our county, State and national officers are also demoralizing. Low wages, low prices for produce, and high prices for manufactured goods, handled by many speculators before they reach the consumers, are demoralizing. We want direct trade from the manufacturer to the consumer at the present prices of our produce. More money is needful to make our produce high. Plant peas for manure, sown one to two bushels per acre, and mow down the hay for stock.

Remarks.—. . . Tobacco is our money crop, and since our products are priced before we plant, the future is quite gloomy. Before the American Tobacco Trust was organized we got much better prices, as we raise bright tobacco in this section; but now the price is just half. Farmers are gloomy, and making no money. We hope to see the time when trusts and futures are to be no more. Money is scarce at this time in this section. I have answered the question as near right as I can, trusting you may be successful in helping us.

DEAR SIR:—These are extra hard times. I have been an employer of labor for many years, and never before saw such hard times. I am still giving full time, full employment, and full pay, but the Lord only knows how long it can last. As to what would be best for our working people, I hardly know what to say. If all could have constant work, that would be a splendid help. Thousands are idle, not of their own choice, but they just can't help themselves. I had rather belong to a country where everybody had work, and everybody *had to* work, than have it as it is. Call it socialism or what you please. Damn a country where there is nobody prosperous but the bond-holder and the money-lender. I want all prosperous—*give all work,* and money enough in circulation to pay for it.

Respectfully,

J. S. RAGSDALE.

DEAR SIR:—Owing to legislation in favor of monopolies our lands are gradually slipping from the hands of the wealth-producing classes and going into the hands of the few. I do not believe God ever intended that a few should own the earth, but that each should have a home. But we cannot take the lands from the rich and give to the poor; no, but let us have legislation to limit a man's freehold, and all that he may own over and above that the law limits him to levy a special tax, something of the nature of an income tax, on it. By this means we could have a revenue for our State that would enable us to educate the children of the State. Three-fourths of our population are tenants, and are not able to buy land at present prices; they are the men who create the wealth and pay the taxes. Let us have legislation that will do justice to all, protect all, and that will bless us as a nation.

Respectfully,

J. A. WILSON.

3. The Ocala Platform, 1890

Proceedings of the Supreme Council of the National Farmers' Alliance and Industrial Union

1. a. We demand the abolition of national banks.

   b. We demand that the government shall establish sub-treasuries or depositories in the several states, which shall loan money direct to the people at a low rate of interest, not to exceed two per cent per annum, on nonperishable farm products, and also upon real estate, with proper limitations upon the quantity of land and amount of money.

   c. We demand that the amount of the circulating medium be speedily increased to not less than $50 per capita.

2. We demand that Congress shall pass such laws as will effectually prevent the dealing in futures of all agricultural and mechanical productions; providing a stringent system of procedure in trials that will secure the prompt conviction, and imposing such penalties as shall secure the most perfect compliance with the law.

3. We condemn the silver bill recently passed by Congress, and demand in lieu thereof the free and unlimited coinage of silver.

This document can be found in Henry Steele Commager, *Documents of American History,* 4/e, vol. II, pp. 142–143. Copyright © 1948 Appleton-Century-Crofts, Inc.

4. We demand the passage of laws prohibiting alien ownership of land, and that Congress take prompt action to devise some plan to obtain all lands now owned by aliens and foreign syndicates; and that all lands now held by railroads and other corporations in excess of such as is actually used and needed by them be reclaimed by the government and held for actual settlers only.

5. Believing in the doctrine of equal rights to all and special privileges to none, we demand—

a. That our national legislation shall be so framed in the future as not to build up one industry at the expense of another.

b. We further demand a removal of the existing heavy tariff tax from the necessities of life, that the poor of our land must have.

c. We further demand a just and equitable system of graduated tax on incomes.

d. We believe that the money of the country should be kept as much as possible in the hands of the people, and hence we demand that all national and state revenues shall be limited to the necessary expenses of the government economically and honestly administered.

6. We demand the most rigid, honest, and just state and national government control and supervision of the means of public communication and transportation, and if this control and supervision does not remove the abuse now existing, we demand the government ownership of such means of communication and transportation.

7. We demand that the Congress of the United States submit an amendment to the Constitution providing for the election of United States Senators by direct vote of the people of each state.

4. Tom Watson's Strategy, 1892

Having given this subject much anxious thought, my opinion is that the future happiness of the two races will never be assured until the political motives which drive them asunder, into two distinct and hostile factions, can be removed. There must be a new policy inaugurated, whose purpose is to allay the passions and prejudices of race conflict, and which makes its appeal to the sober sense and honest judgment of the citizen regardless of his color.

To the success of this policy two things are indispensable—a common necessity acting upon both races, and a common benefit assured to both—without injury or humiliation to either.

The white people of the South will never support the Republican Party. This much is certain. The black people of the South will never support the Democratic Party. This is equally certain.

Hence, at the very beginning, we are met by the necessity of new political alliances. As long as the whites remain solidly Democratic, the blacks will remain solidly Republican.

As long as there was no choice, except as between the Democrats and the Republicans, the situation of the two races was bound to be one of antagonism. The

This document can be found in Thomas E. Watson, "The Negro Question in the South," *Arena,* 1892, vol. VI, p. 548.

Republican Party represented everything which was hateful to the whites; the Democratic Party, everything which was hateful to the blacks.

Therefore a new party was absolutely necessary. It has come, and it is doing its work with marvellous rapidity.

Why does a Southern Democrat leave his party and come to ours?

Because his industrial condition is pitiably bad; because he struggles against a system of laws which have almost filled him with despair; because he is told that he is without clothing because he produces too much cotton, and without food because corn is too plentiful; because he sees everybody growing rich off the products of labor except the laborer; because the millionnaires who manage the Democratic Party have contemptuously ignored his plea for a redress of grievances and have nothing to say to him beyond the cheerful advice to "work harder and live closer."

Why has this man joined the PEOPLE'S PARTY? Because the same grievances have been presented to the Republicans by the farmer of the West, and the millionnaires who control that party have replied to the petition with the soothing counsel that the Republican farmer of the West should "work more and talk less."

Therefore, if he were confined to a choice between the two old parties, the question would merely be (on these issues) whether the pot were larger than the kettle—the color of both being precisely the same.

The key to the new political movement called the People's Party has been that the Democratic farmer was as ready to leave the Democratic ranks as the Republican farmer was to leave the Republican ranks. . . .

The very same principle governs the race question in the South. The two races can never act together permanently, harmoniously, beneficially, till each race demonstrates to the other a readiness to leave old party affiliations and to form new ones, based upon the profound conviction that, in acting together, both races are seeking new laws which will benefit both. On no other basis under heaven can the "Negro Question" be solved.

Now, suppose that the colored man were educated upon these questions just as the whites have been; suppose he were shown that his poverty and distress came from the same sources as ours; suppose we should convince him that our platform principles assure him an escape from the ills he now suffers, and guarantee him the fair measure of prosperity his labor entitles him to receive,—would he not act just as the white Democrat who joined us did? Would he not abandon a party which ignores him as a farmer and laborer; which offers him no benefits of an equal and just financial system; which promises him no relief from oppressive taxation; which assures him of no legislation which will enable him to obtain a fair price for his produce?

Granting to him the same selfishness common to us all; granting him the intelligence to know what is best for him and the desire to attain it, why would he not act from that motive just as the white farmer has done?

That he would do so, is as certain as any future event can be made. Gratitude may fail; so may sympathy and friendship and generosity and patriotism; but in the long run, self-interest *always* controls. Let it once appear plainly that it is to the interest of a colored man to vote with the white man, and he will do it. Let it plainly appear that it is to the interest of the white man that the vote of the Negro should supplement his own, and the question of having that ballot freely cast and fairly counted, becomes vital to the *white man*. He will see that it is done. . . .

Let the colored laborer realize that our platform gives him a better guaranty for political independence; for a fair return for his work; a better chance to buy a home and keep it; a better chance to educate his children and see them profitably employed; a better chance to have public life freed from race collisions; a better chance for every citizen to be considered as a *citizen* regardless of color in the making and enforcing of laws,—let all this be fully realized, and the race question at the South will have settled itself through the evolution of a political movement in which both whites and blacks recognize their surest way out of wretchedness into comfort and independence. . . .

The conclusion, then, seems to me to be this: the crushing burdens which now oppress both races in the South will cause each to make an effort to cast them off. They will see a similarity of cause and a similarity of remedy. They will recognize that each should help the other in the work of repealing bad laws and enacting good ones. They will become political allies, and neither can injure the other without weakening both. It will be to the interest of both that each should have justice. And on these broad lines of mutual interest, mutual forbearance, and mutual support the present will be made the stepping-stone to future peace and prosperity.

5. A Populist Speaker Responds, 1898

[In 1896 the Democrats] said "silver! silver! silver!" and on every breeze and every lip it was silver from every Democratic tongue. They ran that campaign on National issues. Why don't they do it again? Silver is just as urgent an issue now as it was then, certainly so far as Congressmen are concerned. No, they go back to their old cry and say "the white metal and the white man," but they don't say much about the white metal. You can pick up Democratic papers and there is nothing about silver or William J. Bryan in them. They have left it off, and it is just "nigger! nigger! nigger!" forevermore. That is all the politics the Democratic party has in the State now; it is all they had prior to 1896, and they took silver up then because they saw the rank and file of their party would leave them and come to the Peoples Party if they did otherwise. Is there a prominent Democrat here who does not believe that? Why, he knows I am telling the living truth; they all know I am telling the truth. . . .

I saw yesterday morning the Raleigh News and Observer. It had a cartoon in it—a picture you know, of Jim young "a negro politician in Raleigh bossing things at the Blind Asylum" in the city of Raleigh. The Democratic party dares not go before the people of North Carolina on any issue of politics and state its belief upon these issues. It therefore howls "nigger." What has Jim Young got to do with the blind institution in the city of Raleigh? Is he on the board? Not at all. There is not a negro on any institutional board in North Carolina except [institutions] for neg[r]oes, and has not been for a matter of some months, with the single exception of a colored man by the name of Peace on the board of penitentiary directors. In the name of common sense and human suffering, is there no question in North Carolina but the question of "negro?" Is that all; and will the Democratic party persist in it

"Dr. Thompson's Great Speech" taken from the Torrance-Banks Family Papers, Special Collections, Atkins Library, The University of North Carolina at Charlotte.

and insult the intelligence of men and make light of the poverty of the people by injecting this as the one issue in their campaign? . . .

And that is not all. Let's look a little further. You have heard Democrats talk about the town of Greenville having a negro policeman. Well, let's see. There is one there. How did he get there? The town has four colored and two white councilmen. Two of the colored councilmen proposed to elect Mr. Cherry, a white Republican policeman, if Mr. Blow, the Democratic County Chairman, Mr. Jarvis' law partner, and Mr. Brown, the other white co[u]ncilman would vote with them. Blow and Brown refused to do it, so the four negroes voted together and elected a negro. Who is responsible for the negro's election? Blow could have prevented it. They could have prevented it if they had wanted to, but they did not want to prevent it. They wanted it for campaign thunder. Well, was that anything out of the way for them to have a negro policeman in the town of Greenville? As far back as 1878, when the town was Democratic, they always elected William Hamahan a negro, for one policeman, and a white man for the other, and in the case of big crowds, when they had to appoint special policemen, they always appointed as many negroes as whites. . . .

You remember the campaign of 1876 was largely upon the issue of "nigger." It was then the cry of negro equality. Now it is the cry of "negro domination." I state here that the Democratic party does not desire to rid itself of the negro in politics. When the Democratic party in North Carolina removes the negro from politics in North Carolina, the Democratic party goes out of existance in North Carolina. If they had desired to get rid of the negro as a disturbing factor in North Carolina, they acquired the power of 1876, when, contrary to all of their professions upon the stump, and their denunciations of the Republican party for putting negroes in office in North Carolina, they proceeded to elect negro magistrates in New Hanover, in Craven and in other counties in the State. They had it in their power to remove the negro from politics from that day until 1895, and yet they left him for the purpose of future campaigns. When they fail of the negro issue in North Carolina, what issue will the Democratic party have?

Why, when Peg-leg Williams in the days of negro exodus was carrying thousands of negroes out of the State of North Carolina, it was a Democratic legislature that rose up and passed a law stopping the business under a penalty of a thousand dollars. I have heard it said that our friend Captain Kitchen felt so outraged at the lessening of the negro population in the county of Halifax that he assaulted poor old Peg-leg Williams who was carrying his thousands further South.

I continue this charge against the Democratic party. It has always howled the nigger, and yet it has given the negro office when it could, notwithstanding its howl. . . .

[Democrats] are the men in North Carolina who have their quiet conferences with negroes, and openly in their public prints say to the negroes, "you do a majority of the voting; therefore you are entitled to a majority of the offices of your party; demand them!" I read this advice in a paper published over here in Dunn, in the same issue of which I found also an appeal for the formation of white supremacy clubs to beat back the waves of negro domination.

What hypocrits these Democrats be. It is astonishing to me that God Himself lets them live. It is a wonder he does not start out and blast them for their hypocrisy.

✣ E S S A Y S

In the first essay, Dewey W. Grantham emphasizes the role of the Redeemers, who, once in office, created a South so forceful in its solidarity that the fundamental political structure of society did not change for seventy-five years. The Republican party, the Readjusters within the Democratic party of Virginia, the Farmers' Alliances, and the Populist party in the South all proved that important opposition existed, but the strength of the Democratic party was in the creation of a white cultural and political identity, a *Herrenvolk* democracy, which used the ideological struggles of the Lost Cause to prevail against all opposing forces. Edward L. Ayers, in the second essay, shows the difficulties inherent in maintaining cooperation between the black and white Alliances and the subsequent challenge presented by the issue of race in forming the Populist party. He suggests, however, that race relations during hard economic times could be fluid, allowing for political alliances based on class rather than on race. In the end, the Populist party, he writes, was constructed on ideals of economic opportunity and American democracy.

Forging the Solid South

DEWEY W. GRANTHAM

The political solidarity of the twentieth-century South originated in the great sectional conflict of the nineteenth century. In the 1850s a virulent southern sectionalism destroyed the existing party system and created a powerful compulsion toward political consensus in the South. The Civil War itself heightened southern self-consciousness and increased the social solidarity of the region's white inhabitants, despite the divisions and enmities it brought to the surface. "Out of that ordeal by fire," wrote Wilbur J. Cash, "the masses had brought, not only a great body of memories in common with the master class, but a deep affection for these captains, a profound trust in them, a pride which was inextricably intertwined with the commoners' pride in themselves." In the long run, the war did little to undermine the South's political autonomy. As the historian Roy F. Nichols once observed, "Did not the South by its war experience insure what it sought, an autonomy within the nation and a political power which enables it at times, as now, for all practical purposes to control national legislation?"

As a matter of fact, southern white unity was more apparent after the war than it had been during that drawn-out conflict. The divisions over secession were a source of continuing irritation and bitterness among southerners, and during the war years islands of disaffection developed in various parts of the Confederacy. The new government was never able to institute effective political machinery within its jurisdiction. Appomattox had surrendered Robert E. Lee's armies but not the southern cause. . . . The Confederate flag and "Dixie" became strong unifying symbols for most white southerners. Outside the South, of course, the war strengthened the bonds of loyalty to the Republican party. Not surprisingly, the war and its turbulent aftermath infused the nation's politics with sectional appeals and helped perpetuate the sectional alignment of party politics that had developed in the 1850s.

Reconstruction was no less important in the forging of the Solid South. Several developments of that era encouraged political competition in the southern states, and it is conceivable that the process of reconstruction could have contributed to a more rational and enduring political division among white southerners. With the collapse of the Confederacy, for example, many of the South's old Whigs assumed an important role in postwar politics. While this Whiggish element was usually identified with southern interests, it had little liking for Democrats, who had led the section into war. A much greater challenge to southern Democrats came with the organization of the Republican party throughout the South following the inauguration of Congressional Reconstruction in 1867. This brought the enfranchisement of perhaps a million freedmen, virtually all of whom became Republicans, and the formation of political coalitions in every southern state made up of blacks, "carpetbaggers," and "scalawags." Something like a fifth of the southern whites were included in these Republican coalitions.

Most white southerners feared and resented the basic features of Radical Reconstruction, which they viewed as the source of harsh and vindictive policies, of Republican abuse and corruption, and of black effrontery and southern privation. Southern Democrats set about uniting as many whites as possible in the party of opposition. They made use of economic pressure and social ostracism, chicanery and fraud, intimidation and violence, and a shrewd campaign of racial propaganda, as well as more traditional political appeals. These techniques soon proved effective. One reason was the continuing prestige of the old, experienced ruling class in the South. Another factor was the inability of the southern Whigs to retain their identity as a separate group. The Whigs differed among themselves as to policy, and their efforts to secure a moderate reconstruction program received curiously little support from conservative Republicans in the North. Many of them were ultimately driven by their frustration into the arms of the Democrats, whose policies they had so often condemned in earlier years. Radical Republican policies and the blandishments of the Democrats (who resorted to the term *conservative* in some states as a gesture of conciliation toward the Whigs) eventually destroyed the Whigs as a clearly recognizable entity in southern politics, while enhancing the reputation of the Democrats among white southerners generally. The economic plight of the postwar South—its wartime losses and its poverty, one-crop economy, and shortage of money—also played into the hands of the Democrats. . . .

The political hegemony of the conservative Democrats who redeemed the South from Radical Reconstruction was formidable. Having restored all of the ex-Confederate states to home rule, southern Democrats moved to liquidate their Republican opposition in the region. The party of Lincoln, Grant, and Hayes steadily lost strength in the South. One of the party's members, Albion W. Tourgée, reported after the election of 1878 that "the Republican party of North Carolina is dead—dead beyond hope of resuscitation or resurrection!" In the presidential election two years later, the Democrats carried every southern state. The Solid South had emerged in its pristine form, although it would not become a thoroughgoing one-party system for another two decades.

Politics in the southern states from the end of Reconstruction to the early 1890s was dominated by the Redeemers. The original architects of the Solid South, they made an enduring contribution to the character of southern politics in the late nineteenth and early twentieth centuries. The system they inaugurated, while elaborated and perfected by later Democratic leaders, provided the fundamental structure of political solidarity in the region for more than three-quarters of a century. The Redeemers (or Bourbon Democrats) regarded themselves as the "natural leaders" of the South. There was a good deal of truth in this view. The bulk of the section's traditional social and economic leaders, including most men of Whiggish persuasion, was identified with the Democratic party by the late 1870s. A Republican leader in Georgia warned as early as 1868 that recent elections "should teach us as Republicans that it is impossible to maintain the party in this State, or indeed in the South, without a division of the white vote." The Democrats, he conceded, "possess most of the intelligence and wealth of the State, which will always control tenants and laborers."

... One study of 585 former Confederate leaders revealed that no fewer than 418 of them held elective or appointive offices after the war. It was, from the standpoint of the most prestigious political offices, the era of the Confederate brigadier. During the Forty-fifth Congress (1877–79), 77 of 107 members in the House of Representatives from the South had fought in the Confederate armies.

The Redeemers, of course, made good use of the romantic cult of the Lost Cause. They made the most of what David M. Potter has described as a "deeply felt southern nationalism" growing out of "the shared sacrifices, the shared efforts, and the shared defeat" of the war. They helped establish an explicit linkage between Confederate images and religious values, joining with other southerners in making "a religion out of their history." The Redeemers' version of Reconstruction provided another support for political conformity among white southerners. They told a grim story of human suffering and of the southern battle for civilization during Radical Reconstruction. "The slaughter and the sacrifices during our great civil war were terrible indeed," declared Rep. Hilary A. Herbert of Alabama in 1890, "but those dark days were lighted by the shining valor of the patriot soldier; the storm clouds were gilded with glory." In Reconstruction, on the other hand, Herbert could find "nothing but wretchedness and humiliation, and shame, and crime begetting crime. There was no single redeeming feature, except the heroic determination of the better classes in the several states to restore good government." Conservatism, as one scholar has written of postbellum Virginia, "was not only a political party, it was also a social code and a state of mind.". . .

Having redeemed their individual states, Democratic leaders worked hard to maintain white unity and to perpetuate their control. While their tactics varied from state to state, their leadership tended to be oligarchical and conservative. In every southern state, a relatively small number of popular leaders dominated the Democratic party, determined the acceptable candidates for key offices, and decided upon the issues and candidates. The oligarchies moved quickly to secure control of the party organization in their respective states and to make sure that their lieutenants and friends were in charge of the election machinery. The concentration of authority in the hands of governors and legislators enabled these state leaders to appoint important local officials in every county. One of the steps taken by North Carolina Redeemers was to pass a law in 1876 designed to assure white Democratic supremacy throughout the state. It provided that the principal officers in each county would be appointed by justices of the peace, who were themselves to be named by the legislature. Conservative control depended on the popularity of Democratic leaders with white voters, but it also rested upon working alliances between state and local leaders. The latter were often part of what some contemporaries unflatteringly called courthouse "cliques" or "rings." These influential local politicians looked after the interests of the party hierarchy in their towns and counties, particularly the operation of the election system and the selection of local officeholders, including members of the state legislature.

Redeemer dominance was reinforced by an assortment of clever techniques and sharp practices: gerrymandering legislative districts, discriminatory apportionment of seats in party conventions, intricate registration and election laws, and use of fraud and intimidation at the polls. In some cases these New Departure Democrats made use of a kind of "captive black vote" against their opponents, even as they characterized themselves as defenders of white supremacy. Indeed, their use of the race question assumed the quality of a fine art. As one historian says of the situation in Mississippi, conservative Democrats used the black man "unsparingly to crush all incipient revolts against their authority."

Lack of unity among the mass of small farmers and workers also aided the Redeemers. White yeomen in southern Appalachia generally supported the Republican party, as did most blacks throughout the South who continued to vote. The region's exploitative social structure—increasing farm tenancy, the pervasive furnishing system, and the growth of textile mill villages and mining towns—debilitated the political role of more and more small farmers and laborers. Agricultural and industrial workers were the victims of a regional labor market that was shaped by high population growth and isolation from national labor norms and pressures. This condition facilitated the structuring of the work force along the lines desired by the planter-merchant-industrialist interests.

Critics referred to the Redeemers and their successors as "Bourbons," likening them to the reactionary European monarchs who had "learned nothing and forgotten nothing." The term is misleading however, for the southern Bourbons were less inflexible and more innovative than the epithet suggests. "Generally speaking," one historian concludes, "they were innovators in economic matters, moderates in race policy once white supremacy was assured, extremists in politics when their own supremacy was threatened, and profoundly conservative in most matters of social policy." Their control reflected corporate and financial interests, especially those involved in railroad promotion, merchandising, and banking. The state governments under their leadership reduced taxes, starved public service agencies and eleemosynary institutions, and made economy in government a major priority. Yet many of them also advocated railroad subsidies and tax exemptions for new industries.

While proclaiming themselves the guardians of fiscal integrity and of a political climate favorable for economic developers, the Redeemers repudiated much of the Reconstruction debt in the southern states, took part in efforts to regulate railroads and other corporations, and supported appropriations for some state services, particularly to benefit farmers. If the new state constitutions whose drafting and adoption they spearheaded emphasized retrenchment in spending and low ceilings on taxation, they also included restrictions on state aid to private enterprises. Nor were the Bourbon Democrats as honest and fiscally responsible as they pictured themselves. They, too, were guilty in many instances of governmental corruption, financial peculation, and public scandals. Nevertheless, they left a lasting imprint on southern politics and society. Perhaps their greatest contribution was their influence in the cultural sphere—in their efforts to create a united southern people with a distinct cultural identity. Taking advantage of their reputation as natural leaders, they stressed the organic character of white society and appealed to the spirit of "*Herrenvolk* democracy"—a democratic society for whites only. They succeeded in large part because they were regarded as representing the "interests" of a majority of white southerners, who in the early post-Reconstruction years held conventional views on most economic questions and on the proper role of government, who considered race an important aspect of politics, and who were responsive to the pleas for southern white unity.

Although every southern state supported the Democratic presidential ticket in 1880, Republican strength in the South did not decline drastically during the last two decades of the century. Those southerners who belonged to the Grand Old Party in the post-Reconstruction years were largely of two very different and often mutually antagonistic types: the freedmen, who for the most part lived in the low country, and the white inhabitants of the mountainous areas. This Republican coalition of blacks and whites was a powerful political force in the late nineteenth-century South, particularly in Virginia, North Carolina, Kentucky, and Tennessee. But the place of blacks in the party was a divisive issue in southern Republicanism and one that GOP leaders were never able to resolve satisfactorily. "The Republican strategy," one authority observes, "became one of offering their black following just enough to ensure their continued support while emphasizing issues that would attract greater numbers of white voters.". . .

Table 1.   Turnout and Proportion of Adult Males Voting for Each Party in the South in Presidential Elections, 1872–1908

ELECTION	DEMOCRAT	REPUBLICAN	OTHER	TURNOUT
1872	23.35	26.87	0	50.24
1876	38.73	26.70	0	64.94
1880	36.88	23.76	2.90	63.55
1884	37.20	25.70	0.34	62.84
1888	37.94	23.08	1.47	62.49
1892	33.87	14.58	9.71	58.16
1896	33.33	19.83	3.00	56.16
1900	26.54	15.35	1.22	43.10
1904	18.95	8.31	1.35	28.62
1908	19.44	9.58	1.15	30.18

SOURCE: Adapted from J. Morgan Kousser, *The Shaping of Southern Politics: Suffrage Restriction and the Establishment of the One-Party South, 1880–1910* (New Haven: Yale University Press, 1974), p. 12
NOTE: These statistics refer to the eleven ex-Confederate states only.

The persistence of southern Republicanism after 1876 can be attributed in part to GOP efforts at the national level to win support in the region. In an age of extraordinarily close elections, Republican leaders, frequently of Whiggish background and usually conservative in their views, turned naturally enough to their counterparts in the South—to what one Republican politician referred to as "the same class of men in the South as are Republicans in the North"—in seeking to head off radical policies and maintain their control of the national government. Despite the return of home rule and Democratic control, there seemed to be some chance that interparty competition would continue in the South. In the presidential election of 1880, a majority of the black adult males in nine of the eleven ex-Confederate states cast their ballots. The percentage of adult males voting in presidential elections in the South between 1876 and 1896 was as high as 65 percent and never lower than 56 percent.

Seeing the cleavages that divided southern Democrats and recognizing the bankruptcy of their own Reconstruction policies, Republican leaders approached the "southern question" in a growing mood of experimentation. President Hayes, dreaming of a strong Republican party in the South, sought to attract southern conservatives with a generous patronage policy and favorable legislation. As it became more evident that southerners of Whiggish ancestry were finding a comfortable home in the Bourbon Democracy, James A. Garfield and Chester A. Arthur began to encourage independent movements that developed in one southern state after another. Benjamin Harrison attempted to use federal intervention, through the "force bill," to protect the voting rights of blacks and whites in the South. And in the agrarian upheaval of the 1890s, Republican leaders tried to work out successful coalitions with Populists and dissident Democrats.

But success was limited. The most spectacular Republican efforts to perfect coalition politics—in Virginia in the early 1880s and in North Carolina in the 1890s—provoked bitter conflict and recrimination and in the long run diminished the party's strength in the region. Those episodes also revealed the immensity of the obstacles confronting the Republicans. Their party lacked leaders, newspapers, and money in the southern states, and its ranks were torn by recurrent factionalism involving personal rivalry and strife between "black and tan" and "lily-white" groups. "From nearly every Republican county convention," a Tennessee newspaper reported in 1900, "comes the same story: Two conventions, a split and contesting delegations to the state convention." Furthermore, southern whites found the Reconstruction image of Republicanism almost irresistible, and despite the willingness of many GOP leaders to abandon their reliance upon black support, a great many southerners continued to associate the Republican party with fears of Negro domination. Outside the mountainous areas, southern whites were inclined to be contemptuous of Republicans. . . .

Republicans also encountered fraud and intimidation, as well as discriminatory election officials and harshly punitive election laws. Five southern states enacted new poll tax, registration, secret ballot, and other restrictive voting laws between 1889 and 1893. These measures took a heavy toll of black and white voters. Under the circumstances, it was virtually impossible for Republicans to formulate a policy on the national level that would appeal to the enemies of the conservative Democrats in the South and at the same time satisfy powerful GOP interests outside the region. Thus, the overtures President Arthur made to southern independents of a radical stripe proved disquieting to orthodox Republicans. The change of sentiment in the North, reflecting the drift away from Reconstruction idealism as well as the strong influence of business elements in the Republican party, doomed President Harrison's attempt to secure passage of the "force bill." And to complicate matters still further, the very threat of such legislation became an effective weapon in the hands of those who championed white supremacy and the Solid South. . . .

Bourbon leaders were faced, almost from the beginning of their dominance, with intraparty dissension and protest movements that held out the dread possibility of a merger with the Republicans and a transfer of political authority. One of the earliest of these independent movements—and the most significant before the Populist uprising—was the Readjuster campaign in Virginia. This movement was organized in the late 1870s when the state's politics was reshaped on the basis of a struggle between those who insisted upon funding Virginia's large debt and those who demanded its "readjustment." The times were ripe for a political upheaval. The Republican party had been repudiated and was badly disorganized, while the triumphant Redeemers were faced with the problem of guiding an unwieldy party and providing answers to a number of perplexing questions, including the handling of the state debt. Economic conditions were poor, people complained about inequitable taxes, and the schools suffered from inadequate support. Criticism of the conservative Democratic leadership increased, farmers began to see political implications in the Granger movement, and some Virginians were attracted to the inflationary schemes of the Greenbackers. A remarkable political messiah then appeared on the scene to lead the revolt. His name was William Mahone, ex-Confederate general, railroad builder, erstwhile conservative, and political organizer extraordinaire.

The movement that Mahone led reflected the geographic and social composition of Virginia. Realizing the potential influence of an expanded electorate, Mahone appealed directly to the people. The general sought the support of the small white farmers and poorer classes, especially in the western part of the state, and he succeeded in combining those groups with a substantial number of blacks, most of whom lived in the eastern lowlands. The Readjuster leaders were, characteristically, middle-class men on the make who found few opportunities for political distinction in the conservative regime of the Redeemers. The Conservatives, as the Democrats were wont to call themselves, had about them an aura of aristocracy and the Lost Cause, but their fiscal orthodoxy and laissez-faire preachments brought them powerful allies from industrial and urban elements.

Readjuster control lasted only a few years, but it had a pronounced effect on Virginia politics. Capturing the state legislature in 1879, the Readjusters soon dominated every branch of the Virginia government, and at one time they also controlled the two U.S. Senate seats and six seats in the national House of Representatives. They readjusted the state debt, revised the system of taxation, repealed the poll tax, abolished the whipping post, provided liberal appropriations for education, and enacted legislation favorable to labor. At the same time, Mahone created a patronage machine and attempted to combine with the Republicans. The Conservatives, meanwhile, took advantage of Readjuster mistakes and warned loudly of Republican control and black domination. By the mid-1880s, they had redeemed the state from "Mahoneism." But in the process they borrowed some democratic features from the Readjuster program and, like many southern Democrats in the 1890s, sought to broaden their appeal to the white masses.

Although Virginia was the only southern state in which independents wrested control from the Redeemers in the 1880s, almost all of the former Confederate states experienced some degree of independent revolt in the decade following Reconstruction. One measure of this political dissidence is provided by the combined opposition (anti-Democratic) vote in the following gubernatorial elections: North Carolina, 48.7 percent and Georgia, 35.1 percent in 1880; Virginia, 52.8 percent and Mississippi, 40.2 percent in 1881; Texas, 40.5 percent, Alabama, 31.6 percent, and South Carolina, 21 percent in 1882; Tennessee, 48.7 percent, Florida, 46.5 percent, and Louisiana, 32.9 percent in 1884; and Arkansas, 45.9 percent in 1888. Some of this political independence represented conflict over state debts and fiscal policies similar to the controversy in Virginia, although the repudiation or readjustment of Reconstruction debts was generally popular in the South and inextricably connected with the overthrow of Radical rule in most southern states. Opposition to Democratic conservatives frequently developed over such local issues as the unequal division of educational funds, inequitable tax rates, high interest rates, fence laws, business favoritism, the operation of the convict lease system, and local-option elections; but there were widespread charges of machine politics, "ring" rule, and manipulated elections. Dissatisfaction also grew out of the malapportionment of state legislatures and the black belts' use of Negro votes to strengthen their position. The convention system of making nominations and choosing party leaders, moreover, was often linked to the system of representation, which meant that black counties were given delegates far out of proportion to their voting strength. In South Carolina, to take an example given by C. Vann Woodward, "the upland plebeians found they had redeemed the state from the Carpetbaggers only to lose it to the lowland bosses." Yet, as another scholar has written of the situation in North Carolina, "The impulse toward democracy struggled to take form and achieve self-conscious direction; the defense of undemocratic privilege adopted more extreme measures in the face of internal pressure and external shocks."

Independent movements were a real force in the South of the late 1870s and early 1880s. In Georgia an independent campaign elected William H. Felton and Emory L. Speer to Congress but failed in an effort to overturn Bourbon control of the state. In 1878 William M. Lowe was elected to Congress as an independent from a north Alabama district, and in the same year, a Greenback-Labor candidate won a congressional seat in Texas. The Greenbackers made a strong showing in gubernatorial contests in Kentucky, Alabama, and Arkansas during the next two years, and in the early 1880s Democratic politicians reflecting the monetary proposals and economic radicalism of Greenbackism challenged the conservative political control in South Carolina, Texas, and other states. While the Greenback movement failed to obtain a substantial number of votes in most southern states, it mirrored, as did other independent movements of the period, strong dissatisfaction with Redeemer authority as well as the socioeconomic cleavages in southern society that belied the claim of a Solid South.

Yet by the mid-1880s the edge of political insurgency in the South had been blunted. All the old techniques of social and economic pressure perfected in the battles against the Reconstruction Radicals had been employed in ruthless campaigns against party independents. The same methods would be applied even more savagely against Populists in the 1890s. At the same time, the southern economy improved as farm commodity prices increased and as the nation entered into an era of unprecedented railroad construction and industrial expansion. There was a feeling of general satisfaction in the South, moreover, with Grover Cleveland's victory in 1884 and the return of the Democrats to national power early the next year. But the relatively placid years of the mid-1880s were not to last long, and the late 1880s and much of the 1890s witnessed growing agrarian distress, industrial crisis, and political conflict all over the country.

The agrarian revolt marked a decisive stage in the evolution of modern southern politics. While gathering strength from the independent movements and farmer organizations of the 1870s and 1880s, the revolt was fundamentally a protest and a countermovement against the encroachment of modern industrialism upon rural society and rural values. It was a social as well as a political movement. There was, to be sure, a solid basis for the agrarian unrest. Farmers in the South and West for two decades after 1870 had suffered from steadily declining agricultural prices, inequitable taxes, inadequate facilities and high interest charges, a contracting currency, a high tariff on the products they bought, and monopolistic power in business, whether exercised by the middlemen they dealt with firsthand or the railroads and industrial "trusts" somewhat further removed. Nor was that all. During those years farmers frequently experienced a social stagnation and loss of personal dignity and community status that produced widespread despair, resentment, and defiance in the agricultural regions. In the South the situation facing the farmer, especially the millions of small operators and tenants, was even worse since it reflected the postwar revolution that introduced peculiar and regressive arrangements in labor, land tenure, and credit.

Of the numerous agricultural organizations that sprang up in the 1880s, the most important was the National Farmers' Alliance and Industrial Union. Originating in Texas, the Farmers' Alliance spread rapidly through the South in the late 1880s, pulling other farm groups and thousands of unaffiliated farmers into its ranks. By 1890 over a million southerners were members of the Alliance. Among these recruits were farm leaders and substantial landowners as well as small operators. The major source of the organization's popularity was its promise of direct economic relief, particularly through its cooperative program, and the sense of community fostered by its local chapters and activities. It was the Southern Alliance, as it was called, that formulated the economic and political ideas that were soon identified with the People's party and populism. Prominent among these were reform measures looking to currency inflation, government-based credit, land reform, railroad and trust regulation, and democratization of the political process.

Alliances and Populists

EDWARD L. AYERS

The Farmers' Alliance could not avoid the tensions, promises, and dilemmas of the New South. . . .

During the winter of 1891–92, as everyone waited to see what would happen in a long-anticipated convention of reform groups in St. Louis in February, some of the incongruities and impossibilities began to be resolved. Farmers who thought the Alliance had no business even thinking of a third party rushed back to the Democrats. Farmers who considered the subtreasury unconstitutional, too expensive, or politically dangerous dropped out of the Alliance. Farmers who had joined in the hopes of immediate help in the marketplace left as the cooperatives failed. Politicians who had joined the Alliance in the easy days of the late 1880s, when the order asked little of its members, returned to their old party as the stakes got higher.

Those Alliancemen who remained through all these trials made a stronger commitment to the Alliance. Even as the formal Alliance organization lost members in 1891 and 1892, men who had not joined the original movement found themselves attracted by the possibility of a new political party in the South. Even farmers too independent, poor, cheap, isolated, or cynical to join the Farmers' Alliance could and did become excited by the possibilities of a third party in the South. Farmers who lacked the interest or the means to participate in cooperative stores, weekly meetings, theoretical debates, or mass picnics might be engaged by the different sort of emotions and commitments created by an overtly political party. Even men who had originally seen little appeal in the Alliance might well be disgusted at the way the Democrats bullied the opposition in local elections, legislative halls, and newspaper columns in 1891 and 1892. As the Alliance and the Democrats broke into open warfare, many voting farmers watched with mounting interest and excitement.

Black men, balancing an especially precarious set of aspirations and fears, sought to define their place in the movement as well. The Colored Farmers' Alliance had built a formidable organization in the late 1880s with little help from the white Alliance. In the St. Louis convention of 1889 the black Alliance had met separately, though the white Alliance had officially acknowledged the black order by exchanging visitors to committee meetings. The awkward maneuvers between the races continued at the Ocala, Florida, convention of 1890, where the Colored Alliance again held a separate but simultaneous meeting. The black Alliancemen suggested to the whites that representatives of the two organizations create a confederation "for purposes of mutual protection, cooperation, and assistance." The white leaders eagerly agreed and both sides "heartily endorsed" a pledge to work together for "common citizenship . . . commercial equality and legal justice."

It was hard for black people to know which way to turn in the summer of 1891. Over the last year, the white Alliance had publicly professed its support for the Colored Alliance, had funded some of the white organizers of the movement, and had denounced the race-baiting tactics of the Democrats. This show of support gave black farmers confidence in the Alliance, for the white Republican allies of black voters appeared as ready as always to desert their black compatriots at the first opportunity. On the other hand the black and white Alliances did not agree on political matters of key importance to blacks, such as the Lodge elections bill and black office-holding. Just as important, black and white Alliancemen tended to occupy antagonistic positions in the Southern economy, the positions of tenant and landowner. Even a group filled with determination to overcome racial barriers as a matter of principle could not have reconciled those conflicts. The white Farmers' Alliance did not have that conviction.

To top it all off, blacks in the Colored Alliance differed deeply among themselves as well. The tensions, internal and external, erupted in the early fall of 1891 when some within the Colored Farmers' Alliance sought to use its newfound strength to tackle the most pressing problem facing its membership. Over the preceding years the amount paid to cotton pickers had declined. R. M. Humphrey the white general superintendent of the Colored Alliance, suggested that the pickers go on strike on September 6 until planters agreed to pay a dollar a day instead of the prevailing rate of 50 cents. Humphrey claimed that 1,100,000 pickers throughout the South had sworn to strike if called. Other leaders of the Colored Alliance, black men, argued against the plan. In Atlanta, E. S. Richardson, the superintendent in Georgia, argued that "this was not the purpose of our organization; that we were banded together for the purpose of educating ourselves and cooperating with the white people, for the betterment of the colored people, and such a step as this would be fatal." Whites agreed: Leonidas Polk argued that the demand for higher wages was "a great mistake on the part of our colored friends at this time. With cotton selling at 7 and 8 cents, there is not profit in it." The *Progressive Farmer* urged white Alliancemen to leave their cotton unpicked rather than cave in to the black demands.

Many in the Colored Alliance seemed eager to take some concrete action despite these admonitions, and Humphrey allowed his call for a strike to stand, organizing the "Cotton Pickers' League" to lead the effort. A group of black men attempted to begin a strike in East Texas but a planter summarily fired them and announced the conflict "immediately settled." The strike flared up again, though, a week later and several hundred miles away. It was led by Ben Patterson, a thirty-year-old black man from Memphis who traveled to Lee County, Arkansas, to organize the pickers. He won more than 25 men to his side, several of whom combed the area trying to win more converts to the cause. When black workers on one plantation got into a fight with the strikers, two nonstrikers were killed. While a posse went out in search of Patterson and his allies, a white plantation manager was killed and strikers burned a cotton gin. Eventually 15 black men died and another six were imprisoned. The white Alliance immediately sought to dissociate itself from the strike and distanced itself from R. M. Humphrey. The Colored Farmers' Alliance fell into sharp decline. . . .

The beginning of 1892 confronted the Farmers' Alliance with an extraordinarily complicated set of circumstances. The order was losing members every day and remaining cooperatives faced imminent failure. The two most important leaders, Leonidas Polk and C. W. Macune, fell into open disagreement and distrust over tactics and leadership. The Colored Farmers' Alliance had challenged the basic class and racial relations of the rural South, only to be crushed. Democrats and Republicans who had been cautiously receptive to the movement in years past now denounced the movement as a threat to the white South, the black South, the national economy, the national party system, property, democracy, and freedom.

Yet Alliancemen could find reasons for optimism as the order approached the St. Louis convention in February of 1892. Many farmers who had been resistant to the Alliance before now seemed deeply interested in a third-party effort; perhaps an election year was just what the order needed to bring it new life. The People's Party had coalesced the previous year in Cincinnati and many expected the St. Louis convention to witness the merging of the Farmers' Alliance with the nation's other insurgent groups; Terence V. Powderly of the Knights of Labor was in attendance, as was Frances Willard of the Women's Christian Temperance Union. Everything seemed to depend on the movement of the Southern Alliance into a third party, and Leonidas Polk immediately removed any doubts in his opening remarks to the convention: "The time has arrived for the great West, the great South and the great Northwest, to link their hands and hearts together and march to the ballot box and take possession of the government, restore it to the principles of our fathers, and run it in the interest of the people."

In Washington, the two major parties struggled in an especially tumultuous political arena. The control of Congress won by the Republicans in 1888 had soon proven to be a burden for the party. Labeled by their opponents the "Billion Dollar Congress," Republican lawmakers had enacted virtually everything for which they had campaigned. To the great majority of white Southerners each law was anathema or disappointment: the Lodge "force bill," the highest tariff in American history, increased pensions for Union veterans, a bill that would siphon money from the embarrassingly bloated treasury into black schools in the South, a largely ineffectual compromise on the financial system.

Voters elsewhere in the nation were disappointed with the Republican Congress as well, and the Democrats regained control of the House in 1890. With a Republican President and Senate on one side and a Democratic House on the other, the national government accomplished little as the economic condition of the country deteriorated and dissident parties gathered strength. The Democrats could barely wait for the 1892 presidential election. Grover Cleveland began to plan for another run for the White House and it soon became apparent that he would win his party's nomination. The party made no sign of trying to conciliate the Alliance and its demands. . . .

The People's Party—or "Populists," as they came to be called by their opponents and then by themselves—tried to mobilize their forces using the tactics of the Farmers' Alliance. Tom Watson's *People's Party Paper* urged its readers on, conveying an image of the party as a healthy, family-oriented, religious, sane alternative to the bluster of the Democrats. Populists such as Watson spoke in a self-consciously straightforward language that tried to cut through the thick tangle of emotion, memory, self-interest, race pride, and fear that tied white Southern men to the Democrats. Sometimes the voice was intimate, the voice of one friend to another. "Stand by your principles and vote for Sally and the babies," Watson urged in the spring of 1892. "What is 'party' to you?"

The Democrats, though, had tradition and "common sense" on their side. From the viewpoint of regular party men, the Populists were misfits, men who could not hope to win the game if they played by the regular rules of politics. Confronted with the third-party challenge, Democrats suddenly discovered that the perpetually detested Republicans were really not so bad after all—and the Republicans suddenly found a soft spot in their hearts for the Democrats as well. "We are sure there are too many honest Republicans and Democrats to allow this crowd to get there just yet," a Republican upcountry Tennessee paper assured its readers about the Populists. To the Democrats and Republicans, the third party (the demeaning label most frequently used by the Populists' opponents) seemed to want something for nothing. Doggerel in the Atlanta *Constitution* put these words in the mouths of the Populists: "Rah for labor! Smash your neighbor! Ring out the old—Ring in the gold and silver, too! Whiskey free for you and me; Milk and honey. Fiat money; Inflammation and damnation." "Poor, pitiful, sinful cranks!" one Democratic paper commented in mock sympathy for the Populists and their lack of sophistication. "Not one of them were ever inside a bank, and know as little as to how they are managed as a hog does about the holy writ of God."

The national elections of 1892 offered real opportunities and real dangers for the Populists. Events in Washington and the South pushed the party ahead—perhaps faster than it was ready to run. Cleveland's nomination at the head of the Democrats despite his well-known advocacy of the gold standard and the national convention's failure to adopt the Farmers' Alliance platform drove many undecided Democrats into the Populist rush. The Republicans' recent billion-dollar Congress and force bill prevented disenchanted Democrats who might have thought of moving into the Republican party from doing so. Meanwhile, the Southern cotton economy continued to decline. On the other hand, the death of Polk left no one at the head of the national Populist organization to give the movement direction. The Farmer's Alliance deteriorated and Populist policies developed no farther. No one came forward with "some better system" than the subtreasury, and yet that idea, without the nourishment provided by a vital Farmers' Alliance organization, seemed to atrophy. One situation offered both opportunity and danger: despite the attrition of the black vote by legal disfranchisement in several Southern states, a majority of Southern blacks still voted in the late 1880s and early 1890s. Neither white Democrats nor white Populists could afford to ignore the black voters.

Because the arrogance and greed of white Republicans had eroded the bonds between black voters and the party of Lincoln, in the early 1890s black leaders made it known that they would consider switching their allegiance to a party that would grant them a fairer deal. Moreover, the increase in the numbers of propertied blacks in towns and in the country in the 1880s created voters who might be more independent and who might have influence among their compatriots. All these contingencies made the already heated conflict between Democrats and Populists even hotter. There were many precincts, counties, and congressional districts where black votes might swing the election.

White Populist leaders set the tone of any interracial negotiations. While black voters and leaders could respond in a variety of ways to white invitations or threats, they could not publicly initiate interracial politics. White Democrats, for their part, had already staked out their positions, had already struck their deals; they could not appear to be scared or intimidated into making new public overtures to black voters. Populist leaders, on the other hand, were starting from scratch. They had to make their positions on race known and they often experimented to find a rhetoric and a strategy that would permit them to win black votes without losing white ones. As a result, tactics varied widely. Populist candidates in Alabama, Louisiana, Virginia, North Carolina, and Texas, while using the same behind-the-scenes techniques of winning black votes that the Democrats used, made few public statements about black rights and opportunities. Although influential blacks worked among black voters, attended conventions as delegates, and spoke from the same platforms, the Populist press of those states published few accounts of interracial cooperation and said little about the implications of the third-party crusade for black citizens in the 1892 campaign. It was to no white candidate's interest to profess anything in public that could be construed as racial heresy and to no black leader's interest to heighten racial conflict. It was to everyone's interest to be on the winning side, however, and winning often required clandestine dealing. In most states in 1892 the racial struggle surrounding Populism remained a quiet and desperate sort of hand-to-hand combat.

In Georgia, though, the Populists publicly confronted the political meaning of race in the New South in 1892. Tom Watson was both temperamentally inclined and strategically impelled to articulate what others refused to say. Watson had been elected to Congress in 1890 as an outspoken Alliance man from Georgia's Tenth District, running as the Democratic representative of rural counties against the entrenched power of the Democrats in the cotton-mill city of Augusta. The same savagely honest language that got Watson elected kept him in the forefront of the farmers' movement and on the front page of the state's newspapers. An early convert to the third-party strategy after Ocala, Watson clashed so repeatedly with the Georgia Democratic party that he considered himself, with cause, "the worst abused, worst disparaged, worst 'cussed' man in Georgia." In Washington, Watson became the most active and aggressive Populist legislator in the House, introducing bill after bill to keep the demands of Ocala before the nation. He published a book about the Populist challenge whose subtitle was *Not a Revolt; It Is a Revolution*, a book the Democrats attacked on the floor of Congress with blistering criticism.

So when Tom Watson came back to Georgia to campaign for reelection in the spring of 1892, he was the focus of great attention. Crowds lined the railroad track beyond the bounds of his district, and when he got home farmers carried him on their shoulders to a stage. An enormously popular speaker and soon sole owner of the *People's Party Paper,* Watson was never at a loss for an opportunity or a desire to make his opinions known. His opponent, James C. C. Black, seemed the embodiment of the town-based Democrats: a lawyer, a Confederate veteran, and a Baptist deacon. He argued that "it is un-American and un-Christian, arraigning one class against another," that he was "a friend of all classes," and that the farmer's economic troubles were "exaggerated." The campaign was brutal. Watson fumed when Populist [presidential] candidate James Weaver was driven from Georgia by Democratic mobs, and he warned that the intimidation was only a foreshadowing of what was to come in the fall elections. . . .

In the midst of this important campaign, Watson wrestled with the role of race in Southern politics. Both in his speeches and in the columns of his newspaper, Watson discussed what many thought should not be discussed. His appeal to blacks was relatively simple. "There is no reason why the black man should not understand that the law that hurts me, as a farmer, hurts him, as a farmer; that the same law that hurts me, as a cropper, hurts you, as a cropper; that the same law that hurts me, as a mechanic, hurts you, as a mechanic." His guiding idea was that "self interest rules," and that as long as white and black Populists each followed their own—congruent—self-interest, they could work together. As long as blacks were on Watson's side, he would help preserve their vote.

Other Georgia Populists were willing to join him. "Why is it that the Democrats are hallooing negro supremacy so persistently?" a man who signed himself "Hayseeder" wrote to the *People's Party Paper* from Burke County, Georgia. "Are they not citizens of the State, holding the same rights under the law that the white man does? If so, isn't it better to give them representation in the convention [as the Populists did in the Georgia State Convention in 1892], that they may know for whom they are voting, thereby getting them to vote with the white people at home than to ignore them till the day of election and then try to buy or force them to vote, thereby driving them into the Republican party?" The correspondent asked these questions because he was "no politician, but simply an old hayseeder, who was born under a Democratic roof, rocked in a Democratic cradle, sung to sleep with a Democratic lullaby, and have always voted with the Democratic party, but finding, in my humble judgment, that the party had drifted from the landmarks of its founders.". . . .

Such pronouncements were indeed remarkable in the New South. Just a few months earlier, no white would have thought of saying them. The political exigencies of the Populist revolt put good orthodox white men in the position where the racial injustice of their society suddenly appeared to them as injustice. When it was *their* allies attacked and threatened, *their* voters bullied and bought, *their* morality challenged, suddenly things appeared different than when only white Republicans were implicated. The very fact that such language could surface so quickly in the New South is one more indication of the fluidity of the political world and of race relations. We should not be too quick to write off such statements as self-serving campaign tactics or as the idiosyncratic rantings of isolated men. Populist speakers stood on platforms in front of hundreds of hard-drinking, fired-up white men and said these things, stood on platforms alongside black men and said these things. In the context of 1892, they were brave things to say.

There were other things said on those platforms, though, things that were also a part of the white Populist view of blacks. In the same speech where Watson talked of the self-interest that should unite blacks and whites, he also made very clear what he did not mean. "They say I am an advocate of social equality between the whites and the blacks. THAT IS AN ABSOLUTE FALSEHOOD, and the man who utter[s] it, knows it. I have done no such thing, and you colored men know it as well as the men who formulated the slander." The *People's Party Paper* made a point of including the responses of blacks in the audience as a sort of chorus, showing that black men recognized the wisdom of Watson's words. "It is best for your race and my race that we dwell apart in our private affairs. [Many voices among the colored: 'That's so, boss.'] It is best for you to go to your churches, and I will go to mine; it is best that you send your children to your colored school, and I'll send my children to mine; you invite your colored friends to your home, and I'll invite my friends to mine. [A voice from a colored man: 'Now you're talking sense,' and murmurs of approval all through the audience.]" What Watson did not want blacks to do was to vote Republican "just because you are black. In other words, you ought not to go one way just because the whites went the other, but that each race should study these questions, and try to do the right thing by each other." Watson, in other words, wanted blacks to support Populist economic policies but not to expect anything besides economic unity. . . .

It should not be surprising that black voters approached the Populists cautiously. Even a black man who joined Watson on the speakers' stand during the heat of the 1892 campaign gave an extremely wary endorsement of the third-party cause. . . .

It was dangerous for a black man to say more. One of Watson's most assiduous allies was a young black minister, H. S. Doyle. Despite many threats of assassination, Doyle made 63 speeches for Watson. As the campaign drew to a close, Doyle received threats of a lynching. He went to Watson for help, and Watson sent out a call to gather supporters to help protect his black ally. Two thousand men appeared, heavily armed, after hearing rumors that Watson himself was in danger; they stayed for two nights. Watson announced at the courthouse "that the humblest white or black man that wants to talk our doctrine shall do it, and the man doesn't live who shall touch a hair of his head, without fighting every man in the people's party." "Watson has gone mad," a Democratic paper warned. Although the two thousand would not have rushed to save the black man alone, the event took on a momentum and racial meaning of its own. White men, after all, had rallied to support a leader who had boldly breached the wall between the races. . . .

The 1892 elections unleashed tensions and conflicts that had been building for years. . . .

It was hard in 1892 to know just who voted for the Populists, and historians ever since have been trying to untangle that mystery. Class or race interests, already complex, became even more so when refracted through the political system. Southern politics in the age of Populism, despite the apparent simplicities of black versus white, town versus countryside, and rich versus poor, were extraordinarily intricate. A close look at the way voting returns meshed with economic and demographic conditions may reveal patterns not immediately apparent from correspondence and newspaper accounts.

Since there were not enough town folk to outnumber the angry farmers, the question has to be why some farmers voted for the Populists while others did not. The starting place is clear: in most states, especially those of the lower South where the Populists were strongest, the higher the percentage of blacks in a county, the less likely Populists were to win. The most obvious reason for this pattern is that the possibilities for fraud, intimidation, persuasion, and violence directed at black men were much greater in the Black Belt than elsewhere. Voting returns from the Black Belt cannot be accepted at face value for reasons that congressional inquiries and outraged Populist editorials made all too clear.

A large black presence in a county, though, had effects other than the mere opportunity for manipulation by Democrats. Black Belt counties possessed a social and political order quite different from that of other counties in their states. First of all, many whites in heavily black counties tended to be better off because they owned land that black tenants worked for them; these landlords, who often lived in town and were closely tied to the merchant elite, were too satisfied with the status quo to listen to the Populists. Just as important, poorer white men in heavily black counties had fewer opportunites to build autonomous parties and groups. Those whites were often tenants or customers of richer men, often bound by ties of debt, obligation, or gratitude to the bulwarks of the Democratic party. The poorer whites also tended to belong to the same churches and sometimes to the same families as their wealthier neighbors. There were many social and economic reasons, then, for tenants and small farmers in the Black Belt to shun the Populists.

There were political reasons as well. Despite class differences, whites in the Black Belt often felt compelled to maintain political unity, whether by consensus or by force, against the black majority. Blacks, after all, had held political power fifteen or twenty years earlier in those counties and had struggled to maintain a living Republican party in the years since. Those Republicans were often anxious to cut a deal with the Populists to help dislodge the Democrats; they had the power of numbers and organization among black voters to offer the insurgents, and in dozens of counties such coalitions won in the early 1890s. It did not seem inconceivable that black and white Republicans could regain some of their old power if white Democrats let down their guard, if a version of the force bill were enacted, if the Democrats lost the presidency.

As incongruous as it may appear, too, considerable numbers of black men, with varying degrees of willingness and enthusiasm, voted for the Democrats in Black Belt counties. As white Republicans in the nation, state, and county increasingly banded against their black compatriots, it began to seem that black voters might do just as well to forge political alliances with the powerful whites in their own districts. In the short run, the Democrats had far more to offer blacks than did the third party. A Georgia Populist bitterly complained in the wake of the 1892 elections that though the whites in his county voted for the new party, "the negroes voted with the opposition, with some few exceptions. What the promise to have their names on the jury list did not bring into the fold of the 'dear old Democratic party,' the lavish use of 'red-eye' and money did." A black man might well decide that his appearance on a jury in the next session of his county court, or even hard cash in his pocket, was worth more than a hypothetical subtreasury plan that must have seemed far away.

Although a heavily black electorate strengthened the hands of the Democrats, a heavily white electorate was no guarantee of Populist success. In Kentucky, Tennessee, Virginia, and North Carolina, the Populists did best in counties where blacks made up a considerable part of the population and won virtually no support in the almost entirely white mountain districts. White mountain Republicans, long persuaded that the Democrats were a drag on progress—just as the Populists charged—turned to their own party for relief. The same kind of social and economic ties that bound Democratic whites to one another in the Black Belt bound Republican whites to one another in the mountains. As a result, the Populists won few votes in Appalachia even though white farmers there faced none of the racial constraints on their voting confronted by potential white Populists in the Black Belt.

In Georgia and Alabama, on the other hand, upcountry whites proved to be some of the strongest supporters of the Populists. Most Georgia and Alabama upcountry whites—unlike their counterparts in the upper South—had been neither staunch antebellum Whigs nor wartime Unionists and had not been willing to go over to the Republicans after the war. On the other hand, their interests often conflicted with the Democratic powers in Montgomery and Atlanta as well as with the Democratic rings in their county seats, and throughout the 1870s and 1880s the farmers of the Georgia and Alabama upcountry had experimented with ways to exert their own political voice without deserting to the Republicans. Those regions had been strongholds of independent and Greenback movements and were willing to listen to other dissident voices. They listened to the Populists when they arrived on the scene.

Even the strongest statistical likelihood, of course, could be circumvented by a persuasive speaker, the influence of friends, effective organizing, or a particularly obnoxious Democratic employer. Even the most powerful tendencies could be over-ridden by a powerful personality, as when Tom Watson led his heavily black Georgia Tenth District into the forefront of the Populist movement. Such leaders were scarce, though, and if the Populist movement as a whole were to succeed it would have to win in counties without cities and without heavy black majorities. An examination of those predominantly white rural counties in the five most successful states for the Populists—Georgia, Alabama, North Carolina, Arkansas, and Texas—reveals a strong pattern. Populist votes tended to increase in counties where the concentration on cotton was strong but where the land was poor or relatively unimproved.

That does not mean that there was a simple or straightforward connection be-tween the misery cotton caused and Populist voting. Populism was strongest in counties where white farmers still owned the land they farmed, not in counties where the crop lien had stripped land from former owners. Populism does not seem to have been a product of particularly isolated or backward rural counties. The pres-ence or absence of railroads made little difference, and the cumulative size of vil-lage population counted for little in every state except North Carolina—where Populist votes actually increased as town population increased. Stores did tend to be dispersed in Populist counties, which probably reflected a lack of towns. Pop-ulist votes tended to be few where manufacturing was present, though the relation-ship was weak.

Populism, in other words, grew in counties that had seen the arrival of the new order's railroads, stores, and villages but not its larger towns and mills. The Pop-ulists tended to be cotton farmers who worked their own land, though it was land that produced only with reluctance. Living in counties that were predominantly white but had no strong Republican presence, these farmers felt they could, indeed must, break with the Democrats.

The Populists, judging from their words and their backgrounds, wanted a fair shot at making a decent living as it was being defined in the Gilded Age. There is little evidence that Populist voters wanted to return to the "hog and hominy" days of their fathers, abandon railroads, or withdraw from the market. The state with the largest Populist presence of all, Texas, attracted men who took anything but a cautious ap-proach to their economic lives. They had risked everything to move to the farming frontier and were determined that their risks would not be in vain. They were farm-ers, with all the ideological, social, political, and economic connotations of that word—not small businessmen or petty capitalists—and they wanted a fair place in market relations as producers and as consumers. The Populists' language rang with disdain for monopoly capitalism and monopoly politics, for Populists saw both as recent perversions of a political economy that could have been democratic and eq-uitable. The Populists did not urge that their communities return to the way things used to be. Instead, they insisted that the new order be brought into alignment with the ideals of American democracy and fair capitalism.

Such a vision had radical implications in late nineteenth-century America. Far from being conservative, it sought to change the way the government and the economy operated. The Populist campaign revealed the radical component always latent in mainstream American ideals: a persistent and unmet hunger for vital democracy, a constant chafing at the injustices of large-scale capitalism. Those ideals, usually held in suspension by a relatively widespread prosperity and by a wide and expanding suffrage, could, given the right conditions, coalesce into powerful and trenchant critiques of the status quo. The raw material for such critiques lay all around the farmers, in the messages of Christian equality they heard in their churches, in the messages of the Declaration of Independence they heard at political rallies, in the ideals of just and open market relations they knew from Jefferson and Franklin. Amidst the many injustices of the New South and in the context of the Farmers' Alliance and Populist party, these ideals worked their way to the surface. . . .

There was really no bright side to 1896 for the Southern Populists. the momentum built up over the preceding decade dissipated as the movement flew in many directions at once. Even those who believed in the cause with all their hearts could see that the party had suffered a crushing blow with Bryan's defeat and the party's loss of unanimity. "Our party, as a party, does not exist any more," Watson admitted. "Fusion has well nigh killed it. The sentiment is still there, but confidence is gone."

The year of 1896 marked a turning point in Southern politics. A Republican President once again held the White House, espousing doctrines that few white Southerners supported; the Republicans controlled the House, Senate, and presidency for the next fourteen years. The Democrats at home had been badly shaken, discredited by their weakness and by their flagrant injustices at the polls. Many townsmen, manufacturers, and workers lost faith in the old guard Democrats even though they were unwilling to vote for the Populists. The Populists had lost their sense of separate identity but had attained none of their goals. Southern politics churned under the surface.

✢ *F U R T H E R   R E A D I N G*

A. M. Arnett, *The Populist Movement in Georgia* (1922)
Donna A. Barnes, *Farmers in Rebellion* (1984)
Gregg Cantrell, *Kenneth and John B. Rayner and the Limits of Southern Dissent* (1993)
Jeffrey J. Crow and Robert F. Durden, *Maverick Republican in the Old North State* (1977)
Charles Crowe, "Tom Watson, Populists, and Blacks Reconsidered." *Journal of Negro History* 55 (April 1970), 99–116.
Robert F. Durden, *The Climax of Populism* (1966)
Gerald Gaither, *Blacks and the Populist Revolt* (1977)
Lawrence Goodwyn, *Democratic Promise* (1976)
———, *The Populist Moment* (1978)
Sheldon Hackney, *Populism to Progressivism in Alabama* (1969)
Steven Hahn, *The Roots of Southern Populism* (1983)
William Ivy Hair, *Bourbonism and Agrarian Protest* (1969)
Roger L. Hart, *Redeemers, Bourbons, and Populists* (1975)
John D. Hicks, *The Populist Revolt* (1931)
Richard Hofstadter, *The Age of Reform* (1955)

William F. Holmes, "The Southern Farmers' Alliance and the Jute Cartel," *Journal of Southern History* 60 (February 1994), 59–80

Paul Horton, "Testing the Limits of Class Politics in Postbellum Alabama: Agrarian Radicalism in Lawrence County," *Journal of Southern History* 61 (1991), 63–84

Michael Kazin, *The Populist Persuasion: An American History* (1995)

J. Morgan Kousser, *The Shaping of Southern Politics* (1974)

Robert C. McMath, *Populist Vanguard* (1975)

——— , *American Populism: A Social History* (1993)

James Tice Moore, "Redeemers Reconsidered: Change and Continuity in the Democratic South, 1870–1900," *Journal of Southern History* 44 (August 1978), 357–378

Stuart Noblin, *Leonidas Lafayette Polk* (1949)

Walter T. K. Nugent, *The Tolerant Populists* (1963)

Bruce Palmer, *"Man Over Money"* (1980)

Norman Pollack, *The Populist Response to Industrial America* (1962)

Michael Schwartz, *Radical Protest and Social Structure* (1976)

Barton Shaw, *The Wool Hat Boys* (1984)

James Turner, "Understanding the Populists," *Journal of American History* 67 (September 1980), 354–373

Samuel Webb, *Two-Party Politics in the One-Party South: Alabama* (1997)

C. Vann Woodward, *Tom Watson* (1938)

——— , *Origins of the New South* (1951)

Race, Violence, Disfranchisement,

and Segregation

⚓

The struggle for political leadership in the South had dramatic consequences. At first conservatives reacted violently against blacks, and lynchings increased. After the defeat of the Populists, conservative Democrats in state legislatures passed restrictive laws designed to discourage black and white political unity. The result was disfranchisement and the imposition of segregation. Black southerners (along with some poorer whites) lost many of the political rights they had gained during Reconstruction. In addition, a legally mandated system of cradle-to-grave segregation imposed upon southern blacks the stigma of inferiority.

Clearly, this institutionalization of white supremacy was in some ways a culmination of racist trends that had been developing since emancipation or even before. But it also marked a drastic change in the legal, political, and social status of African Americans, who had been voting and had not been legally barred from many areas of southern life. The causes of violence, disfranchisement, and segregation are complex and therefore have generated considerable historical debate. The connection between Populism and segregation, in particular, is an area of significant disagreement among historians today.

What were the roots of disfranchisement and segregation? What role did the politics of the 1890s play in advancing disfranchisement and segregation, and what role did gender play? Which decade saw the greatest number of lynchings? Did segregation have any influence on the gradual decline of lynching? How did the federal government aid in advancing segregation? How did white southerners respond to disfranchisement and segregation? How did African Americans respond to the rising tide of racism and to attempts to impede their voting rights and impose Jim Crow laws? How did the new system affect blacks and Mexican Americans?

⚓ D O C U M E N T S

Causes for lynching, as described by protester Ida B. Wells in Document 1, changed over time, but the rape of a white woman by a black man was often considered the most justifiable reason for violence. In her newspaper, the *Free Speech,* Wells documented that lynchings were more often motivated by economic jealousy. She raised the ire of white citizens in Memphis in 1892 when she suggested that many so-called rapes were in fact voluntary romantic alliances between a white woman and a black man. In Document 2, the actual incidence of lynching is charted by region, by state, and by year. The legal formulas for disfranchisement—literacy tests, poll taxes, and grandfather clauses (used to benefit otherwise unqualified whites)—are illustrated by excerpts from a North Carolina statute in Document 3. Although institutional and political power had swung against them, black leaders protested vigorously, as shown by the remarks of Robert Smalls, a black delegate to South Carolina's 1895 constitutional convention, in Document 4. The U.S. Supreme Court abetted the South's move toward segregation by upholding the concept of "separate but equal" in the case *Plessy* v. *Ferguson,* portions of which are reprinted in Document 5. By the end of the century, white supremacists villified black males, especially as threats to white womanhood, as shown in Document 6 via excerpts from the *Raleigh News and Observer.* The consequence of violent rhetoric was violent action. In Document 7, Walter White, who grew up in Atlanta but later became executive director of the National Association for the Advancement of Colored People, describes how he was affected by the Atlanta race riot of 1906.

1. Ida B. Wells Reports the Horrors of Lynching in the South, 1892

From 1865 to 1872, hundreds of colored men and women were mercilessly murdered and the almost invariable reason assigned was that they met their death by being alleged participants in an insurrection or riot. But this story at last wore itself out. No insurrection ever materialized; no Negro rioter was ever apprehended and proven guilty, and no dynamite ever recorded the black man's protest against oppression and wrong. It was too much to ask thoughtful people to believe this transparent story, and the southern white people at last made up their minds that some other excuse must be had.

Then came the second excuse, which had its birth during the turbulent times of reconstruction. By an amendment to the Constitution the Negro was given the right of franchise, and, theoretically at least, his ballot became his invaluable emblem of citizenship. In a government "of the people, for the people, and by the people," the Negro's vote became an important factor in all matters of state and national politics. But this did not last long. The southern white man would not consider that the Negro had any right which a white man was bound to respect, and the idea of a republican form of government in the southern states grew into general contempt. It was maintained that "This is a white man's government," and regardless of numbers the white man should rule. "No Negro domination" became the new legend on the sanguinary banner of the sunny South, and under it rode the Ku Klux Klan, the Regulators, and the lawless mobs, which for any cause chose to murder one man or a dozen as suited their purpose best. It was a long, gory campaign; the blood chills and the heart almost loses faith in Christianity when one thinks of Yazoo, Hamburg, Edgefield, Copiah, and the countless massacres of defenseless Negroes, whose only crime was the attempt to exercise their right to vote.

But it was a bootless strife for colored people. The government which had made the Negro a citizen found itself unable to protect him. It gave him the right to vote, but denied him the protection which should have maintained that right. Scourged from his home; hunted through the swamps; hung by midnight raiders, and openly murdered in the light of day, the Negro clung to his right of franchise with a heroism which would have wrung admiration from the hearts of savages. He believed that in that small white ballot there was a subtle something which stood for manhood as well as citizenship, and thousands of brave black men went to their graves, exemplifying the one by dying for the other.

The white man's victory soon became complete by fraud, violence, intimidation and murder. The franchise vouchsafed to the Negro grew to be a "barren ideality," and regardless of numbers, the colored people found themselves voiceless in the councils of those whose duty it was to rule. With no longer the fear of "Negro Domination" before their eyes, the white man's second excuse became valueless. With the Southern governments all subverted and the Negro actually eliminated from all participation in state and national elections, there could be no longer an excuse for killing Negroes to prevent "Negro Domination."

Brutality still continued; Negroes were whipped, scourged, exiled, shot and hung whenever and wherever it pleased the white man so to treat them, and as the civilized world with increasing persistency held the white people of the South to account for its outlawry, the murderers invented the third excuse—that Negroes had to be killed to avenge their assaults upon women. There could be framed no possible excuse more harmful to the Negro and more unanswerable if true in its sufficiency for the white man.

Humanity abhors the assailant of womanhood, and this charge upon the Negro at once placed him beyond the pale of human sympathy. With such unanimity, earnestness and apparent candor was this charge made and reiterated that the world has accepted the story that the Negro is a monster which the Southern white man has painted him. And to-day, the Christian world feels, that while lynching is a crime, and lawlessness and anarchy the certain precursors of a nation's fall, it can not by word or deed, extend sympathy or help to a race of outlaws, who might mistake their plea for justice and deem it an excuse for their continued wrongs. . . .

If the Southern people in defense of their lawlessness, would tell the truth and admit that colored men and women are lynched for almost any offense, from murder to a misdemeanor, there would not now be the necessity for this defense. But when they intentionally, maliciously and constantly belie the record and bolster up these falsehoods by the words of legislators, preachers, governors and bishops, then the Negro must give to the world his side of the awful story.

A word as to the charge itself. In considering the third reason assigned by the Southern white people for the butchery of blacks, the question must be asked, what the white man means when he charges the black man with rape. Does he mean the crime which the statutes of the civilized states describe as such? Not by any means. With the Southern white man, any mesalliance existing between a white woman and a colored man is a sufficient foundation for the charge of rape. The Southern white man says that it is impossible for a voluntary alliance to exist between a white woman and a colored man, and therefore, the fact of an alliance is a proof of force. In numerous instances where colored men have been lynched on the charge of rape, it was positively known at the time of lynching, and indisputably proven after the victim's death, that the relationship sustained between the man and woman was voluntary and clandestine, and that in no court of law could even the charge of assault have been successfully maintained.

It was for the assertion of this fact, in the defense of her own race, that the writer hereof became an exile; her property destroyed and her return to her home forbidden under penalty of death, for writing [an] editorial [stating this] which was printed in her paper, the Free Speech, in Memphis, Tenn., May 21, 1892.

2. Lynching in the United States, 1882–1930

Table 1.   Number of Persons Lynched, by Region and by Race for Five-Year Periods, 1889–1928

YEARS	SOUTH	NON-SOUTH	BLACK	WHITE	TOTALS
1889–1893	705	134	579	260	839
1894–1898	680	94	544	230	774
1899–1903	492	51	455	88	543
1904–1908	362	19	354	27	381
1909–1913	347	15	326	36	362
1914–1918	311	14	264	61	325
1919–1923	287	14	273	28	301
1924–1928	95	5	91	9	100

Source: Compiled from data in NAACP, *Thirty Years of Lynching* (New York: NAACP, 1919) and *Supplements* (1919–1928). Southern states are Alabama, Arkansas, Florida, Georgia, Kentucky, Louisiana, Mississippi, Missouri, North Carolina, Oklahoma, South Carolina, Tennessee, Texas, Virginia, West Virginia—the fifteen states in which the ASWPL was active.

Table 2.   Number of Persons Lynched, by States, 1882–1930

STATE	WHITES	BLACKS	TOTAL
Alabama	46	296	342
Arizona	35	1	36
Arkansas	64	230	294
California	42	4	46
Colorado	70	6	76
Connecticut	0	0	0
Delaware	0	1	1
Florida	25	241	266
Georgia	34	474	508
Idaho	16	6	22
Illinois	15	16	31
Indiana	33	19	52

From *Revolt Against Chivalry: Jessie Daniel Hines and the Women's Campaign Against Lynching* by Jacquelyn Dowd Hall. © 1979, Columbia University Press. Reprinted with the permission of the publisher.

STATE	WHITES	BLACKS	TOTAL
Iowa	19	1	20
Kansas	34	18	52
Kentucky	62	151	213
Louisiana	60	328	388
Maine	0	0	0
Maryland	3	27	30
Massachusetts	0	0	0
Michigan	4	4	8
Minnesota	6	3	9
Mississippi	45	500	545
Missouri	53	63	116
Montana	91	2	93
Nebraska	55	5	60
Nevada	12	0	12
New Hampshire	0	0	0
New Jersey	0	1	1
New Mexico	39	4	43
New York	1	1	2
North Carolina	14	85	99
North Dakota	12	2	14
Ohio	9	13	22
Oklahoma	116	44	160
Oregon	22	3	25
Pennsylvania	1	5	6
Rhode Island	0	0	0
South Carolina	5	154	159
South Dakota	34	0	34
Tennessee	44	196	240
Texas	143	349	492
Utah	6	3	9
Vermont	0	0	0
Virginia	16	88	104
Washington	30	0	30
West Virginia	15	35	50
Wisconsin	6	0	6
Wyoming	38	7	45
Total	1,375	3,386	4,761

Source: Monroe Work, ed., *The Negro Year Book: An Annual Encyclopedia of the Negro, 1931–1932* (Tuskegee: Negro Year Book Publishing Co., 1931), p. 293.

3. Literacy Test and Poll Tax, 1899

(Sec. 4.) Every person presenting himself for registration shall be able to read and write any section of the constitution in the English language and before he shall be entitled to vote he shall have paid on or before the first day of March of the year in which he proposes to vote his poll tax as prescribed by law for the previous year. Poll taxes shall be a lien only on assessed property and no process shall issue to enforce the collection of the same except against assessed property.

(Sec. 5.) No male person who was on January one, eighteen hundred and sixty-seven, or at any time prior thereto entitled to vote under the laws of any state in the United States wherein he then resided, and no lineal descendant of any such person, shall be denied the right to register and vote at any election in this state by reason of

This document can be found in the Public Laws of North Carolina, 1899, Chapter 218.

his failure to possess the educational qualification prescribed in section four of this article: *Provided,* he shall have registered in accordance with the terms of this section prior to December one, nineteen hundred and eight. The general assembly shall provide for a permanent record of all persons who register under this section on or before November first, nineteen hundred and eight: and all such persons shall be entitled to register and vote in all elections by the people in this state unless disqualified under section two of this article: *Provided,* such persons shall have paid their poll tax as requ[i]red by law.

4. Black Leaders Fight Disfranchisement, 1895

General Smalls' Speech

Gen. Robert Smalls who is known everywhere as South Carolina's "gullah statesman," then took the floor. He said: . . .

I was born and raised in South Carolina, and today I live on the very spot on which I was born, and I expect to remain here as long as the great God allows me to live, and I will ask no one else to let me remain. I love the State as much as any member of this convention, because it is the garden spot of the south.

Mr. President, this convention has been called for no other purpose than the disfranchisement of the negro. Be careful, and bear in mind that the elections which are to take place early next month in very many of the States are watching the action of this convention, especially on the suffrage question. Remember that the negro was not brought here of his own accord. I found my reference to a history in the congressional library in Washington . . . that he says that in 1619, in the month of June, a Dutch man-of-war landed at Jamestown, Va., with 15 sons of Africa aboard, at the time Miles Kendall was deputy governor of Virginia. He refused to allow the vessel to be anchored in any of her harbors. But he found out after his order had been sent out that the vessel was without provisions, and the crew was in a starving condition. He countermanded his order, and supplied the vessel with the needed provisions in exchange for 14 negroes. It was then that the seed of slavery was planted in the land. So you see we did not come here of our own accord; we were brought here in a Dutch vessel, and we have been here ever since. The Dutch are here, and are now paying a very large tax, and are controlling the business of Charleston today. They are not to blame, and are not being blamed.

We served our masters faithfully, and willingly, and as we were made to do for 244 years. In the last war you left them home. You went to the war, fought, and come back home, shattered to pieces, worn out, one-legged, and found your wife and family being properly cared for by the negroes you left behind. Why should you now seek to disfranchise a race that has been so true to you? . . .

The speech of General Robert Smalls of South Carolina can be found in *The Columbia State,* October 27, 1895.

Since reconstruction times 53,000 negroes have been killed in the south, and not more than three white men have been convicted and hung for these crimes. I want you to be mindful of the fact that the good people of the north are watching this convention upon this subject. I hope you will make a Constitution that will stand the test. I hope that we may be able to say when our work is done that we have made as good a Constitution as the one we are doing away with.

The negroes are paying taxes in the south on $263,000,000 worth of property. In South Carolina, according to the census, the negroes pay tax on $12,500,000 worth of property. That was in 1890. You voted down without discussion, merely by a vote to lay on the table, a proposition for a simple property and educational qualification. What do you want? You tried the infamous eight-box [required poorly educated voters to place ballots correctly in eight separate ballot boxes, one for each office] and registration laws until they were worn to such a thinness that they could stand neither the test of the law nor of public opinion. In behalf of the 600,000 negroes in the State and the 132,000 negro voters all that I demand is that a fair and honest election law be passed. We care not what the qualifications imposed are, all that we ask is that they be fair and honest, and honorable, and with these provisos we will stand or fall by it. You have 102,000 white men over 21 years of age, 13,000 of these cannot read nor write. You dare not disfranchise them, and you know that the man who proposes it will never be elected to another office in the State of South Carolina. But whatever Mr. [Ben] Tillman can do, he can make nothing worse than the infamous eight-box law, and I have no praise for the Conservatives, for they gave the people that law. Fifty-eight thousand negroes cannot read nor write. This leaves a majority of 14,000 white men who can read and write over the same class of negroes in this State. We are willing to accept a scheme that provides that no man who cannot read nor write can vote, if you dare pass it. How can you expect an ordinary man to "understand and explain" any section of the Constitution, to correspond to the interpretation put upon it by the manager of election, when by a very recent decision of the supreme court, composed of the most learned men in the State, two of them put one construction upon a section, and the other justice put an entirely different construction upon it. To embody such a provision in the election law would be to mean that every white man would interpret it aright and every negro would interpret it wrong. I appeal to the gentleman from Edgefield to realize that he is not making a law for one set of men. Some morning you may wake up to find that the bone and sinew of your country is gone. The negro is needed in the cotton fields and in the low country rice fields, and if you impose too hard conditions upon the negro in this State there will be nothing else for him to do but to leave. What then will you do about your phosphate works? No one but a negro can work them; the mines that pay the interest on your State debt. I tell you the negro is the bone and sinew of your country and you cannot do without him. I do not believe you want to get rid of the negro, else why did you impose a high tax on immigration agents who might come here to get him to leave?

Now, Mr. President we should not talk one thing and mean another. We should not deceive ourselves. Let us make a Constitution that is fair, honest and just. Let us make a Constitution for all the people, one we will be proud of and our children will receive with delight.

5. *Plessy* v. *Ferguson*, 1896

BROWN, J[ustice] This case turns upon the constitutionality of an act of the general assembly of the state of Louisiana, passed in 1890, providing for separate railway carriages for the white and colored races. . . .

The constitutionality of this act is attacked upon the ground that it conflicts both with the 13th Amendment of the Constitution, abolishing slavery, and the 14th Amendment, which prohibits certain restrictive legislation on the part of the states.

1. That it does not conflict with the 13th Amendment, which abolished slavery and involuntary servitude, except as a punishment for crime, is too clear for argument. . . .

A statute which implies merely a legal distinction between the white and colored races—a distinction which is founded in the color of the two races, and which must always exist so long as white men are distinguished from the other race by color—has no tendency to destroy the legal equality of the two races, or re-establish a state of involuntary servitude. Indeed, we do not understand that the 13th Amendment is strenuously relied upon by the plaintiff in error in this connection. . . .

The object of the amendment was undoubtedly to enforce the absolute equality of the two races before the law, but in the nature of things it could not have been intended to abolish distinctions based upon color, or to enforce social, as distinguished from political, equality, or a commingling of the two races upon terms unsatisfactory to either. Laws permitting, and even requiring their separation in places where they are liable to be brought into contact do not necessarily imply the inferiority of either race to the other, and have been generally, if not universally, recognized as within the competency of the state legislatures in the exercise of their police power. The most common instance of this is connected with the establishment of separate schools for white and colored children, which have been held to be a valid exercise of the legislative power even by courts of states where the political rights of the colored race have been longest and most earnestly enforced. . . .

It is claimed by the plaintiff in error that, in any mixed community, the reputation of belonging to the dominant race, in this instance the white race is *property,* in the same sense that a right of action, or of inheritance, is property. Conceding this to be so, for the purposes of this case, we are unable to see how this statute deprives him of, or in any way affects his right to, such property. If he be a white man and assigned to a colored coach, he may have his action for damages against the company for being deprived of his so-called property. Upon the other hand, if he be a colored man and be so assigned, he has been deprived of no property, since he is not lawfully entitled to the reputation of being a white man. . . .

So far, then, as a conflict with the 14th Amendment is concerned, the case reduces itself to the question whether the statute of Louisiana is a reasonable regulation, and with respect to this there must necessarily be a large discretion on the part of the legislature. In determining the question of reasonableness it is at liberty to act with reference to the established usages, customs, and traditions of the people, and with a view to the promotion of their comfort, and the preservation of the public peace and good or-

---

This document can be found in Plessy v. Ferguson (163 U.S. 537) in *Cases Argued and Decided in the Supreme Court of the United States,* 163, 164, 165, 166, U. S., Book 41, Lawyer's Edition (Rochester, N.Y.: The Lawyers Cooperative Publishing Company, 1920), pp. 257–58, 260–62, and 264–65.

der. Gauged by this standard, we cannot say that a law which authorizes or even requires the separation of the two races in public conveyances is unreasonable or more obnoxious to the 14th Amendment than the acts of Congress requiring separate schools for colored children in the District of Columbia, the constitutionality of which does not seem to have been questioned, or the corresponding acts of state legislatures. . . .

Justice HARLAN, dissenting. . . . In respect of civil rights, common to all citizens, the Constitution of the United States does not, I think, permit any public authority to know the race of those entitled to be protected in the enjoyment of such rights. Every true man has pride of race, and under appropriate circumstances, when the rights of others, his equals before the law, are not to be affected, it is his privilege to express such pride and to take such action based upon it as to him seems proper. But I deny that any legislative body or judicial tribunal may have regard to the race of citizens when the civil rights of those citizens are involved. Indeed such legislation as that here in question is inconsistent, not only with that equality of rights which pertains to citizenship, national and state, but with the personal liberty enjoyed by every one within the United States. . . .

In my opinion, the judgment this day rendered will, in time, prove to be quite as pernicious as the decision made by this tribunal in the Dred Scott Case. . . . [I]t seems that we have yet, in some of the states, a dominant race, a superior class of citizens, which assumes to regulate the enjoyment of civil rights, common to all citizens, upon the basis of race. The present decision, it may well be apprehended, will not only stimulate aggressions, more or less brutal and irritating, upon the admitted rights of colored citizens, but will encourage the belief that it is possible, by means of state enactments, to defeat the beneficent purposes which the people of the United States had in view when they adopted the recent amendments of the Constitution, by one of which the blacks of this country were made citizens of the United States and of the states in which they respectively reside and whose privileges and immunities, as citizens, the states are forbidden to abridge. Sixty millions of whites are in no danger from the presence here of eight millions of blacks. The destinies of the two races in this country are indissolubly linked together, and the interests of both require that the common government of all shall not permit the seeds of race hate to be planted under the sanction of law. What can more certainly arouse race hate, what more certainly create and perpetuate a feeling of distrust between these races, than state enactments which in fact proceed on the ground that colored citizens are so inferior and degraded that they cannot be allowed to sit in public coaches occupied by white citizens? That, as all will admit, is the real meaning of such legislation as was enacted in Louisiana.

6. Democrats Fight Back: The White-Supremacy Campaign, 1898

The Duty of White Men Today.

No man who loves his State can read the daily occurrences of crime in North Carolina where the negro is the aggressor without trembling for the future of the State.

Taken from the *News and Observer* of Raleigh, North Carolina, September 22, 1898, p. 4.

The Fusion Candidate for the Senate in Edge-combe County.

There have been more assaults upon white women by negro brutes in one year and a half of Republican rule than in twenty years of Democratic rule. There have been more insults to white girls, more wrongs to white men, more lawlessness and more crime committed by negroes in North Carolina during the last twenty months than during the previous twenty years.

More Negro Scoundrelism

Black Beasts Attempt to Outrage the Young Daughter of a Respectable Farmer.

Her Father Swears to It

These items originally appeared in the *Raleigh North Carolina News and Observer—Cartoon*, September 22, 1898, p. 1; "More Negro Scoundrelism" September 23, 1898, p.1.

Attacked on the Public Highway in
Brunswick County While Returning
From Sunday-School—Her Screams
Saved Her From a Fate Worse Than Death.

(Wilmington Star.)

Joseph Gore is an honest and respectable farmer of the county of Brunswick—poor in this world's goods, but esteemed by his neighbors. He has a wife and children, and there is a church and Sunday school near his home which are attended by his family. But he lives in a township where the negroes outnumber the whites more than three to one. This, coupled with the fact, no doubt, that Brunswick county is under Republican-fusion rule, emboldened two beastly negroes to make an attempt to outrage a young girl on the public road, as narrated in the following affidavit.

State of North Carolina,

County of Brunswick.

Personally appeared before me, Geo. H. Bellamy, a Justice of the Peace for Town Creek Township, Brunswick County, Joseph Gore, who being duly sworn, states: "Some days ago my daughter, aged 15 years, was returning from Sunday school, accompanied by her little brother, aged 12 years, about 3 o'clock in the afternoon. When about a quarter of a mile from home, two negro boys, aged about 16 to 18 years, ran after my daughter, with their coats turned over their heads to con-

The Vampire That Hovers Over North Carolina.

ceal their identity, and attempted to take hold of her, and doubtless would have placed their unholy hands on her person; and had it not been for her screams, would have doubtless accomplished their purpose. This was done in Town Creek Township, in broad daylight. The villains have not yet been detected.

(Signed.)   "Joseph Gore."

Signed and sworn to before me, this 19th day of September, A.D., 1898.

Geo. H. Bellamy, J. P.

White men of Brunswick County, can you stand that? Is there one left in the borders of your county who will not now vote against every candidate who consorts with negroes, and who is dependent on them for election? Has it come to this, that your daughters cannot attend church or Sunday school without having a body-guard to protect them from the lustful black brutes who roam through your county?

Rise in your might, white men of Brunswick. Assert your manhood. Go to the polls and help stamp out the last vestige of Republican-populist-negro fusion.

7. Walter White Remembers the Atlanta Race Riot, 1906

There were nine light-skinned Negroes in my family: mother, father, five sisters, an older brother, George, and myself. The house in which I discovered what it meant to be a Negro was located on Houston Street, three blocks from the Candler Building, Atlanta's first skyscraper, which bore the name of the ex–drug clerk who had become a millionaire from the sale of Coca-Cola. Below us lived none but Negroes; toward town all but a very few were white. Ours was an eight room, two-story frame house which stood out in its surroundings not because of its opulence but by contrast with the drabness and unpaintedness of the other dwellings in a deteriorating neighborhood.

Only Father kept his house painted, the picket fence repaired, the board fence separating our place from those on either side white-washed, the grass neatly trimmed, and flower beds abloom. . . . This spic-and-spanness became increasingly apparent as the rest of the neighborhood became more down-at-heel, and resulted, as we were to learn, in sullen envy among some of our white neighbors. It was the violent expression of that resentment against a Negro family neater than themselves which set the pattern of our lives.

On a day in September 1906, when I was thirteen, we were taught that there is no isolation from life. . . .

I had read the inflammatory headlines in the *Atlanta News* and the more restrained ones in the *Atlanta Constitution* which reported alleged rapes and other crimes committed by Negroes. But these were so standard and familiar that they made—as I look back on it now—little impression. The stories were more frequent, however, and consisted of eight-column streamers instead of the usual two- or four-column ones.

From *A Man Called White: The Autobiography of Walter White* (Athens: University of Georgia Press, 1995, 1948), pp. 5–12. Reprinted in edited form by permission of Jane White Viazzi.

Father was a mail collector. His tour of duty was from three to eleven P.M. He made his rounds in a little cart into which one climbed from a step in the rear. I used to drive the cart for him from two until seven, leaving him at the point nearest our home on Houston Street, to return home either for study or sleep. . . . Father told me as we made the rounds that ominous rumors of a race riot that night were sweeping the town. But I was too young that morning to understand the background of the riot. I became much older during the next thirty-six hours. . . .

One of the most bitter political campaigns of that bloody era was reaching its climax. Hoke Smith—that amazing contradiction of courageous and intelligent opposition to the South's economic ills and at the same time advocacy of ruthless suppression of the Negro—was a candidate that year for the governorship. His opponent was Clark Howell, editor of the *Atlanta Constitution,* which boasted with justification that it "covers Dixie like the dew." Howell and his supporters held firm authority over the state Democratic machine despite the long and bitter fight Hoke Smith had made on Howell in the columns of the rival *Atlanta Journal.*

Hoke Smith had fought for legislation to ban child labor and railroad rate discriminations. He had denounced the corrupt practices of the railroads and the state railway commission, which, he charged, was as much owned and run by northern absentee landlords as were the railroads themselves. He had fought for direct primaries to nominate senators and other candidates by popular vote, for a corrupt practices act, for an elective railway commission, and for state ownership of railroads—issues which were destined to be still fought for nearly four decades later by Ellis Arnall. For these reforms he was hailed throughout the nation as a genuine progressive along with La Follette of Wisconsin and Folk of Missouri.

To overcome the power of the regular Democratic organization, Hoke Smith sought to heal the feud of long standing between himself and the powerful ex-radical Populist, Thomas E. Watson. Tom Watson was the strangest mixture of contradictions which rotten-borough politics of the South had ever produced. He was the brilliant leader of an agrarian movement in the South which, in alliance with the agrarian West, threatened for a time the industrial and financial power of the East. . . .

. . . Watson ran for president in 1904 and 1908, both times with abysmal failure. His defeats soured him to the point of vicious acrimony. He turned from his ideal of interracial decency to one of virulent hatred and denunciation of the "nigger." He thus became a naturally ally for Hoke Smith in the gubernatorial election in Georgia in 1906.

The two rabble-rousers stumped the state screaming, "Nigger, nigger, nigger!" Some white farmers still believed Watson's abandoned doctrine that the interests of Negro and white farmers and industrial workers were identical. They feared that Watson's and Smith's new scheme to disfranchise Negro voters would lead to disfranchisement of poor whites. Tom Watson was sent to trade on his past reputation to reassure them that such was not the case and that their own interests were best served by now hating "niggers."

Watson's oratory had been especially effective among the cotton mill workers and other poor whites in and near Atlanta. The *Atlanta Journal* on August 1, 1906, in heavy type, all capital letters, printed an incendiary appeal to race prejudice backing up Watson and Smith. . . .

Fuel was added to the fire by a dramatization of Thomas Dixon's novel *The Clansman* in Atlanta. (This was later made by David Wark Griffith into *The Birth of a Nation,* and did more than anything else to make successful the revival of the Ku Klux Klan.) The late Ray Stannard Baker, telling the story of the Atlanta riot in *Along the Color Line,* characterized Dixon's fiction and its effect on Atlanta and the South as "incendiary and cruel." No more apt or accurate description could have been chosen.

During the afternoon preceding the riot little bands of sullen, evil-looking men talked excitedly on street corners all over downtown Atlanta. Around seven o'clock my father and I were driving toward a mail box at the corner of Peachtree and Houston Streets when there came from near-by Pryor Street a roar the like of which I had never heard before, but which sent a sensation of mingled fear and excitement coursing through my body. I asked permission of Father to go and see what the trouble was. He bluntly ordered me to stay in the cart. A little later we drove down Atlanta's main business thoroughfare, Peachtree Street. Again we heard the terrifying cries, this time near at hand and coming toward us. We saw a lame Negro bootblack from Herndon's barber shop pathetically trying to outrun a mob of whites. Less than a hundred yards from us the chase ended. We saw clubs and fists descending to the accompaniment of savage shouting and cursing. Suddenly a voice cried, "There goes another nigger!" Its work done, the mob went after new prey. The body with the withered foot lay dead in a pool of blood on the street.

Father's apprehension and mine steadily increased during the evening, although the fact that our skins were white kept us from attack. Another circumstance favored us—the mob had not yet grown violent enough to attack United States government property. But I could see Father's relief when he punched the time clock at eleven P.M. and got into the cart to go home. He wanted to go the back way down Forsyth Street, but I begged him, in my childish excitement and ignorance, to drive down Marietta to Five Points, the heart of Atlanta's business district, where the crowds were densest and the yells loudest. No sooner had we turned into Marietta Street, however, than we saw careening toward us an undertaker's barouche. Crouched in the rear of the vehicle were three Negroes clinging to the sides of the carriage as it lunged and swerved. On the driver's seat crouched a white man, the reins held taut in his left hand. A huge whip was gripped in his right. Alternately he lashed the horses and, without looking backward, swung the whip in savage swoops in the faces of members of the mob as they lunged at the carriage determined to seize the three Negroes.

There was no time for us to get out of its path, so sudden and swift was the appearance of the vehicle. The hub cap of the right rear wheel of the barouche hit the right side of our much lighter wagon. Father and I instinctively threw our weight and kept the cart from turning completely over. Our mare was a Texas mustang which, frightened by the sudden blow, lunged in the air as Father clung to the reins. Good fortune was with us. The cart settled back on its four wheels as Father said in a voice which brooked no dissent, "We are going home the back way and not down Marietta."

But again on Pryor Street we heard the cry of the mob. Close to us and in our direction ran a stout and elderly woman who cooked at a downtown white hotel. Fifty yards behind, a mob which filled the street from curb to curb was closing in.

Father handed the reins to me and, though he was of slight stature, reached down and lifted the woman into the cart. I did not need to be told to lash the mare to the fastest speed she could muster.

The church bells tolled the next morning for Sunday service. But no one in Atlanta believed for a moment that the hatred and lust for blood had been appeased. Like skulls on a cannibal's hut the hats and caps of victims of the mob of the night before had been hung on the iron hooks of telegraph poles. None could tell whether each hat represented a dead Negro. But we knew that some of those who had worn the hats would never again wear any.

Late in the afternoon friends of my father's came to warn of more trouble that night. . . .

We turned out the lights early, as did all our neighbors. No one removed his clothes or thought of sleep. Apprehension was tangible. We could almost touch its cold and clammy surface. Toward midnight the unnatural quiet was broken by a roar that grew steadily in volume. Even today I grow tense in remembering it.

Father told Mother to take my sisters, the youngest of them only six, to the rear of the house, which offered more protection from stones and bullets. My brother George was away, so Father and I, the only males in the house, took our places at the front windows of the parlor. The windows opened on a porch along the front side of the house, which in turn gave onto a narrow lawn that sloped down to the street and a picket fence. There was a crash as Negroes smashed the street lamp at the corner of Houston and Piedmont Avenue down the street. In a very few minutes the vanguard of the mob, some of them bearing torches, appeared. A voice which we recognized as that of the son of the grocer with whom we had traded for many years yelled, "That's where that nigger mail carrier lives! Let's burn it down! It's too nice for a nigger to live in!" In the eerie light Father turned his drawn face toward me. In a voice as quiet as though he were asking me to pass him the sugar at the breakfast table, he said, "Son, don't shoot until the first man puts his foot on the lawn and then—don't you miss!"

In the flickering light the mob swayed, paused, and began to flow toward us. In that instant there opened up within me a great awareness; I knew then who I was. I was a Negro, a human being with an invisible pigmentation which marked me a person to be hunted, hanged, abused, discriminated against, kept in poverty and ignorance, in order that those whose skin was white would have readily at hand a proof of their superiority, a proof patent and inclusive, accessible to the moron and the idiot as well as to the wise man and the genius. No matter how low a white man fell, he could always hold fast to the smug conviction that he was superior to two-thirds of the world's population, for those two-thirds were not white. . . .

The mob moved toward the lawn. I tried to aim my gun, wondering what it would feel like to kill a man. Suddenly there was a volley of shots. The mob hesitated, stopped. Some friends of my father's had barricaded themselves in a two-story brick building just below our house. It was they who had fired. Some of the mobsmen, still bloodthirsty, shouted, "Let's go get the nigger." Others, afraid now for their safety, held back. Our friends, noting the hesitation, fired another volley. The mob broke and retreated up Houston Street.

In the quiet that followed I put my gun aside and tried to relax. But a tension different from anything I had ever known possessed me. I was gripped by the knowledge of my identity, and in the depths of my soul I was vaguely aware that I was glad of it.

✝ E S S A Y S

In the first essay, Joel Williamson carefully examines the type and chronology of violence, disfranchisement, and segregation in the South. He places the shapers of southern segregation laws into the categories of Radicals and Conservatives and delineates their differing perspectives. Segregation resulted from issues surrounding race; the consequence, Williamson argues, was the growth of separate cultures in the South, one black and one white, which mentally still interacted with each other although "the frontier between them was not clearly marked." David Montejano, in the second essay, reminds us that the South was not simply biracial, but rather multicultural, especially in Florida and Texas. He examines the makings of race thinking, wherein Anglos justified their belief in Mexican inferiority on the basis of history—not unlike the way Reconstruction history was used in the establishment of Jim Crow laws—and on issues of cleanliness. Montejano argues that the relationship of segregation to land ownership and labor control—that is, class issues—dominated the thinking of both Anglos and Mexican Americans.

A Rage for Order

JOEL WILLIAMSON

The lynching of Negroes by whites in the South has indeed had a strange career. During slavery, Negroes had been lynched, especially after about 1830. But, even then, it was not at all common, and lynching was by no means reserved for blacks. In Reconstruction there were assaults by gangs of whites upon Negroes as individuals, but the pattern differed from what came later. These early attacks were often in response to trivial abuses—an alleged breach of contract, a verbal insult, a push on the sidewalk, or the display of weapons—and rape or the threat of rape played no extraordinary role. Further, white vengeance, even at the height of Ku Klux activities, was often satisfied with whippings that were graded in severity more or less to match the seriousness of the alleged offense. Atrocious as such punishments were, they stopped short of murder. Negroes were killed by whites in Reconstruction, but when this happened, they were usually shot to death instantly, without torture, without ceremony, and because they happened to be black, not because of some alleged individual transgression. It is interesting that the ubiquitous punishment of slavery, whipping, persisted through Reconstruction. It was almost as if white men reared under the peculiar institution were incapable of innovation in doing physical harm to blacks. The ultimate in studied violence against black people, death by lynching, had to wait for a new generation of young whites to grow to adulthood. Like the "new Negro," perhaps the "new whites" had not enjoyed the "civilizing" effects of slavery. Radicals did not feature blacks as children, of course, and certainly not as

From *A Rage for Order: Black/White Relations in the American South Since Emancipation* by Joel Williamson. Copyright © 1986 by Joel Williamson. Used by permission of Oxford University Press, Inc.

their children. In Radical eyes, whipping for blacks was not the ultimate punishment.

For a generation after the Civil War, Southern whites seemed to have no greater fear of black men as rapists than they had of white men committing the same crime. What they did fear, and feared immensely during the first few years after emancipation, was black insurrection, a massive and horrendous upheaval in which vast numbers of whites—men, women, and children—would suffer and die from the black rage. With the rise of Radicalism came the new fear, the fear of the Negro as rapist. With both came interracial violence in a distinctly different mode from any that had gone before. Whites began the practice of lynching as a reaction against the presumed threat of the black beast to white womanhood, but it soon became an appalling habit, applicable to a wide range of offenses, real or imagined.

One of the most striking aspects about the lynching phenomenon was, as we have seen, the suddenness of its appearance in and after 1889 as a distinctly interracial happening in the South. In 1888 there was little indication that in the following year the hysteria would be sweeping through the black belts of the South. Witness, for example, the personal transformation of Marion Butler. Butler became the chairman of the national executive committee of the Populist party in the 1890s. In 1889 he was a recent graduate of the University of North Carolina and had become the editor of the Clinton (Sampson County) *Caucasian*. Sampson County was significantly black, with more than one-third of its population Negro. The *Caucasian* itself, as its name suggested and its banner line candidly declared, was devoted to the cause of white supremacy. But the white supremacy to which it referred was that special style that ended Reconstruction. By 1889 that style of racism was rapidly becoming antique, like the Bourbons who represented it in the nation's capital. However, in Sampson County in that crucial year, Butler's own editorials began to add a sharp new cutting edge to the traditional racial sword. In September, he recommended to his readers Nathaniel S. Shaler's thinking on the Negro. "Prof. Shaler (of 'Cambridge')," he said, "considered that the negro was elevated under the conditions of slavery and he [is] losing that elevation under the experiment of citizenship—sinking back to the conditions of barbaric Africa. Prof. Shaler is the author of the new and probably correct theory for explaining the unprogressivism of the negro, namely that his animal nature so preponderates over his intellectual and moral natures, that in the age of puberty, when the animal nature developes, that the moral and intellectual qualities are clouded by the animal instinct and not only cease to develop but really retrograde." A month later Butler was still able to respond to a lynching in a piedmont county by asking for action "to prevent further taking of human life in the barbarous manner in our State. . . . But two years afterward, an alleged rape by a Negro man of a fifty-five-year-old white woman in his own county brought on what was by then the all too usual lynching and a radically different response from Butler. "This is the first lynching that has occurred in Sampson County within our remembrance," declared the thirty-one-year-old editor, "and though a dangerous precedent, is justified by public sentiment, if not by law. A more fiendish deed has not been attempted in our community in many years."

It is astounding how quickly respectable, intelligent, educated, and leading Southerners turned to support lynching on the basis of the Radical rationale. Butler, whose origins and education would seem to predict an orthodox, conservative view of blacks, executed a perfect about-face within two years. Governor Tillman . . . turned from a pronouncement in September 1891 that lynching would not be tolerated to a promise in the summer of 1892 that he would himself lead a mob to lynch a rapist.

As Radicalism seized the leaders, so, too, did it seize the masses. In the 1890s in fourteen Southern states, an average of 138 persons was lynched each year and roughly 75 percent of the victims were black. From 1900 to 1909, the number of lynchings declined by half, but Negroes were 90 percent of those lynched and the lower South remained its special scene. Between 1885 and 1907 there were more persons lynched in the United States than were legally executed, and in the year 1892 twice as many. . . .

Whatever the numbers, the cold statistics hardly begin to capture the emotional heat generated by the crisis of sex and race in the South in the early 1890s. If rapes had risen in the last few years from practically none to some fearsome number over a hundred each month, as some well-informed contemporaries thought, what was to be expected in the future? If intelligent and informed persons could believe these things, what could minds less sophisticated believe? Clearly, something drastic would have to be done, and done soon.

It is small wonder, then, that lynching increased in the South and very shortly became a regional ritual. . . .

The Separation of the Races

It is fully appropriate that legal disfranchisement and legal segregation be linked. While legal disfranchisement generally ran its course between about 1890 and 1915, legal segregation generally ran its course between about 1889 and 1915. Also, just as disfranchisement was part of a much larger process that might be called the depoliticalization of the Negro, legal segregation was part of a larger process that might be called the separation of the races. . . .

With emancipation came a great increase in the separation of the races. In quantitative terms, probably the most significant area was economics. Domestic servants in freedom fled the households of the white elite; but, more important, the demise of slavery meant the demise of the plantation as it had been both in fact and in mind. . . . [T]he vast majority of plantations, especially among those that had produced cotton or tobacco as their staple, broke down into so many farms. This occurred . . . because black people—not white people—would have it so. Blacks wanted their own farms, and they wanted their own family and no others on their farms. Whether by somehow buying land, renting for cash, or, as was massively the case, by share-cropping, this was their desire. It was a desire that went stubbornly against the strongly expressed wishes of the landed gentry. . . . Whereas black people in slavery had lived together in the very faces of the whites, they were now scattered over the countryside as separate families, relatively removed from the eyes of the whites. This was, in effect, a residential separation of a high order. The very place in which blacks had been proximate to whites before—in their work on the plantations—was now marked by a high level of separation, a separation upon which blacks themselves insisted.

Ordinarily, black people labored on their farms during the week, and on the seventh day they went to church. Here again the pattern went from whatever mixing there might have been in the churching of whites and slaves to a profound separation. Just as black people pulled away from white control on the plantations, so too did they move to pull out of white control in the churches. In the last generation of slavery, several hundred thousand slaves had been enrolled in white churches. Many hundreds of thousands more were supervised in one way or another by white churchmen in separated services. In emancipation, the white connection ended with amazing rapidity as black members withdrew from white churches and established their own. Black churches that had been physically separated but under white supervision also established their independence. In addition many blacks who had never been churched in slavery became so in freedom. Indeed, several hundred thousand black people joined the two great all-black churches, the African Methodist Episcopal Church and the African Methodist Episcopal Church Zion, both of which had often been excluded from the South in the previous generation. . . .

In freedom, there were two areas in which the two races came physically together most often. The first was as domestics, and the second was in the towns and cities and in the public carriers that joined those towns and cities. In the first relation, mixing was very tolerable to whites because the relative condition of each race was clearly fixed. There could be no misunderstanding the fact that the servant was the servant of the master or mistress. Domestic service was tolerable to blacks as a way to earn a living, and they could always move on to another household if need be. Contact in the growing towns and cities where impersonal relations were on the rise was, indeed, a racial frontier. There were not many blacks in urban areas compared with those who remained on the land, but those city dwellers were riding the wave of the future. With federal guarantees of civil rights for all citizens embodied first in the Civil Rights Act of 1866 and then in the Fourteenth Amendment in 1868, urban blacks presumed themselves to have equal rights as citizens, including equal rights to public accommodations. The black codes enacted in the South by the Johnson state governments soon after the war were outlawed, as were a scattering of specifically segregative measures. Very generally, first the military governments and then the Republican governments in the various Southern states in and after 1868 made rules and laws that positively opened all public accommodations to all people. Finally, in the twilight of Reconstruction the federal government enacted the Civil Rights Act of 1875. These acts ruled that streetcars, trains, steam passenger boats, restaurants, theaters, hotels, and all such facilities were open to all persons regardless of race. Even so, the federal and state governments did not make violations of these laws criminal offenses; they were, rather, civil offenses for which the offended party might bring a civil suit and collect damages.

Numerous black leaders asserted their rights under these laws. Apparently, they were often denied in spite of the laws. When they pressed their cases to the end, they usually won. However, the litigation was long and costly, and often damages were awarded in such trivial amounts as to constitute an opinion of the lack of seriousness of these violations. In brief, even in Reconstruction, antisegregation laws were not well enforced, and after Reconstruction were effectually vitiated by the courts. . . .

The one area in which integration in Reconstruction might have taken a great step forward was in the public schools. All over the South a mark of Republican

Reconstruction regimes was to put in place legislation for compulsory education, and in every state some progress was made in the realization of that ideal. Yet, only in New Orleans were the schools integrated in some significant measure. . . .

The failure to integrate public schools in Reconstruction, potentially an area of recurrent and intimate association between blacks and whites, was a great loss to the nation. It was an opportunity to bring up a new generation—a New Negro and a New White—that had at least had contact with one another in formative situations in which the authorities were ostensibly committed to equality. The separation of the races in the schools not only perpetuated a separation of cultures, it promoted the cultivation, the enrichment of each to the exclusion of the other. The failure to integrate was based on a conviction among many black leaders and most influential whites in education that if they integrated the public schools, the whites would stay away and thus cripple the whole effort. Black leadership in South Carolina, for instance, argued the point carefully in a constitutional convention in 1868 and decided for allowing a voluntary separation on the understanding that in time white people in their own schools would be educated up to an acceptance of the civil equality of black people. At the national level, ironically, some of the people who were most effective in promoting both white and black education—indeed, the real leaders in promoting public education in America—took the initiative in deliberately taking the schools out of the bill that was to become the Civil Rights Act of 1875. . . .

The 1880s witnessed a rapid erosion in the legal claims of Negroes to equality of access to public accommodations. In 1883 the Supreme Court vitiated the Civil Rights Act of 1875 in all places except such federal enclaves as the territories, the District of Columbia, and aboard American vessels on the high seas. Beginning with Tennessee in 1882, the various states began to pass laws mandating segregation. In the famous case of *Plessy* v. *Ferguson* in 1896 the Supreme Court ruled constitutional a Louisiana law of 1890 separating the races on most railroads provided that equal accommodations were accorded to Negroes and whites. This "separate and equal rule" would guide the courts in such cases for the next sixty years.

The advent of Radicalism ushered in another era in the separation of the races. It was an era in which separation was legalized. Whereas in Reconstruction there had been laws against segregation, in and after 1889 there were waves of laws passed actually requiring segregation. This change represented no great revolution in physical arrangements because blacks had not been using these facilities in any large numbers anyway. It was a revolution, however, in declarations of intent by governments and the white constituencies they represented. These laws came in three waves: 1889–93, 1897–1907, and 1913–15; and they related to specific areas. The first two waves primarily affected public accommodations, especially common carriers, namely, trains, streetcars, and passenger boats. The third wave related to new industrial and urban situations. Specifically, it segregated facilities in factories, particularly toilets, and set up schemes designed to achieve block-by-block segregation in urban housing. That something new was happening in the separation of the races was indicated by the fact that a new word was required for such occasions. The word "segregation" apparently was not much used before 1899, and when it was used it had no special racial connotations. In and after that time, it was used frequently to refer to the separation of the races, and it seemed to carry with it the idea that the separation referred to was effected by law. The nationalization of the word seemed to occur in 1913 and 1914 with the attention that was focused on the attempt to segregate facilities in Washington, D.C. . . . .

Virginia offers a good example of . . . segregation. There had been . . . troubles on the trains in Virginia in the 1890s. When the reformers got firmly in control for a time after 1900, they passed a segregation law. It set aside facilities for black people, a place where black people could ride by themselves and have dignity as well as comfort. In true Virginia style, it also divided white facilities. Trains that made sufficiently long runs were required to provide not only a separate car for blacks, but also first- and second-class cars for whites. The second-class white car was for the less genteel sort, the people who wanted to do what they used to do in the second-class car, plus those who chose not to or could not afford to pay first-class fare. The first-class car, of course, was for ladies and gentlemen. Just as Virginia reformers were willing to leave some black men enfranchised and were not at all unwilling to disfranchise some white men, so too would they make a place for black people on the trains and segregate less worthy whites in second-class facilities. . . .

By far the most vigorous acts of segregation came in the first two waves. The third wave, in 1913–15, was clearly feeble. Indeed, it was then that segregation was turned back at the borders of the South. Ordinances for affecting residential segregation block-by-block were reversed or failed to pass in Baltimore and Oklahoma City. In Wilmington, Delaware, a move to establish separate windows for black and white citizens to do business with the city was defeated. In the North, attempts to pass legislation based on Radical premises also failed. In 1907, for instance, a proposal by the future mayor of New York City, Jimmy Walker, to pass a law against miscegenation was defeated in the state legislature. Geographically, by 1915, Radicalism had reached its high water marks somewhere south of Wilmington and east of Oklahoma City.

After 1915 the era of legal separation expired. Obviously, segregation laws were passed in considerable numbers thereafter; but they were passed sporadically, spottily, and in a makeshift fashion. Often they came in response to new technology or new institutions. Thus, laws concerning elevators, airplanes, and buses appeared. Here and there laws required that textbooks that had been used in black schools could not be used in white, and separate Bibles were required in the courtrooms upon which to touch and swear.

Unlike laws disfranchising blacks, which at least were well-thought-out and internally consistent within each state, segregation laws within each state were passed over a long period of time, related to different areas, varied widely from state to state, and varied even more widely within each state as towns, cities, villages, and other local communities made their own laws. The results were rather chaotic, especially for a black person traveling. In 1892 a young black man from Raleigh, North Carolina, on his way to enroll in Meharry Medical School in Nashville, Tennessee, came to appreciate that fact. He had just been in railroad stations during his trip in which the drinking fountains were not segregated. Arriving in Chattanooga, he was bending down to drink at the fountain when he sensed some movement behind him. He turned just in time to see a policeman poised to bring his billy club down on his head. He was able to explain to the policeman that he did not know the local law or custom and escape beating and arrest. Again the Radical point was vividly made.

White people made the rules, and they could make them as arbitrarily as they pleased. If black people did not understand the rules, it was but another sign of their non-belonging in a white man's country.

The Separation of Cultures

The deep and peculiar separation of races that came to the South in the twentieth century was a matter of minds as well as bodies, and it had its roots in the separation of black and white cultures. . . .

The process of cultural separation was long in the making, but it was in full flux precisely as the passage of segregating legislation reached a crescendo between 1897 and 1907. In that decade, those multifarious black enclaves that emerged during and after Reconstruction were coming rapidly under the unifying aegis of Booker T. Washington, and in their many parts they carried within them the hard core of black culture for the twentieth-century South. Washington's leadership had many failings, but it did at least raise a flag under which the great mass of black people could rally as distinctly black. However arrived at, the South—and the nation—would soon have a black world on one side and a white world on the other.

The growing separation of cultures in the postwar South was evident in many ways. One clear manifestation was in music. Blues was long considered "race" music; that is, for blacks only. As such, it was often denigrated by jazz musicians of both races. Unalloyed Bluesmen, such as B. B. King, found little audience for their talent outside of the "chitlin circuit," as the round of black clubs and theaters was called.

Cultural separation was also manifested in a separation of language. Black and white language evolved away from each other, and that process was succinctly illustrated . . . in naming practices. In slavery, black people had typically taken names from four sources. In early slavery, African names, such as Sambo, meaning second son, persisted. As creolization occurred, and Africans in America began to generate a new world culture fitted to their lives on this side of the Atlantic, African names sometimes shifted into American variations. Negro children in America in the fifth, sixth, and seventh generations continued to receive African names or variants thereof, not in veneration of Africa, but rather in honor of some older American-born relatives who bore those names. In slavery blacks had also taken Biblical names such as Gabriel, Joshua, and Rachel, classical names such as Bacchus, Scipio, and Phoebe, and British names such as George, Charles, and Mary. In freedom, African-derived and classical names tended to disappear while Biblical and British names remained. Toward the end of the nineteenth century, however, black people began to invent given names that were not at all in the language of whites. For examples, Robert Charles's youngest sister was named Floril, and a younger brother Aliac. Another brother, born in 1869, was named John Wesley, while three older brothers born in slavery were named George, Henry, and Charles. In the twentieth century the tendency became even more pronounced, and one encounters Countee Cullen, Eartha Kitt, Wynonie Harris, and Leontyne Price. Beautiful, euphonious, and close-fitting names, but distinctly not white.

Given two cultures, the issue became not a matter of whether or not there would be separation. It was, rather, a matter of what would be the process and form of separation. There would be prejudice and discrimination on both sides, and there would be responses on both. There would be a white country and a black country, and the frontier would find itself wherever the balance between the needs and power of white people and the needs and power of black people was struck. How was the balance struck? Historically in the South it has been found in a process probably best described as the "etiquette" of race relations. That process has never been a matter primarily of either laws or no laws, and de facto separation is a rather clumsy term, hobbled specially by the fact that it has come to be reflexively juxta-posed to legal separation. Legal separation was embodied in the whole matrix and had no opposite.

In a very real sense, there was no single or unitary race line in the South either before, during, or after the era of segregative legislation. Probably, only a North-erner like the journalist Ray Stannard Baker, who wrote a book on the subject, could imagine that he was following a color line, and he, perhaps, was led to do so by his origins in a North that in 1908 was being flooded to overflowing by ghettoiz-ing immigrants from Southern and Eastern Europe. Just as the attempt to apply class lines derived from European culture does not work well in the homogeneous Old Settled South—indeed does more to confound understanding than it does to promote it—so too with race lines. Race relations in the South have been worked out very much like white relations have been worked out—each case, each event, each meeting between one and another as it occurred. When black met white, the nature of the exchange was negotiated according to the time, the place, and the indi-viduals involved—with sensitivity to generally understood customs. There were guidelines to behavior, but what was to be done in a specific situation was what was most comfortable to the parties concerned. In a specific situation one could err in judgment and act beyond the tolerances of custom. But etiquette itself required for-giveness of the avowedly contrite transgressor. It was always a matter of individual responsibility. The two cultures evolved words to say, gestures to make—a lan-guage in which individuals might negotiate interracial encounters; but each situa-tion was unique, and the solution in each situation personal and creative. There was a black country and a white country, and the frontier between them was not clearly marked and was ever-shifting as if in some undeclared and usually quiet war. The location and nature of the frontier were much more a function of mind than of mat-ter, of white minds and black minds rather than white bodies and black bodies.

The Culture of Segregation

DAVID MONTEJANO

. . . In the minds of most Anglos, there was no question that Mexicans were an infe-rior people. Herschel Manuel pointed out the assumption in a 1930 report on Mexi-can school segregation: "The evidence that in general the Mexicans are considered inferior by non-Mexicans is not hard to find. It is so pronounced and so much a part of general knowledge in the state that it seems superfluous to cite evidence that it

Reprinted from *Anglos and Mexicans in the Making of Texas, 1836–1986* by David Montejano. Copy-right © 1987. Reprinted by permission of the University of Texas Press.

exists. To Texas readers one could almost say, 'Ask yourself,' or 'Consult your own experience.' ". . . [T]he images and ideas of race . . . were offered as common sense, as conventional wisdom, to explain the particular ordering of people and privilege.

My interpretation of race-thinking involves three tasks. The first is to identify the major themes expressed in the mass of racial opinions and beliefs of the Anglo settlers. What specifically did "Mexican" mean as a sign of inferiority? What ideas or images were associated with being Mexican? The second task is to outline how the farm order made the "races" of the region. Although in the 1920s and 1930s it seemed as if these commonsense ideas about Mexican inferiority had always been present—and in some sense, they had been—their emergence as public themes corresponded to the development of commercial agriculture. These ideas, in other words, were closely related to changes in the class order, a point I will discuss in some detail. The final task is to discuss how race ideas outlined the basis for an appropriate relationship between the two communities. Race ideas, in providing explanations for the position of Anglo and Mexican, also provided a basis for control of the Mexican, a critical element for the stability of the new farm order. To the extent that such ideas were accepted by both Anglo and Mexican, they served to legitimize the segregated order.

Ideas of Race or Class?   Playing the part of a devil's advocate, agricultural economist Paul Taylor tested the limits of the segregated order by asking Anglos about "equality with the educated Mexicans." Was segregation more a matter of class or of race? No straightforward answer was possible. Anglos were intransigent in their opposition to equality with Mexicans, and their comments generally made references to both race and class.

On the one hand, the question of skin color made equality with the Mexican, whether educated or not, impossible. A Nueces County professional man, although hedging a bit on the question, gave a typical response: ". . . you crowded me there [with the question]. Not as a rule, you can't give them social equality. Any other dark-skinned, off-color race is not equal to us. I may be wrong . . . but I feel, and the general public here, feels that way. They are not as good as Americans." An "old salt" in Dimmit County handled Taylor's hypothetical question about equality by lecturing the testy young professor on Texas history: "They are a mixture, a mule race or cross-breed. The Spaniard is a cross between a Moor or a Castilian, and the Indian is a cross with them. I know a case in which the father is a mixture of Indian, white and Negro. The mother is Mexican. By intermarriage you can go down to their level but you can't bring them up to yours. You can put that down and smoke it. When you cross five races you get meanness." A ranch manager's wife in the same county was willing to allow for "educating Mexicans" with one condition: "Let him have as good an education but still let him know he is not as good as a white man. God did not intend him to be; He would have made them white if He had." And a West Texas dairy farmer familiar with anthropological theory was in favor of educating Mexicans but noted that they would "never amount to anything . . . [because] they are brunettes. The blondes organize and are at the head in giving directions." The specific racial explanations were diverse and incorporated historical, religious, and scientific arguments.

The Taylor interviews make clear, on the other hand, that these wide-ranging race arguments derived a basic shared meaning from the class structure of the farm societies. The fact that Anglos were the owners and bosses and Mexicans the field workers provided the necessary ground for the elaboration of these various notions of Mexican inferiority. Thus, the dairy farmer never strayed far from the practical importance of his blonde-brunette theory: "Mexican labor is as essential at this degree of latitude as plows. We are blondes. They have pigment to absorb the actinic rays of the sun. . . ." . . . More direct in pointing out the combination of race and class was a newcomer school official in Dimmit County: "We have a high type of American and low class Mexican people. The inferiority of the Mexican is both biological and class. White trash is not superior in intellect to the Mexicans we have here, but we don't have any white trash here." Even religious principles that supported a charitable view were constrained by the sharp class differences that separated Anglo from Mexican. In the words of a Winter Garden housewife: "I try to be a Christian, but whenever it comes to social equality I won't stand for it. Say 'Mr.' or 'Mrs.' to the Mexicans? No sir-ee!! Not to the class we have around here."

In short, the elements of race and class were inextricably interwoven in the minds of Anglo residents. When the pragmatic language of interest or control was not used to explain the segregated order, the language of race entered in a critical way to fill out the details, to paint the color, of the regional society.

Themes in Race-Thinking

While Mexican inferiority was taken for granted by most Anglos, their specific views were complex and belied any appearance of a simple pattern. Mexican inferiority meant different things to different Anglos. Native Texans recalled Texas history or remembered the experiences of long-dead relatives who had fought against Mexicans. Newcomers, who had no easy recourse to Texas history, relied on their own experience with colored peoples in explaining their treatment of Mexicans. Transplanted southerners merely transferred their views of black labor to Mexican labor, and some exmidwesterners saw Mexicans as "domesticated Indians." For those new settlers with no strong racial bias on which to build, assimilation of Texan frontier lore quickly filled the void, and many who initially were taken aback at the conditions they found in South Texas often became, with a few years of residence, more Texan than the old-timers.

In the Winter Garden town of Catarina, for example, the initial reaction of its northern homesteaders was one of shock; they were unaccustomed to the low wages and brutal treatment of Mexican laborers. . . . The comments of a Winter Garden school official, a newcomer, suggested the social adjustments one learned to make: "The newcomer here seldom comes into conversation with the local people. After a few years he takes the views of the older people. At first I felt like doing a lot more for the Mexicans. At the beginning I would not have been opposed at heart to their coming over to the white school, but after I heard the old-timers I felt differently. There is a line between the two towns." The assimilation process worked its magic in the American farm towns. The distinction between old-timer and newcomer, so sharp in the first twenty years of the farm developments, gradually broke down. Despite the reputed arrogance of Texan natives, newcomers showed themselves capable of learning old-timer lessons about "cotton and Mexicans."

From this diverse mass of ideas and images, however, one prominent thread emerges. . . . Old-timer ideas were rooted in frontier memories, in war and battle with Mexicans and Indians. Newcomer ideas, on the other hand, consisted of concern with hygiene and notions of germ theories. These two sets of ideas were not rigidly compartmentalized between the two groups; what separated old-timers and newcomers was the ease with which they referred to one or the other set of images. With the "amalgamation" of newcomer and old-timer, the distinction between historical and hygienic themes gradually became unimportant.

The Old-timer Theme: Remember the Alamo?   One common justification for anti-Mexican prejudice lay in the Anglo-Texan legends and folklore about Texas history. In these popular accounts, the Mexican was portrayed as the enemy that Texans had fought and defeated in several official and unofficial wars throughout the nineteenth century. By the early twentieth century the story of the Alamo and Texas frontier history had become purged of its ambiguities—of the fact that Mexicans and Anglos had often fought on the same side. The exploits of Texas dime novels had become woven into an Anglo-Texan saga, into a history of the triumph of Anglo over Mexican. Texans, according to historian T. R. Fehrenbach, "came to look upon themselves as a sort of chosen race." This legacy, symbolized by the battle cry "Remember the Alamo!" was part of the folk culture, an integral part of school curricula, and the essence of Texan celebrations.

Thus, for native Texans the lessons of history (and the fruits of victory) explained the Mexicans' inferior place. Texas history made the issue of equality with Mexicans a rather absurd proposition, as a native Texan, a schoolteacher, explained: "Maybe some day these greasers can be (elevated) but Mexico is too near, and past Texas history. . . . They look at Texas with covetous eyes. We have border troubles here, and revolutionary cliques. . . . In one Mexican uprising their aim was the King Ranch. We were in fear at night even in Caldwell County. We heard the 'Mexican troops were pressing towards Texas.' " Regardless of which aspect of the Mexican problem was mentioned, Texans frequently injected a historical element in outlining their position. . . .

The point may be stated another way. Texan historical memories played a part similar to that of Reconstruction memories in the Jim Crow South of the same period. As a southerner described the latter (in the 1940s): "Stories of Reconstruction days in the South are kept vividly alive not because of historical interest, but because they provide the emotional set which any good Southerner is supposed to have." In the first forty years of the twentieth century, the story of the Alamo furnished both old-timer and newcomer with the emotional set for being "good Texans." Américo Paredes has summarized the matter well: "The truth seems to be that the old war propaganda concerning the Alamo, Goliad, and Mier later provided a convenient justification for outrages committed on the Border by Texans of certain types, so convenient an excuse that it was artificially prolonged for almost a century. And had the Alamo, Goliad, and Mier not existed, they would have been invented, as indeed they seem to have been in part."

The Newcomer Theme: Mexicans Are Dirty.   Even as the newcomer farmers were assimilated as Anglo-Texans, they transformed the pioneer ranch country into a modern farm world—into a society with new classes, new social relations, new

definitions, new symbols. . . . A more prominent, more relevant appeal among the
farm settlers was a reference to hygiene: Mexicans were dirty. This characterization
constituted the primary language in which segregation was discussed and assessed
among the farmers. Germ theories, in particular, were an excellent vehicle for explaining the separation or quarantine of Mexicans in Texas.

These ideas about dirtiness were imported by the new settlers. "Twenty-five
per cent of the newcomers," estimated Cameron County sheriff Emilio Forto (in
1919), "usually look upon the Mexican as filthy, unsanitary and sickly makeshift."
As a result "everything relative to the Mexican and his habits becomes repulsive to
the American who has been fed on anti-germ theories for a lifetime." The repulsion
was evident in the responses to Taylor's questions about "mixing with Mexicans."
As one Nueces County farmer put it: "I don't believe in mixing. They are filthy and
lousy, not all, but most of them. I have raised two children with the idea that they
are above the doggone Mexican nationality and I believe a man should." A. H.
Devinney, superintendent of Agua Dulce schools in the same county, explained that
Anglos "would drop dead if you mentioned mixing Mexicans with whites. They
would rather not have an education themselves than associate with these dirty Mexicans." Several counties away in Dimmit, a school official noted that such intense
opinions were commonplace: "There would be a revolution in the community if the
Mexicans wanted to come to the white schools. Sentiment is bitterly against it. It is
based on racial inferiority. We have an exaggerated idea of their inferiority. The
Mexicans have head and body lice and don't want to bathe."

Concern with hygiene did not exhaust the meaning of "dirty Mexicans." Anglos commonly used the adjective "dirty" as a synonym for dark skin color and inferiority. Another common but more complex use of dirtiness was as an expression of
the class order in the farm societies. For some Anglos, dirtiness stood as an appropriate description of the Mexican's position as a field laborer. Thus, farmers, when
they talked about dirty Mexicans, generally didn't mean dirty in any hygienic
sense; they meant dirty in the sense of being an agricultural laborer, in the sense of
one who "grubs" the earth. For others who believed, as one bus driver did, that
Mexicans were a "nasty" people who lived in "bunches and shacks," dirtiness referred to the living conditions of Little Mexicos. Mexican dirtiness, in this sense,
was a metaphor of the local class structure.

As a class metaphor, the caricature was supported, on the one hand, by the fact
that farm labor was exclusively the work of Mexicans. On the other hand, the notion of Mexican dirtiness was suggested and reinforced daily by the physical condition of the Mexican towns in Texas. Mexicans did live in "bunches and shacks." In
the Winter Garden, according to a federal survey conducted in the 1930s, the "typical houses of Mexicans" were unpainted one- or two-room frame shacks with single
walls, dirt floors, one or two glass windows, and outdoor toilets. The poorer houses
were "patched together from scraps of lumber, old signboards, tar paper, and flat-
tened oil cans." Some of the families had no stoves, and the women cooked outside
over open fires or, when the weather made it necessary, inside in open washtubs.
Cleanliness was impossible: "Children slept on dirt floors, rolled up in quilts; clothing was kept in boxes under beds or cupboards; and although most of the Mexican
housewives strove for neatness and cleanliness, these were qualities impossible to
achieve in the face of such obstacles."

Given these living conditions, added the federal report, it was not surprising that sickness and disease were common in the Mexican quarter. Serious epidemics of preventable diseases like diphtheria "broke out" occasionally. Tuberculosis, according to a federal official in the area, was extremely high among Mexicans because they "had been undernourished over a long period of years." Such poverty-related diseases, needless to say, validated the fear Anglos had of dirty Mexicans; they enabled, in the psychiatric language of Joel Kovel, "the entire complex of prejudiced fantasies to attain the certification of belief."

In short, the theme of dirtiness resonated with meaning. In the minds of Anglos it referred to the race, work position, and living conditions, as well as hygiene, of Mexicans in Texas. Although these various meanings of dirtiness could generally be found together in segregationist statements, the most respectable way of making the point was through an emphasis on the problem of Mexican hygiene. Thus, the *Report of Illiteracy* in Texas, a University of Texas bulletin issued in 1923, called for separate schools on the basis of cleanliness: for "those who have not seen can scarcely conceive of the filth, squalor, and poverty in which many of the Mexicans of the lower classes live." The report elaborated: "Many of the children are too ill-clad to attend school with other children. The American children and those of the Mexican children who are clean and high-minded do not like to go to school with the dirty 'greaser' type of Mexican child. It is not right that they should have to do so. There is but one choice in the matter of educating these unfortunate children and that is to put the 'dirty' ones into separate schools til they learn how to 'clean up' and become eligible to better society.". . .

In one word, then, the idea of dirtiness portrayed the manner in which the farm settlers thought of the matters of race and class in their new society. . . .

One further point remains to be explored. These race ideas not only were justifications for policies and behavior; they also contained the elements of a new understanding. The segregated order was, of course, ultimately supported through physical force, but much more effective in regulating everyday life were the ideas and values that were taught and reinforced through the reality of segregation. More effective was the word of the superior that passed for truth, for beauty, for honor, for morality. Douglas Foley and his co-authors suggest this type of legitimation in their history of Frio County when they note that "paternalistic kindness and the Mexicano's acceptance of Anglo superiority were far more powerful forms of control than physical violence." To the extent that the notion of dirtiness and other ideas were accepted by Anglo and Mexican as criteria of inferiority, these ideas offered the prospect of an organic reconstitution of the new class society. Having already described the opinions of Anglo adults[,] I can now turn to the opinions of children, particularly Anglo children, and to the opinions of Mexicans with respect to the segregated world in which they lived.

Learning About Supremacy.   The truth about Anglo superiority and Mexican inferiority was taught to the youngest generation of the farm towns. Newcomers into this world, those who migrated as well as those born into it, were taught the morals and rules of living in a segregated society. In a world already divided into compartments, these lessons about the important differences between Anglo and Mexican came in numerous, diverse, and easy ways. Anglo and Mexican children, for example, understood that separate schooling meant separation of superior from inferior. This meaning was taught to them in countless lessons—the Mexican school was physically inferior, Mexican children were issued textbooks discarded by Anglo children, Mexican teams were not admitted to county athletic leagues, Mexican girls could not enter beauty contests, and so on.

The Anglo children readily understood the [catechism] of segregation: Mexicans were impure and to be kept in their place. Anglo children understood this well, of course, because their parents and teachers made it clear to them. One notable demonstration of their comprehension of these tenets occurred in Dimmit County when anxious school authorities found themselves short of books at the Anglo school. They had the Mexican children send over their books but "the American children refused to use any of the books . . . because they said the Mexicans had used them."

It was the lot of Anglo boys, naturally, to maintain and defend social standards. In the Winter Garden, observed an approving official, the Mexicans were considered "almost as trashy as the Negroes," and "the white boys are quick to knock their block off if they [the Mexicans] get obstreperous." In Nueces County, where a similar situation existed, a school official put it this way, "The white child looks on the Mexicans as on the Negro before the war, to be cuffed about and used as an inferior people." In Corpus Christi, where the American high school accommodated a few Mexicans, Mexican students spoke bitterly about hazing and wanted a separate high school. In Dimmit County, many parents, both Anglo and Mexican, believed that separation was necessary to keep the peace, that separation avoided fighting. And some school officials in both Dimmit and Nueces frankly attributed the low attendance of Mexican children to the antagonism they encountered from Anglo students and teachers. Such antagonism, not surprisingly, often relied on the lessons learned from Texas history. One Texas Mexican recalled that "when we were told of the Alamo in school, some of the Mexicans stayed away from school and some never returned.". . .

Learning About Inferiority.   The inferior place of Mexicans, as mentioned previously, could not be maintained by physical force alone. The stability of the segregated order rested on Mexican recognition of their own inferiority. Mexicans had to be taught and shown that they were dirty and that this was a permanent condition— that they could not become clean. How well did the Mexicans learn?

There were diverse responses in the Mexican community to these notions of Anglo supremacy and Mexican inferiority. Mexicans in the Winter Garden, according to Foley's historical account, had "contradictory feelings" of gratitude, anger, frustration, and resignation concerning their experience with Anglos. Some Mexicans accepted Anglo beliefs about Anglo superiority, yet others could never admit such things because they "hated them [Anglos] too much." Mexican youth in the same region displayed their defiance of the racial order with some regularity: heckling, gang rumbles, and other confrontations with Anglo youth were commonplace. And among the small but growing class of professionals and propertied townspeople, the "educated Mexicans" of which Taylor spoke, there were vigorous campaigns against discrimination and prejudice.

Much of the Mexican response to the racial order, however, occurred on the cultural field created by the Anglo settlers. Judging from the campaigns organized by the League of United Latin American Citizens (LULAC), the rhetoric of protest conformed to the dominant ideas of the time. The argument the educated Mexicans wished to make, and they made it forcefully, was that not all Mexicans were dirty. A no less important argument was that American-born Mexicans were loyal, patriotic Americans. Thus, the expressed purpose of the league, which in the 1920s saw itself "as a small nucleus of enlightenment" for the rest of the Mexican community, was "to develop . . . the best, purest and most perfect type of a true and loyal citizen of the United States of America." The standards that the league expected of its exclusive membership were the highest standards of respectability—speak English, dress well, encourage education, and be polite in race relations. Andres de Luna, a prominent leader of the Corpus Christi chapter, explained the approach as follows: "We try to teach our children to be clean and to tell the teachers to send them back home to be cleaned. Some of the other nationalities are dirty too."

In other words, the race ideas of Anglos—ideas of cleanliness, of beauty, of respectability—constituted much of the cultural ground on which segregationist policies were discussed and debated. These ideas were diffused throughout the social order, among young and old, Anglo and Mexican. The notion of Mexican dirtiness, in particular, permeated the opinion of the time, influencing even opposition arguments to segregation. The campaigns of LULAC were one example, but there were others. For instance, sympathy for the Texas Mexican led Professor Herschel Manuel of the University of Texas to take issue with the popular and official opinion about dirty Mexicans. Interpreting the epithet literally, Manuel conducted a comprehensive survey in the region to measure hygienic conditions among Mexican children. He discovered, contrary to the widespread belief, that many schools had no difficulty at all with Mexican dirtiness. In one South Texas school with nearly nine hundred children in the first three primary grades, the "ratio of dirty children to total enrollment" was 3, 2, and 2 percent for the first, second, and third grades, respectively. Head lice was a more serious problem: 62 percent of the first graders, 50 percent of the second graders, and 46 percent of the third had been infected with lice at some point in the school year. In another school, however, the first-grade infection rate had been reduced "from 80 percent in the first month of school to 8 percent in the second month." There was room for optimism, concluded Manuel: "The treatment for lice is a very simple one and very effective unless the child is reinfected." The results of Manuel's study however, do not matter so much; what is important and ironic in this defense of Mexicans was that Manuel had operationalized the idea of "dirty Mexican."

The limits to such hegemonic ideas were always present. The very contrast in living conditions that validated race ideas for the Anglo also ensured permanent questioning by the Mexican. Thus, the idea of cleanliness was constantly in danger of exposure as self-serving rhetoric that justified segregation. Even the ambitious middle-class Mexicans could not reconcile the contradictions between their assimilationist posture and the intransigence of the Anglo community. The editor of the *LULAC News,* F. Valencia, posed the dilemma concisely in describing the problem of securing adequate education for Mexican children in 1931: "But how can we make rapid strides toward this goal, when at every turn we are confronted by the segregation question in various towns? In some towns they say it is for pedagogical reasons. At others they give no reasons, and perhaps don't care to give any, they taking it for granted that the reason is well understood (inferiority as they see it). Such are the obstacles placed before us by the same people whose standards we are trying to adopt." Cleanliness, as the educated Mexicans continually discovered, was simply not enough. . . .

These race ideas, moreover, point to the historically specific character of the class order; in this case, to a society composed of farmers and migratory laborers. The rich, clean, and loyal were of one color, and the poor, dirty, and disloyal of another. But the effectiveness of much racial imagery was based on the politics and culture of a particular class context. Thus, already in the late 1920s, the civil rights campaigns of the small Texas Mexican middle class suggest what the emergence of this class signified for the culture of racism. Although these campaigns were presented in the name of the Mexican community, they were essentially class-specific protests: they pressed for the rights of the respectable educated Mexicans. The aim of these protests was not the abolition of all discrimination or the eradication of the cleanliness standard; the aim rather was to secure an acknowledgment from Anglos that some Mexicans could become clean.

⚓ FURTHER READING

Eric Anderson, *Race and Politics in North Carolina, 1872–1901* (1981)

James D. Anderson, *The Education of Blacks in the South, 1860–1935* (1988)

Theodore W. Allen, *The Invention of the White Race: The Origin of Racial Oppression* (1998)

Armando C. Alonzo, *Tejano Legacy: Rancheros and Settlers in South Texas, 1734–1900* (1998)

Elizabeth Bethel, *Promiseland* (1981)

John W. Blassingame, *Black New Orleans, 1860–1880* (1973)

W. Fitzhugh Brundage, *Lynching in the New South* (1993)

———, ed., *Under Sentence of Death* (1997)

John W. Cell, *The Highest Stage of White Supremacy* (1982)

Helen G. Edmonds, *The Negro and Fusion Politics in North Carolina, 1894–1901* (1951)

Neil Foley, *The White Scourge: Mexicans, Blacks, and Poor Whites in Texas Cotton Culture* (1997)

George Fredrickson, *The Black Image in the White Mind* (1971)

Willard B. Gatewood, *Aristocrats of Color: The Black Elite, 1880–1920* (1990)

Glenda Gilmore, *Gender and Jim Crow* (1996)

Kenneth W. Goings, *Mammy and Uncle Mose: Black Collectibles and American Stereotyping* (1994)

John W. Graves, *Town and Country: Race Relations in an Urban-Rural Context* (1990)

Janette Greenwood, *Bittersweet Legacy: The Black and White "Better" Classes in Charlotte* (1994)

Grace Hale, *Making Whiteness: The Culture of Segregation in the South* (1998)

Louis R. Harlan, *Booker T. Washington: The Making of a Black Leader, 1856–1901* (1972)

Robert C. Kenzer, *Enterprising Southerners: Black Economic Success in North Carolina, 1865–1915* (1997)

J. Morgan Kousser, *The Shaping of Southern Politics* (1974)

Leon Litwack, *Trouble in Mind: Black Southerners in the Age of Jim Crow* (1998)

Gordon B. McKinney, *Southern Mountain Republicans, 1865–1900* (1978)

Neil R. McMillen, *Dark Journey: Black Mississippians in the Age of Jim Crow* (1989)

August Meier, *Negro Thought in America, 1880–1915* (1963)

Pauli Murray, *Proud Shoes* (1956, 1978)

Sydney Nathans, *The Quest for Progress* (1983)
Nell Irvin Painter, *Exodusters* (1977)
Howard N. Rabinowitz, *Race Relations in the Urban South, 1865–1890* (1978)
Donald Spivey, *Schooling for the New Slavery* (1978)
Mildred Thompson, *Ida B. Wells-Barnett: An Exploratory Study of an American Black Woman, 1893–1930* (1990)
George Brown Tindall, *South Carolina Negroes, 1877–1900* (1952)
Vernon Lane Wharton, *The Negro in Mississippi, 1865–1890* (1947)
Shane White and Graham White, *Stylin': African American Expressive Culture* (1998)
Joel Williamson, *The Origins of Segregation* (1968)
———, *The Crucible of Race* (1984)
C. Vann Woodward, *Origins of the New South* (1951)
———, *The Strange Career of Jim Crow,* 3d rev. ed. (1974)

C H A P T E R
7

Southern Religion and
the Lost Cause

Religion remains one of the major characteristics of southern identity. Evangelical Protestantism became central to the perspectives of both black and white southerners, though they responded to its theology in different ways. In the postwar era, many white southerners, despondent over defeat and convinced of God's displeasure, sought solace in evangelical Protestantism, where the focus remained on hoped-for redemption, personally and regionally. African Americans formed evangelical churches, which served to unite, protect, support, and educate freedpeople in a sacramental and social institution. In towns and cities, black churches offered respite from racial discrimination and often provided a base for social protest. African American ministers emerged as powerful leaders who urged their congregations to persevere—and even to protest.

Evangelical Christianity's enthusiastic, joyful style of worship and distinctive preaching, its emphasis on conversion, salvation, and love, its focus on the individual's personal relationship with God, its insistence on funding missions and spreading the gospel, its fascination with sin and the eradication of "sinful vices," its soulful music, its reluctance to engage in social reform, and its preference for large-scale revivals, all contributed to a distinctive and unique religious culture in the South. So dominant was this evangelical culture that one may forget that the South was also home to mainstream Protestant and Roman Catholic churches and Jewish synagogues.

For some, the ideology of the Lost Cause resembled religion—a civil religion. The intertwining of symbol, pageantry, parades, and catechism blended with devotion to the image of an unspoiled Old South and a cause that many believed was noble. Confederate veterans and the United Daughters of the Confederacy carefully nourished Lost Cause ideals, trained the younger generation to revere and respect its mission, and imbued the so-called southern way of life and culture with religious, almost divine, significance.

After the 1890s, many churchmen and churchwomen supported social reforms and considered themselves progressive. The roots of child labor reform, welfare, and even civil rights may be found in the South's religiosity. But the region's distinctive evangelical style remains in place today, as evidenced by the fact that

187

the majority of televangelists are southern. The South is still considered the most religious section of the nation. How can the region's history help explain this? What has been the relationship between southern religion and segregation or between southern religion and reform? Is southern religion a force for inspiring change—or for sanctifying the status quo? How did white southerners use the sacred to enhance the Lost Cause? What role did gender play in the creation of a Lost Cause ideology?

✝ D O C U M E N T S

Evangelical theology is not all of a piece; there are disparate black and white interpretations and numerous differences among the denominations. In black and white sacred music, the past figured significantly, but in contrasting ways. Negro spirituals from the slavery era often had double meanings, as indicated in "Steal Away to Jesus." Hymns in white churches after the Civil War sanctified the Lost Cause, as the 1901 variation on "When the Roll Is Called Up Yonder" in Document 1 reveals. In Document 2, black leader W. E. B. Du Bois reflects on the pervasiveness of religion in the life of African Americans. Document 3, a sermon by John Lakin Brasher, a minister in the evangelical Holiness Movement, indicates with typographical emphasis basic tenets of evangelical Protestantism—each person is a sinner who can be redeemed only through the grace of God. In Document 4 Lillian Smith, well-known author and civil rights advocate, recalls in excerpts from her book *Killers of the Dream* the lessons that southern religion imparted to her. In Document 5, Cornelia Branch Stone, author of the U. D. C. Catechism for Children, outlines the "correct" answers to questions regarding the Old South, the Civil War, and the South in 1912. The term *catechism* is defined as a summary of religious doctrine in the form of questions and answers. Finally, in Document 6, Katharine Du Pre Lumpkin, civil rights supporter and author of *The Making of a Southerner,* recalls with irony and sadness how the Lost Cause was sustained for her and her siblings through family instruction.

1. Two Hymns

"Steal Away to Jesus," a Negro Spiritual, N.D.

Chorus

Steal away, steal away, steal away to Jesus!
Steal away, steal away home,
I ain't got long to stay here.
Steal away, steal away, steal away to Jesus!
Steal away, steal away home,
I ain't got long to stay here.

My Lord, He calls me.
He calls me by the thunder,
The trumpet sounds within-a my soul,
I ain't got long to stay here.

First song can be found in James Weldon Johnson, ed., *The Book of Negro American Spirituals* (New York: Viking Press, 1925), pp. 114–117. Second song can be found in Robert H. Coleman, ed., *The Modern Hymnal: Standard Hymns and Gospel Songs: New and Old for General Use in All Services* (Nashville: Broadman Press, 1926), p. 366.

Chorus

> Green trees a bending, po' sinner stand a-trembling,
> The trumpet sounds within-a my soul,
> I ain't got long to stay here,
> Oh, Lord I ain't got long to stay here.

"When the Roll Is Called Up Yonder," 1901

When this time with us shall be no more and final taps shall sound,
And the Death's last cruel battle shall be fought;
When the good of all the armies shall tent on yonder camping ground,
When the roll is called up yonder, let's be there.

On that mistless, lonely morning when the saved of Christ shall rise,
In the Father's many-mansioned home to share;
Where our Lee and Jackson call us to their homes beyond the skies,
When the roll is called up yonder, let's be there.

If all's not well with thee, my comrades, for thy entrance at the gate,
Haste thy calling and election to prepare;
You will find that precious peace, sweet peace,
When the roll is called up yonder, let's be there.

2. W. E. B. Du Bois on the Faith of the Fathers, 1903

It was out in the country, far from home, far from my foster home, on a dark Sunday night. The road wandered from our rambling log-house up the stony bed of a creek, past wheat and corn, until we could hear dimly across the fields a rhythmic cadence of song,—soft, thrilling, powerful, that swelled and died sorrowfully in our ears. I was a country school-teacher then, fresh from the East, and had never seen a Southern Negro revival. To be sure, we in Berkshire were not perhaps as stiff and formal as they in Suffolk of olden time; yet we were very quiet and subdued, and I know not what would have happened those clear Sabbath mornings had some one punctuated the sermon with a wild scream, or interrupted the long prayer with a loud Amen! And so most striking to me, as I approached the village and the little plain church perched aloft, was the air of intense excitement that possessed that mass of black folk. A sort of suppressed terror hung in the air and seemed to seize us,—a pythian madness, a demoniac possession, that lent terrible reality to song and word. The black and massive form of the preacher swayed and quivered as the words crowded to his lips and flew at us in singular eloquence. The people moaned and fluttered, and then the gaunt-cheeked brown woman beside me suddenly leaped straight into the air and shrieked like a lost soul, while round about came wail and groan and outcry, and a scene of human passion such as I had never conceived before.

Those who have not thus witnessed the frenzy of a Negro revival in the untouched backwoods of the South can but dimly realize the religious feeling of the slave; as described, such scenes appear grotesque and funny, but as seen they are

W.E.B. DuBois on the Faith of the Fathers, 1903. Reprinted by permission.

awful. Three things characterized this religion of the slave,—the Preacher, the Music, and the Frenzy. The Preacher is the most unique personality developed by the Negro on American soil. A leader, a politician, an orator, a "boss," an intriguer, an idealist—all these he is, and ever, too, the centre of a group of men, now twenty, now a thousand in number. The combination of a certain adroitness with deep-seated earnestness, of tact with consummate ability, gave him his preëminence, and helps him maintain it. The type, of course, varies according to time and place, from the West Indies in the sixteenth century to New England in the nineteenth, and from the Mississippi bottoms to cities like New Orleans or New York.

The Music of Negro religion is that plaintive rhythmic melody, with its touching minor cadences, which, despite caricature and defilement, still remains the most original and beautiful expression of human life and longing yet born on American soil. Sprung from the African forests, where its counterpart can still be heard, it was adapted, changed, and intensified by the tragic soul-life of the slave, until, under the stress of law and whip, it became the one true expression of a people's sorrow, despair, and hope.

Finally the Frenzy or "Shouting," when the Spirit of the Lord passed by, and, seizing the devotee, made him mad with supernatural joy, was the last essential of Negro religion and the one more devoutly believed in than all the rest. It varied in expression from the silent rapt countenance or the low murmur and moan to the mad abandon of physical fervor,—the stamping, shrieking, and shouting, the rushing to and fro and wild waving of arms, the weeping and laughing, the vision and the trance. All this is nothing new in the world, but old as religion, as Delphi and Endor. And so firm a hold did it have on the Negro, that many generations firmly believed that without this visible manifestation of the God there could be no true communion with the Invisible. . . .

The Negro church of to-day is the social centre of Negro life in the United States, and the most characteristic expression of African character. Take a typical church in a small Virginian town: it is the "First Baptist"—a roomy brick edifice seating five hundred or more persons, tastefully finished in Georgia pine, with a carpet, a small organ, and stained-glass windows. Underneath is a large assembly room with benches. This building is the central club-house of a community of a thousand or more Negroes. Various organizations meet here,—the church proper, the Sunday-school, two or three insurance societies, women's societies, secret societies, and mass meetings of various kinds. Entertainments, suppers, and lectures are held beside the five or six regular weekly religious services. Considerable sums of money are collected and expended here, employment is found for the idle, strangers are introduced, news is disseminated and charity distributed. At the same time this social, intellectual, and economic centre is a religious centre of great power. Depravity, Sin, Redemption, Heaven, Hell, and Damnation are preached twice a Sunday with much fervor, and revivals take place every year after the crops are laid by; and few indeed of the community have the hardihood to withstand conversion. Back of this more formal religion, the Church often stands as a real conserver of morals, a strengthener of family life, and the final authority on what is Good and Right.

Thus one can see in the Negro church to-day, reproduced in microcosm, all that great world from which the Negro is cut off by color-prejudice and social condition. . . .

Such churches are really governments of men, and consequently a little investigation reveals the curious fact that, in the South, at least, practically every American Negro is a church member. Some, to be sure, are not regularly enrolled, and a few do not habitually attend services; but, practically, a proscribed people must have a social centre, and that centre for this people is the Negro church. The census of 1890 showed nearly twenty-four thousand Negro churches in the country, with a total enrolled membership of over two and a half millions, or ten actual church members to every twenty-eight persons, and in some Southern States one in every two persons. Besides these there is the large number who, while not enrolled as members, attend and take part in many of the activities of the church. There is an organized Negro church for every sixty black families in the nation, and in some States for every forty families, owning, on an average, a thousand dollars' worth of property each, or nearly twenty-six million dollars in all.

3. Sermon of John Lakin Brasher

The Holy Spirit is the only one that can conVICT a sinner. Not in a trial of a thousand years could the church or the singers or the preachers conVICT ONE HUMAN SOUL. He uses singers. He uses preachers. He uses the CHURCH. But He, alone, can convict. Conviction is one hundred percent divine.

He's the only one that can asSIST a sinner to rePENT. Sinner thinks he can repent any time he PLEASES. No, that's a FALlacy. You can only repent when He HELPS you, and if He is grieved and DOESN'T help, no one can repent. His GRACious asSISTance must be GIVen every SOUL or they must perish.

He's the only one that can GIVE a man or a woman a NEW HEART. Not all the sacraments administered by whomsoever can give any man a NEW HEART. It's a fallacy to think that you can get a man out of the world, and bring him and join him into your church, and administer to him the comMUNion, and make a CHRIStian out of him. The only POWER in the HEAVENS or the EARTH that can make a man a NEW HEART is the Holy Ghost.

He's the only one that can tell that man when he HAS done it that it IS done. Nobody can tell you when you are born of God, but the Holy Spirit ALONE can tell you that. For He's the only one that KNOWS, 'til He has reVEALed it to you.

He's the only one that can show a believer that deep, dark, hidden sin, lodged way down in his nature, that CARnal mind, that something that won't be GOOD, that something that can't be made good.

He's the only one that shows its DEPTH, its HEINousness, its UGliness, and its hell-worthiness.

He's the only one that can assist a believer to CONsecrate. Somebody said consecration is one thing, and sanctification is God's part, but it's only half true. You can't consecrate fully to God, DEATHlessly to God, without the assistance of the

From *The Sanctified South: John Lakin Brasher and the Holiness Movement,* by J. Lawrence Brasher. Copyright © 1994 by the Board of Trustees of the University of Illinois. Used with the permission of the University of Illinois Press and the editor.

Holy Ghost. And GOD CANNOT SANCtify you without your choice and faith. It takes BOTH YOU AND GOD to meet these conditions and GIVE you a holy heart.

He's the only one that can tell you when you have GOT a clean heart.

He's the only one that can CLEANSE your heart.

He's the only one that can keep you from FALLing and present you FAULTless before the presence of His glory with exceeding joy. From the time you are awakened to the fact that you are a sinner until you are housed in heaven, it is HIS hand that guides, HIS hand that saves, HIS voice that awakens, HIS Spirit that teaches, for the WHOLE WORK of redemption is NOW in HIS hands. (SR 36)

4. Lillian Smith on Lessons About God and Guilt

Our first lesson about God made the deepest impression on us. We were told that He loved us, and then we were told that He would burn us in everlasting flames of hell if we displeased Him. We were told we should love Him for He gives us everything good that we have, and then we were told we should fear Him because He has the power to do evil to us whenever He cares to. We learned from this part of the lesson another: that "people," like God and parents, can love you and hate you at the same time; and though they may love you, if you displease them they may do you great injury; hence being loved by them does not give you protection from being harmed by them. We learned that They (parents) have a "right" to act in this way because God does, and that They in a sense represent God, in the family.

Sometimes, when we felt weakened by anxieties that we had no words for, and battered by impulses impossible to act out, we tried to believe that God was responsible for this miserable state of affairs and one should not be too angry with parents. At least we thought this as we grew older and it helped some of us make a far more harmonious adjustment to our parents than to God.

As the years passed, God became the mighty protagonist of ambivalence although we had not heard the word. He loomed before us as the awesome example of one who injures, even destroys, in the name of "good" those whom He loves, and does it because He has the "right" to. We tried to think of Him as our best friend because we were told that He was. Weak with fear, we told ourselves that when you break the rules you "should be punished" by Him or your parents. But a doubt, an earthy animal shrewdness, whispered that anyone who would harm us was also our enemy. Yet these whispers we dared not say aloud, or clearly to ourselves, for we feared we might drop dead if we did. Even a wispy thought or two loaded us down with unbearable guilt. As we grew older and began to value reason and knowledge and compassion, we were told that He was wise and all-loving; yet He seemed from Old Testament stories to be full of whimsies and terrifying impulses and definitely not One whom a child could talk to and expect to receive an understanding reply from.

He was Authority. And we bowed before His power with that pinched quietness of children, stoically resigning ourselves to this Force as it was interpreted by the grown folks.

But life seemed a lost battle to many of us only after we learned the lesson on the Unpardonable Sin. Then it was that man's fate, our fate certainly, was sealed. According to this lesson, received mainly at revival meetings but graven on our hearts by our parents' refusal to deny it, God forgave, if we prayed hard and piteously enough, all sins but one. This one sin "against the Holy Ghost" He would never forgive. Committing it, one lived forever among the damned. What this sin was, what the "Holy Ghost" was, no one seemed to know. Or perhaps even grown folks dared not say it aloud. But the implication was—and this was made plain—that if you did not tread softly you would commit it; the best way was never to question anything but always accept what you were told.

Love and punishment . . . redemption and the unpardonable sin. . . . He who would not harm a sparrow would burn little children in everlasting flames. . . . It added up to a terrible poetry and we learned each line by heart.

5. U.D.C. Catechism for Children, 1912

What causes led to the war between the States, from 1861 to 1865?

The disregard, on the part of the States of the North, for the rights of the Southern or slave-holding States.

How was this shown?

By the passage of laws in the Northern States annulling the rights of the people of the South—rights that were given to them by the Constitution of the United States.

What were these rights?

The right to regulate their own affairs and to hold slaves as property.

Were the Southern States alone responsible for the existence of slavery?

No; slavery was introduced into the country in colonial times by the political authorities of Great Britain, Spain, France and the Dutch merchants, and in 1776—at the time of the Declaration of Independence—slavery existed in all of the thirteen colonies.

How many of the colonies held slaves when the federal constitution was adopted, in 1787?

All except one.

Did slavery exist among other civilized nations?

Yes, in most all; and our mother country, England, did not emancipate her slaves until 1843, when Parliament paid $200,000,000 to the owners.

After the first introduction of slavery into the colonies, how was the African slave trade kept up?

By enterprising shipowners of New England, who imported the slaves from Africa and secretly sold their cargoes along the coast, after the States of the North had abolished slavery.

Why did not slavery continue to exist in the States of New England?

Because they found it unprofitable, and they sold their slaves to the States of the South.

Reprinted courtesy of the Rosenberg Library, Galveston, Texas.

What great leader in the Northern army owned slaves?

Gen. U. S. Grant, who continued to live on their hire and service until the close of the war, and after the emancipation proclamation had been published, while he was leading armies to free the slaves of the South.

When the Northern States had sold their slaves to the South, what did they then do?

They organized a party to oppose slavery, called the "Abolition Party," which advocated all means to abolish slavery, with no intention of paying the people of the South for their property.

When did the South become alarmed?

At the election of Abraham Lincoln by this party, which was pledged to take away the slaves and offer no terms of payment to the owners.

Did the people of the South believe that slavery was right?

No, not as a principle; and the colonies of Virginia and Georgia had strongly opposed its first introduction, but after the Constitution of the United States had recognized the slaves as property, and the wealth of the South was largely invested in negroes, they did not feel it was just to submit to wholesale robbery.

How were the slaves treated?

With great kindness and care in nearly all cases, a cruel master being rare, and lost the respect of his neighbors if he treated his slaves badly. Self-interest would have prompted good treatment if a higher feeling of humanity had not.

What was the feeling of the slaves toward their masters?

They were faithful and devoted and were always ready and willing to serve them.

How did they behave during the war?

They nobly protected and cared for the wives of soldiers in the field, and widows without protectors; though often prompted by the enemies of the South to burn and plunder the homes of their masters, they were always true and loyal.

What were the principles of the Southern people?

They believed that each State should regulate her own affairs, according to its best interests, with no meddling with the management of other States, and that each State should loyally support the Constitution of the United States.

Who was most prominent in defining "State Rights?"

John C. Calhoun, of South Carolina.

What steps did the Southern people take after the election of Mr. Lincoln?

They seceded from the Union, and at once took possession of the forts, arms and ammunition within their borders.

Did the forts surrender without resistance?

In nearly all cases.

In what order did the States secede?

South Carolina, December 20, 1860.

Mississippi, January 9, 1861.

Florida, January 10, 1861

Alabama January 11, 1861.

Georgia, January 19, 1861.

Louisiana, January 26, 1861.

Texas, February 1, 1861.

Virginia, April 17, 1861.
Arkansas, May 6, 1861.
North Carolina, May 20, 1861.
Tennessee, June 24, 1861.
Missouri, October 31, 1861.
Kentucky, November 20, 1861.
What other State attempted to secede?
Maryland.
How was this prevented?
The Maryland Legislature was closed by the United States marshal and the secession members were sent to prison on September 18, 1861.
What had happened before this in Baltimore?
Federal troops in passing through that city to invade the South, were attacked on April 19, 1861, by the citizens of Baltimore, and a fight ensued in the streets, and the first blood of the war was there shed.
Did Maryland take any part in the cause of the South?
Yes, most valiant part, by furnishing many regiments of men and other aid for carrying on the war, and those who gave this aid endured persecution and imprisonment by the Federal authorities, as well as from those at home who opposed secession. Maryland was only kept in the Union by force.
What honor did General Lee confer on Maryland officers?
In the last retreat of the world-famed fighting army of northern Virginia he appointed Col. H. Kyd Douglas and Col. Clement Sullivane, two staff officers, one twenty-four years of age, the other twenty-six, to command the rear guard of the two divisions of the little army on its way to Appomattox.
What was the first step taken by the seceded States?
They proceeded to organize a government, by uniting themselves under the name of the Confederate States of America, and adopted a Constitution for their guidance.
Whom did they elect as their President?
Jefferson Davis, of Mississippi, senator from that State in the Congress of the United States, when Mississippi seceded, and already distinguished as a soldier and statesman, having gallantly served in the Mexican war, and as secretary of war under President Pierce, and member of both houses of Congress.
Did he resign his seat in the Senate as soon as his State seceded?
No. His State seceded on January 9th, and he remained in the Senate until January 21st, pleading for some pledge from the North that would secure the interests of the people of the South.
Does it appear from this that he led his people to secession?
No; like General Lee, he was led by the people of his State, obeying their call, and believing that his first duty was to his State. . . .
What purposes have the Daughters of the Confederacy?
To preserve the true history of the Confederacy and keep in sacred memory the brave deeds of the men of the South, their devotion to their country and to the cause of right, with no bitterness toward the government of the United States, under which we now live.
What other purpose have the Daughters of the Confederacy?

To teach their children from generation to generation that there was no stain upon the action of their forefathers in the war between the States, and the women of the South who nobly sustained them in that struggle, and will ever feel that their deathless deeds of valor are a precious heritage to be treasured for all time to come.

For what was the army of the South particularly noted?

For its great commanders—great as soldiers and great as men of stainless character—and for the loyalty of the men in the ranks, who were dauntless in courage, "the bravest of the brave," ever ready to rush into the "jaws of death" at the command of their great leaders.

6. Katharine Du Pre Lumpkin on the Lost Cause

Confederate reunions . . . came infrequently. At least it was so for us children. We must wait until it was the turn of our town again to welcome the old men. Moreover, reunions could not do everything. They could be counted upon to arouse our Southern patriotism to a fervid pitch and spur us on to fresh endeavors. When all was said and done, however, something continuing and substantial should be going on if we children were indeed to fulfill the part our people had set their hearts upon.

My father put it this way. He would say of his own children with tender solemnity, "Their mother teaches them their prayers. I teach them to love the Lost Cause." And surely his chosen family function in his eyes ranked but a little lower than the angels. He would say: "Men of the South, let your children hear the old stories of the South; let them hear them by the fireside, in the schoolroom, everywhere, and they will preserve inviolate the sacred honor of the South."

Many other men like Father—men of his station and kind, men who like him still lived in the days of their lost plantations—also said such words, said them continually. For my home, I know it did not rest at words. I know that Father not alone preached these things. In very fact he lived them, at the same time impregnating our lives with some of his sense of strong mission. . . .

My father devised one special means for teaching us. . . .

Our "Saturday Night Debating Club" was . . . a training ground, although to us it seemed much more an absorbing family game. It was serious business, but never solemnly serious, nor would any of us have been left out of it for anything. Even I was allowed a small part in keeping with my tender years. On most weekdays Father must be away from home attending to the task of making a living. Each Saturday night he would announce the topic for the next meeting, but being away, he left much of our advice in preparation to Mother. She was entirely qualified to give it, although of course when Father was there we naturally turned to him. Indeed, Mother turned us, saying, "Ask your father. He knows about that better than I do." Occasionally the subject for debate would be an old-fashioned query—"Is the pen mightier than the sword?" Usually, and these were our favorites, we argued topics of Southern problems and Southern history. I say "we."

The most I ever contributed were a few lines which Mother had taught me. After that I was audience.

We would hurry through Saturday-night supper and dishes. A table would be placed in the parlor, Father seating himself behind it, presiding. On either side were chairs for the debaters. Mother and I comprised the audience, although at the proper time she would retire with Father to assist in judging. All being assembled, Father would rap firmly for order, formally announce the subject, introduce the first speaker on the affirmative, and the game was on.

And what a game! What eloquence from the speakers! What enthusiasm from the "audience"! What strict impartiality from the chairman! And how the plaster walls of our parlor rang with tales of the South's sufferings, exhortations to uphold her honor, recitals of her humanitarian slave regime, denunciation of those who dared to doubt the black man's inferiority, and, ever and always, persuasive logic for her position of "States Rights," and how we must at all times stand solidly together if we would preserve all that the South "stood for.". . .

There was the glamorous, distant past of our heritage. Besides this, there was the living, pulsing present. Hence, it was by no means our business merely to preserve memories. We must keep inviolate a way of life. Let some changes come if they must; our fathers had seen them come to pass: they might grieve, yet could be reconciled. It was inconceivable, however, that any change could be allowed that altered the very present fact of the relation of superior white to inferior Negro. This we came to understand remained for us as it had been for our fathers, the very cornerstone of the South.

It too was sanctified by the Lost Cause. Indeed, more than any other fact of our present, it told us our cause had not been lost, not in its entirety. It had been threatened by our Southern disaster (we would never concede the word "defeat"). No lesson of our history was taught us earlier, and none with greater urgency than the either-or terms in which this was couched: "Either white supremacy or black domination." We learned how Restoration—or the Redemption, as men still said in their more eloquent moments—had meant this as much as anything to our heritage. "The resounding defeat of the forces of darkness. The firm re-establishment of our sacred Southern principles." To be sure, we learned all this long after we had begun to behave according to the practical dictates of the "sacred principle" of white supremacy.

☧ *E S S A Y S*

In the first essay, historian Paul Harvey writes about black and white southern Baptists, the largest group among evangelical Protestants in the South. He argues that static concepts of evangelical individualism conceal the actual "diversity of southern religious life." He advocates understanding the central role that evangelicalism played in creating "redemption" for white Baptists and liberation for black Baptists. In the next essay, Charles Reagan Wilson explains the connection between the white southerners' religious beliefs, southern history, and the creation of a Lost Cause ideology. In the final essay, Elizabeth Hayes Turner argues that white women, through the United Daughters of the Confederacy, furthered acceptance of the Lost Cause ideology by imbuing their activism with religious and cultural symbolism.

Redeeming the South

PAUL HARVEY

Southern historians have searched for a central theme to bring together the difficult contradictions of the southern past—in particular, the paradox of slavery and freedom. Scholarship on religion in the American South, however, has engaged in little argument on the topic. The central theme of southern religious history in scholarly works remains the rise of evangelicalism, symbolized in the term "Bible Belt" and expressed institutionally in the numerical and cultural dominance of Baptist and Methodist churches. According to this view, the focused moment of salvation has constituted the bedrock of southern religious belief and practice. This evangelical individualism stifled any social ethic, leaving southern churches captive to racism and a dogmatic literalist theology.

Musicians and novelists of the South have recognized the centrality of evangelical Protestantism in a region "haunted by God." William Faulkner, hardly renowned for adherence to evangelical morality, nevertheless acknowledged how he "assimilated" the regional religious tradition, how he "took that in without even knowing it. It's just there. It has nothing to do with how much I might believe or disbelieve—it's just there."

But an overly simple and static use of the concept of evangelicalism hides the diversity of southern religious life. Thomas Dixon Sr. was a conservative Baptist minister in North Carolina. His son Thomas Dixon Jr. also pastored in Baptist churches but branched off into Shakespearean theater and authored the novels *The Leopard's Spots* and *The Clansman*, graphic classics of the popular culture of American racism. The later adaptation of these works into "Birth of the Nation," the 1915 technological wonder of the film world, provided Dixon (and director D. W. Griffith) with a canvas painted with grotesque white supremacist visions of a unified nation. Yet the junior Dixon also served as an advocate of the social gospel, a movement anathematized by many southern evangelicals. His brother, Amzi Clarence Dixon, helped to organize the emerging Fundamentalist movement of the early twentieth century and abhorred Thomas's popular works of fiction as much as Thomas poked fun at Amzi's stuffy theology. The Dixon family of North Carolina illuminates some of the diverse varieties of southern evangelicalism.

In the 1890s, many southern Baptist parishioners heard weekly homilies espousing conformity to a private, domestic evangelicalism and warning of the dangers of radical ideologies such as Populism. At the same time, rural congregants might hear fiery sermons that condemned the plutocrats and "social parasites" of the era. Rural Baptists of the era typically met in a one-room structure in the countryside in congregations of one hundred or fewer, heard a part-time bivocational minister at monthly meetings, and concentrated their religious expression on overcoming sin and achieving salvation. Meanwhile, inside the impressive structure of the First Baptist Church of Atlanta, a congregation of several hundred experienced an ordered and decorous service. The concept of southern evangelicalism thus explains everything and nothing at the same time.

The static use of this paradigm also obscures the dynamic function of black churches in the postbellum era. Booker T. Washington, a black Baptist layperson, found himself appointed as the designated race spokesman after his famous "Atlanta Compromise" speech in 1895, in which he had advised black Americans to "cast down" their buckets where they were—the South. In the minds of white listeners he seemed to accept second-class citizenship for African Americans. Washington found many supporters within the National Baptist Convention, an organization created in the same year of Washington's speech. But the black Baptist church also nourished figures such as Sutton Griggs, a minister, educator, and novelist from Texas who formulated an early form of Afrocentrism, and Nannie Burroughs, a woman who lashed out unflinchingly at racial hypocrisies while fiercely defending middle-class ideals and the rights of African Americans to aspire to them. After Reconstruction these churches rarely challenged the southern racial order in an overt way, providing instead a means of survival for a beleaguered community. This response in itself constituted a rebuke to a southern social order that mercilessly attacked the essential humanity of black people.

The growth of Baptist churches from small outposts of radically democratic plain-folk religion in the mid-eighteenth century into conservative and culturally dominant institutions in the twentieth century illustrates one of the most impressive evolutions of American religious and southern cultural history. . . . By 1910, about 40 percent of white churchgoers and 60 percent of black churchgoers in the South were Baptists. Most of these nearly five million southern Baptists worshiped in churches associated with the Southern Baptist Convention (white) or the National Baptist Convention (black). In the twentieth century, the Southern Baptist Convention (SBC) became the largest Protestant denomination in America, while the National Baptist Convention (NBC) grew to be the largest black religious organization in the world. Both conventions expanded their influence into outside areas, but until the 1920s the great majority of constituent churches for both groups remained in the South. Churches not affiliated with the SBC or NBC usually were connected to Primitive Baptist groups, who rejected larger denominational structures and mission endeavors. Primitive Baptists, concentrated in Appalachia and in up-country regions of the South, made up just over 10 percent of Baptists. Numerous other groups—Regulars, Old Regulars, Independent, Two-Seeds-in-the-Spirit, and so on—made up a rich tapestry of Baptists in Appalachia. Their religious expressions, lovingly described in Deborah McCauley's work, *Appalachian Mountain Religion,* made up an alternative subculture from the mainstream Baptist expressions that form the primary emphasis of this.

Historians now understand southern Baptists as part of the mainstream rather than the exotic fringes of American religious and cultural history. Evangelical Protestantism ordered the lives of millions of common folk in the South long after its central role in other parts of the country had been diminished. The southern evangelical emphasis on direct, immediate, and vibrantly emotional contact with God has given the South its distinctive religious coloration. This emphasis on experience remains firmly in the center rather than on the fringes of religious expression in the region.

Historians also have explored thoroughly the argument that southern churches languished in "cultural captivity." White southern churches rarely sought to overturn the southern social and racial hierarchy but rather reinforced and even defined it. In this sense they remained in bondage to southern culture, at least according to traditional definitions of this term. The cultural captivity thesis highlights the moral failings of white southern religion, as it was originally designed to do. But the argument fails to place southern religious history in a bicultural context. Based on studies of white churches and denominational organizations, the model ignores the presence and agency of black churches. It could just as easily be said, moreover, that southern culture fell captive to southern religion. But which "southern religion" and which "southern culture"? Would it be the southern religion of Thomas Dixon Sr., or his son, the famous novelist Thomas Dixon Jr., or Dixon's fundamentalist brother, Amzi Clarence Dixon? Would it be the southern religion of Martin Luther King Jr.'s father, or of Ned Cobb, the black cotton farmer and activist in the Sharecropper's Union in Alabama? By singularizing the terms southern religion and southern culture, the argument overlooks the multilayered nature of religious and cultural interactions.

Beyond the cultural captivity thesis, there remain deeper questions about the relationship of southern Baptists and southern cultures. Anthropologists have explained how religion provides mythological underpinnings for particular cultures, while it also allows dissident groups a chance to formulate alternative visions for a new order. When this idea is applied to southern religion, it is possible to replace the "captivity" metaphor altogether and use instead anthropological notions of religion and culture as inextricably intertwined. Southern culture has been identified closely with decentralized, localistic, traditionalist patterns of life and with highly persistent cultures. Well into the twentieth century, southern folk remained intensely defensive of local norms and reluctant to break from entrenched practices. They found in both their white and black Baptist churches a powerful theological and ecclesiastical tradition—congregational independence—that taught that God had sanctioned local men and women to run their own spiritual affairs and implied that they were meant to control their own destinies. The fierce localism of southern Baptist churches, the tenacity of rural religious practices, and the conflict between these practices and the centralizing desires of denominational reformers and Progressive Era activists suggest a fresh way to look at the relation of southern religion and southern culture. This same congregational control allowed black Baptists to nourish a unique religious culture that, though politically subdued during the early twentieth century and relentlessly criticized by both white and black Baptist denominationalists, was a wellspring from which flowed later movements for freedom. . . .

The Civil War revolutionized southern religious life for both blacks and whites. Before the war, the white southern ministry reaffirmed the view that "pure religion" involved defining and enforcing the proper behavior of individuals in their divinely prescribed social duties, not questioning the roles themselves. Ministers led in the "sanctification of slavery," realizing that the defense of chattel slavery in a liberal democracy necessitated the divine stamp of approval for "our way of life." The axiom that politics should be left out of the pulpit effectively muffled religious dissent. White southern evangelicalism served conservative ends from the early nineteenth century forward. But this implicit prohibition against ministers engaging in "political-religion" loosened considerably during and after the war. Baptist ministers took an active part in secession discussions, some fervently supporting it, others fearing it as a rash and unwarranted move. The Alabaman Basil Manly Sr. exulted in his prominent role in secession discussions. The genteel Virginian John A. Broadus opposed secession but decided in 1861 that "it would be worse than idle to *speak* against it now" and that he should "resolve to do my duty as a citizen here." Southern political leaders understood the necessity of enlisting the spiritual authority held by Methodist and Baptist clerics for the war effort. A way thus opened for ministers to accept a greater sense of public responsibility. Chaplaincy in the Confederate army deeply informed the consciousness of a younger generation of evangelical ministers. Religious organizations such as the SBC flooded wartime camps with religious literature. After the war, elite ministers such as the Virginia Baptist John William Jones evangelized for the Lost Cause, the worship of Confederate heroes. They preserved the sense of the sacred in white southern history originally learned in the Confederate camps.

"Redemption" (meaning, in the religious sense, "washed in the blood") referred politically to the return of white Democrats to power in the 1870s. It also graphically symbolized the often bloody mixing of religion and politics in the postbellum South. During Reconstruction and into the 1880s, ministers preached a Lost Cause theology. The sacrifice of brave Confederate soldiers, they intoned, cleansed the South of its sin, while the cultural determination of whites after the war ensured the return of a righteous order. Once preached in this idiom—the language of the white evangelical South—this view hardened into an orthodoxy that pervaded southern historical interpretation for a century to come.

The Civil War revolutionized black religious life as well. African Americans interpreted the war as a conflict about slavery long before white political leaders North or South conceded as much. After the war, organizers of African American religious institutions used this biblical interpretation of current history—the war and Reconstruction—to galvanize support for the Republican Party. And the separate religious life that enslaved blacks developed before the Civil War, even while worshiping in white churches, took an institutional form after 1865, as African American believers withdraw from white congregations.

White and black Baptists profoundly influenced each other. Together, and separately, they created different but intertwined southern cultures that shaped Baptists in deep and lasting ways. Southerners of widely varying social groups, from plantation owners to yeoman farmers to enslaved blacks, accepted the evangelical Protestant mythology of mankind's unearned ability to achieve salvation. They rarely questioned the assuredness of salvation for the elect and damnation for the unconverted. They expected and demanded that believers exercise their faith by participating in a community of local Christians and by caring for those who were still "lost." By 1920 these beliefs had undergone challenges and some alteration, but the evangelical template still provided a pattern for the culture. The struggle against modernism marked southern religion as a distinctive element in the national culture. Fundamentalism originated as an intellectual movement in northern seminaries, but in the twentieth century it became identified with a group of southern evangelicals given to gloomy premillennial prophecies.

The congregationalism of Baptist church governance also continued to shape the lives of southern believers and the larger culture. To be a southern Baptist meant to worship in a local congregation that exercised ultimate authority in church matters. It meant voting on who would pastor the church, how the church would expend its funds, and how the church's worship service would be conducted. Local congregational control—termed "Baptist democracy" by denominational apologists—also ensured that southern vernacular styles could be exercised freely in congregational gatherings. The localism and traditionalism so entrenched in southern culture found safe haven within the walls of self-governing congregations, where the people of a community could practice "watchcare" on each other and suspiciously guard against sinful influences from the outside world. Denominational leaders found some success in implanting in their constituency Victorian bourgeois norms of private spiritualities and public behavior, but their "progress" in achieving this was slow. The resistance put up by congregants to the visions of the reformers—whether continuing to sing in southern oral dialect, refusing to cooperate with centrally organized denominational programs, or resisting modernizing trends in theology—demonstrated the tenacity of rural culture in southern Baptist life. This resistance also meant estrangement from an increasingly heterogeneous and urbanized America. But Southern religious forms survived the programmatic piety of denominational reformers and gradually penetrated American popular expressions later in the twentieth century.

Southern religion in the white sense has usually produced a profoundly conservative stance, while southern religion for blacks, though rarely assuming any revolutionary bent in the postwar South, has supported prophetic voices of change. The religious cultures of blacks and whites in the South provided the moral and spiritual force both for the Civil Rights movement and for the dogged resistance to it. Blacks transformed the hymn "Woke up this morning with my mind / Set on Jesus" into the civil rights anthem "Woke up this morning with my mind / Stayed on Freedom." Conservative southern whites adopted southern evangelical strictures and added to them the technology of modernity.

Into the 1940s, when white southern Baptists might be worshiping in a small church in Bakersfield, or black Baptists in scattered congregations in south Chicago, religious styles with rural roots endured and were adapted to new settings. Congregants lined out old hymns, listened to impassioned changed sermons, set aside mourners' benches for the benefit of the unsaved under conviction, and condemned the traditional vices of drinking, dancing, and gambling. Even while many Americans moved to secular ways of perception and action, southern Baptists (many of whom no longer lived in the South) deliberately and proudly remained outside of the national mold set during the era of modernization. They remained instead firmly inside the evangelical consensus of the nineteenth century. By staying where they were, they found themselves in the twentieth century marginalized from the dominant culture. Today, while still seeing themselves as outsiders, their styles have become part of the dominant national culture, and they have claimed a political inheritance denied their forebears. Southern Baptists, white and black, were two peoples divided by religious cultures with different historical roots that ultimately nurtured a tree that sprouted diverse and unique branches.

The Lost Cause as Civil Religion

CHARLES REAGAN WILSON

This is a study of the afterlife of a Redeemer Nation that died. The nation was never resurrected, but it survived as a sacred presence, a holy ghost haunting the spirits and actions of post–Civil War Southerners. Embodying the dream of Southerners for a separate political identity, the Confederacy was defeated by Father Abraham and an apparently more blessed, as well as more self-righteous, Redeemer Nation. But the dream of a separate Southern identity did not die in 1865. A Southern political nation was not to be, and the people of Dixie came to accept that; but the dream of a cohesive Southern people with a separate cultural identity replaced the original longing. The cultural dream replaced the political dream: the South's kingdom was to be of culture, not of politics. Religion was at the heart of this dream, and the history of the attitude known as the Lost Cause was the story of the use of the past as the basis for a Southern religious-moral identity, an identity as a chosen people. The Lost Cause was therefore the story of the linking of two profound human forces, religion and history. . . . It was a Southern civil religion, which tied together Christian churches and Southern culture. . . .

By 1861 Southern churches, like other regional institutions, had . . . laid the basis for secession. For a generation they had preached of slavery's divine nature and the need to protect it. Unionist sentiment did exist among ministers, and those in the border states urged a policy of moderation after Lincoln's election. But in the crisis of secession and the attack on Fort Sumter in the spring of 1861, Southern clergymen and their institutions made clear their commitment to what they believed was God's cause. Like their counterparts in the North, Southern clerics preached that their cause was a holy one: they interpreted battle victories as God's blessings, and defeats as God's punishments for their failings. A recurring phrase in the Confederate religious lexicon was "baptism of blood." In his sermon "Our National Sins," preached on November 21, 1860, before Lincoln's inauguration, the distinguished Presbyterian theologian James H. Thornwell called for secession, even though "our path to victory may be through a baptism of blood." In 1862 the Episcopal Bishop Stephen Elliott observed, "All nations which come into existence at this late period of the world must be born amid the storm of revolution and must win their way to a place in history through the baptism of blood." "A grand responsibility rests upon our young republic," said the Episcopal rector B. T. Lacy in 1863, "and a mighty work lies before it. Baptized in its infancy in blood, may it receive the baptism of the Holy Ghost, and be consecrated to its high and holy mission among the nations of the earth." This evocative, powerful terminology suggested the role of war in

---

From Charles Reagan Wilson, *Baptized in Blood: The Religion of the Lost Cause, 1865–1920* (Athens: University of Georgia Press, 1980), pp. 1, 4–15. Copyright © 1980.

bringing a redemption from past sins, an atonement, and a sanctification for the future. . . .

At the end of the Civil War, Southerners tried to come to terms with defeat, giving rise to the Lost Cause. "The victory over Southern arms is to be followed by a victory over Southern *opinions,*" said the Macon, Georgia, *Christian Index* in March, 1866; others echoed this call for wariness. Fearing that crushing defeat might eradicate the identity forged in war, Southerners reasserted that identity with a vengeance. In *The Lost Cause* (1866), the Richmond editor Edward A. Pollard called for a "war of ideas" to retain the Southern identity. The South's religious leaders and laymen defined this identity in terms of morality and religion: in short, Southerners were a virtuous people. Clergymen preached that Southerners were the chosen people, peculiarly blessed by God. "In a word," says Samuel S. Hill, a leading historian of Southern religion, "many southern whites have regarded their society as God's most favored. To a greater degree than any other, theirs approximates the ideals the Almighty has in mind for mankind everywhere." This attitude helped wed Southern churches to Southern culture. As Hill points out, the "religion of the southern people and their culture have been linked by the tightest bonds. That culture, particularly in its moral aspects, could not have survived without the legitimating impetus provided by religion. Their coexistence helped enable southern values and institutions to survive in the face of internal spiritual contradictions and external political pressures. For the south to stand, its people had to be religious and its churches the purest anywhere." Unfortunately, the self-image of a chosen people leaves little room for self-criticism. This deficiency has led to the greatest evils of the religion-culture link in the South.

Southerners interpreted the Civil War as demonstrating the height of Southern virtue, as a moral-religious crusade against the atheistic North. In light of defeat, the ministers cautioned against decline: they feared throughout the late nineteenth century that their society would not measure up to its past heroic standards of virtue. They feared that, in present and future crises, Southerners would not meet the challenges. They saw that their own age produced only men, not saints—a disturbing thought, when measured against the past. Religious leaders continued the wartime military-political battle for virtue on a new level by the creation of a civil religion. The antebellum and wartime religious culture evolved into a Southern civil religion, based on Christianity and regional history. . . .

Judged by historical and anthropological criteria, the civil religion that emerged in the postbellum South was an authentic religious expression. As Clifford Geertz has said, the anthropological study of religion (in this case, the Lost Cause religion) is a twofold undertaking: first, one must analyze the symbols and the myth of the Southern faith for the meanings they embody; second, one must explore the relationship of these meanings to "social-structural and psychological processes." The South faced problems after the Civil War which were cultural but also religious—the problems of providing meaning to life and society amid the baffling failure of fundamental beliefs, of extending comfort to those suffering poverty and disillusionment, and of encouraging a sense of belonging in the shattered Southern community. The anthropologist Anthony F. C. Wallace argues that religion originates "in situations of social and cultural stress," and for postbellum Southerners

such traditional religious issues as the nature of suffering, evil, and the seeming ir-
rationality of life had a disturbing relevancy. Scholars stress that religion is defined
by the existence of a sacred symbol system and its embodiment in ritual. As Geertz
has said, the religious response to the threat of disorder in existence is the creation
of symbols "of such a genuine order of the world which will account for, and even
celebrate, the perceived ambiguities, puzzles, and paradoxes in human experience."
These symbols create "long-lasting moods and motivations" which lead men to act
on their religious feelings. At the heart of the religion of the Lost Cause were the
Confederate heroes, who came to embody transcendent truths about the redemptive
power of Southern society. In fact, the Lost Cause had symbols, myth, ritual, theology, and organization, all directed toward meeting the profound concerns of postwar Southerners.

In addition to fulfilling the role of religion as, in Geertz's words, interpreter of
"social and psychological processes in cosmic terms," the Lost Cause religion also
fulfilled another function of religion by shaping these processes. Southerners used
the Confederate past for their own purposes in the late nineteenth century. Businessmen and politicians employed the glorious legacy for their own needs; Southern ministers did the same. As the guardians of the region's spiritual and moral
heritage, they used the Lost Cause to buttress this heritage. This study stresses that
Christian clergymen were the prime celebrants of the religion of the Lost Cause.
They were honored figures at the center of the Southern community, and most of
them had in some way been touched by the Confederate experience. Not all Southern preachers were celebrants of the religion of the Lost Cause, but those who were
true believers were frequently prominent church leaders; the phrase "minister of the
Lost Cause" identifies those who were most clearly committed to it. These ministers saw little difference between their religious and cultural values, and they promoted the link by constructing Lost Cause ritualistic forms that celebrated their
regional mythological and theological beliefs. They used the Lost Cause to warn
Southerners of their decline from past virtue, to promote moral reform, to encourage conversion to Christianity, and to educate the young in Southern traditions; in
the fullness of time, they related it to American values. Anthony F. C. Wallace has
speculated that all religions originate as cultural revitalization movements, and it is
clear that Southern ministers and their churches achieved this revitalization by
shaping their culture. While some revitalization movements have been utopian,
looking to the future, the Lost Cause religion was a revivalistic movement, aiming,
as Wallace has said, "to restore a golden age believed to have existed in the society's past."

Race, of course, was of fundamental importance to Southern culture. Indeed,
Samuel Hill argues that Southern "racial traditions and practices have served as the
cement for the South's cultural cohesion," and that white supremacy was the "primary component" of Southern culture. . . . Race was intimately related to the story
of the Lost Cause but was not the basis of it, was not at the center of it. In recent
years the needed concentration on the racial dimensions of religion's relationship to
culture in the South has left the impression that the secular culture entirely modified
and distorted religion. It should now be (and is) historical orthodoxy to assert that
the Southern churches were culturally captive. By focusing on this related but still

separate issue of the role of religion and history in Southern culture, one can see that the churches exploited the secular culture, as well as vice versa. The culture was a captive of the churches.

The Southern civil religion assumes added meaning when compared to the American civil religion. Sociologist Robert N. Bellah's 1967 article on that topic and his subsequent work have focused scholarly discussion on the common religion of the American people. Bellah has argued that "an elaborate and well-institutionalized civil religion" existed, which was "clearly differentiated" from the Christian denominations. He has defined "civil religion" as the religious dimension of a people "through which it interprets its historical experience in the light of transcendent reality." Like Sidney E. Mead, Bellah saw civil religion as essentially prophetic, judging the behavior of the nation against transcendent values. Will Herberg has proposed that the civil religion has been a folk religion, a common religion emerging out of the life of the folk. He has argued that it grew out of a long social and historical experience that established a heterogeneous society. The civil religion came to be the American Way of Life, a set of beliefs that were accepted and revered by Protestants, Catholics, and Jews. "Democracy" has been the fundamental concept of this civil religion. Scholars have identified the sources of the American public faith in the Enlightenment tradition and in the secularized Puritan and Revivalist traditions. Clearly born during the American Revolution, it was reborn, with the new theme of sacrifice and renewal, in the Civil War.

In the post–Civil War and twentieth-century South, a set of values existed which could be designated a Southern Way of Life. Those values constituted the basis for a Southern civil religion which differed from the American civil religion. Dixie's value system varied from the one Herberg discussed—Southerners undoubtedly were less optimistic, less liberal, less democratic, less tolerant, and more homogeneously Protestant. In their religion Southerners stressed "democracy" less than the conservative concept of "virtue." The Enlightenment tradition played no role in shaping the religion of the Lost Cause, while the emotionally intense, dynamic Revivalist tradition was at its center. The secularized legacy of idealistic, moralistic Puritanism also helped form its character. While the whole course of Southern history provided the background, the Southern civil religion actually emerged from Dixie's Civil War experience. Just as the Revolution of 1776 caused Americans to see their history in transcendent terms, so the Confederate experience led Southerners to a profound self-examination. They understood that the results of the Civil War had clearly given them a history distinct from that of the North. The story of the civil religion included the founding of Virginia in the colonial period, the Southern role in the American Revolution and World War I, and the myths of the Old South and Reconstruction. These aspects were adjuncts to the religion of the Lost Cause, which contained ritualistic, mythological, theological, institutional, educational, and intellectual elements that were simply not present in the other aspects of the civil religion. Without the Lost Cause, no civil religion would have existed. The two were virtually the same.

A civil religion, by definition, centers on the religious implications of a nation. The Southern public faith involved a nation—a dead one, which was perhaps the unique quality of this phenomenon. One of the central issues of the American faith has been the relationship between church and state, but since the Confederate quest for political nationhood failed, the Southern faith has been less concerned with such political issues than with the cultural question of identity. Because it emerged from a heterogeneous immigrant society, the American civil religion was especially significant in providing uprooted immigrants with a sense of belonging. Because of its origins in Confederate defeat, the Southern civil religion offered confused and suffering Southerners a sense of meaning, an identity in a precarious but distinct culture.

The institutional aspect is perhaps the most controversial part of the civil religion debate. The civil religion possesses a basic conceptual ambiguity: Has it been a separate religious tradition? Or simply an aspect of other societal institutions? Recent historical studies have cast doubt on Bellah's assumption of the continuing existence of the American public faith in permanent organizations. Scholars increasingly believe the term "civil religion" should be used to denote episodes of religious nationalism, heavily influenced in the nineteenth century by evangelical Protestantism. This study of the religion of the Lost Cause extends the conceptual debate on this controversial issue of the civil religion. Bellah's original insight seems to have qualified validity for the South; the Southern public religion was not a formal religion, but it was a functioning one. It possessed well-defined elements—mythology, symbolism, theology, values, and institutions—which combined to make a religion. Its elements were not unrelated parts, but interactive aspects of a well-organized, multidimensional spiritual movement. Even more than in the North, a strong connection existed between the Southern civil religion and the Protestant churches. Although support of the Lost Cause was indeed a prominent theme of Southern Protestantism, certainly not all religious leaders supported it. This . . . is a study of the Southern civil religion and should not be seen as a study of Southern Protestantism. Its conclusions do not apply to all Southern clergymen; in addition, many important concerns of Southern Protestantism did not touch on the Lost Cause.

The religion of the Lost Cause, moreover, had its own distinctive structure of instructions. John Wilson has shown that voluntary associations have been perhaps the key organizational embodiment of the American public faith, and similar groups (the Confederate veterans' groups and the Ku Klux Klan, as well as the churches and denominational schools) expressed the religion of the Lost Cause. Because of this complex structure of well-defined, interactive institutions, the Southern civil religion, again, should not be seen simply as the equivalent of Southern Protestantism. Southern ministers who believed in the Lost Cause were the indispensable individuals who mediated between their own denominations and the other institutions of the Lost Cause. They were frequently members of these voluntary associations and directed their organizational and ritualistic activities. While they shaped the religion of the Lost Cause in the image of Southern Protestantism, organizationally the two were not precisely the same.

The persistent Bible Belt image suggests that the South has been long regarded as a sacred society. To be sure, secular values have been potent, especially in the twentieth century; nevertheless, the South's historical development resulted in longer dominance of an "old-time religion." The pioneering sociologist Emile Durkheim argued that all societies have a sacred quality, a spiritual dimension, and that members may even regard their society itself as holy. But postbellum Southerners saw their culture, rather than their society, as enduring. The reality of Southern culture's alleged sacredness was less important than the Southerner's conviction that his regional values and cultural symbols were holy. Another of Durkheim's insights helps to clarify further the question of the South's sacred or secular quality. He pointed out that religion divides existence into two realms, the sacred and the profane, based upon the perception of holiness, rather than upon the inherent qualities of the sacred items. Sacredness depends not on the item itself, but on the perception of its holiness by a religious person or group. The South was sacred to its citizens because they saw a sacred quality in it. The religious culture in Dixie, including the Confederate memory, promoted the self-image of virtue and holiness and thus helped maintain the cohesiveness of Southern society in a critical postwar period.

Women, Religion, and the Lost Cause

ELIZABETH HAYES TURNER

United Daughters of the Confederacy

[The] notion that men would abandon the past was especially troubling to women who bore scars from a . . . recent national upheaval, the Civil War. The animus that drove women to join the United Daughters of the Confederacy was . . . the desire to educate the young with proper histories lest they forget the sacrifices of their fathers and mothers, to tend and mark the graves of fallen heroes, and to erect in regal monuments symbolic gestures of gratitude for sacrifices. But there were other concerns for Confederate daughters: aged veterans and female survivors of the war suffering from neglect needed care, and, of course, overarching all was the fact that there had been heroic struggles for nationhood but no ultimate victory. Theirs was a Lost Cause in fact; Confederate Daughters would not let it be a cause lost to memory.

Nothing worried southern women more than to think that southern children might be subjected to "distorted" views contradictory to the "true" picture as presented by the UDC, guardians of the region's past. Mary Hunt Affleck, chairwoman of the textbook committee for the Texas Division of the UDC, exhorted her audience to concern itself with the selection of books for schools and town libraries. "Southern schools should use such books bearing on literature that give proper emphasis to Southern productions; on civics, that discuss the deeper constitutional questions, as did the ante-bellum statesmen and jurists; on history that recognizes the great war of the sixties as a civil war, in which both sides were equally patriotic and both honest defenders of unsolved national questions, and in which neither was in rebellion." Histories that did not make the grade were "condemned," their expulsion from southern schools insisted upon by the UDC and often acted upon by veterans of the Civil War in towns across Texas. Resolutions were passed in 1905 that propelled the Texas UDC, under the guidance of its president, Ida Smith Austin—First Presbyterian Bible class teacher, YMCA auxiliary and future YWCA president—to use its influence "as a body to have books teaching Southern authors and their works . . . in our public schools." The result was a purging from southern

From *Women, Culture, and Community: Religion and Reform in Galveston, 1880–1920* by Elizabeth Hayes Turner. Copyright © 1997 by Elizabeth Hayes Turner. Used by permission of Oxford University Press, Inc.

schools and libraries of books that did not present a "true history for the children of the South."

The Daughters of the Confederacy put substantial pressure on women's clubs in Texas, which were beginning to establish libraries in little towns across the state, to select carefully those histories, biographies, novels, magazines, and volumes of literary criticism that were acceptable to southern views. The report from members of the Fortnightly Club of Brenham, Texas, to the annual meeting of the UDC stated boldly that its members were "true Southern ladies, all of whom are eligible to the Daughters of the Confederacy. Its policy has ever been to place upon the library shelves the very best of Southern literature. Especial attention has been paid to juvenile books pertaining to the growth and true history of our beloved Southland." The urgency Texas clubwomen felt in establishing libraries involved not only educating the public but also educating them according to southern prescriptions. The library movement was propelled by women who maintained a form of censorship over the ideas, literature, and history that might reside upon library shelves.

Open-mindedness that accompanies intellectual inquiry never presented itself for adoption among members of the UDC. Their goal was propagandistic and was aimed at children who had never lived with slaves or experienced the war. UDC members worried that the new generation might at some future point endanger the region's collective memory with views critical of slavery or of the Lost Cause. Hence, the justification of nationhood and secession and the description and adulation of "southern civilization" for the future of the region remained the UDC's most important mission. Mothers were singled out for special admonition. "I urge upon you as Southern mothers the sacred duty of teaching your children the truths of history and ask you to use as a home textbook the UDC Catechism written by our beloved Mrs. Cornelia Branch Stone. Its truths will sink so deeply into their young hearts that their after lives will be firmly imbued with the belief in a cause that was just."

Cornelia Branch Stone, prominent Galveston clubwoman and former president of the General UDC, wrote for the Texas Division a question and answer booklet, the "U.D.C. Catechism for Children." Its sale contributed substantially to the UDC monument fund and was widely used among Galveston households to train and instruct young people in the proper history of the South. Typical passages included:

QUESTION: What causes led to the war between the States?
ANSWER: The disregard on the part of the States of the North, for the rights of the Southern or slave-holding States.
QUESTION: What were these rights?
ANSWER: The right to regulate their own affairs and to hold slaves as property.
QUESTION: How were the slaves treated?
ANSWER: With great kindness and care in nearly all cases, a cruel master being rare, and lost the respect of his neighbors if he treated his slaves badly.
QUESTION: What was the feeling of the slaves toward their masters?
ANSWER: They were faithful and devoted and were always ready and willing to serve them.

QUESTION: How did they behave during the war?
ANSWER: They nobly protected and cared for the wives of soldiers in the field. They were always true and loyal.

To suggest that southern men would unnecessarily lead the region into a disastrous and futile war would bring dishonor on the family; to admit that slaves were mistreated or that they proved their objections to slavery by disloyalty during the war would bring into question the racial order upheld by white supremacy. When viewed from the perspective of racism, as well as of "home and family protection," which southern women upheld as their duty, the dissembling becomes more clear. The notion that southern honor and race superiority were male ideals needs to be broadened to include women, especially given the evidence manifested by members of the UDC. Southern women simply could not admit to themselves or to their children that their forebears had erred or that African Americans had suffered in bondage; to do so would bring shame upon white southerners. The logical extension of this cultural trait was to invest an entire region with glory and honor.

A stereotypical lecture given in 1916 by Mildred Lewis Rutherford, historian general of the UDC, justified, whitewashed, and carefully revised southern history. She baldly stated that "the selling of slaves in the South did not separate mother and child as often or with as much cruelty as did the slave trafic [*sic*] in Africa. . . . There was no such thing as chattel slavery in the South." Reconstruction came in for severe criticism. "This unwise policy [Reconstruction government] was the real blow aimed at the overthrow of the civilization of the Old South. The men of the South were then put under military discipline which actually tied their hands and only the Ku Klux, the 'Chivalry of the Old South,' could break these bonds that fettered them." The seriousness of the fact that southern men perpetrated violence in the form of war and later in vigilante groups compelled southern women (including Galvestonians) to practice a kind of self-delusion, to pretend that the South held no imperfections, to insist that slaves were treated fairly and that violence on the part of whites was fully justified. It was a subterfuge that produced no guilt, for the women were convinced they were correct. Moreover, they again were duty bound by southern cultural traditions to preserve the honor of their ancestors and family. Caught up as they were in the traditions of cultural transmission, white southern women chose to defend, preserve, and protect southern civilization wherein their ancestry, family, and pride resided. The motives for producing shibboleths for southern schools and libraries was a very personal one, bound inextricably with the imperatives of family honor, protection of the home and homeland, and grave site memorialization of loved ones.

Galveston women took seriously the admonition to train children in southern truths. Agnes D. Killough set up in 1910 a children's auxiliary to the local UDC chapter, where children of UDC members attained proper southernizing at least once a month. James S. Hanna recounts that his boyhood was filled with such attempts to construct his thinking along proper channels. Apparently it worked, for he wrote of the "shameful atrocities that occurred during the period of Reconstruction." But his reminiscences betray a certain cynicism toward the method of indoctrination. "I, and my sister Margaret, Dorothy and all of the other children of the prominent Southern families of Galveston were drafted into [the children's auxiliary of the UDC], and for several years had to attend monthly meetings where we were compelled to listen to accounts of the brave deeds of our ancestors, and wind up the meetings singing 'Dixie.'"

Southern songs, ballads, and patriotic anthems were essential to the preservation of oral traditions from the Old South, and members of the UDC, also caught up in the musical culture peculiar to women, understood this better than most. Attempts to revive and bring into popular usage songs of their childhood were facilitated by their own singing and by their admonition to others. Annual meetings rang with renditions of the "Bonnie Blue Flag," whose stanzas repeat "Hurrah for Southern rights," and old ballads such as "Annie Laurie" and "Ben Bolt and Lily Dale." Children needed to learn these songs, the members insisted, for emotional ties to the old homeland are often best bound through music and lyric. They romanticized the "old songs that black mammy crooned to drowsy children, when gray heads were golden, and starlit dusks [were] odorous with lilacs, clove pinks, and old-fashioned Southern roses." "Oh Daughters of the Confederacy," they pleaded, "open your old music books before your descendants, and strike upon the harps of the past, and teach them in home and school, the fireside songs and grand old battle hymns of the Southland, while time plays softly on the pipes of peace." Music had its patriotic uses as well.

The Galveston UDC chapter, known as the Veuve Jefferson Davis chapter, was established in 1895 at the instigation of Mollie Macgill Rosenberg, who remained its president until she died in 1917. Within three years it had enrolled 100 members and by 1908 had reached its peak membership of 390. The timing is notable, for it coincides exactly with the elimination of black male office holders, the disfranchisement of black male voters, the rise of Jim Crow laws, and the transfer of political influence from minority and working-class voters to white women. The UDC and its philosophies, then, provided politically powerful white men and potential women voters with rhetorical assurances that the emergent Jim Crow politics contributed to the restoration of Old South values. By publicly justifying the past violence of whites in the defense of southern civilization, they articulated a rationale for discrimination. Divorced from the actual political process as they were in 1895, women supporters of the Confederacy ideal, nonetheless, employed a falsified version of history to win converts to a political agenda that supported white supremacy. The fact that they did this aggressively, influencing the selection of reading material for libraries, inculcating children with notions of white superiority, and reviving music and memories of a time when whites owned slaves, puts them squarely in the camp with apologists of the emerging racial order.

In this way, members of the UDC used the past to construct elaborate rituals filled with political and gendered meanings. Mollie Rosenberg, widow of financier philanthropist Henry Rosenberg, is best known for two things: for furnishing and supplying the interior artwork in Grace Episcopal Church [Galveston] and for presiding in queenly fashion over the Veuve Jefferson Davis chapter of the Daughters of the Confederacy. Like many of her contemporaries in the UDC, she was born and raised in comfort, living her childhood in the ancestral home in Hagerstown, Maryland. Her family endured deprivation and hardship during the war as four brothers fought under southern skies and as she and her sisters survived Union "occupation."

It was through these experiences that she came to live a life devoted to the perpetuation of southern cultural values. Grace Episcopal Church received the benefits of her spiritual devotion to an aristocratic southern church, and the local UDC gained its most generous and ardent patroness. As if epitomizing a genteel feminine culture, Mollie Rosenberg spread her fortune only among select semiprivate organizations. In both cases, she made sure the emphasis was on women and family. While we cannot pretend that this constitutes a feminist political perspective, it does represent, nonetheless, a concentration on women's values that tended to enrich women's self-esteem while at the same time locking them into an ecclesiastical and regional conservatism.

Mollie Rosenberg expressed her devotion to the Lost Cause through her maternalism over the local chapter. As president she not only presided over meetings and influenced the agenda and activities of the chapter but she also showered the chapter with gifts. Her authority allowed her to play the role of lady bountiful—supplying items from stationery to pianos—without appearing to "buy" the chapter. "Again our gracious president has given us evidence of her continued and generous care, and at her own expense provided official stationery, of beautiful quality, and complete and personal design, for the use of her official family," wrote one grateful member, who saw more in the term "daughters" than simply the official appellation.

Rather than meet in a church parlor or in a home, Rosenberg built a fully furnished meeting hall on her property, named it Macgill Memorial Hall for her parents (her mother's wedding dress remained on display there), and insisted that the chapter conduct its business under her wing. Cornelia Branch Stone best described the scene:

> Her boundless generosity gave no pause, but filled [the hall] with one hundred chairs, a cabinet in oak for relics, a handsome bookcase, a beautiful and convenient desk, . . . and then she crowned this wonderful bounty by the splendid gift of a piano that our lives here may be full of melody. In the corner closet . . . will be found the brooms in two sizes, which is a reminder that royal gifts require royal care.

Symbols of the home abounded: a cabinet for relics, a piano for musical entertainment, and brooms to suggest a tidy house. Karen Blair writes that a movement for clubhouses did not gain momentum until after World War I. Mollie's gift to the local UDC was well ahead of the national trend, but it betokened a need felt by women to pursue their interests in their own space. Most clubhouses became focal points of artistic display, but the Macgill Hall became a reliquary for Mollie's family mementos and a meeting place for members away from individual homes or the impersonal rooms of the YMCA.

Although the officers of the local UDC were elected annually, Mollie Rosenberg's office may as well have been self-perpetuating. One indication of the group's conservatism rests on the fact that no other women's club surviving to the twentieth century allowed one "patron saint" to dominate its activities. Yet, no one dared oust their patroness from her position. In effect, the organization not only revered the culture of the Old South, it practiced it as well, perpetuating a form of matriarchy, and, as long as enthusiasm lasted for the club, a conservative hierarchy among women that would barely be challenged by New South progressivism.

Besides Mollie Rosenberg, the local chapter's two most influential and prominent members were Ida Smith Austin, who became president of the Texas Division of the UDC in 1905, and Cornelia Branch Stone, president-general of the UDC from 1907 to 1909. Ida Austin remained the teacher of the Bible class named for her at the First Presbyterian Church; the class motto, "With God everything; without God nothing," was adopted by the Veuve Jefferson Davis chapter of the UDC, every chapter letterhead containing this imprint. While it is well known that the connection between religion and the Lost Cause found expression in civil religion, in this case the direct transference of the Ida Austin Bible class motto to the Daughters of the Confederacy, surrounded by the symbols of the Confederate flag, confirmed for women the sanctity and religiosity of their cause. Just as Mollie Rosenberg had provided a home so that the Daughters would never be far from the hearth, so Ida Austin reaffirmed their close affiliation to the church and legitimated their mission with the symbols of divine guidance. As heirs and guardians of family traditions, as enthusiastic participants in church endeavors, and as preservers of "southern civilization," the Daughters of the Confederacy wove a conservative tapestry of blue and gray, heavily decorated with gendered symbols of religion, home, and ancestry.

☩ F U R T H E R   R E A D I N G

Fred Arthur Bailey, "Textbooks of the 'Lost Cause': Censorship and the Creation of Southern State Histories," *Georgia Historical Quarterly* 75 (Fall 1991), 507–533
———, "Mildred Lewis Rutherford and the Patrician Cult of the Old South," *Georgia Historical Quarterly* 77 (Fall 1994), 509–535
Kenneth K. Bailey, *Southern White Protestantism in the Twentieth Century* (1964)
Edith L. Blumhofer, *Restoring the Faith: The Assemblies of God, Pentecostalism and American Culture* (1993)
John B. Boles, *The Great Revival, 1787–1805: The Origins of the Southern Evangelical Mind* (1972)
Paul Conkin, *American Originals: Homemade Varieties of Christianity* (1997)
Mark Cowett, *Birmingham's Rabbi: Morris Newfield and Alabama, 1895–1940* (1986)
Leonard Dinnerstein and Mary Dale Palsson, eds., *Jews in the South* (1973)
John Lee Eighmy, *Churches in Cultural Captivity: A History of the Social Attitudes of Southern Baptists* (1972)
Eli N. Evans, *The Provincials: A Personal History of Jews in the South* (1973)
Wilson Fallin, *The African American Church in Birmingham, Alabama, 1815–1963* (1997)
J. Wayne Flynt, "Baptists and Reform," *Baptist History and Heritage* 7 (1972), 211–222
Gaines Foster, *Ghosts of the Confederacy: Defeat, the Lost Cause, and the Emergence of the New South* (1987)
Mary E. Frederickson, "'Each One Is Dependent on the Other': Southern Churchwomen, Racial Reform, and the Process of Transformation, 1880–1940," in Nancy Hewitt and Suzanne Lebsock, eds., *Visible Women: New Essays on American Activism* (1993).
Jean E. Friedman, *The Enclosed Garden: Women and Community in the Evangelical South, 1830–1900* (1985)
Willard B. Gatewood, Jr., *Preachers, Pedagogues and Politicians: The Evolution Controversy in North Carolina, 1920–1927* (1966)
David Edwin Harrell, Jr., *White Sects and Black Men in the Recent South* (1971)
———, *All Things Are Possible: The Healing and Charismatic Revivals in Modern America* (1975)
———, ed. *Varieties of Southern Evangelicalism* (1981)
Merrill M. Hawkins, Jr., *Will Campbell: Radical Prophet of the South* (1998)
Evelyn Higginbotham, *Righteous Discontent* (1993)
Samuel S. Hill, Jr., *Southern Churches in Crisis* (1966)
———, *The South and the North in American Religion* (1980)

E. Brooks Holifield, *The Gentlemen Theologians: American Theology in Southern Culture, 1795–1860* (1978)

Anne C. Loveland, *Lillian Smith: A Southerner Confronting the South* (1986)

Bobbie Malone, *Rabbi Max Heller: Reformer, Zionist, Southerner, 1860–1929* (1998)

Robert F. Martin, "A Prophet's Pilgrimage: The Religious Radicalism of Howard Anderson Kester, 1921–1941," *Journal of Southern History* 48 (1982), 511–530

William E. Montgomery, *Under Their Own Vine and Fig Tree: The African-American Church in the South, 1865–1900* (1993)

Ted Ownby, *Subduing Satan: Religion, Recreation, and Manhood in the Rural South* (1990)

James Sellers, *The South and Christian Ethics* (1962)

Nina Silber, *The Romance of Reunion: Northerners and the South, 1865–1900* (1993)

Shelton Smith, *In His Image, But . . . : Racism in Southern Religion, 1780–1910* (1972)

Vinson Synan, *The Holiness-Pentacostal Tradition* (1971)

Noreen Dunn Tatum, *A Crown of Service: A Story of Woman's Work in the Methodist Episcopal Church South, from 1878 to 1940* (1960)

James J. Thompson, Jr., *Tried as by Fire: Southern Baptists and the Religious Controversies of the 1920s* (1982)

Edward L. Wheeler, *Uplifting the Race: The Black Minister in the New South, 1865–1902* (1986)

Charles Reagan Wilson, ed., *Religion in the South* (1985)

The Progressive South in the Age of Jim Crow: Promise and Paradox

Historians of the South have long grappled with the complexities of southern progressivism. As the nation experienced reform at the city, state, and national levels, so too did the South. The Progressive movement in the South, however, occurred in the context of black disfranchisement (considered a reform measure by white southerners), racial violence, segregation, the Lost Cause, and the rise of a one-party South.

Nonetheless, historians have shown that for at least three decades between 1895 and 1925, a vigorous spirit of reform took root in the South. These included the insistence that government take a larger role in promoting the welfare of its citizens by setting a minimum working age for children in factories; improving public schools; regulating the railroads; ending the convict lease system; eradicating diseases such as hookworm and pellagra; maintaining better oversight and inspection of foods sold in the marketplace; ensuring safe, clean water and public spaces; building better roads and promoting scientific agriculture for farmers; establishing well-baby clinics, antituberculosis hospitals, and parks and playgrounds for children; protecting families through prohibition; and extending rights to women (raising the age of consent, passing married women's property rights, and granting suffrage).

At the same time, progressives paradoxically believed that restricting the right to vote to those who were literate or who could pay a poll tax was a move toward improving the electorate. They believed that segregation ordinances would create harmony between the races, and that the sterilization of mentally deficient individuals (eugenics) would improve humankind. These laws, also a part of the progressive movement, represented a desire to direct southern society in an orderly, efficient, and moral manner. Unlike Populists, the progressives did not offer any radical economic programs; rather, they actively pursued economic development as another method of improving southern society.

The champions of progressive reform came primarily from a new middle class emerging in cities and towns and comprised both men and women, whites and blacks. The movement may be traced to various sources: religion, higher education,

*urbanization, and a national momentum for change, to name just a few. Consider-
ing the South's inherent conservatism, historians have pondered the impact that
southern progressivism may have had on society. Did the promise of progressivism
merely result in an improved version of the status quo? Or were the changes more
fundamental, and did they establish a foundation for future advances in race relations, gender equality, labor, and education?*

⚓ D O C U M E N T S

The documents reflect both the diversity of southern progressivism and its relationship to regional culture. Charles W. Dabney was a leading southern educator and president of the University of Tennessee at the time he wrote "The Public School Problem
in the South" (1901), reproduced here as Document 1. The essay candidly discusses
the "disgrace" of public education in the South and its impact on politics and the regional economy. Dabney's views on disfranchisement and "industrial education" for
blacks were typical of southern progressives. Edgar Gardner Murphy, an Episcopal
priest in Montgomery, Alabama, joined many of his colleagues in the movement by
participating in a wide variety of reform efforts. These included race relations, education, and, as can be seen from Document 2, child labor. The Southern Sociological
Congress was a major organizational response to the progressive movement in the
South. It was founded in Nashville in 1912 and was dedicated to coordinating social
reform efforts. The 1914 meeting in Memphis took as its theme "The Solid South for a
Better Nation," and the excerpts from the conference proceedings presented here as
Document 3 reveal the strong clerical influence on progressive reform, as well as progressives' interest in improving race relations. Georgia's governor Hoke Smith discussed an array of progressive measures in his 1907 inaugural address. His speech,
seen here in Document 4 makes clear how black disfranchisement, paradoxically, fit
well with white progressives' views of reform. Documents 5 and 6 should be read together, as they present the opposing views of the two leading spokesmen for African
Americans in the progressive South—Booker T. Washington and W. E. B. Du Bois. In
1895, as white supremacy movements gained momentum, Booker T. Washington accepted an invitation to speak at the Atlanta Exposition before a white audience. The
text of his speech sheds light on black fears and reveals one leader's strategy for improving race relations. His speech was labeled "The Atlanta Compromise." W. E. B.
Du Bois, Harvard-trained sociologist and cofounder of the NAACP in 1909, challenged Washington's compromise with white southerners and renounced his accom-
modationist policies.

1. Charles W. Dabney on the Public-School
Problem in the South, 1901

The South waiting for education.—Everything in the South waits upon the general
education of the people. Industrial development waits for more captains of industry,
superintendents of factories, and skilled workmen. The natural resources of the

---

Charles W. Dabney, "The Public School Problem in the South," from Capon Springs Conference for Education in the South Proceedings, Raleigh, 1901.

Southern States are great and varied; capital in abundance is ready for investment in them; only men are wanted who can plan, organize, and direct. This is true of all our industries, even of our agriculture. A director of an Agricultural Experiment Station says: "We can do little more to improve the agricultural methods of the farmers until a new generation is educated, who can read our bulletins, apply scientific methods, and keep simple farm accounts."

The colleges for liberal, and institutions for scientific and technical education as well, wait for preparatory schools and high schools. With the same population there were during 1899 in all collegiate and graduate courses in liberal arts only 16,351 students in the Southern States against 30,741 in the North Central States, where they have public high schools. A system of public education is a pyramid; the primary schools are the foundation; the secondary schools and high schools, the normal schools, the technical schools, and the colleges carry up the structure step by step, and the university is the capstone. Our old system of education in the South, so far as we had any, was a Greek column; the university was a beautiful carved capitol of classic design, supported by a slender column of literary colleges and academies, which stood upon a narrow and unsubstantial base of private schools.

The effects of war and reconstruction.—Good government in town and State and intelligent action in national affairs are impossible without educated voters. Pettifogging politicians, selfish demagogues, and corrupt lobbyists will continue to control our legislative and county governments until a majority of the voters can read and think for themselves. The Republic must have an educated citizenship or go down. The question of educating all the people is more critically important to the South than it is to the remainder of the nation. We must educate all our people, blacks as well as whites, or the South will become a dependent province instead of a coordinate portion of the nation. . . . The only remedy for the political situation in the South is to be found in public education. . . .

Believing that the Southern people have at last overcome most of the financial and political results of [the Civil] [W]ar and reconstruction, I hold that the time has come when we must begin seriously upon the work of reconstructing Southern society in all its departments, and that the first thing to do is to establish schools for all the people. . . .

. . . In North Carolina only 30 per cent of the children are in daily attendance upon the schools; less than 60 per cent are enrolled in them, and the annual school term is less than seventy-one days. There are in North Carolina on the average 65 enrolled pupils to each school and 54 to each teacher. The schoolhouse which is supposed to shelter the children is valued at $179.60, and the teacher who has charge of them receives $23.36 a month for seventy and eight-tenths days, or about $77 for the term. The amount expended per year per pupil in attendance is but $1.34, which is only 51 cents per capita. In Tennessee less than half of the children between 5 and 18 years of age are in daily attendance; only 70 per cent are enrolled in the schools; the school term is only ninety-six days, and the enrolled pupils attend an average of only sixty-three days in the year. In Tennessee they are taught in a schoolhouse which cost $426, by teachers who receive an annual salary of $134. The total expense per pupil is $5.17 a year, which is only 87 cents per capita. . . .

The laws designed to disfranchise illiterate whites and blacks are likely to have a beneficent influence upon the educational situation in the South. Such laws, if impartially drawn and fairly carried out, will do almost as much good in promoting the elementary education, of males at least, as compulsory laws. The uneducated people of the Southern States, both whites and blacks, esteem their ballot to a degree that is almost ridiculous. In States like North Carolina, where the educational qualification has been applied, the colored people are already showing an earnest desire to get the little education required to qualify as voters. But these laws, even at best, touch only one-half the population. The only perfect solution of the problem is a compulsory attendance law carefully designed to reach every healthy child. We must put all the children in school, but before we do this we must have the schools and the teachers. . . .

. . . We should consider the negro as a man to be educated for work, independence, and citizenship like other men. Everything I have said applies to him, therefore, just as it does to the white man. The negro is in the South to stay—he is a necessity for Southern industries—and the Southern people must educate and so elevate him or he will drag them down. The human race is an organism, all its members being bound together by natural affinities and ministering to each other by natural law. If history, philosophy, and revelation teach us anything it is the solidarity of all mankind, that "no man liveth to himself" and "no man dieth to himself," but that we are each "his brother's keeper."

I plead for justice and common sense in the education of the negro. The most encouraging thing about public education in the South is the noble, self-sacrificing way in which the Southern people have given of their limited resources for the education of their recent slaves. That they will continue to do for the black man all that their means will permit, I firmly believe. These attacks upon the negro school fund, these proposals to give him for his schools only what he pays in himself, come from short-sighted people who fail to recognize the basal principle underlying all public education, namely, the duty of all the people to educate all the people. They do not represent the opinion of the best people of the South and their proposals will not prevail. The people of the South realize already that this proposal is not primarily an assault upon the black man, but a movement to undermine the foundation of the country's prosperity, progress, and peace. . . .

But we must use common sense in the education of the negro. We must recognize in all its relations that momentous fact that the negro is a child race, at least two thousand years behind the Anglo-Saxon in its development, and that like all other races it must work out its own salvation by practicing the industrial arts, and becoming independent and self-supporting. Nothing is more ridiculous than the programme of the good religious people from the North who insist upon teaching Latin, Greek, and philosophy to the negro boys who come to their schools. Many of our Southern States make a similar mistake in trying to enforce in the schools of the black districts courses of study laid down for whites.

2. Edgar Gardner Murphy on
Child Labor in Alabama, 1901

A Reply to the Committee

On Wednesday, October 30, the following communication appeared in the
***Evening Transcript* of Boston, Massachusetts.**

To the Editor of the *Transcript:* . . .

As treasurer of a mill in that State [Alabama], erected by Northern capital, I am interested in the subject [of child labor]. From the starting of our mill, I have never been
South without protesting to the agent, and overseer of spinning (the only department in
which small help can be employed), against allowing children under twelve years of age
to come into the mill, as I did not consider them intelligent enough to do good work. On
a visit last June, annoyed that my instructions were not more carefully observed, before
leaving I wrote the agent a letter of which the following is a copy:—

"Every time I visit this mill, I am impressed with the fact that it is a great mistake
to employ small help in the spinning room. Not only is it wrong from a humanitarian
standpoint but it entails an absolute loss to the mill. . . . I again express the wish that you
prevent the overseer, as far as possible, from employing children under twelve years of
age. . . .

In defence of our officials, it is doubtless true that the trouble comes largely from
the parents, who make every effort to get their children into the mill, and often because
of refusal, take their families containing needed workers, to other mills, where no objection is made to the employment of children. . . .

Now in regard to the attempted legislation of last winter: The labor organizations at
the North imported from England a very bright and skilful [sic] female labor agitator
and sent her to Alabama. She held meetings at central points, and when the Legislature
convened appeared at Montgomery with her following, and a bill against employing
children was promptly introduced. The manufacturers and other business men of Alabama resented this outside interference, well knowing the source from which it came,
and they were also aware that manufacturers at the North were being solicited for funds
with which to incite labor troubles in the South.

As they recognized that this bill was only the entering wedge, they determined that
action must come from within the State, and not outside. They also felt that the adjoining State of Georgia, having double the number of spindles, should act first. With these
considerations in mind, the manufacturers selected among others our agent, a native Al-
abamian, to appear before the legislative committee, with the result that the bill was defeated. I think it may be said with truth, that the interference of Northern labor agitators
is retarding much needed legislation in all the manufacturing States of the South.

As to our mill and the little town of 2300 people which has grown up around
it, there is nothing within the mill or without, of which any citizen . . . need be
ashamed. . . . From the inception of this enterprise, the purpose has been to build up a
model town that should be an object lesson to the South, and we are assured that its influences have been helpful. In addition to a school supported by public tax, the company
has always carried on a school of its own, with an experienced and devoted teacher, who

---

Edgar Gardner Murphy, *Child Labor in Alabama: An Appeal to the People and Press of New England
with a Resulting Correspondence*, as appeared in the *Evening Transcript* of Boston, Massachusetts, on
October 30, 1901.

has been instructed to make special effort to get in the young children, and thus allure them from the mill. We have built and have in operation a beautiful library—the first erected for this special purpose in the State of Alabama, and we have a church building which would be an ornament in any village of New England, and is in itself an education to our people. We are now building a modern schoolhouse from plans by Boston architects which will accommodate all the children of our community. These are a few of the things we have done and are doing, in our effort to meet the responsibility we have assumed, in dealing with a class of people who have some most excellent traits, and who appeal to us strongly, because many of them have hitherto been deprived of needed comforts and largely of elementary advantages. . . .

J. Howard Nichols,
Treasurer Alabama City Mill, Alabama

A Rejoinder from Alabama

On the afternoon of November 2d, Mr. Edgar Gardner Murphy, of Montgomery, Alabama, the chairman of the Alabama Child-labor Committee, received a copy of the above letter. Mr. Murphy at once wrote and forwarded the following rejoinder:—

To the Editor of the *Transcript:*

I note in your issue of October 30th a reply to a statement to the press and the people of New England, on the subject of child labor in Alabama. Our statement bore the signatures of six representative citizens of Alabama, among them the Superintendent of Public Schools of Birmingham and ex-Governor Thomas G. Jones, of Montgomery. The reply to the address of the committee is signed, not by a disinterested citizen of the State, but by Mr. J. Howard Nichols, Treasurer of the Alabama City Mill, at Alabama City.

I thank you for publishing Mr. Nichols's letter. The well-known citizens of Alabama with whom I have the honor to be associated, have welcomed the discussion of this subject, and they desire the frankest and fullest showing of the facts.

I note, however, with some amazement, that the Treasurer of the Alabama City Mill begins his argument by conceding the two fundamental principles for which we are contending—the social wrong and the economic error of child labor under twelve. He declares that from the starting of that mill he has repeatedly protested against the use of children under this age and that last June he wrote to his local agent that the employment of such help "is not only wrong from a humanitarian standpoint, but it entails an absolute loss to the mill." Now this is substantially, and in admirable form, the whole case of our committee.

Yet what must be our added amazement when, in the next paragraph but one, we read the further admission that, in order to continue this economic and social wrong and in order to defeat a simple and effective remedy for this wrong, the salaried representative of his own mill, during the preceding February, had appeared in this city before our Legislature, in aggressive and persistent antagonism to the protection of little children under twelve! This, in the teeth of protests which Mr. Nichols declares he has made since "the starting" of his mill. Who, then, is the responsible representative of the actual policy of the Alabama City Mill—its Treasurer or its representative before the Legislature? Or is the policy of the mill a policy which concedes the principle, only to deny the principle its fruit? If this be the true interpretation of the conditions, what are we to say to the explanations which are suggested; explanations offered "in defence of our [Mr. Nichols's] officials."

Mr. Nichols assures us that the officials have been put under grave pressure from the parents. Let us concede that this is true. Yet Mr. Nichols himself is not satisfied with this "defence," and he declares wisely and bravely that his officials must take their stand against the pressure of unscrupulous and idle parents. His agents must resist the threat of such parents to leave the Alabama City Mill for mills having a lower standard of employment. Does not Mr. Nichols see that our legislation was precisely directed toward ending this pressure, toward breaking up this ignoble competition, and toward the preservation of the standard of employment which he professes? There could be no pressure to withdraw the children and to enter them in other mills, if such labor were everywhere prohibited by statute. But we are grateful to Mr. Nichols for his declaration. And yet, is he ignorant of the need of legislation in the State at large? His very argument is a confession of knowledge. If the Alabama City Mill is fairly represented by the profession of Mr. Nichols, why should the paid and delegated agent of that mill labor here for weeks to thwart a simple legislative remedy for the abuses he deplores?

Is it sufficient for your correspondent to declare that this legislation met with local opposition simply because such reforms should come "from within the State and not from outside"? This is a strange objection upon the part of one who represents investments from outside. The evils may be supported from the East, but the remedies (sic) must be indigenous! Nor is there the slightest ground for the suggestion that the initiative for our movement of reform came from "a skilful female labor agitator imported from England." We yield sincere gratitude to the American Federation of Labor for their earnest, creditable, and effective coöperation. Their interest in the situation is entirely intelligible. When the younger children are thrust into the labor market in competition with the adult, they contend that the adult wage is everywhere affected. But the agent of the Federation of Labor—earnest and devoted woman that she is—did her work, not in the spirit of interference, but in the spirit of helpfulness. She was not responsible for the beginning of the agitation. The demand for this legislative protection of our children was made by the Minister's Union of Montgomery and by the Woman's Christian Temperance Union of Alabama, before she was ever heard of in the South.

Nothing could be more baseless than the assumption that our local effort for reforms is due to outside forces. But if it were—what of it? There is at stake here to-day the welfare of our little children, the happiness and efficiency of our future operatives; the moral standard of our economic life; and this committee frankly proposes, in every honorable way, to secure all the aid, from every quarter of our common country, which we can possibly command. The criticism of such a policy is a little out of place from the representative of a mill here operated upon investments from Massachusetts. . . .

Mr. Nichols also declares that our reform measure was defeated because it was believed to be "the entering wedge" of other troublesome labor legislation. We must not protect our little children under twelve, we must not do a compassionate and reasonable thing, because, forsooth, somebody might then demand an inconsiderate and unreasonable thing! Do the corporate interests in Alabama wish to predicate their liberties upon such an argument? . . .

I concur in the claim that the Alabama City Mill is in some respects wholly exceptional. Says Mr. Nichols: "I challenge either of the gentlemen from Alabama to mention among the mills of the State . . . any one which compares with ours in the expenditure which has been made for the comfortable housing of the operatives and the appliances introduced for their comfort and uplift." In one breath the friends of this mill ask us to believe it exceptional, and yet in the next breath they ask that the need for reform legislation in relation to all the mills of the State, shall be determined from the conditions it presents! If the Alabama City Mill is so unique, then it is not representative or typical. If it is not representative of the average conditions of child labor in Alabama, it has nothing to do with this argument. . . .

That mill, with its great influences, has led the fight in this State against the protection of our factory children. Will it continue to represent a policy of opposition and reaction? Or, will it represent a policy of coöperation and of progress? . . .

EDGAR GARDNER MURPHY.
Montgomery, Ala., November 2, 1901.

3. The Southern Sociological Congress's Agenda for Reforming the South, 1914

The Social Program of the Congress

The Southern Sociological Congress stands:

For the abolition of convict lease and contract systems, and for the adoption of modern principles of prison reform.

For the extension and improvement of juvenile courts and juvenile reformatories.

For the proper care and treatment of defectives, the blind, the deaf, the insane, the epileptic, and the feeble-minded.

For the recognition of the relation of alcoholism to disease, to crime, to pauperism, and to vice, and for the adoption of appropriate preventive measures.

For the adoption of uniform laws of the highest standards concerning marriage and divorce.

For the adoption of the uniform law on vital statistics.

For the abolition of child labor by the enactment of the uniform child labor law.

For the enactment of school attendance laws, that the reproach of the greatest degree of illiteracy may be removed from our section.

For the suppression of prostitution.

For the solving of the race question in a spirit of helpfulness to the negro and of equal justice to both races.

For the closest co-operation between the Church and all social agencies for the securing of these results.

The Social Mission of the Church to City Life

RABBI EMANUEL STERNHEIM, GREENVILLE, MISS.

True religion insists on human service, and this is the end toward which the real development of religion should be in the present suborned. One of the signs of the times is a new consciousness of others' needs. All men agree that there are rights which have not been recognized and duties which have not been performed. The desire to serve is forcing men to new and sometimes to strange activities, but nevertheless the desire to determine the relation of the individual to the community is a universal one.

These documents can be found in James E. McCulloch, ed., *Battling for Social Betterment: Southern Sociological Congress, Memphis, Tennessee,* May 6–10, 1914 (Nashville: Southern Sociological Congress, 1914), p. 9.

Busy with our trade, and surrounded with the signs of wealth, we, like Jacob, have been met by the angel of our forgotten brother. It is of the struggle of this angel, in the concerted effort to find what we must do for other's needs, that shall make of us princes of God, and enable us to remember that "the rich and poor meet together; the Lord is the maker of them all." . . .

I propose to devote myself to two or three specific duties of the Church about which there is usually some dispute.

The first claim I make is, that it is the duty of the Church to enter into the work of municipal government. There are arguments pro and con about this, but it seems to me to be axiomatic that the minister is a citizen and a man before he is a parson and he cannot be refused the rights of a citizen; but I am not keen on pressing the point, for my argument is to be that it is a comparatively unimportant thing whether the minister sits on the municipal board or not, but it is an essential to righteous city government that the united voices of the churches of the city shall speak through its personnel the demand for a godly and God-fearing administration. . . .

Anticipating much the same objection and giving to it much the same reply, I am going to be sufficiently controversial to advocate the extension of the duty of the church to the domain of education. With a very complete and long experience of the evils of the infusion of religious differences into education, I am nevertheless anxious about the growth of a paramount utilitarian and materialistic education system. . . .

By virtue of the position of the Church in regard to guidance, it should so coöperate with every educational effort in the city that every teacher in the city may thank God and take courage.

The last point with which I shall deal is the duty of the Church with regard to recreation. . . .

What I am advocating here, however, is not so much the erection of the institutional church to which, of course, there can be no objection in the light of the principles enunciated in this address, but rather a conception of the duty of the Church in the fostering and the encouragement of every possible form of clean and wholesome amusement within the city limits. . . .

Finally, it must be the conception of the Church that it is its function to stand for every effort to beautify the city. In the simple yet majestic words of Browning,

> If you get simple beauty and naught else,
> You get about the best thing God invents.

In an ideal city all these things will be. The mission of the Church to the city is to make it ideal, and therefore all these things must be. In an ideal city none will be very rich and none will be very poor; knowledge and good will will join together to give to every child the best education; to render every house and street as healthy as the healthiest hillside in the world; to provide the most comfortable hospital for every one who is sick and to have at hand a friend for every one in trouble.

In our ideal city art will grow out of common life, undisturbed by contrasts of wealth and poverty. The people will have pleasure in their work and leisure to admire what is beautiful.

4. Hoke Smith's Gubernatorial Inaugural Address, 1907

A government fails to reach its highest sphere if it does not protect the right of property, and at the same time constantly broaden opportunities for mental, moral and financial growth to the less fortunate.

A government by the people furnishes the only hope for such a result. To make it sure, ballot boxes must be pure, and legislative halls must be free from the influences of predatory wealth. . . .

Education

The chief object of government should be to prevent special privileges and to give to all equal rights and opportunities. To this the men and women of Georgia are entitled, and you are preparing legislation which insures it to them.

The relation of the state to the children goes much further. It is the duty of the state to see that the children are given an opportunity for all preparation which their probable life work requires.

Education from books alone is not always of much value. It should be accompanied with practical training, having in view the future of the child.

Negro Children

Let me refer to the negro children in this connection. Any plan for the negroes which fails to recognize the difference between the white and black races will fail. The honest student of history knows that the negro had full opportunity for generations to develop before the days of slavery; that the negro race was improved by slavery, and that the majority of the negroes in this state have ceased to improve since slavery. Few have been helped by learning from books. All have been helped who have been taught or made to work.

It is not the difference of environment; it is the difference of race, deep seated, inherited for generations and generations through hundreds of years.

The large majority of negroes are incapable of anything but manual labor and many taught from books spurn labor and live in idleness. Few negroes are willing to work beyond the procurement of the hardest necessities of life.

The negro child should be taught manual labor and how to live. The negro teacher should be selected less by book than by character examinations. The negro school to be useful needs less books and more work. I favor a complete change in the examination of teachers for the negro schools, and for them a different plan of management; I would have the schools help the negro, not injure him. . . .

White Children

The white children of Georgia are prepared for the highest development: but I do not mean by this that they will necessarily obtain it through literary and classical studies.

Hoke Smith's gubernatorial address: Journal of the Senate of the State of Georgia, Executive Minutes of Georgia (Atlanta: Department of Archives and History, 1907), pp. 3–14.

For them it is at this time most important to improve the manual training and agricultural schools, and the rural schools. With a view to progress, I ask you to consider the unorganized condition of the educational work of Georgia.

University and Branches

. . . We must require the corporations in Georgia to pay their just taxes. We must equalize taxation among all the people of Georgia. Who will object to paying taxes when he realizes that the money is to be intelligently spent for the children of the state? Instead of a burden, it should be a great privilege to help in so noble a cause.

5. Booker T. Washington's Atlanta Exposition Address, 1895

Mr. President and Gentlemen of the Board of Directors and Citizens: One-third of the population of the South is of the Negro race. No enterprise seeking the material, civil, or moral welfare of this section can disregard this element of our population and reach the highest success. I but convey to you, Mr. President and Directors, the sentiment of the masses of my race when I say that in no way have the value and manhood of the American Negro been more fittingly and generously recognized than by the managers of this magnificent Exposition at every stage of its progress. It is a recognition that will do more to cement the friendship of the two races than any occurrence since the dawn of our freedom.

Not only this, but the opportunity here afforded will awaken among us a new era of industrial progress. Ignorant and inexperienced, it is not strange that in the first years of our new life we began at the top instead of at the bottom; that a seat in Congress or the state legislature was more sought than real estate or industrial skill; that the political convention or stump speaking had more attractions than starting a dairy farm or truck garden.

A ship lost at sea for many days suddenly sighted a friendly vessel. From the mast of the unfortunate vessel was seen a signal, "Water, water; we die of thirst!" The answer from the friendly vessel at once came back, "Cast down your bucket where you are." A second time the signal, "Water, water; send us water!" ran up from the distressed vessel and was answered, "Cast down your bucket where you are." And a third and fourth signal for water was answered, "Cast down your bucket where you are." The Captain of the distressed vessel, at last heeding the injunction, cast down his bucket, and it came up full of fresh, sparkling water from the mouth of the Amazon River. To those of my race who depend on bettering their condition in a foreign land or who underestimate the importance of cultivating friendly relations with the Southern white man, who is their nextdoor neighbor, I would say: "Cast down your bucket where you are"—cast it down in making friends in every manly way of the people of all races by whom we are surrounded.

Cast it down in agriculture, mechanics, in commerce, in domestic service, and in the professions. And in this connection it is well to bear in mind that whatever other sins the South may be called to bear, when it comes to business, pure and simple, it is in the South that the Negro is given a man's chance in the commercial world, and in nothing is this exposition more eloquent than in emphasizing this chance. Our greatest danger is that in the great leap from slavery to freedom we may overlook the fact that the masses of us are to live by the productions of our hands, and fail to keep in mind that we shall prosper in proportion as we learn to dignify and glorify comman labor and put brains and skill into the common occupations of life; shall prosper in proportion as we learn to draw the line between the superficial and the substantial, the ornamental gewgaws of life and the useful. No race can prosper till it learns that there is as much dignity in tilling a field as in writing a poem. It is at the bottom of life we must begin, and not at the top. Nor should we permit our grievances to overshadow our opportunities.

To those of the white race who look to the incoming of those of foreign birth and strange tongue and habits for the prosperity of the South, were I permitted I would repeat what I say to my own race, "Cast down your bucket where you are." Cast it down among the 8 millions of Negroes whose habits you know, whose fidelity and love you have tested in days when to have proved treacherous meant the ruin of your firesides. Cast down your bucket among these people who have, without strikes and labor wars, tilled your fields, cleared your forests, builded your railroads and cities, and brought forth treasurers from the bowels of the earth, and helped make possible this magnificent representation of the progress of the South. Casting down your bucket among my people, helping and encouraging them as you are doing on these grounds, and to education of head, hand, and heart, you will find that they will buy your surplus land, make blossom the waste places in your fields, and run your factories. While doing this, you can be sure in the future, as in the past, that you and your families will be surrounded by the most patient, faithful, law-abiding, and unresentful people that the world has seen. As we have proved our loyalty to you in the past, in nursing your children, watching by the sickbed of your mothers and fathers, and often following them with tear-dimmed eyes to their graves, so in the future, in our humble way, we shall stand by you with a devotion that no foreigner can approach, ready to lay down our lives, if need be, in defense of yours, interlacing our industrial, commercial, civil, and religious life with yours in a way that shall make the interests of both races one. In all things that are purely social we can be as separate as the fingers, yet one as the hand in all things essential to mutual progress. . . .

Nearly 16 millions of hands will aid you in pulling the load upward, or they will pull against you the load downward. We shall constitute one-third and more of the ignorance and crime of the South, or one-third its intelligence and progress; we shall contribute one-third to the business and industrial prosperity of the South, or we shall prove a veritable body of death, stagnating, depressing, retarding every effort to advance the body politic. . . .

The wisest among my race understand that the agitation of questions of social equality is the extremest folly, and that progress in the enjoyment of all the privileges that will come to us must be the result of severe and constant struggle rather than of artificial forcing. No race that has anything to contribute to the markets of the world is long in any degree ostracized. It is important and right that all privileges of the law be ours, but it is vastly more important that we be prepared for the exercises of these privileges. The opportunity to earn a dollar in a factory just now is worth infinitely more than the opportunity to spend a dollar in an opera house.

In conclusion, may I repeat that nothing in thirty years has given us more hope and encouragement, and drawn us so near to you of the white race, as this opportunity offered by the exposition; and here bending, as it were, over the altar that represents the results of the struggles of your race and mine, both starting practically empty-handed three decades ago, I pledge that in your effort to work out the great and intricate problem which God has laid at the doors of the South, you shall have at all times the patient, sympathetic help of my race; only let this be constantly in mind, that, while from representations in these buildings of the product of field, of forest, of mine, of factory, letters, and art, much good will come, yet far above and beyond material benefits will be that higher good, that, let us pray God, will come, in a blotting out of sectional differences and racial animosities and suspicions, in a determination to administer absolute justice, in a willing obedience among all classes to the mandates of law. This, this, coupled with our material prosperity, will bring into our beloved South a new heaven and a new earth.

6. W. E. B. Du Bois Denounces Washington's Accommodationist Policies, 1903

Easily the most striking thing in the history of the American Negro since 1876 is the ascendancy of Mr. Booker T. Washington. It began at the time when war memories and ideals were rapidly passing; a day of astonishing commercial development was dawning; a sense of doubt and hesitation overtook the freedmen's sons,—then it was that his leading began. Mr. Washington came, with a simple definite programme, at the psychological moment when the nation was a little ashamed of having bestowed so much sentiment on Negroes, and was concentrating its energies on Dollars. His programme of industrial education, conciliation of the South, and submission and silence as to civil and political rights, was not wholly original; the Free Negroes from 1830 up to war-time had striven to build industrial schools, and the American Missionary Association had from the first taught various trades; and Price and others had sought a way of honorable alliance with the best of the Southerners. But Mr. Washington first indissolubly linked these things; he put enthusiasm, unlimited energy, and perfect faith into this programme, and changed it from a by-path into a veritable Way of Life. And the tale of the methods by which he did this is a fascinating study of human life.

It startled the nation to hear a Negro advocating such a programme after many decades of bitter complaint; it startled and won the applause of the South, it interested and won the admiration of the North; and after a confused murmur of protest, it silenced if it did not convert the Negroes themselves.

To gain the sympathy and coöperation of the various elements comprising the white South was Mr. Washington's first task; and this, at the time Tuskegee was

---

Selected portions from *Of Mr. Booker T. Washington and Others* by W.E.B. DuBois. Reprinted by permission.

founded, seemed, for a black man, well-nigh impossible. And yet ten years later it was done in the word spoken at Atlanta: "In all things purely social we can be as separate as the five fingers, and yet one as the hand in all things essential to mutual progress." This "Atlanta Compromise" is by all odds the most notable thing in Mr. Washington's career. The South interpreted it in different ways: the radicals received it as a complete surrender of the demand for civil and political equality; the conservatives, as a generously conceived working basis for mutual understanding. So both approved it, and to-day its author is certainly the most distinguished Southerner since Jefferson Davis, and the one with the largest personal following. . . .

. . . So Mr. Washington's cult has gained unquestioning followers, his work has wonderfully prospered, his friends are legion, and his enemies are confounded. To-day he stands as the one recognized spokesman of his ten million fellows, and one of the most notable figures in a nation of seventy millions. One hesitates, therefore, to criticise a life which, beginning with so little, has done so much. And yet the time is come when one may speak in all sincerity and utter courtesy of the mistakes and shortcomings of Mr. Washington's career, as well as of his triumphs, without being thought captious or envious, and without forgetting that it is easier to do ill than well in the world.

The criticism that has hitherto met Mr. Washington has not always been of this broad character. In the South especially has he had to walk warily to avoid the harshest judgments,—and naturally so, for he is dealing with the one subject of deepest sensitiveness to that section. . . .

Among his own people, however, Mr. Washington has encountered the strongest and most lasting opposition, amounting at times to bitterness. . . . [T]here is among educated and thoughtful colored men in all parts of the land a feeling of deep regret, sorrow, and apprehension at the wide currency and ascendancy which some of Mr. Washington's theories have gained. These same men admire his sincerity of purpose, and are willing to forgive much to honest endeavor which is doing something worth the doing. They coöperate with Mr. Washington as far as they conscientiously can; and, indeed, it is no ordinary tribute to this man's tact and power that, steering as he must between so many diverse interests and opinions, he so largely retains the respect of all. . . .

. . . But Booker T. Washington arose as essentially the leader not of one race but of two,—a compromiser between the South, the North, and the Negro. Naturally the Negroes resented, at first bitterly, signs of compromise which surrendered their civil and political rights, even though this was to be exchanged for larger chances of economic development. The rich and dominating North, however, was not only weary of the race problem, but was investing largely in Southern enterprises, and welcomed any method of peaceful coöperation. Thus, by national opinion, the Negroes began to recognize Mr. Washington's leadership; and the voice of criticism was hushed.

Mr. Washington represents in Negro thought the old attitude of adjustment and submission; but adjustment at such a peculiar time as to make his programme unique. This is an age of unusual economic development, and Mr. Washington's programme naturally takes an economic cast, becoming a gospel of Work and Money to such an extent as apparently almost completely to overshadow the higher aims of life. . . .

. . . Mr. Washington distinctly asks that black people give up, at least for the present, three things,—

First, political power,

Second, insistence on civil rights,

Third, higher education of Negro youth,—and concentrate all their energies on industrial education, the accumulation of wealth, and the conciliation of the South. This policy has been courageously and insistently advocated for over fifteen years, and has been triumphant for perhaps ten years. As a result of this tender of the palm-branch, what has been the return? In these years there have occurred:

1. The disfranchisement of the Negro.

2. The legal creation of a distinct status of civil inferiority for the Negro.

3. The steady withdrawal of aid from institutions for the higher training of the Negro.

These movements are not, to be sure, direct results of Mr. Washington's teachings; but his propaganda has, without a shadow of doubt, helped their speedier accomplishment. The question then comes: Is it possible, and probable, that nine millions of men can make effective progress in economic lines if they are deprived of political rights, made a servile caste, and allowed only the most meagre chance for developing their exceptional men? If history and reason give any distinct answer to these questions, it is an emphatic *No*. And Mr. Washington thus faces the triple paradox of his career:

1. He is striving nobly to make Negro artisans business men and property-owners; but it is utterly impossible, under modern competitive methods, for workingmen and property-owners to defend their rights and exist without the right of suffrage.

2. He insists on thrift and self-respect, but at the same time counsels a silent submission to civic inferiority such as is bound to sap the manhood of any race in the long run.

3. He advocates common-school and industrial training, and depreciates institutions of higher learning; but neither the Negro common-schools, nor Tuskegee itself, could remain open a day were it not for teachers trained in Negro colleges, or trained by their graduates.

This triple paradox in Mr. Washington's position is the object of criticism by two classes of colored Americans. One class is spiritually descended from Toussaint the Savior, through Gabriel, Vesey, and Turner, and they represent the attitude of revolt and revenge; they hate the white South blindly and distrust the white race generally, and so far as they agree on definite action, think that the Negro's only hope lies in emigration beyond the borders of the United States. And yet, by the irony of fate, nothing has more effectually made this programme seem hopeless than the recent course of the United States toward weaker and darker peoples in the West Indies, Hawaii, and the Philippines,—for where in the world may we go and be safe from lying and brute force?

The other class of Negroes who cannot agree with Mr. Washington has hitherto said little aloud. . . . Such men feel in conscience bound to ask of this nation three things:

1. The right to vote.

2. Civic equality.

3. The education of youth according to ability.

They acknowledge Mr. Washington's invaluable service in counselling patience and courtesy in such demands; they do not ask that ignorant black men vote when ignorant whites are debarred, or that any reasonable restrictions in the suffrage should not be applied; they know that the low social level of the mass of the race is responsible for much discrimination against it, but they also know, and the nation knows, that relentless color-prejudice is more often a cause than a result of the Negro's degradation, they seek the abatement of this relic of barbarism, and not its systematic encouragement and pampering by all agencies of social power from the Associated Press to the Church of Christ. They advocate, with Mr. Washington, a broad system of Negro common schools supplemented by thorough industrial training; but they are surprised that a man of Mr. Washington's insight cannot see that no such educational system ever has rested or can rest on any other basis than that of the well-equipped college and university, and they insist that there is a demand for a few such institutions throughout the South to train the best of the Negro youth as teachers, professional men, and leaders.

. . . They do not expect that the free right to vote, to enjoy civic rights, and to be educated, will come in a moment; they do not expect to see the bias and prejudices of years disappear at the blast of a trumpet; but they are absolutely certain that the way for a people to gain their reasonable rights is not by voluntarily throwing them away and insisting that they do not want them; that the way for a people to gain respect is not by continually belittling and ridiculing themselves; that, on the contrary, Negroes must insist continually, in season and out of season, that voting is necessary to modern manhood, that color discrimination is barbarism, and that black boys need education as well as white boys.

✝ E S S A Y S

In the first essay, Dewey W. Grantham summarizes a generation of scholarship on southern progressivism by focusing on the origins, background, and programs of progressives. While acknowledging the cultural boundaries of the progressive movement in the South, Grantham notes that the reform activities were promoted not only by middle-class white men but also by women and African Americans. Grantham sees a reconciliation between southern tradition and progress, which, he argues, helped to establish the promise of change in the region. Historian William A. Link, in the second essay, finds more paradox than promise in the southern progressive movement. He takes the view that southern urban reformers and northern philanthropists were at odds with southern traditionalists, whose values were informed by "an intensely localistic, rural participatory democracy."

The Promise of Southern Progressivism

DEWEY W. GRANTHAM

The April 1946 issue of the *North Carolina Historical Review* contained a pioneering article by Arthur S. Link on "The Progressive Movement in the South,

By Dewey W. Grantham, from "The Contours of Southern Progressivism," in *American Historical Review* 86 (December 1981), pp. 1035–1056. Reprinted by permission.

1870–1914." While noting that most writers "ignore the progressive movement in the South altogether," Link contended that the Southern states were the scene of "a far-reaching progressive movement." At the time the young Princeton historian wrote these words, he had virtually no scholarly literature on which to rely, particularly for developments of the early twentieth century. This was still largely true five years later when C. Vann Woodward's interpretation, "Progressivism—For Whites Only," appeared as chapter 14 of his *Origins of the New South, 1877–1913* (1951). Except for a few scholarly articles and a handful of monographs on such topics as child labor reform and prohibition, Woodward was forced to quarry his building materials from primary sources. But the situation was already beginning to change.

During the 1950s the Progressive era in the South became a new historical frontier. The field attracted a growing number of historians, especially young scholars stimulated by Woodward's seminal volume, and their research merged into the larger historiographical assault on the Age of Reform in the United States. Some of the products of this research are apparent in George B. Tindall's *The Emergence of the New South, 1913–1945* (1967) and in other general studies published by Hugh C. Bailey in 1969 and Jack Temple Kirby in 1972. In the preface to an edition of *Origins of the New South* that appeared in 1971, Woodward spoke of "the outpouring of historical scholarship" during the past twenty years, a statement amply substantiated in the 112-page bibliographical essay prepared for the new edition by Charles B. Dew. The number of books, articles, and essays on the Progressive era in the South continued to mount during the 1970s. Evidence of this historiographical vitality can be found in the selected bibliography published annually in the *Journal of Southern History* and in almost any recent volume of a Southern state's historical journal.

The scholarly writings on the Progressive era in the South are so extensive that it is now possible to think in terms of a comprehensive historical synthesis. This essay attempts to outline the dimensions of such a synthesis. In sketching the contours of Southern progressivism, the essay addresses several questions. First, what were the origins of the progressive impulse in the South? Second, who were the Southern progressives and what were their social values? Third, what were the most important progressive campaigns in the Southern states and what pattern did they assume? Fourth, to what extent did these regional movements eventually become national in orientation? And what effect did Woodrow Wilson's first administration and World War I have on Southern progressivism? Fifth, what of the aftermath of progressivism in the South? Did it have an enduring impact on Southern politics and social attitudes? . . .

Perhaps the most fundamental of the dynamics that contributed to Southern progressivism were changes that had occurred by the end of the nineteenth century in the social landscape of the region, particularly the coming of industry, increasing urbanization, and the growing importance of a new middle class made up of business and professional groups. The increasing economic diversification of the South brought with it what one observer described as "radical changes in the social tendencies" of the section's inhabitants. A spirit of commercialism had become pervasive, and "business" was exalted as never before. Distinct "capitalist" and "laboring" classes were emerging. Social differentiation based on wealth and business success was becoming more pronounced, especially in the cities, and institutions like the church were less "democratic" than in earlier years. The varied forces of economic and social change disrupted many established patterns of life in the South, threatened the stability of the countryside and small town, and precipitated a new awareness of human problems and needs. According to a Vanderbilt professor, writing in 1909, "The most capable business men, lawyers, doctors and preachers are practically all leaving the country for the town and city." This meant that "the great centers of life and influence and authority" were shifting from the country to the city, and "as a result the city is more and more setting the pace of and dominating Southern life and Southern thought."

The expanding role of cities in Southern life brought notable social changes. . . . The city sorted out people along economic and social lines, facilitated the formation of functional organizations, and fostered a heightened concern for social order, stability, and efficiency. New social types were especially prominent in the South's developing cities. . . . A new and growing class of supply merchants and bankers provided credit for farmers. In the larger cities and favorably located rural communities a group of industrial entrepreneurs came into existence, mainly in lumber, food, and textile industries. Many small merchants, salesmen, technicians, and clerical workers entered the South's amorphous but expanding middle class.

The emerging urban-industrial system, in the South as elsewhere, demanded a host of services and skills. These were provided by traditional professions such as law, medicine, engineering, education, and journalism and by a wide range of newer professions and specialities in industry, the service trades, public administration, public health, social work, and so on. The vocational and professional concerns of these increasingly differentiated and specialized groups tended both to isolate them from their local communities and to encourage their organization on the basis of function and skill. Industrialists and businessmen came together in trade associations, merchant organizations, bankers' groups, and chambers of commerce. . . . They turned to collective action, not only to obtain entrepreneurial and professional advantages but also to help control the social environment in which they operated.

Social reform in the early twentieth-century South was also rooted in the idea of Southern progress. . . . It found expression in many ways, most notably in the creed of the New South. The forward-looking ideas of the New South advocates embodied a compelling vision of regional progress. The benefits to be derived from industrialization seemed boundless. The spokesmen for industrialism in Tennessee, for example, "equated prosperity, progress, and civilization with smoking factory chimneys, booming cities, and rising indices of industrial production." . . . Economic advances promised to bring the South "a larger point of view," help diminish "prejudice and emotionalism in southern life," and further national integration.

The idea of Southern progress was promoted not only by the concept of economic development but also by a group of critics who wanted to improve life in the region by reforming various institutions and practices. The new social criticism, more restrained and more hopeful than the searing agrarian indictment of the 1890s, began to have an effect early in the twentieth century. Suddenly, it seemed, ministers, women, professors, writers, and publicists were singling out an assortment of evils in Southern life: in farm conditions, factory work, corporate practices, political life, and so forth. The critics included a liberal sprinkling of crusading journalists, a group of educators and scholars who had recently come out of the new graduate schools, a handful of socially conscious ministers, Southern expatriates like Walter Hines Page and William Garrott Brown, and an occasional politician, usually a state legislator. Some of the critics began to complain about the intolerance—even the tyranny—of public opinion in a section where, as one writer observed, everything must conform to "the Democratic platform, the Daughters of the Confederacy, old General So-and-So, and the Presbyterian creed."

Nevertheless, there was an optimistic note in most of this social commentary. "Here," wrote a contributor to the *South Atlantic Quarterly* in 1905, "is the supreme opportunity of the Southern newspaper, the Southern college, and Southern criticism of today, to learn from the records of the past the essentials of human progress and to bring these lessons of life to bear on the solution of our own particular problems." A few years later a Southern progressive declared, with considerable satisfaction, that the South had become "a laboratory for the study of sociological forces." . . .

Another reform dynamic was incorporated in the growth of a more vigorous humanitarian spirit in the South. The church was the major source of this social compassion. Although Southern Protestantism did far more to conserve than to undermine the dominant culture in the region, Southern churches were agents of change—and reform—as well as of continuity. An impressive number of ministers stood in the vanguard of social reform in the South. The clergy spoke out with greater frequency against social evils, religious bodies showed a deepening interest in the improvement of social conditions, and all of the major Protestant denominations established social action agencies of one kind or another. As Kenneth K. Bailey has written of the three leading white Protestant churches in the South, "Absorbed at the turn of the century in evangelism and little mindful of social needs beyond blue laws and prohibition, they emerged during the next fifteen years as advocates of social justice, proclaiming the Christian obligation to fashion Christ's kingdom on earth." Christian faith continued to center in the gospel of personal redemption, but the churches succeeded in giving a moral-religious tone to much of the region's reformism. The social justice activities of women in the South took shape, appropriately enough, in "church work," particularly in the women's missionary societies and the Woman's Christian Temperance Union. Religion remained "a central aspect" in the lives of many Southern women at the turn of the century, and, as Anne Firor Scott has pointed out, its form gradually changed from "intense personal piety to a concern for the salvation of the heathen and for social problems."

The origins of Southern progressivism can also be traced to the changing political scene and the transformation of Southern politics in the late nineteenth century. The most distinctive attribute of political affairs in the South at the turn of the century was the overwhelming dominance of the Democratic party. Despite the fissures in the section's political solidarity caused by the Populist revolt of the 1890s, Democratic supremacy in the states from Virginia to Texas was more secure than ever before. This meant that the competition for political leadership and public office, the formulation and discussion of political issues, the fate of reform movements, and the outcome of legislative action were all decided within the confines of one-party politics. This simple fact had a profound influence on the nature of Southern progressivism.

Several features of the South's altered political system were especially significant in shaping Southern progressivism. One of these was the drastic shrinkage of the electorate as a result of the restructuring of Southern politics in the 1890s and early 1900s. Disfranchisement and restrictive election laws not only deprived most black Southerners of the ballot but also, in conjunction with the persistence of poverty, illiteracy, and cultural barrenness, sharply limited the political involvement of millions of whites. A second important feature of Southern politics in the Progressive period was the direct primary and other democratic devices, whose adoption introduced new elements into the region's politics and promised changes in the complexion of state government. These innovations contributed to a third notable development in the politics of the South: the vigorous competition in the Democratic party and the prevalence of bifactional cleavages in most Southern states. The implications of these developments for social reform were ambiguous, but such changes facilitated the emergence of interest-group politics and enhanced the political influence of middle-class organizations and professional groups, whether in mobilizing mass support or bringing pressure to bear on legislators and other public officials. Although the remodeled system was restrictive and undemocratic, it nonetheless provided a setting for insurgent political campaigns, for broad appeals to the public, for the open discussion of issues, and for the organization and conduct of reform movements.

The political context in which Southern progressivism developed was also affected by populism. In appealing for solidarity in the white community, Democratic leaders were moved to make some concessions to the agrarian reformers, particularly in their rhetorical obeisance to the ideal of popular government. . . . Populist proposals for stringent railroad regulation, liberal agricultural credit, abolition of convict leasing, and support of public education became part of the reform agenda of the region's progressives. Southern Democrats increasingly accepted the Populist concept of the positive state—of a more active governmental role in promoting economic growth and protecting society—and this notion found fertile ground in the new climate of interest-group politics. . . .

Politics, of course, constituted an essential medium for the waging of progressive campaigns. State and local governments were the primary agencies for the resolution of conflicts in the community and for the regulation of business practices and social behavior, as well as the source of public services. The South's economic growth and diversification increased the demands on state and local governments for franchises, services, and regulations. The expanding cities and towns were confronted with especially troublesome problems, which often required action by state legislatures. With the enhanced role of government came a dramatic enlargement in the part played by economic and professional organizations in the formulation and enactment of public policy. Chambers of commerce, freight bureaus, farmers' organizations, labor unions, professional associations, and scores of other groups were soon participating in local and state politics throughout the region.

All of these tendencies—social change, the emergent ideology of Southern progress, a broadening humanitarianism, and the transformation of politics— converged around the turn of the century to provide a favorable setting for Southern progressivism. The divisions and frustrations of the 1890s formed a somber back-drop for the sunnier outlook of the new decade. The ending of the economic depression lifted Southern spirits, and talk of the South's imminent agricultural and industrial expansion assumed a new animation. With the passing of the political turmoil of the 1890s, the public mood became more relaxed. The threat to the integrity of the "Southern" community had faded away. Democratic hegemony having been re-established, politicians paid greater heed to the widespread revulsion against the political corruption and electoral fraud of earlier years. The "race question" was apparently being settled through disfranchisement and segregation laws. The possibility of outside interference in the politics and social arrangements of the South, despite campaign rhetoric, seemed increasingly remote, and "Northern" opinion was, for the most part, agreeably acquiescent. The South's enthusiastic support of the Spanish-American War appeared to symbolize the final achievement of intersectional harmony and national integration.

Identifying the Southern progressives continues to pose a challenge to historians of reform movements in the early twentieth-century South. . . .

Although the composition of the progressive coalitions in the South remains inadequately analyzed, it is clear that many of them involved what Sheldon Hackney has called "the politics of pluralistic interest groups." These groups were primarily concerned with their own survival and competitive position, but their increasing resort to collective action made them a major consideration in reform politics. The commercial-civic elites and other organized elements often opposed social reforms, of course, and their character differed from state to state. Urban influences were obviously stronger in Tennessee than in Mississippi. Cultural traditions were more significant in Virginia than in Oklahoma politics. Farmer and labor groups were better represented in the politics of the Southwestern states than in the states of the Southeast. In general, however, the politics of pluralistic interest groups reflected the strength and vigor of the new commercial and professional classes centered in the region's cities. These groups included lawyers, editors, teachers, ministers, doctors, businessmen, agricultural scientists, demonstration agents, city planners, labor leaders, social workers, YMCA directors, railroad commission experts, and legislative lobbyists. These middle-class men and women were the quintessential Southern progressives.

Nevertheless, rural Southerners played an important part in the South's progressivism, particularly in legislative enactments and support of such causes as disfranchisement, public education, railroad regulation, and prohibition. . . . The concept of "a continuing and potent agricultural influence," to borrow the phrase James Tice Moore applied to the Age of the Southern Redeemers, may have considerable validity in the case of the Progressive era in the South.

Southern progressives were no doubt a rather disparate collection of social reformers, but they were unified in some measure by common goals and social values. They shared a yearning for a more orderly and cohesive community. Such a community, they believed, was a prerequisite for economic development and material progress. Its realization depended upon the effective regulation of society in the interest of ethical business practices and good government, and in the elimination of political corruption, machine politics, and the insidious power of large corporations and other special interests. Social controls were also indispensable to the preservation of moral values, to the purification of social institutions, and to the protection of men from their own weaknesses. Optimistic about future prospects but alarmed by the tensions and turmoil that pervaded the South in the late nineteenth century, Southern progressives looked toward the creation of a clearly defined community that would accommodate a society differentiated by race and class but one that also possessed unity, cohesion, and stability. . . .

Progressives in the South, like other American reformers in this period, talked about the virtues of "the people," identified morality with majority rule, and urged the desirability of preserving and expanding traditional democratic principles. . . . But well-to-do and middle-class Southerners, including many social reformers, often revealed a deep distrust of the masses, whether black or white. While the social critics and reformers in the early twentieth-century South worked for the education and uplift of the common man, they were fully aware of his prejudices and narrow-mindedness, of his extreme sensitivity to criticism, obsession with the race question, and susceptibility to sentimentalism. Thus, Southern progressives demonstrated a proclivity toward paternalistic solutions in dealing with many social problems. It is significant that progressives sometimes coupled education, which they emphasized as an instrument of material progress and social control, with the need to cleanse the political process and limit participation to those who were prepared for responsible citizenship.

For all of their emphasis on social order and their faith in social controls, many Southern progressives revealed a strong commitment to social justice and the amelioration of human suffering in their communities. A growing number of Southerners were genuinely worried about the consequences of industrialization for ordinary people, aware of the increasing need for social services, and sensitive to the social roles and responsibilities opening up to them as part of an emerging class of trades people, professionals, and experts. The creative response of Southern women to the plight of the poor and disadvantaged was especially notable in the South's uplift campaigns. The cause of social justice in the South was also fostered by the monetary and moral support of Northern philanthropists during the Progressive era.

Most Southern progressives were convinced that much of the South's social distress could be relieved or prevented through economic development. They accepted, like so many contemporary Southerners, the basic assumptions of the New South program of regional progress through rapid economic growth, industrialization, and a more diversified economy. These objectives led directly to an emphasis on efficiency and rationality not only in the production of goods but also in such areas as education, the treatment of criminals, race relations, and the prohibition of alcoholic beverages. The theme of social efficiency was prominent, for instance, in the efforts of Southern progressives to improve farm life, in their approach to industrial labor, in their municipal reforms and innovations, and in their advocacy of a larger role for state governments as promoters, regulators, and arbiters. The search for efficiency in these diverse areas of Southern society, while not exclusively or even primarily a manifestation of social reform, was nonetheless a significant aspect of the progressive mentality and program in the South.

These social values—order, morality, benevolence, efficiency, and development—were not separate categories of progressive concern. Rather they were, as

Sheldon Hackney has written of the Alabama progressives, "interrelated facets of a single, economically self-interested, ethically shaped, middle-class attitude toward life." These areas of social concern and commitment, moreover, were mutually reinforcing, and in seeking to give them effect Southern progressives began to develop an expanded concept of governmental responsibilities. They moved beyond the regulatory state to advocate a broadening array of public services. In other words, Southern progressivism became "a movement for positive government."

Identifying the major movements that comprised Southern progressivism and categorizing them on the basis of their fundamental purposes may be helpful at this point. The reform movements were often interrelated, and in many cases the same reformers were prominent in several progressive campaigns. In Virginia and South Carolina, for example, the educator Samuel Chiles Mitchell was an ardent champion of public schools, child labor reform, prohibition, public health, better roads, improved race relations, and public welfare programs. Furthermore, the progressive endeavors were inspired by a variety of motives; thus, the classification suggested in this essay is somewhat arbitrary. One group of reform efforts appears to have been primarily concerned with governmental regulation and the imposition of social controls in troublesome areas such as race relations. The race settlement of the 1890s and early 1900s was one such manifestation of Southern progressivism. The white consensus that developed during this period reflected a widespread conviction that disfranchisement, segregation, and black proscription not only made up a workable system of racial control but also promised a greater measure of social stability and public calm. Such a milieu, it was said, would make it possible for progressives to address themselves to other pressing social causes. It might also help establish a new national consensus of "enlightened" and "liberal" opinion on the race question.

Prison reform, centering on efforts to abolish the leasing of convicts, to introduce prison farms, and to develop a new system of road work for prisoners, constituted another example of Southern progressivism largely concerned with the application of more efficient social controls. Antimonopolism represented another manifestation of the regulatory impulse among the region's progressives. The movement to control railroads and other large corporations and to destroy their political dominance became a major objective of progressives in many Southern states. Corporate regulation also served as one of the key issues in providing a rallying point for progressive politics in the South. For big business, so often identified with powerful outside interests, entrenched political "machines," unethical business practices, and the destruction of competition, seemed to demand stronger public control no less than did black workers, criminals, and alcoholic beverages. The concentrated attack of Southern governors and legislatures upon railroads and other corporations in 1906 and 1907 soon spent itself, and much of the regulatory force during the next decade found an outlet in the antiliquor crusade, first in the drive for statewide prohibition and subsequently in the campaign for a national law. Prohibition offered a means of moral reaffirmation of traditional values, an assurance of cleaner politics, and a way to employ the power of the state in the pursuit of moral and social progress.

A second significant category of progressive campaigns in the South was dominated by the theme of social justice. One of the principal reform movements in this sphere was devoted to the regulation of child labor. The child-labor cam-paigns brought the section's social reformers together in a common cause, gave them valuable experience in organizing for reform purposes, and stimulated their interest in the establishment of juvenile courts and programs for the care of depend-ent children. No aspect of social reform in the South during the Progressive era touched the immediate lives of more of the region's inhabitants than the great edu-cational awakening soon after the turn of the century. Education was the entering wedge and the sustaining focus for unprecedented Northern philanthropy as well as a major element in the rationale of interregional accommodation that flourished during these years. It was almost always viewed by reformers as a redemptive force in the development of a better South. A third area of social justice concern was the organized charity movement. By the end of the first decade of the twenti-eth century, social welfare in the South had begun to move away from the long-dominant emphasis on relief of the destitute and to put greater stress on casework, surveys, and organization.

The cause of social justice also included an embryonic movement to ameliorate the conditions of black people in the South. During the Progressive period, the pri-mary concerns of white Southerners, including most social reformers, in their ap-proach to the "race problem" were social efficiency and the means of social control. Yet some whites sought to ease the terrible burden of racial injustice borne by the Negro. Their program, as one scholar has recently observed, was based on "an up-dated version of paternalism in which whites would offer blacks help, guidance, and protection in exchange for a commitment to the New South values of thrift and hard work, as well as a continued subservience."

There was also a black approach to racial progress and better social conditions. Given sustenance by an emerging Negro middle class, it envisioned "an expanded concept of social justice, a more efficient pattern of living, and a greater emphasis upon local organizations." Blacks, as John Dittmer has written, "built their own in-stitutions behind the walls of segregation, preaching race pride and practicing self-help." Negro civic organizations, boards of trade, public welfare leagues, and community betterment groups, particularly in the larger cities, labored to extract worthwhile concessions in education and other public services from the white sys-tem, to secure more adequate correctional facilities for black juveniles, to improve housing and sanitation in Negro areas, and to promote moral conduct, social order, and efficiency in the black community. The community work of Negro club women was a prominent feature of this black progressivism. . . .

The progressive campaigns for efficiency in agriculture, municipal govern-ment, and industrial labor led to greater emphasis on scientific knowledge, exper-tise, and effective administration in the public arena. Similar pressures emanated from other reform campaigns, such as the movements for public education, public health, and good roads. The state was increasingly viewed not only as the source of regulatory action but also as the provider of vital new services. This expanded role of government was in harmony with the widespread commitment in the South to economic development and with the entrepreneurial aspirations of diverse groups and specialized organizations representing farmers, industrial workers, and busi-ness and professional men and women. The steadily mounting demand for public services formed an important dimension of Southern progressivism. . . .

By the time Woodrow Wilson assumed the presidency in March 1913, a new stage had arrived in the evolution of Southern progressivism. Reform movements in the Southern states, as in other sections, were increasingly influenced by national organizations, standards, and solutions. This tendency was evident in the formation of the Southern Sociological Congress, a regional civic organization established in Nashville in the spring of 1912. Characterized by a zeal for uplift and an evangelical spirit, the congress was intended to serve as a medium for organizing and coordinating various social reform groups. Its creation reflected the growth of social services in the South during the previous decade, the organization of several state conferences on charities and correction, and a heightened awareness among Southern progressives of social reforms in other parts of the country. The congress stimulated interest in attacking social problems, including racial injustice, encouraged the establishment of other social welfare groups, and exerted some influence in the enactment of social reform legislation in the individual states.

The nationalization of reform after 1912 was apparent in two of the Southern progressives' most vigorous regulatory movements: the campaign to control railroads and the prohibition crusade. The barriers to effective regulation of railroads by state legislatures and commissions, including the inherent problem of dealing with interstate companies and the restraints imposed by federal court decisions and Interstate Commerce Commission rulings, brought a shift from reliance on state regulation to national control. Meanwhile, the vexatious task of enforcing state and local prohibition in dry areas, not to mention the defeat of the antiliquor cause in Florida, Texas, and Alabama, led many Southern reformers to fall in line with the American Anti-Saloon League's call for national prohibition. The tendency to look for national remedies was also evident in numerous other progressive campaigns: in the child labor reform movement; in the demand by the Farmers' Union and other agricultural pressure groups for federal regulations, credit facilities, and farm demonstration programs; and in the willingness of organizations such as the Southern Commercial Congress to turn to Washington for assistance in dealing with problems like flood control. This transition from state to federal action was hastened by the activities of such organizations as the National Child Labor Committee, the American Anti-Saloon League, the Commission on Country Life, and the National Association of Charities and Correction.

The South was slower in lending support to the National American Woman Suffrage Association's efforts to secure the enfranchisement of women through congressional action and a constitutional amendment. Although tiny woman suffrage groups were formed in most Southern states in the 1880s and 1890s, they were feeble and many of them soon disappeared. There was little concerted activity in behalf of the votes-for-women cause before 1910. Nevertheless, the intensity of "the woman's movement" in the region had increased, the feminine involvement in the campaign to regulate child labor, the educational crusade, the prohibition movement, not to mention numerous community projects, indicates the distance the reformers had come since joining the missionary societies and the women's clubs. As time passed this feminist reformism tended to find greater focus in the drive for the suffrage. During the five or six years before the United States entered World War I, Southern suffragists developed statewide associations, organized hundreds of local societies, and launched campaigns to influence legislators and the public. Their objective was to win the vote with favorable decisions in the statehouses, but they encountered formidable resistance. As their strength grew and their frustrations mounted in the wake of setbacks at the state level, Southern suffragists began to work more actively for a federal amendment.

Meanwhile, Southern politics showed signs of increasing involvement in the debate over national issues and elections. In 1910 the Democrats won control of the House of Representatives, and, when the House organized for business in 1911, the seniority rule brought a group of Southerners to prominence as chairmen of important committees. Southern interest in national politics rose to new heights with the nomination and election of Woodrow Wilson as the nation's twenty-eighth president. . . .

Southern congressmen, who dominated the standing committees in both houses of Congress, strongly supported the principal legislation of Wilson's New Freedom. Nevertheless, there was strong Southern opposition to many of the more advanced progressive measures considered during Wilson's first term. For example, Southerners were in the vanguard of the successful opposition in 1914 and 1915 to a constitutional amendment to enfranchise women. The Southern lawmakers were much more inclined to support certain measures of social control, such as national prohibition, immigration restriction, and especially Negro proscription in Washington and the federal service. . . .

In some respects the First World War weakened and redirected the currents of social reform in the United States, particularly after the nation entered the conflict in April 1917. Yet the war also created new opportunities for social planning and even nourished the progressive belief that "by altering the environment it was possible to reconstruct society." The war had a momentous effect on Southern society. It contributed to the region's prosperity, brought an expansion in the functions of government, encouraged civic cooperation, enhanced the role of voluntary groups, and opened new avenues of social control, efficiency, and social justice. Preoccupation with the war effort was evident in virtually every aspect of Southern life. . . .

Some Southern states took advantage of the wartime atmosphere to adopt new social welfare legislation. North Carolina, for example, reorganized its public welfare program during the years 1917–19. The war also brought to fruition three reforms for which Southern progressives had long struggled. One of these was national prohibition, an achievement that owed much to Southern congressmen, state legislators, and public opinion. Another was the adoption of the Nineteenth Amendment enfranchising women. During the war the woman suffrage movement had emerged as a serious reform cause in the South. Although a majority of the Southern congressmen voted against the amendment and it encountered powerful opposition in the section's state legislatures, it was supported by an increasing number of Southerners. The third reform occurred in the search for progress in race relations. The attention given this perennial question by the Southern Sociological Congress and the efforts of people like Willis D. Weatherford, James H. Dillard, and Will W. Alexander helped pave the way for tangible action. Even so, the exigencies and opportunities of the war and its aftermath provided the immediate impetus for the establishment of the Commission on Interracial Cooperation in 1919.

The end of the war and the collapse of the Wilson administration in 1919 and 1920 coincided with and contributed to the disintegration of Southern progressivism. By that time the regional focus of the reformers had been disrupted, and they were no longer united by a common program of social reforms and values. They had also lost much of their élan and optimism as progressives. Social change, accelerated by the war, created new tensions, and the postwar years were exacerbated by sharp conflicts among Southerners and between the South and other sections. The intersectional struggle for control of the Democratic party eroded the progressive balance in the South and added to the saliency of cultural issues like prohibition. In other words, the harmony that had held the major components of Southern progressivism in balance no longer existed. The earlier successes of Southern progressivism may also have contributed to its loss of vitality in the 1920s. There were signs that the progressives had about reached the limits of their concept of reform. A new generation of leaders was coming to the fore. Furthermore, many professional groups were making the transition from "the missionary era to one of institutionalization and professionalism." Caught up in the struggle to develop effective agencies and services in their particular fields and in their professional growth and recognition, they found the old kinds of social reform increasingly irrelevant and unsatisfying. Southern social workers, for example, like their counterparts in the rest of the country, now seemed more concerned with "procedure and the adjustment of the individual to his environment" than in transforming the social environment in which the individual lived.

Nevertheless, progressivism in the South did not disappear in the 1920s. Instead, as George B. Tindall has shown, it was "transformed through greater emphasis upon certain of its tendencies and the distortion of others." One of the surviving strains of Southern progressivism expressed itself in the zealous campaign to enforce prohibition, in the fundamentalist movement, and in other efforts to protect moral standards and traditional cultural values. Another was what Tindall has termed "business progressivism"—the intensified emphasis on "good government," administrative efficiency, and more adequate public services. Racial attitudes and practices provide a third example. Southern reformers, building upon their modest efforts of earlier years to soften the harsh rigidities of race relations and to continue the limited interracial cooperation of the war period, undertook a major reform initiative in this period. The creation of the Commission on Interracial Cooperation represented an organized endeavor for harmonious race relations and, unlike earlier white reformism in this area, pointed to a concrete and realistic mode of action. But at the same time the commission was carefully restricted by the bounds of white orthodoxy.

The Paradox of Southern Progressivism

WILLIAM A. LINK

In 1946, a young scholar of southern history barely out of graduate school advanced a reinterpretation of the Progressive Era South. The stereotype of the region as so

---

Essay, "The Paradox of Southern Progressivism," from "The Social Context of Southern Progressivism, 1880–1930," by William Link from *The Wilson Era: Essays in Honor of Arthur S. Link* edited by John Milton Cooper, Jr. and Charles E. Neu. Wheeling, IL: Harlan Davidson, Inc. © 1991. Reprinted by permission.

"unbelievably backward, economically, politically, and socially" as to be incapable of sustaining any liberal reform movement needed exploding, wrote Arthur S. Link. A common objective of "greater economic, political, and social justice" united southern social reformers as diverse as Grangers, Greenbackers, Alliancemen, and Populists; along with early twentieth-century progressives, they sought to restructure the political system, stabilize the social structure, and extend popular control over the economy through the extension of the role of government. Link's reformers were governors, congressmen, legislators, and newspaper editors, whose primary objectives included state regulation and restrictions on the power of party machines; southern progressivism's culmination came during the presidency of Woodrow Wilson.

Although an admiring portrait, Link's assessment acknowledged "serious deficiencies." Committed to political reform, progressives were concerned neither with such deeply rooted social problems as the increase in farm tenancy nor with, implicitly, meaningful economic change for the mass of southerners. Similarly, they ignored the plight of blacks; while they condemned lynching, they opposed black political rights. "As far as progressive democracy went in the South," he concluded, "it was progressive democracy for the white man." Still, the reformers came out well; according to Link, they articulated the attitudes and political aspirations of most white southerners and led the fight against "conservatives and reactionaries."

Four and a half decades after the publication of this seminal article, scholars continue to debate the origins, motivations, and consequences of reform along the lines just described. By including the category of social alongside political reform, subsequent historians of the Progressive Era South filled in the details of southern progressivism which Link initially sketched out. Still, by focusing on the narrow issue of whether reformers' stated motivations were genuine, the scholarly debate remains limited. Some historians, generally optimistic about the causes and consequences of progressivism, have stressed that reformers were motivated by humanitarian impulses and wanted, as Hugh C. Bailey enthusiastically writes, to "restore the mythical equality of opportunity which supposedly existed in the society of the past." Most of these optimists, like Link, have qualified their praise, but they agree that the reformers, impelled by humanitarianism and their view of regional progress, acted in accord with their announced objectives. Other historians paint a more pessimistic portrait. In his classic *Origins of the New South, 1877–1913,* C. Vann Woodward characterized southern reform as a "paradoxical combination of white supremacy and progressivism" which had little relevance for the "political aspirations and deeper needs of the mass of the people"; despite the heralding of a new era of "washed, wormed, and weeviled Southerners," the condition of the rural masses probably worsened during the Progressive Era.

Recently historians have grown even more critical. David L. Carlton contends that South Carolina child-labor reformers actually sought to extend middle-class control over mill families; their main objective was class stabilization. James L. Leloudis II asserts that while women school reformers in North Carolina espoused a humanitarian rhetoric, their goal was the molding of children into a manageable labor force. Extending this argument to the role of northern philanthropists in southern black education, James D. Anderson argues that their primary motivation in promoting "industrial" education was to develop an "economically efficient and politically stable" southern social system. Taken together, these pessimist historians have turned the optimist orthodoxy about progressivism on its head. Whereas optimist historians take reformers at their word and portray them as well-intentioned, democratic, and responding to documented social problems, pessimists assert that a mask of liberal rhetoric hid darker purposes and intentions. As J. Morgan Kousser writes, reality "differed . . . from the 'progressive' myth," for progressivism was for middle-class whites only.

This essay suggests another model for understanding southern progressivism. Most scholars have examined only one part of southern progressivism—the reformers themselves—while they have neglected the social contexts that reformers encountered. They have assumed, incorrectly, that reform was primarily a personal, political process which can best be comprehended in the setting of elections, legislatures, and governors. Whereas scholars' emphases have been political and biographical, reform had its most important impact outside of politics: on processes, institutions, and communities. Although the traditional approach makes most rural southerners passive participants in reform, they in fact played a dynamic role.

In order to understand the full consequences of reform, we need to know less about the problematic category of motivation and more about reform's social context. In particular, we need to comprehend how social policy functioned in pre-bureaucratic culture; why reformers came to see traditional social policy as inadequate; with what consequences they began to transform it in the early decades of the twentieth century; and, perhaps most important, how rural southerners responded to these policy changes.

Pre-bureaucratic Social Policy and the Emergence of Reform . . .

In the rural South, centuries of isolation helped to form a restrictive definition of community. Localism fused with a rural republican ideology that articulated autonomy and self-reliance, stressed the dangers of concentrated power, and provided a political language for suspicion of outsiders. Southerners were the "historical partisans of personal liberty," explained one observer, and they were "naturally opposed to sumptuary laws of any kind."

Two disparate instances of social policy, public health and liquor licensing, supply examples of the decentralized but also democratic style of pre-bureaucratic governance. Into the early years of the twentieth century, poor sanitary conditions produced major outbreaks of cholera, yellow fever, and smallpox. Mosquitoes, one of many menaces, made nights in Texas "memorable," a nineteenth century visitor remembered; there was no escape from them "except to hang yourself or run away." A Republican governor in Reconstruction Mississippi found his room "full of the hungriest, blood thirstiest crew of mosquitoes that ever presented a bill to me." Going from room to room to escape, he finally slept in his boots to protect his ankles and feet.

Southern public health bureaucracies, despite efforts after Reconstruction to strengthen them, proved nearly powerless in practice. . . .

Even after the discovery of microscopic origins of disease revolutionized public health in the late decades of the nineteenth century, southern state health officials received necessary funds and political support only after epidemic disease had begun its periodic sweep. Few late nineteenth- and early twentieth-century state health officers could do more than gather scattered, inaccurate statistics and make pronouncements about the general condition of health. Even if localities did request help, state health officials were effectively limited to advice. When physicians in a western North Carolina county requested that the state test local dairies, the state health officer replied with undisguised sarcasm that, with an annual budget of only $2,000, he could ill afford "to indulge in 'luxuries.' "

An even more serious problem was the lack of effective local health organization. Although most states provided for some form of local health organizations, in practice these were informal and almost completely powerless. In most states, local health officials performed few duties: periodically visiting the jail, fumigating the courthouse, and examining lunatics—for a minimal salary. They exercised supervisory powers over disease only in times of epidemic. . . .

Local health officials also knew that little support would be forthcoming from state officials. Florida's health bureaucracy came into existence after a devastating outbreak of yellow fever in 1888, when the state legislature provided a State Board of Health with an assured revenue and with authority to restrict the inflow of yellow fever and smallpox from the Caribbean. Even so, the Board's actual power to aid local health officials—and to engage in any form of preventive public health— remained sharply curtailed. . . .

Government's power over alcohol consumption provides another example of the limited scope of pre-bureaucratic southern social policy. The spread of the market economy during the nineteenth century spurred the commercialization of alcohol production, especially of corn whiskey; rising consumption, and excessive drinking, were commonplace in nineteenth-century southern life. In antebellum Mississippi, not only was it common to see "one who reeled as he walked," but only if Mississippians "lay and wallowed" were they regarded as drunk. Despite overdrinking, state and local governments before about 1905 avoided assuming a regulatory function over the distribution, sale, or consumption of alcohol. Although local option spread across the rural South in the post-Reconstruction period, illegal saloons, or "blind tigers," and bootleggers violated the law almost routinely, while federal internal revenue agents regularly collected taxes from dry counties in the South. . . .

. . . Lacking any tradition of state intervention, southern state and local administrators were uniformly unsuccessful in constructing an effective bureaucracy. Instead, local communities held the upper hand. . . . [S]outherners, white and black, were far from passive on the subject of governance. Because of the strength of community power, social policy in the nineteenth century remained decentralized and always required the approval of local communities.

Set in this social context, the emergence of southern progressivism takes on new significance. What reformers often portrayed as problems were actually social and political conditions long taken for granted. What reformers lamented as a decline in "community" was a contentious, intensely localistic, rural participatory democracy. Their prescription for social improvement and the means of enforcing it ran squarely into strong southern traditions of personal liberty and fear of and hostility toward outside intrusions.

If southern social reformers possessed a common characteristic, it was the belief that their region had undergone a serious crisis in the late decades of the nineteenth century and that it faced renewed crises in the near future. To many, the problems were primarily moral rather than political or social, and southern progressivism drew from a grass-roots swell of moral reformers. Beginning in the 1880s, evangelical churchmen began to mobilize against what they perceived as increasing secularization and moral decline in southern society. Post-Reconstruction churchmen witnessed rapid social change that seemed to erode social, racial, and gender order. Assertive children and adolescents, the rising incidence of divorce, and urban-centered evils like dancing, card-playing, theater, and, above all, prostitution, all indicated a moral order in decline.

The menace of alcohol, which embodied both individual and community corruption, became the central issue for moral reformers. To reformers, the connections between the saloon and moral decline were obvious, but they went a step further by linking corruption and moral decline to a passive social policy. . . .

Near the turn of the twentieth century, reformers began to criticize and publicize what they considered evils in existing southern social and political institutions. The national popular press portrayed the South as a problem in need of solution. . . . The South retained a large, mobile, and ever-increasing rural population that would remain its majority well into the twentieth century. Social reformers in the North and Midwest addressed problems of rapid industrialization and the social and economic change that came with it. Not so with southern social critics. They believed that their social crisis came from underdevelopment and poverty, and their solutions were aimed at modernizing an entire people and an entire society. In the South, explained rural sociologist Eugene Cunningham Branson in 1902, isolation and poverty caused "social degeneracy and decay." To avoid stagnation and eventual social and political instability, reformers believed that the South's entrenched patterns of individual and community conduct needed to change. They favored not only expanding railroad and hard-surfaced transportation to the hinterlands, but also extending the values of the outside world: an outward-directed standard of conduct and adherence to a modernized, cohesive "community." In advocating these changes, reformers clashed with rural precepts of personal honor, individualism, and community control that were cardinal principles of the nineteenth-century South. Thus establishing a refashioned notion of community with reinvigorated institutions ultimately meant wrenching those institutions from their social context.

Social reformers inaugurated their assault on traditional social policy with evangelical-style crusades. The first such crusade began in 1901, when reformers established the Southern Education Board (SEB) to coordinate a regional public-school campaign. Other crusades followed: a long campaign, beginning about 1902, to institute prohibition, first by state legislation, then by state constitutional amendment, and finally by federal constitutional amendment; a campaign, organized in 1904, to limit or eliminate child labor in factories; a campaign, inaugurated in 1909, to eradicate hookworm disease; and a campaign, which began in the South in the same year, to grant women the right to vote.

These crusades were closely connected. Educational reform attracted a variety of reformers who saw the schools as vehicles of wider societal changes and who later applied the methods of the educational crusade to other reform campaigns. Edgar Gardner Murphy, executive secretary of the SEB, spearheaded the child-labor crusade; Madeline McDowell Breckinridge, a veteran of Kentucky school reform, became a leading regional and national suffragist; and Wickliffe Rose, a Tennessee university professor and educational reformer, later headed the hookworm crusade and the Rockefeller Foundation's International Health Board.

Studies of southern progressivism have said little about the organizational bases of these crusades and how they mobilized public opinion and translated a crusade into long-term social policies. As several historians have suggested recently, trends in American Protestantism strongly influenced progressive reform, and, in the South, this was nowhere more apparent than in the crusades' style, organization, and objectives. Reformers, themselves suffused with evangelical values, adopted the technique and approach of the religious revival. Like the revival, the reform crusades sought to move public opinion toward a dramatic conviction of social sin. In the case of the educational crusade, the objective was public support for schools and higher local taxes. In the case of the hookworm crusade, the reformers sought to alter public attitudes about public health so as to make parasitic infection impossible.

Careful advance preparations, including consultation with local leaders, assured success and public approval for the crusades. An example of thorough preparation modeled on evangelical methods comes from the Rockefeller Sanitary Commission, which was created in 1909 with a million-dollar endowment and led a five-year crusade to eradicate hookworm in the South. The commission's Administrative Secretary, Wickliffe Rose, endorsed a program of county dispensaries, traveling clinics that treated hookworm sufferers and preached the virtues of sanitation.

Rockefeller operatives laid a solid groundwork for each county crusade. They persuaded prominent citizens to endorse the dispensary and then organized a large delegation to meet with local officials to urge them to appropriate money for the dispensary. Success also depended on a massive publicity campaign, with printed placards and handbills announcing the dispensary and warning of the dangers of hookworms. "Parents who do not use this opportunity to rid their children of this dreaded-disease," read one placard in Alamance County, North Carolina, stood "squarely across their offspring's future, condemning them of times to an early death or a life of misery." These methods enabled the crusaders to reap a harvest of heavy turnout and public approbation.

Among the most sophisticated employers of these evangelical-style methods were the prohibitionists, who conducted their campaign under the auspices of the Anti-Saloon League (ASL). Organized nationally in 1895, the ASL began to penetrate the South after the turn of the century. The league organized state chapters which conducted local campaigns and lobbied state legislatures. Like hookworm campaigners, ASL prohibitionists emphasized advanced preparation and publicity. Relying on donations from local churches, the Virginia league—like all the ASL state chapters, an interdenominational coalition—had an operating budget of $16,000 by 1906, only five years after its founding. As did other southern prohibitionists, the Virginia reformers used these funds to develop a sophisticated system of publicity.

Examples abound of the staged preparation of early twentieth-century reform crusades. . . .

The centerpiece of all these crusades, as for nineteenth-century revivalists, was a public event designed to reverse popular attitudes. Crusaders spread the word through familiar means: a courthouse meeting, often held under a tent, before throngs streaming in from adjoining rural areas. During the early years of the crusade, educational rallies coincided with the visits of outside speakers; during the later years, local school improvement leagues, led and run by women, orchestrated the rallies. The results were often dramatic. Wickliffe Rose described a typical scene at a hookworm dispensary held in Sampson County, North Carolina. "As we neared the place," he wrote, "we met a line of buggies and wagons with whole families coming away; . . . a hundred or more people of both sexes and of all ages [were] waiting for attention."

By the time southern suffragists emerged after 1910, these crusading techniques were well established. Like the other reformers, suffragists employed public events to rally public opinion behind the cause. The suffrage crusaders often organized parades which became, in the setting of southern towns, a startling dramatization of feminine assertiveness. The early suffrage parades occurred more or less spontaneously. Elisabeth Perry Collins remembered that suffragists in Greenville, South Carolina, attempted to join a community parade but were greeted by jeers and taunts. Lila Meade Valentine similarly remembered that it was "considered indecent for women to speak in public" and "to march in processions with their brothers." Yet parades, and other public suffrage demonstrations, soon became commonplace across the South.

Like other crusaders, suffragists sent out visiting speakers, who usually made their addresses at county seats. In some localities, suffragists organized "suffrage schools," which invited speakers and distributed suffragist literature. "Suffrage speakers have been present at the State Fair, most of the County Fairs, Farmers' meetings, and many picnics and other public gatherings and have aided greatly in extending the suffrage 'gospel,' " reported a Virginia suffragist in 1915. The most successful of these meetings featured speeches by suffragists of noted oratorical ability and statewide reputation, such as Lila Meade Valentine of Virginia or Madeline McDowell Breckinridge of Kentucky. . . .

The chief object of the reform revival became a kind of conversion experience through which collective public opinion radically recast its attitudes. The reformers' confidence in revival-based reform was not just based on its organizational style; they were convinced that reform would come suddenly. As in a revival, popular enthusiasm was carefully managed, staged, and manipulated. . . .

By reaching out to public opinion in terms which rural southerners easily comprehended, the crusades reaped a full harvest. Their success provides additional evidence that the mass of southerners, far from passive objects of reform, performed an active role. Without the popular enthusiasm generated by the campaigns, it seems unlikely that political support for reform-oriented legislation would have materialized. And with what appeared to be a public consensus, reformers were able to convince legislators in state capitals to endorse sweeping new legislation that redefined governance and social policy in the South. Yet in redefining social policy, reformers clearly overstepped the mandate of the crusades. For if southern public opinion became aroused at the exposure of social conditions, it remained strongly committed to a pre-bureaucratic conception of governance.

A New Social Policy: Implementation and Resistance

Even as the reform crusades enjoyed early successes, a process had begun that would redefine the role of government in southern society. Early social reformers had criticized governance and endorsed a new degree of activism, but probably not all of them envisioned a full-blown bureaucratic, interventionist state. With the secular revival-crusades, reformers expressed common cultural attitudes and embraced traditional views of local autonomy and the solution of social problems. They believed that by altering public opinion, changed social conditions would follow.

In reality, the experience of implementing southern social reform would prove far more complex. At the root of social change, reformers came eventually to believe, lay the alteration of firmly rooted and popular folkways; democratically executed social policy would mean leaving the status quo unchanged. In taking the process of reform a step beyond the crusade model, then, reformers confronted a thorny dilemma. They discovered that implementing what they believed was a needed social change ran against local traditions and would necessitate the abandonment of community control. Operating within a restricted, disfranchised state made easier the rationalization of antidemocratic methods, as did cultural and attitudinal differences separating reformers and reformed. Yet continued problems in enforcing innovations in governance forced its practitioners to adapt and even to alter the new social policy.

The success of the reform crusades resulted in a host of new legislation. Southern state legislatures responded to the educational revival with new laws increasing state funds for schools and granting stronger powers to state school superintendents. Child-labor reformers persuaded most southern states to enact laws banning the employment of children in factories. Prohibitionists enjoyed a string of victories after 1905 in which statewide prohibition came into force by popular referendum or legislative enactment. Other reformers, operating in urban communities, obtained new laws or pressured municipal governments into enforcing existing ones to limit organized prostitution and ban business transactions on Sunday. In the wake of the hookworm campaign, state health departments experienced a dramatic growth in their coercive and regulatory powers. An offshoot of the general crusade for social betterment was the introduction of responsibility for social work and social welfare as part of state and local governments.

Increasingly, the agencies which these laws revitalized or created exercised centralized, bureaucratic governance. In some instances, as in the case of social efficiency modernizers, the transition from revival to bureaucracy was quick and almost unthinking. These reformers sought to change southern folkways by eliminating rural individualism and localism and substituting urbanized, dynamic values that would make social development along progressive lines possible. Social efficiency policy manifested itself primarily in a revamped approach to public schools and public health. With larger budgets and greater powers, educational and health bureaucracies expanded staff and exerted a supervisory role over local communities. . . .

. . . [I]n state health bureaucracies . . . [m]ost of the new power went to the executive officers of the state boards of health, and from their offices grew new supervisory staffs. Their powers were probably the most coercive of any agency of the new social policy. With new authority to establish quarantine—powers that had before only theoretically existed—state health officials expanded their role in preventive health care. They acquired increased control over public sanitation and, beginning in urban areas, enforced new standards with new rigor. Health officials also began to examine and treat schoolchildren. They introduced new programs of child and maternal welfare, of disease prevention through inoculation and basic sanitation, and participated in energetic programs to combat venereal disease and tuberculosis.

Expansion of the state's welfare role constituted another category of the redefined social policy. The crusade to limit child labor was only one part of a broad effort to transform conceptions of the causes and solutions of poverty, social dislocation, and family disarray. The crusade for woman suffrage could also be lumped, not inappropriately, into this category. Suffragists frequently contended that extending the franchise to women would make government more nurturing and maternal toward its citizens. Suffragists assumed—incorrectly as it turned out—that the vote for women would create a constituency for new legislation to uproot vice, wife-beating, child labor, and bad working conditions for women and to establish an equal role for women within the family.

Another category of revised social policy involved the most ambitious effort to shape moral behavior in American history, state and national prohibition. In the South and elsewhere prohibitionists sought to redefine the relationship between government and the individual through a transformed social policy. Prohibitionists were the first to admit that there was never any time in which either statewide or later national prohibition was completely effective. Continued violations of prohibition, however, did not render it a failure, they argued. All civilized societies banned murder, but there would always be murder; larceny was illegal, yet it would always occur. Similarly, reformers reasoned, continued drinking was hardly an argument for prohibition's failure.

In a different category of social policy, race relations, most white social reformers welcomed disfranchisement and legally enforced racial segregation as necessary. Combined with a paternalism that dominated the thinking of social reformers, their belief in racial hierarchy exposed a dark, almost sinister side to southern progressives. But they also viewed political exclusion and *de jure* segregation as reforms that would stabilize white-black relations—which experienced a crisis of disturbing proportions during the 1890s—and, at least as they saw it, pave the way for black progress. To reformers, the disfranchised, one-party state provided opportunities for moderate, paternalistic racial policies. They believed that unlimited democracy and control by the mass of whites meant complete exclusion; the new administrative state, ironically, offered some benefits and services to blacks, those southerners most disinherited by progressive reform.

On the eve of World War I, then, a new approach to race relations was beginning to gain wider currency. Black education became a vehicle through which white reformers could seek black progress under the Jim Crow system. Programs, such as those which the General Education Board and the Rosenwald Fund sponsored, provided financial resources for the improvement of black schools under the vague rubric of "industrial education." Black educational reform also provided a model for future white southern reformers who accepted segregation while endorsing a program of black progress. By the 1920s, however, white race reformers discovered an erosion of white and black support for industrial education. In the pre–World War I period, white moderates defined the "Negro Problem" primarily in terms of black inadequacy; they believed that industrial education would transform black folkways with an infusion of Victorian standards of thrift and hard work. By the 1920s, moderates allied with the Commission on Interracial Cooperation (CIC), founded in 1919, espoused a different view: the primary problem was "discrimination" and "prejudice," not black inadequacy. Rejecting Victorian racial attitudes, CIC reformers—despite rampant racism and generally bleak prospects for blacks— sought improvements for blacks through the bureaucratic structures erected during the Progressive Era. Increasingly attracted to empirical definitions of racial problems, the CIC turned toward the new social scientists of the South for answers. Will Winton Alexander, the director of the CIC, thus established a close relationship with the Chapel Hill social scientist Howard W. Odum, who relied in turn on Alexander for advice, contacts with northern philanthropic foundations, and a supply of some of the earliest southern students of race relations.

Working closely with other practitioners of a new southern social policy, CIC reformers enjoyed access to the educational and health bureaucracies, and with them, they participated in state interracial groups and conferences. Black public education and public health assumed a greater priority during the 1920s. A new network of social scientists, typified by Odum and Wilson Gee of the University of Virginia, sponsored the incorporation of black welfare work into state social welfare systems. By the end of the 1920s, what Alexander called the "integration of the interracial movement with the official and volunteer social welfare agencies of many communities and states" had already occurred in Alabama, Georgia, the Carolinas, Louisiana, Virginia, and Tennessee. In the remaining states interracialists claimed "close and sympathetic relations" with social welfare agencies.

In attempting to alter some fundamental characteristics of southern life, reformers had traveled a long road during the first three decades of the twentieth century. From the educational revival in 1901 to the triumph of the woman suffrage movement in 1919, a series of regional crusades popularized new ways of identifying and attempting to solve social problems. These crusades enjoyed widespread support from public opinion—a major objective—yet they also betrayed a leadership style whose attitudes and intentions were far removed from those of most rural southerners. It should come as little surprise that reformers—who were infused with the cultural and social values of the new industrial order, who came from self-confident and assertive town classes, and who regarded the traditional village and rural culture with disdain—would favor a new form of interventionism.

That the attempt to implement these changes met frequent opposition supplies still more evidence that rural southerners were more active than passive regarding both reform and its implementation. Although reformers and rural communities converged in the crusades because of their familiarity with rural evangelical traditions, the attempt to introduce bureaucratic governance was another matter. Indeed the introduction of policy innovations began a long struggle between reformers and local communities. Still, the nature of this opposition must be placed in context, for the great majority of those who opposed reform possessed no unifying ideology or group consciousness. Although social distinctions and conflicts affected almost every aspect of southern life, few country folk reacted to social reform and accompanying policy changes exclusively or even primarily in terms of class. Rather, usually viewing the issue as a contest between their community and outsiders, they resisted reforms because they and their parents had always opposed interference in local matters. Significantly, in almost every instance of resistance to southern social reform, the resisters refused to link arms with one another for one very clear reason: they were as suspicious, perhaps even more suspicious, of other rural southerners as they were of outside centralizers. . . .

Resistance was thus strongest wherever communities, especially rural communities, faced the deprivation of traditional autonomy. Benjamin Earle Washburn, who worked with the Rockefeller hookworm campaign and early county health programs in North Carolina, expressed his frustration with local resistance in a fable that he wrote about 1918. Public health conditions in his fictitious Miasma County, North Carolina, like the rest of the rural South, were atrocious. Open surface privies, which sanitarians regarded as public health threats, prevailed; hookworms were of a "ferocious type"; and "everybody took Quinine except the Lady Principal of the County High School and she took Quin-een." Because of the "Rule and Fashion" that governed Miasma County, everyone existed in a "Run Down Condition from these causes" and was "Predisposed to Typhoid and Diarrhea—and these diseases did their part."

Local physicians only abetted Miasma's problems. "Old Doc Richards," who dispensed what was "Technically Known as Hot Air," opposed public health measures because, he claimed, they meant sacrificing personal liberty. As he reminded the locals, he "knew the county Much better than an Outsider could ever know it," and public health meant a tax increase to pay a "Rank outsider,—maybe some Yankee who wouldn't understand Miasma and her ways." The county commissioners appointed Richards as full-time county health officer.

Not surprisingly, Miasma's experiment with public health was brief. Hookworms and mosquitoes "didn't keep their contract with Doc; and Typhoid Fever was about as Gay As Ever and Infant Diarrhea acted like it had never heard of a Health Officer." The county commissioners abolished the failed local health structure, and Washburn's story reached its unhappy conclusion: Miasma County returned to the "Good Old Times when each family took care of itself without having the County or State Meddle with Its Personal Affairs."

Washburn's fable was overdrawn, and it reflected the imperiousness of early twentieth-century health reformers. But it portrayed the frustration of reformers accurately. Countless other southern rural communities were as suspicious as Miasma County of the costly innovation of health reform and of the centralization and coercion that came with it. Rural southerners drew on a deep tradition of fear and anger toward the medical profession and public health measures such as vaccination. Recipients of nineteenth-century medical treatment often fared worse than they would have with no treatment at all, and rural southerners feared that modern public health would bring even more life-threatening ministrations. In fact, it is undeniable that public health measures were sometimes just that. Treatment for hookworm, which involved highly toxic substances such as thymol, carbolic acid, or oil of chenopodium, could result in violent, often fatal reactions, if taken improperly.

Reformers reported widespread indifference or hostility to public health throughout the rural South. Rural Kentuckians, wrote a health official in 1913, possessed no faith in preventive medicine or personal hygiene. Audiences refused to admit "the existence of Hookworm or other parasites; they do not believe that they are infected with these parasites even if they do exist." The Louisiana state health officer in 1916 made a similar observation. It would take a "world of education," he concluded, to persuade rural Louisianans to endorse the "most necessary sanitary reforms." Although post–World War I reformers concluded that rural health depended upon the bureaucratization of county health systems, rural opposition often translated into the unwillingness of local government to finance public health work. In 1915, the Tennessee state health officer observed that funds were "tight, . . . especially in the cotton counties and in mining counties," and the county courts were "not disposed to open the strongbox." Throughout the 1920s, state officials faced local resistance to pay for reforms. . . .

Localism thus forced modernizers to modify their policies. Rather than extending the blessings of modern sanitation all at once, reformers had to introduce it incrementally, and they had their greatest successes where alliances were struck with local communities. Often the price of cooperation was the participation of local physicians. "I have not worked in a state where the citizens . . . were more annoying in their insistence" that local candidates be employed in public health positions, complained an International Health Board official about Louisiana in 1921. Most of these candidates had "some ax to grind," and thus public health work easily became mired in local politics.

The necessity of compromise with localism became just as evident to modernizing school officials. In the cases of school consolidation and compulsory education, southern educators faced hostility and noncooperation. Because they depended even more than health officials upon local participation—through the support of tax revenues and attendance—school officials bowed to local opinion. School consolidation, which involved the closing of community schools and their centralization at some other location, carried a genuine potential for rebellion. . . .

The dilemma of implementing centralization while retaining community cooperation was even more obvious in the instance of compulsory education. Enforcement introduced a strong degree of coercion to local school administration. Although every southern state had enacted effective compulsory education legislation by the end of the 1920s, enforcement still depended on the voluntary participation of local communities. . . .

The primary problem for child-labor reformers, as for health and educational reformers, was to secure local cooperation. A reformer in Alabama wrote in 1913 that local officials exhibited "great laxity" in enforcement of the state's laws against child labor, especially in mill communities. The North Carolina reformer Charles Lee Coon reached a similar conclusion. Close investigation of working conditions, he wrote, revealed that the laws were "flagrantly violated in all sections of the State." In 1914, a National Child Labor Committee field agent discovered that nonenforcement was the rule in the South. . . .

Resistance to child-labor restrictions came not just from mill owners concerned about lower labor costs but also from parents determined to use the labor of their children. Recent studies have shown that child labor was a central part of worker culture and, where given the chance to express their opinions, workers strongly opposed the reform. In 1909, a Macon, Georgia, labor leader, described child-labor reform as "a great joke" because "mill-workers themselves" opposed it. Although reformers usually dismissed worker opposition as indicative of pervasive "feudalism" in the mill village or of the degeneracy of workers' family structure, the noncooperation of workers figured prominently in the failure of child-labor legislation. Nor is there much evidence that children preferred the school to the mill, where most of their friends and family worked. . . . This pattern of reform and resistance also appeared in the case of woman suffrage. What we know about the woman suffrage movement in the South suggests that its base was overwhelmingly urban. The profile of its leaders and supporters resembled the profile of the leaders and supporters of other social reforms—that is to say, it was dominated by an upper middle-class, white, urban Protestant elite. When urban suffragists attempted to extend their base to the rural South, they often encountered indifference or hostility. Rural women in Kentucky treated suffrage "lightly," if at all, as a suffragist complained in 1910. . . .

A comparable problem of inaugurating an unpopular reform confronted prohibitionists. . . .

Probably more than other advocates of a new social policy, prohibitionists experienced the persisting strength of individualism and localism in the rural South. In the Appalachian South, moonshiners engaged in a generation of violent struggle against "revenuers," the federal agents who sought payment of the federal excise tax; subsequently, they continued to do battle against prohibition agents. In many communities, moonshiners enjoyed public approval and support, and enforcement of the law provoked violence. "The moonshine work is get[t]ing to be so [dangerous] you will have to furnish me with a high power rifel [*sic*] or a repe[a]ting shot gun," reported an agent in mountainous Virginia.

This essay has argued that a clearer assessment of early twentieth-century reform requires a reexamination of its social context and consequences. Most historians of southern progressivism have neglected the social environment that reformers sought to change and the impact on it of their policy innovations. By focusing on reformers and their motivations, scholars have placed responsibility for major intergenerational social and political changes on their shoulders.

The real significance of Progressive Era social reform is to be found in the society which reformers confronted: a dispersed, rural population with strong traditions of individualism and localism. What the reformers sought amounted to revolutionary changes in governance and the administration of social policy, and they succeeded in introducing a new measure of interventionism in state and local government, designed to reorient fundamental qualities of southern culture. Popular antagonism to these changes, although not always fully or effectively articulated, frequently imperiled programs of modernization and administrative centralization. The implementation of the reformers' new social policy brought about not only centralized governance, but also localized community resistance. Historians of Progressive Era reform in the South must include both in their analyses.

✣ *F U R T H E R   R E A D I N G*

Raymond Arsenault, *The Wild Ass of the Ozarks: Jeff Davis and the Social Bases of Southern Politics* (1984)

Edward Ayers, *The Promise of the New South: Life After Reconstruction* (1992)

Hugh C. Bailey, *Edgar Gardner Murphy: Gentle Progressive* (1968)

——, *Liberalism in the New South: Southern Social Reformers and the Progressive Movement* (1969)

Paul D. Casdorph, *Republicans, Negroes, and Progressives in the South* (1981)

Bruce Clayton, *The Savage Ideal: Intolerance and Intellectual Leadership in the South, 1890–1914* (1972)

John Dittmer, *Black Georgia in the Progressive Era, 1900–1920* (1977)

W. E. B. Du Bois, ed. *Efforts for Social Betterment Among Negro Americans* (1909)

Elizabeth E. Etheridge, *The Butterfly Caste: A Social History of Pellagra in the South* (1972)

J. Wayne Flynt, *Dixie's Forgotten People: The South's Poor Whites* (1979)

——, *Poor but Proud: Alabama's Poor Whites* (1989)

Dewey W. Grantham, *Southern Progressivism: The Reconciliation of Progress and Tradition* (1983)

Louis R. Harlan, *Separate and Unequal: Public School Campaigns and Racism in the Southern Seaboard States, 1901–1915* (1958)

——, *Booker T. Washington: The Making of a Black Leader* (1972)

——, *Booker T. Washington: The Wizard of Tuskegee, 1901–1915* (1983)

Carl V. Harris, *Political Power in Birmingham, 1871–1921* (1977)

William F. Holmes, *The White Chief: James Kimble Vardaman* (1970)

Jack Temple Kirby, *Darkness at the Dawning: Race and Reform in the Progressive South* (1972)

J. Morgan Kousser, *The Shaping of Southern Politics: Suffrage Restriction and the Establishment of the One-Party South, 1880–1910* (1974)

——, "Progressivism—For Middle-Class Whites Only: North Carolina Education, 1880–1910," *Journal of Southern History* 46 (1980), 169–194

James L. Leloudis, *Schooling the New South* (1996)

David Levering Lewis, *W. E. B. Du Bois: Biography of a Race* (1993)

Alex Lichtenstein, "Good Roads and Chain Gangs in the Progressive South: "The Negro Convict Is a Slave," *Journal of Southern History* 59 (February 1993), 85–110

Arthur S. Link, "The Progressive Movement in the South, 1870–1914," *North Carolina Historical Review* 23 (1946), 172–195

William A. Link, *A Hard Country and a Lonely Place: Schooling, Society, and Reform in Rural Virginia, 1870–1920* (1986)

——, *The Paradox of Southern Progressivism, 1880–1920* (1993)

John Patrick McDowell, *The Social Gospel in the South: The Woman's Home Mission Movement in the Methodist Episcopal Church, South, 1886–1939* (1982)

Thomas R. Pegram, "Temperance Politics and Regional Political Culture: The Anti-Saloon League in Maryland and the South, 1907–1915," *Journal of Southern History* 63 (February 1997), 57–90

Bradley S. Rice, *Progressive Cities* (1977)

Zamir Shamoon, *Dark Voices: W. E. B. Du Bois and American Thought* (1995)

George B. Tindall, *Emergence of the New South, 1913–1945* (1967)

Linda D. Vance, *May Mann Jennings: Florida's Genteel Activist* (1985)

LeeAnn Whites, "The De Graffenried Controversy: Class, Race, and Gender in the New South," *Journal of Southern History* 54 (1988), 449–478

Cary Wintz, ed., *African American Political Thought* (1996)

George C. Wright, *Life Behind a Veil: Blacks in Louisville, Kentucky, 1865–1930* (1985)

Robert I. Zangrando, *The NAACP Crusade Against Lynching* (1980)

New Women, New South, New Prospects

✝

Increasingly scholars have come to recognize the importance of gender in understanding the history of the New South. This is amply demonstrated in the numbers of books and articles published over the last fifteen years. Black and white women in the New South coexisted in communities, formed families and households, bore and raised children, and provided care for aging relatives. Some worked in cotton and tobacco fields, labored in textile and tobacco mills, clerked in stores, cleaned houses, or taught in schools. The resources available to southern women in their private and working lives varied widely, but all shared a common position subordinate to men as prescribed by southern patriarchal traditions. Notions of submission were complicated by issues of race and class, but it was within this environment that southern women struggled to assert themselves, to gain wider opportunities in education and employment, and to share in the shaping of southern culture and government.

Following the Civil War, black and white southern women found that opportunities for public education often depended on private resources, and those who were able to enter the newly established schools of higher education were likely to find open to them careers in education, religion, writing, the arts, and medicine. Southern women became indispensable in voluntary associations, establishing Sunday schools, founding charitable organizations, funding missions, promoting sisterhoods and sororities, and creating women's clubs and civic organizations. In Richmond, Maggie Lena Walker, a black woman, established a savings bank for black clients, the first successful business venture of its kind. In Atlanta, Lugenia Burns Hope cofounded the Neighborhood Improvement Association, while Jessie Daniel Ames of Texas organized the Association of Southern Women for the Prevention of Lynching. Reformers abounded among black and white women: Both joined the Woman's Christian Temperance Union, the Young Women's Christian Association, and the Commission on Interracial Cooperation; both worked for juvenile welfare, community improvement, and equality of rights, although in race-specific contexts. Twentieth-century reforms such as the campaign against lynching, labor organizing, and the civil rights movement could not have gained much momentum without the support and active leadership of women.

The conservative nature of southern history and politics meant that many women also supported white supremacy and racial segregation; some opposed woman suffrage before 1920, joined the Auxiliary to the Ku Klux Klan, participated in the Red Scare of the 1950s, campaigned against the integration of public schools in the 1960s, and brought defeat to the Equal Rights Amendment in the 1980s. Still, historians continue to ask how the South's culture, with its unique blend of politics and race relations, influenced women in their public and private roles. Were churches and synagogues promoters or inhibitors of women's public activism, and if so, in which direction? What role did race play in developing opportunities for women? How were women affected by urbanization and industrialization in the South? What were the results of women's political activism?

✣ D O C U M E N T S

The Woman's Christian Temperance Union (WCTU) in 1881 became the South's first national women's organization. Although hesitant at first to publicly promote temperance and later prohibition, southern women defended their activism on the grounds that drinking tempted children, caused violence in the home, and led to penury and debasement for wives of alcoholic husbands. Rebecca Latimer Felton, wife of a Georgia politician and an activist in her own right, as seen in Document 1, argued for prohibition before the Georgia assembly by using the rhetoric of motherhood and home protection. Anna Julie Cooper, a North Carolina educator, wrote in *Voice from the South*, Document 2, that black women were confronted "by both a woman question and a race problem." Here she spoke of the valuable contributions that could be made by women but for the difficulty of black women's claiming sex equality when issues of political and economic rights consumed the black community. Document 3, a memoir from Charleston, South Carolina, describes the evening that Mary Church Terrell, first president of the National Association of Colored Women, came to encourage and enlist African American women in civic reform. Document 4, a political cartoon published in the *Dallas Morning News* following Independence Day, depicts suffragists from the Congressional Union for Woman Suffrage exhorting President Woodrow Wilson to endorse the Susan B. Anthony Amendment. His refusal in 1914 encouraged southern antisuffragists, who raised their cry of alarm, as seen in Document 5, by bringing in issues of race and memories of "black rule" during Reconstruction. The logical result of extending the franchise—in Texas, women could vote in 1918—was for women to run for public office. Document 6 is a campaign broadside for Annie Webb Blanton, who ran for Texas state superintendent of public instruction in 1918 and won.

1. Rebecca Latimer Felton Endorses Prohibition, 1895

Address Delivered Before Joint Committee, House and Senate, November 1895.

There Were 100,000 Copies Printed and Circulated Over Georgia.

――――――

Mrs. Felton's Appeal.

The following is the address of Mrs. Felton before the joint committee of the house and senate on Nov. 7th. We are sorry we haven't the space to publish the able ad-

――――――

Rebecca Latimer Felton, *Country Life in Georgia in the Days of My Youth.* Copyright © 1919 by Rebecca Latimer Felton.

dresses of other leading prohibitionists on this occasion. We will however give some of them later on.

"We come before you today," said she, "to present the appeal of the mothers of the state of Georgia, who are praying every day that the barroom may be removed from their midst and their children delivered from such temptation and the destruction that follows.

"As I look in the faces of those honorable gentlemen and remember that you are commissioned to be the guardians of the best interest of the women and children in the state, I make free to present this appeal as a matter of right, as well as of courtesy. While you are called upon to protect cities and counties that have police and authority to protect themselves, I come to bespeak protection for mothers.

"I remember something else that touches my heart, namely, that each and every one of you had once a mother. Whether your mother, like mine, is still with you, trembling with three score and ten years of feebleness and loss of strength, or has passed to the reward beyond the Jordan of death I can safely say that you know and I know that there is no more unselfish love and self-sacrificing devotion than our mothers have given to their children.

"I now ask you to turn in your thoughts upon the homes and firesides of this country and then tell me if there is any class of citizenship, or order of human beings, any sex or species, that have superior claims upon this country for protection in their homes and protection to their offspring.

"I am not here to detail the results of intemperance. It would be like illustrating your prison walls to show the prisoners that jails were the legal lodging place for criminals and murderers. The reality is so much worse than I could picture in words that it beggars description.

"The question that I bring to you to decide upon today is a very plain and simple one, namely: Do you consider the saloon keepers of Georgia of superior importance to the mothers of this country and the safety of their offspring?

"There can be no temporizing, no hesitation in the decision you will make—you will either prefer one or the other. Which shall be?

"When the Almighty Father placed the burden of maternity upon women—made her the custodian of the infant in the critical period of its life.—He said to the father train up that child in the way it shall go; and when it is old it will not depart from it. The Lord blessed Abraham, His servant because he would command his children and his household after him, that they should keep the way of the Lord to do justice and judgment.

"The burden of motherhood lies upon the woman, but the burden of protection and good example lies upon man—that the offspring shall be able to do justice and judgment to the Maker and others.

The issue is clearly stated, and I am here to say to you, measuring my words, in the sight of God and the presence of this assembly, no child should be thrust upon an unfriendly world that is denied the privilege of a sober home to be borne into, with clean blood in its veins, unstained by hereditary diseases that follow upon drunkenness. Anything which disregards this vested right is rank injustice to the child which comes here without its consent. Anything less than this protection to the mother who goes down into the valley of the shadow to give an immortal soul its being is wanton cruelty to the innocent and deserving that must and will bring retribution upon its perpetrators and authors. All other duties and obligations pale into insignificance when the eternal destiny of the human race is thus involved and this question cannot be evaded when it is proposed to perpetuate crime factories and the sinkholes of perdition—that nobody ever claims will elevate or make prosperous the votaries of the saloon.

"It cannot be disputed that protection from the dramshop means more to the mothers of this country than any other class or condition of our people. Deprivation of protection and the lack of restraining laws also mean more of injured mother love than any other loss or deprivation that it ever encounters.

"Motherhood should be carefully protected, guarded and defended as no other interest, no matter what it may represent, can deserve or demand.

"To state this fact is simply to affirm it. For the sake of those yet to come as well as for those already here, every known avenue of crime, temptation and evil suggestion should be rigidly closed to the child whose moral and physical traits are molded or branded by the unerring laws of heredity, as well as the circumstances of environment.

The bearing, nursing and training of the coming millions are the problems of the age.

"This high and holy estate of motherhood should appeal to you and all others as no influence may equal or surpass. . . .

"Barrooms are always a constant menace to the peace and happiness of these mothers. With blandishing enticements they are sure to gloat over victims in plenty, as the poor wretches yield one after another, their character and happiness, disappear in the gilded saloons and their money passes into the pockets of the liquor seller.

"Now, gentlemen, which will you choose? Which is more valuable to Georgia, these children [or] the saloons? Will you protect these women or will you soil your palms with license money, turning over these mothers and their children to the destroyer? . . .

["]Can you stand in your places, sworn to do your duty, in the fear of God and the presence of all Georgia, and choose the saloon in preference to the protection of mothers and all they love and cherish in their homes? Shall we lean upon you as our protectors or will you leave us defenseless?["]

2. Anna Julia Cooper's "Voice from the South," 1892

There is to my mind no grander and surer prophecy of the new era and of woman's place in it, than the work already begun in the waning years of the nineteenth century by the W. C. T. U.* in America, an organization which has even now reached not only national but international importance, and seems destined to permeate and purify the whole civilized world. It is the living embodiment of woman's activities and woman's ideas, and its extent and strength rightly prefigure her increasing power as a moral factor.

From *The Voice of Anna Julia Cooper,* edited by Charles Lemert and Esme Bhan. Copyright © 1998, Rowman & Littlefield Publishers, Inc. Reprinted by permission of the publisher.

*W.C.T.U.: Woman's Christian Temperance Union, an organization of women that crusaded against saloons and the drinking of alcohol.

The colored woman of to-day occupies, one may say, a unique position in this country. In a period of itself transitional and unsettled, her status seems one of the least ascertainable and definitive of all the forces which make for our civilization. She is confronted by both a woman question and a race problem, and is as yet an unknown or an unacknowledged factor in both. While the women of the white race can with calm assurance enter upon the work they feel by nature appointed to do, while their men give loyal support and appreciative countenance to their efforts, recognizing in most avenues of usefulness the propriety and the need of woman's distinctive co-operation, the colored woman too often finds herself hampered and shamed by a less liberal sentiment and a more conservative attitude on the part of those for whose opinion she cares most. That this is not universally true I am glad to admit. There are to be found both intensely conservative white men and exceedingly liberal colored men. But as far as my experience goes the average man of our race is less frequently ready to admit the actual need among the sturdier forces of the world for woman's help or influence. That great social and economic questions await her interference, that she could throw any light on problems of national import, that her intermeddling could improve the management of school systems, or elevate the tone of public institutions, or humanize and sanctify the far reaching influence of prisons and reformatories and improve the treatment of lunatics and imbeciles,—that she has a word worth hearing on mooted questions in political economy, that she could contribute a suggestion on the relations of labor and capital, or offer a thought on honest money and honorable trade, I fear the majority of "Americans of the colored variety" are not yet prepared to concede. It may be that they do not yet see these questions in their right perspective, being absorbed in the immediate needs of their own political complications. A good deal depends on where we put the emphasis in this world; and our men are not perhaps to blame if they see everything colored by the light of those agitations in the midst of which they live and move and have their being. The part they have had to play in American history during the last twenty-five or thirty years has tended rather to exaggerate the importance of mere political advantage, as well as to set a fictitious valuation on those able to secure such advantage. It is the astute politician, the manager who can gain preferment for himself and his favorites, the demagogue known to stand in with the powers at the White House and consulted on the bestowal of government plums, whom we set in high places and denominate great. It is they who receive the hosannas of the multitude and are regarded as leaders of the people. The thinker and the doer, the man who solves the problem by enriching his country with an invention worth thousands or by a thought inestimable and precious is given neither bread nor a stone. He is too often left to die in obscurity and neglect even if spared in his life the bitterness of fanatical jealousies and detraction.

And yet politics, and surely American politics, is hardly a school for great minds. Sharpening rather than deepening, it develops the faculty of taking advantage of present emergencies rather than the insight to distinguish between the true and the false, the lasting and the ephemeral advantage. Highly cultivated selfishness rather than consecrated benevolence is its passport to success. Its votaries are never seers. At best they are but manipulators—often only jugglers. It is conducive neither to profound statesmanship nor to the higher type of manhood. Altruism is its *mauvais succès* and naturally enough it is indifferent to any factor which cannot be worked into its own immediate aims and purposes. As woman's influence as a political element is as yet nil in most of the commonwealths of our republic, it is not surprising that with those who place the emphasis on mere political capital she may yet seem almost a nonentity so far as it concerns the solution of great national or even racial perplexities.

There are those, however, who value the calm elevation of the thoughtful spectator who stands aloof from the heated scramble; and, above the turmoil and din of corruption and selfishness, can listen to the teachings of eternal truth and righteousness. There are even those who feel that the black man's unjust and unlawful exclusion temporarily from participation in the elective franchise in certain states is after all but a lesson "in the desert" fitted to develop in him insight and discrimination against the day of his own appointed time. One needs occasionally to stand aside from the hum and rush of human interests and passions to hear the voices of God. And it not unfrequently happens that the All-loving gives a great push to certain souls to thrust them out, as it were, from the distracting current for awhile to promote their discipline and growth, or to enrich them by communion and reflection. And similarly it may be woman's privilege from her peculiar coigne of vantage as a quiet observer, to whisper just the needed suggestion or the almost forgotten truth. The colored woman, then, should not be ignored because her bark is resting in the silent waters of the sheltered cove. She is watching the movements of the contestants none the less and is all the better qualified, perhaps, to weigh and judge and advise because not herself in the excitement of the race. Her voice, too, has always been heard in clear, unfaltering tones, ringing the changes on those deeper interests which make for permanent good. She is always sound and orthodox on questions affecting the well-being of her race. You do not find the colored woman selling her birthright for a mess of pottage. Nay, even after reason has retired from the contest, she has been known to cling blindly with the instinct of a turtle dove to those principles and policies which to her mind promise hope and safety for children yet unborn. It is notorious that ignorant black women in the South have actually left their husbands' homes and repudiated their support for what was understood by the wife to be race disloyalty, or "voting away," as she expresses it, the privileges of herself and little ones.

It is largely our women in the South to-day who keep the black men solid in the Republican party. The latter as they increase in intelligence and power of discrimination would be more apt to divide on local issues at any rate. They begin to see that the Grand Old Party regards the Negro's cause as an outgrown issue, and on Southern soil at least finds a too intimate acquaintanceship with him a somewhat unsavory recommendation. Then, too, their political wits have been sharpened to appreciate the fact that it is good policy to cultivate one's neighbors and not depend too much on a distant friend to fight one's home battles. But the black woman can never forget—however lukewarm the party may to-day appear—that it was a Republican president who struck the manacles from her own wrists and gave the possibilities of manhood to her helpless little ones; and to her mind a Democratic Negro is a traitor and a time-server. Talk as much as you like of venality and manipulation in the South, there are not many men, I can tell you, who would dare face a wife quivering in every fiber with the consciousness that her husband is a coward who could be paid to desert her deepest and dearest interests.

3. Mary Church Terrell Speaks on the Role of Modern Woman

Mamie and I joined the City Federation [Charleston, S.C.] together. It was Mrs. Ida Green, wife of Reverend Nathaniel Green, Centenary's pastor, who organized the city. But it was Mrs. Mary Church Terrell who really brought the excitement to us. I'll never forget the night she spoke. It was at Mt. Zion A.M.E. Church. And it seemed like everybody in Charleston got there early, then packed into the pews so tight until you had to put even the smallest purse on the floor, between your toes. In a short time, you could hardly turn your head to see who was behind you. And, with all the people, it was hot. Although you had a pasteboard fan in the hymnal rack in front of you, the people sat so close that you could only work it back and forth in front of you—side to side, you were liable to elbow your neighbor. That's to show you how the city turned out to hear this fine educator from Washington, D.C. We sat in the heat, dresses clinging to us, ladies' hats almost touching, fans just a-going—*flickflick-flickflick.* All of Charleston was waiting to hear what Mrs. Terrell would say about the role of the Modern Woman. Oh, my, when I saw her walk onto that podium in her pink evening dress and long white gloves, with her beautifully done hair, she *was* that Modern Woman. And when her voice went out over that huge crowd—no microphones back then—the fans stopped flicking. No one wanted to miss a word.

We have our own lives to lead, she told us. We are daughters, sisters, mothers, and wives. We must care for ourselves and rear our families, like all women. But we have more to do than other women. Those of us fortunate enough to have education must share it with the less fortunate of our race. We must go into our communities and improve them; we must go out into the nation and change it. Above all, we must organize ourselves as Negro women and work together. She told the story about a letter that a Southern white man sent to England, insulting us all, which was the cause of starting the Federation. "Let us turn in our numbers to face that white man and call him *liar,*" she said, and she had a wonderfully resonant voice. Every word could be heard clearly from the very front pew downstairs to the very last one in the gallery. When she raised her voice to say "LIAR," you could almost feel it on your skin.

She walked back and forth across the podium. In fact, she didn't walk, she *strode.* Regal, intelligent, powerful, reaching out from time to time with that long glove, she looked and sounded like the Modern Woman that she talked about. "And who were the Negro women who knew how to carry their burden in the heat of the day?" she asked looking right at this one and then right at that one in the audience. Harriet Tubman knew. Harriet wore a bandanna on her head and boots on her feet, a pistol on her hip and a rifle in her hand. Mrs. Terrell talked until we could almost see Harriet Tubman rescuing slaves right there and then, in front of our eyes. And then, what about Sojourner Truth, not armed with a rifle or a pistol but with the truth spoken:

Ain't I a woman?

That man over there says, a woman needs to be helped into carriages and lifted over ditches, and to be given the best place everywhere. Nobody ever helped me into a carriage. I rode in one mule wagon and enjoyed it. I got out in the muddy places and jumped over. Ain't I a woman?*

She went on quoting and telling about the great women who'd done their work in the yesteryears. Well now, what about us, the women who were sitting in the Mt. Zion Church, the women coming after our great ancestresses? "WHO OF YOU KNOW HOW TO CARRY YOUR BURDEN IN THE HEAT OF THE DAY?" Mrs. Terrell demanded. And then she stopped talking altogether for a good little while, time enough for everybody there to ask herself, "Do I?" Then she told us a quiet "Good evening." The women hardly knew what to do when Mrs. Terrell got through speaking. We felt so stirred up, nobody wanted to wait till morning to pick up our burden again. Everywhere you might look, there was something to do.

4. Women Urge President Woodrow Wilson to Endorse Suffrage, 1914

THE PRESIDENT IS INTERVIEWED

Reprinted by permission from *The Dallas Morning News.*

5. Antisuffragists Raise the Race Issue

Men of the South: heed not the song of the suffrage siren! Seal your ears against her vocal wiles. For, no matter how sweetly she may proclaim the advantages of female franchise,—*Remember,* that *Woman Suffrage* means a reopening of the entire *Negro* Suffrage question; loss of State [*sic*] rights; and another period of reconstruction horrors, which will introduce a set of female carpetbaggers as bad as their male pro-totypes of the sixties. *Do Not Jeopardize* the present prosperity of your sovereign States, which was so dearly bought by the blood of your fathers and the tears of your mothers, by again raising an issue which has already been adjusted at so great a cost. Nothing can be gained by woman suffrage and much may be lost.

6. Annie Webb Blanton Runs for State Office, 1918

Concerning the Race for State Superintendent of Public Instruction

Why you SHOULD vote for Annie Webb Blanton for State Superintendent of Public Instruction.

1. She has actually taught in every grade of the public schools, rural and urban, and has first-hand practical knowledge of their needs.

2. For seventeen years she has been engaged in training teachers in the North Texas Normal College at Denton.

3. She is a graduate of the University of Texas, and has done graduate work in the University of Chicago.

4. She has the absolute confidence of the teachers of the State, as was evidenced when they elected her, by an overwhelming majority, president of the State Teachers Association, the only woman accorded that honor in the last 39 years.

5. She has wonderful natural endowment, is a born leader, a splendid public speaker, whom Mr. Doughty—her opponent—steadfastly, and perhaps intelligently, refuses to meet on the stump during this campaign, although she challenged him to do so.

6. She will remove the State Department of Education from connection with every form of machine politics, and put the great Public School system of Texas solidly in the "American" column. She has no hyphenated connections.

Why you SHOULD NOT vote for W. F. Doughty for State Superintendent of Public Instruction.

1. He was on the "Red" list of the breweries—that is, O. K.'d by them, which secret alliance was disclosed on pages 1547–1559, record of the Sulphur Springs brewery case.

2. The breweries were allied with the German-American Alliance, whose declared purpose was to control the public schools and Universities in the interest of German *kultur.*

This document can be found in the Romulus A. Nunn Papers, North Carolina Division of Archives and History, Raleigh, North Carolina.

This document can be found in the Annie Webb Blanton Vertical File, Center for American History, University of Texas at Austin.

3. If he was acceptable to the breweries, was he not acceptable to the German-American Alliance? (See U. S. Senate Subcommittee report, Sixty-fifth Congress, page 647).

4. He appeared on the platform with James E. Ferguson when Ferguson called the University of Texas professors a lot of "two-bit" thieves, endorsing by his silence this statement, which he knew to be slanderous, for he is himself a graduate of the University and had for years been befriended, helped, and taught by these same men, whom he suffered to be called "two-bit thieves," when he knew them to be honest and upright. The head of the educational interests of Texas should be a person with enough nerve to defend its educational institutions from slander.

5. Declaring that he has had the "privilege" of serving with the "honorable" James E. Ferguson, he refuses to make a public statement of his position on the Ferguson issue, in spite of the impeachment and conviction of the former governor [Ferguson].

✢ E S S A Y S

When Frances Willard, president of the WCTU, made her organizing tour of the South in the 1880s, she opened for many black and white middle-class women unprecedented opportunities for leadership, civic activism, and interracial cooperation. In the first essay, Glenda Gilmore explains the vital importance of institutions of higher education for women of both races and the reasons why after 1881 such women were encouraged to cooperate as social and political activists through the WCTU. Gilmore argues that interracial cooperation, tenuous at best, failed in the 1890s with the advent of black disfranchisement. Jacqueline Anne Rouse, in the second essay, provides a history of Atlanta's Neighborhood Union, founded by Lugenia Burns Hope, community activist and wife of Morehouse College president John Hope. When segregation came to Atlanta, African American women received little help from city government for school or community betterment. Instead, Hope and others employed their own creative resources to achieve neighborhood improvements. The third essay, by Marjorie Spruill Wheeler, explains the rise of a woman's political movement—woman suffrage—in the nation's most conservative region. When she refers to the "inhospitable South," she alludes to the difficulties associated with women's struggle for the right to vote in a region where antisuffragists flourished and where voting rights for African Americans had been severely limited by white supremacists.

Womanhood, Race, and the WCTU, 1881–1898

GLENDA ELIZABETH GILMORE

The Woman's Christian Temperance Union [WCTU] joined women of both races who sought to impose new values on southern life. . . .

. . . [T]he monumental statewide prohibition referendum of 1881 set the stage for the WCTU's entry into the state. In the midst of the 1881 prohibition campaign,

From *Gender and Jim Crow: Women and the Politics of White Supremacy in North Carolina. 1896–1920* by Glenda Elizabeth Gilmore. Copyright © 1996 by the University of North Carolina Press. Used by permission of the publisher.

Frances Willard visited Wilmington to mobilize women and encourage them to join the WCTU. Willard worried about how southern white women would receive a northern woman, but her nervousness did not prevent her from advocating temperance work among African Americans. To Willard's surprise, southern white women embraced her suggestion with enthusiasm. She observed: "Everywhere the Southern white people desired me to speak to the colored." Willard was not the only white woman reaching out to black women; for example, when a "ladies' prohibition club" met at the Methodist church in Concord, the white women reported that "the galleries of the church were set apart for our colored friends." Black men's votes and black women's political influence mattered in the temperance election.

Statewide prohibition failed in North Carolina in 1881, and many whites blamed blacks, despite the nearly unanimous endorsement of prohibition by the black press. Reports from across the state declared that African Americans had voted overwhelmingly in favor of whiskey, probably because many blacks kept small shops in which liquor sold briskly. White prohibitionists, mostly Democrats, charged that liquor interests bought black votes to tip the election. After 1881, temperance strategy centered on local-option elections, and the WCTU attempted to win prohibition town by town, county by county. To that end, the white women began to organize and support black WCTU chapters throughout the state that reported to the white statewide officers.

The Woman's Christian Temperance Union mattered so much to southern black women reformers of the late nineteenth century because it promoted a working model of finer womanhood that meshed with their own ideals. The union joined black women's religious and class values to their activism, even as it provided a safe forum for agitation. Black women welcomed its legitimation of a public role for women, a role they knew would be necessary for racial uplift. Through the telescope of the WCTU, southern African Americans could gaze upward past vacuous white southern belles to solid white women such as Frances Willard, WCTU national president. . . .

For black women and a growing number of educated white women from poor families, class identity was a lesson to be learned and one they bore a responsibility to teach, and the WCTU facilitated that task. Black women reformers tried to impose upon uneducated women and men sobriety, thrift, purity, and a love for learning; if a woman embraced those values, they embraced her, regardless of the trappings of her life or her origins. Abna Aggrey Lancaster, whose mother and father taught at Livingstone College, recalled that it was not money that made a difference between people—"we were all poor"—but "training." Mary Lynch, who trained Lancaster in temperance, herself learned and taught class standing. Born just after Reconstruction to poor parents, Lynch attended Scotia Seminary and began teaching at Livingstone in 1891. One hundred years later, a male Livingstone student recalled her from the 1920s as the professor of "finer womanhood." Teaching and learning "finer womanhood" became a strategy black women deployed to counter white supremacy.

On the other hand, many southern white women initially found the WCTU's public duties a challenge to their sense of propriety. The WCTU asked its members to step beyond the pale of southern white ladyhood. It encouraged them not only to visit jails but to break bread with the prisoners, black and white; to spend

Thanksgiving at the county poor farm with its biracial conglomeration of demented alcoholics, lice-ridden wayward girls, and toothless, tobacco-spitting old women; to throw up a beribboned gauntlet at that most raucous of masculine preserves, the polling place, buttonhole voters who tried to elbow past, and glare at them while they voted. Once white women overcame their fears, WCTU work probably changed their lives a great deal more than they changed the lives of the recipients of their beneficence. One reflected on her lunch with two white and six black men in the Winston-Salem jail: "The power of the Holy Spirit rested upon all. . . . It was a melting time."

In the 1880s and 1890s, the North Carolina WCTU undertook a novel experiment in interracial contact. Black women hoped to find common ground with white women in the WCTU to construct a cooperative venture joined by class and gender ties, one capable of withstanding the winds of white supremacist rhetoric. For several years in the 1880s, women worked as members of separate black and white chapters within a single statewide structure, the first postbellum statewide biracial voluntary organization in North Carolina. Under the heat of temperance fever, racial boundaries softened ever so slightly.

Historians have argued that the WCTU's chief attraction for women was its critique of the drunken father and husband and that its activism sprang from belief in "feminine moral superiority." White female temperance activists linked drinking with male profligacy, domestic physical abuse, and women's economic dependence. They drew on the doctrine of separate spheres to confer on women moral authority in family matters, even if the exercise of that power necessitated a temporary foray into the public sphere. Thus, among whites, temperance became increasingly a woman's issue, an expression of "female consciousness." Black women's participation in the WCTU, however, meant something more than "home protection." Although domestic issues certainly mattered to southern African American women, participation in the WCTU also folded into the cause of racial uplift.

To counteract whites' blindness to the realities of middle-class black life, African American women used the WCTU to point up black dignity, industriousness, and good citizenship. Since many whites predicted that the absence of the "civilizing" influence of slavery would result in the extinction of African Americans, occasions of black drunkenness generated self-satisfied notice among whites. When white southern tobacco farmers came to town to tie one on, no one suggested that their drinking sprees foretold the racial degeneracy of the Anglo-Saxon "race." But a drunken black man staggering home from a saloon might inspire an "I-told-you-so" editorial in the local white newspaper replete with Darwinistic predictions of the extinction of the black race in a single generation. Thus, black women temperance activists worried not just about the pernicious effects of alcohol on the family but also about the progress of the entire race, and temperance activities bolstered African Americans' contested claims to full membership in the polity.

Moreover, black women saw in the WCTU a chance to build a Christian community that could serve as a model of interracial cooperation on other fronts. If, through white women's recognition of common womanhood and shared class goals, black women could forge a structure that encouraged racial interaction, they might later build on that structure. The WCTU represented a place where women might see past skin color to recognize each other's humanity. One source of black women's optimism sprang from Frances Willard's family background. As a child, her abolitionist parents opened their home as a stop on the Underground Railway, and her father was a Free-Soiler. Willard had the confidence of Frederick Douglass and William Lloyd Garrison, both members of an older generation of abolitionists.

White women, however, envisioned interracial cooperation as a partnership in which the women they referred to as "our sisters in black" were junior partners, participating in a segregated structure that reported to white women. They believed the power relations of a biracial WCTU should mirror the racial hierarchy of society at large. Nonetheless, founding a biracial organization, even one separated internally, required courage and a vision of the future that differed from the white male perspective. By organizing black WCTU chapters, white women recognized gender and class as binding forces that mitigated racial differences.

In the late nineteenth century, African Americans and whites used the term "interracial cooperation" to signify working across racial lines to solve common problems: Black women undertook interracial cooperation without illusions of sisterhood because they believed racial progress depended on it as long as whites controlled southern institutions. Nothing about the term implied a common commitment to civil rights, to racial equality, to working together cheerfully, or even to working together with civility. There was never a point in the two decades of inter-racial cooperation within the WCTU when white women could not be characterized according to today's standards as "racist." Yet such a characterization reveals little about actual practice and obscures a more important truth: racism is never a static phenomenon. . . .

It was black political power that convinced white women to work with African American women, whose support they needed in local-option campaigns. In 1883, Frances Willard returned to North Carolina, where she spoke again to black audiences, including one at Livingstone College, and brought the existing WCTU chapters into a statewide organization. Within the state structure, "Work amongst the Colored People" became one of six departments, and all black chapters were subordinated to the white female department head. Despite the separate chapters and the reporting structure, the biracial WCTU was a dramatic departure from the past. For a brief period, black and white women in the WCTU circumvented the racial conventions of their time.

Most of the white women who volunteered to organize black WCTU chapters were already involved in interracial educational or religious work. Rosa Steele, the wife of Wilbur Steele, the white president of Bennett College, an institution for African Americans, headed the statewide "Work amongst the Colored People" department. Steele bridged two worlds, and she had already earned a reputation among blacks as a "zealous" woman. A Methodist and native New Englander, Rosa Steele lived in the college community surrounding Bennett. The Steeles regularly dined with African American friends, causing the white press to dub Wilbur "Social Equality Steele." . . .

White women like Steele saw temperance work among African Americans as missionary labor, uplifting for the white women as well as the black women. Clearly Steele used the WCTU to promote her own agenda: "uplifting" the black race under white direction. The fact that black women continued to work for temperance without the supervision of white women worried her. "They have many workers of their own and many teachers doing this temperance work among them," Steele noted, but she added that white women must take the lead by supervising chapters. She advised white women to attend "each meeting to keep the organization on its proper line of work." Although her belief in the superiority of white leadership indicated the distance she perceived between herself and blacks, Steele's racial attitudes represented those of the most liberal white women in the South. Southern white communities generally ostracized white women who promoted black education, but the WCTU accepted and used their talents in order to achieve its goals.

African American women drew upon their long experience in temperance, and they chafed at the patronizing missionary approach of whites. Steele's exhortations inspired white women who had never attempted interracial work to try to organize black WCTU chapters in their hometowns. They often complained that when they approached African American women, "they were looked upon suspiciously by those whom they desired to help." The racial dynamics baffled white women, who could not fathom black women's reactions. The white women who wanted to bring African Americans to the temperance cause were not able to recognize black women's capabilities. The black women were understandably resentful, and the gap between them loomed large. To make matters worse, most white women approached black women only during local-option elections, neglecting the work the rest of the time. Steele admonished white women not to view African Americans opportunistically or to cultivate them just for political purposes. Temperance would succeed only if whites showed a "real live interest in the colored man, not born of a disire [*sic*] to win his vote at election time," she argued.

In many cities and towns, however, no white women came forward to head the "Work amongst the Colored People," and black women organized their own WCTU chapters. The experience of Mary Lynch and the Charlotte chapter illustrates how African American women came to the temperance cause and built their own statewide organization. A student at Scotia Seminary in Concord during the prohibition campaign of 1881, Lynch was caught up in the fever of the biracial ladies' temperance meetings and influenced by her teachers' participation in the WCTU. Upon graduation, she moved to Charlotte to teach in the graded school, where she joined a sixty-member black WCTU chapter that formed in 1886. That year, the Charlotte chapter sent delegates to the state convention who addressed the assembled white women. . . .

In 1888, after five years of appealing to white women to organize black temperance chapters, Rosa Steele tried a new tactic that produced extraordinary results: she invited Sarah Jane Woodson Early, the African American superintendent of "Colored Work for the South" for the national WCTU, to North Carolina. Early spent five weeks in the state. She entered the local prohibition battles raging in Raleigh and Concord and encouraged African American women to join the campaign. One African American woman from Concord wrote that she had lobbied hard for black male votes and felt sure that "Christians will vote as they pray." Early's African American audiences financed her trip, and by the time she left the state, fourteen black WCTU chapters stood on solid ground.

The next year, building on Early's organizing campaign, African American WCTU leaders seceded from the state organization. Ultimately, black women found the racial hierarchy embedded in the WCTU structure contradictory on its face. If all WCTU members were temperance women, they must be equally worthy, sisters in the family of God. Because their temperance work involved multiple goals, African American women refused to trade equality for interaction. With secession, they rejected their status as a subordinate department under white direction. The black women made this clear when they named their organization the WCTU No. 2 and announced, "We cautiously avoided using the word colored . . . for we believe all men equal." The white "Colored Work" committeewomen reported to their organization that the African Americans "desire to attain their full development and think this can best be done in an independent organization . . . with the department work under their own control." The new African American WCTU reported directly to the national WCTU and achieved organizational status equal to the white group, holding separate statewide conventions in 1890 and 1891.

As North Carolina's black women organized the WCTU No. 2, black women across the South replicated their experience. Prior to the organization of the National Association of Colored Women's Clubs in 1896, the WCTU represented the principal interdenominational voluntary association among black women. Black WCTU organizations flourished in the North and the West, and black women in five southern states managed statewide unions. Southern African American women traveled to national and international temperance conferences, published newspapers, and learned skills of self-presentation that they took back to their churches and women's clubs.

Throughout the 1890s in North Carolina, the WCTU No. 2 continued under the direction of African American women. In 1891, when Mary Lynch became a professor at Livingstone College, she found the campus branch of the Young Woman's Christian Temperance Union (YWCTU) languishing. Lynch immediately revitalized it and invited Anna Julia Haywood Cooper to speak to the group. From her post at Livingstone, Lynch threw herself into temperance work; within five years, she formed connections with the nation's leading African American women and became president of the WCTU No. 2. Meanwhile, the group that Lynch oversaw at Livingstone flourished. One of Lynch's protégées was Annie Kimball, a student in the classical department. Kimball led the union in early-morning Sunday prayer meetings. Peer pressure to join must have been strong, for an observer reported, "Every girl, without an exception, [who was a] boarder in the school . . . has signed the pledge and become a member." . . .

Kimball brought both racial and female consciousness to temperance work. She argued eloquently that where whites found black degeneracy, she found hope. The only trait becoming extinct among African Americans, she charged, was "the spirit of unmanly and unwomanly servility and fawning." Kimball exhorted her female classmates to lift "the banner of purity . . . around every home," and she predicted that the "dram-shop and all other places of ill-repute" would soon fall to "school houses, and churches of the living God." Then, she predicted, those whites who "maligned and slandered" blacks would be "utterly put down by a more enlightened and healthy public sentiment." On a May day in 1894, Annie Kimball graduated as salutatorian of her class, gave the commencement address in Latin, and, that afternoon, married an AME Zion minister, George Clinton. . . . The Clintons made their home in Charlotte, where she became state president of the YWCTU. . . .

When the WCTU No. 2 seceded, the white organization initially realized they should replace their outreach to African Americans with cooperation with the African American chapters. They appointed a committee to work with the black leaders, whom they called "genuine W.C.T.U. women." But after a year, the whites again formed a committee on "Colored Work" that haltingly described its mission as "continu[ing] to work to assist in completing the work of organizing" African Americans. . . .

. . . Black women must have resented white women who sought "co-operation" while assuming they knew best. The white women's efforts found some success among African American youth, in schools or prisons, all captive audiences, but only rarely did they form an organization of adult black women under white control after secession.

Why did white women continue to try to establish black chapters even as they acknowledged the autonomy of the WCTU No. 2? There are at least two reasons. Except for a few leaders like Rosa Steele, most white women knew very little about, and discounted the abilities of, educated black women. Hence, they presumed that a black union would do better work under white leadership. Most importantly, however, the white women wanted very much to control the politics of the black temperance workers. They were not altogether sure that African Americans, because of their political allegiance to the Republican Party, could be trusted to vote for prohibition. Moreover, they believed that blacks proved easy prey for corrupt politicians and sinister forces. For example, after the formation of the WCTU No. 2, a white temperance worker announced an imminent Catholic peril among African Americans. She reported that Catholics, the archnemeses of prohibitionists, had spread out "propagating Catholicism among the *blacks* of the *South*." She asked, "Is it to *save souls* this new movement is made to Catholicise the negroes, or is it that he has a *vote* and now, that he is free, can aid in extending papal dominion in the United States?" (emphasis in original). White women reasoned that, left on their own, black women might not serve as political allies in local prohibition elections. Indeed, a primary duty of the white superintendents after secession was to distribute white ribbons signifying prohibition support to black women when a local-option election seemed threatening. . . .

. . . [F]lawed but significant interracial contacts continued between black and white WCTU women in North Carolina. . . . North Carolina's white WCTU convention condemned lynching in 1896, a symbolic but nonetheless important gesture, particularly considering that more than twenty years would elapse before southern white women moved again in an organized way against lynching. Delegate exchanges continued between the black and white WCTUs as well. For example, when the black women met in statewide convention in Salisbury in 1896, white WCTU delegates attended a session. That year, black women renamed their union the Lucy Thurman WCTU, honoring the black national organizer, and elected Mary Lynch state president. In 1897, Lynch presided over thirteen unions, attending the white state convention, and spoke at the national meeting, following Anthony Comstock and Anna Shaw. The next year, she gave the opening prayer at the national WCTU convention marking the organization's twenty-fifth anniversary.

In 1896, a black-supported coalition of Republicans and Populists won control of state government, giving African Americans their greatest political voice since Reconstruction and reordering the politics of temperance work. That year, Belle

Kearney, a white Mississippian with North Carolina roots, delivered an address to the North Carolina white WCTU convention, the same one that condemned lynching, entitled, "Why the Wheels Are Clogged." Mary Lynch sat in the audience as a delegate from the Lucy Thurman WCTU and listened to Kearney tell the delegates that prohibition would never pass while 250,000 blacks voted in the South. Quickly white women's local temperance strategies shifted to complement the Democratic Party's white supremacist platform. WCTU women helped organize mock elections limited to whites to demonstrate that prohibition would pass if blacks could not vote in temperance elections. In 1898, the white WCTU ceased its work among African Americans forever, and delegate exchanges between the two WCTUs ended abruptly. For the next few years, temperance, which had once held such promise for interracial understanding, would serve white supremacy.

It was a force beyond the control of women—party politics—that obliterated interracial contact within North Carolina's WCTU. Temperance was above all a political issue, and the WCTU solicited prohibition votes. As Democrats began to seek to exclude African Americans from the electoral process, white women were no longer concerned with black temperance and readily recast their former allies as part of the "Negro problem." Although the experience of the WCTU points up the difficulty of transcending difference, it also shows that as long as African Americans had political rights, women's interaction continued because black votes mattered. Electoral politics, then, had a powerful impact upon the lives of those normally cast as the group with the least direct involvement in the process— women. By the end of the decade, the political winds gathered strength until they swept through every corner of black women's lives, leaving few spaces untouched.

The Atlanta Neighborhood Union, 1908–1924

JACQUELINE ANNE ROUSE

By the turn of the century Atlanta was the most segregated city in Georgia. As early as 1890 Atlanta had instituted Jim Crow laws that separated the city into distinctive Black and white areas. . . .

Atlanta's Black community numbered sixty-three thousand by 1900. Most lived in varied pockets throughout the city. The Fourth Ward and Auburn Avenue had for some time housed the older Black Atlantans who composed the city's Black aristocracy. Mainly of mulatto ancestry, this upper class consisted of entrepreneurs and businesspeople whose clientele was predominantly white. By 1900 a new group of Blacks, mostly in-migrants to Atlanta, made up this professional and business group. This new group of professionals never accounted for more than 4 percent of the population, however, for the majority of Black Atlantans were poor residents who lived in slum areas with dilapidated houses and schools and who were mainly unskilled or semiskilled laborers. The women worked in domestic and personal services. Urban employers usually hired Black men only for the duration

Essay, "The Atlanta Neighborhood Union," by Jacqueline Anne Rouse, from *Lugenia Burns Hope: Black Southern Reformer.* Athens: University of Georgia Press. Copyright © 1989. Reprinted by permission of Georgia Press and the author.

of a particular construction project or contract. As Jacqueline Jones has noted, "These sporadic wage-earning opportunities guaranteed . . . low wages and long periods of enforced idleness." So Black women became the breadwinners of their families, working in white households, as laundresses and washerwomen, and as sellers of vegetables, fruits, and flowers. Women of the upper and middle classes were generally seamstresses and schoolteachers. (The latter became the promoters of racial consciousness and the organizers of women's clubs.)

Black Atlanta also had a notable artisan class that dominated brickmasonry, carpentry, and barbering, yet by 1900 these skilled laborers had lost their positions and patronage to white laborers. Throughout the South, management used Blacks as strikebreakers to destroy the union movement. . . .

Though deplorable living conditions for Blacks in Atlanta were stimulus enough to unite neighborhoods and to spark them into action, the specific incident that led to the Neighborhood Union's development was the death of a young woman in the community immediately surrounding the college campuses on the West Side. . . .

Lugenia [Burns Hope], who learned about the tragedy soon afterward, saw the opportunity to organize the community. The incident had occurred, she believed, because of the absence of neighborly feelings. The result was a meeting of the neighbors and the development of an organization.

On Thursday evening, July 8, 1908, Lugenia called a meeting of her neighbors to discuss "whether those assembled thought it needful to have settlement work in the community, and to solicit their cooperation." The idea was accepted; those in attendance believed that such work would benefit the neighborhood. The women decided to develop an organization whose objective would be the "moral, social, intellectual, and religious uplift of the community and the neighborhood in which the organization or its branches may be established." They elected Lugenia president, Hattie Watson secretary, and Dora Whitaker treasurer. Their target area, they decided, would be the immediate community, bounded by the streets Ashby, Walnut, Green's Ferry, and Beckwith. This section was designated a district and divided into subsections. . . .

Reports returned to the union at its second meeting showed that there were major needs in the area that no one, including the city, was working to alleviate. Attendance at this second meeting was double that at the first. The women voted to name their group the Neighborhood Union, to adopt "Thy Neighbor as Thyself" for their motto, and to raise "the standard of living in the community and to make the West Side of Atlanta a better place to rear our children."

Aided by students of Morehouse, the union conducted house-to-house surveys in order to introduce the organization to the community. Union members canvassed one hundred families around the college, informing the residents that their purpose was to organize and to provide for the children of the area. The union stressed the welfare of children over that of adults: the children were viewed as future citizens, and measures taken on their behalf were to be preventive rather than remedial. The union intended to provide services needed by the community until a permanent agency—whether city, state, or federal—was developed to take over the work.

The survey disclosed that streets were in need of improvement, that lighting was insufficient, that there were few if any sewage facilities, that the water supply was mainly from surface wells (which were uncovered and thus hazardous to children), that juvenile delinquency and houses of ill repute were present, that school buildings were dilapidated and inadequate, that garbage was seldom collected and never covered, that unscreened surface toilets were common, that housing (even that under construction) was poor, that there were no recreational areas, and that families experienced a great deal of disorganization. These results were reported to the union members at the July 23 meeting. In order to attack the evils of the community "to which the boys and girls were exposed," the members defined for themselves a number of lofty aims: to provide playgrounds, clubs, and neighborhood centers for physical, moral, and intellectual development; to develop a spirit of helpfulness among neighbors; to establish lecture courses for the purpose of encouraging habits of cleanliness; to promote child welfare; to impart a sense of cultural heritage; to abolish slums and houses of immorality; to improve the sanitation of homes and streets; to bring about efficiency in general homemaking; to cooperate with the Associated Charities and the Juvenile Court; and to cooperate with city officials in suppressing vice and crime. The ultimate goal of the union was to organize neighborhoods in each section of the city and establish settlement houses in each neighborhood, where the "people could gather for their meetings, clubs and classes and feel that they were their very own."

To implement these goals, the union divided the city into zones; with each zone under a chairperson elected by the neighborhood. The zones were further divided into neighborhoods and the neighborhoods into districts. Each district was supervised by a neighborhood president whose duty it was to organize the neighborhood and to preserve records for the union, and by a director chosen from among the key women who had aided the union during its initial survey. Directors were required to conduct house-to-house surveys and visits to acquaint their districts with the plan for neighborhood improvement, relief, and solidarity. Familiarity with the economic and social status of her district's residents was of course essential for each director. The findings of the neighborhood president and the director were reported back to the union.

The directors of the districts were organized into a Board of Directors, of which the president of the Neighborhood Union was chairperson. The work of the city as a whole was to be supervised by the Board of Managers, consisting of zone chairpersons, department heads, and presidents of the various neighborhood branches. This board was the governing force, with the power to appoint committees that conducted other aspects of the union's work and to set up additional branches in other localities. This board was also required to make annual reports to the members of the union. By 1911, the year of the union's incorporation, it had expanded beyond the West Side into four additional communities: Pittsburg, Summerhill, the Fourth Ward, and South Atlanta. By 1914 branches were established throughout the city.

Membership was open to all members of "worthy" families within a given branch's boundaries who would organize under its direction. The membership fee was set at ten cents per month per family, but moneys for the work of the union came mainly from donations and fund-raisers like carnivals, apron sales, bake sales, baseball games, track meets, and bridge tournaments. When the union became a member of the Community Chest in 1924, its annual budget of five thousand dollars gained a monthly subsidy of twenty-five dollars; a year later, however, the union was dropped from the larger organization in an economy move.

Under Lugenia's leadership, the union was divided into four departments. The Moral and Educational Department sponsored lectures, special meetings, and a large number of projects; the Literary Department secured good books; the Musical Department cultivated a love for good music, particularly Black music; and the Arts Department secured teachers and materials for classes, made out schedules, and arranged the work.

The Arts Department recruited teachers from Morehouse, Spelman, Atlanta University, and Tuskegee Institute (and student teachers from Morehouse) to offer classes in sewing, cooking, basketry, embroidery, woodworking, millinery (taught by Lugenia), textiles, food preparation, gardening and yard beautification, folk dancing, housecleaning, storytelling and song, dressmaking, pattern drafting, and fitting. At the time the union was founded the city's public schools offered no vocational classes for Black boys and girls. These classes offered by the union were therefore vigorously promoted until the schools added vocational classes to their curricula.

Clubs, including reading and painting circles, were established through the relevant departments for boys and girls between the ages of eight and twenty-two. Union members believed that "wholesome recreation and cultural education" were essential "for the people of the community," and parents were taught to "entertain their children in order to keep them off the streets." Specific entertainments and activities were planned for older girls. Young male teachers instructed the neighborhood boys in manual training, military tactics, and athletics. Student dues of ten cents a month were instituted to cover the costs of these programs.

Much of the work of the union fell under the auspices of the Moral and Education Department. One of its functions was to sponsor public gatherings to "arouse group mindedness and to secure cooperation through lectures and mass meetings." Lectures by people of national reputation, like Margaret Murray Washington and Mary McLeod Bethune, covered topics in health, morals, education, citizenship, child welfare, and general culture. . . .

As early as the 1908 surveys, the union began confronting the city of Atlanta with the urgent needs it was uncovering. Union members petitioned the mayor, the City Council, and the Sanitation and Health departments to improve facilities. They went to court to ask for better health and housing programs, better streets, and more streetlights to prevent crime. They approached individual councilmen, trying to win their goodwill. As a result, the city welfare worker, Phillip Weltner, invited a committee from the union to meet with City Hall to discuss common problems. He then asked the committee to coordinate the union's settlement work with the city's. Later the city turned over to the union all of the settlement work for Blacks in Atlanta.

Providing recreational centers and a health care program were among other important early efforts of the union. As noted, the first playground for the city's Black children was donated by Atlanta Baptist College. Later Spelman donated a plot for supervised play. These lots soon filled, and the union members began to use vacant lots as supervised play areas.

The union offered classes in nursing, home hygiene, bathing the sick, prenatal care, and infant care. Instructions were disseminated on the identification and treatment of hookworm, typhoid, pellagra, and tuberculosis. The first clinics set up were for adults, but as the adults became more responsible for their health needs the union's attention turned increasingly to the children. Monthly mothers' meetings taught facts about tuberculosis and their children's need for medical care. A group of lectures on teeth and their care led to the establishment of an ongoing dental clinic for the children. Infant and preschool children's clinics were set up as well. At the Anti-Tuberculosis Clinic, patients were referred to specific physicians. Volunteer nurses and doctors visited homes, clubs, and churches. The union's report for July 1910 stated that over 135 such visits had been made, and "the 'follow up' work of this clinic will show that 99% of those patients have followed the instructions given them at the Neighborhood Union Clinic this month."

During the year in which the union was receiving funding from the Community Chest the union mounted a successful fund-raising campaign for its health program. . . .

The first union health clinic location was a house at the corner of West Fair and Mildred Streets, purchased from a friend of one of the members on October 14, 1908. Funds raised from bake sales and donations were used to make a partial payment. Soon this property was sold and plans were made to acquire a permanent structure. The union then bought property on Lee Street, later selling it for $1,500. In June 1914 the union purchased the property at 41 Leonard Street from Spelman and opened a center. The Woman's American Baptist Home Mission Society appropriated a monthly salary for a matron, and the union hired Carrie Bell Cole from New York. In its first year the center served over four hundred patients. The center operated successfully at this location until 1926, when the Leonard Street property was sold to the Leonard Street Orphanage and the union purchased a lot on West Fair Street.

In 1926, under the supervision of Ludie Andrews, a registered nurse and the Neighborhood Union's president, the union opened its new Health Center at 706 West Fair Street. The opening was a grand event: Margaret Murray Washington dedicated the building and poet Georgia Douglass Johnson delivered the main address. The union operated at this location until 1934, when the federal government offered to purchase the lot to build federal housing for Blacks. The government offered $5,370 for the property and guaranteed to build a center for the union in the housing project. The union's rental fee was approximately 4 percent of the cost of the property. Repairs and security—a hired watchman—for the new center were to be provided by the government. The Executive Committee of the union agreed to sell the property in order to aid governmental efforts at slum clearance. Following necessary expenditures, the balance was deposited in the Citizen's Trust Company, the local Black-owned bank, and the new center was opened.

At the dedication of University Homes, Harold L. Ickes, secretary of the interior, praised the residents' thorough organization and their "systematic work towards the improvement of the housing conditions over a long period of years." The union's secretary recorded this as a historic acknowledgment of the union, which was the one organization in the West Fair area that had worked for

> twenty-five years to improve living conditions among blacks, taking its fight to city council, to churches, and finally to the real estate agents, themselves, through a survey of their property. Hence, the Neighborhood Union is due the credit . . . for the choosing of the Federal Government of the Beaver Slide Slum District for its first national housing project.

From its inception, members of the Neighborhood Union had agreed that an essential goal of the organization would be the welfare of the children of the area. Programs designed to provide services and facilities for the children were begun at once. Yet paramount for the members was the quality of education these children were receiving in the Black public schools of Atlanta. In 1913 the union began an investigation of the city's Black schools. The Women's Civic and Social Improvement Committee, chaired by Lugenia, was organized "to investigate conditions with a view of remedying the evils." To substantiate the handicaps that resulted from operating the schools in double sessions, the committee received from each school principal the names and addresses of absentees from their schools during a particular month. Members secured a list of responsible parents, who testified that their children's health was impaired by crowded conditions in the public schools. Physicians gave an estimate of the extent of ill health among teachers owing to overwork and poor conditions in the schools. Churches gave estimates of the number of children who could not enter school because of the limited seating capacity.

For six months this committee of "one hundred leading women of Atlanta" investigated and inspected the twelve Black schools in the city. Overall conditions were found deplorable: sanitary conditions were unhealthy; lighting and ventilation were unusually poor, with many children consequently suffering eyestrain and sickness; classrooms were crowded; and there were double sessions with the same teacher for both sessions. For the year 1913–14, there was a seating capacity in the Black schools of 4,102 but an enrollment of 6,163, so that the number of pupils served by each double session was around 3,081.

The committee contacted every influential white woman in the city, including members of the Board of Lady Visitors of the Board of Education, soliciting their support. Some of these white women visited the schools and saw at first hand the actual conditions. The committee also interviewed each member of the City Council, the mayor, the members of the Board of Education, Black ministers, members of Black women's clubs, and members of other Black organizations. They solicited help from influential Black men (including their husbands). Committee members spoke before Black congregations, explaining the nature of their project and urging parents to pay their personal taxes and to have their children vaccinated. The committee reached other members of the community by persuading insurance agents to inform their clients of the committee's work as they made their collections. Using newspapers and mass meetings, the committee publicized the deplorable conditions it had discovered by its surveys. Pictures of these conditions were published in local newspapers.

The women were given permission by the Board of Education to have a committee of six at each school on the first day of the term to collect the names and addresses of those children who had not been vaccinated. The members then visited the children's parents and saw to it that the children were vaccinated and returned to school the following school day. The women kept up a running campaign for better conditions, posting placards and giving illustrated lectures to show the problems. They drew up a petition to attack the inadequacies of the schools and forwarded it to the Board of Education. . . .

The board discussed possible remedies to the reported conditions: bonds, a special tax, new allocations from existing city funds. All met with varying degrees of disapproval. Board member James L. Key reacted by stating that he believed the conditions had been exaggerated and that "this agitation is going to do the schools more harm than good." He had formerly made it known to the committee members that teachers—"the girls"—were not compelled to teach double sessions but wanted to, and he thought "it better to have poor schools than have the children out of school." . . .

Though the women's committee did not solve the complex problems of inadequate school facilities for Black children in Atlanta, this was the first organized effort to investigate and confront the blatant racism of the City Council and the Board of Education. The union kept up its challenge of segregation in the public school system in Atlanta, and these efforts eventually contributed to the opening of Atlanta's first Black high school, Booker T. Washington, in 1924.

The Woman Suffrage Movement in the Inhospitable South

MARJORIE SPRUILL WHEELER

In 1892, Laura Clay of Kentucky sent a warning to the leaders of the National American Woman Suffrage Association in a letter to *The Woman's Journal:* "Since we claim to be national let us never forget that the South cannot be left out of our calculations. You have worked for forty years and you will work for forty years more and do nothing unless you bring in the South." Clay's letter was both insightful and prophetic. The woman suffrage movement, she realized, had begun in the Northeast in 1848 and had spread to a certain extent to other sections of the nation, but its leaders had made little effort to organize in the South. Yet the NAWSA, which hoped to enfranchise women throughout the United States, would have to "bring in" supporters in all regions if it wanted to achieve a "national" victory. After all, a federal suffrage amendment would have to be approved by three-fourths of the states; the suffragists would need some southern states in order for the amendment to be ratified. When victory finally came in 1920, it was won with the support of four southern states that broke ranks with the otherwise "Solid South" and ratified the Nineteenth Amendment: Kentucky, Texas, Arkansas, and the famous thirty-sixth state, Tennessee.

"Bringing in" the South, however, was a difficult task that was never fully accomplished. In the 1890s, under Clay's leadership and with strong support from the NAWSA, a small but determined group of elite white women became suffragists and sought enfranchisement, primarily through the new state constitutions of that era. Between 1909 and 1916, a much larger contingent of southern suffragists sought the vote through amendments to their state constitutions. When these efforts failed, most but not all southern suffragists joined national leaders in supporting the federal amendment. Southern hostility to the suffrage movement frustrated southern suffragists in their efforts to become enfranchised through either state or federal

From *Votes for Women! The Woman Suffrage Movement in Tennessee, the South, and the Nation* edited by Marjorie Spruill Wheeler. Knoxville: University of Tennessee Press. Copyright © 1995 by The University of Tennessee Press.

action, however. Prior to the ratification of the Nineteenth Amendment in 1920, southern women gained full enfranchisement in *no* southern state and partial suffrage in only four. Southern politicians managed to block passage of the federal suffrage amendment in Congress for many years and, once it was submitted to the states, made a concerted effort to prevent ratification—despite the pleas of regional favorite son President Woodrow Wilson to support the amendment for the sake of the National Democratic Party. Of the ten states that failed to ratify, *nine* were south of the Mason-Dixon line. Several southern states passed "rejection resolutions" denouncing the federal amendment variously as "unwarranted," "unnecessary," "undemocratic," and "dangerous." Indeed, the South is notorious in the history of the woman suffrage movement as the region that afforded the movement the greatest resistance and the least success.

. . . This overview of the woman suffrage movement in the South examines the obstacles to the movement, its development despite these obstacles, and the profound impact of the race and states' rights issues. The primary focus is upon the ideas and actions of the movement's most prominent leaders and the strategies they devised in order to cope with the "peculiar institutions" of their region.

The fierce opposition of most white southerners to the woman suffrage movement resulted from several interrelated cultural, political, and economic factors. The southern suffrage movement took place in a period, from 1890 to 1920, in which white southerners were passionately devoted to the preservation of a distinct and, they believed, superior "Southern Civilization." As one leading minister put it, they were eager that the "victory over Southern arms" not be followed by "a victory over Southern opinions." A key element of this Southern Civilization they wished to preserve was a dualistic conception of the natures and responsibilities of the sexes that precluded the participation of women in politics and cast "The Southern Lady" in the role of guardian and symbol of southern virtue. Charged with transmitting southern culture to future generations, as well as inspiring current statesmen to serve as their noble defenders, southern womanhood had a vital role to play in preserving the values of "the Lost Cause." A leading "Lost Cause" minister, Albert Bledsoe, urged southern women to shun the fruit offered by the women's rights movement and take as their "mission," not to "imitate a Washington, or a Lee, or a Jackson," but to "rear, and train, and educate, and mould the future Washingtons, and Lees, and Jacksons of the South, to protect and preserve the sacred rights of woman as well as of man." That representatives of the burgeoning industries of the New South, particularly the textile industry, wished southern women to confine their beneficent influence to the home rather than vote for child labor legislation and other encumbrances was an additional and potent obstacle to the success of woman suffrage in the South.

In the eyes of white southerners, the cornerstone of this Southern Civilization was white supremacy, and their determination to restore white supremacy in politics—and then defend the state sovereignty thought necessary to preserve it—also presented a tremendous obstacle to the southern suffrage movement. In the late nineteenth and early twentieth centuries, white southerners were generally contemptuous of the women's rights movement as yet another unfortunate product of an inferior northern culture that they were trying to resist, as an offshoot of abolitionism led by northern women with the same "naive" and dangerous belief in equality that had characterized the abolitionists. Southern suffragists were scolded for playing into the hands of social "levelers" who had no understanding of the crucial social distinctions of gender and race that accounted for the superiority of Southern Civilization; moreover, suffragists were accused of unwittingly complicating the South's efforts to restore and protect white supremacy. The suffragists, charged the "antis," failed to recognize that the proposed federal woman suffrage amendment was nothing more than a "reaffirmation of the Fifteenth Amendment" and that its ratification by the South would signal acceptance of black suffrage and concede the right of the federal government to determine suffrage qualifications in the states. . . .

The southern women who were willing to embrace woman suffrage, indeed to become the leaders of such an unpopular cause, were formidable individuals. In their 1923 reflective, *Woman Suffrage and Politics,* Carrie Chapman Catt and Nettie Shuler observed, "No stronger characters did the long struggle produce than those great-souled southern suffragists. They had need to be great of soul." Catt and Shuler meant, of course, that advocacy of woman suffrage in such an inhospitable climate was character-building; but the leaders of the woman suffrage movement in the southern states had to have unusual self-confidence and determination in order to take up this cause in the first place.

Certainly it was no coincidence that most of the leaders of the southern suffrage movement were descended from the South's social and political elite. These included Laura Clay, the so-called "Susan B. Anthony of the South," the crucial intermediary between northern and southern suffragists; the Gordon sisters, Kate and Jean, of New Orleans, "silk-stockinged reformers" who were leaders of the states' rights suffragists; Nellie Nugent Somerville of Mississippi, the impressive leader of the suffragists in her state whose father was revered by white Mississippians for his role in restoring "home rule" in the state and ending Reconstruction; FFV Lila Meade Valentine of Richmond, leader of the Virginia suffragists; her close friend and associate, the famous novelist and descendent of Confederate heroes, Mary Johnston; Rebecca Latimer Felton of Georgia, whose husband served several terms in the state legislature and in the United States Congress; Madeline McDowell Breckinridge of Kentucky, granddaughter of Henry Clay and wife of Desha Breckinridge (who was the great-grandson of Thomas Jefferson's attorney-general, the son of a congressman, and the editor of the *Lexington Herald*); Pattie Ruffner Jacobs of Alabama, a star among the younger suffragists and wife of a wealthy Birmingham industrialist; and Tennessee's socialite suffragist Anne Dallas Dudley, to name a few. . . .

Indeed, the decisions of these suffrage leaders to take up this unpopular cause resulted from a combination of personal characteristics and experiences that made them receptive to feminism. The attitudes and example of family members were very important in shaping the views of these women. . . .

. . . Contacts with suffragists from the North, the West, from other countries, and with suffragists from other southern states were also crucial in the decisions of these women to become advocates of women's rights. And once recruited, they interested scores of other southern women in the cause. Like all reformers, southern suffragists came to feel themselves part of a supportive subculture and to judge themselves according to the precepts of that group rather than those of the larger society they were trying to reform.

Nevertheless, these white southern suffragists identified strongly with their region and shared many of the attitudes of the men of their race and class. Though they were quite clearly "New Women" who sought expanded rights and privileges for themselves and their gender, they took pride in their heritage as Southern Ladies, accepting the traditional duties if not the restrictions that role entailed. Their opponents called them "unconscious agents" of northern saboteurs, but they fully understood what they were doing and why. For the most part, they considered their movement to be supportive rather than destructive of Southern Civilization. Yet they were clearly weary of their indirect, supportive role in politics, which, they had concluded, not only denied their individuality but also had proven to be inadequate for the protection of their interests or that of their "constituency," the "unprivileged" of the South—particularly women and children.

Drawn from the region's social and political elite, the women who led the southern suffrage movement fully supported the 1890s campaign led by the men of their race and class to return government to the so-called "best people." They took it for granted that it was the duty of the "most qualified" to guide and protect the rest, but they believed themselves to be among the best qualified. Indeed, their goal in fighting for suffrage was to add maternalism to paternalism, to carry the traditional role of the Southern Lady into politics, to offer their services and unique feminine insights to the governing of their region. They sought, in fact, to restore and preserve elements they believed had once been integral in southern politics but were missing in the politics of the New South: morality, integrity, and the tradition of noblesse oblige.

Indeed, one important characteristic shared by all of these white southern suffrage leaders that inspired them to take up this unpopular cause and continue working for it despite so many defeats was their low opinion of the current management of the New South. All of the suffrage leaders had friends or relatives in public office. They believed, however, that southern politics since the Civil War had degenerated to the point that too few honest and intelligent men were willing to serve. . . .

Rebecca Latimer Felton's long struggle for Prohibition and against the convict lease system convinced her that women must be enfranchised; she was well aware of the "Liquor Interest's" eagerness to contain woman's influence. When criticized for meddling in politics, she insisted that men's failure to give "sober homes to women and children" made it necessary for women to become involved. . . .

Involvement in charitable work and reform societies led these women to a greater knowledge of social ills and a conviction that many of the social and economic problems that were formerly addressed by the private sector now required governmental attention. . . . [T]he suffragists believed that, in their eagerness to promote economic development, the leaders of the New South were willing to offer up the South's working class for northern exploitation. . . .

Their own indirect influence seemed negligible compared to that exercised by the brewers, the "cotton men," the railroad barons, and other industrialists. As they grew increasingly frustrated by legislative resistance to the reforms they supported, the suffragists grew increasingly cynical about the celebrated chivalry of southern men and denounced the southern woman's enforced reliance upon indirect influence as degrading as well as inefficient.

Many were converted to what Jean Gordon called "a belief in the potency of the ballot beyond that of 'woman's influence' " after the defeat of child labor legislation. Gordon recalled that the failure of a child labor bill heartily supported by New Orleans clubwomen—including the wives of many legislators—caused many of the women to question the efficacy of indirect influence. We learned, she said, "what we had suspected," that "the much-boasted influence of the wife over the husband in matters political was one of the many theories which melt before the sun of experience." . . .

Considering that indirect influence was still their only weapon with which to pry suffrage from a reluctant South, the suffragists tried to make their demand for power as unthreatening as possible. They *did* invoke "natural rights" arguments, insisting that, as Rebecca Latimer Felton put it, "I pay taxes and obey the laws, and I know the right belongs to me to assist in selecting those who rule over me." Somerville denied a statement by an editor who said that the suffragists' chief argument was that enfranchised womanhood would "bring about great reforms." "The orthodox suffragists," she wrote, "do not base their claims on any such argument. We stand upon the Declaration of Independence, 'governments derive their just powers from the consent of the governed.' Any argument based on results is merely incidental and not fundamental."

Yet, like suffragists all over the nation, they argued for equal partnership in governing with the men of their race and class by emphasizing the differences in the interests and responsibilities of the sexes—a nice and less challenging way of saying that the interests of women and children would never be adequately represented as long as women were relying upon men to protect them. . . .

. . . Most southern suffragists strenuously avoided association with the National Woman's Party, publicly denouncing their "unseemly," "fanatical," and "misguided" tactics including picketing the White House and burning Woodrow Wilson's speeches in Lafayette Square. Lila Meade Valentine begged the public not to "condemn the suffrage cause as a whole because of the folly of a handful of women" and urged Virginia suffragists to avoid all "spectacular tactics." . . .

White southern suffragists, who spoke eloquently of the inalienable right of women as citizens to self-government, nevertheless advocated or at least acquiesced in the restoration of white supremacy that took place contemporaneously with the southern woman suffrage movement. Rebecca Latimer Felton, an open racist, declared in a 1915 suffrage speech:

> Freedom belongs to the white woman as her inherent right. Whatever belongs to the freeman of these United States belongs to the white woman. Her Anglo-Saxon forefathers, fleeing from English tyranny won this country from savage tribes and again from English bayonets, by the expenditure of blood and treasure. Whatever was won by these noble men of the Revolution was inherited alike by sons and daughters. Fifty years from now this country will hold up hands in holy horror that . . . any man or set of men in America should assume to themselves the authority to deny to free-born white women of America the ballot which is the badge and synonym of freedom.

Like most white southerners of their class, but also like a growing number of white, native-born Americans all over the nation in the late nineteenth century, the suffragists believed that voting was *not* a right of all citizens but the privilege and duty of those best qualified to exercise it. Indeed, the contemporary meaning of the phrase "the negro problem" to white southern suffragists was not the use of the race issue against their cause—though this concerned them greatly—but the enfranchisement after the Civil War of several million blacks considered by southern whites to be ignorant, purchasable, and unfit for political participation. . . .

There was a range of opinion within this group of southern suffrage leaders, ranging from negrophobes such as Kate Gordon, Belle Kearney, and Rebecca Latimer Felton who spoke of African Americans as though speaking of another, inferior species, to Mary Johnston, who denounced the use of racist tactics by suffragists, saying, "I think that as women we should be most prayerfully careful lest, in the future, that women—whether colored women or white women who are merely poor, should be able to say that we had betrayed their interests and excluded them from freedom." The "liberal" position among white southern suffragists (most clearly articulated by Madeline Breckinridge) was that white supremacy in politics was only a temporary necessity until "undesirable" voters became "desirable" through education and gradual social progress—advancements that elite whites were morally obligated to guide and support (through noblesse oblige), and that, meanwhile, "qualified" blacks should be allowed to vote. Still, most southern suffragists employed racist arguments to promote woman suffrage, some aggressively and enthusiastically and others defensively and reluctantly. African Americans were systematically excluded from all white-led suffrage organizations and meetings as the suffragists sought to distance their movement from its historic association with advocacy of the rights of black Americans.

One of the most fascinating aspects of the relationship between the southern suffrage movement and the South's "negro problem" is the crucial role of the latter in determining the strategy, the rhetoric, and even the timing of the woman suffrage movement in the South. Though historians usually focus upon the race issue as a prime obstacle to the suffragists' success, there is considerable evidence to indicate that the race issue was also a major *causative* factor in the development of the southern suffrage movement in the 1890s—not in causing southern women to *want* suffrage, but in giving them a *reason to expect that they could win it*. An organized regional movement with strong national support came into existence in the 1890s because many leading suffragists—both southern and northern—believed the South's "negro problem" might be the key to female enfranchisement.

It is one of history's many ironies that this idea was originally conceived by Lucy Stone's husband, Henry Blackwell, a former abolitionist. He began presenting this idea to southern politicians in 1867 and, by 1890, was able to persuade delegates to the Mississippi Constitutional Convention of 1890 to give it serious consideration. This impressed Laura Clay, whose pleas for woman suffrage as "justice" were falling upon deaf ears, as well as the leaders of the NAWSA, who launched a major campaign based on Blackwell's southern strategy. Indeed, many of them, including Carrie Chapman Catt, shared the indignation of these elite, white southern women that their social "inferiors," whether African Americans in the South or immigrants in the North, had become their political "superiors."

Late-nineteenth-century suffragists found it quite difficult to believe that the federal government would, as it did, abandon the defense of black suffrage and allow the South to solve its "negro problem" by disfranchising African-American men. They believed that should southern states attempt to disfranchise voters protected by the Fifteenth Amendment, Congress would invoke the amendment's enforcement clause, or the Supreme Court would rule the disfranchisement provisions unconstitutional. However, solving "the negro problem" by *extending* the franchise to *women* (with property requirements that would ensure that the vast majority of new voters would be white) would, they predicted, be seen as a *liberalization,* rather than a restriction, of suffrage and provide the means to preserve white political supremacy without risking congressional retribution or an unfavorable ruling by the Supreme Court. Throughout the 1890s, many southern suffragists believed that as the men of their class cast about for a means of countering the effects of black suffrage, they might resort to enfranchising white women—just as conservatives in the West had made use of woman suffrage to consolidate their political position.

The 1890s movement to restore white supremacy and Democratic hegemony, like the Progressive movement that came after it, gave white southern suffragists grounds to argue that the enfranchisement of women was expedient to society. But unlike the Progressive movement, which was relatively weak in the South and inspired no great hopes for success on the part of national suffrage leaders, the zealous campaign of the self-proclaimed best classes of whites to regain hegemony in southern society encouraged southern suffragists and their northern co-conspirators to believe the South would actually lead the nation in the adoption of woman suffrage.

By 1910 it was clear, however, that the dominant southern politicians had managed to solve "the negro problem" without resorting to woman suffrage and that the federal government was going to allow them to get away with disfranchising African-American men. In the second stage of the suffrage movement in the South, southern suffragists rarely raised the race issue and were almost exclusively on the defensive in regard to the race issue against opponents who claimed that state or federal woman suffrage amendments would endanger the newly established white dominance in politics. Suffragists insisted that the race issue was now irrelevant to the woman suffrage issue; "negresses" would be disfranchised by the same provisions that applied to "negroes."

On the race issue, white suffragists presented a united front. Those who questioned the use of racist tactics or disapproved of the wholesale exclusion of blacks from the electorate kept such sentiments to themselves or at least out of the public arena; they had no desire to confirm the widespread perception that suffragists were advocates of black political power. But there was no such consensus or show of solidarity regarding the states' rights issue; and in the last decade of the suffrage movement, as the federal suffrage amendment gained momentum elsewhere in the nation, differences of opinion over the state sovereignty issue divided southern suffragists into warring camps as the National American Woman Suffrage Association [NAWSA], the newly formed National Woman's Party [NWP], and a new southern organization—the Southern States Woman Suffrage Conference—followed separate strategies and competed for the loyalty of southern suffragists. The controversy over strategy strained, and in some cases, severed long-standing friendships and added to the difficulties the woman suffrage movement faced in the South. . . .

A minority of southern suffragists, of course, could not bring themselves to support a federal suffrage amendment. When in 1913 the National, prodded into action by Alice Paul and her associates, renewed its campaign for a federal suffrage amendment, Kate Gordon decided it was time that southern suffragists go their own way. A disgruntled former NAWSA officer and a committed states' rights advocate, Gordon led in the establishment of the Southern States Woman Suffrage Conference (SSWSC). She and her followers insisted that the southern states would never allow a federal amendment to be passed by Congress; even if it were passed, the SSWSC would remain solid against ratification and thus block any possibility of enfranchisement through federal action. . . .

Most southern suffragists, however, did not follow Gordon's lead. Few were willing to renounce federal suffrage when it might be necessary to secure their enfranchisement. In fact, after one of her tirades against NAWSA leaders, Gordon achieved the notoriety of being formally reprimanded by not one but two southern state suffrage organizations. Led by Sue Shelton White and Pattie Ruffner Jacobs, respectively, the state suffrage organizations of Tennessee and Alabama rebuked Kate Gordon and her presumptuous claim to speak for southern suffragists. Tennessee's resolution, drafted by White, declared that "the Convention of the Tennessee Equal Suffrage Association go on record as disapproving the action of Miss Kate M. Gordon in undertaking to dictate to the NAWSA or its Congressional Committee in regard to its policy, methods, or plans . . . and in her presuming to speak for the women of the South; and that the Recording Secretary of this convention be instructed to immediately notify the National officers and the Chairman of the Congressional Committee of such action. ". . .

After 1916, when many pleas for state suffrage amendments had been made and rejected throughout the South, and the National was fully committed to securing enfranchisement through federal action, the majority of southern suffragists campaigned actively for a federal woman suffrage amendment. Some, including Nellie Nugent Somerville, set aside reservations about federal intervention in the affairs of states and labored to convince fellow southerners that the federal amendment held "no menace for the institutions of any State or any group of States." . . .

When in June 1919 Congress finally submitted the proposed Nineteenth Amendment to the states for ratification, the leaders of the woman suffrage movement in the southern states found themselves fighting one another as well as the antis—a situation that did nothing to help the cause. In Virginia, there was open hostility between the NAWSA loyalists led by Valentine and the state's chapter of the NWP. In Mississippi, Somerville and her associates endured the bitter experience of sitting in the gallery while Kate Gordon, in Jackson at the invitation of the *Clarion-Ledger,* denounced the federal amendment as a threat to state sovereignty and the constitution. In Louisiana, the Gordons and other advocates of woman suffrage through state action combated a coalition of federal amendment supporters *and* the antisuffragists, creating a three-way struggle in which no form of woman suffrage was adopted. In Tennessee, both Gordon sisters and Laura Clay actually campaigned against ratification of "this hideous amendment" though Clay had "a great distaste" at being publicly associated with the despised antis.

As the end of the long struggle for woman suffrage approached, those southern suffragists who opposed the Nineteenth Amendment were bitter, disappointed in their fellow suffragists, and dismayed that the success of woman suffrage for which they had worked for so many years helped undermine another cherished political ideal—state sovereignty. Most southern suffragists, however, were jubilant when ratification came at last and grateful to Tennessee for, in the words of Virginia suffragists, "redeeming the honor of the country." . . .

White southern suffragists, with their elite cadre of leaders who shared many of the ideas of other southerners of their race and class, offered no thoroughgoing indictment of their society. They did not challenge the idea that many within the region needed the "guardianship" of the more enlightened citizenry, but they objected to the idea that *they* needed such guidance and protection. These suffragists were "radical" for their region only in their advocacy of women's rights—their support for important changes in the relations between the sexes and their insistence upon expanding and improving woman's lot in southern society.

None of these reforms, however, were as threatening to the social order as woman suffrage; reforms short of suffrage could still be seen as evidence of male protection of women and children, secured through "indirect influence." The request for the vote, on the other hand, was interpreted as a challenge to the fundamentally hierarchical and paternalistic political structure of the region as well as to the sovereignty of the states; and however nicely the suffragists tried to put it, demanding the power to represent their own interests constituted an indirect accusation of failure that southern politicians understood and did not appreciate.

The South was never, as Laura Clay hoped, fully "brought in" to the suffrage fold—even though sufficient numbers of southern states ratified for the Nineteenth Amendment to become law. And in rejecting woman suffrage, southern politicians made it clear that they still found much about the old pattern of relations between the sexes quite attractive. After 1920, southern women would still have far to go in their quest for equality in the South.

✢ *F U R T H E R   R E A D I N G*

Shirley Abbott, *Womenfolks: Growing Up Down South* (1983)

Virginia Bernhard et al., *Southern Women: Histories and Identities* (1992)

———, *Hidden Histories of Women in the New South* (1994)

Kathleen M. Blee, *Women of the Klan: Racism and Gender in the 1920s* (1991)

Janet Coryell et al., *Beyond Image and Convention: Explorations in Southern Women's History* (1998)

Debbie Cottrell, *Pioneer Woman Educator: The Progressive Spirit of Annie Webb Blanton* (1993)

Elizabeth York Enstam, *Women and the Creation of Urban Life: Dallas, Texas, 1843–1920* (1998)

Elna C. Green, *Southern Strategies: Southern Women and the Woman Suffrage Question* (1997)

Beverly Guy-Sheftall, *"Daughters of Sorrow": Attitudes Toward Black Women, 1880–1920* (1990)

Jacquelyn Dowd Hall, *Revolt Against Chivalry: Jessie Daniel Ames and the Woman's Campaign Against Lynching* (1974)

Joanne Hawks and Sheila Skemp, eds., *Sex, Race, and the Role of Women in the South* (1983)

Nancy A. Hewitt and Suzanne Lebsock, eds., *Visible Women: New Essays on American Activism* (1993)

Darlene Clark Hine, "Black Women's History, White Women's History: The Juncture of Race and Class," *Journal of Women's History* 4 (Fall 1992), 125–133

Dolores Janiewski, *Sisterhood Denied: Race, Gender, and Class in a New South Community* (1985)

Jacqueline Jones, *Labor of Love, Labor of Sorrow: Black Women, Work and the Family from Slavery to the Present* (1985)

Elisabeth Lasch-Quinn, *Black Neighbors: Race and the Limits of Reform in the American Settlement House Movement, 1890–1945* (1993)

James L. Leloudis, "School Reform in the New South: The Woman's Association for the Betterment of Public School Houses in North Carolina, 1902–1919," *Journal of American History* 69 (March 1983), 886–909

A. D. Mayo, *Southern Women in the Recent Educational Movement in the South* (1892)

Judith N. McArthur, *Creating the New Woman: The Rise of Southern Women's Progressive Culture in Texas, 1893–1918* (1998)

Jacquelyn M. McElhaney, *Pauline Periwinkle and Progressive Reform in Dallas* (1998)

Cynthia Neverdon-Morton, *Afro-American Women of the South and the Advancement of the Race, 1895–1925* (1989)

Dorothy Salem, *To Better Our World: Black Women in Organized Reform, 1890–1920* (1990)

Anne Firor Scott, *The Southern Lady: From Pedestal to Politics, 1830–1900* (1970)

———, *Natural Allies: Women's Associations in American History* (1992)

Stephanie Shaw, *What a Woman Ought to Be and to Do: Black Professional Women Workers During the Jim Crow Era* (1996)

Anastatia Sims, *The Power of Femininity in the New South* (1997)

Roslyn Terborg-Penn, *African American Women in the Struggle for the Vote, 1850–1920* (1998)

Mary Martha Thomas, ed., *Stepping Out of the Shadows: Alabama Women* (1995)

Mildred Thompson, *Ida B. Wells-Barnett: An Exploratory Study of an American Black Woman, 1893–1930* (1990)

Elizabeth Hayes Turner, *Women, Culture, and Community: Religion and Reform in Galveston, 1880–1920* (1997)

Pam Tyler, *Silk Stockings and Ballot Boxes: Women and Politics in New Orleans, 1920–1963* (1996)

Marsha Wedell, *Elite Women and the Reform Impulse in Memphis, 1875–1915* (1991)

Marjorie Spruill Wheeler, *New Women of the New South: The Leaders of the Woman Suffrage Movement in the Southern States* (1993)

Margaret Ripley Wolfe, *Daughters of Canaan: A Saga of Southern Women* (1995)

In Search of the Modern South

In a 1917 article, journalist and critic H. L. Mencken referred to the South as "the Sahara of the Bozart," ridiculing the South's lack of "beaux arts." By the 1940s, this had changed; millions of Americans read the novels of Thomas Wolfe, Zora Neale Hurston, Lillian Smith, and William Faulkner. Sociologist Howard W. Odum and his colleagues at the University of North Carolina had established national reputations for their social-scientific explorations of southern problems; and a creative group at Vanderbilt University, the Nashville Agrarians, had offered a stunning critique of urban-industrial society.

In fact, the South was changing. The literary renaissance and the accompanying developments in critical thought and the social sciences demonstrated that southerners were capable of insightful self-analysis and creative genius. Cities, which had always brought fresh ideas to a region, were growing in the South, fostering better education and employment opportunities for residents away from their rural roots. By 1920, women had the right to vote and the social freedom to smoke, drink, and raise their hemlines. Southerners bought automobiles and began to see the region from a new perspective. Educators, influenced by the theories of Charles Darwin and others, sought more scientific methods for explaining their world. Black veterans, home from the front, questioned the place of segregation in a democracy.

While intellectuals and modernists waged a campaign of words over southern culture, some southerners, fearful of change and made nervous by gender and race expectations, revolted against modernism. In their opinion, secular values were undermining traditional evangelical beliefs. Through legislation and extra-legal violence, antimodernists attempted to recapture the "safety" of the traditional South. Fundamentalist Christianity, a northern religious innovation that made enormous headway in the South, flourished in some evangelical churches, adding a moralistic tone to antimodernist rhetoric. Such events as the rise of the Ku Klux Klan and the Scopes "Monkey" trial indicate the level of disturbance felt by traditionalists in the South.

Scholars today still ask why the cultural renaissance occurred in the 1920s. How did the growth of cities, increasing public opportunities for women, rising secularization, and new ideas from World War I shape the direction of the modern South? What were the consequences of antimodernist impulses for the South?

✣ D O C U M E N T S

To many southerners, the pundits' ridicule of the region was aimed at their agrarian as opposed to industrial way of life. The Nashville Agrarians, in their manifesto entitled *I'll Take My Stand,* warned that modernization of the South would destroy some important regional values. In Document 1, Vanderbilt University English professor John Crowe Ransom, who wrote the introduction to *I'll Take My Stand,* criticizes the negative effects of the industrial society in contrast to the South's traditional agrarian folkways. Although Ranson portrayed the South as primarily rural, in fact, its urban population had increased substantially, as indicated by Document 2, which shows the leading southern cities. Even in the South, the image of the "New Woman" took many forms; one that incensed supporters of traditional codes of decency was the southern beauty pageant, shown here in Document 3. Sinister in their white apparel, as shown in Document 4, members of the Ku Klux Klan used secrecy, intimidation, and violence against Catholics, Jews, blacks, labor union organizers, and whites who violated traditional moral codes. Few causes stirred evangelical zeal in the 1920s more than the attempt to outlaw the teaching of evolution. In Document 5, a sermon delivered in Raleigh, North Carolina, the Reverend Amzi Clarence Dixon attributes an array of global evils, including World War I and divorce, to Darwin's theory. Finally, in Document 6, William L. Poteat, Baptist president of Wake Forest College, concludes that fundamentalism and its insistence on the divorce between scientific evidence and the biblical story of creation "is compromising Christianity before the intelligence of the world."

1. John Crowe Ransom Takes a Stand for the Agrarian Way of Life, 1930

Nobody now proposes for the South, or for any other community in this country, an independent political destiny. That idea is thought to have been finished in 1865. But how far shall the South surrender its moral, social, and economic autonomy to the victorious principle of Union? That question remains open. The South is a minority section that has hitherto been jealous of its minority right to live its own kind of life. The South scarcely hopes to determine to other sections, but it does propose to determine itself, within the utmost limits of legal action. Of late, however, there is the melancholy fact that the South itself has wavered a little and shown signs of wanting to join up behind the common or American industrial ideal. . . . The younger Southerners, who are being converted frequently to the industrial gospel, must come back to the support of the Southern tradition. They must be persuaded to look very critically at the advantages of becoming a "new South" which will be only an undistinguished replica of the usual industrial community.

But there are many other minority communities opposed to industrialism, and wanting a much simpler economy to live by. The communities and private persons sharing the agrarian tastes are to be found widely within the Union. Proper living is a matter of the intelligence and the will, does not depend on the local climate or ge-

Reprinted by permission of Louisiana State University Press from *I'll Take My Stand: The South and the Agrarian Tradition,* by Twelve Southerners. Copyright © 1930 by Harper & Brothers. Copyright renewed 1958 by Donald Davidson. Introduction copyright © 1962, 1977 by Louis D. Rubin, Jr. Biographical essays copyright © 1962, 1977 by Virginia Rock.

ography, and is capable of a definition which is general and not Southern at all. Southerners have a filial duty to discharge to their own section. But their cause is precarious and they must seek alliances with sympathetic communities everywhere. The members of the present group would be happy to be counted as members of a national agrarian movement.

Industrialism is the economic organization of the collective American society. It means the decision of society to invest its economic resources in the applied sciences. But the word science has acquired a certain sanctitude. It is out of order to quarrel with science in the abstract, or even with the applied sciences when their applications are made subject to criticism and intelligence. The capitalization of the applied sciences has now become extravagant and uncritical; it has enslaved our human energies to a degree now clearly felt to be burdensome. The apologists of industrialism do not like to meet this charge directly; so they often take refuge in saying that they are devoted simply to science! They are really devoted to the applied sciences and to practical production. Therefore it is necessary to employ a certain skepticism even at the expense of the Cult of Science, and to say, It is an Americanism, which looks innocent and disinterested, but really is not either.

The contribution that science can make to a labor is to render it easier by the help of a tool or a process, and to assure the laborer of his perfect economic security while he is engaged upon it. Then it can be performed with leisure and enjoyment. But the modern laborer has not exactly received this benefit under the industrial regime. His labor is hard, its tempo is fierce, and his employment is insecure. The first principle of a good labor is that it must be effective, but the second principle is that it must be enjoyed. Labor is one of the largest items in the human career; it is a modest demand to ask that it may partake of happiness.

The regular act of applied science is to introduce into labor a labor-saving device or a machine. Whether this is a benefit depends on how far it is advisable to save the labor. The philosophy of applied science is generally quite sure that the saving of labor is a pure gain, and that the more of it the better. This is to assume that labor is an evil, that only the end of labor or the material product is good. On this assumption labor becomes mercenary and servile, and it is no wonder if many forms of modern labor are accepted without resentment though they are evidently brutalizing. The act of labor as one of the happy functions of human life has been in effect abandoned, and is practiced solely for its rewards.

Even the apologists of industrialism have been obliged to admit that some economic evils follow in the wake of the machines. These are such as overproduction, unemployment, and a growing inequality in the distribution of wealth. But the remedies proposed by the apologists are always homeopathic. They expect the evils to disappear when we have bigger and better machines, and more of them. Their remedial programs, therefore, look forward to more industrialism. . . .

Religion can hardly expect to flourish in an industrial society. Religion is our submission to the general intention of a nature that is fairly inscrutable; it is the sense of our rôle as creatures within it. But nature industrialized, transformed into cities and artificial habitations, manufactured into commodities, is no longer nature but a highly simplified picture of nature. We receive the illusion of having power over nature, and lose the sense of nature as something mysterious and contingent. The God of nature under these conditions is merely an amiable expression, a superfluity, and the philosophical understanding ordinarily carried in the religious experience is not there for us to have.

Nor do the arts have a proper life under industrialism, with the general decay of sensibility which attends it. Art depends, in general, like religion, on a right attitude to nature; and in particular on a free and disinterested observation of nature that occurs only in leisure. Neither the creation nor the understanding of works of art is possible in an industrial age except by some local and unlikely suspension of the industrial drive.

The amenities of life also suffer under the curse of a strictly-business or industrial civilization. They consist in such practices as manners, conversation, hospitality, sympathy, family life, romantic love—in the social exchanges which reveal and develop sensibility in human affairs. If religion and the arts are founded on right relations of man-to-nature, these are founded on right relations of man-to-man.

Apologists of industrialism are even inclined to admit that its actual processes may have upon its victims the spiritual effects just described. But they think that all can be made right by extraordinary educational effects, by all sorts of cultural institutions and endowments. They would cure the poverty of the contemporary spirit by hiring experts to instruct it in spite of itself in the historic culture. But salvation is hardly to be encountered on that road. The trouble with the life-pattern is to be located at its economic base, and we cannot rebuild it by pouring in soft materials from the top. The young men and women in colleges, for example, if they are already placed in a false way of life, cannot make more than an inconsequential acquaintance with the arts and humanities transmitted to them. Or else the understanding of these arts and humanities will but make them the more wretched in their own destitution. . . .

The tempo of the industrial life is fast, but that is not the worst of it; it is accelerating. The ideal is not merely some set form of industrialism, with so many stable industries, but industrial progress, or an incessant extension of industrialization. It never proposes a specific goal; it initiates the infinite series. We have not merely capitalized certain industries; we have capitalized the laboratories and inventors, and undertaken to employ all the labor-saving devices that come out of them. But a fresh labor-saving device introduced into an industry does not emancipate the laborers in that industry so much as it evicts them. Applied at the expense of agriculture, for example, the new processes have reduced the part of the population supporting itself upon the soil to a smaller and smaller fraction. Of course no single labor-saving process is fatal; it brings on a period of unemployed labor and unemployed capital, but soon a new industry is devised which will put them both to work again, and a new commodity is thrown upon the market. The laborers were sufficiently embarrassed in the meantime, but, according to the theory, they will eventually be taken care of. It is now the public which is embarrassed; it feels obligated to purchase a commodity for which it had expressed no desire, but it is invited to make its budget equal to the strain. All might yet be well, and stability and comfort might again obtain, but for this: partly because of industrial ambitions and partly because the repressed creative impulse must break out somewhere, there will be a stream of further labor-saving devices in all industries, and the cycle will have to be repeated over and over. The result is an increasing disadjustment and instability.

It is an inevitable consequence of industrial progress that production greatly outruns the rate of natural consumption. To overcome the disparity, the producers, disguised as the pure idealists of progress, must coerce and wheedle the public into being loyal and steady consumers, in order to keep the machines running. So the rise of modern advertising—along with its twin, personal salesmanship—is the most significant development of our industrialism. Advertising means to persuade the consumers to want exactly what the applied sciences are able to furnish them. It consults the happiness of the consumer no more than it consulted the happiness of the laborer. It is the great effort of a false economy of life to approve itself. But its task grows more difficult every day.

It is strange, of course, that a majority of men anywhere could ever as with one mind become enamored of industrialism: a system that has so little regard for individual wants. There is evidently a kind of thinking that rejoices in setting up a social objective which has no relation to the individual. Men are prepared to sacrifice their private dignity and happiness to an abstract social ideal, and without asking whether the social ideal produces the welfare of any individual men whatsoever. But this is absurd. The responsibility of men is for their own welfare and that of their neighbors; not for the hypothetical welfare of some fabulous creature called society.

Opposed to the industrial society is the agrarian, which does not stand in particular need of definition. An agrarian society is hardly one that has no use at all for industries, for professional vocations, for scholars and artists, and for the life of cities. Technically, perhaps, an agrarian society is one in which agriculture is the leading vocation, whether for wealth, for pleasure, or for prestige—a form of labor that is pursued with intelligence and leisure, and that becomes the model to which the other forms approach as well as they may. But an agrarian regime will be secured readily enough where the superfluous industries are not allowed to rise against it. The theory of agrarianism is that the culture of the soil is the best and most sensitive of vocations, and that therefore it should have the economic preference and enlist the maximum number of workers.

These principles do not intend to be very specific in proposing any practical measures. How may the little agrarian community resist the Chamber of Commerce of its county seat, which is always trying to import some foreign industry that cannot be assimilated to the life-pattern of the community? Just what must the Southern leaders do to defend the traditional Southern life? How may the Southern and the Western agrarians unite for effective action? Should the agrarian forces try to capture the Democratic party, which historically is so closely affiliated with the defense of individualism, the small community, the state, the South? Or must the agrarians—even the Southern ones—abandon the Democratic party to its fate and try a new one? What legislation could most profitably be championed by the powerful agrarians in the Senate of the United States? What anti-industrial measures might promise to stop the advances of industrialism, or even undo some of them, with the least harm to those concerned? What policy should be pursued by the educators who have a tradition at heart? These and many other questions are of the greatest importance, but they cannot be answered here.

For, in conclusion, this much is clear: If a community, or a section, or a race, or an age, is groaning under industrialism, and well aware that it is an evil dispensation, it must find the way to throw it off. To think that this cannot be done is pusillanimous. And if the whole community, section, race, or age thinks it cannot be done, then it has simply lost its political genius and doomed itself to impotence.

2. Leading Southern Cities, 1920

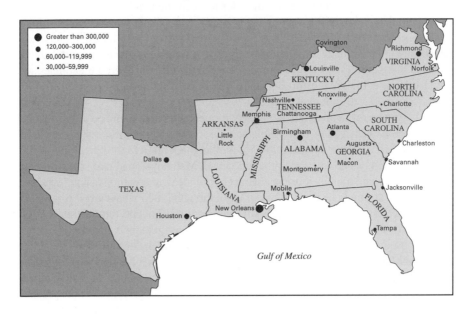

3. First International Pageant of Pulchritude, Galveston, Texas, c. 1926

Map reprinted by permission of Louisiana State University Press from *Cotton Fields and Skyscrapers*, by David R. Goldfield. Copyright © 1982 by Louisiana State University Press.

First International Pageant of Pulchritude & Seventh Annual Bathing Girl Review at Galveston, Texas (Library of Congress)

4. Ku Klux Klan Propaganda

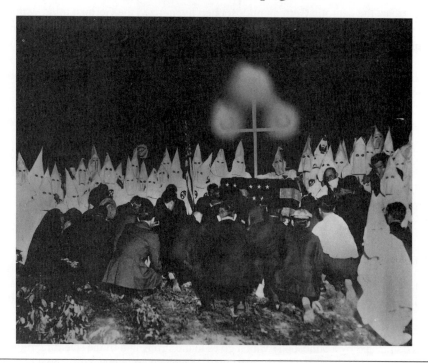

A Ku Klux Klan Night Ceremony Inducting New Members in 1915. (UPI/Corbis-Bettmann)

5. The Reverend Amzi Clarence Dixon on the Evils of Evolution, 1922

Evolution with its "struggle for existence" and "survival of the fittest," which gives the strong and fit the scientific right to destroy the weak and unfit is responsible for the oppression and destruction of the weak and unfit by the strong and fit. It has fostered autocratic class distinctions and is no friend to those who stand for the protection of the weak against the oppression of the strong. The greatest war in history, which has drenched the world with blood and covered it with human bones, can be traced to this source. If the strong and fit have the scientific right to destroy the weak and unfit, that human progress may be promoted, then might is right, and Germany should not be criticized for acting upon this principle.

"Dr. Dixon Claims Evolution Started in Unscientific Age," as appeared in *Raleigh News & Observer,* December 31, 1922, p. 5.

The "Superman"

Nietzsche, the neurotic German philosopher, hypnotized the German mind with his Pagan brute philosophy. "The weak and botched," said he, "shall perish; first principle of humanity. And they ought to be helped to perish. What is more harmful than any vice? Practical sympathy with the botched and weak Christianity." "If what I publish be true," he wrote to an invalid woman, "a feeble woman like you would have no right to exist."

"Christianity," he said, "is the greatest of all conceivable corruptions, the one immortal blemish of mankind." And he hated it because of its sympathy with the botched and weak. He glorified his ideal "blond beast" and gave to the world a "superman," one-third brute, one-third philosopher. Under the spell of his daring brutality, Germany adopted the motto, "Corsica has conquered Galilee." Nietzsche's philosophy of beastliness has its roots in the evolutionary assumption that the strong and fit, in the struggle for existence, have the scientific right to destroy the weak and unfit.

The Super-Nation

Under the spell of Nietzsche's "superman" there came into the heads of the German politicians and militarists the vision of a super nation, with the scientific right to destroy weaker nations and build its throne upon their ruins. . . .

I tremble for the future of the world if the millions of China are to be moulded and dominated by a philosophy which gives to the strong and fit the scientific right to destroy the unfit. It is easy for the patriotism of any nation to make its people believe that they are the fittest nation in the world; only, if China with the conviction should become conscious of her strength, she could become, under masterful military leadership, the menace of the future. Any nation that teaches this pernicious delusion to its youth is now a menace to the peace of the world; and if all nations teach it, war will be the normal method of settling all disputes. Universal peace can never come until nations turn from this voice of the jungle to the song of the angels floating from the skies above the plain of Bethlehem: "Peace on earth among men of good will."

If the home is to be preserved as a sacred institution, the Bible which teaches that marriage came down from God and not up from the beast must be believed. The jungle theory as to the origin of marriage is today keeping busy the divorce courts of the civilized world. If government came down from God, so that "the powers that be are ordained of God," law will rule in righteousness and courts will mete out justice, but if the basis of government came from the jungle where brute force prevails, the Bolshevist rule by bullet and bayonet is scientific and the scientific mind ought to accept it. This jungle origin of government is today a world-wide peril. If the Bible is a revelation from God through inspired men, its teaching is authoritative and its truths have in them an irresistible dynamic, but if the Bible is a mere record of human experience as men have struggled upward from their jungle origin, its teaching has no authority and its sayings are to be accepted or rejected by the inner consciousness of men, which is itself a product of the jungle.

If man came down from God, created in His image and has been wrecked by sin, then sin is an intrusion, an enemy that ought to be expelled; but, if man came up from the beast through the jungle, sin is "embryonic goodness," "righteousness in process of formation," even a search after good; of course such sin has no guilt and may be condoned, if not coddled. Such a delusion makes it easy to believe that sin has no existence and all things, even theft, falsehood and murder are good, because there is no evil in the world.

If the church came down from God in the sense that its members are "born from above," we have on this world a unique spiritual organism, of which Jesus Christ is the head, endued with an irresistible dynamic, "power from on high." But if the church came up from the beast through the jungle and is the expression of man's struggle out of beastliness into spirituality, we have simply one earth-born institution among many and cannot be optimistic regarding its destiny.

If Christ came down from heaven, as He says He did, "the only begotten Son of God" in the sense that He is the only one in the universe begotten of God in a virgin's womb, "God manifest in the flesh," "the Word made flesh and dwelling among men," we have in Him a unique personality; God, who is a Spirit, made concrete, thinkable, approachable and lovable; God, lowering Himself to our level, that He may lift us to His level. But if Christ is the expression of humanity's struggle up from the beast through the jungle, we have in Him simply a combination and culmination of jungle life in body, soul and spirit, detached from heaven, on the same plane with others, with little power to lift or transfigure.

The Beast-Jungle theory of evolution robs a man of his dignity, marriage of its sanctity, government of its authority, the church of her power and Christ of His glory.

6. Dr. William L. Poteat Criticizes Fundamentalism, 1925

We subject religious doctrine and the interpretation of the Bible to the test of the rational faculty, just as we apply that test to all other bodies of literature and doctrine. And however partial and dangerous it may be to rely upon one of our faculties and ignore the rest, many among us add to the habit of rationalism the offensive attitude of bigotry. The rationalism of science will set down as absurd what it is unable to explain or handle with its apparatus of the foot-rule, the clock, and the balance. So Reinach will declare that "religion is a collection of scruples which impede the free exercise of our faculties." The rationalism of orthodoxy will deny any fact which does not fit neatly into its system without deranging it, will go beyond what is written and seek to enforce with anathemas subscription to the decrees of an alien logic. So Mr. [William Jennings] Bryan will say that evolution is "a false, absurd, and ridiculous doctrine without support in the written Word of God and without support also in nature."

Fundamentalism. An interesting phenomenon in the religious thought of to-day springs out of this Western and modern tendency to rationalize the religious experience. Fundamentalism is an active movement which it is impossible to ignore, even if one wishes to do so. In so far as it succeeds it is likely to impose on popular

"Dr. William L. Poteat Criticizes Fundamentalism, 1925," by William Louis Poteat from *Can a Man Be a Christian Today?* © 1925 by the University of North Carolina Press.

opinion the view that religion and science cannot dwell together in peace in the same mind. Such a practical result the propaganda does not seek, but it follows of necessity. The gentlemen who are promoting this movement appear to have learned nothing from history, illustrating a saying of the German author of the "Philosophy of History" that we learn from history that men never learn anything from history. They are loyal to a closed logical system and are repeating a blunder against which the past is full of warnings, and they are courting the disaster which has invariably followed the blunder,—the disaster of raising a perilous issue and later pulling it down. After a bitter resistance Christian theology in England came to see that the discovery of the method of creation did not dispense with the Divine agency in creation, and along with other human disciplines accepted and incorporated the great conception of evolution. That modus, as we have seen, was established some forty years ago. But only yesterday a few gentlemen, sincere, devout, and capable, old enough to remember it if they were even slightly in touch with the thought of that period, waked up to find, as they thought, the scientists secretly digging out the foundations of Christianity. Their excitement and alarm spread rapidly and widely. Trained for the most part in pre-laboratory days, they could not be expected to have the scientific habit or attitude. Invoking a man-made theory of inspiration most unfair to the precious documents of our faith, and committed to a bald literalism of interpretation, they take the rôle of defenders of the faith and in its name propose, by ecclesiastical and legislative enactment, by executive order, by organized propaganda, by inquisition and the refinements of modern torture, to crowd the eagle back into the shell and then, in Voltaire's famous phrase, crush the infamous thing. An organ of the movement announces that its purpose is "to drive out of all tax-supported schools every evolution teacher and every book teaching evolution. It is going to mean war to the knife, knife to the hilt." Once more the old slogan comes out of retirement—"religion or science," "Moses or Darwin." These earnest but misguided men are producing no effect whatsoever upon scientific opinion. Their solicitude comes in the wrong century. It might have been more effective in the nineteenth. In another direction, however, Fundamentalism is not without influence, and there lies the tragedy of it. It is compromising Christianity before the intelligence of the world. The young men and women who are trained in the laboratories of our colleges and universities, so far as they are affected at all, will find it difficult, under this interpretation, to keep their place in the Christian communion, or unpromising to enter. Without intending it, these ardent propagandists are, in reality, scattering thorns in the path of the young Greeks of our day who would see Jesus. We are witnessing another case of conservatism putting in jeopardy the cause which it seeks to save. The spectacle is amazing and disheartening.

Modernism in its newer phase is the reaction from Fundamentalism. As there are extreme Fundamentalists, so there are extreme Modernists. If the one says he believes everything in the Bible from cover to cover, including the covers,—everything read as it was written, interpreted with severest literalism, the other says he believes nothing in the Bible, interpreted with never so much freedom of figure and allegory: science has displaced religion as religion displaced magic. These two categories are neither exclusive nor exhaustive. Most intelligent Christians decline both labels. In French and other legislative assemblies three groups of members are recognized,—the Right or conservatives, the Left or radicals, and the Center, the group holding intermediate or moderate views. The Center is most likely to be both clear and dependable. A great artist once said to me, "Perfection lies midway between perfection and barbarism."

⚓ E S S A Y S

In the first essay, historian Richard H. King asserts that the key to understanding the southern literary renaissance and its participants lies in examining how the writers perceived and dealt with the past. Whereas King writes of extraordinary intellectuals willing to break the bonds of traditional thinking, Nancy Maclean, in her history of the Ku Klux Klan, writes about the ordinary middle-class southerners, including pastors, who became klansmen. Hannah Arendt's phrase the banality of evil becomes appropriate when looking at Klan membership and ideology. In the final essay, Willard Gatewood documents the effects of the Scopes trial on southern laws regarding the teaching of evolution in schools and the lingering adherence in the South to fundamentalist principles.

Explaining the Southern Renaissance

RICHARD H. KING

What then was the Southern Renaissance? Put briefly: the writers and intellectuals of the South after the late 1920s were engaged in an attempt to come to terms not only with the inherited values of the Southern tradition but also with a certain way of perceiving and dealing with the past, what Nietzsche called "monumental" historical consciousness. It was vitally important for them to decide whether the past was of any use at all in the present; and, if so, in what ways? Put another way, the relationship between present and past which the Renaissance writers explored was fraught with ambivalence and ambiguity. . . .

One of the chief problems was that the South had neither a strong "enlightenment" tradition nor mass tradition of intellectual or educational concern. The Jeffersonian ideal of intellectual curiosity about whatever bore on man's fate had long since faded. By the 1930s the Jeffersonian legacy was a rather tame affair, something honored more in the breach than observance. Virginius Dabney's attempt to show the pervasive influence of Jeffersonian liberalism served mainly to show how weak and amorphous it had been. And of course no better example exists than the Scopes "Monkey" trial in Dayton, Tennessee, in 1925, about the teaching in public schools of Darwin's theory of evolution. . . .

On the institutional level, the university tradition in the South was notably weak, though by the 1920s several departments of history and sociology (along with Vanderbilt's English department) were beginning to make their mark. As Howard Odum would note in *Southern Regions* (1936), no Southern university belonged in the top rank of American universities. There was but a small and rather precarious space of freedom within which to consider, much less advocate, new ideas. . . .

In addition, Southern cities such as Atlanta or Birmingham, New Orleans or Charleston, lacked strong, dissident artistic communities or influential universities. While black scholars such as W. E. B. Du Bois, earlier at Atlanta, and Charles Johnson at Fisk did important sociological work, the black minority lacked the power or opportunity to be a major factor in Southern intellectual ferment. . . .

And yet, as [W. J.] Cash might have said, something began happening in the 1920s. The "introspective revolution" of the 1930s and 1940s was prepared by a series of historical events which had profound symbolic reverberations among Southern writers and intellectuals. These events served as historical precipitates, crystallizing cultural themes and solidifying individuals into groups, thus setting the stage for much of the *Kulturkampf* in the 1930s.

The first of these events was World War I itself, which marked the end of a century of European peace and the stable bourgeois order which marked that period. Though less so than among the intellectuals of the European nations, the war profoundly affected American writers. The center did not hold. For sensitive Southerners, World War I represented the occasion for the South, as Allen Tate put it, to "rejoin the world."

Nor was the effect of that war lost on young Southern writers such as William Faulkner, who wrote of the disillusionment of the returning veteran in *Soldier's Pay* and *Sartoris*. William Alexander Percy, then a young poet, was later to write in *Lanterns on the Levee* of the exhilaration of combat—and then the sense of being adrift after his return from the trenches. Many young Southerners must have seen World War I not only as a great adventure but also as a sort of historical second chance. Having grown up in a Southern tradition powerfully shaped by the Civil War and Reconstruction, young Southerners saw World War I as a chance to demonstrate the heroism which had been drummed into them as one of the transcendent virtues of the Southern tradition. In the long run the war's cultural reverberations gave a final blow to the genteel tradition in literature. In this sense the Southern Renaissance, at least in its literary manifestations, drew less from the Depression experience than from the cultural impact of the war.

In these years the most frontal (and notorious) assault on Southern cultural esteem came from H. L. Mencken. His "Sahara of the Bozart" (1917) was read by many devoted Southerners, including liberals, as an unfair attack by an outsider. It is less well known that Mencken did not attack only to withdraw and gloat at the havoc he had wreaked. Rather, he helped keep alive fledgling literary magazines such as *The Double Dealer* in New Orleans and *The Reviewer* in Richmond, and later opened the pages of *The American Mercury* to young Southerners, such as W. J. Cash and Gerald Johnson, who were critical of the region's cultural aridity. For him, as for the poets associated with *The Fugitive* in Nashville, the enemy was the genteel tradition, New South boosterism, and the cultural wasteland of rural society. . . . It was in response to Mencken's attack on the South in Dayton that poets and intellectuals in Nashville readied the counterattack which was to appear in 1930 as *I'll Take My Stand.*

By then even for defenders of the Southern tradition, not to mention its critics, the tradition had become an "entity" which could not be simply assumed; it had to be reappropriated. Accompanying this reification of the tradition was an upsurge in historical self-consciousness, a sign itself of the distance between self and tradition. As Allen Tate was to write in 1930, "[T]radition must, in other words, be automatically operative before it can be called tradition." The very act of trying to re-present the tradition pointed to its absence. In fiction and poetry the tradition was often symbolized in the portraits of the heroic generation, the presiding presences of the tradition, who had wrested the land from the Indians and defended it against the Yankees and the aggressions of Reconstruction. The portraits of these men—stern, untroubled, and resolute—hung in the entrance halls or the parlors of the homes; and from there they judged the actions of their successors. Their example was a standing rebuke to a decline in energy and will. The next generation was of necessity less heroic; charismatic origins were institutionalized, perpetuated by hard work, and marked by less glamor, for the generation between the heroic one and the one that experienced the tradition as absent had to live in the world rather than die heroically. They were too near their sons to be quite heroic. The meaning of the Civil War was, in Donald Davidson's words:

> Something for grandfathers to tell
> Boys who clamor and climb.
> And were you there, and did you ride
> With the men of that old time?
>
> ("Sequel of Appomattox")

And yet, a crucial segment of the third (and in some cases fourth) generation, which was born around the turn of the century and lived through the cultural crisis of World War I, came to feel increasingly estranged from the tradition. That tradition loomed distressingly distant and overpoweringly strong, insupportable yet inescapable. . . .

Certainly of the rehashing of old verities there was no end in the 1930s. One thinks here of the Agrarians or of William Alexander Percy. Calling upon the past to aid the present, they attempted to revitalize the tradition by turning it into a conservative, even reactionary ideology. Some, like Percy, realized that the tradition could not be revitalized in any binding, collective way and that it had become "merely" a personal code by which they could at least live.

Nor was violence far from the surface of much of the writings in the 1930s. One thinks here of Tate's call for violence to reclaim the lost Southern tradition or his evocation of the lost possibility of an expansionist slave empire in his biography of Jefferson Davis. And no matter how far removed they were from the ideological violence of contemporary European fascism, the fictional fantasies of Faulkner's Gail Hightower in *Light in August* or the lacerating self-destructiveness of Bayard Sartoris in *Flags in the Dust* and the sophisticated poetry of Tate or Donald Davidson in his "Lee in the Mountains," all testified to the barely submerged violence that threatened to surface in the Southern tradition at its time of dissolution.

Certainly [Hannah] Arendt's description of reality become "fantastic" could stand as a general characteristic for much of the literature of Renaissance, a sort of modernist gothic style. What else is Faulkner wrestling with in his work up through, say, *Absalom, Absalom!*? And surely W. J. Cash and Lillian Smith were preoccupied with the fantastic aspects of Southern culture, the ways in which historically shaped desires and their inverse, self-destructiveness, had woven a texture which stifled rather than gave comfort. Though the question of when a culture becomes fantastic is terribly complicated, not least because all cultures are based upon certain fantasies, a provisional answer might apply the pragmatic criterion: when it no longer "works." Themes and motifs split off and become isolated from the whole; they are spun out into whole visions. One might also say, following Freud, that in fantasy there is a refusal to acknowledge that we must die, that we have a body which imposes certain limits on us, and that we must live in a world with other people. In cultures grown fantastic, the regression or reactionary form of memory is dominant. Time is denied. . . .

But in the Southern Renaissance a second movement of memory despaired of the repetition which marked the culture of melancholy and set about scrutinizing the tradition of the family romance itself. As seen in Faulkner's Quentin Compson of *Absalom, Absalom!* and in Tate's work, beginning with "Ode to the Confederate Dead" and culminating in *The Fathers,* this form of historical consciousness ends in a tragic confusion between past and present, fantasy and reality. Neither repetition nor recollection can triumph. What recollection reveals is the violence and horror at the heart of the tradition itself, or its weakness and contradictions. Time becomes an obsession, and the founding of the tradition and the costs thereby incurred are emphasized.

The third mode of historical consciousness moved toward a reconstitution of "reality" after having carried through on a demystification of the family romance. Building upon the agonized analysis of the second stage, it incorporated and transcended the Southern tradition as previously conceived. As seen in Faulkner's "The Bear" and the writings of W. J. Cash and Lillian Smith, memory emerges from the trap of fantasy which is organized around the judgments of the founding fathers. Recollection triumphs over repetition; not only the impossibility but the undesirability of resurrecting the tradition become clear.

These three stages of historical consciousness present analogies to the unfolding and transformation of memory in psychoanalysis. In both instances, the past is problematic: now overpowering, now completely absent from memory, it is debilitating. What had been assumed as "mine" now appears as "other" and strange. In the final stage this "otherness" is demystified and reassimilated after having been worked through. It is incorporated into a new synthesis. The movement is from incapacitating repetition to recollection and then to self-consciousness, from identity to estrangement and back to incorporation at a higher level. Beyond Nietzsche's monumental and critical forms of historical consciousness, a new form—the analytic or the ironic—emerges. One awakens from the nightmare of history.

Thus the modes of historical consciousness which emerged in the 1930s and 1940s were manifestations of the ambivalent spirit of cultural modernism. The prototypical historical consciousness of the modern period is obsessed with the past and the precarious possibilities of its survival. In addition, the preoccupation with the past among Southern writers and intellectuals in this period was typically Southern. Still, they were by no means united in their attitudes toward the past in general or toward the family romance in particular. The decades after 1930 were to see a reassessment of the Southern tradition.

Mobilizing the Invisible Army

NANCY MACLEAN

If there were such a thing as a typical Klan meeting, the klonklave held by the Athens Klan on the night of September 15, 1925, would qualify. Exalted Cyclops *J.P. Mangum,** a fifty-two-year-old policeman, called the meeting to order at 8:30 in the Klan's klavern (meeting hall). Presiding over the evening's events with *Mangum* was a full complement of twelve "terrors" (officers). In many regards, the meeting resembled one any other organization might hold: minutes read and approved, new members voted in, dues collected, plans laid for a recruitment campaign, an educational discussion, and even niceties: members received thanks from *Mangum* for having visited him when he was sick and from the board of stewards of a local church for having attended its recent revival meeting with a contribution.

Yet, mundane as the proceedings were, a few signs indicated that this club differed from others—notwithstanding the order's policy of not allowing discussions in meetings of "any subject, which, if published, would reflect discredit upon our great movement." Among the humdrum bills paid, for example, was one for labor and materials for a "fiery cross." Then there were the applications to join, some from previous members, that the Klansmen in attendance voted to reject. The chapter had recently reorganized due to a public scandal over the use of extralegal methods to combat vice, and it seems these men were viewed as possibly disloyal— "loose-mouth," "weak-kneed," or "traitors," in Klan parlance. Finally, one brief item in the minutes hinted at why absolute loyalty was so necessary. *L.S. Fleming,* the chapter Klokan (investigator), reported the case of a man who had been brought to the Klan's attention for failing to support his family. Not a few such delinquents found themselves kidnapped and flogged by crews of masked men in the 1920s.

Such blending of the ordinary and the extreme was common in the Klan of the 1920s; indeed, the blurring proved a source of strength. . . .

The second Klan's founder, William Joseph Simmons, had not explicitly included such things among the Klan's goals when he established the order in 1915. The son of a poor Alabama country physician, Simmons was a man chronically on the make. Having tried his hand at farming, circuit-riding as a Southern Methodist Episcopal Church preacher, and lecturing in Southern history at Lanier University, by 1915 he had settled into a mildly lucrative position as the Atlanta-area organizer for the Woodmen of the World, a fraternal benefit society. Unsatisfied, Simmons dreamed of reviving the hooded order his father had served in as an officer after the Civil War.

For years, he thought about creating a new Ku Klux Klan. By October of 1915, he was ready to unveil the plans to a group of like-minded friends. Together, the group petitioned for a charter from the state. Then, on Thanksgiving night, they met atop Stone Mountain, an imposing several-hundred-foot-high granite butte just outside Atlanta. With a flag fluttering in the wind beside them, a Bible open to the

*Names in italics have been changed.

twelfth chapter of Romans, and a flaming cross to light the night sky above, Simmons and his disciples proclaimed the new Knights of the Ku Klux Klan. Their passion for ceremony was not matched by a talent for organizing, however. Unclear about exactly what their message was, Simmons and his partners floundered over how to spread it. By early 1920, they had only enrolled a few thousand men.

That would soon change. In June of that year, Simmons signed a contract with Mary Elizabeth Tyler and Edward Young Clarke, partners in the Southern Publicity Association. Having organized support for the Red Cross, the Anti-Saloon League, the Salvation Army, and the War Work Council, the two had mastered the art of modern propaganda. Hiring a staff of seasoned organizers, they set to work to amass a following for the Klan and a small fortune for themselves. Within a few months, membership jumped to an estimated 100,000. A wife at age fourteen and a widowed mother at fifteen who went on to make a career as a businesswoman, Tyler had a knack for turning adversity to advantage. When in 1921 the *New York World* set out to destroy the Klan by documenting over one hundred and fifty separate cases of vigilante violence charged to it—an exposure so damning that it prompted a congressional investigation of the order—Tyler turned both into recruiting opportunities. In the four months after the *World*'s exposé, the Klan chartered two hundred new chapters; overall membership leapt to some one million.

Seasoned promoters, Tyler and Clarke knew not only how to sell, but what would sell. To Simmons' initial blend of white supremacy, Christianity, and the male-bonding rituals of fraternalism, they added elements geared to tap the fears of many white contemporaries in the anxious years after the Great War. Declaiming against organized blacks, Catholics, and Jews, along with the insidious encroachments of Bolshevism, the order put itself forward as the country's most militant defender of "pure Americanism." It stood for patriotism, "old-time religion," and conventional morality, and pledged to fend off challenges from any quarter to the rights and privileges of men from the stock of the nation's founders. The message took. Although Tyler and Clarke had expected only Southerners to respond, men from all over the country did. "In all my years of experience in organization work," Clarke told Simmons, "I have never seen anything equal to the clamor throughout the nation for the Klan." . . .

Following a strategy devised by the Atlanta-based national office, Athens Klan promoters worked existing networks in the community to accumulate members. They looked to two areas in particular where it seemed their message might be well-received: fraternal orders and Protestant churches. The Klan presented itself to prospective members as the active embodiment of "the principles of the better class of lodges." Simmons, a member of fifteen other fraternal organizations himself, rallied men with odes to "the united powers of our regal manhood." To enhance the Klan's mystique, he designed a special alliterative lexicon for the movement. And he painstakingly worked out the details of elaborate rituals whereby members advanced in the order by obtaining "degrees" as they did in other fraternal orders. When he first came to Athens to advertise the new order in 1915, Simmons in fact emphasized "its unrivaled degree work." Many local Klansmen took the bait; they delighted in impressing their fellows with their mastery of Klan ritual.

In presenting their order thus, Klan organizers staked a bid for the loyalties of participants in the long tradition of fraternal association. The country had over six

hundred secret societies by the mid-1920s; together, they enlisted over thirty million people. The Klan curried support from a number of these groups, especially
those of common mind. It endorsed the *Fellowship Forum,* an anti-Catholic publication that claimed a readership of one million white, Protestant fraternalists. The
Junior Order of United American Mechanics (JOUAM), an anti-Catholic, nativist
fraternity whose better-known members included populist leader Tom Watson and
President Warren Harding, was also known as "a close ally" of the Klan. Indeed, the
Georgia JOUAM shared its weekly Atlanta-based publication, *The Searchlight,*
with the Klan until the Klan formally took it over in October of 1923. The distinction between the two was moot in any case, since Klan leader J. O. Wood edited the
newspaper.

Klan leaders cultivated their common ground with fraternal orders to reap a
bumper crop of recruits. . . .

The strategy worked. Even the meager records available for local fraternal orders reveal that a minimum of 120 Athens Klansmen, or twenty-nine percent, belonged to at least one. Among those that shared members with the Klan were the
Woodmen of the World, the Elks, the Masons, the Odd Fellows, the Knights of
Pythias, and the Shriners. Several Clarke County Klansmen also held office in these
groups. . . .

. . . Nationwide, the Klan boasted that 500,000 Masons had joined by 1923.
Along with members of other fraternal organizations, they often formed the backbone of local chapters.

. . . Throughout the country, evangelical Protestants in particular flocked to the
Klan, primarily Baptists, Methodists, and members of the Church of Christ, the
Disciples of Christ, and the United Brethren. Men in more élite or liberal denominations, in contrast, such as Unitarians, Congregationalists, Lutherans, or Episcopalians, appeared less likely to join. . . . Even the patchy church records available
showed that at least forty-three percent of Athens Klansmen belonged to a church—
about the same proportion as that of all white county residents. Of these, thirty-
seven percent were Baptists; thirty percent, Methodists; and smaller proportions
scattered among other denominations.

Many Athens Klan laymen helped lead their churches. At least forty-six held
positions such as deacon, elder, steward, committee member, usher, or Sunday
School participant. Twelve Klansmen took part in the Men's Sunday School class at
First Methodist Church alone. Some members advanced the cause in other ways.
Klansman *L. T. Curry* served as Treasurer of the Businessmen's Evangelistic Club,
while *N. O. Bowers* championed "personal evangelism" among young people
through the Christian Endeavor Society. The wives and mothers of many local
Klansmen, for their part, participated in the women's missionary societies of their
churches.

Like laymen, many clergymen cooperated with the Klan. Of the thirty-nine national lecturers working for the Klan at one point, two-thirds were said to be Protestant ministers. Each Klan chapter, meanwhile, had its own kludd (chaplain). By
1924, the Klan boasted that it had enrolled 30,000 ministers. In that year, the Klan
also claimed as members three-quarters of the 6,000 delegates to the Southeastern
Baptist Convention. In Clarke County, most of the white Protestant churches had
some connection to the Klan. Either their pastors belonged, or they allowed

announcements of Klan meetings or robed visits of Klansmen during services, or they accepted Klan aid in evangelistic efforts. . . .

Through such channels, the Klan built up its numbers. By 1923, its ranks included "three hundred of the finest men in Clarke County." Confident of their future, they began building a new klavern to hold their meetings. Members proudly announced that the hall would sport a forty-foot-tall electric cross. With its membership hovering around three hundred the next few years, the local chapter was a "baby Klan," as *The Searchlight* put it. The chapter drew in approximately one in ten of the native-born, Protestant white men eligible for membership—a considerable proportion, but small relative to some of its counterparts.

Statewide, the Klan also thrived in the first half of the decade. Since Atlanta hosted the Klan's national office, or Imperial Palace, Georgia always played a significant role in Klan affairs. The Atlanta Klan enrolled upwards of fifteen thousand members and boasted the largest fraternal hall in the city. By the mid-'twenties, chapters blanketed the state. . . .

In the nation as a whole, Georgia ranked eighth among states in estimated membership. Among regions, the North Central and Southwestern states enrolled the most members, followed by the Southeast, the Midwest and Far West, and, finally, the North Atlantic states. By mid-decade, the total reached perhaps as high as five million, distributed through nearly four thousand local chapters. Yet the numbers barely suggest the reach of the Klan's tentacles. If its membership claims were true, the order enrolled as many members as the American Federation of Labor at the peak of its strength. . . .

But their effect was enhanced by the kind of men the Klan was able to attract. The typical member, in Athens as elsewhere, was not the uprooted angry young man one might expect; he was middle-aged, married, and probably a father as well. Ninety-two percent of Athens Klan members were married men; more than two-thirds were fathers, with an average of between three and four children. While most local Klansmen were family men, not a few were civic leaders. . . .

Just as the Klan recruited men from the mainstream, so it boosted members' morale with the kinds of family and community activities that clubs and churches also sponsored. Although excluded from the Klan itself, Klansmen's wives and sons could join parallel orders: the Women of the Ku Klux Klan, created in 1923, and the Junior Klan, created in 1924. Here, without distracting attention from the leading roles of their menfolk, family members might work for shared ends. Athens Klanswomen and men thus cooperated to reward a visiting minister with an automobile for his leadership of a successful revival at East Athens Baptist Church in 1926, winning themselves the gratitude of the church's chairmen and deacons. The following year, they collaborated on a fund-raiser whose end was "to place a Flag and Bible" in the city high school.

Klan chapters promoted sociability and mutual aid as well. At Klan picnics such as the "Great Klan Barbecue" hosted by Athens Klansmen in 1928, members gathered with their families and friends for afternoons of music, sports, and swimming, along with speeches. Sometimes, Klan rallies featured weddings of members, public rituals that interwove personal and political commitments. More important, fellow Klansmen were on hand in times of trouble. . . . How much such courtesies meant was evident when the mother of two local Klansmen and grandmother of another passed away. Her six children and their spouses, "representing forty grand-children and twenty great-grandchildren," joined to thank the Athens Klan and ask "God's richest blessings" for each of its members.

And yet Klansmen were not just Odd Fellows in robes and hoods. For all the ties that bound Klansmen to commonplace community networks and habits, the Klan was different. Leaders reminded members that their organization was "not a lodge," but "an army of Protestant Americans." As a *"mass movement"* to secure the alleged birthright of Anglo-Saxon Americans, it could achieve that goal only through "an aggressive application of the art of Klan craft." That required winning the confi-dence of the community by recruiting respected local men and making the Klan a *"civic asset."* In short, breaking into church and fraternal networks was part of a larger strategy to accrue power. And that power would be used toward ends some people in these networks might balk at.

Signs that the second Klan would be more than just another community or-ganization were there from the beginning, not least in its name. The first call to re-establish the Klan came, not from William Joseph Simmons, but from Tom Watson. The foremost leader of Georgia's Populist movement in the 1890s, Watson had long since given up the struggle for interracial economic justice. Recently, he had turned his attention to Catholic and Jewish subversion. In August of 1915, he informed readers of his Georgia-based *Jeffersonian* magazine that "another Ku Klux Klan may have to be organized to restore Home Rule." Georgia's governor had just com-muted the death sentence of Leo Frank, a Jewish factory supervisor convicted of the murder of Mary Phagan, a young white woman in his employ. The governor's mercy enraged those who believed Frank guilty, Watson among them. Four days af-ter he issued his incitement, a body of men calling themselves the Knights of Mary Phagan kidnapped Frank from the state prison farm, took him to her home town, and hanged him from a tree.

Three months later, Simmons resurrected the Knights of the Ku Klux Klan in Atlanta, where Frank's alleged crime and his trial had taken place. The Frank case has often been cited as a catalyst for the creation of the second Klan, whose found-ing members, according to popular myth, included some of the Knights of Mary Phagan. In fact, no one has ever documented a direct connection between the two. The "truth" of the link lay less in personnel than in a common vigilante spirit. An appeal to that spirit would always be part of the Klan. Its promise of swift and secret vengeance, more than anything else, distinguished it from contemporary organiza-tions with whom it shared ideas, rituals, and members.

Nothing in the early years helped more to make that promise come to life than D. W. Griffith's film extravaganza, *Birth of a Nation,* released in the same year as the second Klan's creation. In this racist epic of the Civil War, Reconstruction, and the restoration of white rule, Griffith harnessed all the emotive power of modern film-making technique to convince viewers that black men were beasts and white vigilantes were the saviors of American civilization. Given the right to vote and hold office, the film averred, African-American men dragged society into chaos; worse, they used such power to stalk white women. Griffith left no doubt about how this fate had been averted. In the final, climactic scene, the hooded and robed mem-bers of the Ku Klux Klan rode in to save his young white heroine from rape—by castrating and lynching her black would-be assailant. Their act ended sectional fratricide among white men and gave birth to a reunited America.

For the Klan, the film proved a boon. When it came to Atlanta for a three-week showing, record-breaking white crowds packed the theaters to cheer on the white-robed crusaders. Recognizing an opportunity, Simmons ran newspaper advertisements for the revived order next to those for the film. Thereafter, the Klan routinely exploited showings of *Birth of a Nation* to enlist new members, for it sent the message the Klan wanted delivered. "No one who has seen the film," commented journalist Walter Lippmann in 1922, "will ever hear the name [Ku Klux Klan] again without seeing those white horsemen." Not surprisingly, the NAACP sought—in vain—to have the film removed from circulation.

Black Americans in fact understood from the beginning that the second Klan was different, even from other racist organizations. In the view of many, it was an immediate threat. One month after the second Klan's founding ceremony, Georgia Republican leader Henry Lincoln Johnson begged the governor to make the order change its name, on the grounds that the Klan's re-establishment would encourage "mob outlawry." "My people (the colored people)," Johnson predicted, "will be the helpless, and often vicarious, victims." He was right. "Nobody knows," complained a Black Atlanta lodge officer to the NAACP in 1921, "the great destress" that this "great evil" had brought upon the black people of Georgia. The state's leading African-American newspaper, *The Atlanta Independent,* for its part, said of the second Klan that, like the first, its "aim and purpose is to terrorize helpless black men and women." "The epitome of race hatred and religious intolerance," it constituted "the most dangerous menace that ever threatened popular government."

Outside Georgia, members of other groups the Klan pitted itself against made it clear that they, too, saw the order as outside the framework of ordinary politics. The editor of the *Catholic World,* for example, warned in 1923 that if the Klan were allowed to persist and the state failed to protect Catholic citizens from its provocations, they would employ "self-defense, even to the extent of bloodshed." In that year, in fact, Catholics were the leading force in organizing a militant anti-Klan group called the "Red Knights," or "Knights of the Flaming Circle." The group welcomed anyone opposed to the Klan and not a Protestant, and was said to be recruiting well in Pennsylvania and West Virginia, and later in the industrial cities of Ohio as well. In several parts of the country, often under the auspices of the Red Knights, Catholics responded to the Klan's provocations with mass, armed counterattacks so determined that the National Guard was called out on at least one occasion.

Some radical farmers and unionists shared the Red Knights' assessment of the novel danger posed by the Klan. Iowa farmers charged a Klan meeting with pitchforks; their counterparts in the Arkansas mountains turned shotguns on Klan intruders, killing one and wounding several. The United Mine Workers of America (UMWA), a renegade in the contemporary craft-dominated labor movement because of its commitment to interracial industrial unionism, tried to close ranks against the Klan. In 1921, while leaders of the American Federation of Labor equivocated, refusing a black delegation to its national convention the right to introduce a resolution calling for the suppression of the Klan, the UMWA barred from its ranks miners who joined the Klan. Although unable to rid the union of Klan influence, many militants tried. Oklahoma UMWA members spied on a Klan meeting and expelled the miners who attended, while their Pennsylvania counterparts put union members suspected of Klan membership on trial.

The imminent dangers perceived by the Klan's targets offer a clue to why the order did not take off until 1921. For one thing, an organized national vigilante movement would probably have seemed superfluous before that. . . .

The Espionage and Sedition Acts of 1917 and 1918 backed community pressures for "one hundred percent Americanism" with censorship and possible prison terms for dissenters. Insulating the war effort from criticism was only part of their purpose; suppressing domestic labor struggle and left-wing radicalism was as important. These strictures had barely been lifted before the postwar Red Scare, the most extensive peacetime violation of civil liberties in United States history, began. Its climax was the Palmer Raids of January 1920, a nationwide dragnet against radicals named for the Attorney General under whose direction they proceeded. As national leaders gradually began to breathe more freely after 1920 and favor a return to normal methods of rule, so did many local élites. Then the kind of methods they had recently endorsed came to seem excessive, even illegitimate.

In Athens, some became nervous when the Klan sought to keep the wartime spirit alive for its own purposes. When the Klan returned to Athens in 1921 and promoted itself as a force for "law and order," the implicit promise was that it would enforce its concept of order in a manner similar to its namesake's. Recoiling, some one hundred "good citizens" signed a petition against it. Their numbers included many prominent civic and business leaders. The signers declared that the "announced purposes of the Ku Klux Klan . . . have the approval of all good citizens." They took issue with the order on only one point: its usurpation of the powers of lawfully "constituted authorities." The Klan may have performed a necessary service during Reconstruction, they argued, but "no such necessity exists now." Hence its re-establishment was "ill advised," and its "self-constituted guardians of the peace, working at night and in disguise" were mistaken in their zeal. However timid their criticism of the Klan, the signers did understand its penchant for violence. To silence them, Klan leaders rounded up more imposing voices. . . .

. . . [T]he Klan steamrollered opposition and gained influence in Georgia. Broker of the votes of an estimated 100,000 of the state's 300,000 Democrats by 1923, the Klan held "the balance of power" in state politics, as even a reporter who sought to play down its domination had to admit. The order enrolled such well-placed officials as Governor Clifford Walker, Chief Justice of the State Supreme Court Richard B. Russell, Sr., State Attorney General George M. Napier, Atlanta Mayor Walter A. Sims, Solicitor General (district attorney) of Fulton County John M. Boykin, and Fulton Superior Court Judge Gus H. Howard, in addition to many less strategically placed men. Some evidence suggests that the roster also included Georgia's United States senators Tom Watson, Walter George, and William J. Harris; United States congressman and past president of the Anti-Saloon League W. D. Upshaw, and President of the Georgia State Senate Herbert Clay.

Similar patterns prevailed elsewhere. In 1923, for example, at least seventy-five congressional representatives were said to owe their seats to the Klan; at the annual conference of state governors the year before, only one was willing to discuss, let alone condemn, the Klan. The reason was not hard to find. The Klan held sway in the political life of many states; it dominated some outright, such as Indiana and Colorado; and it swept anti-Klan governors from office in a number of others, most spectacularly in Oregon and Kansas.

The ability to dispose of opponents so handily where it had the requisite numbers gives an indication of why Klan leaders put such a high premium on electoral politics. "It is of vital importance that our friends be placed in office," Georgia's Grand Dragon explained; "the life of our organization" might hinge upon the outcome of elections. . . .

But it was back at home that the insulation mattered most. With it, the Klan could fend off measures that might have made its night-riding operations more difficult, such as a 1922 bill—aimed at the Klan—to prevent the wearing of masks on Georgia's public highways. The order went on to deliver one of the biggest electoral defeats in state history to the governor who proposed it, Thomas W. Hardwick. His successor, Clifford Walker, a Klansman himself, learned the lesson. As governor, he consulted Klan leaders before introducing new initiatives to the state assembly. On the local level, prosecution of Klan violence was hardly likely when municipal governments, police departments, and courts were rife with Klan members and sympathizers. "Everybody in the courthouse belonged to the Klan" in Atlanta, recalled a local city attorney; "virtually every judge, the prosecuting officers . . . all the police and the mayor and the councilmen." If he exaggerated, it was not by much. With the cards thus stacked in its favor, the Klan could act with impunity.

Indeed, newspaper editors in the South, like politicians, tended to quaver in the face of Klan's power. Clearly, they did not view the order as an innocent analogue of other fraternal lodges. While local papers boosted these, most maintained an eerie silence regarding the Klan's activities. Few offered outright support, yet neither would they investigate or expose it. With the notable exceptions of the *Columbus Enquirer-Sun* and eventually the *Macon Telegraph,* no Georgia newspapers condemned the Klan until the second half of the decade, when its power had begun to wane. The Athens press was no exception. . . . "Nothing unpleasant must ever be printed" seemed to be the operating principle of most newspapers, observed one Athens educator and resident; another later recalled, "they put only nice things in the *Banner-Herald.*"

Night-riding and inciting hatred were not nice; neither were they "newsworthy" if their targets were blacks or poor whites. The topic was just too ticklish to touch. Coverage of the Klan's activities, after all, might deter outside investors, agitate blacks, and stimulate discord among whites—to say nothing of losing subscriptions. Yet, uneasiness about the Klan's methods remained. The Athens press thus gave editorial support to two area judges who came out against the Klan in 1926 for its "lawlessness," its efforts "to intimidate men and . . . dominate who shall run for office," and its habit of "trying men in secret." Throughout the South, in fact, the most commonly stated rationale for élite opposition to the Klan was, in the words of one Texas judge, that society could not abide "two systems of government for punishing crime," one "working at night with a bucket of tar and a sack of feathers."

After Scopes: Evolution in the South

WILLARD B. GATEWOOD, JR.

Whether the so-called monkey trial at Dayton, Tennessee, in July 1925 was a decisive moment in the history of Christianity as William Jennings Bryan suggested or "an obscenity of the very first calibre" as Henry L. Mencken believed, it was the biggest and best newspaper story in the decade after World War I. On hand to witness the trial of John Thomas Scopes, the local football coach and high school teacher accused of violating Tennessee's new law against the teaching of Darwin's theory of evolution, was a larger contingent of newsmen than covered the naval limitation conference in Washington four years earlier. The principal attraction in the sleepy town in the Tennessee hills—"forty miles from the nearest city and a million miles away from anything urban, sophisticated and exciting"—was not young Scopes, but rather two nationally known verbal pugilists, William Jennings Bryan, whom the World's Christian Fundamentals Association dispatched to assist the prosecution, and Clarence Darrow, who headed the legal team sent by the American Civil Liberties Union to defend Scopes.

The Scopes trial quickly took its place alongside the Ku Klux Klan as a standard ingredient in the version of a Benighted South that emerged in the 1920s. That the South was the scene of a succession of well publicized battles over Darwin's theory and the only region of the country that kept monkey laws on the statute books for over forty years lent credence to the view that militant opposition to biological evolution was as southern as racism and states' rights. In one form or another the idea that campaigns against Darwin were rustic capers by ignorant religious zealots of the southern hinterlands has persisted since the 1920s. Such a view, while not without elements of truth, tends to distort the role of the South in the controversies over evolution that have periodically erupted in the twentieth century and to obscure the scope and meaning of these struggles.

To interpret the disturbances over Darwin as rural in origin, much less as mere regional phenomena, is to fly in the face of considerable evidence to the contrary. The antievolution campaigns, whether in the form of laws banning the theory from public schools in the 1920s or of acquiring "equal time" for creation science more than a half century later, were not isolated local efforts by a handful of untutored clerical zealots hostile to science per se. Rather they represented the most publicized aspect of a larger, more complex movement known as fundamentalism, a version of evangelical Protestantism that emerged in the late nineteenth century. Northern and urban in origin, fundamentalism was a supernatural, biblically-based faith, often with a premillenialist orientation and always militantly opposed to liberal theology and the cultural changes it accommodated. Constituting a formidable coalition by the end of World War I, fundamentalists embarked upon a nationwide

Willard B. Gatewood, in *The South Is Another Land: Essays on the Twentieth Century South,* B. Clayton & J. Salmond, eds (Greenwood Press, Westport, CT, 1987). Copyright © 1987 by Bruce Clayton and John A. Salmond. Reprinted with permission.

offensive in the 1920s that for a time filled the air with the sounds of ferocious combat and that polarized American Protestantism into warring camps.

. . . The fundamentalist theology that came to maturity in the era of World War I was in many respects similar to what Victor I. Masters, a prominent southern Baptist, described in 1915 as "the Anglo-Saxon evangelical faith" of the South. Essential in both was a belief in a divinely inspired, errorless Bible as the source of all that was "decent and right in our civilization." For fundamentalists, their battle for the Bible was a battle for civilization. In the South, where the "Anglo-Saxon evangelical faith" was linked with cultural conservatism, the battle for the Bible easily became a battle for the southern way of life. . . .

The strong antimodernist impulse, evident throughout southern Protestantism, early identified Darwin's theory as a threat to the integrity of the errorless Scriptures. Among the victims of the bias against evolution in the late nineteenth century was James Woodrow, an uncle of Woodrow Wilson, who in 1886 was dismissed from the Southern Presbyterian Seminary in South Carolina for insisting that evolution was compatible with the book of Genesis. Concern about the dangers of the "new theology" that accompanied the emergence of fundamentalism not only caused southerners to be on guard against its appearance in their midst but also prompted greater attention to what was viewed as a critical component of that theology, namely evolution. . . .

In a region so proud of its reputation as "the stronghold of orthodox Christianity in this country" and traditionally hostile to Darwin, the antievolutionist rhetoric proved extraordinarily effective in galvanizing public opinion in favor of statutes to outlaw evolution. The crusade against evolution in the South, as Wilbur J. Cash observed, was not the work of a "small, highly organized pressure group," but rather "an authentic folk movement.". . . Ultimately five states—Oklahoma, Florida, Tennessee, Mississippi and Arkansas—enacted antievolution measures. More remarkable, perhaps, in view of the regional obsession with Darwin, was the failure of similar legislation elsewhere in the South.

If evolution was the issue that allowed organized fundamentalism to attract a mass audience and broad support for a time, it was also the issue on which the movement foundered. The ridicule and derision heaped upon fundamentalists in the wake of the Scopes trial, coupled with the loss of their most popular and prestigious spokesman with the death of Bryan shortly afterward, disrupted their coalition and diminished their influence. Diffused among rival organizations and individuals with a penchant for the sensational and bizarre, fundamentalism began to conform to its new image as the representative of "the forces of organized ignorance."

Emerging from the struggles of the 1920s without capturing control of a single major denomination and stereotyped as combative eccentrics existing on the fringes of modern culture, fundamentalists were no longer newsworthy by the early 1930s. Contrary to pronouncements by some liberal religious journals, neither fundamentalism nor hostility to evolution disappeared. The latter for a time went into "remission," but fundamentalism put down roots outside the mainline denominations and ultimately developed into what has been termed "a second wing of Protestantism" whose growing numerical strength and influence went largely unnoticed in the secular press until after World War II. Nor did fundamentalism remain static. In the decades after the 1920s it came to include a succession of separatist groups that continued to wear with pride the "fundamentalist" label and nurtured other, more moderate elements known as evangelicals. . . .

. . . Viewing themselves as a faithful remnant surrounded by infidels and false prophets and no more reconciled to Darwin's theory than their forebears, fundamentalists in the South as elsewhere concentrated their energies on establishing an institutional base outside the major denominations. Rather than mounting crusades against evolution, they dedicated themselves to organizing churches, seminaries, colleges and Bible schools, mission programs, and publishing and broadcasting concerns. The results, by any standard of measurement, were spectacular.

. . . Preeminent among fundamentalist institutions of higher education in the South were Bob Jones University and Dallas Theological Seminary, both founded in the 1920s, which exerted influence far beyond the boundaries of the Old Confederacy. . . .

During the fifty years following the Dayton Affair the South witnessed the emergence of numerous independent churches, sects, and religious organizations of a fundamentalist variety. The separatist tendencies that prompted the exodus of fundamentalists from the major denominations persisted in the continual division and subdivision within their own ranks later. . . .

Magazines, tracts, and various other publications that poured forth from fundamentalist presses in the region, sometimes in multiple printings of more than one hundred thousand copies, regularly reminded the faithful of the dangers inherent in Darwin's theory. For a generation beginning in 1934, for example, John R. Rice, a Baptist revivalist and radio preacher with headquarters in Murfreesboro, Tennessee, waged war on the theory, especially in his publication *The Sword of the Lord* and in the tracts and books published by his Sword of the Lord Press. The author of 124 books and pamphlets with a combined circulation of thirty-six million, Rice consistently argued that evolution was an "infidel guess" and a "part of the doctrine and ideology of Communism."

Individuals active in the antievolution crusade of the 1920s who continued to oppose Darwin's theory throughout the quarter of a century afterward kept the issue alive and prepared the soil in which creation science would flourish in the 1970s. . . . [One who was] significant was the flamboyant, controversial J. Frank Norris of Texas, editor of *The Fundamentalist* and "the epitome of the independent fundamental Baptist" who exerted a powerful influence in fundamentalist circles for almost three decades after the Scopes trial. A whole generation of preachers and evangelists were "inspired by his example" and "hundreds of churches" organized through his influence. By his own admission one of his most notable achievements was his war on evolution that resulted in the purging of the Baylor University faculty of "seven evolution professors." The ever broadening base of southern fundamentalism and the virile legacies bequeathed by . . . Norris and others insured the survival of antievolution sentiment in the South.

Class differences tended to obscure the substantial areas of agreement that existed between conservatives in the mainline southern churches and the more militant, separatist fundamentalists. Although those independent Baptists outside the Southern Baptist Convention viewed those inside as "false prophets" or compromisers, the southern Baptist fold itself as well as other mainline denominations included many whose beliefs and attitudes intersected at various points with those of their more separatist-oriented fundamentalist brethren. Their similarities became evident in 1968 in a book entitled *Why I Preach the Bible Is Literally True,* written by W. A. Criswell, the pastor of the First Baptist Church in Dallas and president of the Southern Baptist Convention. The point was that many southern churchmen, though repelled by the bizarre antics of some fundamentalists and resentful of the ridicule heaped upon the South as a result of the Scopes trial, were nonetheless in sympathy with the intent of antievolution legislation, which in the words of the Tennessee governor in 1925 was "to protest the tendency to exalt science and deny the Bible." . . .

. . . By 1931 five southern states required Bible reading and six others permitted it. Except for Louisiana, where a large Catholic population precluded a Protestant consensus, Bible reading became virtually a universal practice in public schools throughout the South. While the pattern in regard to the teaching of biological evolution was probably less uniform, there is substantial evidence to indicate that Darwin's theory was a topic that teachers in the region either chose to ignore altogether or to approach with great caution.

After the enactment of the Arkansas antievolution measure in 1929, which marked the end of legislative activity for almost fifty years, a common observation, especially by apologists for the South, was that the existence of monkey laws in three states posed no threat and were in fact meaningless. . . .

The mere existence of antievolution laws not only acted as a deterrent to free discussions of evolution, but they also made available to disgruntled citizens legal instruments for disciplining teachers and administrators they found objectionable on other grounds. In 1929, for example, a high school principal in Fentress County, Tennessee, who incurred the enmity of two citizens because he suspended their children from school for a fireworks prank, was brought to trial and accused, among other things, of teaching evolution. Although the evolution charge was obviously added in an attempt to arouse community opinion against the principal, he was ultimately cleared of all charges. "It must now appear plain," the Memphis *Commercial Appeal* editorialized regarding the Fentress County case, "that the [antievolution] law is not going to be permitted to enjoy a dead letter status." Somewhat similar to the Fentress County case was a suit filed in 1967 by a group of taxpayers in Izard County, Arkansas, charging the superintendent with misusing funds and with "allowing textbooks that teach evolution in the schools in violation of the law." Again evolution "was thrown in to add comfort to the other charge" against the superintendent. . . .

The widespread acceptance of such a view in the South was sufficient to intimidate teachers and administrators who were sympathetic to evolution. The UABS survey revealed that biology teachers from North Carolina, a state that defeated evolution laws in the 1920s and prided itself in being in the vanguard of southern progressivism, were acutely aware of the risks involved in frank discussions of evolution in the classroom. Darwin's theory was, according to one teacher in the state, "a taboo subject to most people in the state"; others agreed and indicated that they avoided any treatment of it in order not "to stir up trouble." In 1971, thirty years after the UABS survey, popular hostility to Darwin's theory may have subsided but had scarcely disappeared in North Carolina. In that year Gaston County school officials summarily dismissed George Ivey Moore, a student teacher in a junior high school, "for having responded to students' questions with answers approving the Darwinism theory, indicating personal agnosticism and questioning the literal interpretation of the Bible." Moore filed suit in federal court and won. The judge ruled that Gaston County school authorities had violated the establishment clause of the First Amendment by officially approving, in effect, "local orthodoxy" in regards to Darwin's theory of evolution. As the judge noted, the very word "evolution" still "struck a nerve" in Gaston County.

In view of the lucrative market in school textbooks it is hardly surprising that publishers were careful to avoid striking the same nerve. As a result, during the decades following the Scopes trial high school biology textbooks underwent significant revision in deference to antievolution opinion in the United States. . . .

Throughout the fifty years after the Scopes trial various individuals and organizations, including scientific and academic groups, attempted in vain to secure the repeal of the monkey laws in Tennessee and Arkansas. . . .

A bill to repeal the Tennessee antievolution law in 1929 met with no more success than those in Arkansas. Later efforts to repeal the Tennessee measure in 1931, 1935, 1939, 1951, and 1961 also failed but not before sparking legislative debates remarkably similar in content and tone to those during the 1920s. Legislators favoring repeal spoke as advocates of liberty and enlightenment who deeply resented the injury to "the good name of the state" prompted by the antics of what they called "a few narrow, prejudiced religious fanatics." Those who opposed repeal included some who preferred to leave the monkey law "quietly and peacefully sleeping" rather than remind the world of its existence. But the majority of the opponents still believed that Darwin's theory was incompatible with their religious faith and a serious threat to morality, ethics, and decency. "If this act is repealed," a Tennessee legislator declared in 1931, "we may as well close our Bibles, turn our backs on Christian people and let this state go to hell." Thirty years later Tennessee legislators, among many others throughout the South, voiced identical sentiments.

In the half century after the Scopes trial the South underwent dramatic social and economic changes; industrialization, urbanization, a steady climb out of education deprivation, a Second Reconstruction that destroyed the legal foundations of racial segregation and prompted references to a "post-racial south," and increased per capita wealth substantially reduced some of the statistical disparities that traditionally distinguished the region from the rest of the nation. Much of the progress in education that commentators in the 1920s considered essential to overcome public hostility to evolution in the South had been achieved by a half century later, but somehow more and better public schools failed to eradicate opposition to Darwin's theory. Notwithstanding the preference of chambers of commerce and other regional boosters for the label "sunbelt," the South remained the Bible Belt. A sociologist writing in 1972 concluded that there was no substantial decrease in "Southern religious peculiarity in the recent past and no prospects for the decrease in the near future." In 1925 Henry L. Mencken observed while returning to Baltimore from Dayton that one could throw a brick out of the train window anywhere in route and hit a fundamentalist on the head. Allowing for Mencken's imprecise use of "fundamentalist" as a pejorative term for a broad spectrum of southern churchmen, his observation possessed considerable validity—and still did a half century later. The typical nonsouthern image of southern Baptists as late as 1967, according to a denominational paper, was that of "fundamentalists and hillbillies," devoted to "ideas and practices of day-before-yesterday," but who somehow appeared "too well dressed." Southern fundamentalists in the 1960s and 1970s were, in fact, different from those of Mencken's era: their ranks exhibited greater affluence and respectability, higher levels of education and sophistication, a broader institutional base, and an increasing political consciousness. The fundamentalism bequeathed by the generation at the turn of the century that was primarily northern and urban in origin lost something and gained something in its sojourn in the South. Hence, the fundamentalism that the South fed back to the nation after World War II, while deeply indebted to those who had formulated the doctrinal statements known as "the fundamentals," was not quite the same. From the ranks of this southern-type fundamentalism emerged the likes of Billy Graham, Jerry Falwell, Oral Roberts, and others who presided over expensive, nationwide religious empires and whose collective influence resulted, to an extraordinary degree, in what David Edwin Harrell, Jr., has termed "the southernization of American evangelicalism." Their message and style revealed the unmistakable influence of those who battled modernism and evolution in the generation of the Scopes trial. The idea of the South as "the nursery, the training ground, the granary, the source of supplies" for evangelizing America and the world was thoroughly familiar for them. Although Graham and most others associated with the post–World War II religious revival in the United States largely ignored Darwin's theory, they contributed significantly to a cultural milieu that nourished antievolutionism. . . .

Although the South was the scene of noisy struggles over Darwin's theory and the only section of the country to invoke the coercive power of the state to ban it from the classroom, the region was never monolithic in its hostility to evolution. Those in the South intent upon enacting monkey laws encountered strong opposition from some conservative churchmen, including Southern Baptists, as well as from academic, scientific, and diverse other groups. Among Southern Baptists there were always leaders who boldly and eloquently opposed antievolution statutes as inconsistent with the denomination's historic commitment to religious liberty and to the principle of church-state separation. But the popularity of the antievolution position in the South meant that those who spoke against such laws, especially elected officials, did so at considerably greater risk than those elsewhere. In the South one was almost certain to be condemned and ostracized as a cultural scalawag who had sold out to alien forces bent on obliterating the southern way of life. Most opponents of antievolution legislation in the region recognized, as did Wilbur J. Cash, that such measures were usually "the focal point of attack for a program, explicit or implicit, that went far beyond evolution laws."

Despite a tendency to identify opposition to Darwin as "an anachronistic movement limited to a few backward Southern states," popular hostility to his theory has never been confined to the South. In 1927 Maynard Shipley, an indefatigable foe of fundamentalists, antievolutionists, and others whom he classified as the "forces of obscurantism," estimated that more than half of the total church membership in the United States, or twenty-five million Americans, found Darwin's theory unacceptable. The results of nationwide public opinion polls conducted during the next half century, which indicated substantial increases in fundamentalist influence and the persistence of antievolutionist sentiments among a broad spectrum of the American population, suggests that Shipley's estimate may have been conservative. In 1968 Howard Zinn insisted that southern fundamentalism and the antimodernist impulse that it so dramatically exhibited on occasion represented "only an intense form" of what existed in the entire nation.

Yet the fact remained that the South's response to evolution has been more intense, noisier, and more productive of coercive legislation than that of the rest of the country. Explanations of the region's exceptionalism on this particular issue have usually included references to two of the three R's of southern distinctiveness in general, ruralism and religion, and on rare occasions to the third R, race. Undoubtedly the South's rural character, low church, Bible centered, individualistic Protestantism, relatively low level of literacy and traditional educational deficiencies, as well as the existence in the region of a populist bias against established authority and elitism, have influenced its reaction to the theory of evolution. Perhaps more important, however, has been the peculiar relationship between regional faith and culture, a relationship in which consensual attitudes have been equated with a divinely ordained order of things. Whatever else antievolution and scientific creationist laws may have symbolized, as Clarence Cason observed in 1935, southerners perceived them as devices "to conserve their customs" and protect "the church about which their social patterns, their essential culture, foregathered to an important extent."

✢ *F U R T H E R   R E A D I N G*

Kathleen M. Blee, *Women of the Klan: Racism and Gender in the 1920s* (1991)

Joseph Blotner, *Faulkner: A Biography,* 2 vols. (1974)

John M. Bradbury, *Renaissance in the South: A Critical History of the Literature, 1920–1960* (1963)

Wayne D. Brazil, *"Social Forces* and Sectional Self-Scrutiny," in Merle Black and John Shelton Reed, eds., *Perspectives on the American South: An Annual Review of Society, Politics and Culture,* vol. 2 (1984), 73–104

Cleanth Brooks, *William Faulkner: The Yoknapatawpha Country* (1963)

Wilbur J. Cash, *The Mind of the South* (1941)

David Chalmers, *Hooded Americanism* (1965)

Paul K. Conkin, *The Southern Agrarians* (1988)

David Herbert Donald, *Look Homeward: A Life of Thomas Wolfe* (1987)

Paul D. Escott, ed., *W. J. Cash and the Minds of the South* (1992)

Ray Ginger, *Six Days or Forever* (1958)

E. Stanley Godbold, Jr., *Ellen Glasgow and the Woman Within* (1972)

Robert A. Goldberg, *Hooded Empire* (1981)

William C. Harvard and Walter Sullivan, eds., *A Band of Prophets: The Vanderbilt Agrarians After Fifty Years* (1982)

Thomas S. Hines, *William Faulkner and the Tangible Past* (1996)

Fred C. Hobson, Jr., *Serpent in Eden: H. L. Mencken and the South* (1974)

———, *Tell About the South: The Southern Rage to Explain* (1983)

Hugh C. Holman, *Three Modes of Southern Fiction: Ellen Glasgow, William Faulkner, Thomas Wolfe* (1966)

Anne Goodwyn Jones, *Tomorrow Is Another Day: The Woman Writer in the South, 1859–1936* (1981)

Michael Kreyling, *Inventing Southern Literature* (1998)

Lawrence Levine, *Defender of the Faith: William Jennings Bryan* (1965)

David Minter, *William Faulkner: The Writing of a Life* (1980)

Leonard Moore, *Citizen Klansmen* (1991)

Jack Nelson, *Terror in the Night* (1993)

Michael O'Brien, *The Idea of the American South, 1920–1941* (1979)

William Alexander Percy, *Lanterns on the Levee: Recollections of a Planter's Son* (1941)

Darden Asbury Pyron, *Southern Daughter: The Life of Margaret Mitchell* (1991)

Elizabeth Robeson, "The Ambiguity of Julia Peterkin," *Journal of Southern History* 61 (1995), 761–786

Louis D. Rubin, Jr., *Writers of the Modern South: The Faraway Country* (1963)

———, *The Wary Fugitives: Four Poets and the South* (1978)

———, ed., *The American South: Portrait of a Culture* (1980)

Louis D. Rubin, Jr., and Robert D. Jacobs, eds., *Southern Renascence: The Literature of the Modern South* (1959)

Ernest Sandeen, *The Roots of Fundamentalism* (1970)

Milton C. Sernett, *Bound for the Promised Land: African American Religion and the Great Migration* (1997)

Patsy Sims, *The Klan* (1996)

Daniel J. Singal, *The War Within: From Victorian to Modernist Thought in the South, 1919–1945* (1982)

———, *William Faulkner: The Making of a Modernist* (1997)

John David Smith, ed., *Disfranchisement Proposals and the Ku Klux Klan* (1993)

Walter Sullivan, *A Requiem for the Renascence: The State of Fiction in the Modern South* (1976)

George B. Tindall, "The Significance of Howard W. Odum to Southern History: A Preliminary Estimate," *Journal of Southern History* 24 (1958), 285–307

Susan Millar Williams, *Devil and Good Woman, Too: The Lives of Julia Peterkin* (1997)

Joel Williamson, *William Faulkner and Southern History* (1993)

Turning Points? The New Deal and World War II

When the Great Depression struck, the South was already reeling from agricultural and industrial miseries. By 1932, the meager financial resources of states and localities had disappeared under the avalanche of unemployment and low crop prices. A few years later, the southern economy was scarcely better, but posters bearing the likeness of President Franklin D. Roosevelt seemed to be tacked to every tobacco barn, county courthouse bulletin board, and filling station in the South. The New Deal gave southerners some work and much hope.

 The Roosevelt administration did not intend to change the region's society and traditions. Southern politicians held important committee posts in the U.S. Congress and Senate and were wary of massive federal expenditures that could short-circuit their control over some whites and most blacks. But with $4 billion of federal money poured into programs, accompanied by the upheaval in farm prices and the dislocation of farm workers, change was bound to happen. What did it mean to long-time farming families and to rural traditions to leave the land? What did it mean to farmers to receive a paycheck from the federal government instead of from the plantation or local store owner? Scholars are sorting out the extent of these changes and especially their legacy for the modern South.

 More important, many historians have argued, was the impact of World War II on the South. The migration from farms to cities and factories, sparked by federal defense factory jobs, increased employment opportunities. The war heightened the aspirations of women, who found that they could be fully employed if they so desired, and of blacks, who hoped for racial progress in the courts, on the battlefields, at polling places, and in their towns. The South was on the move: Millions left their communities to work in distant cities or fight in remote places. What impact these changes had on the South and on its future is a question debated by historians today. Some believe that World War II brought greater change to the South than had the Civil War. As with the New Deal, it is not yet clear whether the war was a watershed or the continuation of earlier trends in southern society.

Southern labor responded actively to the economic and policy changes of the 1930s. One of the most famous, and bloody, strikes of the decade occurred in coal-mining Harlan County, Kentucky, in 1931. Florence Reece, a local balladeer whose husband was a member of the striking National Miners Union, wrote "Which Side Are You On?" on the back of a calendar. This song, Document 1, became a classic protest song for the American labor movement. The grim conditions on the farms and in the mines and factories played a role in thrusting the author of Document 2, Louisiana governor and senator Huey P. Long, into the national spotlight. The "Kingfish," as he was known, was a dyed-in-the-cotton demagogue in a region already famous for the genre, but his deeds matched his rhetoric more closely than others. This selection demonstrates why he generated such loathing and love in the South and elsewhere. The Great Depression muted the brash boosterism of the 1920s, and the federal government laid out the truth about the region's poverty. Document 3, the President's Emergency Council Report, details how far the South lagged behind the rest of the country in economic, educational, and social development. For the children of tenants and sharecroppers, the Great Depression was an especially difficult time. Document 4 is an excerpt from *Mothers of the South,* the result of research into the lives of southern tenant farm women conducted by sociologist Margaret J. Hagood. For girls, poverty, lack of education, and male privilege left lasting scars. The Farm Security Administration sent photographers, including Dorothea Lange, into the South during the late 1930s to capture the impact of the New Deal and to record what remained to be accomplished. Lange hoped that these photographs would help the nation understand the continuing needs in the South. W. T. Couch, director of the University of North Carolina Press, commissioned a book written by African Americans designed to explicate their aspirations during and after the war. The resulting manuscript, edited by Howard University history professor Rayford W. Logan with writings by veteran black educator Gordon B. Hancock are excerpted here as Document 6. They reflect a less patient generation of blacks, who sought national solutions to regional racial problems. Finally, Document 7 gave blacks considerable cause for hope. The decision in *Smith* v. *Allwright,* involving a challenge to the white primary in Texas by a black Houston dentist, held the potential of opening up the most important election in the southern states—the Democratic party primary—to black voters.

1. Florence Reece's "Which Side Are You On?", 1931

Come all of you good workers,
Good news to you I'll tell,
Of how the good old union
Has come in here to dwell.

REFRAIN: Which side are you on?
Which side are you on?

We've started our good battle,
We know we're sure to win,

Because we've got the gun thugs
A-lookin' very thin.

They say they have to guard us
To educate their child;
Their children live in luxury
Our children's almost wild.

With pistols and with rifles
They take away our bread,
And if you miners hinted it
They'd sock you on the head.

They say in Harlan County
There are no neutrals there;
You either are a union man
Or a thug for [Sheriff] J. H. Blair.

Oh workers, can you stand it?
Oh tell me how you can.
Will you be a lousy scab
Or will you be a man?

My daddy was a miner,
He is now in the air and sun [blacklisted and without a job]
He'll be with you fellow workers
Until the battle's won.

2. Huey Long, "Every Man a King," 1933

The increasing fury with which I have been, and am to be, assailed by reason of the fight and growth of support for limiting the size of fortunes can only be explained by the madness which human nature attaches to the holders of accumulated wealth.

What I have proposed is:—

The Long Plan

1. A capital levy tax on the property owned by any one person of 1% of all over $1,000,000; 2% of all over $2,000,000 etc., until, when it reaches fortunes of over $100,000,000, the government takes all above that figure; which means a limit on the size of any one man's fortune to something like $50,000,000—the balance to go to the government to spread out in its work among all the people.

2. An inheritance tax which does not allow any one person to receive more than $5,000,000 in a lifetime without working for it, all over that amount to go to the government to be spread among the people for its work.

Huey P. Long, "The Maddened Fortune Holders and Their Infuriated Public Press," in *Every Man a King: The Autobiography of Huey P. Long* (New Orleans: National Book Co., 1933), pp. 338–340.

3. An income tax which does not allow any one man to make more than $1,000,000 in one year, exclusive of taxes, the balance to go to the United States for general work among the people.

The foregoing program means all taxes paid by the fortune holders at the top and none by the people at the bottom; the spreading of wealth among all the people and the breaking up of a system of Lords and Slaves in our economic life. It allows the millionaires to have, however, more than they can use for any luxury they can enjoy on earth. But, with such limits, all else can survive.

That the public press should regard my plan and effort as a calamity and me as a menace is no more than should be expected, gauged in the light of past events. According to Ridpath, the eminent historian:

> The ruling classes always possess the means of information and the processes by which it is distributed. The newspaper of modern times belongs to the upper man. The under man has no voice; or if, having a voice, he cries out, his cry is lost like a shout in the desert. Capital, in the places of power, seizes upon the organs of public utterance, and howls the humble down the wind. Lying and misrepresentation are the natural weapons of those who maintain an existing vice and gather the usufruct of crime.
>
> —Ridpath's History of the World,
> Page 410.

In 1932, the vote for my resolution showed possibly a half dozen other Senators back of it. It grew in the last Congress to nearly twenty Senators. Such growth through one other year will mean the success of a venture, the completion of everything I have undertaken,—the time when I can and will retire from the stress and fury of my public life, maybe as my forties begin,—a contemplation so serene as to appear impossible.

That day will reflect credit on the States whose Senators took the early lead to spread the wealth of the land among all the people.

Then no tear dimmed eyes of a small child will be lifted into the saddened face of a father or mother unable to give it the necessities required by its soul and body for life; then the powerful will be rebuked in the sight of man for holding that which they cannot consume, but which is craved to sustain humanity; the food of the land will feed, the raiment clothe, and the houses shelter all the people; the powerful will be elated by the well being of all, rather than through their greed.

Then, those of us who have pursued that phantom of Jefferson, Jackson, Webster, Theodore Roosevelt and Bryan may hear wafted from their lips in Valhalla:

EVERY MAN A KING

3. The President's Council Reports on Southern Economic Conditions, 1938

The President's Letter

To the Members of the Conference on Economic Conditions in the South: My intimate interest in all that concerns the South is, I believe, known to all of you; but this

---

From The President's Council Reports on Southern Economic Conditions, 1938.

interest is far more than a sentimental attachment born of a considerable residence in your section and of close personal friendship for so many of your people. It proceeds even more from my feeling of responsibility toward the whole Nation. It is my conviction that the South presents right now the Nation's No. 1 economic problem—the Nation's problem, not merely the South's. For we have an economic unbalance in the Nation as a whole, due to this very condition of the South.

It is an unbalance that can and must be righted, for the sake of the South and of the Nation.

Without going into the long history of how this situation came to be—the long and ironic history of the despoiling of this truly American section of the country's population—suffice it for the immediate purpose to get a clear perspective of the task that is presented to us. That task embraces the wasted or neglected resources of land and water, the abuses suffered by the soil, the need for cheap fertilizer and cheap power; the problems presented by the population itself—a population still holding the great heritages of King's Mountain and Shiloh—the problems presented by the South's capital resources, and problems growing out of the new industrial era and, again, of absentee ownership of the new industries. There is the problem of labor and employment in the South and the related problem of protecting women and children in this field. There is the problem of farm ownership, of which farm tenantry is a part, and of farm income. There are questions of taxation, of education, of housing, and of health.

FRANKLIN D. ROOSEVELT.

THE WHITE HOUSE

Washington, D.C., July 5, 1938.

Report to the President

Population

The population of the South is growing more rapidly by natural increase than that of any other region. Its excess of births over deaths is 10 per thousand, as compared with the national average of 7 per thousand; and already it has the most thickly populated rural area in the United States. Of the 108,600,000 native-born persons in the country in 1930, 28,700,000 were born in the Southeast, all but 4,600,000 in rural districts.

These rural districts have exported one-fourth of their natural increase in sons and daughters. They have supplied their own growth, much of the growth of southern cities, and still have sent great numbers into other sections. Of these southerners born in rural areas, only 17,500,000 live in the locality where they were born, and 3,800,000 have left the South entirely.

This migration has taken from the South many of its ablest people. Nearly half of the eminent scientists born in the South are now living elsewhere. While some of these have been replaced by scientists from other sections of the country, the movement from the South has been much greater than this replacement. The search for wider opportunities than are available in the overcrowded, economically undeveloped southern communities drains away people from every walk of life. About one child of every eight born and educated in Alabama or Mississippi contributes his life's productivity to some other State.

The expanding southern population likewise has a marked effect on the South's economic standards. There are fewer productive adult workers and more dependents per capita than in other sections of the country. The export of population reflects the failure of the South to provide adequate opportunities for its people.

The largely rural States of the South must support nearly one-third of their population in school, while the industrial States support less than one-fourth. Moreover, in their search for jobs the productive middle-age groups leave the South in the greatest numbers, tending to make the South a land of the very old and the very young. A study of one southern community in 1928 showed that about 30 percent of the households were headed by women past middle age. Since 1930 most of these women, formerly able to live by odd jobs and gardening, have gone on relief. Relief studies in the eastern Cotton Belt have shown recently that 15 percent of the relief households were without a male over 16 years of age and 15 percent more, or 31 percent altogether, were without any employable male. Even if the southern workers were able, therefore, to secure wages equal to those of the North on a per capita basis dollar for dollar, a great gap would still remain between the living standards of southern families and those of other regions. . . .

Private and Public Income

Ever since the War between the States the South has been the poorest section of the Nation. The richest State in the South ranks lower in per capita income than the poorest State outside the region. In 1937 the average income in the South was $314; in the rest of the country it was $604, or nearly twice as much.

Even in "prosperous" 1929 southern farm people received an average gross income of only $186 a year as compared with $528 for farmers elsewhere. Out of that $186 southern farmers had to pay all their operating expenses—tools, fertilizer, seed, taxes, and interest on debt—so that only a fraction of that sum was left for the purchase of food, clothes, and the decencies of life. It is hardly surprising, therefore, that such ordinary items as automobiles, radios, and books are relatively rare in many southern country areas.

For more than half of the South's farm families—the 53 percent who are tenants without land of their own—incomes are far lower. Many thousands of them are living in poverty comparable to that of the poorest peasants in Europe. A recent study of southern cotton plantations indicated that the average tenant family received an income of only $73 per person for a year's work. Earnings of share croppers ranged from $38 to $87 per person, and an income of $38 annually means only a little more than 10 cents a day.

The South's industrial wages, like its farm income, are the lowest in the United States. In 1937 common labor in 20 important industries got 16 cents an hour less than laborers in other sections received for the same kind of work. Moreover, less than 10 percent of the textile workers are paid more than 52.5 cents an hour, while in the rest of the Nation 25 percent rise above this level. A recent survey of the South disclosed that the average annual wage in industry was only $865 while in the remaining States it averaged $1,219. . . .

Since the South's people live so close to the poverty line, its many local political subdivisions have had great difficulty in providing the schools and other public services necessary in any civilized community. In 1935 the assessed value of taxable property in the South averaged only $463 per person, while in the nine Northeastern States it amounted to $1,370. In other words, the Northeastern States had three times as much property per person to support their schools and other institutions.

Consequently, the South is not able to bring its schools and many other public services up to national standards, even though it tax the available wealth as heavily as any other section. In 1936 the State and local governments of the South collected only $28.88 per person while the States and local governments of the Nation as a whole collected $51.54 per person.

Although the South had 28 percent of the country's population, its Federal income-tax collections in 1934 were less than 12 percent of the national total. These collections averaged only $1.28 per capita throughout the South, ranging from 24 cents in Mississippi to $3.53 in Florida.

So much of the profit from southern industries goes to outside financiers, in the form of dividends and interest, that State income taxes would produce a meager yield in comparison with similar levies elsewhere. State taxation does not reach dividends which flow to corporation stockholders and management in other States; and, as a result, these people do not pay their share of the cost of southern schools and other institutions.

Under these circumstances the South has piled its tax burden on the backs of those least able to pay, in the form of sales taxes. (The poll tax keeps the poorer citizens from voting in eight southern States; thus they have no effective means of protesting against sales taxes.) In every southern State but one, 59 percent of the revenue is raised by sales taxes. In the northeast, on the other hand, not a single State gets more than 44 percent of its income from this source, and most of them get far less. . . .

Women and Children

Child labor is more common in the South than in any other section of the Nation, and several Southern States are among those which have the largest proportion of their women in gainful work. Moreover, women and children work under fewer legal safeguards than women and children elsewhere in the Nation.

Low industrial wages for men in the South frequently force upon their children as well as their wives a large part of the burden of family support. In agriculture, because of poor land and equipment, entire families must work in order to make their living.

The 1930 census, latest source of comprehensive information on child labor, showed that about three-fourths of all gainfully employed children from 10 to 15 years old worked in the Southern states, although these States contained less than one-third of the country's children between those ages. . . .

In a region where workers generally are exploited, women are subjected to an even more intense form of exploitation. Many women work more than 50 hours a week in cotton and other textile mills, and in the shoe, bag, paper box, drug, and similar factories in certain Southern States.

The South has two of the four states in the entire Nation that have enacted no laws whatever to fix maximum hours for women workers. Only one of the Southern States has established an 8-hour day for women in any industry. Only four of the Southern States have applied a week as short as 48 hours for women in any industry.

Reports for a number of industries, including cotton manufacturing, have shown wage earners receiving wages well below those estimated by the Works Progress Administration as the lowest which would maintain a worker's family.

Women's wages ordinarily amount to less than men's. However, only two of the Southern States have enacted a law providing a minimum wage for women, though several others are attempting to pass such legislation. Recent pay-roll figures show women textile workers in an important southern textile State receiving average wages 10 percent below the average outside the South. Other figures show that a week's wage of less than $10 was received by more than half the women in one State's cotton mills, and by a large part of the women in the seamless hosiery plants of three States and in the men's work-clothes factories of two States.

Many women, even though employed full time, must receive public aid because their wages are insufficient to care for themselves and their children. The community thus carries part of the burden of these low wages and, in effect, subsidizes the employer.

One condition tending to lower women's wages is the system by which factories "farm out" work to be done in homes. Women have been found at extremely low pay doing such work as making artificial flowers, sewing buttons on cards, clocking hosiery, embroidering children's clothing, stuffing and stitching baseballs. Although this is a relatively recent tendency in the South, there are indications that such work is increasing. Usually the pay is far below that paid in the factory. A study of industrial home work on infants' wear disclosed that the women worked much longer hours than in the factory, though half of them received less than $2.73 for their week's work.

A low wage scale means low living standards, insufficient food for many, a great amount of illness, and, in general, unhealthful and undesirable conditions of life.

4. The Tenant Child

The story of the tenant child begins more than a quarter of a century ago. On Monday ten-year-old Mollie [Goodwin] woke up when her mother lifted the stove lid and began making the fire. She slipped from underneath the cover easily, so as not to disturb her little brother, and took down her last year's red dress, which had been fleecy and warm, but now was slick and thin. Their bed was in the log kitchen of the Goodwin's two-room cabin, which would be warm enough in a half hour for the sickly knee-baby, who slept with Mollie, to face the December morning.

From *Mothers of the South: Portraiture of the White Tenant Farm Woman* by Margaret Hagood. Copyright © 1939 by the University of North Carolina Press, renewed 1967 by Margaret Benaya. Used by permission of the publisher.

Mollie's father came from the main room of the cabin to lace up his shoes in front of the kitchen stove. He never made the fire unless his wife was sick in bed, but he got up at the same time she did to go out to the smokehouse and measure out the day's allowance of meat. Ben Goodwin was a saving man who could not abide waste. He made his share of the proceeds from the small, cotton tenant farm buy the annual fall clothing supply for his family of seven and run them through the winter and spring until midsummer or later. Even then, he kept his account at the country store the lowest of any family's in the neighborhood, doing all the buying himself and measuring out the rations every morning.

Mollie's plump arms stretched tight the seams of her outgrown dress, and as she leaned over to pick up fresh wood for the fire, she felt her dress split at the shoulder. She wondered what she would do the washing in if she couldn't get into the old dress next Monday or the one after that. Her father's rule was that her two new dresses of the same cotton fleece lined material, one red and one blue, must never be worn except for school or Sunday School. She had no sisters to hand down clothes to her, for the other four children were boys. Some girls she knew wore overalls for working, but her father would not allow that either. A wicked thought came to her mind—maybe if she had nothing to wear to wash in next Monday, she wouldn't have to wash and instead could go to school with her brothers. She could iron on Tuesday inside the house in her underwear—then a vision of her mother bending over the wash tubs, moaning with the pain in her back, made her put aside the daydream of a washless Monday.

After breakfast Mollie's older brother cut wood and started a fire under the wash pot while she and the brother next younger drew and carried water from the well. Then the boys left for the mile walk to the one-teacher school and Mollie started back for the house to get up the clothes. She lingered on the way, debating whether her father's overalls, stiff with a week's accumulation of winter mud and stable stains, were harder to wash than the baby's soiled diapers. They *were* harder, but the odor from the diapers made you feel you couldn't go on. It was a sensory symbol of babies, of her sick mother, of crying, little brothers, and now was vaguely mixed with her distaste for what two girl friends had told her at recess last week about how babies come. Mollie tried not to think about this and hoped she never had any babies.

The school bell's ringing interrupted her musing and reminded Mollie of how much she wanted to be there. Her dress was as new as any in school and its color still bright. The teacher had smiled approvingly at Mollie last week when the visiting preacher pinched her dimpled cheek and said, "Miss Grace, you have a fine looking bunch of little girls." Mollie thought now of having, when she was grown, a dress like Miss Grace's Sunday one. The bell stopped ringing and Mollie resolved to stop thinking and to work very hard and fast. Once before she had finished all the washing in time to go back with the boys after dinner. And so she scrubbed with all her force against the washboard and paid no attention to the pain from her knuckles scraped raw.

By dinner time all the clothes were on the line and the first ones out already frozen stiff. Mollie, numbed by cold and fatigue, ate peas, fat pork, and cornbread without joining in the family talk. When she got up from the table, her back ached—she wondered how many years of washing it would take to make it as bent over as her mother's. She changed to her new dress in time to set off for the afternoon session of school. She pulled herself together to respond to the teacher's beaming look of approval for having come to school that afternoon, and then relaxed into a lethargy from weariness and missed words she knew in the Third Reader and was spelled down quickly. . . .

Mollie's play had to be largely with her brothers because the only close neighbor had no daughters. In summer she would go to the creek with them and, if no other boys were along, go in swimming with them, too. The boys wore nothing but she wore her oldest dress. They were good to her and often let her play ball with them. Once in the spring the three children stayed after school to watch a baseball game and when they got home at dark, Ben Goodwin was beside himself with anger. They had neglected work and had watched a baseball game, which was against his religious principles. He whipped them all severely, even Mollie. They never went to a baseball game again. . . .

Mollie liked summer time best after the cotton had been chopped, hoed, and laid by. Once or twice a week she was allowed to go spend the afternoon with Mrs. Bynum, the nearest neighbor, who had no daughters. They sat on the front porch and rocked and talked. This was a treat for the little girl because her own mother always had to lie down when she could stop working, and pain limited her words to necessary instructions. One summer Mrs. Bynum bought some flowered dimity and made Mollie a visiting dress. They used to hitch up her horse to the buggy and drive four miles to visit a sister who had twelve children, most of them girls. The older girls let Molly try on hats and brooches and Mollie loved these afternoons. On the trip Mrs. Bynum taught Mollie to drive the horse. In her own family's wagon there were always boys who claimed this privilege.

One stormy winter night three months before Mollie was twelve, she was put to bed early. Her father moved the trundle bed from the main room and all the children went to sleep in the kitchen—all but Mollie. She had a terrible feeling of impending disaster to her mother and herself. When she had asked her mother about babies not long before, her mother had told her she was going to have another and that something would happen to Mollie soon, too. From the front room Mollie heard groans and knew her mother was suffering. Her own body began to ache. Her mother's sounds grew louder and each time an anguished scream reached Mollie's ears, a shooting pain went through her. Hardly daring, Mollie reached down under the cover and felt that her legs were wet. All the boys were asleep and so she drew back the cover and in the moonlight saw black stains which had come from her body. Suddenly she thought she was having a baby. She tried to scream like her mother, but the terror of the realization paralyzed her. Fright overwhelmed her until she was no longer conscious of pain. She remained motionless for a long time, knowing and feeling nothing but a horrible fear of disgrace and dread. Then she became aware that the moaning in the next room had stopped and that someone had unlatched the kitchen door. Trembling, she eased out of bed and crept into her mother's room. There was a new baby lying on one side, but she slipped into the other side of the bed and nestled against her mother. The relaxing warmth and comfort of another's body released the inner tensions and Mollie melted into tears and weak, low sobs. Her mother stroked her but said nothing. She lay there for some minutes until the Negro "granny" said she must leave her mother and led her back to bed. Early in the morning she hid the soiled bedclothes in a corner until she could wash them secretly in the creek and found some cloths in her mother's drawer which she asked for without giving any reason. Not for two years, when a girl friend told her, did she have any instruction about how to fix and wear sanitary pads.

5. Dorothea Lange Photographs the Depression

Shacktown, Elm Grove, Oklahoma, 1936. (Dorothea Lange/Library of Congress)

Ex-Slave Outside of Her Home in Alabama, 1937. ((c) Dorothea Lange Collection, The Oakland Museum of California, The City of Oakland. Gift of Paul S. Taylor.)

6. Perspective on "What the Negro Wants," 1944

Gordon B. Hancock on a Southern Solution to Race Relations

The Durham Conference

What is probably the most constructive departure in race relations since the emancipation of the Negro was made in the historic conference held at Durham, North Carolina, October 20, 1942. Sixty of the most influential Negroes of the South representing all shades of thought and occupational affiliation met of their own free will and accord—and at their own expense—and drew up a statement now known as the Durham Manifesto, which has had a far reaching effect on the thought and thinking of this country. Six thousand copies of the printed statement have been sent upon request to every state of the Union where interested persons are seeking more intimate knowledge of a document that has had such dramatic reception throughout the country. The conferees not only brought forth the statement, but as-

From *What the Negro Wants* by Rayford W. Logan. Copyright © 1944 by the University of North Carolina Press, renewed 1974 by Rayford W. Logan. Used by permission of the publisher.

sumed the financial responsibility for its publication. This forthright statement by a group of Southern Negroes caught the imagination of the country and the first edition of seven thousand copies is nearing exhaustion. A prominent churchwoman recently requested sufficient copies to supply the missionary circles of her entire state where it is to be used for study groups. In the *Statement of Purpose* we read:

> The inception of this conference hinges about the tragedy that took place at the close of World War I, when returning Negro soldiers were met not with expressions and evidences of the democracy for which they had fought and for which thousands of their fellow race men had died. Instead, there was a sweeping surge of bitterness and rebuff that in retrospect constitutes one of the ugliest scars on the fair face of our nation. Interracial matters were left adrift and tragic was our experience and distressing was our disillusionment. Today the nations are again locked in mortal combat and the situation is desperate and dangerous, with the scales of fortune so delicately poised that we dare not predict what a day may bring forth; but this we know, that the Negro is again taking the field in defense of his country. Quite significant also is the fact that whereas the pronounced anti-Negro movement followed the last war, it is getting under way before the issues of the current war have been decided. In an hour of national peril, efforts are being made to defeat the Negro first and the Axis powers later. Already dire threats to throw again the Negro question into the politics of the South is becoming more and more dangerous. This is a direct challenge to the Negroes of the South who have most to gain if this threat is throttled and most to lose if it is fulfilled.
>
> The purpose then of this conference is to try to do something about this developing situation. We are proposing to set forth in certain "Articles of Cooperation" just what the Negro wants and is expecting of the postwar South and nation. Instead of letting the demagogues guess what we want, we are proposing to make our wants and aspirations a matter of record, so clear that he who runs away may read. We are hoping in this way to challenge the constructive cooperation of that element of the white South who express themselves as desirous of a New Deal for the Negroes of the South.
>
> In our "Articles of Cooperation" we are seeking for a common denominator of constructive action for the Negroes and this element of whites who are doing many of the things that we want done, and cannot do ourselves. In other words, we are proposing to draft a "New Charter of Race Relations" in the South. The old charter is paternalistic and traditional; we want a new charter that is fraternal and scientific, for the old charter is not compatible with the manhood and security of the Negro, neither is it compatible with the dignity and self-respect of the South. It ever leaves the South morally on the defensive! The Negro has paid the full price of citizenship in the South and nation, and the Negro wants to enjoy the full exercise of this citizenship, no more and no less.

The Durham Manifesto broke down the whole area of race relations into seven categories relating to political and civil rights, industry and labor, service occupations, education, agriculture, military service, social welfare and health. The statement was widely and favorably received throughout the nation, with white and Negro press not only lavish in their praise of the document but generous in the space allotted to its publicity. By its very nature it presupposed a like conference of the Southern whites which met in Atlanta, April 8, 1943, attended by over a hundred representatives from all the Southern states. The righteousness of the Negro's cause and contentions were readily conceded and full assurances of cooperation given in any reasonable plan for the achievement of the objectives outlined in the Durham Manifesto. Members of a Collaborating Committee were named to meet with a like committee representing the Durham Conference. The Collaboration Conference was held in Richmond, June 16, 1943, attended by sixty-six committeemen representing the Durham and Atlanta conferences. The Durham statement was heartily indorsed and was accepted as the "blue print" for the improvement of race relations in the South. The profound and sympathetic understanding evinced by the participating conferees can best be appreciated by an excerpt from the final report which reads in part:

> This is the problem of two great peoples caught up in the midst of transition between the powerful heritage of the past and the mighty pull of the future. For here is the white South, a great people often doing little things and good people often doing bad things. And here is the Negro South, caught as always between the upper and nether millstones of conflicting forces and as also paying the price of extraordinary transition from level to level of cultural achievement, and needing plenty of understanding and cooperation. And here is the white South inexorably conditioned by cultural complexes, suffering terribly, too, and needing sympathy and help as few peoples have ever needed in the annals of man. And, even more important, the two, white South and black South, are part and parcel of the nation whose people need, scarcely less than the two regional peoples, the sense of time and wisdom. . . .
>
> This is a rare challenge to the leadership of the South; to the white leadership to find new ways of cooperation and to justify increased confidence of Negro leadership in the white South; to sense the difficulties involved and to meet increasing demands without slowing down their essential efforts.

. . . All things considered, it is safe to say that the ground work for some constructive developments in race relations has been laid by the Durham, Atlanta and Richmond Conferences and that great things are possible if ways and means and moral courage can be found to implement the spirit of these pronouncements. If the South can be organized by states and counties into councils on race relations committed to the implementation of this spirit of the new South, there are evidences that we are heading somewhere in particular in the area of race relations.

7. *Smith* v. *Allwright*, 1944

Mr. Justice Reed delivered the opinion of the Court: . . .

Primary elections are conducted by the party under state statutory authority. The county executive committee selects precinct election officials and the county, district or state executive committees, respectively, canvass the returns. These party committees or the state convention certify the party's candidates to the appropriate officers for inclusion on the official ballot for the general election. No name which has not been so certified may appear upon the ballot for the general election as a candidate of a political party. No other name may be printed on the ballot which has not been placed in nomination by qualified voters who must take oath that they did not participate in a primary for the selection of a candidate for the office for which the nomination is made.

This document can be found in Smith v. Allwright: 321 U.S. 757 (April 3, 1944).

The state courts are given exclusive original jurisdiction of contested elections and of mandamus proceedings to compel party officers to perform their statutory duties.

We think that this statutory system for the selection of party nominees for inclusion on the general election ballot makes the party which is required to follow these legislative directions an agency of the state in so far as it determines the participants in a primary election. The party takes its character as a state agency from the duties imposed upon it by state statutes; the duties do not become matters of private law because they are performed by a political party. . . . When primaries become a part of the machinery for choosing officials, state and national, as they have here, the same tests to determine the character of discrimination or abridgment should be applied to the primary as are applied to the general election. If the state requires a certain electoral procedure, prescribes a general election ballot made up of party nominees so chosen and limits the choice of the electorate in general elections for state officials, practically speaking, to those whose names appear on such a ballot, it endorses, adopts and enforces the discrimination against Negroes, practiced by a party entrusted by Texas law with the determination of the qualifications of participants in the primary. This is state action within the meaning of the Fifteenth Amendment. . . .

The United States is a constitutional democracy. Its organic law grants to all citizens a right to participate in the choice of elected officials without restriction by any state because of race. This grant to the people of the opportunity for choice is not to be nullified by a state through casting its electoral process in a form which permits a private organization to practice racial discrimination in the election. Constitutional rights would be of little value if they could be thus indirectly denied. . . .

The privilege of membership in a party may be . . . no concern of a state. But when, as here, that privilege is also the essential qualification for voting in a primary to select nominees for a general election, the state makes the action of the party the action of the state.

✢ *E S S A Y S*

Professor of history Martha H. Swain argues that the New Deal represented a partial turning point for southern women. The number of professional women working for New Deal agencies in the South increased and programs such as the School Lunch Project and the Historic Records Survey proved successful, but racial discrimination and customary attitudes toward women's inability to do "heavy" labor kept many relief clients from well-paid jobs or from training in skilled trades and professions. Swain points out that however well-intentioned New Deal providers might have been, they often "made policies that worked against southern populations on relief." Professor James C. Cobb takes the long view of the impact of the New Deal and World War II on the South. He sees evidence of the "changes in southern agriculture, the outmigration of blacks, and the move to industrialize" beginning before World War I. But New Deal programs and massive federal expenditures on defense pushed the South down the road to moderate prosperity. Cobb's depiction of the South's turning point includes economic, cultural, literary, racial, and political changes, although he also points to the limitations of change brought on by World War II.

A New Deal for Southern Women

MARTHA H. SWAIN

Long before the full impact of the Great Depression that began late in 1929 hit the South, the region's women ranked lower than men on economic indices of income and employment. By 1933 unemployment, poverty, and need for basic sustenance were facts in the lives of countless women, both urban and rural. But by the year's end in 1933 there was hope for improved circumstances through a new women's work program, under way with the Federal Emergency Relief Administration (FERA) and directed by Ellen Sullivan Woodward and virtually all-female national and state staffs. There were a number of administrative strictures common to all work relief projects that mitigated against women seeking work assignments. The prejudice of the lay public and local officials, particularly against minority women, presented additional difficulties. Nonetheless, Woodward's division made notable inroads against the obstacles it faced. From 1933 to 1943, women held "made work" jobs under three successive New Deal agencies on projects whose legacies remain until the present.

During the so-called years of the locust, 1929–33, women's economic opportunities declined further than their previous lows. Urban workers lost jobs when the downturn reached their municipalities. Women workers in a range of mills and industries, most particularly textiles, suffered worse than even in previous years, as did sharecropper and tenant farm wives. From Arkansas, where the extreme drought of 1930–31 wrought unbelievable hardship, one despairing widow wrote to the Red Cross, "I wish if you will please send me some clothes. Just enough to wear to the cotton patch," while a mother wrote, "I am near my row's end." Julia Kirk Blackwelder had documented the "quiet suffering" among women in Atlanta, New Orleans, and San Antonio, where blacks bore the brunt of layoffs and harsh work.

When local governments proved unable or unwilling to assist women, they wrote to Lou Henry Hoover, wife of President Herbert Hoover. Among the thousands of supplications mailed to the First Lady from 1929 to 1932, many were from the South. From Alabama came a request for used garments; similar pleas came from Louisiana and Kentucky. A Sandersville, Georgia, woman begged for "some money to buy us some clothes and shoes"; some requests were for employment. . . . The letters were no different from those Lou Hoover's successor as First Lady received after March 1933.

Mrs. Hoover was correct in responding that only limited resources were available from the hard-strapped states or private charities. Even states that could have provided monetary aid had no governmental mechanism in place to do so. Documented cases point to the poverty of Alabama women whose direct assistance amounted to no more than $2.60 every two weeks. In Mississippi, of the only thirty-four families that drew pensions in 1931, thirty were headed by widows. No real help was forthcoming under two organizations set up by President Hoover, the

President's Emergency Committee on Employment (PECE) and the President's Organization for Unemployment Relief (POUR). Each had a women's division, but like the parent organization, it relied strictly on the voluntary cooperation of local municipalities, charities, churches, or women's clubs.

What proved to be of some merit were the ideas generated by the women's divisions of PECE and POUR to create employment opportunities for women, albeit on a voluntary basis. For Ellen S. Woodward, secretary of the Mississippi units of the two committees, it was instructive to study the work plans of other states and the periodic bulletins from the national women's program that came across her desk outlining "made work" endeavors.

Harry Hopkins, the head of the FERA since its inauguration in May 1933, was greatly influenced by Eleanor Roosevelt and was determined to create a women's work program. In late August he appointed Woodward to direct the new Women's Division within the FERA. He accepted Woodward upon the recommendations of colleagues who knew of her work as executive secretary of the Mississippi State Board of Development, her involvement in the new State Board of Public Welfare, her direction of the PECE and POUR activities in Mississippi, and her related social welfare activities. He needed a woman administrator who was an effective organizer, able to manage diverse personalities and present his relief program in a favorable light to politicians. There is no evidence that he found her work wanting, for he retained her as an assistant administrator in the short-lived Civil Works Administration (CWA) from 1933 to 1934, and the Works Progress Administration (WPA), established in 1935.

The challenge of putting to work a vast number of needy, unemployed women, especially those in the South, became evident to Woodward soon after she arrived in Washington in September 1933. At a White House Conference on the Emergency Needs of Women on November 20, the stark reality of the task ahead became apparent. Representatives of women's organizations in attendance reported on conditions existing in their locales. Alabama activist Patti Ruffner Jacobs had informed the Women's Bureau of the United States Department of Labor that there were six thousand unemployed clerical workers in Birmingham alone. Additionally, she reported that a new department store received five thousand applications for seventy-five advertised jobs. The need of Alabama women for income was no greater than that of women throughout the South. Women's Bureau studies documented the low wages of workers in the hard-hit clothing and textiles industries, the depletion of what little savings women had accumulated, and the fact that resources of social service bureaus were inadequate to assist destitute women, circumstances common to the unemployed throughout the country, but exacerbated in the South.

Woodward's first task was to create a Women's Division within each state, consisting of a state director, state supervisors for each approved statewide work project, and supervisors of designated districts in each state. State directors were women representing a range of experience that provided a sense of professionalism to the entire Women's Division. Some of the most effective programs in New Deal work relief had developed by the time the WPA began in 1935, because of the extent of need and the past experiences of the state directors. . . .

For many young women of the South, work relief social services offered an entrée into a new career. The task of administering means tests to relief applicants and certifying needy persons for work inundated state FERAs, necessitating the employment of trained social workers. Scholarships enabled a sizable number of young women to obtain graduate degrees in social work. The initial assignment given Marie L. Hoffman, the first person in the Mississippi FERA to hold a master's degree, was to supervise twelve graduate students entering Tulane University, where she had received her advanced degree in 1933. She became a pioneering FERA district supervisor and later an assistant director in the state WPA office. In South Carolina, thirty-one-year-old Alice Norwood Spearman, as director of the Social Service Department of the Marion County Relief Administration, was the first South Carolina woman to administer a county relief program. From Alabama, a child welfare worker, Loula Friend Dunn, became the FERA regional supervisor for eleven southern states and, after 1937, commissioner of public welfare for Alabama.

While the FERA and CWA Women's Division heads competed with the men's construction work for project approval, it was at the county level that less-noticed foot dragging went on. "Women are not getting a fair share of the work," reported the Mississippi federated clubs president in January 1934. The CWA women's work leader in a southern Mississippi county met the kind of rebuff common to others. For three weeks her office was no more than a "big manilla envelope carried under her arm," for she was granted no office space. She concluded that it "was thought dangerous for a woman to be around the CWA headquarters."

Under the FERA and the CWA, questions loomed, as they would in the WPA, about what constituted "woman's work." Woodward insisted that women "could and should work wherever work is," including manual labor, especially when it paid "men's wages," more remunerative than most of the women's service programs. A Leflore County (Mississippi) women's work official complained that the state CWA head had ruled that landscaping projects involving raking were "too hard for women," but he would approve projects "where the work is light, such as washing windows and scrubbing floors and walls." The disapproving office could have added that the pay for "light" women's work was lower. Similarly, a North Carolina women's project leader was aghast to learn that CWA men directors ruled that furniture making was too strenuous for women. She knew many women who spent "weary days at such back-breaking work as plowing, chopping wood, scrubbing floors, dragging babies around, or bending over a wash tub for hours on end." State officers appeared not to know what skills women possessed. Ethel Payne commented, "Every man has the idea that if a woman is trained, she is a stenographer, but if she isn't she can sew."

In actuality, many women could not sew and had no skills at all. . . .

Critics of the "traditional" women's work done on many of the FERA-CWA-WPA service (women's) projects would do well to recognize that it broke tradition and long-established patterns for masses of uneducated, often illiterate women with no prior work history other than in the fields to be employed at nonagricultural tasks away from home. The women's work program was supposed to enable women to maintain skills during the economic emergency or train them for employment when the Depression ended. The truth is that the majority of women certified for work relief were so bound to their families as household heads that they had virtually no mobility; thus movement into new lines of work was not promising. "The

fact that a very large number of first priority women are unskilled creates many difficulties in trying to achieve a diversified program," Woodward informed Hopkins
late in 1935, as the WPA got under way.

Project designers in the Division of Women's and Professional Projects (WPP),
as Woodward's section was reconstituted after 1936, were beleaguered by recurring
problems inherent in administering effective projects for unskilled and semiskilled
women, who accounted for 79.5 percent of all women on relief in 1935. The fact
that in southern cities between 70 and 80 percent of women on relief jobs were unskilled weighted that figure. Defenders of sewing activities rebutted detractors who
scorned the projects as "female ditch-digging." Woodward feared that the "only alternative [for the unskilled] seems to be their return to direct relief," that is, the
dole. She was determined that such women have the same opportunity as educated
and professional women to earn work relief wages. Files on sewing projects offer
glimpses into the lives of workers. After a small unit at Artesia, Mississippi, closed,
its supervisor wrote President Franklin D. Roosevelt of one worker who with her
five children subsisted on bread and water for two weeks while waiting for another
assignment. Displaced women in North Carolina, a sympathetic congressman wrote
to a constituent, "must have something to eat, some kind of roof over their head and
some fuel to keep . . . warm."

Most male WPA state chiefs frowned on sewing projects but offered no ideas
about how to place small clusters of rural women in work accessible to their homes
and under requisite supervision. As one North Carolina administrator put it,
"Frankly our hearts don't palpitate over sewing rooms." But even Lorena Hickok,
Harry Hopkins's roving reporter who never minced words in pointing up shortcomings she saw in the WPA, saw merit in the projects. After visiting sewing rooms in
Florida, she wrote, "I don't think you have any idea what they have done to women
themselves. . . . Working in pleasant surroundings, having some money and food
have done wonders to restore their health and morale." A sharecropper's boast that
the $21 his wife drew at a WPA sewing room "just about takes care of everything"
speaks volumes about the low standard of living of many clients.

Sewing projects were enormously productive in their output of clothing and
household items distributed to needy families. In Memphis, for example, between
1936 and 1938 sewers who annually added $200,000 to the city's payroll produced
clothing worth $250,000. Atlanta women by the late 1930s had distributed over four
million garments to individuals and public institutions. When tornadoes devastated
towns in Mississippi and Georgia in 1936, WPA output supplied welfare families
who had lost everything. Ethel Payne reported from her state that the WPA clothing
room at Tupelo "looks like Sears Roebuck." Of the eight million items produced in
Kentucky by 1943, many had gone to children in rural and mining communities so
that they could attend school.

Still, as one of the most highly visible production-for-use WPA activities,
sewing was a target for vociferous critics. Woodward could reasonably answer
some, such as those from private manufacturers who charged unfair competition.
After all, relief recipients of WPA-made articles hardly constituted a ready market
for stores on Main Street. Woodward had more persistent difficulty in dealing with
repeated assertions that minority women suffered discrimination. Even though
sewing was developed for the unskilled or semiskilled, at a time when the WPA

load in May 1940 in eleven southern states consisted of 22.9 percent blacks, only 7.4 percent of sewing wage earners were black women. They were given work assignments at more difficult tasks, for instance, stitching heavy fabrics instead of lighter textiles, or cleanup chores not expected of whites. They were the first to be released when congressional cutbacks closed projects, or else they were transferred to menial and demeaning work. In one of many such cases, Fayetteville, North Carolina, supplicants wrote of the "rampant discrimination" in the reassignment of sixteen black sewing project workers to yard cleanup. Honest efforts to investigate legitimate complaints led to dead ends. Local officials denied the charges, and victims of certain abuse feared reprisal if they were identified as complainants. Moreover, projects for black and Mexican American women were curtailed when congressmen received rebukes from employers, whether landowners or housewives, who resented the loss of their cheap labor to better-paying government relief jobs.

Women's Division personnel developed two activities primarily to provide wages for black women, the Housekeeping Aide Project and Household Demonstration. Both were intended to ease the high unemployment among women who classified their occupation as "servant," a category claimed in 1934 in seventeen southern cities by fifty-two thousand blacks and only five thousand whites. Kentucky, for example, reported in 1933 that more than half its black women were out of work, three-fourths of them in domestic service. As housekeeping aides, women who had minimal domestic skills gained training sufficient to send them into homes of needy families as "surrogate mothers" so that the caregiver there could work herself or children held home to nurse a sick family member could attend school. In the South most aides were black. Despite constant watchfulness from Washington, some local officials abused the system. San Antonio furnished one example where women, in this instance white, were sent to do "dirty and exhausting" work in homes of wealthy families.

But where the program was properly run, it won praise as a genuinely humane social service that aided women household heads whose families were hard hit by illness or some other calamity that had halted income. At the same time it provided FERA or WPA wages to women who were unable to obtain assignments on other activities for which quotas were filled. Texas observers claimed that infant mortality had been reduced; Tennessee's final report emphasized the sheer relief to human suffering that housekeeping "Good Samaritans" rendered.

In 1935 an Arkansas native, Alfred Edgar Smith, who was an investigator on black affairs for Harry Hopkins, began work for Woodward's office. In successive reports, he explored appropriate work opportunities for untrained black women "for which Federal, state, and local administrative officials admit having no solution." The challenge led Woodward to conclude that training projects could be a function of her division that would make its program distinct from that for men. In 1935, with the express encouragement of Eleanor Roosevelt, the Women's Division launched the first of three Household Workers' Training Projects to set up centers to upgrade skills of domestic workers. In the South, where a preponderance of the projects existed, the centers were segregated and a vast majority of trainees were minorities. In Mississippi and Louisiana, all enrollees were black, but then the nationwide figure was 93 percent. The history of the program proves that Roosevelt, Woodward, and other reformers, including the liberal congressman from Texas, Maury Maverick, were wrong to believe that training household workers could actually increase wages and improve work conditions. It is a lamentable fact that New Deal federal work relief was limited in what it could do to raise wages in the private sector. But the greatest failure of the Household Workers' Training Project is captured in Jane Van De Vrede's terse comment to Lorena Hickok, "The only trouble is that [blacks] won't go for it. They don't want to learn how to be servants."

Both Congress and President Roosevelt made policy that worked against southern populations on relief. "Sponsors," either local organizations or state agencies, always underfunded in the best of years, had to meet most nonlabor costs. For the WPA women's projects, the sponsor was often a women's club or the local parent-teacher associations, organizations that either had limited resources or were too often dominated by provincial viewpoints about what segments of society should first be served. When Gay Shepperson, Georgia's WPA chief and the only woman to head a state program until Arizona appointed a woman head, tried to give blacks greater assistance, she alienated sponsors and was forced to back down or else cancel projects. Hence, blacks had no choice but to accept "half a loaf" or none at all. Similarly, when the Georgia Women's Democratic Club complained about integrated sewing centers, the practice was curtailed. Florida laws forbade whites from teaching blacks and vice versa, a stricture that hampered efforts toward mixed-race supervision in training in most other southern states as well.

Finally, there were circumstances within black families that made it difficult for women to prove they were household heads, a firm requisite for certifying individuals for work relief. A husband was often absent so much he provided no assistance, yet he remained the legal household head. The seasonal nature of WPA programs for men inflicted hardships on a wife, who could not be accepted for WPA work even while none was available at the time for the husband. Those and other concerns were explored at a special White House conference in April 1938 instigated by Mary McLeod Bethune and conducted by Eleanor Roosevelt and Ellen Woodward. Attended by a number of representatives of southern black women's organizations, the Conference on Participation of Negro Women and Children in Federal Programs adopted resolutions that were only perfunctory. Had Congress ever appropriated sufficient funds for the WPA to operate independent of state or private sponsorship, work relief could have been conducted without deference to regional prejudices. It never happened, and in fact as the 1930s went on, Congress made deep cuts in federal relief that worsened problems with the states.

Difficulties and discriminations that beset work relief for southern women assigned to sewing or training should not cloud the success of other projects that employed almost half of women on relief. Probably the most popular of all Women's and Professional Projects activities was the School Lunch Project and its allied Gardening and Canning Projects. School lunches for undernourished and needy children came into their own under the WPA and were nowhere as welcome as in the South. Virginia's record was as impressive as that of any state: between January 1937 and April 1939, women on relief served nine million lunches. In Texas at the program's peak in 1941–42, 7,000 project workers were serving 250,000 lunches daily in 2,500 schools. Little wonder that local esteem for the WPA lunch ran as high in Texas as everywhere else in the South, and school officials touted the gains in student health, attendance, and demeanor. Probably more than any other Goods Production project, WPA feeding programs left a true legacy and did much to augment passage in 1946 of the National School Lunch Act.

WPA nurses performed a myriad of duties: bedside care of mothers, promotion of oral hygiene, maintenance of clinics to treat specific diseases, and location of crippled children for therapy. Georgia's project bore the stamp of Jane Van De Vrede: by 1936 (in less than one year of WPA service), workers had immunized 184,000 persons against typhoid, 2,300 against smallpox, and 26,000 against diphtheria. WPA public health and nursing personnel replicated such work in all southern states. Extensive library projects, popular in all southern states, were the cornerstones of eventual statewide library systems encompassing every county. It was in the South that librarians on relief delivered books by intrepid means: by packhorse in Kentucky, by flatboats in the Mississippi, Arkansas, and Louisiana Delta, and by houseboats that plied the streams in backwater counties. There is no question that library service under the WPA was institutionalized and made permanent all over the South at the demise of work relief.

Women on relief performed other work that remains useful to the present. They worked at Historic Records Surveys and wrote local histories under the Historical Research Project. A Vital Statistics Survey, which operated under the nomenclature of Public Administration and under the Women's and Professional Projects division, employed women to check back records of births and deaths, work that was of considerable value to state departments of public health and for Social Security applicants after 1935. Independent of the WPA Divisions of Emergency Education and Recreation, Woodward's program included extensive nursery and recreation projects. Women mounted displays and performed research for public museums and schools and created traveling exhibits. All of this does not even touch upon the employment of women in the Four Arts Projects for Art, Music, Writers, and the Theatre. Historian Douglas L. Smith has concluded that "in terms of human impact," the women's service programs in the South "in some way touched almost everyone in every locality where they operated."

Accurate figures for the total number of southern women employed by the WPA are difficult to obtain since final reports do not list numbers by region. Moreover, the WPA was chary of reporting employment on population groups by race or ethnicity. Until June 1940, women constituted between 12 and 18 percent of those on WPA rolls. If an internal count for the Women's and Professional Projects made in mid-July 1937, showing an average of 27.6 percent women as WPA employees in twelve southern states compared to a national average of 18.2 percent, represented usual loads, then it seems likely that women consistently made a better showing in the South. (The matter of hourly wages is another thing.) Because many workers were dropped from projects and others hired, or women were removed from relief rolls when they became eligible for assistance under Social Security, monthly WPA totals cannot tell how many *different* individuals drew relief wages.

Beyond work relief, southern women were beneficiaries of the New Deal in other ways that have not yet been explored to any extent. Women received homeowner loans and worker's and literacy education; they signed contracts as landowners under the Agricultural Adjustment Administration and benefited extensively, and gratefully, from rural electrification. They moved to new locales through rural resettlement and lived on subsistence homesteads. They won at least small gains under wage and hour clauses of the National Industrial Recovery Act and the Fair Labor Standards Act. Younger women enrolled in National Youth Administration work that replicated that of work relief in many ways.

Gender and race distinctions limited women to less assistance in the vast work programs of the FERA-CWA-WPA than that given men. Nevertheless, lasting gains resulted for many women from the multifaceted federal programs in the 1930s. Unlike the imprimaturs left on many of the construction projects, women's work relief has few monuments that testify to its consumer goods and services. Mississippi's Ethel Payne thoughtfully asked near the end of 1939 how to equate the lasting value of linear feet of paved sidewalks and airstrips with linear feet of books on a WPA library shelf. For a time, women's work relief was the salvation of workers and their families, and their communities benefited in incalculable ways.

The Impact of World War II on the American South

JAMES C. COBB

While it was difficult at the end of the 1940s to look back much beyond the War itself, the perspective of the 1990s both affords us the luxury of the longer view and requires that we take it. When we do, we can see that, to some extent, the changes in southern agriculture, the outmigration of blacks, and the move to industrialize were actually rooted in conditions and trends visible as early as or even before World War I. In fact, the years from the boll weevil invasion of the early twentieth century through the beginnings of the Great Migration of blacks to the North and the descent into the Great Depression might be seen as the harbingers of a great turning period, a protracted drama for which the New Deal and World War II constituted the final acts.

Most scholars have argued that of the two acts, World War II clearly deserves top billing, but it is virtually impossible to assess the impact of the New Deal and World War II separately. Both the New Deal and the war contributed heavily to the modernization of southern agriculture and the South's subsequent efforts to industrialize. While the New Deal's acreage-reduction programs rendered much of the old farm labor force marginal, if not superfluous, however, the war offered alternative employment opportunities and threatened to create a labor scarcity sufficient to boost farm wages above levels that southern landlords were willing to pay. Meanwhile, although the war seemed ultimately to undermine southern liberalism and strengthen anti-New Deal conservatism, the conflict did not cancel the Roosevelt administration's stated commitment to improving economic conditions in the South and arguably even facilitated it by removing the restrictions on spending that had hampered New Deal recovery efforts.

The $52 billion paid out on just the ten largest government defense contracts between 1940 and 1944 was roughly equivalent to total government expenditures

Essay, "The Impact of WWII on the American South," by Jim Cobb from *Remaking Dixie: The Impact of WWII on the American South* edited by Neil R. McMillen, (Jackson, MS.: University Press of Mississippi). Copyright © 1997. Reprinted by permission of the publisher.

between 1932 and 1939. Not surprisingly, southern manufacturing employment grew by 50 percent during the war, and annual wages climbed by 40 percent between 1939 and 1942 alone as war-induced competition for labor quickly rendered the New Deal's Fair Labor Standards minimums obsolete in some southern industries. For all the undue influence still wielded by reactionary southern politicians, the Roosevelt administration also seized numerous wartime opportunities to exempt the South from its official "hold the line" policy on wages while affording significant support to organized labor as well. Although the South remained a decidedly low-wage region, it emerged from the conflict with an expanded industrial labor force and a markedly more affluent consumer pool which became a crucial part of the region's postwar attraction for market-oriented industries. If it is correct to credit the war with finishing what the New Deal started, it seems reasonable as well to think of World War II functioning, at least in part, as a sort of unarticulated Third New Deal, one freed from some of the most severe economic constraints that hampered the first two.

Wartime spending created many new job opportunities for southerners, although not all enjoyed equal access to them. On any construction site, as one black southerner who spoke from experience explained, "If a white man and a black man both walk up for an opening and it ain't no shovel in that job, they'd give the job to a white man." This generalization applied to black veterans as well. Promiseland, South Carolina, veteran Isaac Moragne angrily rejected a Veterans Administration staffer's recommendation that he apply for a common laborer's position, explaining later, "I was a staff sergeant in the Army, . . . traveled all over England . . . sat fourteen days in the English Channel . . . I wasn't going to push a wheel barrow.". . .

During the war, men and women left the South's farms for its factories in almost equal numbers, and in many cases, employers preferred to hire the women. This was especially true when the choice lay between a white woman and a black man. In some instances, defense employers simply drew on the existing textile labor pool where white women were heavily represented and blacks hardly at all. Although many of these white women withdrew or were pushed out of the industrial workforce when the war ended, postwar economic expansion soon afforded them new opportunities to return to the factories while the concomitant shrinkage of the South's agricultural sector often made such a move a matter of absolute necessity. In Mississippi, the number of women employed in manufacturing increased by nearly 60 percent between 1940 and 1950, a rate nearly twice as high as that for their male counterparts. At the same time, continuing discrimination forced blacks of both sexes to pursue wartime opportunities in the North.

In both the short and long terms, the war's impact on worker mobility was crucial in a number of ways. At the national level, while 12 million Americans were being shipped overseas, another 15 million moved to cities elsewhere in the nation, with half of these moving to different states. Meanwhile, between 1940 and 1945, three times as many people left the South each year as had departed during the preceding decade. A total of 1.6 million civilians moved out of the South during the war, and almost as importantly, three times that many moved elsewhere within the region. Prior to the war, southern workers had been far less mobile, sticking close to home either because they could not afford to move, had no incentive to move, or simply could not bring themselves to move. This labor market inflexibility was far less pronounced in the postwar South as outmigration, inmigration, and intraregional migration continually responded to and shaped economic, racial, political, and cultural trends.

Among the cultural trends most affected by this newfound mobility and other war-induced changes was the evolution of southern music. . . . Country music went both national and international thanks not only to the proliferation of country radio programming in response to the outmigration of southern whites but to the Armed Forces Radio Network, which carried what had once been seen as strictly regional "hillbilly" music all over the world. The major beneficiary of this was Grand Ole Opry star Roy Acuff, whose distinctive voice became so well known in the steamy jungles of the South Pacific that some Japanese troops reportedly spurned "banzai" in favor of "To Hell with Roy Acuff.". . . A second beneficiary of wartime developments was the Texas Troubadour, Ernest Tubb, who pioneered in a musical style known as "honky tonk," which drew its name from establishments known for drinking and dancing and not infrequently fighting and shooting as well. The repeal of prohibition, the sense of rootlessness and transiency and the loosening of morals and family constraints occasioned by economic expansion and population redistribution shaped both the thematic and stylistic contours of honky tonk. The loud, twangy pedal steel guitar was a perfect accompaniment for tunes such as "What Made Milwaukee Famous Made a Loser Out of Me," and it also allowed the song to be heard over the clamor of the laughing, cursing, and fighting that filled the bars and beer joints where it was most often played. . . .

During the war and after, younger and more urbane black audiences readily demonstrated their preference for the amplified dance-oriented stylings that became known as "rhythm and blues." Researchers who studied black life during the war had discovered a marked trend toward secularization as rural blacks acquired radios, automobiles, and telephones and generally transcended the barriers that had once insulated them from mass-society influences. Disgusted by the changes she observed, lifelong Mississippi Delta churchgoer Matilda Mae Jones complained, "Songs they sing in church now feel like fire burning. . . . all fast and jumpy and leapy like. . . . that's just the way these swing church songs are now." Jones's complaint foreshadowed a trend that would see performers like Clarksdale-born gospel singer Sam Cooke, who began his career singing songs such as "Jesus Gave Me Water," go on to fame as a rhythm and blues superstar with hits like "Chain Gang" and "Everybody Loves to Cha Cha Cha." Cooke's career paralleled those of countless others, such as James Brown and Otis Redding and Ray Charles, who, in succeeding years, not so much left gospel music as took it with them when they entered the secular, sensual world of rhythm and blues. . . .

Writing in 1935, Greenville writer David L. Cohn described the Mississippi Delta as a land of "complete detachment," explaining that "change shatters itself on the breast of this society as Pacific breakers upon a South Sea reef." "Disturbing ideas" might "crawl like flies around the screen of the Delta," wrote Cohn, but "they rarely penetrate." In the wake of World War II, Cohn painted a decidedly different portrait, however, noting that "many changes have occurred in the life of the Mississippi Delta as elsewhere. We had scarcely emerged from a shattering economic depression before we were plunged into man's most catastrophic war. The foundations of our faith are severely shaken. We no longer believe, as we once did, in the inevitability of progress. Our compass is aberrant, our course erratic. We are more than a little fearful that we shall not make our landfall."

Cohn's observation seemed to bear out George Orwell's contention that "if the war didn't kill you, it was bound to start you thinking," but in reality, southerners were already thinking, particularly about the South, well before World War II. The region once dubbed "The Sahara of the Bozart" by H. L. Mencken could by 1941 boast of having the nation's most dynamic literary community. The pivotal member of that community, William Faulkner, sought vainly to enlist in the military during World War II but wound up sitting out the war as a screenwriter in Hollywood, working on *Battle Cry, God Is My Co-Pilot,* and a number of other patriotic films. Still, Faulkner revealed his emotional involvement in the conflict in a letter to his stepson who was then serving in the military: "A change will come out of this war. If it doesn't, if the politicians and people who run this country are not forced to make good the shibboleth they glibly talk about freedom, liberty, human rights, then you young men who have lived through it will have wasted your precious time, and those who don't live through it will have died in vain." Looking beyond the war, Faulkner could only hope that there "will be a part for me, who can't do anything but use words, in the rearranging of the house so that all mankind can live in it."

Ironically, some literary scholars now quote these eloquent lines as they mark World War II as the beginning of the end for Faulkner as a great writer, arguing, with *Intruder in the Dust* as a case in point, that his subsequent fiction became more didactic and mechanical and less open ended and artistically valid. Whether Faulkner was a less gifted writer is of less significance for our purposes than the fact that after the war he was far more widely read and appreciated. The contradictions raised by World War II and subsequently magnified by the tensions of the Cold War focused national and international attention on the South's deficiencies. World War II brought more than twice as many Yankee soldiers to the South as the Civil War and their wartime experiences often yielded specific and personal testimony to the South's backwardness. . . . The result was the creation of what Sosna called "a bull market . . . for regional exposure, explanation, and analysis."

Certainly, the war years inspired and nurtured a host of writers of both fiction and nonfiction who wrote with the clear purpose of focusing attention on the South's problems and stressing the urgency of finding solutions. Serving as a Naval officer in India, young historian C. Vann Woodward was struck by his visit with the leader of India's untouchables who "plied me with questions about the black 'untouchables' of America and how their plight compared with that of his own people." Already the author of a revisionist biography of Populist Tom Watson, Woodward returned from the war to write a sweeping reinterpretation of the Redeemer Era South and then to pen *The Strange Career of Jim Crow,* an enormously influential volume that struck at both the legal and emotional underpinnings of segregation.

Meanwhile, Woodward contemporary John Hope Franklin, who had just received his Ph.D. from Harvard, offered his services as a historian to the War Department. Because he was black, he was rebuffed without receiving serious consideration. Then, responding to Naval recruiters' appeals for clerical personnel, Franklin was again rejected solely on the basis of his race. Finally, ordered to report for a draft physical, Franklin was subjected to further indignities, leading him to conclude that "the United States did not need me and did not deserve me." Consequently, he spent the rest of the war outwitting the draft board and "feeling nothing but shame for my country—not merely for what it did to me, but for what it did to the millions of black men and women who served in the armed forces under conditions of segregation and discrimination." Franklin went on to revise the traditional historical view of Reconstruction and of the role of blacks in southern history and to serve (as did Woodward, in a lesser capacity) as an adviser to the NAACP Legal Defense Team representing the plaintiffs in the *Brown* v. *Board of Education* case.

Franklin's wartime experience reflected the ambivalence and frustration with which many black intellectuals approached the conflict. Determined to link the fighting abroad to the struggle for racial justice at home, poet Langston Hughes exulted in "Jim Crow's Last Stand" that "Pearl Harbor put Jim Crow on the run/That Crow can't fight for Democracy/And be the same old Crow he used to be." Hughes also urged black soldiers to get those "so bad, evil and most mad, GO AND GET THE ENEMY BLUES." As segregation continued to flourish throughout the war effort, however, a disappointed Hughes also mocked, "Jim Crow Army and Navy, Too/Is Jim Crow freedom the *best* I can expect from you?"

By the time the war began, Richard Wright's angry fiction had already established him as the nation's preeminent black writer. As an increasingly disenchanted member of the Communist Party, however, Wright found himself zigging and zagging in response to a party line that was zigging and zagging as well. In the wake of the Nazi-Soviet Pact, he insisted that the conflict was "Not My People's War," pointing out that "the Negro's experience with past wars, his attitude towards the present one, his attitude of chronic distrust, constitute the most incisive and graphic refutation of every idealistic statement made by the war leaders as to the alleged democratic goal and aim of this war." After Hitler's invasion of Russia, however, the party suddenly had no more use for Comrade Wright's pacifism, and slightly more than a week after Pearl Harbor, a frustrated Wright pledged his "loyalty and allegiance" to the American cause, promising that "I shall through my writing seek to rally the Negro people to stand shoulder to shoulder with the administration in a solid national front to wage war until victory is won."

Meanwhile, irreverent novelist and folklorist Zora Neale Hurston had drawn consistent criticism from Richard Wright and other black intellectuals for her failure to use her writings as a weapon in the struggle against racism and Jim Crow. Yet for all her apparent reluctance to devote her energies to solving the race problem, in the original manuscript for her autobiographical *Dust Tracks on a Road,* she pointed out that "President Roosevelt could extend his four freedoms to some people right here in America. . . . I am not bitter, but I see what I see. . . . I will fight for my country, but I will not lie for her." Like several others, this passage was subsequently excised after Hurston's white editor deemed it "irrelevant." After the war, however, writing in *Negro Digest,* Hurston cited Roosevelt's reference to the United States as "the arsenal of democracy" and wondered if she had heard him correctly. Perhaps he meant "arse-and-all" of democracy, she thought, since the United States was supporting the French in their effort to resubjugate the Indo-Chinese, suggesting that "the ass-and-all of democracy has shouldered the load of subjugating the dark world completely." Hurston also announced that she was "crazy for this democracy" and would "pitch headlong into the thing" if it were not for the numerous Jim Crow laws that confronted her at every turn.

World War II also stiffened white crusader Lillian Smith's resolve to fight against segregation. She insisted in 1943 that fighting for freedom while acquiescing to Jim Crow amounted to "trying to buy a new world with Confederate bills." Condemned by Georgia governor Eugene Talmadge as "a literary corn cob," Smith's 1944 novel *Strange Fruit* was a searing story of miscegenation and murder that concluded with the lynching of an innocent young black man. It lay bare the pain and suffering caused by white racism and the hypocrisy and sexual repression that festered just beneath the surface of the southern way of life.

The uncompromising Smith was hardly more contemptuous of those who defended Jim Crow than those who urged moderation in the fight against it. Yet, with external pressures mounting as the Supreme Court struck down the white primary in 1944, many white southerners who had once seemed most dedicated to racial justice found themselves urging the proponents of desegregation to slow down. Ardent and courageous spokesmen like Hodding Carter and Ralph McGill insisted that ending segregation would take time, and when they bristled at northern critics—members of the "hit-and-run school of southern writing," as Carter called them—they sounded a great deal like Faulkner's Gavin Stevens in *Intruder in the Dust* and Faulkner himself a few years thereafter. As Numan V. Bartley observed, in the wake of the war "the very word 'liberal' gradually disappeared from the southern political lexicon, except as a term of opprobrium." Meanwhile, although the contradictions raised by Jim Crow were inconsistent with the United States's rise to free-world leadership, the anti-Communist hysteria of the early Cold War years made even northern liberals initially reluctant to encourage antisegregation litigation and protests. . . .

Even before World War II, some southern intellectuals were beginning to behave according to a pattern that now seems fairly typical of emerging or developing nations around the world, agonizing about their region's backwardness but also expressing their fears about the loss of cultural identity and virtue that might accompany the accelerating effort to modernize their society. No writer struggled more painfully or brilliantly with the persistence of the South's deficiencies or the decay of its virtues than William Faulkner. In the wake of World War II, Faulkner's fictional Jefferson was already experiencing what Walker Percy later called "Los Angelization," its "old big decaying wooden houses" giving way to antiseptic one-story models crammed into subdivisions "with their neat plots of clipped grass and tedious flowerbeds" and its housewives "in sandals and pants and painted toe nails," puffing "lipstick-stained cigarettes over shopping bags in the chain groceries and drugstores." Meanwhile, mechanization of agriculture brought a dramatic change in the rhythm of southern rural life as machines came between men and women and the land and further separated them from the product of their labors. "I'd druther have a mule fartin' in my face all day long walkin' de turnrow than dem durned tractors," a Delta farmhand told David Cohn. "There ain't nothing about a tractor that makes a man want to sing," complained another worker. "The thing keeps so much noise and you so far away from the other folks.". . .

In his semi-autobiographical novel *The Year the Lights Came On,* Terry Kay described the postwar scene in Royston, Georgia: "The cotton mill placed an advertisement in *The (Royston, Ga.) Record,* seeking employees. A sewing plant was officially opened by His Honor the Mayor. Farmers began to listen to what county agents had to say about subsoiling, land testing, seed treating, or about planting kudzu and lespedeza to stop topsoil from washing away in the ugly scars of erosion. The sound of John Deere tractors stuttered even at night." In Royston, no less than elsewhere, Kay believed "everyone seemed aware of being embraced by a new history of the world, and everyone knew it would be a history never forgotten."

Like Kay and [Flannery] O'Connor, Walker Percy was also witness to the destabilizing effects of urbanization, industrialization, and agricultural mechanization in the postwar South. Even as O'Connor worried that the changes sweeping across her region might purge the South "not only of our many sins but our few virtues," Percy was noting the "growing depersonalization" of southern social relations and suggesting that northernization of southern life would mean a society "in which there is no sense of the past, or of real community, or even of one's own identity." Percy would ultimately emerge as one of the dominant literary figures in the post–World War II South, and a new generation of writers such as Richard Ford and Josephine Humphreys now explore in their own work the validity of Percy's insistence that modern life subjects southerners, like all other Americans, to "deep dislocation in their lives that has nothing to do with poverty, ignorance, and discrimination."

Expressing similar concerns, John Egerton worried in 1974 that the "Americanization of Dixie" simply meant that the South and the nation were "not exchanging strengths as much as they are exchanging sins." In his 1995 study of the pre–Civil Rights generation in the South, however, Egerton was more upbeat, crediting World War II with bringing the South into "the modern age" by turning "hard times into hopeful times," moving "people up and out," and changing "our ways of thinking and working and living. Practically everything about this war," Egerton believed, "from the way we got into it to the way we got out of it, suggested transformation."

Confirming Egerton's assessment of the war as a watershed, Bertram Wyatt-Brown insisted in 1991 that "the South [W. J.] Cash knew has largely disappeared. In matters of economic prosperity, racial demography, urbanization, and politics, the fact is that the region has altered much more since the early 1940s than it did between 1865 and 1941."

Few contemporary observers seem inclined to dispute Egerton or Wyatt-Brown, but if we are to understand the full impact of World War II on our region, we must take into account not only the magnitude but the limitations of the changes induced by the war. Upon close examination, we can also see that although the War is responsible for many of the differences between the South that Cash saw in 1940 and the South we see today, it also contributed to some of the similarities as well. For example, if the war made the South more attractive to industrial investors, its failure to destroy the region's heavy concentration in low-wage industries helped to explain why the postwar South retained a cheap-labor appeal that those investors still find significant. In addition, the war's stimulus to industrial mobility and to southern efforts to attract new and better industries meant that the South ultimately went from offering thousands of dollars in subsidies to underwear plants to offering hundreds of millions of dollars in subsidies to automobile plants.

On another front, the war's acceleration of black migration from states where blacks could not vote to states where they could played a key role in spurring the

Democratic Party's advocacy of civil rights, but in doing so, it also fed the nation-wide white blacklash that all but derailed the civil rights movement. Similarly, if the war-inspired Civil Rights revolution allowed southern blacks to claim the political rights and influence so long denied them, it also triggered the massive exodus of racially conservative southern whites from the Democratic Party, the cumulative result being a South that quickly amassed the nation's largest concentration of black officeholders while becoming its most predictably Republican region in presidential elections and a growing number of lesser contests as well.

While Cash would have found officeholding by Republicans or blacks almost equally startling, he would probably have been even more amazed to see that the changes set in motion or intensified by the war had rendered his version of the southern mind essentially obsolete, replacing it with a more heterogeneous and less exclusionary model, one open to anyone who saw themselves as southerners regardless of race or gender or even regional or national origin. Not only were blacks just as likely as whites to identify themselves as southerners by the 1990s, but in many cases, they actually seemed more confident of what that meant. Enduring taunts and threats and all manner of abuse from those who sought to preserve Cash's South, Charlayne Hunter-Gault had broken the color barrier at the University of Georgia in 1961. In 1988 she returned to Athens to deliver the commencement address, embracing the South as "my place" and paying tribute to southerners of both races whose "tumultuous" but shared history had melded them into the nation's only "definable people." Numerous such examples along with contemporary polls identifying Robert E. Lee and Martin Luther King as the South's most revered historical figures seem to point to a southern mind dramatically different though hardly less paradoxical or contradictory than the one that tormented Cash.

Confirming the anxiety Cash had felt in 1940, Morton Sosna concluded that the South had emerged from World War II as "an arena where the forces of good and evil, progress and reaction, rapid change and seemingly timeless continuity were about to engage in a battle of near mythological proportions." As Sosna indicated, for the South, the end of the war meant not peace but another quarter century of struggle. More than any single preceding event, World War II helped to shape not only the contours of this struggle but its outcome, an outcome that finally allowed us to contemplate a South whose virtues, if they did not tower over its faults, were at least no longer totally obscured by them. All of this seems to have come out far better than Cash dared to hope. Yet, before we credit World War II with unloosing forces that destroyed Cash's South, we should first take note of the racism, violence, anti-intellectualism, and social indifference that now permeate American society at large and ask how the postwar historical context so clearly conducive to mitigating these characteristic vices of the southern mind in 1940 could have also set the stage for their ominous emergence as defining features of the national mind in 1996.

✠ *F U R T H E R   R E A D I N G*

Anthony J. Badger, *Prosperity Road: The New Deal, Tobacco, and North Carolina* (1980)
Roger Biles, *Memphis in the Great Depression* (1986)

————, *The South and the New Deal* (1994)

George T. Blakey, *Hard Times and New Deal in Kentucky, 1929–1939* (1986)

James A. Burran, "Urban Racial Violence in the South During World War II: A Comparative Overview," in Walter J. Fraser, Jr., and Winfred B. Moore, Jr., eds., *From the Old South to the New: Essays on the Transitional South* (1981), 167–177

Dominic J. Capeci, Jr., "The Lynching of Cleo Wright: Federal Protection of Constitutional Rights During World War II," *Journal of American History* 72 (1986), 859–887

Dan T. Carter, *Scottsboro: A Tragedy of the American South* (1969)

James C. Cobb, *The Selling of the South* (1982)

James C. Cobb and Michael V. Namorato, eds., *The New Deal and the South* (1984)

Pete Daniel, *Breaking the Land: The Transformation of Cotton, Tobacco, and Rice Cultures Since 1880* (1985)

————, *Standing at the Crossroads* (1986)

Keith Dix, *What's a Coal Miner to Do?* (1988)

Alan Draper, "The New Southern Labor History Revisited: The Success of the Mine, Mill and Smelter Workers Union in Birmingham, 1934–1938," *Journal of Southern History* 62 (February 1996), 87–108

Anthony P. Dunbar, *Against the Grain: Southern Radicals and Prophets, 1929–1959* (1981)

Charles W. Eagles, *Jonathan Daniels and Race Relations: The Evolution of a Southern Liberal* (1982)

John Egerton, *Speak Now Against the Day: The Generation Before the Civil Rights Movement in the South* (1994)

Gilbert C. Fite, *Cotton Fields No More: Southern Agriculture, 1865–1980* (1984)

Frank Freidel, *FDR and the South* (1965)

John Temple Graves, *The Fighting South* (1943)

Donald H. Grubbs, *Cry from the Cotton: The Southern Tenant Farmers' Union and the New Deal* (1971)

William Ivy Hair, *The Kingfish and His Realm: The Life and Times of Huey P. Long* (1991)

Ronald L. Heinemann, *Depression and New Deal in Virginia: The Enduring Dominion* (1983)

John W. Hevener, *Which Side Are You On? The Harlan County Coal Miners, 1931–1939* (1978)

James A. Hodges, *New Deal Labor Policy and the Southern Cotton Textile Industry, 1933–1941* (1986)

Donald Holley, *Uncle Sam's Farmers: The New Deal Communities in the Lower Mississippi Valley* (1975)

Preston J. Hubbard, *Origins of the TVA: The Muscle Shoals Controversy, 1920–1932* (1961)

Glen Jeansonne, *Messiah of the Masses: Huey P. Long and the Great Depression* (1993)

————, ed., *Huey at 100: Centennial Essays on Huey P. Long* (1995)

James Jones, *Bad Blood: The Tuskegee Syphilis Experiment* (1992)

Robin D. G. Kelley, *Hammer and Hoe: Alabama Communists During the Great Depression* (1990)

Jack Temple Kirby, *Rural Worlds Lost: The American South, 1920–1960* (1987)

Thomas A. Krueger, *And Promises to Keep: The Southern Conference for Human Welfare, 1938–1948* (1967)

Michael J. McDonald and John Muldowny, *TVA and the Dispossessed: The Resettlement of Population in the Norris Dam Area* (1982)

Paul Mertz, *New Deal Policy and Southern Rural Poverty* (1978)

H. L. Mitchell, *Mean Things Happening in This Land: The Life and Times of H. L. Mitchell, Co-Founder of the Southern Tenant Farmers Union* (1979)

Chester M. Morgan, *Redneck Liberal: Theodore G. Bilbo and the New Deal* (1985)

Robert J. Norrell, "Caste in Steel: Jim Crow Careers in Birmingham, Alabama," *Journal of American History* 73 (December 1986), 669–694

Nell Painter, *The Narative of Hosea Hudson: His Life as a Negro Communist in the South* (1979)

Richard Polenberg, *War and Society: The United States, 1941–1945* (1972)

Merl E. Reed, "The FEPC, the Black Worker and the Southern Shipyards," *South Atlantic Quarterly* 74 (1974), 446–467

———, "FEPC and Federal Agencies in the South," *Journal of Negro History* 66 (1980), 43–56

John A. Salmond, *A Southern Rebel: The Life and Times of Aubrey Willis Williams, 1890–1965* (1983)

Harvard Sitkoff, *A New Deal for Blacks: The Emergence of Civil Rights as a National Issue,* vol. 1: *The Depression Decade* (1978)

John R. Skates, "World War II as a Watershed in Mississippi History," *Journal of Mississippi History* 37 (1975), 131–142

Morton D. Sosna, *In Search of the Silent South: Southern Liberals and the Race Issue* (1977)

Patricia Sullivan, *Days of Hope: Race and Democracy in the New Deal Era* (1996)

Martha Swain, *Ellen Woodward: New Deal Advocate for Women* (1955)

Tom Terrill and Jerrold Hirsch, eds., *Such As Us: Southern Voices of the Thirties* (1979)

Nancy J. Weiss, *Farewell to the Party of Lincoln: Black Politics in the Age of FDR* (1983)

T. Harry Williams, *Huey Long* (1969)

Nan Elizabeth Woodruff, *As Rare as Rain: Federal Relief in the Great Southern Drought of 1930–31* (1985)

Race Relations and
Freedom Struggles

⚓

Historians of the South have labeled the civil rights movement the Second Reconstruction. It attempted to accomplish what the first Reconstruction movement failed
to do, which was to give enduring civil rights to black southerners. In terms of its
importance to the history of the South, the civil rights movement ranks with the
Civil War and World War II. There is no doubt that the war's theme of greater
diplomacy challenged white supremacists, who reacted with intimidation and violence, especially after the U.S. Supreme Court's Brown decision in 1954. Black
southerners acted too: They pressed to desegregate schools, reenstate voting rights,
and end segregation in public accommodations through boycotts, sit-ins, freedom
rides, and protest marches.

Freedom struggles begin with those who envision justice and courageously act
to secure it. The movement to gain freedom and democracy stemmed in part from
black churches, which had fostered solidarity and had brought forth pastors such as
Martin Luther King, Jr., Fred Shuttlesworth, and Andrew Young and lay leaders
such as Ella Baker and Fannie Lou Hamer. Black colleges and universities became
proving grounds for civil rights activists, men and women, faculty and students
alike. The NAACP, the Southern Christian Leadership Conference (SCLC), the Congress of Racial Equality (CORE), and the Student Non-Violent Coordinating Committee (SNCC) were among the many organizations founded to ensure that the
movement for civil rights would not lose momentum. These groups and individuals
in communities across the South took the freedom struggle to the courts, to the
streets, and to the jury of public opinion; thousands of volunteers learned to practice
nonviolent direct action, which often led to abuse from white supremacists, arrest,
and even death. Thousands of citizens in towns and cities found their own ways to
protest.

Segregation finally began to fall across the South with the 1964 Civil Rights
Act, and, after a series of bloody demonstrations in Mississippi and Alabama, Con-
gress in 1965 enacted the Voting Rights Act. That same year the nation ratified the
Twenty-fourth Amendment to the Constitution, ending poll taxes. The integration of
schools through busing and the desegregation of neighborhoods followed as the U.S.
Supreme Court further defined the term civil rights. Liberation movements for one

*group often inspire others to take action. It is well known that the movement for
civil rights led to a renewed national movement for women's rights as many women
volunteers for civil rights found themselves discriminated against even by their own
colleagues.*

*The historiography of the movement has changed since scholars began writing
its history. Until the early 1980s, most authors concentrated on national figures and
the major sites of the movement. More recently, studies at the state and community
levels have examined the movement from the viewpoint of local people, demonstrated the existence of factions within the movement, and showed the diversity of
actors—black and white, male and female, young and old. Still, questions remain
to be answered. What role did the federal government play in promoting civil
rights? What was the nature of white resistance, and where has white supremacy
found expression today? What was the relationship between local activists and
protest movements and regional and national civil rights organizations? What has
been the legacy of the movement for women's rights. What has the civil rights movement brought to the nation?*

✢ D O C U M E N T S

Document 1 is a personal recollection written by historian Melton McLaurin, who grew
up in Wade, a small town in North Carolina. There he learned (and repudiated) the
meaning of white supremacy. In this selection, he illustrates how profoundly whites believed in the inferiority of blacks and how in one afternoon he came to the full realization of its importance in his own life. By the mid-1950s segregation was beginning to
be fully challenged. Since the 1930s, the U.S. Supreme Court had been eroding the
Plessy v. *Ferguson* (1896) ruling, which held that separate but equal accommodations
were constitutional. In May 1954, the Court decisively overturned that precedent in
Brown v. *Board of Education of Topeka*, declaring that segregation was inherently unequal. A portion of Chief Justice Earl Warren's opinion appears in Document 2. This
decision and subsequent protests by southern blacks provoked strong reaction in the
South, fueled in part by opportunistic politicians. As white supremacy increasingly became the litmus test for officeholding and as the courts continued to rule in favor of
black plaintiffs, a period of massive resistance emerged in the South. Document 3, popularly known as the Southern Manifesto, marked an important stage in this resistance.
Signed by almost all southern senators and congressmen, it aimed to demonstrate white
southern solidarity and thereby forestall federal efforts to implement the *Brown* decision. The Supreme Court unwittingly aided segregationists when it decided in *Brown II*
that schools should desegregate "with all deliberate speed." Many whites responded
with "Never." In 1955, tired of waiting for change, Rosa Parks, a seamstress with a history of civil rights involvement, refused to give up her seat in a Montgomery bus, was
arrested, and thereby helped to initiate the activist stage of the civil rights movement.
Document 4, a memoir by Jo Ann Gibson Robinson, an English professor at Alabama
State College and president of the Women's Political Council, explains how women activists in Montgomery worked through the night to create a successful bus boycott.
This resulted a year later in the end of Jim Crow buses. In 1963 the movement came to
Birmingham, where many members of the SCLC led boycotts and marches to protest
the city's segregated stores and facilities. Martin Luther King, Jr., stirred the ire of the
white clergy, who wrote a letter to the *Birmingham News* asking him to stop the
demonstrations, here reprinted as Document 5. In Document 6, we see excerpts from
his reply. "Letter from Birmingham Jail" has since become one of the classic pieces of

civil rights literature. King began the letter while imprisoned for violating a court injunction; he used religious principles, a stubby pencil, and the margins of a newspaper to discuss the reason why blacks could no longer wait for civil rights. With logic he explained how nonviolent direct action was necessary to "create such a crisis and establish such creative tension that a community that has constantly refused to negotiate is forced to confront the issue." Document 7, written anonymously by women civil rights workers, illustrates the sometimes difficult racial, gender, and class relations that characterized the movement. Equating prejudice against women in the movement with prejudice against African Americans, this SNCC position paper heralds the beginning of the women's rights movement of the late 1960s and 1970s.

1. Melton McLaurin Recalls Segregation

In the South of my youth "good breeding" was still extremely important. Adults who abused blacks "for no good reason" were held in contempt by my family, and as late as the 1950s the older generation talked disparagingly about whites who "treated their colored people mean," as if whites still owned blacks and were compelled by some social code to handle their laborers gently. *Nigger* was a word poor whites used, a term they hurled at blacks (whom the adults in my family always referred to as "colored people") the way my childhood friends from less affluent families hurled pieces of granite from the railway track beds at hapless black children their age or younger. Despite linguistic niceties, however, all whites knew that blacks were, really, servants. It was their destiny to work at menial tasks, supervised, of course, by benevolent whites. All this was according to God's plan and was perfectly obvious to all but dimwitted Yankees and Communists. As a young child I could sit in church with the other white children of the village and sing "Jesus loves the little children . . . Red and yellow, black and white" and never wonder why no black children were in our group. Until I began to work at the store the thought that they should have been in church with us never occurred to me. It also probably never occurred to the adult church members, including the minister.

Race, then, was something I rarely thought about and never pondered—that is, until a single incident, a commonplace occurrence involving Bobo, made me aware of the tremendous impact a segregated society had upon my life. Unlike schoolmates like my best friend, Howard Lee Baker[,] . . . Bobo was never an important part of my life. Bobo was merely there, a child whom I saw frequently and played with on occasion, but who was of no real consequence to me. Because of his relative unimportance, because I had known him all my life, because he had been a part of my childhood environment in the same way as the trees and the school playgrounds and the dusty streets, because, like them, he had always been there, Bobo changed that comfortable, secure racist world for me. He did so unintentionally, yet irrevocably, in the fall of my thirteenth year. . . .

There was certainly nothing extraordinary about physical contact with Bobo. As a child I played football and basketball with him, wrestled with him, and competed against him in other games that were actually boyhood tests of physical strength. . . .

We each enjoyed the physical nature of the contest, the straining of muscles and the measuring contact of young bodies, the sense of manliness that such exertions evoked. . . . Such racial innocence, or perhaps naiveté, soon departed, and with its departure came the realization that segregation fundamentally affected everyone in Wade, whites and blacks, that no one was immune, and that it was a constant force, controlling our present and dictating our future.

The realization occurred in a comfortable, familiar setting on the playground. It was one of those uncommon common incidents of ordinary life which, because of some inexplicable turn of events or perhaps because of their timing, unmask some aspect of our life that we have always accepted as a given, place it in another perspective, and cause it to assume an entirely different face. Often such perceptions are not a result of either education or training but are instead mere happenstances, accidents of understanding, and are as unwelcome as they are unintended.

A basketball court was as appropriate as any place to gain some understanding of the larger implications of segregation and racism. In Wade basketball was the premier sport, played continually by boys, black and white, from September through May. . . .

Pickup games between integrated teams were nothing unusual; in fact, they were the norm when blacks and whites played on the same court. . . . Although race was not completely ignored on the courts, it rarely influenced the conduct of a game. In all the years I played in such integrated contests, I never saw a fight provoked for racial reasons, though disputes over fouls, out-of-bounds plays, and other technicalities occurred with monotonous regularity during practically every game. The lack of racial tensions on the court probably stemmed from the fact that the society accepted, and in many ways encouraged, the practice of integrated play. Young southern males had traditionally engaged in integrated informal sports events, especially such outdoor sports as hunting and fishing. Integrated pickup basketball games, as opposed to organized play, were merely an extension of this practice. It was only contact with females of the opposite race that was proscribed, and that only after puberty. . . .

One fall Saturday afternoon six of us were matched in a hotly contested game, neither of the equally untalented threesomes able to gain much of an advantage. Howard Lee and I, the only whites in the game, were joined by an awkward young black named Curtis, whose reasonably accurate jump shot was negated by his general lack of coordination. Bobo played on the other team, opposite me as usual. . . .

We were using Howard Lee's ball, which presented a challenge because it leaked air and had to be reinflated every thirty minutes or so. Since there was an air compressor at the store, I was charged with keeping the ball inflated. Although we played on a black playground, the white kids controlled the situation because we controlled the ball. None of the black players had a ball, so without us there was no game. . . .

We played into the afternoon, our play interrupted by frequent trips to the air compressor. When enough air leaked from the ball to cause it to lose its bounce and begin to interfere with the game, I would take it to the air compressor to pump it up.

... When we reached the air compressor I pulled from my pocket the needle required to inflate the ball and without thinking handed it to Bobo.

The procedure followed for inserting a needle into a basketball had long been sanctioned by the rituals of kids playing on dirt and asphalt courts. First, someone wet the needle by sticking it into his mouth or spitting on it. Thus lubricated, the instrument was popped neatly into the small rubber valve through which the ball was inflated. This time chance dictated that playground procedure would fail; we couldn't insert the needle into the valve. Bobo stuck the needle in his mouth, applied the usual lavish amount of saliva, and handed it to Howard Lee, who held the ball. Howard struggled to push the needle into the valve, with no luck. Irritated by what struck me as their incompetence and anxious to return to the game I decided to inflate the ball myself. I took the ball from Howard, pulled the needle from the valve, and placed it in my mouth, convinced that my spit would somehow get the needle into the ball and us back onto the court. A split second after placing the needle in my mouth, I was jolted by one of the most shattering emotional experiences of my young life. Instantaneously an awareness of the shared racial prejudices of generations of white society coursed through every nerve of my body. Bolts of prejudice, waves of prejudice that I could literally feel sent my head reeling and buckled my knees.

The realization that the needle I still held in my mouth had come directly from Bobo's mouth, that it carried on it Bobo's saliva, transformed my prejudices into a physically painful experience. I often had drunk from the same cup as black children, dined on food prepared by blacks. It never occurred to me that such actions would violate my racial purity. The needle in my mouth, however, had been purposely drenched with Negro spit, and that substance threatened to defile my entire being. It threatened me with germs which, everyone said, were common among blacks. These black germs would ravage my body with unspeakable diseases, diseases from the tropics, Congo illnesses that would rot my limbs, contort my body with pain. . . . Those awful African diseases, I now imagined, would claim me as a victim.

The tainted substance on the needle also threatened, in a less specific but equally disturbing manner, my white consciousness, my concept of what being white meant. Bobo's spit threatened to plunge me into a world of voodoo chants and tribal drums. Suddenly the *Saturday Evening Post* cartoon world of black savages dancing about boiling cauldrons filled with white hunters and missionaries seemed strangely real. I felt deprived of the ability to reason, to control the situation. All threats to mind and body, however, failed to compare to the ultimate danger posed by the saliva on the needle. It placed in jeopardy my racial purity, my existence as a superior being, the true soul of all southern whites. . . .

. . . The urge to gag, to lean over and vomit out any of the black saliva that might remain to spread its contamination throughout my body, was almost unbearable. Yet I could neither gag nor vomit, nor could I wipe my mouth with the back of my hand. Ironically, the same prejudices that filled me with loathing and disgust also demanded that I conceal my feelings. The emotional turmoil exploding inside me had to be contained, choked off. Not for a second could I allow Bobo to suspect that I was in the least upset, or to comprehend the anguish his simple act of moistening the needle with his saliva had caused me. . . . More than the poison of Bobo's saliva I feared the slightest indication of loss of self-control, the merest hint that this black child I knew so well had the power to cut me to the emotional quick, to reach the innermost regions of my being and challenge the sureties of my white world. He could never be allowed to cause me to deviate in the least from the prescribed pattern of white behavior. . . .

Yet my vindication of white supremacy was incomplete. While I had asserted my superiority and my right to that status because of my skin color, I still felt defiled. The thought that some residual contamination, some lingering trace of the essence of Bobo's blackness remained with me became an obsession. I could feel his germs crawling through my body, spreading their black pestilence from head to toe. I had to cleanse myself—to purify my body of Bobo's contaminants and to rid my person of any remaining trace of his negritude. Only then could I fully reclaim my racial purity and restore my shaken sense of superiority. And I had to do so quickly, without the knowledge of others, before I could return to the game.

. . . From the side of the building protruded a faucet, used by thirsty ball players who had no money for Cokes. Bending over, I turned the tap and watched the clear, clean water burst from the spigot and spatter into the sand. I cupped my hands beneath the flow, watched them fill with the crystal liquid, then splashed it to my face, felt it begin to cleanse me of Bobo's black stain. Bending farther, I placed my mouth against the grooved lip of the faucet. . . . I let the cleansing stream trickle through my mouth, removing any remaining Negro contaminant. I splashed more water over my face and head, then washed my hands and forearms. Finally, I swallowed a large gulp of water, felt it slide down my throat, and in my mind's eye saw it wash away the last traces of Bobo's blackness. My rite of purification was completed. With this baptism of plain tap water I was reborn, my white selfhood restored. I stood straight, shook the water from my face and hands, and walked back to rejoin the game.

. . . What I remember is an awareness that things had changed. I knew that Bobo was black, that he would always be black, and that his blackness set him apart from me in ways that I had never understood. I realized, too, that his blackness threatened me, that in a way I did not comprehend it challenged my most securely held concepts about who I was and what I might become. . . . I also knew that there was something very wrong, even sinister, about this power Bobo held over me, this ability to confound my world simply because he was black. None of it made much sense at the time. But the knowledge, the understanding that segregation was so powerful a force, that it could provoke such violent emotional responses within me, for the first time raised questions in my mind about the institution, serious questions that adults didn't want asked and, as I would later discover, that they never answered.

2. *Brown* v. *Board of Education of Topeka, Kansas,* 1954

Mr. Chief Justice Warren delivered the opinion of the Court. . . .

This document can be found in Brown v. Board of Education: 349 U.S. 483 (May 17, 1954).

Today, education is perhaps the most important function of state and local governments. Compulsory school attendance laws and the great expenditures for education both demonstrate our recognition of the importance of education to our democratic society. It is required in the performance of our most basic public responsibilities, even service in the armed forces. It is the very foundation of good citizenship. Today it is a principal instrument in awakening the child to cultural values, in preparing him for later professional training, and in helping him to adjust normally to his environment. In these days, it is doubtful that any child may reasonably be expected to succeed in life if he is denied the opportunity of an education. Such an opportunity, where the state has undertaken to provide it, is a right which must be made available to all on equal terms.

We come then to the question presented: Does segregation of children in public schools solely on the basis of race, even though the physical facilities and other "tangible" factors may be equal, deprive the children of the minority group of equal educational opportunities? We believe that it does.

In *Sweatt* v. *Painter* . . . , in finding that a segregated law school for Negroes could not provide them equal educational opportunities, this Court relied in large part on "those qualities which are incapable of objective measurement but which make for greatness in a law school." In *McLaurin* v. *Oklahoma State Regents,* . . . the Court, in requiring that a Negro admitted to a white graduate school be treated like all other students, again resorted to intangible considerations: ". . . his ability to study, to engage in discussions and exchange views with other students, and, in general, to learn his profession." Such considerations apply with added force to children in grade and high schools. To separate them from others of similar age and qualifications solely because of their race generates a feeling of inferiority as to their status in the community that may affect their hearts and minds in a way unlikely ever to be undone. The effect of this separation on their educational opportunities was well stated by a finding in the Kansas case by a court which nevertheless felt compelled to rule against the Negro plaintiffs:

> Segregation of white and colored children in public schools has a detrimental effect upon the colored children. The impact is greater when it has the sanction of the law; for the policy of separating the races is usually interpreted as denoting the inferiority of the negro group. A sense of inferiority affects the motivation of a child to learn. Segregation with the sanction of law, therefore, has a tendency to [retard] the educational and mental development of Negro children and to deprive them of some of the benefits they would receive in a racial[ly] integrated school system.

Whatever may have been the extent of psychological knowledge at the time of *Plessy* v. *Ferguson,* this finding is amply supported by modern authority. Any language in *Plessy* v. *Ferguson* contrary to this finding is rejected.

We conclude that in the field of public education the doctrine of "separate but equal" has no place. Separate educational facilities are inherently unequal. Therefore, we hold that the plaintiffs and others similarly situated for whom the actions have been brought are, by reason of the segregation complained of, deprived of the equal protection of the laws guaranteed by the Fourteenth Amendment.

3. The Southern Manifesto, 1956

The unwarranted decision of the Supreme Court in the public school cases is now bearing the fruit always produced when men substitute naked power for established law.

The Founding Fathers gave us a Constitution of checks and balances because they realized the inescapable lesson of history that no man or group of men can be safely entrusted with unlimited power. They framed this Constitution with its provisions for change by amendment in order to secure the fundamentals of government against the dangers of temporary popular passion or the personal predilections of public officeholders.

We regard the decision of the Supreme Court in the school cases as a clear abuse of judicial power. It climaxes a trend in the Federal Judiciary undertaking to legislate, in derogation of the authority of Congress, and to encroach upon the reserved rights of the States and the people.

The original Constitution does not mention education. Neither does the 14th amendment nor any other amendment. The debates preceding the submission of the 14th amendment clearly show that there was no intent that it should affect the system of education maintained by the States.

The very Congress which proposed the amendment subsequently provided for segregated schools in the District of Columbia.

When the amendment was adopted in 1868, there were 37 States of the Union. Every one of the 26 States that had any substantial racial differences among its people, either approved the operation of segregated schools already in existence or subsequently established such schools by action of the same law-making body which considered the 14th amendment.

As admitted by the Supreme Court in the public school case (*Brown* v. *Board of Education*), the doctrine of separate but equal schools "apparently originated in *Roberts* v. *City of Boston* (1849), upholding school segregation against attack as being violative of a State constitutional guarantee of equality." This constitutional doctrine began in the North, not in the South, and it was followed not only in Massachusetts, but in Connecticut, New York, Illinois, Indiana, Michigan, Minnesota, New Jersey, Ohio, Pennsylvania and other northern States until they, exercising their rights as States through the constitutional processes of local self-government, changed their school systems.

In the case of *Plessy* v. *Ferguson* in 1896 the Supreme Court expressly declared that under the 14th amendment no person was denied any of his rights if the States provided separate but equal public facilities. This decision has been followed in many other cases. It is notable that the Supreme Court, speaking through Chief Justice Taft, a former President of the United States, unanimously declared in 1927 in *Lum* v. *Rice* that the "separate but equal" principle is "within the discretion of the State in regulating its public schools and does not conflict with the 14th amendment."

This interpretation, restated time and again, became a part of the life of the people of many of the States and confirmed their habits, customs, traditions, and way of

---

This document can be found in *Southern School* News, April, 1956.

life. It is founded on elemental humanity and common-sense, for parents should not be deprived by Government of the right to direct the lives and education of their own children.

Though there has been no constitutional amendment or act of Congress changing this established legal principle almost a century old, the Supreme Court of the United States, with no legal basis for such action, undertook to exercise their naked judicial power and substituted their personal political and social ideas for the established law of the land.

This unwarranted exercise of power by the Court, contrary to the Constitution, is creating chaos and confusion in the States principally affected. It is destroying the amicable relations between the white and Negro races that have been created through 90 years of patient effort by the good people of both races. It has planted hatred and suspicion where there has been heretofore friendship and understanding.

Without regard to the consent of the governed, outside agitators are threatening immediate and revolutionary changes in our public-school systems. If done, this is certain to destroy the system of public education in some of the States.

With the gravest concern for the explosive and dangerous condition created by this decision and inflamed by outside meddlers:

We reaffirm our reliance on the Constitution as the fundamental law of the land.

We decry the Supreme Court's encroachment on rights reserved to the States and to the people, contrary to established law, and to the Constitution.

We commend the motives of those States which have declared the intention to resist forced integration by any lawful means.

We appeal to the States and people who are not directly affected by these decisions to consider the constitutional principles involved against the time when they too, on issues vital to them, may be the victims of judicial encroachment.

Even though we constitute a minority in the present Congress, we have full faith that a majority of the American people believe in the dual system of government which has enabled us to achieve our greatness and will in time demand that the reserved rights of the States and of the people be made secure against judicial usurpation.

We pledge ourselves to use all lawful means to bring about a reversal of this decision which is contrary to the Constitution and to prevent the use of force in its implementation.

In this trying period, as we all seek to right this wrong, we appeal to our people not to be provoked by the agitators and troublemakers invading our States and to scrupulously refrain from disorder and lawless acts.

4. Jo Ann Gibson Robinson on the Montgomery Bus Boycott, 1955

In the afternoon of Thursday, December 1, a prominent black woman named Mrs. Rosa Parks was arrested for refusing to vacate her seat for a white man. Mrs. Parks

From *The Montgomery Bus Boycott and the Woman Who Started It: The Memoir of Jo Ann Gibson Robinson,* edited by David J. Garrow. Copyright © 1987 by The University of Tennessee Press.

was a medium-sized, cultured mulatto woman; a civic and religious worker; quiet, unassuming, and pleasant in manner and appearance; dignified and reserved; of high morals and a strong character. She was . . . respected in all black circles. By trade she was a seamstress, adept and competent in her work.

Tired from work, Mrs. Parks boarded a bus. The "reserved seats" were partially filled, but the seats just behind the reserved section were vacant, and Mrs. Parks sat down in one. . . . More black and white passengers boarded the bus, and soon all the reserved seats were occupied. The driver demanded that Mrs. Parks get up and surrender her seat to a white man, but she was tired from her work. Besides, she was a woman, and the person waiting was a man. She remained seated. In a few minutes, police summoned by the driver appeared, placed Mrs. Parks under arrest, and took her to jail.

It was the first time the soft-spoken, middle-aged woman had been arrested. She maintained decorum and poise, and the word of her arrest spread. Mr. E. D. Nixon, a longtime stalwart of our NAACP branch, along with liberal white attorney Clifford Durr and his wife Virginia, went to the jail and obtained Mrs. Parks's release on bond. Her trial was scheduled for Monday, December 5, 1955.

The news traveled like wildfire into every black home. Telephones jangled; people congregated on street corners and in homes and talked. But nothing was done. A numbing helplessness seemed to paralyze everyone. Very few stayed off the buses the rest of that day or the next. There was fear, discontent, and uncertainty. . . .

Thursday evening came and went. Thursday night was far spent, when, at about 11:30 P.M., I sat alone in my peaceful single-family dwelling on a quiet street. I was thinking about the situation. Lost in thought, I was startled by the telephone's ring. Black attorney Fred Gray . . . was returning the phone message I had left for him about Mrs. Parks's arrest. Attorney Gray, though a very young man, had been one of my most active colleagues in our previous meetings with bus company officials and Commissioner Birmingham. . . .

Tonight his voice on the phone was very short and to the point. Fred was shocked by the news of Mrs. Parks's arrest. I informed him that I already was thinking that the WPC [Women's Political Council] should distribute thousands of notices calling for all bus riders to stay off the buses on Monday, the day of Mrs. Parks's trial. "Are you ready?," he asked. Without hesitation, I assured him that we were. With that he hung up, and I went to work.

I made some notes on the back of an envelope: "The Women's Political Council will not wait for Mrs. Parks's consent to call for a boycott of city buses. On Friday, December 2, 1955, the women of Montgomery will call for a boycott to take place on Monday, December 5."

Some of the WPC officers previously had discussed plans for distributing thousands of notices announcing a bus boycott. Now the time had come for me to write just such a notice. I sat down and quickly drafted a message and then called a good friend and colleague, John Cannon, chairman of the business department at the college, who had access to the college's mimeograph equipment. . . . Along with two of my most trusted senior students, we quickly agreed to meet almost immediately, in the middle of the night, at the college's duplicating room. We were able to get three messages to a page, greatly reducing the number of pages that had to be mimeographed in order to produce the tens of thousands of leaflets we knew would be needed. By 4 A.M. Friday, the sheets had been duplicated, cut in thirds, and bundled. Each leaflet read:

> Another Negro woman has been arrested and thrown in jail because she refused to get up out of her seat on the bus for a white person to sit down. It is the second time since the Claudette Colvin case that a Negro woman has been arrested for the same thing. This has to be stopped. Negroes have rights, too, for if Negroes did not ride the buses, they could not operate. Three-fourths of the riders are Negroes, yet we are arrested, or have to stand over empty seats. If we do not do something to stop these arrests, they will continue. The next time it may be you, or your daughter, or mother. This woman's case will come up on Monday. We are, therefore, asking every Negro to stay off the buses Monday in protest of the arrest and trial. Don't ride the buses to work, to town, to school, or anywhere on Monday. You can afford to stay out of school for one day if you have no other way to go except by bus. You can also afford to stay out of town for one day. If you work, take a cab, or walk. But please, children and grown-ups, don't ride the bus at all on Monday. Please stay off of all buses Monday.

Between 4 and 7 A.M., the two students and I mapped out distribution routes for the notices. . . . We outlined our routes, arranged the bundles in sequences, stacked them in our cars, and arrived at my 8 A.M. class, in which both young men were enrolled, with several minutes to spare. We weren't even tired or hungry. . . .

After class my two students and I quickly finalized our plans for distributing the thousands of leaflets so that one would reach every black home in Montgomery. I took out the WPC membership roster and called the former president, Dr. Mary Fair Burks, then the Pierces, the Glasses, Mrs. Mary Cross, Mrs. Elizabeth Arrington, Mrs. Josie Lawrence, Mrs. Geraldine Nesbitt, Mrs. H. Councill Trenholm, Mrs. Catherine N. Johnson, and a dozen or more others. I alerted all of them to the forthcoming distribution of the leaflets, and enlisted their aid in speeding and organizing the distribution network. . . .

Then I and my two student helpers set out. Throughout the late morning and early afternoon hours we dropped off tens of thousands of leaflets. Some of our bundles were dropped off at schools, where both students and staff members helped distribute them further and spread the word for people to read the notices and then pass them on to neighbors. Leaflets were also dropped off at business places, storefronts, beauty parlors, beer halls, factories, barber shops, and every other available place. Workers would pass along notices both to other employees as well as to customers.

During those hours of crucial work, nothing went wrong. . . . The action of all involved was so casual, so unconcerned, so nonchalant, that suspicion was never raised, and neither the city nor its people ever suspected a thing! . . . And no one missed a class, a job, or a normal routine. Everything was done by the plan, with perfect timing. By 2 o'clock, thousands of the mimeographed handbills had changed hands many times. Practically every black man, woman, and child in Montgomery knew the plan and was passing the word along. No one knew where the notices had come from or who had arranged for their circulation, and no one cared. Those who passed them on did so efficiently, quietly, and without comment. But deep within the heart of every black person was a joy he or she dared not reveal.

5. Letter from Alabama Clergy, 1963

April 12, 1963

We the undersigned clergymen are among those who, in January, issued "An Appeal for Law and Order and Common Sense," in dealing with racial problems in Alabama. We expressed understanding that honest convictions in racial matters could properly be pursued in the courts, but urged that decisions of those courts should in the meantime be peacefully obeyed.

Since that time there had been some evidence of increased forebearance and a willingness to face facts. Responsible citizens have undertaken to work on various problems which cause racial friction and unrest. In Birmingham, recent public events have given indication that we all have opportunity for a new constructive and realistic approach to racial problems.

However, we are now confronted by a series of demonstrations by some of our Negro citizens, directed and led in part by outsiders. We recognize the natural impatience of people who feel that their hopes are slow in being realized. But we are convinced that these demonstrations are unwise and untimely.

We agree rather with certain local Negro leadership which has called for honest and open negotiation of racial issues in our area. And we believe this kind of facing of issues can best be accomplished by citizens of our own metropolitan area, white and Negro, meeting with their knowledge and experience of the local situation. All of us need to face that responsibility and find proper channels for its accomplishment.

Just as we formerly pointed out that "hatred and violence have no sanction in our religious and political traditions," we also point out that such actions as incite to hatred and violence, however technically peaceful those actions may be, have not contributed to the resolution of our local problems. We do not believe that these days of new hope are days when extreme measures are justified in Birmingham.

We commend the community as a whole, and the local news media and law enforcement officials in particular, on the calm manner in which these demonstrations have been handled. We urge the public to continue to show restraint should the demonstrations continue, and the law enforcement officials to remain calm and continue to protect our city from violence.

We further strongly urge our own Negro community to withdraw support from these demonstrations, and to unite locally in working peacefully for a better Birmingham. When rights are consistently denied, a cause should be pressed in the courts and in negotiations among local leaders, and not in the streets. We appeal to both our white and Negro citizenry to observe the principles of law and order and common sense.

C.C.J. Carpenter, D.D., L.L.D., Bishop of Alabama; Joseph A. Durick, D.D., Auxiliary Bishop, Diocese of Mobile-Birmingham; Rabbi Milton L. Grafman, Temple Emanu-El, Birmingham, Alabama; Bishop Paul Hardin, Bishop of the Alabama-

West Florida Conference of the Methodist Church; Bishop Nolan B. Harmon, Bishop of the North Alabama Conference of the Methodist Church; George M. Murray, D.D., L.L.D., Bishop Coadjutor, Episcopal Diocese of Alabama; Edward V. Ramage, Moderator, Synod of the Alabama Presbyterian Church in the United States; Earl Stallings, Pastor, First Baptist Church, Birmingham, Alabama.

6. Martin Luther King, Jr.'s Letter from Birmingham Jail, 1963

My dear Fellow Clergymen,

While confined here in the Birmingham city jail, I came across your recent statement calling our present activities "unwise and untimely." Seldom, if ever, do I pause to answer criticism of my work and ideas. If I sought to answer all of the criticisms that cross my desk, my secretaries would be engaged in little else in the course of the day, and I would have no time for constructive work. But since I feel that you are men of genuine good will and your criticisms are sincerely set forth, I would like to answer your statement in what I hope will be patient and reasonable terms.

I think I should give the reason for my being in Birmingham, since you have been influenced by the argument of "outsiders coming in." I have the honor of serving as president of the Southern Christian Leadership Conference, an organization operating in every southern state, with headquarters in Atlanta, Georgia. We have some eighty-five affiliate organizations all across the South—one being the Alabama Christian Movement for Human Rights. Whenever necessary and possible we share staff, educational and financial resources with our affiliates. Several months ago our local affiliate here in Birmingham invited us to be on call to engage in a nonviolent direct-action program if such were deemed necessary. We readily consented and when the hour came we lived up to our promises. So I am here, along with several members of my staff, because we were invited here. I am here because I have basic organizational ties here.

Beyond this, I am in Birmingham because injustice is here. Just as the eighth century prophets left their little villages and carried their "thus saith the Lord" far beyond the boundaries of their hometowns; and just as the Apostle Paul left his little village of Tarsus and carried the gospel of Jesus Christ to practically every hamlet and city of the Graeco-Roman world, I too am compelled to carry the gospel of freedom beyond my particular hometown. Like Paul, I must constantly respond to the Macedonian call for aid.

Moreover, I am cognizant of the interrelatedness of all communities and states. I cannot sit idly by in Atlanta and not be concerned about what happens in Birmingham. Injustice anywhere is a threat to justice everywhere. We are caught in an inescapable network of mutuality, tied in a single garment of destiny. Whatever affects one directly affects all indirectly. Never again can we afford to live with the narrow, provincial "outside agitator" idea. Anyone who lives in the United States can never be considered an outsider anywhere in this country.

You deplore the demonstrations that are presently taking place in Birmingham. But I am sorry that your statement did not express a similar concern for the conditions that brought the demonstrations into being. I am sure that each of you would want to go beyond the superficial social analyst who looks merely at effects, and does not grapple with underlying causes. I would not hesitate to say that it is unfortunate that so-called demonstrations are taking place in Birmingham at this time, but I would say in more emphatic terms that it is even more unfortunate that the white power structure of this city left the Negro community with no other alternative.

In any nonviolent campaign there are four basic steps: (1) collection of the facts to determine whether injustices are alive, (2) negotiation, (3) self-purification, and (4) direct action. We have gone through all of these steps in Birmingham. There can be no gainsaying of the fact that racial injustice engulfs this community.

Birmingham is probably the most thoroughly segregated city in the United States. Its ugly record of police brutality is known in every section of this country. Its injust treatment of Negroes in the courts is a notorious reality. There have been more unsolved bombings of Negro homes and churches in Birmingham than any city in this nation. These are the hard, brutal and unbelievable facts. On the basis of these conditions Negro leaders sought to negotiate with the city fathers. But the political leaders consistently refused to engage in good faith negotiation.

Then came the opportunity last September to talk with some of the leaders of the economic community. In these negotiating sessions certain promises were made by the merchants—such as the promise to remove the humiliating racial signs from the stores. On the basis of these promises Rev. [Fred] Shuttlesworth and the leaders of the Alabama Christian Movement for Human Rights agreed to call a moratorium on any type of demonstrations. As the weeks and months unfolded we realized that we were the victims of a broken promise. The signs remained. Like so many experiences of the past we were confronted with blasted hopes, and the dark shadow of a deep disappointment settled upon us. So we had no alternative except that of preparing for direct action, whereby we would present our very bodies as a means of laying our case before the conscience of the local and national community. We were not unmindful of the difficulties involved. So we decided to go through a process of self-purification. We started having workshops on nonviolence and repeatedly asked ourselves the questions, "Are you able to accept blows without retaliating?" "Are you able to endure the ordeals of jail?" We decided to set our direct-action program around the Easter season, realizing that with the exception of Christmas, this was the largest shopping period of the year. Knowing that a strong economic withdrawal program would be the by-product of direct action, we felt that this was the best time to bring pressure on the merchants for the needed changes. Then it occurred to us that the March election was ahead and so we speedily decided to postpone action until after election day. When we discovered that Mr. [Eugene "Bull"] Connor [Birmingham's Public Safety Commissioner] was in the run-off, we decided again to postpone action so that the demonstrations could not be used to cloud the issues. At this time we agreed to begin our nonviolent witness the day after the run-off.

This reveals that we did not move irresponsibly into direct action. We too wanted to see Mr. Connor defeated; so we went through postponement after postponement to aid in this community need. After this we felt that direct action could be delayed no longer.

You may well ask, "Why direct action? Why sit-ins, marches, etc.? Isn't negotiation a better path?" You are exactly right in your call for negotiation. Indeed, this is the purpose of direct action. Nonviolent direct action seeks to create such a crisis and establish such creative tension that a community that has constantly refused to negotiate is forced to confront the issue. It seeks so to dramatize the issue that it can no longer be ignored. I just referred to the creation of tension as a part of the work of the nonviolent resister. This may sound rather shocking. But I must confess that I am not afraid of the word tension. I have earnestly worked and preached against violent tension, but there is a type of constructive nonviolent tension that is necessary for growth. Just as Socrates felt that it was necessary to create a tension in the mind so that individuals could rise from the bondage of myths and half-truths to the unfettered realm of creative analysis and objective appraisal, we must see the need of having nonviolent gadflies to create the kind of tension in society that will help men to rise from the dark depths of prejudice and racism to the majestic heights of understanding and brotherhood. So the purpose of the direct action is to create a situation so crisis-packed that it will inevitably open the door to negotiation. We, therefore, concur with you in your call for negotiation. Too long has our beloved Southland been bogged down in the tragic attempt to live in monologue rather than dialogue.

One of the basic points in your statement is that our acts are untimely. Some have asked, "Why didn't you give the new administration time to act?" The only answer that I can give to this inquiry is that the new administration must be prodded about as much as the outgoing one before it acts. We will be sadly mistaken if we feel that the election of Mr. Boutwell will bring the millennium to Birmingham. While Mr. Boutwell is much more articulate and gentle than Mr. Connor, they are both segregationists, dedicated to the task of maintaining the status quo. The hope I see in Mr. Boutwell is that he will be reasonable enough to see the futility of massive resistance to desegregation. But he will not see this without pressure from the devotees of civil rights. My friends, I must say to you that we have not made a single gain in civil rights without determined legal and nonviolent pressure. History is the long and tragic story of the fact that privileged groups seldom give up their privileges voluntarily. Individuals may see the moral light and voluntarily give up their unjust posture; but as Reinhold Niebuhr has reminded us, groups are more immoral than individuals.

We know through painful experience that freedom is never voluntarily given by the oppressor; it must be demanded by the oppressed. Frankly, I have never yet engaged in a direct action movement that was "well-timed," according to the timetable of those who have not suffered unduly from the disease of segregation. For years now I have heard the word "Wait!" It rings in the ear of every Negro with a piercing familiarity. This "Wait!" has almost always meant "Never." It has been a tranquilizing thalidomide [a drug that caused birth defects], relieving the emotional stress for a moment, only to give birth to an ill-formed infant of frustration. We must come to see with the distinguished jurist of yesterday that "justice too long delayed is justice denied." We have waited for more than 340 years for our constitutional and God-given rights. The nations of Asia and Africa are moving with jetlike speed toward the goal of political independence, and we still creep at horse and buggy pace toward the gaining of a cup of coffee at a lunch counter. I guess it is easy for those who have never felt the stinging darts of segregation to say, "Wait." But when you have seen vicious mobs lynch your mothers and fathers at will and drown your sisters and brothers at whim; when you have seen hate-filled policemen curse, kick, brutalize and even kill your black brothers and sisters with impunity; when you see the vast majority of your twenty million Negro brothers smothering in an airtight cage of poverty in the midst of an affluent society; when you suddenly find your tongue twisted and your speech stammering as you seek to explain to your six-year-old daughter why she can't go to the public amusement park that has just been advertised on television, and see tears welling up in her little eyes when she is told that Funtown is closed to colored children, and see the depressing clouds of inferiority begin to form in her little mental sky, and see her begin to distort her little personality by unconsciously developing a bitterness toward white people; when you have to concoct an answer for a five-year-old son asking in agonizing pathos: "Daddy, why do white people treat colored people so mean?"; when you take a cross-country drive and find it necessary to sleep night after night in the uncomfortable corners of your automobile because no motel will accept you; when you are humiliated day in and day out by nagging signs reading "white" and "colored"; when your first name becomes "nigger" and your middle name becomes "boy" (however old you are) and your last name becomes "John," and when your wife and mother are never given the respected title "Mrs."; when you are harried by day and haunted by night by the fact that you are a Negro, living constantly at tiptoe stance never quite knowing what to expect next, and plagued with inner fears and outer resentments; when you are forever fighting a degenerating sense of "nobodiness"; then you will understand why we find it difficult to wait. There comes a time when the cup of endurance runs over, and men are no longer willing to be plunged into an abyss of injustice where they experience the blackness of corroding despair. I hope, sirs, you can understand our legitimate and unavoidable impatience.

You express a great deal of anxiety over our willingness to break laws. This is certainly a legitimate concern. Since we so diligently urge people to obey the Supreme Court's decision of 1954 outlawing segregation in the public schools, it is rather strange and paradoxical to find us consciously breaking laws. One may well ask, "How can you advocate breaking some laws and obeying others?" The answer is found in the fact that there are two types of laws: there are *just* and there are *unjust* laws. I would agree with Saint Augustine that "An unjust law is no law at all."

Now what is the difference between the two? How does one determine when a law is just or unjust? A just law is a man-made code that squares with the moral law or the law of God. An unjust law is a code that is out of harmony with the moral law. To put it in the terms of Saint Thomas Aquinas, an unjust law is a human law that is not rooted in eternal and natural law. Any law that uplifts human personality is just. Any law that degrades human personality is unjust. All segregation statutes are unjust because segregation distorts the soul and damages the personality. It gives the segregator a false sense of superiority, and the segregated a false sense of inferiority. To use the words of Martin Buber, the great Jewish philosopher, segregation substitutes an "I-it" relationship for the "I-thou" relationship, and ends up relegating persons to the status of things. So segregation is not only politically, economically and sociologically unsound, but it is morally wrong and sinful. Paul Tillich has said that sin is separation. Isn't segregation an existential expression of man's tragic separation, an expression of his awful estrangement, his terrible sinfulness? So I can urge men to disobey segregation ordinances because they are morally wrong.

Let us turn to a more concrete example of just and unjust laws. An unjust law is a code that a majority inflicts on a minority that is not binding on itself. This is difference made legal. On the other hand a just law is a code that a majority compels a minority to follow that it is willing to follow itself. This is sameness made legal.

Let me give another explanation. An unjust law is a code inflicted upon a minority which that minority had no part in enacting or creating because they did not have the unhampered right to vote. Who can say that the legislature of Alabama which set up the segregation laws was democratically elected? Throughout the state of Alabama all types of conniving methods are used to prevent Negroes from becoming registered voters and there are some counties without a single Negro registered to vote despite the fact that the Negro constitutes a majority of the population. Can any law set up in such a state be considered democratically structured?

These are just a few examples of unjust and just laws. There are some instances when a law is just on its face and unjust in its application. For instance, I was arrested Friday on a charge of parading without a permit. Now there is nothing wrong with an ordinance which requires a permit for a parade, but when the ordinance is used to preserve segregation and to deny citizens the First Amendment privilege of peaceful assembly and peaceful protest, then it becomes unjust.

I hope you can see the distinction I am trying to point out. In no sense do I advocate evading or defying the law as the rabid segregationist would do. This would lead to anarchy. One who breaks an unjust law must do it *openly, lovingly* (not hatefully as the white mothers did in New Orleans when they were seen on television screaming, "nigger, nigger, nigger"), and with a willingness to accept the penalty. I submit that an individual who breaks a law that conscience tells him is unjust, and willingly accepts the penalty by staying in jail to arouse the conscience of the community over its injustice, is in reality expressing the very highest respect for law.

Of course, there is nothing new about this kind of civil disobedience. It was seen sublimely in the refusal of Shadrach, Meshach and Abednego to obey the laws of Nebuchadnezzar because a higher moral law was involved. It was practiced superbly by the early Christians who were willing to face hungry lions and the excruciating pain of chopping blocks, before submitting to certain unjust laws of the Roman Empire. To a degree academic freedom is a reality today because Socrates practiced civil disobedience.

We can never forget that everything Hitler did in Germany was "legal" and everything the Hungarian freedom fighters did in Hungary was "illegal." It was "illegal" to aid and comfort a Jew in Hitler's Germany. But I am sure that if I had lived in Germany during that time I would have aided and comforted my Jewish brothers even though it was illegal. If I lived in a Communist country today where certain principles dear to the Christian faith are suppressed, I believe I would openly advocate disobeying these anti-religious laws. I must make two honest confessions to you, my Christian and Jewish brothers. First, I must confess that over the last few years I have been gravely disappointed with the white moderate. I have almost reached the regrettable conclusion that the Negro's great stumbling block in the stride toward freedom is not the White Citizen's Counciler or the Ku Klux Klanner, but the white moderate who is more devoted to "order" than to justice; who prefers a negative peace which is the absence of tension to a positive peace which is the presence of justice; who constantly says, "I agree with you in the goal you seek, but I can't agree with your methods of direct action"; who paternalistically feels that he can set the timetable for another man's freedom; who lives by the myth of time and who constantly advised the Negro to wait until a "more convenient season." Shallow understanding from people of good will is more frustrating than absolute misunderstanding from people of ill will. Lukewarm acceptance is much more bewildering than outright rejection. . . .

I wish you had commended the Negro sit-inners and demonstrators of Birmingham for their sublime courage, their willingness to suffer and their amazing discipline in the midst of the most inhuman provocation. One day the South will recognize its real heroes. They will be the James Merediths, courageously and with a majestic sense of purpose facing jeering and hostile mobs and the agonizing loneliness that characterizes the life of the pioneer. They will be old, oppressed, battered Negro women, symbolized in a seventy-two-year-old woman of Montgomery, Alabama, who rose up with a sense of dignity and with her people decided not to ride the segregated buses, and responded to one who inquired about her tiredness with ungrammatical profundity: "My feet is tired, but my soul is rested." They will be the young high school and college students, young ministers of the gospel and a host of their elders courageously and nonviolently sitting-in at lunch counters and willingly going to jail for conscience's sake. One day the South will know that when these disinherited children of God sat down at lunch counters they were in reality standing up for the best in the American dream and the most sacred values in our Judeo-Christian heritage, and thusly, carrying our whole nation back to those great wells of democracy which were dug deep by the Founding Fathers in the formulation of the Constitution and the Declaration of Independence. . . .

I hope this letter finds you strong in the faith. I also hope that circumstances will soon make it possible for me to meet each of you, not as an integrationist or a civil rights leader, but as a fellow clergyman and a Christian brother. Let us all hope that the dark clouds of racial prejudice will soon pass away and the deep fog of misunderstanding will be lifted from our fear-drenched communities and in some not too distant tomorrow the radiant stars of love and brotherhood will shine over our great nation with all of their scintillating beauty.

Yours for the cause of Peace and Brotherhood,

Martin Luther King, Jr.

7. SNCC Position Paper: Women in the Civil Rights Movement, 1964

1. Staff was involved in crucial constitutional revisions at the Atlanta staff meeting in October. A large committee was appointed to present revisions to the staff. The committee was all men.
2. Two organizers were working together to form a farmers['] league. Without asking any questions, the male organizer immediately assigned the clerical work to the female organizer although both had had equal experience in organizing campaigns.
3. Although there are women in the Mississippi project who have been working as long as some of the men, the leadership group in COFO is all men.
4. A woman in a field office wondered why she was held responsible for day-to-day decisions, only to find out later that she had been appointed project director but not told.
5. A fall 1964 personnel and resources report on Mississippi projects lists the number of people in each project. The section on Laurel, however, lists not the number of persons but "three girls."
6. One of SNCC's main administrative officers apologizes for appointment of a woman as interim project director in a key Mississippi project area.
7. A veteran of two years' work for SNCC in two states spends her day typing and doing clerical work for other people in her project.
8. Any woman in SNCC, no matter what her position or experience, has been asked to take minutes in a meeting when she and other women are outnumbered by men.
9. The names of several new attorneys entering a state project this past summer were posted in a central movement office. The first initial and last name of each lawyer was listed. Next to one name was written: (girl).
10. Capable, responsible, and experienced women who are in leadership positions can expect to have to defer to a man on their project for final decision making.
11. A session at the recent October staff meeting in Atlanta was the first large meeting in the past couple of years where a woman was asked to chair.

Undoubtedly this list will seem strange to some, petty to others, laughable to most. The list could continue as far as there are women in the movement. Except that most women don't talk about these kinds of incidents, because the whole subject is not discussable—strange to some, petty to others, laughable to most.

. . . Assumptions of male superiority are as widespread and deep-rooted and every much as crippling to the woman as the assumptions of white supremacy are to the Negro. Consider why it is in SNCC that women who are competent, qualified, and experienced are automatically assigned to the "female" kinds of jobs such as: typing, desk work, telephone work, filing, library work, cooking, and the assistant kind of administrative work but rarely the "executive" kind.

The woman in SNCC is often in the same position as that token Negro hired in a corporation. The management thinks that it has done its bit. Yet, every day the Ne-

---

gro bears an atmosphere, attitudes, and actions which are tinged with condescension and paternalism, the most telling of which are seen when he is not promoted as the equally or less skilled whites are. . . .

This paper is presented . . . because it needs to be made known that many women in the movement are not "happy and contented" with their status. It needs to be made known that much talent and experience are being wasted by this movement, when women are not given jobs commensurate with their abilities. It needs to be known that just as Negroes were the crucial factor in the economy of the cotton South, so too in SNCC, women are the crucial factor that keeps the movement running on a day-to-day basis. Yet they are not given equal say-so when it comes to day-to-day decision making. . . .

Maybe the only thing that can come out of this paper is discussion—amidst the laughter—but still discussion. (Those who laugh the hardest are often those who need the crutch of male supremacy the most.) And maybe some women will begin to recognize day-to-day discriminations. And maybe sometime in the future the whole of the women in this movement will become so alert as to force the rest of the movement to stop the discrimination and start the slow process of changing values and ideas so that all of us gradually come to understand that this is no more a man's world than it is a white world.

✢ E S S A Y S

In the first selection, historian David L. Chappell takes a look at the Montgomery bus boycott of 1955 and 1956 and argues that the black leaders of the movement for civil rights and freedom understood the divisions and differences within the white community. While white southerners sympathetic to the movement eventually came forward with support, white segregationists and racists, lacking the unity that prevailed among the protesters, bumbled and failed. Even violence, such as bombings and police harrassment, failed to work against the carefully coordinated tactics of Montgomery's black leaders. White southerners came to see that segregation, which had been implemented fifty years before for the sake of order, no longer prevented social conflict; instead, it contributed to it. In the second essay, Clayborne Carson, editor of the Martin Luther King Jr. papers, takes issue with traditional approaches to the study of reform movements in general and the black freedom struggle of the 1960s in particular. He urges scholars to become aware of the number and nature of sustained protest movements in communities across the South in which local problems of political power and economic equality often took precedence over issues of national legislation.

White Southerners and the Montgomery Bus Boycott

DAVID L. CHAPPELL

In the middle of the 1950s, a handful of black preachers found an opportunity to lead the white South away from the demagogues who had dominated racial politics

David L. Chappell, *Inside Agitators: White Southerners in the Civil Rights Movement.* © 1994 Johns Hopkins University Press. Reprinted by permission of the publisher.

since the end of the Populist revolt in 1896. These preachers knew that those who dominated politics never represented the whole white South, yet they also knew that the dissenters only complained ineffectually against the demagogues or, more often, kept a glum silence. They observed the white dissenters, unable to lead, spending a good deal of their time blaming the South's ills on the absence of proper leadership. Though white dissenters undoubtedly expected proper leadership to emerge from the ranks of the educated white elite, it emerged instead from an educated black elite, among the preachers, in the mid-1950s. A central question in the history of southern white dissenters was how they responded to this surprising development.

Two representatives of the dissenting tradition, Clifford and Virginia Durr of Montgomery, Alabama, were called upon quite directly to respond to the new black leadership. The character of the call did not seem new at first, however, for black leaders had been calling on the Durrs for many years. Clifford, who had been assistant counsel to the Reconstruction Finance Corporation in Washington, was a white lawyer who had a reputation for helping black clients. He was a close friend of Aubrey Williams, the white southerner who headed the National Youth Administration, one of the few New Deal agencies that defied state laws by operating without racial discrimination in the South. Virginia was perhaps even better known as a Democratic National Committeewoman, who had been active in the campaign to abolish the poll tax. . . .

Through E. D. Nixon [head of the Montgomery NAACP], Virginia Durr also met Rosa Parks, secretary of the local NAACP. Durr hired Parks as a seamstress, and the two became friends. There was nothing unusual about this friendship in Durr's mind. Herself an upper-class lady from a long line of Alabama gentry, she found Rosa Parks to be "one of the gentlest" women she had ever met—"the epitome of what you'd call the southern lady."

Through the poll tax crusade, Virginia Durr had become well connected to other dissenters from racial orthodoxy across the South, particularly those with socialist leanings and ties to organized labor. One of her favorites was Myles Horton, a poor white sharecropper turned theologian, who studied under Reinhold Niebuhr at Union Theological Seminary and then, in 1932, established the Highlander Folk School at Monteagle, Tennessee. Patterned on a Danish model that was influenced by the settlement house work of Jane Addams and the educational ideas of John Dewey, Highlander was an interracial training center for labor, socialist, and religiously oriented community organizers in the South. Through his support of unionization and his fights against racism, Horton had also become friends with E. D. Nixon, who had been an organizer for the Sleeping Car Porters. Clifford Durr and Aubrey Williams were among the financial sponsors of the Highlander School.

Virginia Durr thought her seamstress could use a vacation from the Deep South and that she was a perfect candidate for Horton's program at Highlander—and perhaps that Highlander could benefit from her. So she arranged for Parks'[s] pilgrimage to Monteagle in the summer of 1955. There, as Parks traded ideas about political action with other organizers, she experienced life without segregation for the first time.

Parks returned to Montgomery a changed woman, saying, in July 1955, that she hoped to attend another workshop at Monteagle soon, eager as she was "to make a contribution to the fulfillment of complete freedom for all people." She got her opportunity at home, though, on the first of December. When she refused a driver's order to give up her seat for a white man, the driver summoned the police, having no idea what his action would lead to. As Irene West mused, "If the man who had called the cop had known it would come to this, he would have been willing to let her sit in his lap."

Bertha Butler, another member of the Women's Political Council who happened to be on the bus, got off and went immediately to tell E. D. Nixon what had happened. Nixon first called Fred Gray, one of two black lawyers in Montgomery, but Gray was out of town. Nixon then called the police station and asked what charges Parks was being held on. The desk sergeant told him that was none of his business. Needing a lawyer, he called Clifford Durr. Durr made a few inquiries and called Nixon back to tell him that Parks was charged with violating the state segregation laws. He volunteered to accompany Nixon to the station and post Parks'[s] bond. Nixon came right over to pick him up and took Virginia Durr along, too.

The three of them got Parks released and took her home to discuss using her as the plaintiff for the test case for which they had all been waiting. Her husband was against it, telling her, "The white folks will kill you, Rosa. . . . Don't do anything to make trouble, Rosa." Her mother did not like the idea either. But Rosa Parks elected to go ahead with it, encouraged by Nixon and the Durrs.

Soon the local NAACP representatives, Nixon and Parks, joined forces with the Women's Political Council; both groups had been toying with the idea of direct action to supplement the attack on segregation through the courts. The WPC contacted nearly all of Montgomery's ninety-two black clergymen, urging them to inspire their congregants to stay off the buses the following Monday. The preachers and their flocks came together to form the Montgomery Improvement Association, with a new young preacher in town, Martin Luther King, Jr., at its head. Both of the Durrs continued to give legal, financial, and moral support to the MIA throughout the boycott and after.

Other white southerners heard the call of the new black leadership of the South less directly than the Durrs. There was one major black church in Montgomery that Nixon and the WPC did not notify: the Reverend Robert Graetz's Trinity Lutheran Church. Graetz heard about the boycott only as a rumor, not too differently from the way the police heard about it. He was in the odd position of being a white pastor to an all-black church. His congregation would not tell him about the boycott when he asked them. Though white folks in Montgomery shunned him, he was not fully welcomed into the confidence of his black congregants, some of whom openly stated that they did not want a white man leading them, especially on risky matters like a boycott. By coincidence, though, he knew Rosa Parks. She was not a member of his congregation, but he had participated in her NAACP activity. He called her to see if she could substantiate the rumor that someone had been arrested and that a boycott was planned in protest. Parks told him the rumor was true and that she was the one who had been arrested.

Graetz wanted to support Rosa Parks all he could. The day after speaking with her, he preached a sermon giving the boycott, scheduled to begin the following day, his blessing. He knew where *he* would be tomorrow, he told his flock. He would be ferrying boycotters all over the city in his car. He warned them sternly of the hazards of disunity: "Let's try to make this boycott as effective as possible," he said, "because it won't be any boycott if half of us ride the buses and half of us don't ride. If we're going to do it, let's make a good job of it." . . .

Graetz soon became a member of the executive board of the MIA, and a year after the boycott ended, he became the organization's secretary. Coretta King said that Graetz "paid dearly" for all his activity in support of the movement. Apart from almost nightly telephone threats and broken windows, the police jailed and threatened him for helping the carpool. In August 1956, while he was at Highlander teaching boycott strategy to future protesters, his house was bombed.

Within two months of its founding, another white southerner, the Reverend Glenn Smiley, had become a prime mover in the Montgomery Improvement Association. Smiley was then a staff member of the Fellowship of Reconciliation [FOR], A. J. Muste's pacifist organization, which Aldon Morris classifies, along with Horton's Highlander School, as one of the "movement halfway houses"—an institution that provided vital organizational support to the movement but, unlike the main movement organizations such as the MIA, did not grow out of the southern black communities.

Like both of the Durrs, Smiley was raised as a southern segregationist. His father owned a cotton plantation in west Texas which employed seasonal labor, mostly braceros from Mexico and black migrants from Arkansas. His mother, from east Tennessee, occasionally retained "colored help" around the house, when the family could afford it, and treated them with warmth and condescension in public; the warmth grew and the condescension diminished in private, but the two never seemed inconsistent with each other. Smiley was aware of racial barriers very early and was taught not to cross or question them. He studied religion in college and became a minister in the Southern Methodist Conference. . . .

. . . Smiley, on the FOR staff in Los Angeles after . . . 1945, helped establish the CORE chapter there.

When the Montgomery bus boycott broke out in December 1955, Bayard Rustin, then on the CORE and FOR staffs, decided he had to go there to indoctrinate the ranks in the principles of nonviolent warfare. But Rustin had to leave town shortly after he arrived. King told Rustin he needed someone to fill in, and Rustin told King to send for Smiley: "Why I don't know," Smiley said, "except I [had] some experience and I was a southerner, which they felt might have helped." On February 14, 1956, Smiley showed up at King's house and attended a press conference there that day. He said King was already imbued with the ideas of nonviolent direct action; all he lacked was experience, and it was Smiley's job to bring the experience of CORE and the FOR to bear on the day-to-day crises of the Montgomery boycott.

"I had two assignments with Dr. King," Smiley said. "One was every mass meeting in which I was in town, I was given a spot on the program to discuss tactical nonviolence. Then, I was supposed to go around to the different churches and meet with small groups and try to whip the clergy and laity into line about nonviolence. My other assignment was to make every contact possible in the white community and attempt to do the same thing, to get them to understand and try to meet with Negroes." In the latter capacity, Smiley says he acted as "a sort of intelligence service as to what people, including the White Citizens' Council and others, were saying. The fact that I was white and could speak and act like a southerner gave me access to public meetings of the WCC and even the Klan."

Smiley supervised the training program in nonviolence which built up the discipline of the mass protesters in Montgomery (and subsequently in other southern cities). The last effort he led in Montgomery was a "workshop" in Ralph Abernathy's church of some five thousand black protesters on the eve of the victory celebration—the boarding of buses on a nonsegregated basis on December 21, 1956, after more than a year of siege. Smiley directed this dress rehearsal. The purpose was to anticipate acts of violence on the newly desegregated buses. Black people had to play all the white parts, as Smiley was the only white person there, and they played the most hostile, intransigent hoods they could imagine; others rehearsed nonviolent appeals to their consciences (with less success than was to be the case in real life the following day).

. . . Smiley's picture, in King's account of the boycott, *Stride toward Freedom,* is featured on the last page of photos, headed "The End," with King's caption, "The first non-segregated bus rides down the streets of Montgomery with Glenn Smiley, a white Southerner, sharing a seat with M. L. King." The bus driver made an unscheduled stop in front of Graetz's home and honked the horn to summon Graetz to board the bus on its way to meet the crowd of thousands who had assembled downtown to meet the dawn of the new day in person. . . .

The white people of Montgomery were not initially united against the boycott. Much had happened already to prepare them for the incremental change being demanded by the boycotters. Black leaders had pressed demands and won concessions, with little calamity resulting. . . .

These usually quiet, behind-the-scenes changes were so incremental and so few as to seem mere tokenism. But other signals from local whites suggested the time was ripe for a frontal assault on white supremacy. Rosa Parks had defied bus drivers before. If she had never gone so far as to refuse a direct order to give up her seat, she and others had refused to follow the unusually insulting rule that required black passengers to pay their fare at the front of the bus, get off, and reenter at the rear. She was not arrested for that. One of the reasons segregation could not command wholehearted moral support was that, however rational and right most whites believed it to be in principle, obeying its rules on a day-to-day basis involved so many such contortions that southerners, never a punctiliously law-abiding people, got in the habit of winking at a humane bending of the rules now and then. Another reason it could not command wholehearted support was that those who did rigorously uphold the rules were typically tiresome, if not cruel and unusual, types. . . .

Though segregation commanded widespread southern white support in the abstract, its actual enforcement in so many instances was so clearly a gratuitous insult to black people (and sometimes to white people) that it was vulnerable to political attack. The critics could attack the specifics of enforcement rather than the principle, the means rather than the end, and tap into a huge reservoir of inarticulate sympathy.

Thus it was not against ironclad resistance that the leading black churches of Montgomery rose up in December 1955. In the first mass meeting of the boycott, Martin Luther King electrified the crowd with righteous impatience. The phrase "there comes a time" punctuated his speech, and the time was unmistakably now. Black people as a whole would never again appear meek and cowering to the white people in Montgomery.

But King's demands in retrospect appear quite mild. The main "demand" was simply to let black people sit from back to front, white people from front to back, with no one ever having to vacate a seat unless (if the passenger was black) an empty seat existed farther back or (if white) farther forward; in no circumstances should whites and blacks sit in the same seat. Two ancillary demands, the hiring of black drivers to serve on predominantly black routes, and "courtesy" from all drivers, did not threaten "the southern way of life." Nor, in substance, did the seating demand, as the MIA took pains to point out in negotiations and public statements: state law required only separate seating. It did not require evicting seated passengers or forcing black passengers to stand when empty seats to the front of seated whites were available. . . .

Grover Hall, Jr., the editor of Montgomery's morning paper, the *Advertiser,* initially took the position that white Montgomery should accept the movement's demands— despite his negative opinion of the new black leadership. When Smiley, on a good will mission to the *Advertiser,* asked Hall what he thought of King, Hall replied, "Dr. King is a dangerous communist son of a bitch." King was less harsh toward Hall. King said that Hall, like the vast majority of white southerners, liked segregation but could not stomach segregationists, whose tactics extended to bombing the houses of preachers.

Hall and his paper did not support the boycott, but having the editor of the leading newspaper in town against the movement's enemies, if not in favor of the movement, was a form of lukewarm support as valuable as the more wholehearted support of the Durrs and Graetz. . . .

Several white people, especially women, wrote letters to the editor in defense of the boycott. Frances P. McLeod confessed on December 9, 1955, "The treatment of Negroes on our city buses has caused us to bow our heads in shame." She did not see any reason why Montgomery could not meet the black demands, which would give Montgomery's bus system the same kind of seating arrangements that prevailed by law in such eminently southern centers as Nashville, Richmond, and Mobile. . . .

A Mrs. E. R. J. told *Advertiser* readers on Christmas day, 1955, "I was born and reared in the Black Belt of Alabama, but I, like a lot of others, have been forced to do a lot of thinking on the race question lately. I am afraid the Negro is not now, nor has ever been, as happy and content with his place as we southern white people have believed. There has been peace, true, but some of it has been peace imposed by fear. Such peace always brings its dangers." . . .

Grover Hall duly printed such letters, along with what seem to have been, at least initially, less frequent letters denouncing the boycott or calling for more "time." The mail received by the *Newsletter* of the Alabama Council on Human Relations (an organization that worked quietly for better understanding between black and white leaders), while hardly representative of white opinion in general, is significant: it ran five to one in favor of the MIA position on bus seating. . . .

The motive behind much of the white help to carpooling—which white drivers did not always refer to, or even recognize, as such—was simple self-interest: white women needed their maids and there was no other way to get them. Such motivation did not, of course, bother the boycott leaders, who understood . . . that people can be counted on to do the right things for the wrong reasons. But there is evidence that at least some of the white aid to the boycott was a deliberate and purposeful expression of support, if always given on the sly. This evidence consists of the letters that many local white people sent to King and the accounts and rosters of the mass meetings which show local white carpool drivers in attendance from time to time.

Many local white people also gave money to the MIA. Though financial contributions were probably more helpful to the cause, they were less risky than driving (of which the police and vigilantes began to take note as the boycott wore on) because they could be covert. The fundraising apparatus was designed to make the contributors' identities impossible to trace, not to protect white dissidents' reputations but to protect the black contributors who were far more vulnerable to reprisals, and whose contributions were, in the minds of the initial planners of the boycott, far more crucial. That white contributors benefited from the diffusion and secrecy of fundraisers, and that the boycott benefited from their contributions, were unexpected side effects. . . .

These contributions were almost all secret. [MIA treasurer Irene] West said she collected a hundred dollars from a white man (an unusually large contribution) but she couldn't tell his name. She just had to say " 'a friend.' " Rosa Parks said that white people typically sent their contributions "with a preference to remain anonymous." Georgia Gilmore, a black cook, midwife, and mother of six, was one of the mainstays of the movement. In addition to providing food for the ranks, at the only eatery in town where blacks and whites could be served (illegally) at the same table, she headed the famous "Club from Nowhere." Next to the plate passings at church, this was the greatest source of MIA funds: tiny contributions—typically fifty cents or a dollar—given anonymously by often terrified black people and, she said, a substantial number of white people. . . .

Apart from practical assistance, such contributions gave concrete evidence that there were many white people in Montgomery who were willing to see the system change. A segregated society was not some abstract, alien thing to the black participants in the movement but a form of degradation and insult maintained by a particular group of white people in the name of all white people. The white community was not some abstract category but a number of flesh and blood persons the black protesters had known, between them, all their lives. The protesters knew that if pressed, many of those persons would gladly give the system up, with all its pretenses and inconveniences. . . .

In Montgomery, however, sympathetic white people did not prevail. The resistance of such white leaders as bus company lawyer Jack Crenshaw and the new police and fire commissioner Clyde Sellers, who (with a 43 percent plurality) had defeated

Dave Birmingham in a race-baiting campaign in March 1955, kept such sentiments from influencing the local government and bus company. . . .

Thus the elected leaders of Montgomery took every possible precaution not to appear soft on integration. They pitched rumors about Martin Luther King at black audiences. (He was an uppity troublemaker who rode in fancy cars, paid for by their contributions, while they got blisters on their feet walking to work.) They denounced King, who was from Georgia, as an outsider. Then all three commissioners hosted a rally for Mississippi senator Jim Eastland, on February 10, 1956. Eastland taunted his hosts with such lines as "I am sure you are not going to permit the NAACP to control your state." He warned all white citizens of the need to "organize and be militant." . . .

The White Citizens' Council put an ad in the *Advertiser* a year later which summed up its position and its frustration: "There are only two sides in the Southern fight—those who want to maintain the Southern way of life or those who want to mix the races. . . . Whites must stand by whites just as Negroes are standing by Negroes. . . . There is no middle ground for moderation . . . that middle ground has been washed away by the actions of the NAACP in seeking to destroy the freedoms of the Southern white man." This was typical of segregationist appeals. The WCC and other such organizations called for unity among the white people, in increasingly exasperated tones, because no such unity existed. The efforts of Crenshaw and Sellers were aimed at achieving unity through the political agency and authority of the local state. The conversion of all three city commissioners to WCC membership suggested that they were well on the way to achieving their goal. . . .

The commissioners' "get tough" policy brought police harassment of boycotters and supporters. As could be expected from any crackdown against such a large and diffuse form of defiance, enforcement was so haphazard that many innocents, including some white people, were detained. This further hardened the black resistance and thinned the ranks of segregationist support. On February 21, 1956, a Montgomery grand jury, empaneled as part of a secret investigation that had begun on January 11, indicted eighty-nine of Montgomery's most respected black leaders for violating an antiboycott law (an old antiunion measure passed in 1921 to fight Birmingham steelworkers). The eighty-nine indicted included twenty-four clergymen, one of whom was Martin Luther King. The Human Relations Council expressed moderate whites' exasperation by commenting that King's arrest only sealed his "martyrdom." This recognition must have eroded the white community's confidence in the ability of its leaders to handle themselves in a crisis; their efforts to restore order persistently had the opposite effect. . . .

The city commission, meanwhile, began to exhort the white masses to take a much more militant stance than they were willing to take. Mayor Gayle tried to goad the employers of domestics (a large proportion of bus passengers) by announcing that the disruption could end in one day if the white women would refuse to drive their maids back and forth to work. According to Virginia Durr, the reaction of the white women in Montgomery was, "If Tacky Gayle wants to nurse my children, if Tacky Gayle wants to wash my clothes, if Tacky Gayle wants to wash my dishes, if Tacky Gayle wants to clean my house, let him do it. In other words, they absolutely refused to give up their maids and they wouldn't listen to him." The movement leaders had no illusions about the innate goodness of people, white southerners or any others. They could make do turning the self-interests of others to their advantage. Durr did not think any of the white mistresses drove their maids "from any desire to help the boycott. They did it from the fact that they didn't want . . . to have to do their own work." . . .

When the police started systematically arresting white women for transporting their maids, a few days later, they only added injury to insult. Next, Mayor Gayle appealed to white businessmen, trying to "get them to fire anybody that drove" or had anything to do with the boycott. "That also fell flat, because nobody wanted to give up their labor." Of course this de facto white opposition to the segregationists' policy required an elaborate justification, which the ranks of the black movement were only too happy to provide. The black and white women of Montgomery "carried on a kind of a game," Virginia Durr said. "The maids would tell their white mistresses that they didn't ride the bus because they were scared that the hoodlums would beat them up. . . . The white women said, 'well now of course *my* maid is not a part of the boycott.' And the maid, you know, would lie to her. And it was, you know, just this terrific game that went on." Underneath the game was the inescapable reality. The mutual dependence that gave southern black folks an intimate, strategic knowledge of their white folks also gave them a measure of direct power. The white people of Montgomery could not "give up the labor of the Negro community," Durr said. Segregationist solidarity "splintered on that rock. . . . If everybody fired everybody that was connected with the boycott, maybe they would have broken it, but they weren't willing."

The few who were willing to make sacrifices for segregation inadvertently divided their ranks by increasing resort to guerrilla tactics. On January 30, 1956, someone threw a stick of dynamite on King's porch. When King arrived at his house that night, Mayor Gayle and Commissioner Sellers were on the scene and getting increasingly nervous about the black crowd that had gathered in front of it. Both men expressed their regret to King that such an incident had taken place in their city. One of King's deacons, expressing a view widespread among the crowd, replied to the mayor, "You may express your regrets, but you must face the fact that your public statements created the atmosphere for this bombing. This is the end result of your 'get tough' policy." According to King, "Neither Mayor Gayle nor Commissioner Sellers could reply." Two days later, someone threw a dynamite cap into E. D. Nixon's yard. If the city leaders were sincere in their condemnation of violence, they had lost control of their movement.

The bombings at once revealed the desperation and futility of the segregationist cause. The commissioners offered a reward for the names of the offenders. There was a certain duplicity here: in later public statements, the commissioners countenanced a segregationist rumor that the MIA itself had planted the bombs as media stunts to elicit financial aid from northern liberals. But such rumors remained at the level of hint and innuendo: Gayle and Sellers never could identify themselves publicly with bombing and other extralegal tactics. . . .

The segregationists' resort to desperate measures increased the commitment of the black community to the continuation of protest. One MIA board member said, "Our protest showed signs of weakening, but the bombings and the indictments came just in time to bring us back together." Since all this took place, increasingly, before the eyes of the world, black protesters had an added incentive to maintain their resolve—out of responsibility to a larger cause, and concerns about their reputation. . . .

King and other leaders found reinforcement for that conviction in their relationships with white southerners throughout the boycott. The MOM [Men of Montgomery, a white booster club] and the *Advertiser*'s Grover Hall saw the indictments of virtually every prominent black leader in Montgomery in late January as above and beyond the call of sanity. Bombings further alienated moderate white opinion, which held social peace in higher regard than segregation itself. The bombs damaged more than the investment climate. They exploded in the homes of the upstanding, well-dressed black leaders who were well known to influential white leaders; one did not have to be a pacifist or a civil rights supporter to find this selection of targets counterproductive. The bomb that went off in the home of a white man, Graetz, broadcast the message that no white person who had given support to the boycott was safe. The "get tough" policy condemned even passive, innocent, or self-interested support.

The black movement's self-disciplined and dignified appeals to biblical and constitutional principles provided a stark contrast to the crassness and clumsiness of the segregationists. The White Citizens' Council forced a polarization by taking an extreme and often wildly impulsive position. That was a recipe for defeat. The movement leaders, recognizing the inbred conservatism of white southerners, knew their only hope was to appear on the opposite side of disorder. As the struggle continued and both sides became more determined, the movement became more disciplined and the segregationists became sloppier. That dynamic made it easier and easier for white southerners in the middle camp to slip over into sympathy for the protesters. Even those who did not slip over into sympathy had less and less confidence in the segregationist leaders, at a time when the segregationists demanded more and more polarization and closing of ranks.

That was the pattern Montgomery established. The black leaders and disciplined ranks would strike at a vulnerable point in the segregation system. A handful of white sympathizers would support them, usually in private, but in crucial instances in public also. Caught off guard, the militant segregationists would cast about for different tactics of response and usually find them insufficient. Frustration would drive them to intransigence and scattershot attacks that would scare away more allies than opponents. Competition for alternative leadership among white people would grow and exacerbate divisions in the segregationist ranks. "Compromise" leaders would emerge from "moderate" quarters of the white elite, and if these failed to settle the dispute, they certainly helped build the movement's hopes as they stole legitimacy from the segregationist leadership.

All these developments contributed to the feeling of futility that segregationism increasingly took on. The civil rights movement's action made it clear to enough white southerners that segregation—which their ancestors had adopted as a moderate measure to stave off social conflict—was not living up to its promise. That was not quite enough to kill the institution of segregation, but it was enough to hobble it—and the entire society built around it—to the point that the federal government, which alone had the power to kill the institution, could no longer avoid moving in. Most important, this process determined which side the federal government took when it did move in.

Black Freedom Struggles

CLAYBORNE CARSON

Social movements ultimately fail, at least in minds of many committed participants. As radicals and revolutionaries have discovered throughout history, even the most successful movements generate aspirations that cannot be fulfilled. Activists, particularly those in social movements that are driven by democratic ideals, often do not regard the achievement of political reform as conclusive evidence of success. Their activism drives them toward values that cannot be fully implemented except within the activist community. Thus, although American social movements provided a major impetus for the extension of civil rights to previously excluded groups, many abolitionists struggled for more radical transformation than was achieved through the Fourteenth and Fifteenth Amendments, and many feminists wanted more than the Nineteenth Amendment or the Equal Rights Amendment. Similarly, many black activists of the 1960s came to see themselves as seeking more than the civil rights acts of 1964 and 1965.

Because the emergent goals of American social movements have usually not been fulfilled, scholars have found it difficult to determine their political significance. Institutionalized political behavior rather than mass movements are the central focus of studies on American politics. Historians have portrayed social movements as important forces on behalf of reform but not as the decisive shapers of the reforms themselves. They typically devote little attention to the internal processes of social movements and view activists only as harbingers of change—colorful, politically impotent, socially isolated idealists and malcontents who play only fleeting roles in the drama of American political history.

Center stage is reserved for the realistic professional reformers who remain at the edges of movements and for politicians who respond to mass activism by channeling otherwise diffuse popular energies into effective reform strategies. Abolitionist activists, historians have suggested, did not free blacks from bondage through moral suasion or through other distinctive forms of antislavery militancy; instead, the Republican Party transformed abolitionist sentiments into a viable political program. Similarly, historians have noted that the initial Populist platform, itself a tepid manifestation of late-nineteenth century agrarian radicalism, was enacted by later generations of unradical reformers. Historians, in short, typically view social reform movements from a distance and see mass activism as significant only to the extent that it contributes to successful reform efforts using institutionalized strategies and tactics.

This view of mass activism reflects sociological approaches to the study of social movements that downplay their political functions. American sociologists of the 1950s and 1960s explained that social movements served to relieve widely shared discontents that resulted from strains in the social system. Implicit or explicit in most sociological studies of American social movements was the notion that they were more likely to serve psychological rather than instrumental functions, that they manifested inchoate, individual discontent rather than serious, even if unsuccessful, political strategies involving organized groups. Historians influenced by sociological studies of social movements have argued, for example, that the abolitionists were psychologically abnormal or that populists were reacting against the passing of a familiar agrarian society.

Until recent years, the classical sociological view of social movements prevailed in the study of what is generally called the civil rights movement. Use of the term "civil rights" itself is based on the assumption that the southern black movements of the 1960s remained within the ideological boundaries of previous civil rights activism. Many social scientists studying black protest participation insisted that activism resulted from a distinctive psychological state that was shared by activists. According to an extensive literature, based largely on survey data rather than field observation of ongoing struggles, protest participation was most likely among blacks who had become increasingly aware of the discrepancies, or dissonance, between their conditions of life and the alternatives made possible by the rapidly changing surrounding society. As one sociologist put it, black protesters were distinguished from other blacks by a "higher awareness of the wider society" which made them "more prone to develop the particular set of attitudes and perceptions that lead to protest."

Social scientists found it much easier to offer such analyses of the black struggle during the first half of the 1960s, when there were few signs of dissension within the movement over integrationist goals. During the last half of the decade, however, it became increasingly difficult to explain black power militancy as the outgrowth of the frustrated integrationist desires of blacks. Nevertheless, the classical sociological perspective continued to dominate scholarly writings regarding black militancy. If mass black activism could not be understood as a somewhat unwieldy tactic for achieving longstanding civil rights objectives, it was still possible to portray it as a politically unproductive or even counterproductive expression of mass frustration. Few scholars have been willing to study the internal dynamics of black social movements or to examine their varied and constantly changing strategies, tactics, and styles of leadership. As the nonviolent struggles of the early 1960s gave way to the violent racial conflicts of the late 1960s, the understandable reluctance of scholars, most of whom were white, to study black movements close up rather than from afar became more and more evident.

Thus, until recently, the civil rights literature was comprised mainly of studies of the major national civil rights leaders and their organizations. Following the lead of sociologists, most historians assumed that the black insurgences of the decade after the Montgomery bus boycott could best be understood within the context of a national campaign for civil rights reform. They saw mass activism among blacks as an extension of previous institutionalized civil rights reform efforts. To be sure, historians recognized that the new activism went beyond the once dominant NAACP tactics of litigation, lobbying, and propagandizing, but they saw increased black activism as a new tactic within a familiar strategy based on appeals to power. Protest was a product of widespread black dissatisfaction with the pace of racial change rather than with underlying strategies to achieve change. Instead of viewing mass activism as an independent social force, with its own emergent values and ideology, scholars were more likely to see it as an amorphous source of social energy that could be directed by the leaders of national civil rights organizations.

Indeed, some historical accounts have stressed the decisive role of white politicians rather than civil rights leaders in guiding the effort to achieve civil rights reforms. Thus, Arthur M. Schlesinger's account of the Kennedy presidency illustrated a common theme in surveys of the 1960s when it described Kennedy as a leader seeking to "keep control over the demand for civil rights" through timely concessions which would "hold the confidence of the Negro community." In broader terms, Schlesinger portrays Kennedy as moving "to incorporate the Negro revolution into the democratic coalition and thereby [helping] it serve the future of American freedom." More recently, Carl M. Brauer gave more attention to the black protest movement as an independent force for change, but he too concluded that Kennedy usually maintained the initiative, driven by his need "to feel that he was leading rather than being swept along by events." When black militancy threatened to get out of hand in the spring of 1963, Brauer recounts, the President "boldly reached out to grasp [the reins of leadership] once again."

Studies of civil rights organizations and their leaders understandably give more emphasis to the role of these organizations and their leaders than do studies of presidential leadership, but nonetheless these writings are ambiguous regarding the extent to which organizations and leaders were able to mobilize and direct the course of black militancy. They have focused on the strategies developed by national civil rights groups, while portraying mass activism as a new instrument in the arsenal of national civil rights leaders. The result has been that we have many studies of national civil rights leaders, particularly Martin Luther King, Jr., but few that attempt to determine the extent to which civil rights leaders reflected the aspirations of participants in black struggles.

This failure to clarify the shifting relationship between leadership and mass struggle is a glaring deficiency of studies that imply that national civil rights organizations and leaders played decisive roles in mobilizing southern blacks as a force for change during the 1950s and 1960s. Although the scholarship of the last five years has begun to rectify this deficiency, the perspective of the previous civil rights literature continues to reflect as well as shape the prevailing popular conception of the black struggle.

Embedded in this literature is the assumption that the black struggle can best be understood as a protest movement, orchestrated by national leaders in order to achieve national civil rights legislation. As already noted, use of the term civil rights movement, rather than such alternatives as black freedom struggle, reflects the misleading assumption that the black insurgences of the 1950s and 1960s were part of a coordinated national campaign. Viewing the black struggle as a national civil rights reform effort rather than a locally-based social movement has caused scholars to see Birmingham in the spring of 1963 and Selma in the winter and spring of 1965 as the prototypical black protest movements of the decade. In reality, however, hundreds of southern communities were disrupted by sustained protest movements that lasted, in some cases, for years.

These local protest movements involved thousands of protesters, including large numbers of working class blacks, and local organizers who were more concerned with local issues, including employment opportunities and political power, than with achieving national legislation. Rather than remaining within the ideological confines of the integrationism or King's Christian-Gandhianism, the local movements displayed a wide range of ideologies and proto-ideologies, involving militant racial or class consciousness. Self-reliant indigenous leaders who headed autonomous local protest organizations have been incorrectly portrayed as King's lieutenants or followers even when they adopted nonviolence as a political weapon rather than a philosophy of life and were clearly acting independently of King or of the Southern Christian Leadership Conference, which he headed.

At present, few detailed studies of these sustained local movements have appeared, but William Chafe's study of Greensboro and Robert J. Norrell's study of the Tuskegee black movement, to cite two examples, reveal that local black movements were unique and developed independently of the national civil rights organizations. Blacks in these communities developed their own goals and strategies which bore little relation to national campaigns for civil rights legislation. King was the pre-eminent national black leader, the exemplar of Gandhian ideals, but in Greensboro, Tuskegee, and many other communities, local leaders and organizers played dominant roles in mobilizing blacks and articulating the emergent values of the local struggles.

Careful examinations of local movements, therefore, challenge the assumption that national leaders, notably Martin Luther King, orchestrated local protest movements in their efforts to alter national public opinion and national policy. There is much to suggest that national civil rights organizations and their leaders played only minor roles in bringing about most local insurgences. It was more often the case that local black movements produced their own distinctive ideas and indigenous leadership rather than that these movements resulted from initiative of national leaders.

The Montgomery bus boycott, for example, began in 1955 as the result of an unplanned act of defiance by Rosa Parks. Martin Luther King, Jr., emerged as a spokesman and as a nationally-known proponent of nonviolent resistance only after Montgomery blacks had launched their movement and formed their own local organization—the Montgomery Improvement Association. King's organization, the Southern Christian Leadership Conference, was formed only after the boycott ended. To be sure, the Montgomery struggle was an extension of previous civil rights reform efforts, but it began as an outgrowth of local institutional networks rather than as a project of any national civil rights organization.

Similarly, no national organization or leader initiated the next major stage of the black struggle, the lunch counter sit-ins of 1960. SCLC, CORE, and the NAACP attempted to provide ideological and tactical guidance for student protesters after the initial sit-in in Greensboro, but student activists insisted on forming their own local groups under student leadership. Even the Student Nonviolent Coordinating Committee, which was founded by student protest leaders, was unable to guide the sit-in movement—a fact that contributed to SNCC's subsequent support for the principle of local autonomy.

CORE initiated the Freedom Rides of 1961, but this desegregation effort did not become a major social movement until CORE abandoned the rides after protesters were attacked by whites in Alabama. Student militants formed their own organizations. Hundreds of student freedom riders then brought the movement into Mississippi and later to other parts of the South.

The Freedom Rides provided a stimulus for the massive Albany protests of December 1961, which became a model for mass mobilizations of black communities elsewhere in the South. Each of the national civil rights organizations tried to offer guidance for the mass marches and demonstrations which culminated in the Birmingham protests of spring 1963, but by the summer of that year it had become clear to national black leaders that the black struggle had acquired a momentum over which they had little control. A. Philip Randolph, the black leader who proposed a march on Washington, told President Kennedy, "The Negroes are already in the streets. It is very likely impossible to get them off. If they are bound to be in the streets in any case, is it not better that they be led by organizations dedicated to civil rights and disciplined by struggle rather than to leave them to other leaders who care neither about civil rights nor about nonviolence?" Malcolm X recognized and identified with the local black leadership that mobilized the black insurgences of 1963: "In Cambridge, Maryland, Gloria Richardson; in Danville, Virginia, and other parts of the country, local leaders began to stir up our people at the grass-roots level. This was never done by these Negroes of national stature."

Even this brief discussion of the early history of the southern black struggle should reveal a major weakness of studies that assumed that King played a dominant initiating role in southern protests. These studies have not determined the extent to which King was actually able to implement his nonviolent strategy in specific places. Studies focused on civil rights leaders and organizations, rather than on local movements, often give the impression that King was not only the major national spokesman for the black struggle but also its prime instigator.

During the period from 1956 to 1961, however, King played only a minor role as a protest mobilizer as opposed to his role as a national symbol of the black struggle. Acknowledgement that King had limited control over the southern struggle should not detract from his historical importance as a heroic and intellectually seminal leader; recognition of King's actual role instead reminds us that his greatness was rooted in a momentous social movement. Numerous black communities organized bus boycotts and, later, sit-in movements with little direct involvement by King, who was seen by many black activists as a source of inspiration rather than of tactical direction. Even in Albany, where he played a major role in the 1961 and 1962 protests, he joined a movement that was already in progress and worked alongside indigenous leaders who often accepted but sometimes rejected his advice. In St. Augustine, Birmingham, and Selma, he also assisted movements that had existed before his arrival. In numerous other communities, movements arose and were sustained over long periods with little or no involvement by King or his organization.

Moreover, these local movements should not be viewed as protest activity designed to persuade and coerce the federal government to act on behalf of black civil rights. There was a constant tension between the national black leaders, who saw mass protest as an instrument for reform, and local leaders and organizers who were often more interested in building enduring local institutions rather than staging marches and rallies for a national audience. Local black leadership sought goals that were quite distinct from the national civil rights agenda. Even in communities where King played a major role, as in Albany, Birmingham, and Selma, he was compelled to work with local leaders who were reluctant, to say the least, to implement strategies developed by outsiders.

Black communities mobilized not merely to prod the federal government into action on behalf of blacks but to create new social identities for participants and for all Afro-Americans. The prevailing scholarly conception of the civil rights movement suggests a movement that ended in 1965, when one of the last major campaigns led by a civil rights organization prompted the passage of the Voting Rights Act. The notion of a black freedom struggle seeking a broad range of goals suggests, in contrast, that there was much continuity between the period before 1965 and the period after. Contrary to the oft-expressed view that the civil rights movement died during the mid-1960's, we find that many local activists stressed the continuity between the struggles to gain political rights for southern blacks and the struggles to exercise them in productive ways. Rather than claiming that a black power movement displaced the civil rights movement, they would argue that a black freedom movement seeking generalized racial advancement evolved into a black power movement toward the unachieved goals of the earlier movement.

In summary, scholars have portrayed the black struggle as an augmentation of traditional civil rights reform strategies directed by national civil rights organizations. They have stressed the extent to which national civil rights leaders were able to transform otherwise undirected mass discontent into an effective instrument to speed the pace of reform.

This conception of the black struggle has encountered a strong challenge from a new generation of scholars who have closely examined the internal dynamics of the black struggle in order to determine its sources and emergent norms. As suggested above, previous scholarly studies become increasingly deficient in explanatory power as scholars move nearer to the black struggle itself. If the black struggle were to be seen as a series of concentric circles, with liberal supporters on the outside and full-time activists at the center, the older scholarly literature would appear adequate in its description of dramatic, highly-publicized confrontations in Albany, Birmingham, and Selma and its treatment of the impact of these confrontations on public opinion and the national government. But the literature fails, for the most part, to explain what occurred at the core of the black struggle where deeply committed [activists] sustained local movements and acquired distinctive tactics, strategies, leadership styles, and ideologies. It was among activists at the core of the struggle that new radical conceptions of American society and black identity emerged. The scholarly literature helps in explaining why a black person gained new rights, but this literature has been less successful in explaining why a black person is now likely to bring quite different attitudes to whatever he or she does than would have been the case before the black struggle began.

✢ *F U R T H E R   R E A D I N G*

Numan V. Bartley, *The Rise of Massive Resistance: Race and Politics in the South in the 1960s* (1969)

Numan V. Bartley and Hugh D. Graham, *Southern Politics and the Second Reconstruction* (1975)

Jack Bass, *Unlikely Heroes: The Southern Judges Who Made the Civil Rights Revolution* (1981)

Mark K. Bauman and Berkley Kalin, *The Quiet Voices: Southern Rabbis and Black Civil Rights 1880s–1990s* (1997)

Taylor Branch, *Pillar of Fire, America in the King Years, 1963–65* (1998)

Robert Frederick Burk, *The Eisenhower Administration and Black Civil Rights* (1984)

Eric R. Burner, *And Gently He Shall Lead Them: Robert Purris Moses and Civil Rights in Mississippi* (1994)

Stewart Burns, ed., *Daybreak of Freedom: The Montgomery Bus Boycott* (1997)

Clayborne Carson, *In Struggle: SNCC and the Black Awakening of the 1960s* (1981)

William Chafe, *Civilities and Civil Rights: Greensboro, NC, and the Black Struggle for Freedom* (1980)

Melinda Chateauvert, *Marching Together: Women of the Brotherhood of Sleeping Car Porters* (1998)

E. Culpepper Clark, *The Schoolhouse Door: Segregation's Last Stand at the University of Alabama* (1993)

Thomas R. Cole, *No Color Is My Kind: The Life of Eldrewey Stearns and the Integration of Houston* (1997)

Robert Coles, *Children of Crisis: A Study in Courage and Fear* (1964)

Vicki Crawford et al., eds., *Women in the Civil Rights Movement* (1990)

Constance Curry, *Silver Rights* (1995)

Jane Sherron De Hart, "Second Wave Feminism(s) and the South: The Difference That Differences Make," from Christie Anne Farnham, eds., *Women of the American South* (1997), 276–292

Dennis C. Dickerson, *Militant Mediator: Whitney M. Young Jr.* (1998)

John Dittmer, *Local People: The Struggle for Civil Rights in Mississippi* (1994)

Glenn Eskew, *But for Birmingham: The Local and National Movements in the Civil Rights Struggle* (1997)

Sara Evans, "Women's Consciousness and the Southern Black Movement," *Southern Exposure* 4 (1976), 10–17

Adam Fairclough, *To Redeem the Soul of America: The SCLC and Martin Luther King, Jr.* (1987)

———, *Race and Democracy: The Civil Rights Struggle in Louisiana, 1915–1972* (1995)

Cynthia Griggs Fleming, *Soon We Will Not Cry: The Liberation of Ruby Doris Smith Robinson* (1998)

Tony Freyer, *The Little Rock Crisis: A Constitutional Interpretation* (1984)

David Garrow, *Protest at Selma: Martin Luther King, Jr., and the Voting Rights Act of 1965* (1978)

David R. Goldfield, *Black, White, and Southern: Race Relations and Southern Culture, 1940 to the Present* (1990)

Hugh Davis Graham, *The Civil Rights Era: The Origins and Development of National Policy* (1990)

John A. Hardin, *Fifty Years of Segregation* (1997)

Russell J. Henderson, "The 1963 Mississippi State University Basketball Controversy and the Repeal of the Unwritten Law: 'Something More than the Game Will Be Lost,' " *Journal of Southern History* 63 (November 1997), 827–854

John Howard, ed., *Carryin' On in the Lesbian and Gay South* (1997)

Elizabeth Jacoway and David R. Colburn, eds., *Southern Businessmen and Desegregation* (1982)

Martin Luther King, Jr., *Stride Toward Freedom: The Montgomery Story* (1958)

Richard Kluger, *Simple Justice: The History of* Brown v. Board of Education *and Black America's Struggle for Equality* (1976)

Steven F. Lawson, *Black Ballots: Voting Rights in the South, 1944–1969* (1976)

———, *Running for Freedom: Civil Rights and Black Politics* (1991)

John Lewis, *Walking with the Wind: A Memoir of the Movement* (1998)

Manning Marable, *Race, Reform, and Rebellion: The Second Reconstruction in Black America* (1991)

Doug McAdam, *Freedom Summer* (1988)

Gerald D. McKnight, *The Last Crusade: Martin Luther King, Jr., FBI, and the Poor People's Campaign* (1998)

Neil R. McMillan, *The Citizens' Council: Organized Resistance to the Second Reconstruction* (1971)

August Meier and John H. Bracey, Jr., "The NAACP as a Reform Movement, 1909–1965: 'To Reach the Conscience of America,' " *Journal of Southern History* 59 (February 1993), 3–30

Sherie Mershon and Steven Schlossman, *Foxholes and Color Lines: Desegregating the U.S. Armed Forces* (1998)

Kay Mills, *This Little Light of Mine: The Life of Fannie Lou Hamer* (1993)

Anne Moody, *Coming of Age in Mississippi* (1968)

Aldon D. Morris, *The Origins of the Civil Rights Movement: Black Communities Organizing for Change* (1984)

Gunnar Myrdal, *An American Dilemma* (1944)

Thomas R. Peake, *Keeping the Dream Alive: A History of the Southern Christian Leadership Conference* (1987)

Julie L. Pycior, *LBJ and Mexican Americans* (1997)

Howell Raines, *My Soul Is Rested: Movement Days in the Deep South Remembered* (1977)

William T. Martin Riches, *The Civil Rights Movement: Struggle and Resistance* (1997)

Armstead L. Robinson and Patricia Sullivan, eds., *New Directions in Civil Rights Studies* (1991)

James Silver, *Mississippi: The Closed Society* (1964)

Harvard Sitkoff, *The Struggle for Black Equality, 1954–1980* (1980)

Morton Sosna, *In Search of the Silent South: Southern Liberals and the Race Issue* (1997)

J. Mills Thornton III, "Challenge and Response in the Montgomery Bus Boycott of 1955–1956," *Alabama Review* 33 (1980), 163–235

Nancy J. Weiss, *Whitney M. Young, Jr., and the Struggle for Civil Rights* (1989)

Frederick M. Wirt, *"We Ain't What We Was": Civil Rights in the New South* (1998)

CHAPTER
13

Race, Politics, and Religion in the Recent South

In the years after the passage of the 1965 Voting Rights Act, millions of formerly disfranchised blacks became voters. At the same time, however, the major civil rights organizations disintegrated into warring factions, the Vietnam War overwhelmed the domestic mission of the Johnson administration, and the politics of rage, heralded by such flamboyant figures as George Wallace, dominated the news. Richard Nixon and his Republican followers became more interested in appealing to southern whites than in maintaining the gains of the 1960s. In the South, the annealing had occurred, and the healing was beginning. The southern caterpillar was transformed into a Sunbelt butterfly, and the business of business soon overshadowed lingering racial tensions.

Gains for African Americans were most visible in southern politics. By 1975, blacks held more political offices in the South than in any other region. Race baiting virtually disappeared from campaigns, and many leaders who emerged during the 1970s owed their election in great part to the expanding black electorate. The Democratic party, which had once based its power on white supremacy, came to rely heavily on black votes. In employment, gains for blacks also came, although more slowly, as barriers to jobs, education, and entry to the professions declined.

The Republican party gained converts among southern white conservatives and retained the allegiance of migrating northerners. As a result, for a time, the era of one-party politics was over. By the 1980s, however, the Republican party, with Ronald Reagan at its head, brought about one of the most powerful political revolutions in American history. The region once more became nearly the Solid South—the solid Republican South. And Newt Gingrich, spokesman for southern Republicans as well as majority leader in the House, negotiated a "Contract with America." This transformation in party loyalty arose in part because many white southerners were uncomfortable with the advances of the civil rights movement, affirmative action, and women's rights, including abortion. On another front, evangelical religious leaders, who in theory eschewed politics, found that their followers favored a conservative political agenda, one that could give power to a growing Religious Right. Because of population growth in the Sunbelt South, the region now greatly influences national politics.

386

Historians, who normally study issues only after a space of fifty years, are relying on studies by political scientists and sociologists, and are beginning to ask questions related to recent changes in the South. What happened to the civil rights movement? What happened to white supremacy? How significant and lasting are the political and economic advances for African Americans? Why, with the changes brought about by the freedom struggles, does poverty still exist among southerners, especially blacks? How has the rise of the Religious Right influenced southern politics?

✥ D O C U M E N T S

Jimmy Carter, the first southerner to win the presidency after the Voting Rights Act, represented the new southern Democratic party. The message of his 1971 inaugural speech as governor of Georgia, reprinted here as Document 1, was that the old days of blatant white supremacy were over. The racial bifurcation of southern political parties, however, implies a more subtle but nonetheless important indication of the persistence of race in regional life and politics, as shown in Document 2. This selection is a reprint of two interviews—with a southern Republican official and a Democratic congressman, respectively—conducted by political scientist Alexander Lamis, indicating candidly how white supremacists used coded language to achieve their goals and how savvy southern politicians responded to their constituents. Document 3 is a political cartoon from the pen of *Charlotte Observer* (and now *New York Newsday*) cartoonist Doug Marlette. Andrew Young has been one of the nation's most prominent black officials during the past two decades. As he began his final year as mayor of Atlanta in January 1989, he took a retrospective view of Atlanta politics. His address, Document 4, drew upon the booster spirit of the old politics with some reference to the social conscience of the new. In the secession crisis leading to the Civil War, southern Baptists had split away from the national denomination over the issue of slavery, creating their own denomination, the Southern Baptist Convention. One hundred and fifty years later, the SBC, in a Declaration of Repentance, apologized for its racist stance against African Americans, as indicated in Document 5. By 1980 the Republican revolution had engulfed the South, and, as the photographs in Document 6 indicate, the Religious Right, led by Moral Majority leader Jerry Falwell, helped to boost southern support. In 1992, before the Republican National Convention in Houston, George Bush actively courted the Christian Coalition, while the Religious Right and pro-life advocates such as Phyllis Schlafly and Rush Limbaugh swayed the party in the direction of family values. Document 7, by Chicago Tribune cartoonist MacNelly, gives an ironic touch to the notion of a Republican Solid South. Finally, Document 8 demonstrates the advance of Republican party strength in the South.

1. Jimmy Carter's Gubernatorial Inaugural Address, 1971

This is a time for truth and frankness. The next four years will not be easy ones. The problems we face will not solve themselves. They demand from us the utmost in

---

This document appeared in the *Atlanta Constitution*, January 13, 1971.

dedication and unselfishness from each of us. But this is also a time for greatness. Our people are determined to overcome the handicaps of the past and to meet the opportunities of the future with confidence and with courage.

Our people are our most precious possession and we cannot afford to waste the talents and abilities given by God to one single Georgian. Every adult illiterate, every school dropout, every untrained retarded child is an indictment of us all. Our state pays a terrible and continuing human financial price for these failures. It is time to end this waste. If Switzerland and Israel and other people can eliminate illiteracy, then so can we. The responsibility is our own, and as Governor, I will not shirk this responsibility.

At the end of a long campaign, I believe I know our people as well as anyone. Based on this knowledge of Georgians North and South, Rural and Urban, liberal and conservative, I say to you quite frankly that the time for racial discrimination is over. Our people have already made this major and difficult decision, but we cannot underestimate the challenge of hundreds of minor decisions yet to be made. Our inherent human charity and our religious beliefs will be taxed to the limit. No poor, rural, weak, or black person should ever have to bear the additional burden of being deprived of the opportunity of an education, a job or simple justice. We Georgians are fully capable of making our judgments and managing our own affairs. We who are strong or in positions of leadership must realize that the responsibility for making correct decisions in the future is ours. As Governor, I will never shirk this responsibility.

Georgia is a state of great natural beauty and promise, but the quality of our natural surroundings is threatened because of avarice, selfishness, procrastination and neglect. Change and development are necessary for the growth of our population and for the progress of our agricultural, recreational, and industrial life. Our challenge is to insure that such activities avoid destruction and dereliction of our environment. The responsibility for meeting this challenge is our own. As Governor, I will not shirk this responsibility.

In Georgia, we are determined that the law shall be enforced. Peace officers must have our appreciation and complete support. We cannot educate a child, build a highway, equalize tax burdens, create harmony among our people, or preserve basic human freedom unless we have an orderly society. Crime and lack of justice are especially cruel to those who are least able to protect themselves. Swift arrest and trial and fair punishment should be expected by those who would break our laws. It is equally important to us that every effort be made to rehabilitate law breakers into useful and productive members of society. We have not yet attained these goals in Georgia, but now we must. The proper function of a government is to make it easy for man to do good and difficult for him to do evil. This responsibility is our own. I will not shirk this responsibility.

Like thousands of other businessmen in Georgia, I have always attempted to conduct my business in an honest and efficient manner. Like thousands of other citizens, I expect no less of government.

The functions of government should be administered so as to justify confidence and pride.

Taxes should be minimal and fair.

Rural and urban people should easily discern the mutuality of their goals and opportunities.

We should make our major investments in people, not buildings.

With wisdom and judgment we should take future actions according to carefully considered long-range plans and priorities.

Governments closest to the people should be strengthened, and the efforts of our local, state and national governments need to be thoroughly coordinated.

We should remember that our state can best be served by a strong and independent governor, working with a strong and independent legislature.

Government is a contrivance of human wisdom to provide for human wants. Men have a right to expect that these wants will be provided by this wisdom.

The test of a government is not how popular it is with the powerful and privileged few, but how honestly and fairly it deals with the many who must depend upon it.

William Jennings Bryan said, "Destiny is not a matter of change, it is a matter of choice. Destiny is not a thing to be waited for, it is a thing to be achieved."

Here around me are seated the members of the Georgia Legislature and other State Officials. They are dedicated and honest men and women. They love this state as you love it and I love it. But no group of elected officers, no matter how dedicated or enlightened, can control the destiny of a great state like ours. What officials can solve alone the problems of crime, welfare, illiteracy, disease, injustice, pollution, and waste? This control rests in *your* hands, the people of Georgia.

In a democracy, no government can be stronger, or wiser, or more just than its people. The idealism of the college student, the compassion of a woman, the common sense of the businessman, the time and experience of a retired couple, and the vision of political leaders must all be harnessed to bring out the best in our State.

As I have said many times during the last few years, I am determined that at the end of this administration we shall be able to stand up anywhere in the world—in New York, California, or Florida and say "I'm a Georgian"—and be proud of it.

I welcome the challenge and the opportunity of serving as Governor of our State during the next four years. I promise you my best. I ask you for your best.

2. Interviews with a Republican and a Democratic Leader, 1981, 1982

Interview with Unidentified Republican Official, 1981

Official. As to the whole Southern strategy that Harry Dent [Republican strategist from South Carolina] and others put together in 1968, opposition to the Voting Rights Act would have been a central part of keeping the South. Now [the new Southern strategy] doesn't have to do that. All you have to do to keep the South is for Reagan to run in place on the issues he's campaigned on since 1964 . . . and that's fiscal conservatism, balancing the budget, cut taxes, you know, the whole cluster. . . .

Questioner: But the fact is, isn't it, that Reagan does get to the [George] Wallace voter and to the racist side of the Wallace voter by doing away with Legal Services, by cutting down on food stamps . . . ?

[The official answered by pointing to what he said was the abstract nature of the race issue today.]

Official: You start out in 1954 by saying "Nigger, nigger, nigger." By 1968 you can't say "nigger"—that hurts you. Backfires. So you say stuff like forced busing, states' rights, and all that stuff. You're getting so abstract now [that] you're talking about cutting taxes, and all these things you're talking about are totally economic things and a by-product of them is [that] blacks get hurt worse than whites. And subconsciously maybe that is part of it. I'm not saying that. But I'm saying that if it is getting that abstract, and that coded, that we are doing away with the racial problem one way or the other. You follow me—because obviously sitting around saying, "We want to cut this," is much more abstract than even the busing thing *and* a hell of a lot more abstract than "Nigger, nigger." . . .

Interview with U.S. Representative David R. Bowen (D-Miss.), 1982

Yes, it was a little bit [like walking a tightrope]. Of course, I had a lot of very conservative white people supporting me, a lot of conservative farmers and businessmen, people like that. And at the same time a large bloc of the black community. I think if you don't have a hard-core doctrinaire position on something in which you lock yourself in by saying, "I am a liberal and I believe in a liberal program, which is the following," and therefore you sort of announce that "I am going after labor votes and black votes and that's that and if I can pick up any more on friendship or personal charm or on whatever, well, I'll get a few more someplace else." That's one way.

Or you can go to the other side and say, "I am a conservative and I am going to get business votes and wealthy farmer votes and I am going to pick up any others wherever I can." Obviously, I was not either of those two extremes. . . . And I had no particular reason to be. . . .

It's easy enough when you are in [the first] campaign to make everybody happy because you never had to vote on anything . . . but how'd you stay in office for ten years? I think I just didn't do anything to alienate either of those two blocs that I had put together. Obviously, there were a lot of white votes I didn't get. Because if my high-water mark was 70 percent of the votes and I was getting maybe 90 percent of the black votes, there were a lot of white votes I was not getting. But my voting record was often on the conservative side, but it varied across the middle of the board. It was not far right or far left. In all these national organizations that rate you, I might range from 35 to 85. . . . My ADA [Americans for Democratic Action] and liberal-type votes were usually in the low numbers. The conservative organizations were more often in the high numbers, but usually in the middle ranges somewhere.

So it was not a very doctrinaire sort of pattern. You could look at it and you could say, "I don't know whether it falls under liberal or conservative." That's pretty much the way it was. No one could really stamp me as a liberal or a conservative. I never did anything to alienate the black support that I had. I never did anything to alienate the business support that I had. There were never very many issues that came along which were kind of no-win issues where you would totally outrage half the people whatever you did. . . .

Take things like food stamps. . . . Theoretically, a lot of the people who do not receive food stamps are against them. Of course, almost all the black community is for them as well as a lot of the whites. I'm on the Ag[riculture] Committee and I have to write food stamp legislation. Of course, blacks stayed with me because I voted for food stamps. And [to] the whites, I was able to explain that I was tightening up the legislation, improving it. And it would have been a lot more costly and a lot less efficient if I were not in there trying to put amendments in there to improve it—conditions that require recipients to register for work and accept work if it is offered and to make sure that people don't draw food stamps who are able-bodied and unwilling to work. So, generally those conservatives who would cuss and holler about food stamps all the time would say, "Well, David's doing a good job trying to improve the program. They are going to pass the thing . . . anyhow. He's in there trying to improve it, trying to tighten it up, trying to cut out the fraud, the waste." But I would certainly vote for the program after I got through tightening it up.

So, . . . what makes good politicians, I guess, is someone who can take whatever his vote is and do a good job of explaining it. . . . If you can explain it to those who are against it and make them like it, even though you voted for it, and then, of course, let the ones who are for it know that you voted for it . . . then you are in good shape. And I think that is probably what I did. . . . It's just kind of a matter of personal skill and packaging what you do and explaining it.

3. Cartoonist Doug Marlette's View of Political Segregation, 1985

Political cartoon by Doug Marlette, New York Newsday Creators Syndicate. Reprinted by permission of Doug Marlette.

4. Andrew Young's State of the City Address, 1989

The past seven years have been among the most exciting of my life. The opportunity to serve the citizens of this city during what I believe is truly the golden age of growth and development in Atlanta has been perhaps the most rewarding chapter to date in my more than three decades of public service. I cannot claim sole credit for the advances we have made in this city during the 1980's, instead I must look to the past and recognize the business, government and religious leaders who laid the foundation for the rewards which we currently reap. . . .

A Philosophy for Governing

In 1982, as I took the oath of office from Judge Osgood Williams and became Atlanta's 55th mayor, the example of leadership set by this community gave me the confidence to say that, *"Atlanta is not now rising from the ashes. It is rocketing into orbit from a solid foundation."*

On that cold and sunny day in January, as over 8,000 Atlantans joined me in a candle-lit inaugural ceremony at the Omni, I knew that challenges which awaited this city were great. I also knew that, *"the American southland has been at the forefront of the struggle against poverty and racism, and Atlanta has always led the way in the South."*

With that knowledge—and with the lessons which I learned by serving the citizens of this city, this region and this nation, in the civil rights movement, the United States Congress, and at the United Nations—I was confident in 1982 that all the ingredients existed here for propelling Atlanta into the 1990's as a true economic, social and cultural leader among the cities of the world.

When I was elected mayor, I felt as though an era was coming to an end. In fact, the banks in this city were all in a state of shock, there was anxiety about the investment climate and a fear that investment was moving out of our city. There was, at the same time, a concern and a fear that the government funds upon which we had depended so much in the 1950's, 1960's, and 1970's were not going to be present for us in the 1980's.

It was with some fear and trembling that I declared my candidacy for mayor, but it was also in a hope that we might find new, alternative sources of revenue. I knew that together we might chart a course that would continue our city's growth and development in spite of the private sector decline that was characteristic of the moment and the decline in government funds which was foreshadowed by a rising government debt burden.

We have seen a diminishing of government funds. We have almost seen the end of revenue sharing. We have seen some $30–$40 million in government funds that used to come into the city now dwindle to less than $10 million, and yet we have been able to find a way to help our city grow.

I contend that that was not just an accident. I contend that as we began to look around us and as we began to decide how we would meet the shortfall, we deter-

Andrew Young's State of the City Address, 1989. Atlanta History Center, Atlanta, Georgia.

mined that only through attracting private capital could we continue to meet the needs of our citizens. Indeed, I think we have developed something which I call **Public Purpose Capitalism,** a pragmatic philosophy in which we have attempted to attract private capital for public purposes.

Quite different from anything that had happened in the 1950's and 1960's, when it was largely government money that drove our growth and development, we knew that in the 1980's more and more of our development had to come from the private sector. Immediately, we embarked upon a strategy which I think is going to be even more important in the years to come, because even though we have tapped private sources of capital, government sources of capital continue to dry up and there seems to be little or no hope of getting more funds from the federal or the state government. What we are going to have to do is to continue to evolve this system of public purpose capitalism, to attract private capital to public purposes which are beneficial to the total growth of our community.

. . . I knew [in 1982] that the challenge of the '80's was economic—jobs—and that Atlanta had to once again point the way in the economic arena just as we had in the social and political spheres.

In order to meet that challenge, I outlined several areas which would receive top priority and emphasis during my administration. They included developing a close working relationship between city hall and the business community, encouraging business investment and expansion, ensuring the public safety of all our citizens, creating downtown entertainment and housing opportunities, promoting Atlanta as a regional center for international finance and export trade, developing a genuine partnership with our state government and the governments of surrounding counties, safeguarding our reputation for minority participation and civil rights, and demanding honest and efficient government at the lowest possible cost to the taxpayer.

5. Southern Baptists Apologize for
Slavery and Racism, 1995

Declaration of Repentance

Resolution No. 1: On Racial Reconciliation on the 150th Anniversary of the Southern Baptist Convention

WHEREAS, Since its founding in 1845, the Southern Baptist Convention has been an effective instrument of God in missions, evangelism, and social ministry; and

WHEREAS, The Scriptures teach that Eve is the mother of all living (Genesis 3:20), and that God shows no partiality, but in every nation whoever fears him and works righteousness is accepted by him (Acts 10:34–35), and that God has made from one blood every nation of men to dwell on the face of the earth (Acts 17:26); and

WHEREAS, Our relationship to African-Americans has been hindered from the beginning by the role that slavery played in the formation of the Southern Baptist Convention; and

WHEREAS, Many of our Southern Baptist forbears defended the right to own slaves, and either participated in, supported, or acquiesced in the particularly inhumane nature of American slavery; and

WHEREAS, in later years Southern Baptists failed, in many cases, to support, and in some cases opposed, legitimate initiatives to secure the civil rights of African-Americans; and

WHEREAS, Racism has led to discrimination, oppression, injustice, and violence, both in the Civil War and throughout the history of our nation; and

WHEREAS, Racism has divided the body of Christ and Southern Baptists in particular, and separated us from our African-American brothers and sisters; and

WHEREAS, Many of our congregations have intentionally and/or unintentionally excluded African-Americans from worship, membership, and leadership; and

WHEREAS, Racism profoundly distorts our understanding of Christian morality, leading some Southern Baptists to believe that racial prejudice and discrimination are compatible with the Gospel; and

WHEREAS, Jesus performed the ministry of reconciliation to restore sinners to a right relationship with the Heavenly Father, and to establish right relations among all human beings, especially within the family of faith.

Therefore, be it RESOLVED, that we, the messengers to the Sesquicentennial meeting of the Southern Baptist Convention, assembled in Atlanta, Georgia, June 20–22, 1995, unwaveringly denounce racism, in all its forms, as deplorable sin; and

---

"Resolution No. 1–On Racial Reconciliation on the 150th Anniversary of the Southern Baptist Convention," from *The Annual of Southern Baptist Convention, 1995*. Reprinted by permission.

Be it further RESOLVED, that we affirm the Bible's teaching that every human life is sacred, and is of equal and immeasurable worth, made in God's image, regardless of race or ethnicity (Genesis 1:27), and that, with respect to salvation through Christ, there is neither Jew nor Greek, there is neither slave nor free, there is neither male nor female, for (we) are all one in Christ Jesus (Galatians 3:28); and

Be it further RESOLVED, that we lament and repudiate historic acts of evil such as slavery from which we continue to reap a bitter harvest, and we recognize that the racism which yet plagues our culture today is inextricably tied to the past; and

Be it further RESOLVED, that we apologize to all African-Americans for condoning and/or perpetuating individual and systemic racism in our lifetime; and we genuinely repent of racism of which we have been guilty, whether consciously (Psalm 19:13) or unconsciously (Leviticus 4:27); and

Be it further RESOLVED, that we ask forgiveness from our African-American brothers and sisters, acknowledging that our own healing is at stake; and

Be it further RESOLVED, that we hereby commit ourselves to eradicate racism in all its forms from Southern Baptist life and ministry; and

Be it further RESOLVED, that we commit ourselves to be doers of the Word (James 1:22) by pursuing racial reconciliation in all our relationships, especially with our brothers and sisters in Christ (1 John 2:6), to the end that our light would so shine before others, that they may see (our) good works and glorify (our) Father in heaven (Matthew 5:16); and

Be it finally RESOLVED, that we pledge our commitment to the Great Commission task of making disciples of all peoples (Matthew 28:19), confessing that in the church God is calling together one people from every tribe and nation (Revelation 5:9), and proclaiming that the Gospel of our Lord Jesus Christ is the only certain and sufficient ground upon which redeemed persons will stand together in restored family union as joint-heirs with Christ (Romans 8:17).

6. The Religious Right Joins the
Republican Party, 1980–1992

In its first electoral outing, the Religious Right hitched its star to candidate Ronald Reagan. Though Reagan's personal life was not as religiously oriented as Jimmy Carter's, he championed the "family values" agenda that [Jerry] Falwell and others espoused. But when his administration failed to follow through, the Religious Right began learning the compromises of political involvement. (AP/Wide World Photos)

From: William Martin, *With God on Our Side: The Rise of the Religious Right in America* (New York: Broadway Books, 1996).

Just before the 1992 presidential election, George Bush made a series of last-minute out-reach appearances to rally the support of conservative groups. Seen here at the Christian Coalition's Road to Victory Conference in September of that year, he received a standing ovation when he told his audience, "I join with you in committing to uphold the sanctity of Life." (Courtesy, George Bush Presidential Library and Museum)

7. The Solid South, 1996

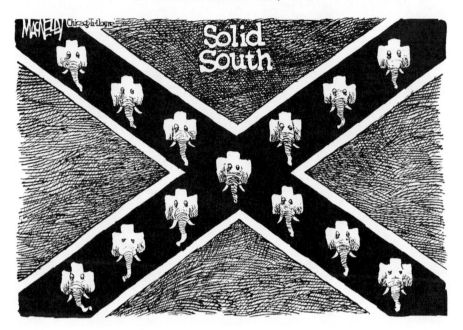

8. Republican Party Advances in the South, 1980–1998

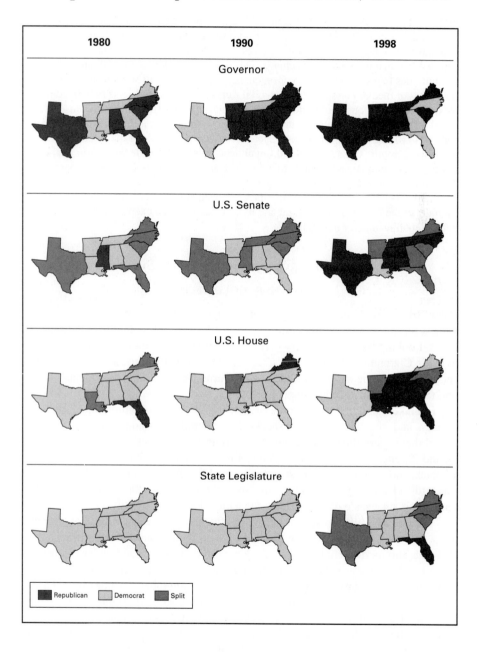

From the National Conference of State Legislators, *Almanac of American Politics. The New York Times,* March 16, 1998.

✣ E S S A Y S

In the first essay, historian David Goldfield reflects on the consequences of court-ordered desegregation. He cites a significant resegregation of public schools in the South as whites sent their children to private schools, moved to suburban districts, or enrolled in urban neighborhood schools. This left civic leaders with a dilemma: Should communities focus on integration or on quality education for all students and teachers regardless of race or class? In the post–civil rights South, the problems remain complex, but race relations, Goldfield argues, have never been better, in part because of the moral influence of the South's evangelical religious traditions. Political scientists Earl and Merle Black, in the second essay, note the effects of the rise of the Republican party in the South. The nearly "Solid Republican South" has made the region vital to any political candidate who wants to hold national office. The South, they declare, "now shapes the trends and sets the pace of national political outcomes and processes." The final essay, by political scientists Mark J. Rozell and Clyde Wilcox, defines the contours of the New Christian Right and its constituency, and examines its connection to the Republican party in Virginia.

Beyond Race in the Modern South

DAVID R. GOLDFIELD

Harry Briggs remembers the long, weary, dangerous battle. It began with a simple request for a school bus and culminated with a historic ruling by the U.S. Supreme Court. Looking back nearly forty years later, Briggs, in his early seventies and still living in Clarendon County, South Carolina, contrasted the hope and striving of his generation with the careless attitude of the current group of black students. "They don't seem to value an education," he said.

But take a walk down to Scott's Branch High School in Summerton, Clarendon County, and see the run-down shacks and dilapidated trailers surrounding the school that is periodically inundated by the runoff from Scott's Branch, and maybe the indifference is more understandable. Take a look at the 590 students—they are all black, and so poor that almost everyone qualifies for free lunches. On a national standardized reading and math exam, the school's tenth-grade class averaged a score of six on a scale of ninety-nine; the national average is fifty.

The county built the school hurriedly after the 1954 *Brown* decision, hoping that a new facility would satisfy blacks and deter them from seeking entrance into all-white Summerton High School. They persisted, however, and under a court order, a few blacks were allowed to attend Summerton High by the mid-1960s. The all-white school board (in a county where blacks outnumbered whites by a ten-to-one margin) refused to go beyond this token gesture, so in 1970 the NAACP filed yet another suit, and a federal district court ordered the county to desegregate its school system totally. The board closed Summerton High, and when the school term began only a half-dozen white children attended the other public schools in the county. A private school, Clarendon Hall, opened to accommodate the white students, leaving the public school system entirely black. The town of Summerton declined along with the public schools, reflecting in part the demise of King Cotton, and in part the reluctance of new industries to come into the county because of the school situation. Harry Brigg's modest and moral proposal forty years ago has ended in bitterness, division, and decay.

The Resegregation of Public Education:
A Microcosm of Southern Race Relations

Public education in the modern South exemplifies both the promise and problems of contemporary race relations in the region. As late as 1968, fourteen years after the *Brown* decision, approximately 18 percent of the region's black schoolchildren attended integrated schools. In Atlanta, roughly 90 percent of school-aged blacks remained in segregated schools. Atlanta journalist Ralph McGill complained to a Birmingham audience in 1968, "I am weary of the old hanging on of the dual school systems and the excuses and the evasion. Must we forever keep on? Must a nation which has put a man in space still argue about where and whether a colored child shall go to school?"

Not only McGill but black parents and the federal courts were losing their patience over the dilatory pace of school desegregation. In 1968, the U.S. Supreme Court ruled in a Virginia case, *Green* v. *New Kent County School Board,* that so-called "freedom-of-choice" plans allowing limited numbers of blacks to attend white schools were no longer appropriate means of complying with the *Brown* decision. School boards were now obligated to "come forward with a plan that promises realistically to work . . . until it is clear that state imposed segregation has been completely removed." The *Green* case established a more specific standard than "all deliberate speed" and foreshadowed even stricter guidelines in future decisions.

The following year, the High Court heard a school desegregation suit originating in Mississippi. The Nixon administration, as part of its "southern strategy," had promised a cautious, if not obstructive approach to the issue of school desegregation; accordingly, the Department of Health, Education, and Welfare had granted thirty-three school districts in Mississippi a one-year delay in implementing desegregation plans. The NAACP challenged the delay, and in *Alexander* v. *Holmes County Board of Education,* the Supreme Court ordered these school districts "to terminate dual school systems at once." The Court specifically abandoned the "all deliberate speed" standard as "no longer constitutionally permissible." School boards could not create plans that guaranteed tokenism while delaying complete integration for an indefinite period.

The Court remained silent, however, on the means school boards could employ to comply with the *Alexander* ruling. A suit adjudicated in Charlotte, North Carolina, that same year established a far-reaching precedent on the appropriate method for achieving school desegregation "at once." Darius Swann, a black Presbyterian missionary who returned to Charlotte from an assignment in India during the early 1960s, attempted in 1965 to enroll his six-year-old son in an all-white elementary school. Though Charlotte was operating under a "freedom of choice" plan that allegedly allowed any student to change schools, the transfers mostly involved white students seeking to escape integration. School officials denied Swann's request, and lawyer Julius Chambers filed suit against the Charlotte-Mecklenburg County Board of Education (the city and county school systems had consolidated in the early 1960s) in January, 1965. The suit prompted the school board to initiate a new desegregation plan that would approve freedom-of-choice transfers for all students within specific geographic areas. The U.S. District Court approved the plan rendering the case moot.

But most (66 out of 109) of the schools in the system remained segregated, and Chambers refiled in 1968. Federal judge James B. McMillan heard the arguments and rendered his decision for the plaintiff in the context of the *Green* and *Alexander* cases. From a legal standpoint, his ruling was not difficult: a plan was necessary to desegregate the entire system immediately. Judge McMillan appointed a prominent educator, Dr. John Finger, to draw up a comprehensive desegregation plan for Charlotte-Mecklenburg, and ordered the school system to adopt a busing program. Busing was nothing new to Charlotte-Mecklenburg children—23,600 students rode buses an average of fifteen miles one way—but busing to achieve racial integration was another matter. As Judge McMillan defended his action, "though seemingly radical in nature, if viewed by people who live in totally segregated neighborhoods, it may, like surgery, be the most conservative solution to the whole problem and the one most likely to provide a good education at minimum cost." The school board appealed, and in May, 1971, the U.S. Supreme Court upheld Judge McMillan's decision in *Swann* v. *Charlotte-Mecklenburg Board of Education*. The era of busing to achieve school desegregation was underway.

Many in the white community vilified the judge and his decision, but he was philosophical about the rebuffs and hate mail. As he told a *Time* reporter in 1971, "a judge would ordinarily like to decide cases to suit his neighbors," but he had a legal and moral duty to uphold the law: "Constitutional rights will not be denied here simply because they may be denied elsewhere. There is no Dow Jones average for such rights." . . .

School desegregation had been a festering controversy in the South for more than fifteen years, but the Supreme Court decisions between 1968 and 1971 left school boards no room for evasion. White parents, confronting what they now knew was inevitable, reacted swiftly and in some cases, as in Charlotte and Greensboro, constructively. Maggie Ray, a white homemaker from an affluent Charlotte neighborhood, helped form the Citizens Advisory Group that participated in preparing a pupil assignment system. The involvement of the city's white community at the initial stage of the desegregation process defused a considerable degree of adverse reaction. In Greensboro, a small group of women led by Joan Bluethenthal decided to study the school situation for their "Great Decisions Club," which worked with Doris Hutchinson of the city school system to initiate a series of weekend retreats for students, parents, teachers, and administrators during the spring of 1971. The retreats became the training ground for hundreds of citizens who began to work for the smooth transition to a totally integrated school system. The climax of the club's efforts was "Public School Sunday," a combination fair and public information program. As historian William Chafe summarized the club's impact, "within days a new world of busing, integrated PTAs and biracial student governments had become routine."

But some places, especially in the Deep South and rural areas, were not so well organized for smooth and uneventful change. Even in these locations, however, few white political leaders advocated resistance, and none advanced veiled warnings of violence. Time had proved the futility of such opposition, and, besides, blacks were becoming a potent political factor. Also, disruption could threaten economic development. Some white leaders even took a forceful stand in support of court-ordered busing. Florida governor Reubin Askew, for example, warned a state PTA conference in 1971 that "we cannot achieve equal opportunity in education by passing laws or constitutional amendments against busing—they could deny us what I believe is the highest destiny of the American people . . . to achieve a society in which all races, all creeds, and all religions have learned not only to live with their differences—but to *thrive* upon them." Extreme protest with respect to racial matters was no longer fashionable in the South, and southerners were always careful to conform their public behavior to the prevailing norm. But there were other ways to register discontent.

For one, whites abandoned public school systems and fled to more homogeneous schools or systems. Private schools—"seg academies" as some called them—proliferated. In the first three years after the *Swann* decision, the number of private schools in Memphis, for example, more than doubled from forty to eighty-five. White parents generally denied racial motives, citing the issue of "quality education" as the stimulus for change, but as Mississippi school superintendent Richard Boyd charged, the private school movement was "100% racial." For those parents who could not afford private school tuition, flight to the suburbs was another alternative. The white withdrawal from the Atlanta school system was indicative of a trend throughout the South: in 1960, Atlanta's segregated school system of 100,000 pupils was evenly divided between black and white, but in 1973, after busing effected integration, white enrollment dropped to 20,000 and black students comprised nearly 80 percent of the total school population. As the black population of southern cities continued to grow during the 1970s, the proportion of black pupils in the public school system advanced even more.

Sometimes white flight involved considerable hardship to working-class white parents, who could not afford to send their children to private academies. In 1970, the Ridgecrest neighborhood in Montgomery, a white working-class area, came under the Carver High School catchment district as a result of a new court-ordered desegregation plan. Rather than have their children attend Carver, formerly an all-black school, many white parents fled the city. The Montgomery *Advertiser* reported "a drastic turnover of housing" in Ridgecrest during the summer and fall of 1970. Citywide, the plan had pushed 4,000 white children into private schools, but many Ridgecrest homeowners could not afford the cost of a private education and so sold out to eager realtors who fueled the panic selling. One white homeowner lamented to a reporter: "This is our home and we love it, but we just can't stay here any more. We can never replace what we had here . . . we can't buy another house as good as this for the price of this one but we are willing to make the sacrifice." The extent of white flight in Ridgecrest upset the desegregation plan, forcing the school board to redraw district lines less than four years later. The Carver district now included another white working-class area, Bellingrath, and the wave of real estate transfers resumed. By 1980, the school district boundaries had become racial boundaries as well. Never before had Montgomery been so segregated in terms of residence by race. . . .

The re-emergence of segregated education had a significant impact on busing. Increasingly in many cities of the South, busing has become irrelevant since there are no longer sufficient numbers of whites to integrate schools. In 1973, the Supreme Court heard a complaint from Richmond city schools that the only way to

avoid a total resegregation of its increasingly black system was to inaugurate a busing plan with the predominantly white Henrico County School system. In a tie vote
(Justice William Powell abstained because he had represented the city of Richmond
in the lower courts), the Court decided that the *Swann* ruling did not extend to
cross-county busing. The implication of this decision and the more sweeping case
involving the Detroit school system, *Milliken* v. *Bradley,* was that suburban whites
should not be penalized for a city problem. Accordingly, by the late 1970s, urban
school districts were scrambling to maintain their white enrollment while at the
same time satisfying court desegregation orders. Busing routes were drawn and re-
drawn, but whites continued to leave the city public school systems. . . .

When cross-town busing began in Norfolk in 1971, the city's school system
was 60-percent white. By the time the Norfolk school board unanimously approved
a neighborhood school plan in April, 1986, the schools were 60-percent black. The
city's black school superintendent, Gene Carter, a strong supporter of the plan,
stated that "we are committed to having a stable desegregated system." During the
fifteen years of busing, whites had left for private schools and for suburban school
districts in nearby Virginia Beach or Chesapeake. Of course, white city residents
left Norfolk for many reasons aside from the school situation, but the net effect was
to complicate busing routes and increase the likelihood of a resegregated system in
the near future. So the city's school officials acted to stem the erosion of white support by abandoning busing for its elementary-school students and creating thirty-
five neighborhood elementary schools, ten of which were to be black. Prior to the
neighborhood plan there were no all-black elementary schools in the city. School
board chairman Thomas Johnson expressed his regret in creating segregated
schools, but "I think the facts tell us we're losing the middle class in this city." The
local NAACP leader held a different perspective: "They might use fancy, deceptive
terms like 'neighborhood schools,' but the bottom line is segregation." . . .

Early returns from the Norfolk experiment are not encouraging. The white
school population has not increased, nor have the number and length of bus rides diminished. Black parental involvement in the resegregated schools, one of the objectives of the plan, has not materialized. The city has spent $454 more per pupil for
materials, teachers, and maintenance in the resegregated schools. Test scores have
been disappointing: four of the black schools had lower scores than any school during the year prior to the shift. The scores reflected problems deeper than racial composition. As one teacher said, "the school system bought us nice science books and
nice social studies books, but my children couldn't 'Turn to page 138,' because they
didn't know what 138 was. We didn't open the science books." Instead, she spent
$800 of her own to purchase or make more appropriate materials. Another teacher
complained that the children in these schools were not receiving reinforcement at
home. Homes lacked crayons or pencils; pupils did not know the meaning of
marshmallow or *cherry* on standardized tests because they had never seen either.
And students often could not go on field trips because they did not have the fifty-
cent admission price for a museum. Teachers also noted a deterioration of discipline, perhaps indicating that middle-class children were better role models for
deportment and work habits. . . .

Some whites have commented that black students tested the waters of integrated education and found the going too rough, choosing instead to pull back into
the traditional sanctuary of their own institutions. Or perhaps, as Harry Briggs im-

plied, the current generation of black students are unwilling to duplicate the tenacity and courage of their predecessors; to contemporary black youngsters an integrated education is nothing to fight for and maybe even something to fight against. Their experiences with integrated education may have reinforced the view that except for athletic teams there is little interaction with whites socially and, in some cases, academically as well. They may have gone to school in Anson County, North Carolina, and have held separate reunions for their classes; or have seen the beauty pageant at Parker High School in Greenville, South Carolina, where a white contestant withdrew after she discovered that a black ROTC cadet was to escort her during the program; or have read about the cross-burning on Sorority Row at the University of Alabama in protest of the pending move of a black sorority to the vicinity; or have heard of the racial hazing of black cadets at The Citadel in Charleston, South Carolina.

But the struggle over school desegregation, as with voting rights and public accommodations, was always broader than the question of access—it concerned intangibles that have become submerged in the current discussion about quality. Integration of schools, even if superficial, involved some contact: seeing blacks in classrooms lessened the surprise of seeing blacks in boardrooms, and thereby increased the likelihood of black economic mobility. For all its dynamism, a good deal of the southern economy is honeycombed with a good-ole-boy network that extends back to college days and beyond, especially in small and medium-sized urban communities. A segregated education for blacks is not likely to enhance economic opportunities. In addition, the absence of contact tends to feed stereotypes. In 1971, a black girl commented on her first days at newly integrated Americus High School: "After all these years now, we realize the whites are just human beings, not supermen without any faults or weaknesses. . . . Why, a boy in one of my classes, he just sits there all the time eating on pencils—yeah!" Though these revelations are unlikely to occur today—another measure of how far we have come— the danger of resegregation is that perceptions will grow and fester in a vacuum. Schools remain the greatest contact points for black and white southerners. . . .

The point is that community mores, even in rural parts of the South, have shifted with respect to race. Southerners have usually been concerned with doing the right thing, especially for an audience. Race-related shrines and commemorative events are among these proper displays, as are extirpations of improper behavior, violent or rhetorical. Again, these exercises might strike some as empty formalism, but in the South they are integral to a way of life.

A Southern Legacy: To Attempt Things
That Might Fail . . .

Ultimately, this was a religious movement—not surprising in an evangelical region where biblical rhetoric and imagery suffuse daily speech and writing, and where *redemption* is both a biblical and a political term, and now perhaps even a social term as well. What saved the South may well have been its religion, which had long served as a helpmate for the racial status quo, but which possessed within it the character for change and salvation. This religious element made the movement a moral crusade, lifted it to a higher plane. Southern religion also carried with it the notion of forgiveness. It would have been understandable for blacks to lapse into bitterness and hatred, but they endured the Freedom Rides, the children's crusade in Birmingham, the church bombing, and the voting-rights murders strengthened by their religious convictions. Their fervor filled their songs of freedom, imbued their leaders with resolve, and challenged the beliefs of whites. Martin Luther King wrote in 1965 that "in the quiet recesses of my heart, I am fundamentally a clergyman, a Baptist preacher." That was the essence of his leadership, firmly grounded in evangelical Protestantism, the folk religion of the South.

The moral, religious fervor of the crusade has dissipated, much as the crusade itself has changed. "We must leave the racial battleground," Jesse Jackson implores, "and find the economic common ground." Perhaps economy does not easily lend itself to a moral framework, especially in a prosperous region, but one of the many legacies of the civil rights movement in the South has been to recharge regional theology for moral change. Black churches have historically been dedicated to this end in theory, if not always in practice, and now there is the possibility that white religious institutions can combine with black counterparts to lend a moral framework to the search for "the economic common ground." The successes of the earlier crusade depended to a great extent upon the religious context of rhetoric and action. Perhaps southern religion, white and black, can work similar miracles through a rededication to the moral precepts of evangelical theology. . . .

At the 1984 Democratic National Convention, Jesse Jackson, in a typical rhetorical flourish, claimed that blacks have "come from disgrace to Amazing Grace." The same observation could be applied to the South. In 1940, black life in the region was circumscribed by segregation, exclusion, and an elaborate and demeaning racial etiquette. That is mostly gone now, but the South isn't, and southern blacks were largely responsible for both the exorcism and the preservation. Though the agenda of race relations in the South is filled with unfinished business, it is now possible to move beyond race and include such items as part of a larger new crusade for economic justice. If that seems to be a tall order, recall that few southerners, black or white, imagined a new racial order just a short generation ago. The task may be more difficult today less because of the problem than because of our prevailing smugness. It is well to remember Jimmy Carter's admonition in a 1985 interview: "When we . . . are satisfied with what we have accomplished in the eyes of God, we are already far from God. Unless we are attempting things that might fail, we have too little faith—in ourselves or in God."

For the crusade against economic injustice, southern blacks and whites are likely to be partners. Just as the problems are no longer necessarily racial in the South, the means for their solution require an interracial alliance, a connection that already finds a common ground of past, place, religion, and manners, as well as a legacy of ameliorating what Gunnar Myrdal called "The American Dilemma." Perhaps the South can become, after all, that beacon of hope that Faulkner and Dabbs and others predicted decades ago. Perhaps black and white together can descend from "the mountaintops of hope," as Urban League president John Jacob put it in 1985, to "the green valleys of complete equality and justice." That would be the most fitting legacy of the crusade for black equality in the South.

The Vital South

EARL BLACK AND MERLE BLACK

National Consequences of Change in the South

The emergence of a Solid Republican South has been a pivotal event in modern presidential politics. From 1880 through 1948 the Republican party essentially wrote off the South. Eisenhower's 1952 and 1956 campaigns were highly success-ful when measured against the Republicans' previous inability to penetrate the South, but neither Nixon in 1960 nor Goldwater in 1964 had Eisenhower's popular appeal. In terms of electoral votes, Nixon was as competitive in the three-way race of 1968 as Eisenhower had been in 1952. With the collapse of the Wallace move-ment in 1972, the Republicans were finally positioned to win the substantial white majorities they required to sweep the South's electoral votes. In every subsequent election save 1976 a new Solid South appeared, this time under Republican auspices.

Once the South contributed no electoral votes at all to Republican presidential campaigns. Commencing with Eisenhower's races, however, the South began to provide a small portion of the electoral college votes needed for a Republican ma-jority. In 1952, for example, Eisenhower's southern breakthrough gave the Republi-cans 21 percent of the electoral votes necessary for victory. Since 1968 the South's contribution to Republican control of the White House has increased enormously. Southern states alone gave Nixon 48 percent of the electoral votes he needed to win reelection in 1972. The South's contribution to Republican presidential candidates slipped to 4 percent in Ford's 1976 loss to Carter, rose to 44 percent in Reagan's victory in 1980, and amounted to a slight majority—51 percent—of the electoral votes needed to elect Reagan in 1984 and Bush in 1988. A completely solid Repub-lican South in the presidential elections of the 1990s would provide 54 percent of the electoral votes needed to win the presidency. Its unmatched size and potential unity make the South the grand regional prize of presidential elections.

The creation of a Solid Republican South in most recent presidential elections has revolutionized the regional dynamics of presidential campaigns. Because of its southern gains, the Republican party has not needed northern electoral majorities to control the presidency. Increasing Republican competitiveness in the South from 1952 through 1968 reduced the Republicans' northern electoral vote target to much smaller majorities (50 to 55 percent). The decisive change occurred in the aftermath of the Great Society. Beginning in 1972 the Republicans usually could win the pres-idency with only a small minority—33 percent in 1984 and 1988—of the northern electoral vote. A Solid Republican South, if it can be retained, gives the Republi-cans the luxury of targeting key northern states (California being the most obvious) while compelling the Democrats to win 69 percent of the northern electoral vote, an extremely difficult task in "normal" political times.

Between the New Deal and the present the Republicans' northern target has been cut roughly in half. Aside from the GOP's close defeat in 1976, the Republicans have exceeded their northern goals by substantial margins. Winning the South thus makes it much easier for the Republicans to succeed in the North. By understanding and fully exploiting the dynamics of southern politics, the Republicans have thus far succeeded in building and rebuilding the large white majorities necessary to carry the South. Southern victories have in turn given Republican presidential candidates a vital hedge against possible northern defeats.

A final point needs to be made about the role of the South in presidential politics. The best political base is the one that can be repeatedly secured with the least expenditure of time and money. Just as the South had traditionally functioned as a cheap and safe Democratic base in presidential politics, so the South today usually serves as an inexpensive and promising Republican stronghold. It is no small advantage to Republican campaigns to be able to pour extra resources into key northern states on the reasonable assumption that the southern states are relatively safe. . . .

As the largest and usually most cohesive region in the nation, the South often controls the votes that influence which parties dominate the executive and legislative branches of the national government. Whether the region will continue to produce Republican landslide white majorities in presidential elections while it produces Democratic biracial majorities in many congressional and senatorial contests is among the most compelling and critical questions confronting the nation.

Today, one looks at the South and sees America. There is abundant reason to pay close attention to future political developments in the South, for it now shapes the trends and sets the pace of national political outcomes and processes. Above all, this is the portrait of a *vital* South, a region once again at the center of struggles to define winners and losers in American politics.

The New Christian Right in Virginia

MARK J. ROZELL AND CLYDE WILCOX

The Christian Right and Its Target Constituency

To conceptualize the relationship between the Christian Right and the Republican party in Virginia, it is first important to understand the Christian Right. [Here] the term *Christian Right* refers to organizations that attempt to mobilize orthodox Christian religious views behind a very conservative political agenda, and to the members and supporters of these organizations. We include pro-life organizations among Christian Right groups in Virginia, mindful that in many parts of the country pro-life groups attract sizable contingents of moderates and even a few liberals. Nationally, pro-life moderates are generally Catholics or are from the "peace and justice" evangelical churches, but in Virginia, Catholic pro-life activists tend to be conservative, and there are few adherents of the liberal evangelical churches. When we refer to pro-life groups as part of the Christian Right[,] . . . we are not referring

---

Mark J. Rozell and Clyde Wilcox. *Second Coming: The New Christian Right in Virginia Politics.* Copyright ©1996 Johns Hopkins University Press. Reprinted by permission of the publisher.

to the small contingent of Feminists for Life or elements of the Seamless Garment Network, but rather to Christian social conservatives who emphasize the abortion issue over all others but are generally conservative on other social and moral issues as well.

Organizations such as the Moral Majority and Christian Voice in the 1980s, and the Christian Coalition and Family Foundation in the 1990s, have sought to organize Christian social conservatives into political action. That action is almost always Republican. In his insightful book on the Pat Robertson and Jesse Jackson presidential candidacies, Allen Hertzke notes that the Christian Coalition views victories by Republicans as victories for Christians. He quotes Oliver Thomas, counsel for the Baptist Joint Committee, as noting that when he announced to a Christian Coalition gathering that his own brother was a "Democratic officeholder and a fine Christian layman," the audience was stunned into silence.

It was not always so. The first Christian Right crusades in the twentieth century were focused on opposition to the teaching of evolution in schools. The chief political spokesperson for this movement was William Jennings Bryan, a perennial Democratic presidential candidate who took decidedly leftist positions on economic issues. But the next generation of the Christian Right, in the 1950s, a collection of Christian anticommunist organizations, was strongly Republican and endorsed the Goldwater presidential campaign with enthusiasm. Although we will see that Virginia's Christian Right first attempted to organize within the Democratic party, by the time the major fundamentalist groups such as the Moral Majority and Christian Voice were fully active in the early 1980s, they almost exclusively backed Republicans. The mobilization efforts of the Christian Right during the 1980s and 1990s are often referred to as the *New* Christian Right, to distinguish them from these earlier efforts. . . . [W]e will also distinguish between the first wave of mostly fundamentalist New Christian Right organizations and a second generation of groups, such as the Christian Coalition, that formed or grew during the late 1980s and early 1990s.

It is important to understand that the Christian Right is distinct from its potential constituency—evangelical Christians and other Christian social conservatives. Some evangelicals support the Christian Right, but a majority do not. Although some journalists persist in referring to born-again or evangelical Christians as the Christian Right, they are more appropriately conceived as the Christian Right's primary target constituency. Thus, newspaper accounts that interpret the strength of the Christian Right based on the percentage of an electorate who are "born again" make a fundamental error and exaggerate the power of the Christian Right.

Robert Zwier described the target constituency of the Moral Majority as "the approximately 50 million evangelicals in this country, and in particular the fundamentalist wing of that community. The aim from the beginning was to mobilize a group of people who had traditionally avoided politics because they saw it as dirty, corrupt business . . . by convincing them that political involvement was a God-given responsibility." Evangelicals can be identified by the churches they attend or by their doctrinal beliefs. Many denominations are members of the National Association of Evangelicals, and thus members of these churches can be considered evangelicals. Lyman Kellstedt, a leading analyst of evangelical politics, suggests that the core of evangelical doctrine is a belief in the divinity of Christ, acceptance of Christ as the only way to attain eternal life or salvation, belief in an inerrant

Bible, and a commitment to spreading the Gospel. For most evangelicals, the act of accepting Christ as their savior is described as becoming "born again," often in an intensely emotional experience.

Evangelicals compose by some estimates a quarter of the American public, but they are a diverse lot. Perhaps the most important distinction is between white and African-American evangelicals. Although black evangelical churches frequently preach conservative messages on issues such as abortion and sexual behavior, they also emphasize the importance of equality and human liberation. While black evangelicals who attend church frequently are actually slightly *more* likely than other African Americans to favor equal roles for women, white evangelicals, reading from the same inerrant Bible, are less likely to support gender equality than other whites. There are other political differences as well. Many African-American evangelical pastors tell their congregants that their religious convictions lead them to support Democratic candidates, while many white evangelical pastors endorse Republicans.

In addition, there are important theological distinctions within the evangelical community, particularly among whites. Three broad groupings are frequently identified: fundamentalists, pentecostals and charismatics, and neoevangelicals. Fundamentalists are most often found in independent Baptist and nondenominational churches. Most fundamentalists believe that the Bible is literally true, word for word, and that when Christians seek to divine God's will they should consult "the Book." Fundamentalists study the Bible and memorize verses. Some also occasionally seek inspiration by opening it at random and reading. Nancy Ammerman provides an amusing account of a man who was troubled by a pending decision about whether to buy another tent from Sears, for the last one he had purchased there had leaked. He opened the Bible at random and read in Deuteronomy 14:5 that Jews were permitted to eat a "roebuck," which he interpreted as divine guidance to give Sears a second chance. Of course, most fundamentalists consult their Bibles for far more important decisions and thoughtfully seek guidance. For fundamentalists, the Bible is the ultimate source, and God through the Holy Spirit guides its interpretation. Fundamentalists generally carry well-worn Bibles with plenty of markings in the margins and markers throughout. They carefully comb the Scriptures, and cross-reference themes and topics. Jerry Falwell is the most visible political actor among fundamentalist Christians.

Pentecostals and charismatics also believe that the Bible is an important tool in understanding God's will, but they emphasize the importance of the active guidance of the Holy Spirit. The Spirit gives gifts, such as the ability to prophesy or to heal by faith, and imparts upon the believer ecstatic religious experiences such as speaking in tongues or being slain in the Spirit. Where the fundamentalists emphasize study of the text, pentecostals and charismatics emphasize direct communication with God. A fundamentalist church service generally involves a sermon heavily laced with Scripture; pentecostal and charismatic services may be punctuated by individuals shouting in the "language of the angels," or falling to the floor in religious rapture. Although there are some doctrinal differences between pentecostals and charismatics, the main difference is denominational. Pentecostals are found in distinctive denominations such as Assemblies of God, but charismatic caucuses exist in most Christian churches, including Episcopalians, Presbyterians, Methodists, and Roman Catholics. Marion (Pat) Robertson is a visible spokesman for pentecostal and charismatic Christians.

Finally, neoevangelicals tend to take more moderate positions on both the Bible and spiritual gifts. Most neoevangelicals believe that the Bible is the inerrant word of God, but they may question a literal interpretation of some passages. For example, some neoevangelicals read the account in Genesis of the universe being created in seven days as a somewhat metaphorical measurement of time. They may believe that the process took seven billion years, for example, not seven twenty-four-hour days, because "one day is with the Lord as a thousand years." They also generally recognize that spiritual gifts exist but hold that these gifts are rarer and more private than the pentecostals would maintain. Billy Graham is probably the best-known neoevangelical preacher.

When scholars or journalists refer to evangelicals, they may mean the neo-evangelicals just described, or they may be referring to the larger set of orthodox Christians that encompasses fundamentalists, pentecostals, charismatics, and neo-evangelicals. Each of these groups is part of the Christian Right target constituency.

The theological differences among these groups may seem quite subtle to those outside of the theological traditions, but they are quite important within the evangelical community. In particular, the relationship between fundamentalists and pentecostals has frequently been a hostile one, due in part to the early competition between fundamentalist and pentecostal churches in the early twentieth century for roughly the same potential clientele. The hostility has been somewhat one-sided, fundamentalists being more antagonistic toward pentecostals than vice versa. One early fundamentalist pastor called pentecostals the "last vomit of Satan," and, although the rhetoric has cooled somewhat in the intervening years, fundamentalist pastors continue to condemn pentecostals and charismatics in strong language. Falwell has written that fundamentalists "violently reject the Pentecostal/Charismatic movement" and that those who speak in tongues "ate too much pizza last night."

The theological divide among evangelicals contributed to the failures of the Moral Majority and other fundamentalist groups of the 1980s. Studies of Moral Majority state organizations showed them to be composed primarily of Baptist Bible Fellowship congregants. The reason for this concentration in a single denomination was evident at one Ohio Moral Majority meeting that one of us attended in 1982. The theme of the sermon that preceded the meeting was "Roman Catholic Church: Harlot of Rome." In addition to Catholics, the preacher lambasted mainline Protestants, evangelicals, pentecostals, and charismatics. By the end of the sermon, it was apparent that this minister believed that heaven, like the Ohio Moral Majority, would primarily contain Baptists, and only one Baptist denomination at that.

These divisions among evangelicals also hurt Pat Robertson's 1988 presidential campaign. A variety of studies showed that Robertson's support was largely confined to pentecostal and charismatic Christians and that fundamentalists and neoevangelical ministers and congregants were at best neutral and occasionally hostile to his campaign. Yet Robertson himself evidenced greater religious tolerance: David Harrell quotes him as saying, "In terms of the succession of the church, I'm a Roman Catholic. As far as the majesty of worship, I'm an Episcopalian; as far as the belief in the sovereignty of God, I'm Presbyterian; in terms of holiness, I'm a Methodist; in terms of the priesthood of believers and baptism, I'm a Baptist; in terms of the baptism of the Holy Spirit, I'm a Pentecostal. So I'm a little bit of all of them." Robertson's *700 Club* television program was not a fundamentalist sermon like Falwell's *Old Time Gospel Hour,* but instead a religious talk show with a black co-host and with guests from a variety of religious backgrounds, including Catholics and Jews.

By January 1989, it appeared that the Christian Right was in retreat. Falwell had disbanded the Moral Majority because of a lack of funds, Christian Voice had ended its political action committee and was generally moribund, and Robertson was back on television and not a part of the new Bush administration. This apparent failure was not because of ebbing public support. Polls showed that the Christian Right had enjoyed the support of a relatively constant 10–15 percent of the general public throughout the 1980s. Instead, the Christian Right of the 1980s failed because of broader political and economic forces. Direct mail revenues for conservative groups declined after Reagan's reelection campaign, which showed fuzzy pictures of a Norman Rockwell America and told voters that it was "Morning in America." It became increasingly difficult to persuade the older women who constituted the financial base of the Moral Majority that their donations of $25 were urgently needed to fight liberalism when Reagan had assured them that all was fine with the world. Moreover, America's two-party system constrained Robertson's role in politics: he could only contest the Republican nomination and then return to his religious television program. In a multiparty parliamentary system, he would doubtlessly head a small religious party with 10 percent of the seats in the legislature.

Yet Christian Right leaders were not despondent, for they had already decided on a new strategy—broader coalitions in grass-roots mobilization. In part, this new strategy was born of necessity. The large, direct mail–funded efforts of the 1980s had failed, and a wave of scandals involving televangelists had made many Christians reluctant to send donations to television preachers. But the new strategy also reflected the reality of decentralization in American politics. Many of the decisions that most profoundly affect the lives of the average citizen are made at the state and local level, and this is especially true of the one issue that has long been most central to the Christian Right—education policy.

The Christian Right organizations that formed and grew in the early 1990s were more focused on grass-roots activity and on fostering interdenominational coalitions. The best known was the Christian Coalition, formed by Pat Robertson and headed by Ralph Reed, Jr., a skillful organizer and publicist. Many other groups . . . were active as well. The Christian Coalition and other "second generation" Christian Right groups seek to appeal to white evangelicals, black evangelicals, Catholics, and even to a few conservative Jews. Together, these organizations seek to move Christian social conservatives into Republican political activism. . . .

The Christian Right as a Party Faction. Despite their occasional willingness to help Democratic candidates, by the 1990s, most activists in the Christian Right were clearly associated with the Republican party. In Virginia, movement activists hold important party positions on the Republican State Central Committee and on county party committees. We can, therefore, also conceive of the Christian Right as a faction within the Republican party. . . .

If some portion of the Christian Right exists as an issue faction within the Republican party, then we should focus on its ability to provide a mass base, an ideo-

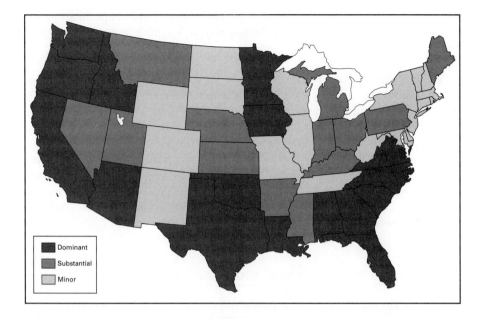

Figure 1. Christian Right influence in state Republican parties as of September 1994. Data from *Campaigns and Elections*. (Alaska and Hawaii, not shown, fall into the Dominant category.)

logical format, and an organizational matrix. Clearly the Christian Right supplies all three. Over the past two decades, Christian social conservatives have become a very regular source of Republican votes in state elections. Christian Right supporters in the Republican party offer a more distinctive ideology than do party centrists. The Christian Right provides an organizational matrix with clearly identifiable faction leaders who give cues to other movement activists. In 1995, the state party chairman was a supporter of the Christian Right, as were more than a third of the State Central Committee. Clearly the Christian Right is not merely a movement outside of the party but a coherent segment of Virginia Republicans. . . .

Yet, in Virginia, the Christian Right's activism has sometimes led to heated factional fighting that has harmed the Republican party. In Fairfax County, one Christian Right activist ran as a third-party candidate for the Board of Supervisors, siphoning off enough support to allow the Democratic candidate to defeat the moderate Republican nominee. In 1994, newly moderate Republican Marshall Coleman ran as an independent against Republican nominee Oliver North. . . .

The existence of a substantial Christian Right faction in Virginia has had other negative consequences for Virginia Republicans. These new elites may move the party further from the average party supporter and average voter and therefore produce candidates who are less electable. The defeats of Michael Farris and Oliver North in years that were marked by statewide and nationwide Republican landslides, and of Elaine McConnell in Fairfax County in 1995 . . . were produced by large countermobilizations by Democratic and independent voters and substantial defections of Republican moderates to the Democratic candi-

dates. Quite simply, the new Christian Right elites have staked out positions on social issues that are unacceptable to the majority of Virginian voters in most elections. . . .

In Virginia, the Christian Right continues to be in transition. There exists a loose
network of activists and organizations that is best characterized as a social movement, but some of these organizations have developed sufficient internal structure
to function as interest groups, and a number of activists have sufficiently penetrated
the party structures to serve as a party faction. Much as interstellar gas and other
matter eventually form a well-defined set of stars and planets, so the social movement of the Christian Right is gradually developing into a set of institutionalized interest groups and party factions. Moreover, just as the process of stellar formation
uses some but not all available matter, so the institutionalization of the Christian
Right may never fully incorporate all activists.

⚓ F U R T H E R   R E A D I N G

Carl Abbott, *The New Urban America: Growth and Politics in Sunbelt Cities* (1981)
Howard Ball et al., *Compromised Compliance: Implementation of the 1965 Voting Rights Act*
    (1982)
Numan V. Bartley, "Another New South?" *Georgia Historical Quarterly* 65 (1981), 119–137
Numan V. Bartley and Hugh D. Graham, *Southern Politics and the Second Reconstruction*
    (1975)
Jack Bass and Walter De Vries, *The Transformation of Southern Politics: Social Change and
    Political Consequences Since 1945* (1976)
Joan Turner Beifuss, *At the River I Stand: Memphis, the 1968 Strike, and Martin Luther King*
    (1985)
William C. Berman, *America's Right Turn: From Nixon to Bush* (1994)
Earl Black, *Southern Governors and Civil Rights: Racial Segregation as a Campaign Issue
    in the Second Reconstruction* (1976)
Peter G. Bourne, *Jimmy Carter: A Comprehensive Biography* (1997)
Dan T. Carter, *The Politics of Rage* (1995)
———, *From George Wallace to Newt Gingrich* (1996)
Robert Dallek, *Flawed Giant: Lyndon Johnson and His Times, 1961–1973* (1998)
Chandler Davidson, ed., *Minority Vote Dilution* (1984)
Chandler Davidson and Bernard Grofman, *Quiet Revolution: The Impact of the Voting Rights
    Act in the South* (1994)
Paul Delaney, "A New South for Blacks?" in John B. Boles, ed., *Dixie Dateline: A Journalis-
    tic Portrait of the Contemporary South* (1983)
Marvin Dunn, *Black Miami in the Twentieth Century* (1997)
Gary M. Fink, *Prelude to the Presidency: The Political Career and Legislative Leadership
    Style of Governor Jimmy Carter* (1980)
Frye Gaillard, *The Dream Long Deferred* (1988)
David Goldfield, *Region, Race, and Cities: Interpreting the Urban South* (1997)
Carl Grafton and Anne Permaloff, *Big Mules and Branchheads: James E. Folsom and Politi-
    cal Power in Alabama* (1985)
Dewey W. Grantham, *The Life and Death of the Solid South: A Political History* (1988)
Melissa Fay Greene, *Praying for Sheetrock* (1991)
Edward R. Haas, *De Lesseps S. Morrison and the Image of Reform: New Orleans Politics,
    1946–1961* (1974)
William C. Havard, ed., *The Changing Politics of the South* (1972)
Alexander Heard, *A Two-Party South?* (1952)

Burton Ira Kaufman, *The Presidency of James Earl Carter, Jr.* (1993)

Martin Luther King, Jr., *Where Do We Go from Here: Chaos or Community* (1967)

Alexander P. Lamis, *The Two-Party South* (1984)

Harold H. Martin, *William Berry Hartsfield: Mayor of Atlanta* (1978)

William Martin, *With God on Our Side: The Rise of the Religious Right in America* (1996)

Kevin E. McHigh, "Black Migration Reversal in the United States," *Geographical Review* 77 (1987), 171–182

Frank R. Parker, *Black Votes Count: Political Empowerment in Mississippi* (1990)

Richard A. Pride and J. David Woodard, *The Burden of Busing: The Politics of Desegregation in Nashville, Tennessee* (1985)

John Shelton Reed, "Up from Segregation," *Virginia Quarterly Review* 60 (1984), 377–393

John Rozier, *Black Boss: Political Revolution in a Georgia County* (1982)

Robert Sherrill, *Gothic Politics in the Deep South* (1968)

Robert P. Steed, et al., *Party Organization and Activism in the American South* (1998)

David M. Tucker, *Memphis Since Crump: Bossism, Blacks, and Civic Reformers, 1948–1968* (1980)

Amy Wells and Robert Crain, *Stepping Over the Color Line: African American Students in White Suburban Schools* (1997)

William Julius Wilson, *The Declining Significance of Race: Blacks and Changing American Institutions* (1978)

Raymond Wolters, *The Burden of Brown: Thirty Years of School Desegregation* (1984)

CHAPTER
14

The South Lives (Moves) On

Will the South live on as a culturally distinct region, or has it begun to move on to become more like the rest of the United States? To paraphrase historian George B. Tindall, the South has had more lives than a cat. Some writers have argued that despite momentous changes in the South since World War II, many elements of southern culture persist. Its cities and industries, for all their superficial resemblance to their counterparts elsewhere, reflect some enduring traditions. While the South has dispatched its peculiar racial customs such as segregation and disfranchisement, it is not clear whether the region is settling into the racial patterns of the rest of the nation or, influenced by its history, is in the process of charting totally new directions in race relations. And while the South is now a two-party region, political scientists point to the power of the Republican party in tones that recall the "Solid South." There are other manifestations of southern endurance—its music, food, idioms and patterns of speech, religion, family life, and above all its remembrance of the past.

Some scholars are skeptical of the South's cultural persistence. They cite statistics and behavior patterns and point out that while some aspects of regional life remain different, the South as a distinctive entity has vanished. The South and the rest of the nation have at last reached a compromise. With so many northerners and westerners moving south and so many shopping malls and skyscrapers going up, southern metropolitan areas could be mistaken for any other place. In education, per capita income, job opportunities, and nouvelle cuisine, the South is approaching the rest of the nation.

Is it time to write an epitaph for Dixie? Or is the South still alive and distinctively well?

✛ ESSAYS

In the opening essay, Bruce J. Schulman notes the dramatic changes that have occurred in the South since the New Deal. He credits a good deal of the change to federal economic policies that boosted the South out of poverty and into the national mainstream. Raymond Arsenault, in the second essay, points to another dimension of southern change since World War II—climate control through air conditioning. Air conditioning not only has contributed to migration to the more comfortable South, but also has brought about a decline in mortality rates and an increase in industrialization and ur-

416

banization, along with changes in family life, architecture, and the incidence of vio-lence. Arsenault contends that although air conditioning has diminished southerners' sense of place, it has not changed everything. The South is still "a land apart." Howard Preston, in the third essay, maintains that while the future South will become less and less distinct, enduring trends of regionalism still exist in the South.

From Cotton Belt to Sunbelt

BRUCE J. SCHULMAN

In the two decades after 1962, the South seemed truly to become an integral piece of the national polity and economy, a part of the main. The contemporary South, many commentators maintained, skipped the intermediate stage in America's pas-sage from rural to urban to suburban nation, from agrarian to industrial to service economy, but rejoined America's post-industrial mainstream. Long-term economic processes—the mechanization of the cotton culture, the steady swelling of cities, the high-technology boom, the ever-narrowing income gap between the regions, the northward migration of poverty—knit the regions together and brought the South a two-party political system, even if those processes by-passed large segments of the South.

Certainly, such "natural" processes played a large role in the South's postwar economic transformation. The oil economy, with its cycle of boom in the 1970s and bust in the 1980s, dominated the fortunes of the Southwest. The long, sustained pe-riod of postwar prosperity produced what economists call "spread effects." That is, continuously strong demand stimulated the expansion of plant[s], while other fac-tors encouraged that new capacity to locate away from the old manufacturing belt. This industrial de-concentration especially benefited the South in the 1950s and 1960s.

The postwar era also witnessed the rise of so-called footloose industries. For these firms, unlike the old heavy industries, geographic proximity to supplies of raw materials was unnecessary. They could readily take advantage of the South's appealing business climate. Footloose industries included the high-tech lines, but also many highly competitive, traditional southern industries like textiles. But, of course, high technology produced few jobs for local residents, and footloose low wage plants moved frequently. Many southern communities found themselves just as dependent as ever on the local mill, and just as vulnerable when that employer departed for another locale.

Tourism and retirement also emerged as major postwar businesses, flooding the warm South with tourists and retirees. Florida led the way in both respects, but by the 1970s, hillside resorts and retirement condominiums had emerged even in Ap-palachia. Tourism development, however, provided little direct benefit to southern-ers. Aged southerners were less likely than elderly Americans to collect social security benefits, and aged black southerners the least likely to do so because domestics and agricultural workers did not participate in social security before the 1960s.

But these basic economic processes . . . owed much of their potency to the federal government. Macroeconomic policy sustained postwar prosperity and pushed industry toward the South. Tourism and the retirement business depended on social security, interstate highways, and airports. Pipeline development and tax policies nourished the oil patch.

"Cotton is going West, Cattle are coming East, Negroes are going North, and Yankees are coming South." That popular southern quip, Frank Smith noted in 1965, captured "a great many of the changes through which the South is passing in these middle years of the twentieth century." The national government figured prominently in all of those epic migrations. The AAA reorganized southern agriculture, reducing cotton production in the Deep South and diminishing the tenancy that sustained it. At the same time, the revised economics of southern agriculture and the vicissitudes of the farm program encouraged the cultivation of livestock. Along with the demise of sharecropping, federal wage policy catalyzed a reorganization of southern manufacturing. The effect was to dry up low wage, unskilled employment and send black workers to northern cities. At the same time, war and space industry and high-tech spin-offs of the defense state attracted educated Yankees below the Mason-Dixon line. They fueled the rise of business-oriented politics. In the 1970s the South's booming cities captured the imagination of the American press as its poverty had in the 1930s. Tales of Sunbelt prosperity replaced stories of Cotton Belt woe in the national consciousness. Even as the Sunbelt boom slowed in the 1980s, the southern economy continued to outpace the national average in employment growth and other indicators, and journalists wondered at the reverse migration of blacks toward the region so many had once fled.

The region's boosters believed the South's new politics consonant with its economic development. They numbered the end of one-party Democratic rule as just another instance of southern progress. That might have been the case. Even the liberal Democrats of the 1930s looked forward to a future South of two-party competition. The shadows on the Sunbelt, however, exposed the folly of unqualified celebration of southern progress. The South, for all its changes, remained a place apart in the 1980s. Poverty persisted, especially in the rural areas. Education still lagged. Public health facilities remained inadequate. Blacks had yet to enter the economic mainstream and the tax structure remained notoriously regressive. The Southern Growth Policies Board was wise to concede in 1986 that the South had journeyed only halfway down the highway to economic prosperity.

The federal government largely paved the way. The South's odyssey from Cotton Belt to Sunbelt, however tortuous and incomplete, depended on national policy. It also dramatized the evolution of postwar national policy, the shift from economic programs to defense-related expenditures. Aid to underdeveloped regions gave way to a competitive scramble for the fruits of federal spending.

In the 1930s, FDR had punctuated nearly every speech about his hopes for regional development by lecturing southerners on their need to truly join the nation. He had echoed Howard Odum and the Depression-era southern liberals, calling for an end to sectionalism and the birth of a South with closer economic and political bonds to the rest of the nation. Luther Hodges picked up Roosevelt's theme when he arrived in Washington in the 1960s: "We Southerners don't want to saw off any part of America, and we are sick and tired of hearing people talk as if they wanted to saw us off, to isolate us from the mainstream of American progress and prosperity." Roosevelt's dreams of a vitalized southern economy were realized but, in the perverse way of dreams, the newest New South appeared not so much as FDR had envisioned it, but as Luther Hodges had.

The Air Conditioner and Southern Culture

RAYMOND ARSENAULT

In 1979 *Time* magazine columnist Frank Trippett took the American intellectual community to task for ignoring the social and cultural significance of air conditioning. Scholars and pop sociologists have been keenly aware of "the social implications of the automobile and television," he observed, but for some reason they have not gotten around "to charting and diagnosing all the changes brought about by air conditioning." Trippett's complaint is valid, and strange as it may seem, nowhere is this more evident than in the field of southern history. When the journalist Pat Watters called the air conditioner the "unsung hero" of the modern South in 1963, he knew what he was talking about. With few exceptions, historical works on the twentieth-century South published during the last forty years make no mention of air conditioning or, for that matter, of anything related to climate or climate control. The recently published *The Encyclopedia of Southern History* contains 2,900 articles, covering everything from "Abbeville" to "Zwaanendael," but incredibly it has no article on "air conditioning." Even the broader subject of southern climate is dismissed in three paragraphs—less space than is devoted to "reptiles and amphibians."

This scholarly neglect is surprising because it goes against the grain of common sense and popular culture. Ask any southerner over thirty years of age to explain why the South has changed in recent decades, and he may begin with the civil rights movement or industrialization. But sooner or later he will come around to the subject of air conditioning. For better or worse, he will tell you, the air conditioner has changed the nature of southern life. Some southerners will praise air conditioning and wonder out loud how they ever lived without it. Others will argue that the South is going to hell, not in a hand basket, but in an air-conditioned Chevy. As one Florida woman recently remarked, "I hate air conditioning; it's a damnfool invention of the Yankees. If they don't like it hot, they can move back up North where they belong."

Southern historians' lack of interest in the social history of climate control cannot be easily explained, but one suspects that, to a great degree, it represents a reaction to the excesses of an earlier generation of scholars. During the first three decades of the twentieth century environmental determinism was a powerful force

Raymond Arsenault, "The End of the Long Hot Summer: The Air Conditioner and Southern Culture," *Journal of Southern History,* L (November 1984), pp. 597–628. Copyright ©1984 by the Southern Historical Association. Reprinted by permission of the Managing Editor. The notes for this piece have been omitted.

in American social science. This was the age of Walter Prescott Webb, Ellsworth Huntington, and Ulrich Bonnell Phillips, when the link between climate and culture was often thought to be a simple relationship of cause and effect. The southern climate, in particular, was credited with producing everything from plantation slavery to the southern drawl. "Let us begin by discussing the weather, for that has been the chief agency in making the South distinctive," was the opening line of Phillips's 1929 classic *Life and Labor in the Old South.* According to Phillips, the hot, humid southern climate "fostered the cultivation of the staple crops, which promoted the plantation system, which brought the importation of negroes, which not only gave rise to chattel slavery but created a lasting race problem. These led to controversy and regional rivalry for power, which produced apprehensive reactions and culminated in a stroke for independence. Thus we have . . . the Confederate States of America." So much for the complexity of history.

Modern scholars have wisely rejected this kind of monocausal climatological determinism, a determinism that was frequently tied to racist and colonialist preconceptions. Unfortunately, they have tended to overreact, throwing out the baby with the bath water. Climate may not be the key to human history, but climate does matter. In some areas, such as the American South, it matters a great deal, or at least it did until the coming of the air conditioner. "Because the air conditioner, the airplane and television have smoothed out harsh differences in climate, nearly abolished distance and homogenized popular taste," a 1970 New York *Times* editorial argued, "Americans are becoming much less regionally diverse. . . . The census sketches a nation that has become one people with much the same problems and expectations everywhere. The regions fade. The urbanized nation strides on." Perhaps so, but the *Times* editor would not be the first person to have been a bit premature in pronouncing the death of southern regionalism. The truth is that no one really knows what impact air conditioning has had on southern life and culture because no one, to this point, has undertaken an in-depth study of the subject. This essay represents a modest first step toward such a study. . . .

The so-called "air conditioning revolution" . . . was actually an evolution—a long, slow, uneven process stretching over seven decades. The air conditioner came to the South in a series of waves, and only with the wave of the 1950s was the region truly engulfed. What had been largely a curiosity in the pre–World War II South became an immutable part of southern life in the postwar era. After the air conditioner invaded the home and the automobile, there was no turning back. By the mid-1970s air conditioning had made its way into more than 90 percent of the South's high-rise office buildings, banks, apartments, and railroad passenger coaches; more than 80 percent of its automobiles, government buildings, and hotels; approximately two-thirds of its homes, stores, trucks, and hospital rooms; roughly half of its classrooms; and at least a third of its tractors. Virtually all of the region's newer buildings, regardless of type or function, were equipped with air conditioning. The South of the 1970s could claim air-conditioned shopping malls, domed stadiums, dugouts, greenhouses, grain elevators, chicken coops, aircraft hangars, crane cabs, off-shore oil rigs, cattle barns, steel mills, and drive-in movies and restaurants. In Chalmette, Louisiana, aluminium workers were walking around with portable air conditioners strapped to their belts. In Nashville a massive air-conditioning plant was being fueled by a steady flow of city garbage. And in Richmond local officials could control the air conditioning in scores of public buildings from a single console. Farther north in Virginia, at Lake Anne Village, an entire town was fully air-conditioned by one central cooling plant. At several amusement [parks] in Texas and Florida even the outdoor queuing areas were air cooled. Predictably, the South's most air-conditioned state was Texas, where even the Alamo had central air. In Houston alone the annual cost ($666 million) of air conditioning exceeded the annual gross national product of several Third-World nations in 1980. . . .

It is important to keep the "air conditioning revolution" in perspective. Despite the best efforts of government, industry, and Madison Avenue, the air conditioner has not conquered all. The South still has more than its share of sun and sweat. And contrary to the claim of one air-conditioning industry spokesman, it is still possible to "escape air conditioning." Not all southerners live in air-conditioned homes, ride in air-conditioned cars, or work in air-conditioned buildings. Among rural and working-class blacks, poor whites, migrant laborers, and mountaineers, air-conditioned living is not the norm. On the other hand, nearly everyone in the region spends at least part of his or her life in an air-conditioned environment. In varying degrees virtually all southerners have been affected, directly or indirectly, by the technology of climate control. Air conditioning has changed the southern way of life, influencing everything from architecture to sleeping habits. Most important, it has contributed to the erosion of several regional traditions: cultural isolation, agrarianism, poverty, romanticism, historical consciousness, an orientation towards nontechnological folk culture, a preoccupation with kinship, neighborliness, a strong sense of place, and a relatively slow pace of life. The net result has been a dramatic decline in regional distinctiveness. In combination with other historical forces—such as the civil rights movement, advances in communication and transportation technology, and economic and political change—the air conditioner has greatly accelerated what John Egerton has called "the Americanization of Dixie."

Perhaps most obviously, air conditioning has had a major impact on southern population growth. The population density of the South (86.3 persons per square mile in 1980) has doubled since 1930. Some of this growth can be attributed to a high birth rate, some to a declining death rate, and some to migration. For the most part, the demographic impact of air conditioning has been limited to the latter two phenomena. Although a number of southerners have adopted the colloquialism "heir conditioning," and during the early 1960s one survey researcher reported a positive correlation between air-conditioned living and fertility, there is no reason to believe that air conditioning has had a significant impact on the region's fertility. A high birth rate was characteristic of the South long before the advent of mechanical cooling. Moreover, despite the rising popularity of air-conditioned bedrooms, the southern birth rate, like the national birth rate, has declined in recent decades.

The link between air conditioning and declining mortality is much more substantial. Prior to the twentieth century the nonmountain South was a relatively unhealthy place. Generally speaking, southern mortality rates were much higher than those of other areas of the United States. And as David Hackett Fischer has recently pointed out, the southern climate, which fostered yellow fever, malaria, and other semi-tropical diseases, was a primary determinant of the region's high mortality. Significantly, since the beginning of the twentieth century regional mortality rates have converged, and the southern population is much healthier today than it was a century ago. The proliferation of air conditioning is one of the reasons. In addition to making millions of hospital patients more comfortable, air conditioning has reduced fetal and infant mortality, prolonged the lives of thousands of patients suffering from heart disease and respiratory disorders, increased the reliability and sophistication of micro-surgery, facilitated the institutionalization of public health, and aided the production of modern drugs such as penicillin. On the other side of the ledger, critics of air conditioning claim that it causes allergies and that it is partially responsible for the pervasiveness of the common cold. Some researchers have even argued that air conditioning contributes to mental illness by disturbing the balance between positive and negative ions in the air. Nevertheless, even if these charges have some merit, the net effect of air conditioning on southern health and life expectancy has been positive.

Climate control has had an even greater impact on migration patterns. In a variety of ways the air conditioner has helped to reverse an almost century-long southern tradition of net out-migration. Between 1910 and 1950 alone, the South's net loss was more than 10 million people. It is more than a coincidence that in the 1950s, the decade when air conditioning first engulfed the South, the region's net out-migration was much smaller than in previous decades and that in the 1960s, for the first time since the Civil War, the South experienced more in-migration than out-migration. Although the net gain during the 1960s was modest—less than half a million people—its very existence was startling. This sudden demographic reversal was partly a function of the success of the civil rights movement and the decline of massive resistance. But it was also a by-product of air conditioning. The 1970 census, according to the New York *Times,* was "The Air-Conditioned Census." "The humble air-conditioner," a 1970 *Times* editorial concluded, "has been a powerful influence in circulating people as well as air in this country. In the last ten years it has become almost as common a device in the warmer sections of the United States as the automobile and the television set. Its availability explains why increasing numbers of Americans find it comfortable to live year around in the semitropical heat. . . ." The 1960s were, of course, only the beginning. Between 1970 and 1978, 7 million people migrated to the South, twice the number that left the region. By the end of the decade, the "sunbelt" era was in full swing.

Because of air conditioning an undetermined but clearly substantial number of southerners who might otherwise have left the South have remained in the region. Insofar as it has promoted personal contentment, employment opportunities, and improved working conditions, the air conditioner has helped to stem the tide of out-migration. This reduction in out-migration has influenced southern political and economic life. But its qualitative impact on regional culture has been somewhat limited. The cultural transformation that has rocked the South in recent years is essentially an outgrowth of the other side of the migration equation. Abetted by millions of tourists, northern migrants have brought new ideas and new lifestyles to the South, disrupting the region's long-standing cultural isolation. The cultural intrusions of the New Deal and World War II which shocked so many southerners forty years ago have been expanded and deepened by the massive northern influx of the 1960s and 1970s. During the last twenty years the southern population has become increasingly heterogeneous, and the concept of the Solid South—long a bulwark of regional mythology—has all but faded from view.

Air conditioning also has played a key role in the industrialization of the modern South. After decades of false starts and inflated promises, industry came to the South in a rush after World War II. The number of southerners employed in manufacturing exceeded those in agriculture for the first time in 1958, and by 1980 the region's manufacturing work force was more than three times as large as its agricultural work force. For better or worse, Henry Grady's "New South" had finally arrived. Some commercial and industrial growth would have occurred in the post–World War II South with or without the air conditioner. But the magnitude and scope of economic change in a non-air-conditioned South would have been much smaller. ". . . can you conceive a Walt Disney World over in the 95-degree summers of central Florida without its air-conditioned hotels, attractions and shops?" a southern columnist asked in 1978, "Can you see a Honeywell or Sperry or anyone else opening a big plant where their workers would have to spend much of their time mopping brows and cursing mosquitoes?" Climate control has not only brought new factories and businesses to the region. It has also brought improved working conditions, greater efficiency, and increased productivity. As numerous controlled studies have demonstrated, an air-conditioned workplace invariably means higher productivity and greater job satisfaction. One of air conditioning's most telling effects has been its positive influence on southern economic growth.

This economic growth has led in turn to a rising standard of living for many southern families. Real wages have increased substantially during the postwar era, and per capita income in the South has risen from 52 percent of the national average in 1930 to almost 90 percent today. Although this increased income has been unevenly distributed across the region—Texas, Florida, and Virginia registered the biggest gains—few areas have been left unaffected. Maldistribution of wealth remains a serious regional problem, but the proportion of southerners living in Tobacco Road–style poverty has declined significantly in recent decades. Thus, in an indirect way, air conditioning has helped to ameliorate one of the post–Civil War South's most distressing characteristics. The social and cultural implications of the decline in southern poverty are immense, because, as C. Vann Woodward noted in 1958, "Generations of scarcity and want constitute one of the distinctive historical experiences of the Southern people. . . ."

Air conditioning has also fostered the urbanization of the South. Since 1940 the South "has been the most rapidly urbanizing section of the country." During this period the proportion of southerners living in urban areas has nearly doubled, from 36.7 percent in 1940 to almost 70 percent today. Although the South remains the most rural area of the United States, the gap between the region and the rest of the nation is closing fast. How much of this recent urbanization can be attributed to air conditioning is difficult to say. But a number of observers have credited the air conditioner with being a major factor behind the rise of the urban South. According to the journalist Wade Greene, "Two of the country's fastest growing cities, Houston and Dallas, would probably be provincial backwaters today without air conditioning." In a similar vein, Frank Trippett has argued that "Sunbelt cities like Phoenix, Atlanta, Dallas, and Houston . . . could never have mushroomed so prosperously without air conditioning . . . ."

Air conditioning has promoted the growth of the urban South in a variety of ways: by encouraging industrialization and population growth; by accelerating the development of large public institutions, such as universities, museums, hospitals, sports arenas, and military bases; by facilitating the efficient use of urban space and opening the city to vertical, high-rise development; and by influencing the development of distinctively urban forms of architecture. Without air conditioning, sky-scrapers and high-rise apartments would be less prevalent (indeed, they would not exist in their present form); urban populations would be smaller; cities would be more spread out; and the physical and architectural differences between inner cities and suburbs would be less striking (even though as an integral component of en-closed shopping malls, air conditioning has contributed to urban sprawl). In sum, the size, shape, and character of urban centers would be vastly different.

In the South urbanization is a matter of no small importance. The stakes go well beyond aesthetics, economics, and demographics. Although its influence has sometimes been exaggerated, few historians would deny that self-conscious agrarianism has been a key element of southern distinctiveness. With the passing of the rural South such things as the Populist heritage, the plantation experience, and the mythic world of the Vanderbilt Agrarians have lost much of their meaning. The region's rural legacy is still a force to be reckoned with, but it is no longer the prime mover of southern life. The locus of power and activity in the South has moved to Main Street, and air conditioning is one of the reasons why.

In a related development, climate control has altered southern attitudes toward nature and technology. Specifically, air conditioning has taken its toll on traditional "folk culture," which, as David Potter once pointed out, "survived in the South long after it succumbed to the onslaught of urban-industrial culture elsewhere. It was an aspect of this culture," Potter observed, "that the relation between the land and the people remained more direct and more primal in the South than in other parts of the country." The South has always been an elemental land of blood, sweat, and tears—a land where personalism and a curious mixture of romance and realism have prevailed. As W. J. Cash noted in 1941, southern elementalism and romanticism have been mutually reinforcing traditions. "The influence of the Southern physical world" was, in Cash's words,

> a sort of cosmic conspiracy against reality in favor of romance. The country is one of extravagant colors, of proliferating foliage and bloom, of flooding yellow sunlight, and, above all perhaps, of haze. Pale blue fogs hang above the valleys in the morning, the at-mosphere smokes faintly at midday, and through the long slow afternoon cloud-stacks tower from the horizon and the earth-heat quivers upward through the iridescent air, blurring every outline and rendering every object vague and problematical. I know that winter comes to the land, certainly. I know there are days when the color and the haze are stripped away and the real stands up in drab and depressing harshness. But these things pass and are forgotten. The dominant mood, the mood that lingers in the memory, is one of well-nigh drunken reverie. . . .

Cash's idyllic statement is part hyperbole, but his central point is well taken. If we remove climate from the historical equation, the South is not the South. At the very least, climate control has taken the edge off of the region's romantic elementalism. As the southern climate has been artificially tamed, pastoralism has been replaced by technological determinism. In escaping the heat and humidity, southerners have weakened the bond between humanity and the natural environment. In the process, they have lost some of what made them interesting and distinctive. Of course, not all southerners would agree that air conditioning has removed them from the natural world. A 1961 profile of a Florida household claimed that "living an air-conditioned life doesn't mean shutting oneself off from beautiful Florida summers. It means enjoying them more. . . . air conditioning provides relaxing intervals between the recreational, business and household activities that take them outdoors." As the father of the house explained, "Our living is about the same as before, only more comfortable and enjoyable. We go swimming as often but it's for the fun of being in the water, not just to cool off." Similarly, a couple in Washington, D.C., insisted that air conditioning added new meaning to their flower garden. "We enjoy gardening," they said, "but even more we enjoy being able to sit indoors comfortably and look out at our garden." Although such testimonials are revealing, it seems clear that, on balance, human interaction with the natural environment has decreased significantly since the advent of air conditioning. To confirm this point, one has only to walk down almost any southern street on a hot summer afternoon, listen to the whir of compressors, and look in vain for open windows or human faces. As Frank Trippett put it, air conditioning has "seduced families into retreating into houses with closed doors and shut windows, reducing the commonality of neighborhood life and all but obsoleting the front-porch society whose open casual folkways were an appealing hallmark of a sweatier America."

In many cases the porch is not simply empty, it's not even there. To the dismay of many southerners, air conditioning has impinged upon a rich tradition of vernacular architecture. From the "dogtrot cabin" with its central breezeway to the grand plantation house with its wrap-around porch, to the tin-roofed "cracker" house up on blocks, traditional southern architecture has been an ingenious conspiracy of passive cooling and cross-ventilation. . . . Historically, these techniques have been an important element of an aesthetic and social milieu that is distinctively southern.

The science of passive cooling, which was refined over several centuries of southern history, was rendered obsolete in less than a decade, or so it seemed before the onset of the energy crisis. With the proliferation of residential air conditioning, vernacular architecture gave way to the modern tract house, with its low ceilings, small windows, and compact floor plan. . . . Many southerners, of course, continue to live in traditionally designed houses. But their numbers are thinning with each passing year.

Residential air conditioning has not only affected architectural form; it has also influenced the character of southern family life. Since strong family ties have long been recognized as an integral characteristic of southern culture, this is a matter of some importance. During the 1950s and 1960s the air conditioner was often portrayed as the savior of the American family. In 1955, for example, one observer claimed that residential air conditioning was changing "the family living pattern back to the days before the automobile took Americans out of their homes." "With comfort in its own living room," he argued, "the family tends to stay home and enjoy each other's society in relaxed evenings of reading, sewing, television, or card-playing." . . .

The alleged benefits of residential air conditioning ranged from better dispositions to increased family privacy. In retrospect, such expansive claims seem naive and misleading. Air-conditioned living may have made many individual family members happier, but it does not necessarily follow that the family unit was strengthened in the process. As numerous social critics eventually pointed out, end-less hours of television watching often detracts from meaningful family life. In any event, the popularity of the air-conditioned living room was soon counterbalanced by the lure of air-conditioned shopping malls, bowling alleys, and other amuse-ments. Of course, even if, on balance, residential air conditioning strengthened the nuclear family, the impact on wider kinship networks probably went in the opposite direction. . . . As more than one observer has noted, the vaunted southern tradition of "visiting" has fallen on hard times in recent years. This is an important point, be-cause the essence of southern family life has always been its semi-extended nature. Thus, the overall effect of chilled air on traditional ties of blood and kin has been, at best, contradictory.

The same could probably be said for air conditioning's effect on patterns of ag-gression and violence. Throughout much of its history, the South has been the most violent section of the United States. In 1934 H. C. Brearley aptly described the South as "that part of the United States lying below the Smith and Wesson line." More recently, Sheldon Hackney and Raymond D. Gastil have used homicide and suicide rates to document the South's "regional culture of violence." Interest-ingly, few students of southern violence have paid much attention to climatic forces. Instead, they have concentrated on such factors as a lingering frontier tradi-tion, adherence to an aristocratic code of honor, white supremacist ideology, racial demography, rurality, poverty, and an endemic "siege mentality" related to the na-ture of southern history. On occasion, however, climate has been cited as an impor-tant determinant of southern violence. In 1969 the historian Albro Martin insisted that the region's propensity for violence was largely a function of climate. And in 1977 Joseph C. Carroll's statistical analysis of homicide and suicide rates in 100 American cities uncovered a strong positive correlation between heat and humid-ity and both homicide and suicide. If these assessments are accurate, what does one make of the fact that southern homicide rates have increased since the advent of air conditioning? Would the rates have increased even more rapidly in a non-air-conditioned South? Unfortunately, the answers to these questions await further study. We know that southern and nonsouthern homicide rates have converged in recent decades, but at this point it is almost impossible to determine the extent to which this convergence is a function of climate control. Available evidence is con-tradictory and consists of little more than speculation. Proponents of indoor cooling have often argued that air conditioning invariably makes people less irritable and hence less violent. On the other hand, several critics of air conditioning, including René Dubos and Frank Lloyd Wright, have claimed that artificial cooling is a phys-iologically dangerous process which reduces human adaptability to stress. . . . If Wright is correct, climate control may be one of the factors behind the rising tide of violence that has engulfed the United States in recent years. . . .

A more immediate threat is the air conditioner's assault on the South's strong "sense of place." Southerners, more than most other Americans, have tied them-selves to local geography. Their lives and identities have been rooted in a particular piece of turf—a county, a town, a neighborhood, a homestead, a family graveyard. Yet in recent years, thanks in part to air conditioning, southern particularism has been overwhelmed by an almost endless string of look-alike chain stores, tract houses, glassed-in high-rises, and, perhaps most important, enclosed shopping malls. The modern shopping mall is the cathedral of air-conditioned culture, and it symbolizes the placelessness of the New South. As William S. Kowinski recently observed, "these climate-controlled bubbles" are designed "to create timeless space. Removed from everything else and existing in a world of its own, a mall . . . is a placeless space." As such, it is the antithesis of traditional southern culture. To quote Kowinski, "can you imagine William Faulkner writing about the Yoknapatawpha Mall?"

At one level or another, air conditioning has affected nearly every aspect of southern life. But it has not changed everything. Although climate control has done its best to homogenize the nation and eliminate regional consciousness, the South remains a land apart—a land that still owes much of its distinctiveness to climatic forces. Of course, how long this will remain so is an open question. Perhaps, as it has done so often in the past, the southerner's special devotion to regional and local traditions will ensure the survival of southern folk culture. But this time it will not be easy: General Electric has proved a more devastating invader than General Sherman. As long as air conditioning, abetted by immigration, urbanization, and broad technological change, continues to make inroads, the South's distinctive character will continue to diminish, never to rise again.

Will Dixie Disappear?

HOWARD L. PRESTON

Ever since Waylon Jennings changed his duck-tail hair style to the blow-dry look of a Hollywood movie star, and the nation elected a president from the Deep South who referred to Italians as "Eye-talians," rumor has had it that the South is over. Reports of the region's demise and alleged cultural extinction have, in fact, circulated for years. The most acclaimed came a little over a generation ago, when C. Vann Woodward of Yale University asked, "Is there nothing about the South that is immune from the disintegrating effect of nationalism and the pressure for conformity?" In his award-winning book, *The Burden of Southern History* (1960), Woodward recalled the righteous myths invented by southerners to fend off unwanted social change and surmised that because of stresses dictated by modernization and nationalism, younger southerners "may come to feel as uprooted as the immigrant." The only thing that the renowned southern historian could think of that offered any hope of avoiding total assimilation within the national culture was "the collective experience of Southern people," even if that experience was one of shared defeat, poverty, and ultimately guilt.

In the decades since Woodward pondered this question, and especially since Vietnam and Watergate, much about the South has changed, and I wonder if Woodward's inquiry about the effects of modernization might be more appropriate now than when he voiced it. Today, the region can no longer be defined solely in terms of its social, political, and economic eccentricities. The late-twentieth-century

South is as much a part of the American mainstream as any other section of the country. Writers who once focused primarily on the region's tumble-down housing and poorly educated school children as evidence of backwardness now direct attention to the gleam and glitter of new Sunbelt South cities where prospects for the future appear bright and optimistic.

But does this mean that southernness is extinct, that the region has finally become a cultural colony of somewhere else, or that, as Hodding Carter III has announced, "the South is purely and contemporaneously mainstream American"? Has the South, well known for its racism, poverty, and penchant for religious fundamentalism and violence really disappeared and, like magic, in its place appeared the shiny, successful, surrealistic Sunbelt? To what extent have southerners weathered the storm of nationalism that Woodward saw eroding the region's provinciality? In the midst of the massive changes that the South has experienced, have southerners managed to retain their regional identity, or have they become the proverbial uprooted citizens that Woodward thought possible in 1960? And, in attempting to rid themselves of the worst aspects of their past, have southerners unwittingly embraced an entirely different set of myths, more national in scope, that have homogenized the South's culture and promise to remake the region into what Marshall Frady called "the inconclusive grumpiness of everywhere else?"

The one provincialism invariably identified as the most characteristic of the South is race. In 1928 the historian Ulrich Bonnell Phillips, a native Georgian, raised the ire of many when he wrote in the *American Historical Review* that slavery was the central theme of southern history, and not surprisingly, that being a white southerner simply meant being a racist. In the 1930s, the North Carolina journalist Wilbur J. Cash came to a similar conclusion. In his famous study *The Mind of the South,* Cash observed that, among other things, race-baiting by political demagogues, which "whipped up the tastes and passions of [southern Democrats] with ever more personal and extravagant representations of the South in full gallop against . . . the Negro," could be singled out as the most firmly established aspect of the region's political history, all the way back to Andrew Jackson. . . .

Since the mid-1960s, however, this has proven to be hardly the case. Richard Arrington, a black man, is mayor of Birmingham, the very seedbed of white [resistance] in the former Confederate states during the early years of the civil rights movement. One hundred sixty-six other cities and towns spread out across the South, including Charlotte, New Orleans, and Richmond, also elected black mayors. Blacks sit on county and city councils in both rural and urban areas of the South. They have been elected to school boards and to the judiciary, appointed to planning commissions, and entrusted with the responsibility of policing large cities and small towns as well as administering local governments.

The issue of race in the South has also been muted by riots that took place during the late 1960s in American cities located far outside the South, by the racial unrest over school desegregation in the 1970s in South Boston, by the bigotry on display in Howard Beach that made headlines in newspapers across the country, and ultimately by the decision of many blacks, who lived elsewhere, to make the South their home. In 1975 only 43 percent of black Americans lived in the South, a decline since 1900 of 35 percent. By the mid-1970s, *Time* reported that this trend had been reversed and that countless well-educated, middle-class blacks were moving south in search of better educational opportunities for their children, a higher standard of living, and better jobs. By 1988, 55.9 percent of the nation's black population lived in the South, a 3.7 percent increase since 1980, and demographers believe that this emerging pattern of reverse migration will come into much sharper focus after the 1990 census. "I suspect," said Larry Long, chief analyst at the Census Bureau's Center for Demographic Studies, "that we will discover that the black middle class has such strong ties to Southern roots that they will retire to traditional areas of the rural South."

Blacks and whites in the South are relating to one another today in the same way that Martin Luther King, Jr., did in the mid-1960s when he addressed Lyndon B. Johnson as "my fellow southerner." But while de jure segregation is a thing of the past, while a certain mutuality in recent years has grown between whites and blacks in the South, and while some blacks enjoy an unprecedented measure of economic prosperity, the region is by no means socially integrated. The highly visible success of some blacks who have done well in business or achieved recognition through election to public office has given rise to an indifference on the part of many whites to the continuing problems the vast majority of blacks in the South still face. . . .

Note the recent election of L. Douglas Wilder as governor of Virginia. In 1986, Wilder, the grandson of slaves, distinguished himself as the first black person to be elected since Reconstruction to a statewide political office—lieutenant governor of Virginia—in the South. Wilder ran a middle-of-the-road gubernatorial campaign, "re-thinking" his position on many sensitive issues like capital punishment along the way. Polls taken just prior to the 1989 fall election indicated that Wilder would win comfortably. But the election proved to be anything but comfortable, and Wilder's victory was not assured until the last precinct was counted. Apparently, as one observer put it, "some of Virginia's white voters are still racially prejudiced and, what's more, anxious to conceal it from pollsters." Wilder's narrow victory may very well be the handwriting on the wall for other blacks in the South, like Andrew Young of Georgia, Harvey Gantt of North Carolina, and Mike Espy of Mississippi, who aspire to statewide political office. . . .

Nationally, the number of black elected officials increased by 5.8 percent in 1988, a change the Washington-based Joint Center for Political Studies attributed in part to an Alabama court decision that eliminated that state's at-large election system. Since the ruling, 252 blacks have been elected to seats in the 180 municipal and county jurisdictions mandated to abandon at-large elections. As of the fall of 1989, Alabama had the largest number, 694, of black-elected office-holders, followed closely by Mississippi with 646, Louisiana with 521, Georgia with 483, North Carolina with 449, Arkansas with 318, and Texas with 312. In South Carolina, 373 blacks were in publicly elected positions, an increase of 5.9 percent over 1988. Considering that the Palmetto State has the second largest black population in the nation, this modest improvement, however, is misleading. The ratio of blacks in public office to the total black population of the state is still exceptionally low, and observers attribute this situation to an unwillingness on the part of white voters to accept black candidates and to a failure by black office-seekers to broaden their political appeal to include whites.

Another example of the stubbornness of racism in the South can be seen in rural Sumter County, Alabama, located in the western part of the state, adjacent to Mississippi. Sumter County school children were as racially segregated in 1989 as they were the day the United States Supreme Court handed down its landmark *Brown v. Topeka Board of Education* decision. Black students in Sumter County attend a poorly funded public school system, and whites attend a network of private Christian academies. . . .

But even in some school districts in the Deep South where integrated classrooms have been the norm for almost twenty years, the vestiges of race consciousness are still apparent. At rural Pleasant Hill High School in Georgetown County, South Carolina, about thirty miles west of Myrtle Beach, for example, blacks and whites have been attending classes together harmoniously since 1970, the year the school integrated. In the spring of 1989, however, when the school hosted its annual "Magical Midnight Hour" prom, only blacks attended. The all-white Members Only club held its own private party in Myrtle Beach. . . .

In recent years race has also figured into the decisions that major corporations, lured to the South by tax exemptions, cheap land, and cheap labor, have made in determining where in the region to build their branch plants and offices. Because of a belief that blacks pose a greater threat for unionization than whites, many of these industries have sought out "whiter" areas of the South in which to relocate. A 1983 Commission on Civil Rights report found that industry had rejected sixteen predominantly black counties in western Alabama as possible sites for factories. That same year, the Southern Growth Policies Board documented that between 1977 and 1982 employment grew more than twice as fast in non-metropolitan counties in the South that were more than 75 percent white than in counties that were more than 50 percent black. Cases in point are the location of the Saturn automobile assembly plant in Maury County, Tennessee, and the decision by Toyota to build its facility in Scott County, Kentucky. The white populations of both of these counties are 93 percent and 83 percent respectively. Furthermore, a poll taken in South Carolina for the *State* (Columbia) newspaper revealed that the majority of blacks and whites surveyed thought that racial discrimination and segregation still existed. Most believed that more progress toward racial equality in housing, employment, and political representation was needed, and perhaps this same point of view applies to the entire South.

The vitriolic rhetoric of demagogues like James Vardaman and Theodore Bilbo of Mississippi, Lester Maddox and Eugene Talmadge of Georgia, and Cole Blease and Benjamin Tillman of South Carolina, which fanned the fires of racism and gained those who employed it untold political support, is politically extinct. Many whites who live in the South today are genuinely embarrassed by racial slurs against blacks and adamantly deplore the radical activities of racially motivated hate groups. As one writer put it, "the babykissing backwoodsman who drove his mules up to the court house square to quote the Bible, cuss the niggers, and claim the votes is an anachronism." But race cannot be dismissed as no longer culturally distinctive of the South. Certainly it seems no longer important politically in Atlanta or Charlotte, but church attendance for the most part throughout the region remains strictly segregated, and so are funeral homes and cemeteries. Despite protests of black students attending the University of Mississippi, the Confederate Battle

Flag and the song "Dixie," the very symbols of white supremacy, remain the official emblems of the university at sporting events. Gerrymandering and at-large elections to county and municipal public offices continue to keep many black southerners politically voiceless in certain areas. Unarguably, the issue of race remains a persistent ingredient of southern culture and continues to play an important role in southern life and politics. The issue of race as a factor influencing day-to-day activities in much of the region is still, and will remain, very much alive. And in this respect at least, the South is not over, not by a long shot!

If race is one of the most distinguishable cultural characteristics of the South, two others are antebellum romanticism and southern cooking. In the nineteenth century, writers and artists cultivated a romantic image for the South as a place where the forces of industrialization had been kind, an image still very much a part of the region's identity. According to the myth, charm and social grace remain a functional part of everyday life below the Mason-Dixon line. Indicative of this century-old understanding of the South is the way in which the region continues to promote itself. For example, an advertisement by the Georgia Visitors' Bureau that appeared in a leading national magazine beckoned tourists with a scene of two wicker rocking chairs sitting empty on the veranda of a white-columned antebellum mansion. Carefully chosen words accompanied this romantic reminiscence: "A Look at the Side of Georgia That's Almost Gone With the Wind."

To many Americans the South is not so much a place as it is a state of mind, and each year the seemingly insatiable appetite of those who want to relive the glories of the Lost Cause is fed a steady diet of third-rate novels and television serials. *Gone With the Wind* is the most popular movie ever shown on television. . . . It is therefore apparent that, in the future, the image of the romantic Old South is not likely to lose its prominence atop the list of ways Americans want to remember and understand the region.

Also a part of the South's romantic image is its legendary hospitality, which many outsiders find most in evidence at dinnertime, when a feast of victuals is laid before them. Southern cooking is known worldwide and calls attention to a lifestyle of abundance that is [unencumbered] by want or modernization. Every serious cook, housewife and househusband alike, has at least one southern cookbook, and county fairs and church bake sales are famous for the fine food they display.

Joe Gray Taylor has written at length about the cultural idiosyncracies of southern cooking and has shown that as much as anything else, modernization has affected southerners' palates. According to Taylor, southerners' diet changed very little between the Civil War and the end of World War II, but since the war, greater mobility, in addition to radio and television, has introduced new products that have changed southern food preparation and eating habits. . . . He finds [however,] that "the southern tradition in food has not disappeared. . . . The very fact that fried chicken is the most popular fast food," he allowed reassuringly, "is evidence of the survival of southern tastes. Standing along side the hamburger palaces, especially in the upper South, are little restaurants that still offer 'all the catfish you can eat' at a reasonable price. And that favorite of southerners, barbecue, is still to be had." . . .

. . . From the standpoint of the kitchen, therefore, the South still exists as a distinctive part of the country. And despite efforts to capture a small measure of the region's culture in a bottle of barbecue sauce to market nationwide, southern cooking is not likely to disappear as a highly recognized and respected measure of life in the South.

Following race, romanticism, and cooking as persistent manifestations of cultural distinctiveness in the South is the widely held perception that the region remains by and large the most backward, isolated, and rural part of the country. No doubt there are places in the South that remain untouched by many aspects of modernization, but this widely held notion of backwardness has been given credence by the unsavory way that the South and southerners have been depicted in such popular films as *Deliverance* (1972) and *Mississippi Burning* (1988), and in such numerous long-running television programs as "The Real McCoys" (1958–62), "The Beverly Hillbillies" (1962–70), "Mayberry R.F.D." (1968–71), and "The Dukes of Hazzard" (1979–84). These and other programs, shown over and over again as reruns, portray southerners as intellectually backward and dim-witted, and their communities, if not politically corrupt, then lazy and devoid of progress.

The two seemingly contradictory cultural characteristics that have long offered outsiders proof of the South's chronic backwardness are the bent southerners have for violent behavior and their long-standing zeal for fundamental religion. The notion that southerners are prone to become violent more often than residents of other parts of the country "is so pervasive," wrote the historian Sheldon Hackney, "that it compels the attention of anyone interested in understanding the South." Scholars have found evidence of violent behavior on the part of southerners at every stage of the region's development. During the colonial period, eye-gouging was commonplace among backwoodsmen, and more "civilized" citizens settled differences by dueling. In the antebellum South the violence carried out by masters and overseers attempting to keep slaves in line was an integral part of the master-slave relationship, and following the Civil War, the night-riding, hooded Ku Klux Klan, along with "Judge Lynch," appeared to keep "uppity," newly emancipated blacks "in their place."

To W. J. Cash, the South by the turn of the century had become so "solidly wedded to Negro-Lynching" that southerners observed the heinous practice ceremoniously as "an act of racial and patriotic expression, an act of chivalry, an act, indeed, having a definitely ritualistic value in respect to the entire southern sentiment." By 1934, when Clemson Agricultural College sociologist H. C. Brearley tabulated the number of lynchings that had occurred in the United States between 1900 and 1930, this so-called "ritualism" had grown to monstrous proportions. Ninety percent of the 1,886 lynchings in the nation occurring during that thirty-year period were carried out in the eleven former Confederate states and Kentucky, and blacks were almost always the victims.

In explanation of southerners' violent tendencies, Brearley postulated that certain European feudal traditions were somehow more valued by southerners than by those who resided outside the region. He theorized that in the South this so-called "cavalier spirit" was manifest in southerners' loyalty to family, to class, and to community. In a society in which the preservation and perpetuation of these values was given highest priority, aggressive behavior was an attribute. . . .

During the depression, feuds over moonshining rights and other nefarious activities hatched by one backwoods, trigger-happy white family against another lent additional credence to Brearley's theory. Toward the middle of the twentieth century, as the South became more industrial, he saw little reason to believe that southerners would outgrow their violent predilections. "When industrial warfare occurs in a region where the participants are already predisposed to deeds of violence . . . such conflicts may be expected to be especially destructive." . . .

In the 1950s and 1960s, as wide-eyed Americans watched on television, the South proved itself conclusively to be the most violent section of the nation and its citizens to be the most unreasonable. School and church bombings in Birmingham, the riotous night of destruction at the University of Mississippi in Oxford over the enrollment of James Meredith that cost two journalists their lives, the brutal police attack against the civil rights marchers on the Edmund Pettus Bridge near Selma, the shooting of two students on the campus of South Carolina State College in Orangeburg, and ultimately the assassination of Martin Luther King, Jr., in Memphis galvanized public opinion against the region and confirmed what many Americans already suspected: southerners were undeniably the most violent of Americans.

The national attention that these and other events of the early civil rights movement received has had a mitigating effect on conspicuous displays of violence in the South. Overt violent behavior has become less tolerable, and although the rate of homicide and gun ownership in the region continues to be among the nation's highest, many residents rationally eschew private displays of violence as socially unacceptable. This does not necessarily mean that violence has vanished as a cultural characteristic of the South and that the region can no longer be identified as the most violent nationally. The sociologist John Shelton Reed found that in 1980 ten of the eighteen states with the highest rates of homicide were southern states, and that a better question than Is the South still the most violent part of the United States? might be, How much like the South has the rest of the country become?

Although it is impossible to document scientifically the way sociologists calculate rates of homicides and per capita gun ownership, some observers have found the decline of criminal violence and the simultaneous upsurge of the popularity of football in the South to have an interesting correlation. "*Southern* football," commented writer Peter Schrag in 1972, "knows levels of meaning, intensity, and violence entirely foreign to other regions." Reflecting on the many football games he had witnessed between the University of Texas Longhorns and the University of Oklahoma Sooners, Willie Morris compared the gridiron confrontation of these two institutions each autumn in Dallas's Cotton Bowl to "the clashes of contemporary armies" and wrote that this particular rivalry has "the flow of history behind [it]."

Since 1980, the universities comprising the Southeastern Conference have come closer to filling their football stadiums to capacity—98.5 percent in 1983—than any other major athletic federation in the country. . . . "Football is a passion around which we order our lives," allowed one University of Alabama fan. "Football holds us together—especially when we beat one of those big Northern schools." . . .

It is not clear to what extent southerners, in their passion for football, are acting out a need to express themselves in a violent manner. What is clear is that one of the most violent sports played in the United States enjoys its greatest success and has its greatest following in the one region that has historically embraced violence as an accepted means of self-expression. The South may well be, as University of Georgia sociologist Ira Robinson believes, "a phoenix dying to resurrect itself and foot-ball is for those who are dying." But it remains a matter of speculation how closely related southerners' vicarious enjoyment of Saturday afternoon gridiron violence is to other historical forms of violence like lynching, which also had great spectator appeal in the South. . . .

While southerners have often in their history expressed violent tendencies, they have employed evangelical religion to temper their aggressiveness and quell their combative spirits. During the twentieth century this provincial theology has contin-ually come under attack, and southerners have had to guard it defiantly against the erosive influences of the outside world. The struggle began as soon as improved roads reached into the isolated, back-wash communities where fundamentalism was practiced in earnest. The fear that contemporary thought is subversive and some-how leads to the destruction of evangelical Christendom is the cornerstone of this literal-minded faith. Central to its brand of theology, therefore, has been the firm belief that individual salvation is the highest religious priority and that a steadfast [resistance] is necessary against the encroachment of any kind of social gospel.

In the past, old-time southern religion was acted out with great zeal and inten-sity, and one need only read some of the stinging articles of H. L. Mencken in the 1920s to recall what it was like. In general, Mencken believed that organized reli-gion stifled individual freedom and was a direct threat to those who sought new knowledge and enlightenment. The patent religious orthodoxy of the South, there-fore, that denounced the reading of any book save the Holy Scriptures, that held gambling and dancing to result surely in damnation, that proclaimed any education beyond Bible study to be apostasy, and that even attacked Coca-Cola "as a levantine and Hell-sent narcotic" was fertile ground for Mencken's caustic pen. Speaking in tongues, holy dancing, emotional outbursts, highly charged sermons, and even snake handling—practices that Mencken labeled as tribal—continue to be a part of religious observances in the South, but they are not in the mainstream and are con-fined primarily to the Pentecostal church. Southerners subject to the cosmopolitan influences of urbanization, education, mass communication, and greater mobility have long since dispensed with them as unsophisticated and idolatrous. "It is all but impossible to conceive of [a] sweat-drenched child of God," wrote Thomas D. Clark in the early 1960s, "sitting in the sedate pews of a seminary-trained minister." What has remained a consistent part of religious life in the South is that it continues to be overwhelmingly Protestant, philosophically fundamental, and profoundly evangelical. In 1976, *Time* estimated that of the thirty-two million Protestants in the South, twenty million considered themselves to be evangelicals. "Southerners are the most church-going people in the nation," the weekly news magazine allowed, "and from camp meeting through riverside baptisms to huge urban congregations, the tone and temper of Southern Protestantism is evangelical." . . .

Where the evils of alcohol, tobacco, dancing, and gambling . . . were once the primary blasphemies of southerners' orthodoxy, new and more portentous secular demons have appeared more recently that threaten the faithful and occupy evangel-icals' attention. Rock music and magazines, public school textbooks that teach evo-lution but fail to give equal attention to the biblical version of creation, prayer in public schools, and above all, abortion are the current issues of greatest importance.

In the summer of 1986, Jimmy Swaggart, broadcasting from his Louisiana church studios, lashed out at Wal-Mart, K-Mart, and grocery stories for selling rock magazines that he claimed were demonic and could be purchased by children of any age. The widely known fundamentalist preacher opposes rock and roll of any kind— even the lyrics of the Christian vocalist Amy Grant—and is on record as saying, "You cannot claim the message of the annointed *with the music of the Devil!*" Shortly thereafter, Swaggart met with Wal-Mart executives and convinced them to remove all rock magazines from the shelves of the chain's more than nine hundred stores in twenty-two states.

While fundamentalists have busied themselves fighting demonic rock and roll, three southern states have been embroiled in litigation over the issue of creationism versus evolutionism. In 1982 the Louisiana state legislature passed the Balanced Treatment for Creation-Science and Evolution-Science Act, which required the teaching of creationism whenever evolution was taught. The Louisiana statute defined the theory of "scientific creation" as "the belief that the origin of the elements, the galaxy, the solar system, of life, of all species of plants and animals, the origin of man, and the origin of all things and their processes and relationships were created *ex nihilo* and fixed by God."

A United States district court did not even need a trial to declare this law contradictory to the Establishment Clause of the First Amendment, and after the Fifth Circuit Court of Appeals upheld the lower court's opinion, the United States Supreme Court, in a 7–2 decision, finalized the matter. Writing for the majority, Associate Justice William J. Brennan, Jr., stated that the law had a nonreligious purpose and was clearly an intent on the part of the Louisiana state legislature to advance a particular religious point of view. . . .

. . . In 1985, *U.S. News & World Report* found that the issue of abortion was "spurring a new fundamentalism," not only in the South but also across the nation, and Catholics and Protestants alike had united in vehement opposition to the Supreme Court's 1973 decision in *Roe* v. *Wade* legalizing abortion. Opposition to abortion, in fact, was found to be stronger in the Northeast, where one in three was against it, compared to one in five in the South. "Across the nation," reported the weekly news magazine, "abortion foes claim vocal allies in Southern-based TV preachers such as Jerry Falwell, Pat Robertson and Jimmy Swaggart."

The electronic ministries of these and other fundamentalist preachers based in the South have breathed new life into Christian evangelism and have helped rally support against abortion and for other evangelical causes. This particular aspect of modernization, therefore, has helped to preserve rather than to erode Christian evangelism in the South. Televangelists' ability to reach directly into viewers' homes gives them enormous power, and their daily broadcasts, watched by millions, have helped blunt the forces of change and, to a certain extent, kept the old-time religion alive. Whenever Jimmy Swaggart or Ernest Angley launches into an agitated, fretful sermon, one cannot help but be reminded of Mencken's description of the emotionally charged preacher he encountered at a camp-site service in the woods outside Dayton, Tennessee, in 1925. . . .

In the last quarter century, rather than being weakened by modernization, Christian evangelism nationwide has experienced a resurgence that some foresee as eventually being as powerful as the great religious upheavals that rocked American society during the eighteenth and nineteenth centuries. Every five years since 1965, while more liberal Protestant denominations suffered a near 5 percent decline in membership, evangelical churches won converts at an average rate of 8 percent. Millions of Americans, including former Surgeon General C. Everett Koop, former Secretary of the Interior Donald Hodel, and pollster George Gallop, Jr., consider themselves born-again Christians. In a society tortured by questions regarding sexuality, alcoholism, and drug abuse, the evangelical message that gives emphasis to the traditional values of family, home, temperance, and community indeed seems plausible to many less fundamental Christians. Consequently, like the old days in the South when concerned evangelists flocked to their politicians to lobby for laws prohibiting the teaching of scientific evolution, the sale of liquor, or retail business on Sunday, we are still seeing, and are likely to see in the future, similar delegations of solicitous evangelists—and not just in southern states—approaching local lawmakers for protection against the corrupting magnetism of modernization.

Nowhere has modernization been more evident in the South than in the region's economy. The South remains the most rural part of the nation, but during the 1980s, this same traditionally agricultural region, where farmers within recent memory plowed their fields straight up and down hills instead of along landscape contours, grew into the most highly industrialized part of the country. This transformation came not so much with the growth of existing textile, tobacco, and paper-product industries, but in the diversification to new industries that produced petrochemicals, electronic parts, and aerospace equipment. More than 25 percent of the rural work force in the South held manufacturing jobs during the mid-1980s, compared to slightly more than 19 percent of labor nationally; and in 1987, 54 percent of the nation's counties that relied on manufacturing as their primary source of income were located in the rural South. . . .

When the South suddenly became the new American industrial frontier, many expected a marked improvement in the region's economy. But after almost two decades . . . , southerners are anything but prosperous. North Carolinians, for example, may brag that their state has the nation's most industrialized labor force, but at the same time, they have to accept the dismal fact that Tarheel workers are the lowest paid of any industrial laborers in the country. More recently, rather than seeking new manufacturing firms, the rural South has found itself trying to hold onto the ones that it has attracted. As Jonesville sought to lure its first major manufacturer, many, many other communities in the piedmont were losing theirs. Between 1979 and 1985, the rural South found itself in bitter competition for industry with third-world developing nations. The irony here, as James C. Cobb has pointed out, is that cost-conscious corporate executives have discovered that, when compared to places like Thailand and Sri Lanka, the rural South, with all its incentives designed to attract industry, is not as attractive as it once seemed to be. What has emerged from the shift in economic fortunes from North to South, and now overseas, is what has been referred to as "a picture of progress and poverty existing side by side—with a widening gap between the winners and losers."

. . . Thus, in the wake of industrialization, rural southerners, traditionally the poorest group in the country, have been able to raise their per capita income only to a mere 75 percent of the national average. The median annual wage for full-time workers in the South is $1,468 less for white males, $1,050 for white females, $6,678 for black males, and $2,263 for black females.

Historically, this has meant poorly funded education programs and miserably inadequate public facilities. . . . No doubt, in this respect, the image of backwardness branded on the South cannot be disputed, for the region remains a colonial economy of the highest order. Between 1969 and 1976, 70 percent of the manufacturing companies that either relocated or built branch plants in the South were controlled from the North, and the newest carpetbaggers hail from overseas.

The South in the 1980s has gained more jobs than it has lost, but this gain has not changed the financial situation for many southerners whose standard of living remains the lowest in the nation. Despite the South's new-found national dominance in manufacturing, the economic well-being that contemporary southern recruiters hoped would accompany industrialization, not unlike the experiences of their late-nineteenth- and early-twentieth-century predecessors, has been thus far only a pipe dream. Recent industrialization has not re-made the South into the vision of independence and progressiveness that prophets of the New South, past and present, said it would. If trends continue, this new industrial livelihood promises to make the region even more dependent, not only on the North for economic nourishment, but also on foreign countries. Perhaps too much has been given away in terms of low wages, guarantees against unionization, and tax exemptions to achieve for the rural South even a measure of the prosperity found elsewhere in the country. . . . In this sense, at least, the future seems more like the past.

Because it has been historically agricultural and slow to industrialize, the South has retained a certain small-town, rural identity long since swept away by modern forces of change in other parts of the country. Historiographically, the region has been portrayed predominantly from a rural perspective, and only recently have southern cities received the national acclaim, as well as the scholarly attention, that they deserve. Woodward's own observation in 1951 that "the sum total of urbanization in the South was comparatively unimportant" is indeed reflective of this long-established perception of the South as primarily agrarian and identifiably small-town.

At the turn of the twentieth century, only one city in the South had grown to a population exceeding one hundred thousand. That was New Orleans, and although the last ninety years have brought sweeping changes to the urban South, citadels like Atlanta, Houston, and Dallas still do not epitomize the region as Boston does New England, Chicago the Midwest, or Los Angeles and San Francisco the West Coast. Twentieth-century metropolises with their gleaming skyscrapers and sprawling suburbs may very well characterize the ever-elusive Sunbelt South, but small towns with populations of 7,500 or fewer, whose pasts, in many cases, reach back into the eighteenth and early-nineteenth centuries, remain most culturally characteristic of the region. "The South is still an aggregate of small communities . . . that form the backbone of the region," claimed *Time* in 1976. "Both pilloried and praised by native writers, the small town remains the custodian of the Southern lifestyle." . . .

The importance southerners assign place includes not only the built environment, but also the natural environment. Many writers have eloquently described Dixie's storybook landscape and referred to the reverence shown for the land. From

William Faulkner and Eudora Welty to Reynolds Price and Olive Ann Burns, the land has played a prominent role in the region's literature. The characters of these and other southern writers caress the red, overworked soil with their hands and water it with the sweat of their brows. The land is something that has been fought over, died on, and relied upon for a living by generation after generation. The land, the soil, the out-of-doors, nature, or whatever southerners choose to call it, gives them a way to keep in touch with their past and even provides them with a means of geographically defining the contemporary South. By the very lay of the land, one contributor to the "Southern Journal" section of *Southern Living* magazine sublimely claimed that she could actually pinpoint where the North ended and the South began.

This homage for the land has been attributed to the South's agrarian heritage, but it penetrates southern culture much deeper and with much broader definition. Southerners, both black and white, rich and poor, place enormous value on land ownership. Owning land deeded from one generation to members of the next has helped to reinforce all-important kinship loyalties and has provided a way for families to maintain a continuity with the past. Sydney Nathans has documented this phenomenon in his study of three generations of one black family that began in the 1840s, when 109 slaves were forced to leave their North Carolina home and migrate across South Carolina and Georgia to a newly opened cotton plantation in Alabama. After the Civil War, some of these 109 slaves eventually were granted title to a portion of the Alabama plantation and willed it to their children and grandchildren. After 150 years, according to Nathans, the community of blacks who own this land is still "marked by a notable continuity." From this homeplace dozens of family members have begun their lives. The land, according to one community resident, has been like a "plant bed," and by holding on to it rather than succumbing to pressures to sell it, this particular black community has carried on a long and valuable family tradition. A tendency, therefore, exists on the part of many southerners to view the land as something more than just real estate to be bought and sold. . . .

Other observers, and even song writers, have alluded to southerners' love of the land by describing their obsession with hunting and fishing. One North Carolinian has written that, in the South, "a youngster of whatever education or social background expects to learn to hunt as a part of growing up. I suspect that what keeps calling the hunter to the field and the fisherman to the river may not be so much the meat as the chance of communion with the land." In the hard-driving song "Dixie on My Mind," country musician Hank Williams, Jr., came to a similar conclusion. Complaining of being stranded in New York City, where life is "one big hassle," and anxious to return home to the South, he lamented:

> The thing, you know, that I miss most of all,
> Is the freedom of the rivers and the pine,
> They don't do much huntin' and fishin' up here, you know,
> But I have met a few squirrels and one porcupine.
> If this is the Promised Land,
> Then I've had all that I can stand,
> And I'm headed back below that Dixie line. . . .

This South is one of the heart, one that people long for, return to, and strive to preserve for future generations to enjoy and from which to glean their own identity.

It seems reasonable to assume, therefore, that like the historic preservation movement that had its beginning in the South and is vital and growing, the importance southerners attach to place will last for many years to come and embrace future southerners just as it has those past and those present.

A large percentage of the residents of metropolitan areas like Atlanta and Houston are assimilated southerners. Residing in predominantly Republican suburbs and commuting to jobs located in landscaped office parks, the acquisition of any identification with the traditional South has not come as easily as it has to those born and raised in the region, if indeed it has come at all. To this growing group of affluent people, southern culture is something that can be consumed. . . . Neither born nor raised in the region, the migration of these "outsiders" to the South has greatly watered-down regional distinctions and replaced them with a national cultural predictability and a mass-produced surrogate southernness. "The South is being etherized," wrote Marshall Frady in 1972, "subtly rendered pastless, memoryless, and vague of identity. What we are talking about is the passing of a sensibility—an event perhaps too wispy to define, but no less seismic . . . in its effect on the inner lives, the folk-geist, of a people. . . . Massively and uncomplainingly, the whole land is being trivialized. . . . The old pipe-organ range of prodigal possibilities for life there [in the South]—both gentle and barbarous, good and evil—has contracted to the comfortable monotone note of middle C." . . .

In 1964 Howard Zinn wrote that the South was a regional embodiment of basic Americanism. The South's shortcomings, in other words, were really a microcosm of the nation's deficiencies, and the best description, according to Zinn, of the relationship between the South and the nation was that of "mirror-image" twins. If he was right, and Americans have all along been "latent southerners," then it is not difficult to understand why southern culture has been so easily exported and is so resilient. Vietnam left many Americans with feelings of defeat, guilt, and repression. The South lived with this malaise long before the first American infantryman set foot in Southeast Asia, and this may also help to explain the adaptability of the region's culture. Still a place where people seem more in touch with their past, the region is commonly understood to be an anachronism where certain sensibilities associated with home, community, and family remain central to everyday life. In a seemingly rootless society caught up in drug addiction, fear of AIDS, public distrust of government, and rampant crime, many Americans have sought to reaffirm contact with traditional values and have looked to rural, small-town America to find some measure of reassurance. The song "Americana" by country musician Moe Bandy, about a forlorn trucker who forsakes the interstate highway for a less-traveled backroad and discovers the "real" America, perhaps best expresses these feelings. "Here's for courtin' at the Rexall soda fountain," he croons, "Like we did before they built the shopping mall. I saw so many reasons why I love this country, you know some things never really change at all."

Inevitably, the future South will be less distinct than it is and will come to resemble more and more freeze-dried, fast-food, suburban America. Its unique regionalism, however, promises not to evaporate altogether and be replaced entirely by a national sameness, or even by an ersatz southernness. What seems more plausible is that like ethnic cultures elsewhere in the United States, attributes, customs, mannerisms, and even attitudes traditionally ascribed to the South will endure in the midst of a more dominant national or possibly even global culture. Thus the answer to Woodward's question seems to be "yes." There are things about the South that have withstood and will continue to withstand the tests of time and the pressures of conformity. Perhaps the most significant of these is the lasting recognition and steadfast conviction on the part of many that the South is indeed different. And this, more than anything else, may help the region to maintain a measure of its stubborn singularity.

✢ F U R T H E R   R E A D I N G

Harry S. Ashmore, *An Epitaph for Dixie* (1957)
Nelson M. Blake, *Land into Water—Water into Land: A History of Water Management in Florida* (1980)
James C. Cobb, *The Selling of the South: The Southern Crusade for Industrial Development, 1936–1980* (1982)
———, *The Most Southern Place on Earth* (1992)
Albert E. Cowdrey, *This Land, This South: An Environmental History* (1983)
Fifteen Southerners, *Why the South Will Survive* (1981)
Joel Garreau, *The Nine Nations of North America* (1981)
Robert L. Hall and Carol B. Stack, eds., *Holding on to the Land and the Lord: Kinship, Ritual, Land Tenure, and Social Policy in the Rural South* (1982)
Robert G. Healy, *Competition for Land in the American South: Agriculture, Human Settlement, and the Environment* (1985)
Florence King, *Southern Ladies and Gentlemen* (1975)
E. Blaine Liner and Lawrence K. Lynch, eds., *The Economics of Southern Growth* (1977)
Randall M. Miller and George E. Pozzetta, eds., *Shades of the Sunbelt: Essays on Ethnicity, Race, and the Urban South* (1988)
Raymond A. Mohl, ed., *Searching for the Sunbelt* (1989)
William Least Heat Moon, *Blue Highways* (1982)
Thomas H. Naylor and James Clotfelter, *Strategies for Change in the South* (1975)
John Shelton Reed, *The Enduring South* (1972)
———, *One South: An Ethnic Approach to Regional Culture* (1982)
Charles P. Roland, "The Ever-Vanishing South," *Journal of Southern History* 48 (1982), 3–20
John David Smith and Tom Appleton, eds. *A Mythic Land Apart: Reassessing Southerners and Their History* (1997)
Carol Stack, *Call to Home: African Americans Reclaim the Rural South* (1996)
Rupert B. Vance and Nicholas J. Demerath, eds., *The Urban South* (1954)
Sandra Vance and Roy Scott, "Sam Walton and Wal-Mart Stores, Inc.: A Study in Modern Southern Entrepreneurship," *Journal of Southern History* 58 (May 1992), 231–252.
Bernard L. Weinstein and Robert E. Firestine, *Regional Growth and Decline in the United States: The Rise of the Sunbelt and the Decline of the Northeast* (1978)
David E. Whisnant, *Modernizing the Mountaineer: People, Power, and Planning in Appalachia* (1980)